THE PELICAN HISTORY OF ART

Founding Editor: Nikolaus Pevsner

Joint Editors: Peter Lasko and Judy Nairn

George Heard Hamilton

THE ART AND ARCHITECTURE OF RUSSIA

George Heard Hamilton has been a member of the history of art faculty at Yale University, and a curator of modern art at the Yale University Art Gallery. From 1966 to 1977 he was Director of the Sterling and Francine Clark Art Institute in Williamstown, Massachusetts, and Professor of Art at Williams College. He is a trustee of the Museum of Modern Art in New York, a member of the International Association of Art Critics, and a past president of the College Art Association of America. In 1971–2 he was Slade Professor at Cambridge, and in 1978–9 Kress Professor at the National Gallery, Washington. He has also written the volume on *Painting and Sculpture in Europe: 1880–1940* in the *Pelican History of Art* series.

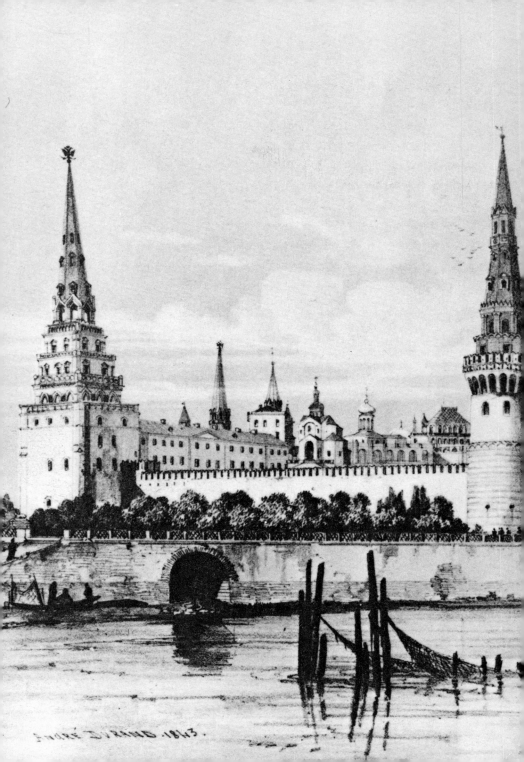

André Durand 1843.

George Heard Hamilton

The Art and Architecture of Russia

Penguin Books

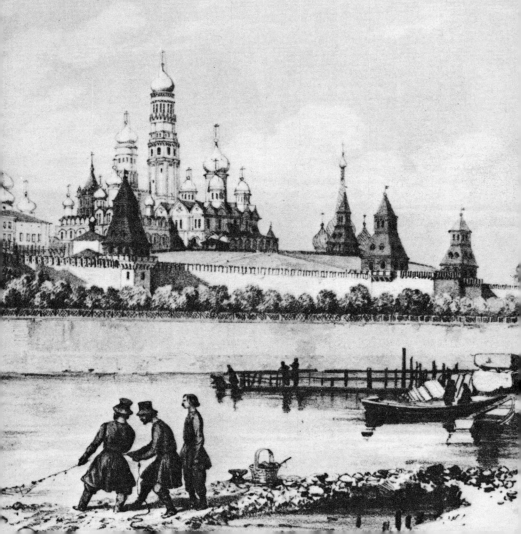

Penguin Books Ltd, Harmondsworth, Middlesex, England
Viking Penguin Inc., 40 West 23rd Street, New York, New York 10010, U.S.A.
Penguin Books Australia Ltd, Ringwood, Victoria, Australia
Penguin Books Canada Limited, 2801 John Street, Markham, Ontario, Canada L3R 1B4
Penguin Books (N.Z.) Ltd, 182–190 Wairau Road, Auckland 10, New Zealand

First published 1954
Second edition 1975
Third (integrated) edition 1983
Reprinted 1987

LIBRARY OF CONGRESS CATALOGING IN PUBLICATION DATA
Hamilton, George Heard.
    The art and architecture of Russia.
(The Pelican history of art)
    Bibliography: p. 449.
    Includes index.
    1. Art, Russian—History. 2 Architecture—Russian S.F.S.R.—History. I. Title.
II. Series: Pelican history of art.
N6981.H34   1982   709'.47   81-10583
ISBN 0 14 0561.06 4 (U.K. and U.S.A. paperback)
ISBN 0 14 0560.06 8 (U.K. hardback)

Printed and bound in Great Britain by
Butler & Tanner Ltd, Frome and London
Set in Monophoto Ehrhardt

Series designed by Gerald Cinamon
This volume designed by Judith Gordon

TO MY WIFE

CONTENTS

The history of a people's art, embracing a thousand years in time and a vast continental space, is not easily or adequately encompassed in a single volume. To cover such a period, from the Christianization of Russia in 988 to the fall of the Empire in 1917, and to consider only the more remarkable artistic manifestations, entailed a process of stringent selection, perhaps always a part of the writing of history. This account is limited to the arts of architecture, painting, and sculpture, as they have been created in the territories of European Russia by the Russian people. Within this programme the parts are not uniform, in content or chronology, but are related to the broad divisions of artistic expression as they have developed in time. The first part is concerned with architecture and painting in the oldest settlements of Kiev, Novgorod, and Suzdalia, from the later tenth century to the Mongol conquest; the second is devoted to icon painting through the fifteenth century; the third to the culture of Muscovy through the seventeenth century; the fourth treats of the architectural development of St Petersburg; and the last of more modern art, especially the development of painting, the dominant artistic manifestation in the nineteenth century. Regretfully, I have only hinted at the existence of other arts in the belief that the reader familiar with the churches and icons of medieval Russia will be in a position to understand enamels and embroideries, the most characteristic Russian contributions to the decorative arts. Peasant or folk crafts present fewer difficulties, originating as they do on a less complex cultural level; their forms and uses are comprehensible to those who have studied similar manifestations elsewhere. For those who wish further information on the decorative arts, a selected list of illustrated books has been provided in the bibliography.

In preparing the text and in selecting the illustrations I have not sought to emphasize either the likeness or unlikeness of Russian art to similar or contemporary expressions in Western Europe. I have tried to explain the characteristic elements as they have appeared in time, and to indicate how influences from outside Russia may have helped to shape such forms. I contend, with Catherine the Great, that 'Russia is a European State', and I have tried to explain Russian art in the terms used for the study of European art. I have assumed that the reader interested in studying Russian art has some knowledge of Russian political and social history and of the principal masters and movements in European art, but that he does not read the Russian language. If he commands it, the annotation of the text will send him to my sources should he wish to amplify or to correct my argument.

This book is intended as a history of the formal structure of a national art, rather than as an exercise in criticism. I have tried to avoid impressions which could not be supported by fact, and with the facts I have tried to tell a story according to the principles of modern historical research. When a project for such a book was raised, I had thought it would be possible to verify my hypotheses by an examination of the monuments. When that expectation faded, it seemed wasteful to abandon the undertaking. I am minded now to repeat the words with which John Milton closed the preface to his *Brief History of Muscovia*, published in 1682:

What was scatter'd in many volumes, and observ'd at several times by Eye-witnesses, with no cursory pains I laid together, to save the Reader a far longer travaile ... that so many things remarkable, dispers'd before, now brought under one view, might not hazard to be otherwise lost, nor the labour lost of collecting them.

My own labours in collecting these materials could not have been concluded without the unfailing assistance of the administrators and staffs of the libraries whose resources made this study possible, especially the several libraries of Columbia and Yale Universities, the Frick Art Reference Library, the Library of Congress, the New York Public Library, and the library of the Metropolitan Museum of Art. For assistance with the illustrations I am grateful to Vera Andrus, Alfred H. Barr, Jnr, Kenneth Conant, W. G. Constable, Charles C. Cunningham, Samuel Galpin, George Hann, John B. Hills, Henry La Farge, Frederic G. Ludwig, the late Elizabeth Naramore, and Warren A. Peterson. Finally, I would express my gratitude to George Vernadsky, Professor of Russian History at Yale University. Ten years ago he generously guided my first studies in Russian culture. If in the following pages the plan and purpose are mine, they would nevertheless have not been at all without his friendship and inspiration at the start.

New Haven, Conn.
1 June 1951

PREFACE TO THE SECOND EDITION

In transliterating the Russian alphabet into the Roman inconsistencies inevitably occur if one accepts certain conventional spellings of proper names rather than arbitrarily holding to a correct but often awkward phonetic parallelism. The new spellings, however logical (Chaikovskii for Tchaikowsky is the most familiar), can cause as much confusion as they would eliminate. Therefore I have tried, on the whole, to adhere to the first two of the four systems proposed by the Library of Congress. For the text I have used System I, suggested for works of a general nature 'directed to any audience whose interest is not primarily in Russian studies ... [or] is not composed of specialists in such studies'. Such persons, I assume, are most likely to read this book. System II, which is recommended for citations of bibliographical material, has generally been used in the notes and bibliography in order that those who wish to pursue any subject in Russian language works, may find them the more readily in library catalogues and other indices.

Among the thirty-three Russian letters and six combinations of letters, there are only four differences between the two Systems. In System I, Й is read as y, rather than i; Ю as yu rather than iu; Я is spelled ya instead of ia; and кc is represented by x rather than ks. I have, however, preferred ya to ia throughout as representing a sound closer to the correct pronunciation. Contrariwise, I have used System II's e, rather than yo, for the Russian ё in proper names (principally Andrey Rublev's) in an attempt to avoid confusion for the reader to whom the spelling Rublyov might be taken as a different name (this disregard for the exact phonetic equivalent is generally followed in the Western press as well).

I have also preferred transliterations of Russian names occurring in history before 1700, but the usual English spelling for such names after 1700 (Alexandr and Andrey before 1700; Alexander and Andrew afterwards). The watershed, of course, corresponds to Peter the Great's drastic Westernization of many aspects of Russian life. When certain names, principally those of the saints, occur simultaneously in Western European and Russian history I have retained the English spelling; thus Andrew and John, rather than Andrey and Ivan or Ioann. In defence of these decisions, I can only plead that I do not recall having yet seen a completely consistent system which was also coherent for any but the specialist.

In preparing this second edition I have had the advantage of visiting the Soviet Union. As a consequence certain errors have been eliminated, and much information and more qualitative judgements have been added.

In Williamstown Selma Sabin has coped with my erratic typescripts and the exasperatingly unusual spellings now for several years. In London I am in debt to Mrs Rose-Smith and her predecessors for finding new photographs which are immeasurably better than those which of necessity had to be used in the first edition twenty years ago, and, beyond hope of redemption, to Mrs Nairn for her exemplary patience and incomparable editorial skills.

Williamstown, Mass.
1 October 1973

PREFACE TO THE THIRD EDITION

The text, in so far as it embodies my thoughts on the origin and development of Russian art and architecture, is substantially as it has been. Thirty years ago my intention was to write 'a history of the formal structure of a national art', but I hope that now it has also become more like what I then eschewed, 'an exercise in criticism'. I have tried to indicate the artistic quality of these strange, unusual, sometimes even familiar forms. To do this I have occasionally altered words, phrases, sentences, sometimes whole paragraphs, less to change the meaning than to strengthen the interpretation.

Still and all the whole is a history, not a handbook or a guide. Yet from the first an intrepid few who took the weighty volume to the Soviet Union returned to tell me of its usefulness. I am glad that now it appears in paperback for those who make that notable artistic journey.

Once again I have inexpressible debts: in London to Mrs Nairn and her staff for their patience and good humour, and of course for their exceptional talents; here at home to the staff of the library of the Sterling and Francine Clark Art Institute, and to Edith Howard for her faultless typing.

The dedication, with my deepest love and admiration, remains the same.

Williamstown, Mass.
1 October 1980

THE ART AND ARCHITECTURE OF RUSSIA

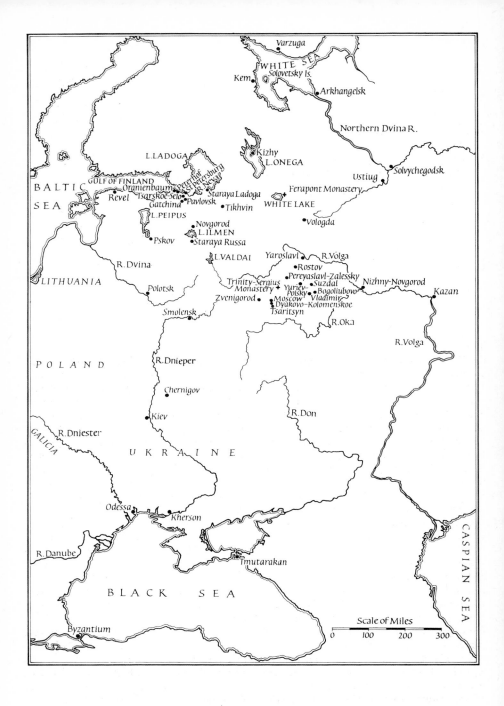

Varzuga

WHITE SEA
Kem Solovetsky Is.
Arkhangelsk

Northern Dvina R.

L.LADOGA
Kizhy
L.ONEGA
Ustiug
Solvychegodsk

BALTIC
GULF OF FINLAND
Peterhof
Oranienbaum
St.Petersburg
R.Neva
Ferapont Monastery
SEA
Revel
Tsarskoe-Selo
Staraya Ladoga
Gatchina
Pavlovsk
WHITE LAKE
Tikhvin
L.PEIPUS
Vologda
Novgorod
L.ILMEN
Pskov
Staraya Russa

R.Dvina
L.VALDAI
Yaroslavl
R.Volga

LITHUANIA
Rostov
Pereyaslavl-Zalessky
Nizhny-Novgorod
Polotsk
Trinity-Sergius
Monastery
Suzdal
Kazan
Zvenigorod
Moscow
Polsky
Bogoliubovo
Yuriev-
Vladimir
Smolensk
Dyakovo-Kolomenskoe
Tsaritsyn
R.Oka

POLAND
R.Dnieper
R.Volga

Chernigov
R.Don

Kiev

GALICIA
R.Dniester

U K R A I N E

CASPIAN SEA

Odessa
Kherson

R.Danube
Tmutarakan

B L A C K   S E A

Scale of Miles
0   100   200   300

Byzantium

PART ONE

KIEVAN RUSSIA

The horses neigh beyond the Sula, the glory echoes at Kiev,
the trumpets blare at Novgorod, the banners stand fast at Putivl

The Tale of the Armament of Igor
(Late Twelfth Century)

CHAPTER I

THE PAST OF KIEV

The study of Russian art properly begins with the Christianization of Russia late in the tenth century. The reason for the appearance of that Christian culture may be better understood by considering the origins of the ancient Russian State. The peoples who were later to be known as Russians, and who can first be described as Eastern Slavs, are thought to have left their homeland in the Carpathian mountains and to have been living, by the third century A.D., in the territory between the Baltic and the Black Seas, and the Don and Danube rivers.[1] This vast sweep of land included the forest and steppe zones where the different natural environments went far to define later Russian culture. In the northern forests, where a living was precariously obtained by clearing the trees and working the soil with primitive instruments, trapping and hunting were the main occupations. Here lived isolated tribes and clans, principally Finns. In the South the forest gave way to the endless grass-covered plains of rich, deep soil, the so-called 'black earth'. The steppes permitted not only thriving agricultural settlements, but also the un-paralleled movement of peoples in the absence of any natural barriers. Up to the limits of the forest zone swept continuous waves of nomads, pushed out of Asia by over-popula-tion and economic distress. The early history of ancient Russia is in part the story of how the Slavic tribes met, countered, or accepted invasions by non-Slavic peoples from the East.

After the shadowy Cimmerians, who con-trolled southern Russia from approximately 1000 to 700 B.C., the first important inhabi-tants to appear in history are the Scythians of Iranian stock, known to Herodotus in the fifth century B.C. for their trade relations with the Greek colonies on the shores of the Black Sea. Judging by the objects found in their tomb-barrows, the Scythians were highly civilized and provided a lively market for luxury wares exported from Greece or manufactured in the Chersonesus.[2] In the early fourth century the Scythians were disturbed by another Iran-ian people, the Sarmatians. Members of one of the most important Sarmatian tribes were known as Alans, originally nomads and renowned as horsemen, who turned in time to an agricultural life and settled among the East Slavic tribes. The Caucasian Alans were called As or Os – hence the modern Ossetians. The name of one of their clans was Rukhs-As, 'the light, or brilliant Alans', which may be the origin of Ros or Rus (Russia, Russians).

Meanwhile Slavic tribes, known in the earliest literature as Antes, whether indigenous or having migrated from western Europe, had been living in southern Russia, where by at least the third century A.D. they had developed a high degree of social and cultural organization. They practised agriculture, animal husbandry, weaving, ceramics, and metal-working. In the sixth and seventh centuries two more tribes, the Avars and the Altaic Turks, appeared out of the East and overran southern Russia. The Avars eventually passed through Pannonia, where they subjugated the peoples of that region and the Balkan Slavs as well, while the Turks settled on the steppes between the lower Volga and the Don and in the northern Caucasus. There the mixture of Turk, Hun, and Caucasian aborigine produced a new people, the Khazars, who by the middle of the seventh century had developed a prosperous state.

During the eighth and ninth centuries the Khazar state reached its greatest extent and power, and the Antes and Slavs of the lower Don and Azov region, the old As or Rus tribes, participated in the first of the empires to be established on Russian soil. Khazar power reached from the Caspian Sea and lower Volga to the Dnieper and Black Sea. The Khazars developed one of the great trade routes of history, stretching from the upper reaches of the Volga to the Caspian and on to the Near and Middle East into the lands of the Arabs.

So far we have considered only the constant movement of peoples and the passage of power in southern Russia as it was determined by invasions from the East. There had been, however, considerable activity in the North. In the sixth and seventh centuries the inhabitants of Scandinavia, in particular the Swedes, had explored the eastern Baltic regions and, travelling up the Dvina, had reached the upper Volga and Oka rivers. If the history of southern Russia had been written in the movement of nomadic tribes across the endless plains, the history of northern Russia was decided by the interminable network of waterways through the forests. At the meeting point of steppe and river, of forest and plain, of northern adventurers and nomadic hosts would be created the first essentially Russian culture.

After 825, when the Khazars were attacked by the Arabs, the Swedish-Russian chiefs defied the Khazars and established an independent Russian Kaganate with a capital presumably at Tmutarakan on the Taman Peninsula. This Kaganate took over the control of the international trade route. Scandinavian metal-work and Russian furs were transported from the northern trading-post of Staraya Russa (Old Rus, a town still in existence, thirty-six miles south of Novgorod), down the Oka, Volga, and Don rivers to Byzantium and the East. The extent of this activity is seen in the presence in Baghdad of Russian merchants in the ninth century. When the Khazars appealed to the Byzantine Emperor for assistance, engineers were sent to build fortresses, notably that of Sarkel on the lower Don. The Khazars then controlled the Russian trade routes to the East and simultaneously broke the connexions between Taman Rus and northern Russia and, after conquering the Slavs of the Oka region, established their Magyar vassals in the area of Kiev.

The effect of the Khazar interruption of the trade route was also felt in northern Russia. Force was required to resolve the crisis which had developed in the south. But the Swedish-Russian outposts in the north, in the region of Staraya Russa and Lake Ilmen, possessed few troops, and help was sought from abroad. Such in effect would seem to have been the reasons for the 'calling of the Varangians from over the Sea', in the middle of the ninth century, traditionally considered the beginning of modern Russian history.[3]

About 856 the Norseman, Rurik, famous as an adventurer and the ruler of South Jutland and Friesland, arrived in northern Russia and established himself in Ladoga and Novgorod.

He showed little concern for the south, apparently because his possessions in western Europe were in jeopardy and required his presence. Two of his followers, Askold and Dir, ventured down the Dnieper and took Kiev in 858 under an agreement with the Magyars. From there they reached the Taman Russians and joined in an attack on Constantinople, apparently in protest against the assistance given the Khazars. The attack was militarily ineffective, but it had the important consequence that the Byzantine patriarch Photius sent missionaries after the Russians, many of whom were later baptized, and in 867 the first Russian bishopric was established at Tmutarakan. In 873 Rurik died and was succeeded by Oleg, who was more interested in the south. In 882 Oleg entered Kiev, killed Askold and Dir, and declared himself an independent ruler. So, at the hands of a Norseman, a 'Varanger', began the history of Kievan Russia.

The character of the new state was primarily military and commercial, and its independence was assured by control of the waterways linking the Baltic with the Black Sea by way of the Gulf of Finland, the river Neva and Lake Ladoga, the river Volkhov and Lake Ilmen, to the headwaters of the Dnieper near Smolensk, and finally down the Dnieper to the sea, and so to Constantinople. Portages were rarely required, the most dangerous being around the rapids which blocked the Dnieper at its furthest eastern bend 300 miles below Kiev. During the winter at the northern trading-stations were collected quantities of the staples of Kievan trade, furs, wax, and honey, as well as slaves from the hinterland, sometimes taken as prisoners of war. These goods were brought to Kiev, where the traders made up their flotilla of small boats for the trip down-river in April when the ice broke. Military protection against the hostile tribes molesting the remoter reaches of the waterway, especially the Pechenegs, who were frequently lying in ambush near the rapids, was provided by the prince and his retinue of warriors, the druzhina. Once arrived in Constantinople, the merchants spent the summer trading their goods for fine wines and eastern silks.

With the establishment of regular mercantile relations with Constantinople the Russians were more susceptible to the influence of Christianity, and the Greeks were not unaware that it was to their advantage to bring the unruly merchants of Kiev under their spiritual as well as economic influence. The chronicler relates that after the signing of the treaty of 911, which concluded Oleg's successful campaign against Byzantium, the Emperor Leo arranged for his vassals to show the Russian envoys 'the beauties of the churches' and to instruct them in 'the true belief'.

Yet what might have been a gradual process was given sudden impetus by the appearance of an extraordinary personality, Olga, the wife and widow of Igor and the first of the women rulers so conspicuous in Russian history. After Igor, who succeeded Oleg and ruled from 913 to 945, had been slain in a campaign against a Slav tribe, the Drevlianians, Olga ruled Kiev during the minority of her son Svyatoslav. After destroying the Drevlianian threat, with clever and brutal tricks, she went to Constantinople, where she is said to have been instructed by the Patriarch and baptized by the Emperor himself. She was unable, however, to convert Svyatoslav, who seems to have been afraid of the ridicule of his druzhina if he adopted Christianity.

It is possible that Svyatoslav's desire to rule over the whole land of Russia and even beyond made him realize that he must not yet abjure the old gods. During his personal reign, from about 962 to 972, he spent most of his time campaigning, leaving the internal administration of Kiev to his mother. By 965 Svyatoslav had overcome the Khazars and occupied their chief towns, including the fortress of Sarkel on the Don and Itil at the mouth of the Volga. Immediately afterwards he turned westward, and in 968 overthrew the Bulgars on the Danube and occupied their city of Pereyaslavets, which he decided to make his permanent residence. Svyatoslav's realm was of tremendous extent, stretching from the Volga to the Danube and including the forest areas of Novgorod and the north. But this mighty empire was of short duration. In 971 Svyatoslav was defeated by the Byzantines, and after returning to Kiev perished the next year when his army was surprised by the Pechenegs.

The history of Kievan Russia for the next 250 years is the account of the gradual dismemberment of Svyatoslav's great empire before successive waves of invasion from the east, complicated by the progressive degeneration of the political situation in a series of fratricidal civil wars among the numerous princes of the ruling house, and culminating in the fall of Kiev to the Tartars in 1240. But if politically the period lacks the epic urgency of the ninth-century Russian Kaganate or of Svyatoslav's military brilliance in the tenth century, it saw the formulation of the first specifically Russian art and architecture. These achieved definite expression in three centres of ancient Russia: in Kiev, 'the mother of Russian cities', where Byzantine art was first introduced; in Novgorod, the northern and very ancient 'New City', where the Byzantine style was modified by distance from Byzantium and proximity to Russia's western neighbours; and in the north-eastern principality of Vladimir-Suzdal, strongly tinged with eastern influences from the Caucasus.

In the cultural development of Kievan Russia, Christianity is an understandably dominant force. Whether or not we are to read the stories in the chronicles about the conversion of Olga and her grandson Vladimir as history or as myth, they are at least consonant with what we may believe were the actual circumstances. Not the least interesting aspect of these stories is the frequent reiteration of the beauty of Byzantine church architecture and church ritual which impressed the Russians. Here was an immediate, sensuous attraction which proved irresistible to a people which has always been noted for its love of colour, sound, and movement, whether in terms of ecclesiastical liturgy, imperial pageantry, or folk arts. In 980, according to the chronicle, after Vladimir had secured for himself the throne of Kiev by treacherously overthrowing his brother Yaropolk, he 'set up idols on the hill outside the castle'. His morals, too, were what are more usually described as pagan than Christian; according to the chronicler, he was 'insatiable in vice'. Subsequently Vladimir was visited by learned men of various faiths who expounded to him the advantages of Mohammedanism, Judaism, and of Roman and Greek Catholicism. He was impressed by the Greek scholar who instructed him in world history according to the Old Testament, but he was still uncertain and sent emissaries into various lands to study the ritual worship of various faiths. Again the Greeks proved themselves the most adroit proselytizers. In 987 the Emperor himself took the Russian envoys into the church 'and placed them in a wide space, calling their attention to the beauty of the edifice, the chanting and the offices of the archpriest and the ministry of the deacons, while he explained to them the worship of his God'. The chronicler added: 'The Russians were astonished and in their wonder praised the Greek ceremonial'. When the envoys returned to Vladimir they reported that they had been among the Bulgarians and the Germans (Latins), and 'saw them performing many ceremonies in their temples; but we beheld no glory there'. The peerless churches of Constantinople exercised their ineluctable spell. 'Then we went on to Greece, and the Greeks led us to the edifices where they worship their God, and we knew not whether we were in heaven or on earth. For on earth there is no such splendour or such beauty, and we are at a loss how to describe it. We only know that God dwells there among men, and their service is fairer than the ceremonies of other nations. For we cannot forget that beauty.' Although he was impressed with this description of the Greek faith, Vladimir withheld his formal acquiescence until he could put such an important step to political use. A year later he besieged and captured the Greek city of Kherson near the mouth of the Dnieper, which he threatened to destroy unless he were given the Emperors' sister as a wife. Basil II and Constantine VIII refused to send their sister Anna unless Vladimir were baptized, to which he agreed providing that Anna herself brought priests with her to perform the office. Vladimir was thereupon baptized in Kherson and departed for Kiev, taking with him his new wife, priests, relics, and sacred vessels for the service. In Kiev Vladimir overthrew the idols of Perun and the other gods and coerced the population into mass baptism in the Dnieper. The people of Novgorod were similarly, although more reluctantly, converted.

The consequences of Vladimir's conversion were soon felt. Many of the cultural advantages which had been unknown to pagan Russians became available to them as Christians. The most important, perhaps, was the new opportunity for education. Vladimir himself established schools for 'the children of the best families', probably somewhat like Charlemagne's palace schools, to assure an educated aristocracy called by birth to positions of authority in civil affairs. The Church, too, required educated men for the priesthood. With the church books, which had been brought from Constantinople and translated into Slavonic, in an alphabet devised by St Cyril and St Methodius for the Slavs, came the principles of Byzantine law, later incorporated in the first Russian code, the eleventh-century *Pravda Russkaya*. With the Church came monastic institutions. The first and for long the most famous was the Kievan Monastery of the Caves, the Pecherskaya Lavra, where not only sanctity but also a high level of intellectual labour was maintained. The latter found expression in the writing of the Russian chronicles, which by the beginning of the twelfth century had grown from a mere list of yearly wonders to a systematic study of history within the framework of religious thought. And, finally, for palace, church, and monastery alike Vladimir and his successors called into existence the buildings and their decoration which constitute the first Russian art.

In Kievan Russia, where the sovereign power was vested in the family of Rurik's descendants rather than in an individual, the principle of succession led to endless and disastrous strife. Only occasionally, as with Vladimir Monomakh (ruled 1113–25), grandson of Yaroslav and through his mother reputedly a grandson of the Byzantine Emperor Constantine IX Monomachus, could an individual of unusual presence and gifts dominate the unruly family. With the decay of the central authority in Kiev, the homogeneity of Oleg's and Vladimir's river-realm declined. Barbarian raids more frequently cut the routes between Kiev and Constantinople, so that the Russians were unable to depend upon trade for a living and turned to agriculture and the exploitation of natural resources. Consequently a new population came into being, centred in towns and depending upon the outlying regions for farm produce, grown on the estates of the wealthy boyars, a term usually understood to mean the landed proprietors among the prince's druzhina. By the middle of the twelfth century a number of local centres had emerged. In addition to Kiev and Novgorod, the Galician principality to the west, bordering on Poland, and the principality of Vladimir-Suzdal in the forests north-east of Moscow came to prominence.

As other cities and religious centres developed, different milieus were created which found distinct expression in art and architecture, as well as in political and social institutions. While Kiev continued until its downfall to stand as the political and spiritual capital of Russia, closely related to the Greek culture of Byzantium, the cities of Novgorod and of Vladimir-Suzdal were soon affected by influences from the East and West. Suzdalia succumbed to the Tartars ahead of Kiev, but before 1237 its rulers had created a princely, aristocratic environment, expressed in a series of magnificent churches and now-vanished palaces which were the wonders of the age. Through the proximity of Suzdalia to the trade-route to the Caspian, and through the marriage of its rulers to Caucasian princesses, Eastern influences early appeared as factors in its art. In Novgorod, at the northern end of the trade-route, western merchants were established from a very early date, and helped to foster a commercial spirit which found political expression in the democratic institution of the town meeting or veche. The painters and architects of Novgorod absorbed western influences and created a vigorous popular style which endured through the century of Tartar domination until the rise of Moscow in the fifteenth century.

From even this brief summary of the first millennium of Russian history certain constant factors emerge for the history of Russian culture. The first may be defined as mobility. We in the twentieth century often consider ourselves the first to move widely and rapidly through the world, but the history of pre-Kievan Russia reveals a constant succession of armies, peoples, and individuals moving as widely, if not so swiftly, as similar groups today. Such a situation implies a variety of influences working in any one place through a period of time which should dispel the notion that such early cultures were fixed or rigid in their forms. Kiev itself, and before Kiev, Tmutarakan, important cities on great trade routes, attracted travellers from the whole world. To this record of the movements of peoples, whether as nations or as individuals, we must add the fact that in the tenth and eleventh centuries Russia was part of two great empires, those of the Byzantines and of the Norsemen. Through their relations with Byzantium, the Russians were in contact with an already old and still potent imperial state. Through the Varangian heritage, Kiev and Novgorod were part of that intensely mobile and brilliant civilization which the Vikings established on the coasts of northern Europe, the Mediterranean, and the Russian waterways in the tenth and eleventh centuries. Thus the Russia of Kiev and Novgorod was politically and culturally a part of Europe to a degree not again achieved until the end of the sixteenth century, and at the beginning of the nineteenth. To think of Kiev and Novgorod as outposts on a strange and savage frontier looking less westward to Greece and Rome than eastward into the fearful distances of Asia, is to misconstrue the historical situation. The Kievan dynasty was allied by marriage more often to the rulers of the West than it was to the imperial family in Constantinople.[4] Indeed, Yaroslav may be considered a European sovereign through the marriages he contracted for himself and his family. Three of his daughters – Elizabeth, Anna, and Anastasia – became queens of Norway, France, and Hungary, and other children married into the royal houses of Sweden, Denmark, and Poland. His wife was a daughter of King Olaf of Sweden. His grandson, Vladimir Monomakh, married Harold II's daughter, Gyda of England, who had taken refuge in Sweden after the Battle of Hastings. The causes which drew Kievan Russia into the orbit of world civilization in the tenth and eleventh centuries outweighed those which might have isolated her from western European culture. Far more than her geographical situation or her acceptance of Orthodox Christianity, it was the Mongol domination from the thirteenth to the end of the fifteenth century which contributed to Russia's subsequent isolation from Europe, making of her a province of Tartary just at the time when the high medieval and early Renaissance revival of learning, discovery of scientific method, and flowering of artistic individualism brought the European nations further political differentiation and cultural interdependence. When the Great Princes of Muscovy, or the Tsars and Emperors of Russia, Ivan III, Alexey Mikhailovich, or Peter the Great, looked to the West for political, scientific, or artistic conceptions, they found that they were separated from their contemporaries by a gulf in time more difficult to bridge than any extent in space.

CHAPTER 2

THE ARCHITECTURE OF KIEV

990–1240

When Vladimir returned to Kiev in 989 after his conquest of Kherson and imposed conversion upon his subjects, one of his first tasks was to supply his chief cities with adequate houses of worship. Christians and Christian churches had existed before this. The chronicles in 882 record a Church of St Nicholas built by Olma over the tomb of Askold and Dir, and the Church of St Elias is mentioned in the Byzantine treaty of 945 as 'a cathedral church since many of the Varangians were Christians'. But these would certainly have been inadequate for the increased demands of the new faith. Vladimir's first act, after throwing down the idols of Perun and Volos which he had previously erected, was to build a church dedicated to St Basil, his patron, upon the site where the idols had stood. These first Kievan churches presumably were wooden structures which soon disappeared; they may have been burned in a fire which swept Kiev in 1017.[1]

Far more important was Vladimir's second church, the Cathedral of the Dormition of the Virgin (Uspensky Sobor) [1], known as the Desyatinnaya or Church of the (Virgin of the)

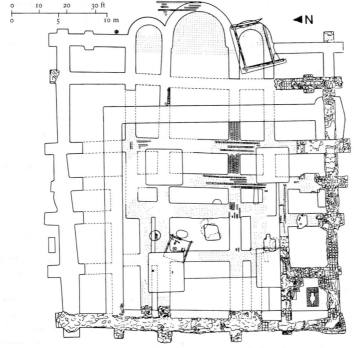

1. Kiev, Desyatinnaya, founded 989, consecrated 996 (or 994), rededicated 1039, plan

Tithe from the fact that Vladimir, in regulating the ecclesiastical institutions of Russia, dedicated to it a tithe of his income.[2] The church was founded in 989, consecrated in 996 (or 994), and rededicated by Theopomptos, the first Metropolitan, in 1039. The reasons for the rededication are unknown, but it is possible that the ceremony was required by rebuilding after the fire of 1017. The Desyatinnaya was pillaged by rebellious Kievan princes in 1169 and 1203, and wrecked in 1240, when the vaults collapsed under the weight of the populace which had retreated there with their household goods during the Tartar siege. The ruins were used for building materials until the seventeenth century, when the Metropolitan Peter Mogila attempted to preserve the remaining fragments by including them in a small chapel he built in the south-west corner. After 1828, during the construction of a new church occupying some two-thirds of the original site, parts of the foundations were uncovered; they were further studied after the demolition of the nineteenth-century church in 1926. Unfortunately the first excavations were hasty, poorly reported, and subsequently spoiled, so that conclusions based upon early drawings of the foundations must be accepted with reservations. At best the evidence disclosed is scanty and contradictory, especially since the fragments of the old walls and floors have now all but disappeared. The discovery beneath these foundations of the remains of a wooden structure and of stone tombs lacking any Christian symbols suggests that Vladimir built his church on the site of a pre-Christian pagan temple.[3] The Desyatinnaya must also have been the palace chapel. Excavations in the neighbourhood have uncovered the foundations of other buildings of granite, stone, and brick. Traces of elaborate architectural ornament, as well as of frescoes, and mosaic and majolica pavements, suggest that Vladimir's palace lay immediately to the south.

From the apparent absence at the east end of the church of piers or of a chain wall for the support of a dome it has been argued that the Desyatinnaya was a basilica with nave and aisles ending in three semicircular apses and that it was roofed in wood. The basilica plan, however, was out of fashion in Constantinople in the tenth century, and was not used later in Russia. Its singular appearance in Kiev in 991 would imply some influence from the West, possibly from Bulgaria, where the three-apsed basilica without domes is found in such churches as St Sophia in Ochrida, founded well before 1018, or from the East, from Kherson, where small churches of the basilican plan with three apses have been uncovered. Neither of these hypotheses can be dismissed, given the close relations between the Russian and Bulgarian Churches in this period. The Russian Church adapted its language – Church Slavonic – from the Bulgarian, and Vladimir built the Desyatinnaya soon after his return from Kherson accompanied by priests from that city. Yet, conversely, the galleries flanking the aisles, and an additional western bay, even if added after 1017, created a five-aisled church closely resembling, in plan at least, the now destroyed churches of St George (1037–51) and St Irene (c. 1050), which were of almost the same dimensions. Since St Irene was a five-domed church with incomplete chain walls, the Desyatinnaya may have been completed after the fire of 1017 as a vaulted five-domed cruciform church. Whatever the original covering was, it must have been supplied with masonry vaults, probably after 1017, judging by the episode in 1240 when the people took refuge on the roof.[4] Such a conclusion would seem justified given the Desyatinnaya's position as the eldest of Kiev's large masonry structures, and Vladimir's favourite church. According to the chronicle in 989: 'After he had begun to build, and the structure was completed, he adorned it with images, and entrusted it to Anastasius of Kherson. He appointed Khersonian priests to serve in it, and bestowed upon this church all the images, vessels, and crosses which he had taken in that city.' Subsequently as his burial-place the church grew in veneration.

Although the Khersonian background of the Desyatinnaya is historically established, there were other influences at work in its creation. The chronicle adds that 'with the intention of building a church dedicated to the Holy Virgin, [Vladimir] sent and imported artisans from Greece'.

Vladimir's earlier memories of the basilican churches of Kherson may later have been modified by information brought by these Greek workmen, and more particularly by the Greek priests who accompanied his Byzantine bride, the Princess Anna. Vladimir, as a Christian and the brother-in-law of the Emperors, would have considered himself closely allied with the imperial house. And he or his wife may well have had in mind the palace church in Constantinople, Basil I's long-lost Nea Ekklesia (consecrated 881), as the model for their own. It is perhaps significant that the Desyatinnaya, like the Nea Ekklesia, was a palace church dedicated to the Virgin and both were in a sense personal donations. If, then, the Desyatinnaya was a cruciform rather than a basilican structure, whether originally or through modifications after 1017, as the progenitor of the later churches of southern Russia it appears in a more logical and coherent relation to Yaroslav's St Sophia. Both structures thereby approach more closely a possible Byzantine prototype such as the Nea Ekklesia, which in turn inspired many Constantinopolitan and provincial churches of the tenth and early eleventh centuries.

However inadequate our attempts to recapture the original appearance of the Desyatinnaya may be, the few surviving fragments of white marble columns, carved capitals, tessellated pavements, mosaics, and fresco-painting, all in the best Byzantine manner, indicate that Vladimir spared neither trouble nor money to make this church a proper monument to his new faith. As a proving ground for Russian art and architecture of the future, it must have been of the utmost significance. Whether the builders were Greeks, or Russians instructed by Greeks,[5] the decorators certainly came from the capital. Russian mason and painter could now learn the new techniques just as, from the Kherson and Byzantine clergy, craftsman and Christian were learning the expressive possibilities of the new religion. The workshops of the Desyatinnaya must have been the schools where the Russians studied who were going to assist in the construction and decoration of St Sophia.

Vladimir's son, Yaroslav the Wise, after overthrowing his brother, the cruel and treacherous Svyatopolk, reigned in Kiev from 1019 to 1054. He continued and even amplified Vladimir's building programme, investing the city with an almost imperial splendour. Even the names of his buildings recalled Byzantium, and from a chronicle of 1037 it is apparent how profound was Yaroslav's interest in the development of a Kievan, Christian culture: 'During his reign the Christian faith was fruitful and multiplied, while the number of monks increased, and new monasteries came into being. Yaroslav loved religious establishments and was devoted to priests, especially to monks. He applied himself to books, and read them continually day and night. He assembled many scribes, and translated from Greek into Slavic. He wrote and collected many books through which true believers are instructed and enjoy religious education.'[6]

The date of the foundation of Yaroslav's supreme achievement, the Cathedral of St Sophia, so-called in emulation of Justinian's incomparable Hagia Sophia (Church of the Holy Wisdom) in Constantinople, has been contested.[7] Since under the year 1036 the chronicle states that Yaroslav met and defeated the Pechenegs 'on the spot where the metropolitan Church of St Sophia now stands', the mention of the church in 1037 in the list of Yaroslav's foundations has been taken to mean that it was begun in that year. Its construction would therefore have occupied the latter years of Yaroslav's reign. It happens, however, that the First Novgorod Chronicle states, in 1018, that St Sophia was founded in that year. If to this is added the statement of the Kievan chronicle that in 1017 when Yaroslav occupied Kiev 'the churches were burned', construction may have been begun about 1018 and been carried well towards completion by 1037 when the list of Yaroslav's accomplishments was set down.[8] The earlier date may also be implied in the words of Hilarion, the first native-born Metropolitan of Russia, who in his *Discourse on Law and Grace*, a sermon preached before Yaroslav some time between 1037 and 1050, apostrophized the Prince as the successor of Vladimir: 'He who is finishing thy unfinished works, as was done for David by Solomon; he who has built in his wisdom a great and holy house of God, and it stands there for the consecration and adornment of thy city; he who has adorned it with every beauty, with gold and silver and precious stones and sacred vessels.'[9] From the tone of this address it would seem that the church not only was finished, especially in so far as its internal decoration was concerned, which would scarcely have

been possible had it been begun only in 1037, but that Yaroslav may possibly have been carrying to completion a building intended, if not actually commenced, by Vladimir and designed to surpass the Desyatinnaya.

St Sophia, the greatest monumental religious structure in Russia and the source from which the long line of Orthodox masonry churches for the next nine centuries was to proceed, is almost as difficult to describe in its original condition as Vladimir's Desyatinnaya. While the one vanished completely, the other disappeared beneath successive destruction and restoration. Damaged in the numerous sacks of Kiev, culminating in the capture of the city by the Tartars in 1240, and abandoned by its clergy during the Middle Ages, the church lay in majestic, almost forgotten, desolation until the seventeenth and eighteenth centuries, when it was internally repaired and externally reconstructed (1685–1707) in the style of the Ukrainian Baroque.

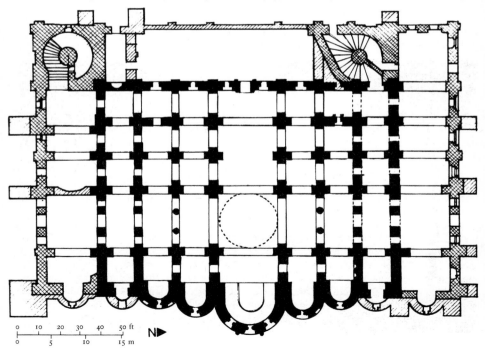

| 0 | 10 | 20 | 30 | 40 | 50 ft |
| 0 | | 5 | | 10 | | 15 m |

The addition of eight new domes, making a total of twenty-one, and the reconstruction of all the cupolas in an intricate baroque form gave it a bizarre appearance totally at variance with what we may conceive the original to have been. Only within the last century have the frescoes and mosaics been recovered from beneath layers of seventeenth-century whitewash, and only in the present century has anything approaching a systematic examination of the fabric begun to yield answers to the many problems it presents.

The nine-aisled plan [2] represents less the original intentions of the builders than a progressive modification and multiplication of elements developing from the basic cruciform plan with adjoining galleries, first stated in the Nea Ekklesia and modified in the Desyatinnaya. Originally St Sophia had a nave and four aisles, ending in eastern apses with a tribune over the outer aisles. An open arcade was then added on three sides, upon which galleries were subsequently constructed and an additional one-storey arcade added to the north and south [3].[10] Early in the eleventh century a stair-tower was erected at either end of the west façade providing access to the adjoining palaces of the Prince and the Metropolitan. In the seventeenth century a gallery was added over the second, outer arcade. This gave the church a cubical appearance and accentuated the fact that its breadth had gradually become greater than its length. At the same time the domes were increased in height and number, so that the present exterior bears no relation to the original structure except on the east, where the distribution and proportions of the three central apses have been preserved [4]. Although the chronicles contain no mention of the origin of the workmen, the construction, in *opus mixtum* composed of alternating courses of thick reddish quartzite and thin buff brick, bound in pink mortar, recalls contemporary Byzantine practice.[11]

2 and 3. Kiev, Cathedral of St Sophia, *c.* 1018–37, plan (*opposite*) and outer galleries (*below*) added towards the end of the century (restored view from the east)

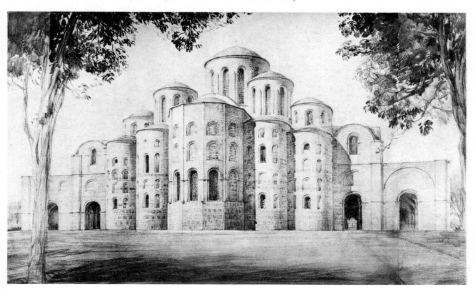

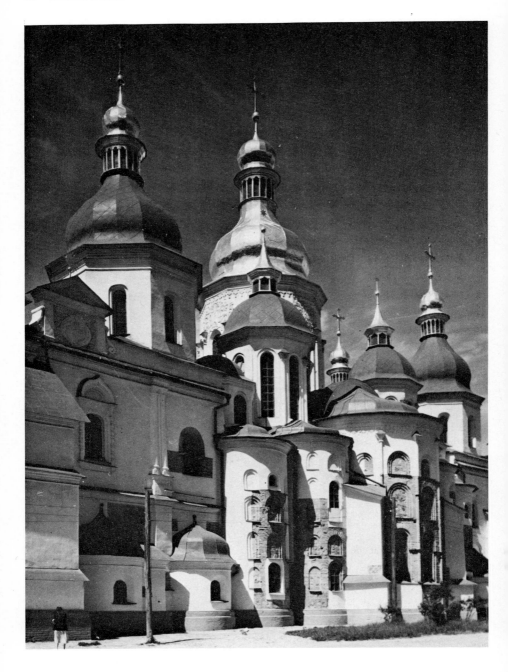

The most spectacular aspect of St Sophia, that in which it departed notably from any Byzantine prototype, was its culminating arrangement of thirteen cupolas, the number signifying Christ and His twelve Apostles. These cupolas, consisting of low domes placed on high and narrow drums, were possibly suggested by a Russian precedent, worked out in a material unfamiliar to Byzantine architects. In 991 Vladimir, after imposing Christianity on the citizens of Novgorod, had founded there the Cathedral of St Sophia (pages 39–43). This wooden church was destroyed by fire in 1045, but it was conspicuous during its brief existence and in the memory of the chroniclers for its thirteen 'tops' (vierkhi). Whether these were roofs, gables, spires, or, as would seem quite unlikely, wooden cupolas, is not clear.[12] But these thirteen crowning elements may have suggested to Yaroslav, who had been Prince of Novgorod before reigning in Kiev, the possibility of surpassing the fine new masonry domes which may have been building above his father's Desyatinnaya, just as the masons were called to his new church.

If the picturesque pyramidal outline of St Sophia can be related to the silhouette of its wooden predecessor in Novgorod, the church to that extent may be taken as a specifically Russian departure from Byzantine principles, and so to mark the beginning of a native tradition in masonry construction. But the plan and organization of space upon which this silhouette was based are more difficult to explain. The primary core of the church – a cross in plan formed by the intersection of three bays of the nave with the bays to the north and south of the space beneath the central dome – was undeniably related to Byzantine tradition. A line might be traced from St

Sophia through such Constantinopolitan structures as the north church of the Fenari-Isa Čami or Djami (the Church of Constantine Lips)[13] of about 930 [5], to the conjectural

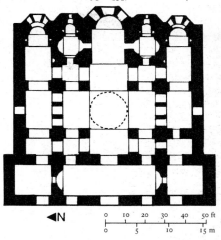

plan of the Nea Ekklesia (881). The somewhat similar plans of the sixth-century church at Meiafarquin in Mesopotamia and the eleventh-century church of Mokvi in the Caucasus [6] may indicate the presence among

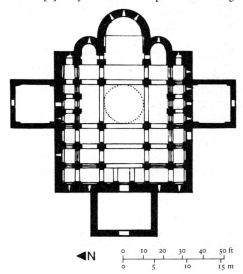

4 (*opposite*). Kiev, Cathedral of St Sophia, *c.* 1018–37, east façade

5 (*above right*). Constantinople, Fenari-Isa Čami or Djami, *c.* 930, plan

6 (*below right*). Mokvi, church, eleventh century, plan

the builders of St Sophia of Greek or even Russian masons familiar with eastern Byzantine architecture.[14] It is worth recalling that although the chronicle specifically states that Vladimir 'sent and imported artisans from Greece' for the Desyatinnaya, there is no mention of Yaroslav having done so. Possibly, therefore, the gangs working on St Sophia included some of the Greek artisans come to Kiev twenty years before, just as they must have numbered among them local craftsmen trained in the shops of the Desyatinnaya.

To predicate a sole source for St Sophia in Asia Minor or the Caucasus would be to build too much upon a few and infrequent resemblances which may have been due as much to chance as to choice, as well as to ignore what must have been the intention of Yaroslav and his contemporaries to recapture if not to surpass the grandeur of Constantinople. In their acceptance of Greek Christianity, in the names of their buildings, and in their dynastic affiliations the Kievan princes, and following them the people, were looking not eastward towards the outposts of the Empire, but towards the city on the Bosphorus whence came their conception of religious and secular culture. And this culture they knew either by personal experience or by frequent contact with travellers, priests, and artisans. To insist on the many similarities between Kievan art and architecture of the tenth and eleventh centuries with other provincial centres is to burden the historical process with too many coincidences. The admittedly inexplicable relationships among the plans, structure, and ornamental details of the early churches of Kiev and the later churches of Suzdalia and those of Georgia, Armenia, and Bulgaria, may best be accounted for by the fact that even in a stylistic environment so extensive and authoritarian as Byzantium and its dependencies, local deviations would not only occur, but would be transmitted by itinerant artisans from one region to another. The fact that among the workmen imported to erect St Sophia there may have

been some who were familiar with Transcaucasian architecture does not make the monument any the less Byzantine. It may perhaps be described by a musical analogy: as a variation, in a provincial key and not without minor eastern harmonies, on a major Byzantine theme.

Within and without, the building was an evocation of Greece. The high crossing under the central dome resembled a courtyard surrounded by a two-storeyed portico whence the space passed through the nave and tribunes into the outer arcades. On the exterior the majestic breadth of the structure, surrounded by open galleries crowned by broad terraces, must have seemed to Yaroslav and his courtiers fair to rival the palaces of Tsargrad ('the Emperor's City'), as the Russians called Constantinople. Yet in the absence of conclusive documentary or pictorial evidence we can only surmise what may have been the original appearance of the huge church, set at the head of a broad square and flanked by the princely and episcopal palaces. Hilarion must have spoken truly when he declared that St Sophia was 'wondrous and glorious to all adjacent countries, and another like it will not be found in all the land of the North from east to west.'

The interior of St Sophia presented a similar departure from, as in other respects it was a more faithful reflexion of, Byzantine models [7]. The many large piers, more massive than in Greece, tended to break up the interior space into numerous small compartments and to accentuate the vertical proportions. The interior was higher and narrower than its Byzantine prototypes, possibly owing to the necessity of providing adequate supports for the thirteen domes. Although the total enclosed space was actually only a third that of Hagia Sophia in Constantinople, the interior may not have originally been so dark when the galleries on the sides were open. Important for subsequent architectural development was the treatment of the external walls with rows of blind recessed windows divided by colonnettes

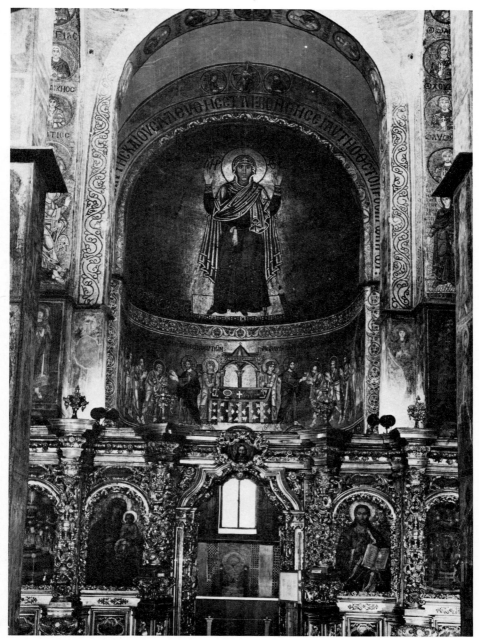

7. Kiev, Cathedral of St Sophia, *c.* 1018–37, interior

or pilasters, but the tiled roof laid directly on the vaults in the Byzantine manner, a device suitable for a warm, dry climate, was soon discovered to be disastrous in the damp Russian weather. The rhythmical effect produced by the multiplication of semicircular elements, in the windows, on the walls and drums, in the arches of the arcades, and in the undulating juncture of roof with walls, became characteristic for later architecture in the north and north-east.

By 1100 St Sophia had achieved its definitive form. The construction of the outer galleries in *opus mixtum* indicates that they were completed before the end of the eleventh century. Also, the upper walls apparently threatened to collapse after the domes had been set in place. To offset this danger, six large quarter-circular buttresses were set at right angles to the walls. Since they interrupt the frescoes in the galleries, it is obvious that they were erected after the church had been decorated, probably early in the twelfth century.

More grandiose than the Desyatinnaya or the contemporary Cathedral of the Transfiguration at Chernigov, the pyramidal mass of St Sophia, with its thirteen domes and glittering polychromatic fabric, became the first great symbolic expression in Russian architecture. Even as it proclaimed the spiritual authority of the Metropolitan of Kiev, and the magnificence of the princely court declaring its attachment to the conception of secular splendour learned in Byzantium, it established a new architectural silhouette which would become implicit in subsequent Russian church buildings, however far they might appear to depart from the original Byzantine model.

Even in ruins, in the hands of the enemy, neglected by its clergy and forgotten by its own people, the church impressed the traveller with its monumental scale. At the end of the sixteenth century a German visitor, Heidenstein, secretary to Sigismund III, King of Poland, admired the western portico then still preserved with its columns of porphyry, marble, and alabaster.[15] To a seventeenth-

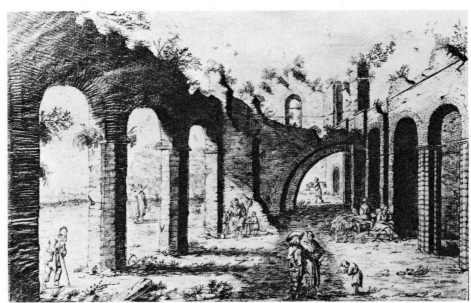

8. Kiev, Cathedral of St Sophia, the outer south gallery in 1651. From a drawing by A. van Westerveldt

century Dutch artist, Abraham van Westerveldt, is due the credit for revealing through his meticulous drawings how well they built who first successfully on Russian soil erected a structure of truly imperial monumentality.[16] Among van Westerveldt's drawings two are of particular interest. One shows the western façade, which was still in ruins, although the eastern end of the church, which was in better condition, had already been restored by Peter Mogila. The interior of a frescoed baptistery, added in the twelfth century, can be seen beside the later south-western stair tower. In another drawing the point of view is taken from the east looking westward down the outer south aisle [8]. The buttresses inserted to support the vaults are conspicuous.

The Desyatinnaya and St Sophia, with the destroyed churches of St George and St Irene,[17] formed an important group of multiple-aisled churches in southern Russia. The continuous pressure on Kiev by the barbarians from the East interrupted the construction of such buildings. Under the circumstances it was perhaps inevitable that a simpler plan and less elaborate structural system should have been evolved to meet the changing requirements of church building. A first indication of the new type appeared in the Cathedral of the Transfiguration (Spaso-Preobrazhensky Sobor) in Chernigov [9], founded about 1017 by Mstislav of Tmutarakan, Prince of Chernigov and younger brother of Yaroslav, with whom he had disputed the Kievan succession. At the

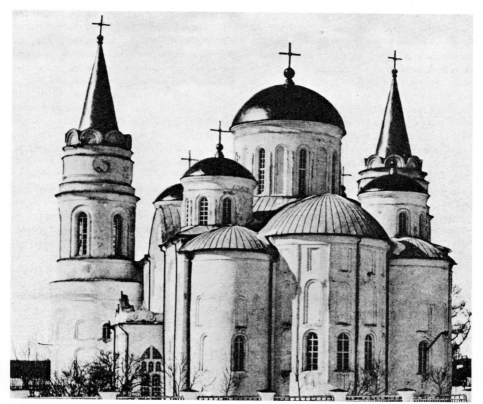

9. Chernigov, Cathedral of the Transfiguration, founded *c.* 1017, view from the east

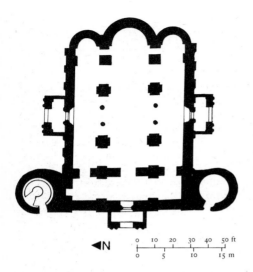

10 (*left*) and 11 (*right*). Chernigov,
Cathedral of the Transfiguration, founded *c.* 1017,
plan and interior

extra bay to the east. One can, as in the Desyatinnaya and St Sophia, but with even more assurance, predicate an eastern influence. The plan of the ruined ninth-century church at Dere Agzi in south-western Asia Minor, with its unmistakable reminiscences of Justinian design, resembles Chernigov, especially in the pairs of columns flanking the central space below the dome.[19] And the transmission of influences to Chernigov from Asia Minor is not improbable, since Tmutarakan, Mstislav's appanage, at the entrance to the Sea of Azov into which flows the Don, had long been a port of entry for trade between the East and Kievan Russia. The Cathedral of Chernigov also suffered severely in the troubled times from the end of the eleventh century, and was even more drastically rebuilt in the seventeenth century, restored in the nineteenth, and finally all but destroyed in the Second World War.

Like the Desyatinnaya, the Chernigov Transfiguration was richly decorated with marbles and frescoes, of which few traces are left. Perhaps of more significance was the treatment of the exterior walls with a series of blind arches, decoratively placed to accentuate the grouping of the various elements rather than as an expression of the structure. From many points of view the church stands as an intermediary between the Desyatinnaya and St Sophia, and between the latter and its provincial variants in the next century. In some respects, notably in the disposition of the central piers, the high space below the central dome, the columns supporting the tribune on the north and south sides of the crossing, and the external arcades, we can trace the older Byzantine tradition. In others, such as the reduction in depth of the apses and the relatively unencumbered space of the nave and aisles recalling the longitudinal distribution of earlier basilican plans, we see in Chernigov the beginning of the line of development which leads

time of Mstislav's death in 1034 (or 1036) the church, built of thin bricks laid in thick mortar according to Kievan practice, had risen 'to a point higher than a man could reach with his hand'.[18] Yaroslav then completed his brother's work, adding a decorative enrichment second only to his own church in Kiev. The plan represents a stage intermediary between the Desyatinnaya and St Irene. The same system of five domes over a nave and aisles where the four piers support the central dome defines the Greek cross both externally and in plan [10]. The presence at the crossing of columns rather than piers as supports for the gallery above the nave is another echo of Greek practice [11]. Such columns, which are found in the Novgorod as well as the Kievan St Sophia, disappear after the eleventh century. There are also indications that, like St Sophia and the Desyatinnaya, it may have had open arcades on the north and south sides. Indeed, here the specifically Russian rectangular plan was more prominent than in any of the contemporary churches of Kiev. The compromise is subtle; the length of the basilica is incorporated within the compact centrality of the domed cross by the addition of a narrow

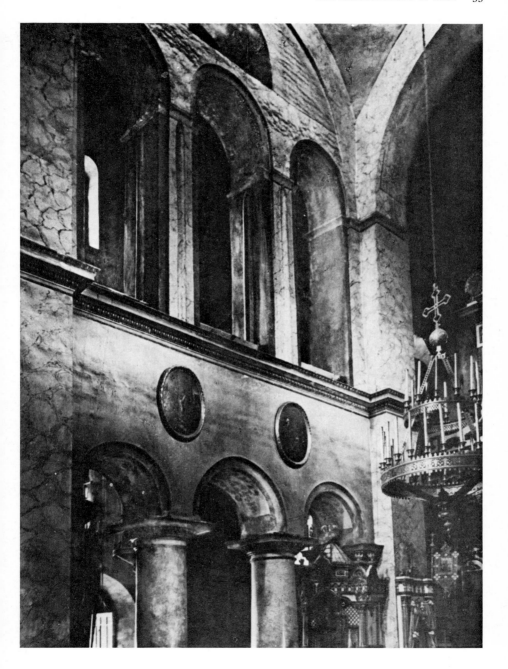

to the simpler churches of northern Russia in later centuries.

In Kiev itself the Cathedral of the Dormition in the Monastery of the Caves (Pecherskaya Lavra) high above the river to the south of the city was begun by St Theodosius, the second abbot, in 1073.[20] This first and most famous monastic establishment in Russia, where the monks lived in caves dug out of the clay banks along the Dnieper, had prospered to such an extent that buildings above ground were required. The cathedral, finished in 1078 and decorated by 1089, was damaged by fire in 1484 and 1718, reconstructed and redecorated in the baroque manner later in the eighteenth century, and destroyed in the Second World War. As with St Sophia, only the eastern façade, in the distribution and proportion of the apses, provided any clue to its original appearance. The simplified plan resembled Chernigov, with the addition of aisles in the eighteenth century. Originally the church had only one dome over the crossing, supported on four masonry piers, an arrangement which soon became customary for church architecture. According to the Lavra chronicles the interior was decorated, beginning in 1083, by artists from Constantinople, but the original mosaics and frescoes were destroyed in the Middle Ages. The interesting remains of a mosaic workshop, discovered in 1951 in the monastery grounds, may now be seen in the Historical Museum. The original core of the tiny Church of the Trinity (1106–8), above the principal gate to the monastery, can still be detected beneath its baroque exterior. The frescoes within of 1734 are interesting examples of an uneasy compromise between eastern iconography and western stylistic devices (see below, Chapter 18). Not far from the Lavra are the remains, amounting to a third of the original structure, of the Church of the Redeemer in the Birch Wood (Spas na Berestovo), built by Vladimir Monomakh about 1100 as a burial church for his dynasty. The well-preserved brickwork of the lower walls is an excellent example of the Russian adaptation of Greek technique.[21]

The church of the Yeletsky Monastery near Chernigov, again with a modern exterior, St Basil at Ovruch, restored in 1908, and in Kiev the Michael church in the monastery of St Michael with the Golden Roofs (so called because of its seven gilded domes), founded before 1051 but demolished in 1935, represented progressive modifications and simplifications of the multiple plan and complex massing of the Desyatinnaya and St Sophia, working towards the definitive simplified form of a cubical mass surmounted by a central cupola supported internally by pendentives on four central piers.[22] The exterior walls were frequently ornamented with arches on pilasters. Although such pilasters, or more rarely colonnettes, were placed opposite the thrust of the vaults within, their purpose was decorative rather than structural, because they were too slender to serve as effective buttresses. All these churches have been so much reworked externally that the treatment of the roof and domes must remain in doubt. But if we deduce a progression from the typical Byzantine domes of the tenth century to the twelfth- and thirteenth-century churches of Vladimir-Suzdal, where the domes and cupolas are in a better state of preservation, it would seem that the Kievan architects worked from the Byzantine flattened saucer dome on a low drum towards the slender high drum and helmet dome of the typical Russian church of the later Middle Ages.

Since Vladimir's and Yaroslav's churches were designed to make Kiev a brilliant city reminiscent of Constantinople, secular architecture of comparable dignity must have been required. In the tenth century the chronicles mention two palaces, one 'in the city', which is to say inside the citadel, and another called 'the castle with the hall' outside the walls.[23] The Desyatinnaya was probably a palace church; excavations have revealed two long masonry halls near it. Similarly, a princely and an episcopal residence were built beside St Sophia. But all these structures vanished long ago, so that it is difficult to hazard even a conjecture about their appearance. Nevertheless, such masonry buildings would have accounted for only a small fraction of the total architecture of Kiev and other princely cities. Wood, for the working of which a sophisticated technology seems already to have been in existence, was the principal structural material, and was to remain so for centuries to come. Unfortunately all traces of the earliest wooden architecture of Kiev, which would have included all but a few of some four hundred churches remarked in the early eleventh century by a German historian, Dietmar of Merseburg, disappeared in the fires which so frequently ravaged the ancient cities of Russia.[24]

CHAPTER 3

THE ARCHITECTURE OF NOVGOROD AND PSKOV

990–1500

At the northern terminus of the 'road between the Varangians and the Greeks', extending along both banks of the river Volkhov four miles below Lake Ilmen, was the city of Novgorod ('New Town'). In spite of its name this was a most ancient settlement which by the tenth century had already become an important centre for trade and the defence of the waterway. Although Novgorod was to remain independent long after Kiev had fallen to the Tartars, its prestige and power depended less on its cultural and ecclesiastical position than on its commercial relations, especially with the territories to the north and west of Russia. The townspeople not only took part in the annual collection of staple goods, furs, honey, and wax, for transportation to the south, but also maintained relations with Scandinavia and Germany through the continuation of the waterway along the Volkhov to Lake Ladoga and so down the Neva to the Gulf of Finland. To the south-west the citizens of the younger city of Pskov at the head of Lake Peipus were no less busy. From Pskov it was only a short journey overland to the Gulf of Riga, and so by water to the countries bordering the Baltic. In this way the merchants of Novgorod and Pskov early came in contact with western culture, especially through their relations with German traders. By the middle of the twelfth century direct commerce with Bremen and Cologne was established, and in 1195 a commercial treaty was concluded between Novgorod and the Germans, Gotlanders, and 'every Latin (Roman Catholic) nation'.[1] In the city itself the district on the right bank of the river where the foreign merchants had their own shops, houses, and churches became known as the Commercial Quarter (Torgovaya

Storona). Travelling along the inland waterways to the north and east, Novgorod traders subdued the Finnish tribes of the forest lands, and by the twelfth century may have penetrated as far as the Urals and beyond. Much later the members of a merchant family of Novgorod, the Stroganovs, were instrumental in effecting the discovery and exploitation of Siberia in the sixteenth and early seventeenth centuries.

Such a culture, where the success or failure of the individual depended on his own exertions quite as much as on his membership in a class or group, led very early to a separatist attitude which found expression in one of the first democratic political organizations in ancient Russia. As early as the mid eleventh century Yaroslav the Wise, who had been Prince of Novgorod before gaining Kiev, granted the city a charter, the first obtained by any Russian town. The princely rule of succession, whereby Kiev went to the eldest or most powerful of the family with Novgorod granted as an appanage to his eldest son, produced such a constant change of governments that the citizens soon were accustomed to take matters into their own hands. Their will was expressed through a general town-meeting or common council, called the veche, known in the history of other Russian cities, but nowhere attaining such continuous and effective influence in municipal affairs as in Novgorod. From the decisions of the veche the princes and posadniks, whose office corresponded to that of mayor, demurred at their own risk. Even in spiritual affairs the citizens of Novgorod frequently took matters into their own hands. As early as 1156 the chronicle records that when Bishop Nifont died, 'the whole town of people gathered together, and decided to appoint as bishop for themselves Arkady, a man chosen of God'. The Metropolitan of Kiev later confirmed him but henceforward his assent was taken for granted for candidates elected by the people.

Novgorod was the only important city of Russia which escaped destruction by the Tartars, who were deterred from taking it by the flooded marshes during the unusually wet spring of 1238. It was also brilliantly defended by its famous prince, Alexander Nevsky, whose title, 'of the river Neva', was bestowed for his defeat of the Swedes on the Neva in 1236. Alexander matched such military victories as this and his rout of the German Knights on Lake Peipus in 1242 with his skilful bargains with the Tartars, to whose court at Batu he had to journey no less than four times. As a result of its geographical good fortune and political astuteness, Novgorod was unmolested through the thirteenth and fourteenth centuries. Long experience in compromise gained in commercial transactions with traders from abroad stood her in good stead. In return for actual independence, the city acknowledged the nominal overlordship of the Tartars and through long years regularly paid tribute.

Rich, independent, and proud, Novgorod took to herself the style and title of 'Lord Novgorod the Great' and defied her enemies with the ringing challenge 'Who can stand against God and Great Novgorod?' Such boasts are dangerous; they arouse antagonism, especially when the spirit in which they are expressed seems so intractable. The end of Novgorod's long independence came in 1475, when Ivan III, determined to bring the city and its vast north-eastern possessions under the control of Muscovy, revoked the ancient charter and removed many of the leading families to Moscow. Even the great bell which in old days had been rung to summon the veche was carried off to the Kremlin. A century later the last embers of its pride were extinguished when Ivan IV, 'the Terrible', took the city in 1570 and destroyed its com-

mercial significance with the fearful execution of some 60,000 citizens.

The architecture of Novgorod in the first period of its history derived from Kiev, and is to be understood as a provincial variant of the Kievo–Byzantine style.[2] But from the first certain factors appeared in the activity of the Novgorod builders which were constant throughout its artistic history. The historical continuity of Novgorod itself was of the first importance. Until the rise of Moscow after 1400 Novgorod remained the only great free city in Russia, maintaining constant contacts with the West through the important German trading establishments, and acting as a centre for the continuous importation and diffusion of art and influences from Constantinople. The fourteenth century, which for the rest of Russia was a period of doubt and confusion, saw the emergence at Novgorod of a style of architecture distinct in plan and structure and the development of important schools of icon and fresco-painting, at times under the direction of masters come from Greece, at others the work of local artists. Until quite recently the reputation of Novgorod, in the absence of adequate information about the history of Kiev, Vladimir-Suzdal, and Moscow, was so great that attribution to the 'Novgorod School' was sufficient to indicate work of the highest quality in painting and the minor arts. Alone of the ancient cities Novgorod had retained its complement of early medieval churches which lent it an architectural prestige, certainly in excess and somewhat to the disadvantage of other centres.

For the extent and quality of this activity the republican mercantile character of the city's traditions and institutions were in large measure responsible. The wealthier citizens, members of a powerful middle class, had not their like elsewhere in medieval Russia as patrons of art and were the primary instigators of the city's tremendous architectural activity. In one century alone, from 1103 to 1207, the chronicles record the construction of no fewer than sixty-eight churches. For forty-one the names of the founders are preserved; fifteen were the work of private individuals or groups of merchants, while sixteen were built by the Archbishops of Novgorod. In contrast to Kiev and Suzdalia, where almost all church construction was initiated by the Prince, only ten churches in this century were so constructed, and the decline in princely power is shown by the fact that of these, six were built in the first thirty-two years, from 1103 to 1135, but only four in the remaining seventy-three.[3]

This volume of building provided unexampled opportunities for change and experiment. Unlike the princely or ecclesiastical authorities, private patrons were less inclined to follow traditional types, and since as merchants they came frequently into contact with foreign traders visiting or resident in Novgorod, they and their architects would more readily accept ideas not encountered in strictly local and inherited traditions. Quite as much as by the climate which required steep roofs for the speedy removal of accumulated snow and ice, the vertical, gabled character of later Novgorod architecture can be explained by influences reaching northern Russia from Germany, particularly from the cities of the Hanseatic League. It is certainly significant that on four occasions between 1115 and 1207 churches were erected in Novgorod by 'foreign merchants'. Although they disappeared long ago, they were designed for the services of the Latin rite and undoubtedly incorporated western Romanesque elements, whatever the material of which they were constructed.

It is necessary also to recall that the men of Novgorod had long been noted for their carpentry, and that wooden churches stood side by side with those of brick and stone. The chronicles more often than not are silent about the material of which a given church was constructed; during the twelfth century only four wooden churches are mentioned, while nine were said to be of stone. But the frequent total destruction of large numbers of churches by fire is an indication that many more were built of wood. The presence of so much construc-

tion, wherein change and experiment were immediately possible, furthered the development of the characteristic Novgorod structure in the course of the thirteenth and fourteenth centuries.

Another and most considerable factor, which must be remembered in evaluating the character of this style, was the rapidity with which churches were erected in Russia. To be sure, they were never very large; only the two Cathedrals of St Sophia approach the dimensions of the great buildings of western Europe, and even they, it is worth noting, were substantially completed within twenty years. On the other hand, the smaller parish churches were erected very quickly. Of the forty-one built in Novgorod during the twelfth century for which the dates of foundation and of completion or consecration are preserved, the period of construction averaged three years. The shortest time recorded was seventy days, for the Church of the Annunciation built between 21 May and 25 August 1179, a masonry structure which survived to modern times.[4]

Such speed was possible only when plan, structure, and decorative effects had been standardized, and the history of Novgorod architecture is in large part the search for a progressive simplification which would permit such easy and rapid execution. Thus in the course of time the six-piered, five-domed plan of Kiev and Vladimir was abandoned in favour of four piers supporting a single central dome. Although three apses were retained throughout the twelfth century, they were most commonly all of equal height. The projection of the apses became less and less salient, until by the end of the twelfth century much of the space originally contained in the semicircular apses was incorporated within the body of the church. In the fourteenth century only one apse was customary, attaining but half the height of the eastern façade.

The technical and formal evolution of architecture in Novgorod and Pskov was hastened by a change in materials. Where Kiev clung to the familiar Byzantine methods of brick and mortar, and Vladimir-Suzdal developed a splendid architecture in white stone, Novgorod soon began to use less costly materials. In any case good stone was hard to find in northern Russia. Instead the masons set odd-sized uneven blocks in thick mortar, almost in the manner of rubble, with brick for pilasters and cornices. The whole surface was then covered with stucco and given a coat of white paint. Such coarse materials, which could be worked very quickly, have been an integral part of the Russian building tradition, even to the present day. Visual appearance was very much a part of Novgorod architecture; the rough surfaces, uneven lines, and frequent departure from the vertical lend many of the smaller churches the effect of having been moulded like potter's clay, of having been 'hand-made'. Contrast was provided by the crisp accents of the brick trim around the cornices and drums.

Wood was early and pre-eminently the most accessible and practicable material in northern Russia. So true was this that from early days the men of Novgorod were even derided by the Kievans as 'carpenters'. When Yaroslav of Novgorod reached Kiev in 1016 to dispossess his half-brother Svyatopolk, the latter's chief of staff, riding along the river bank, taunted the men of Novgorod: 'Wherefore have you come with that builder of wooden houses? You are carpenters and we shall make you build houses for us.'[5] Wood-workers they were, for they already had to their credit the 'first truly Russian church of monumental character',[6] the Cathedral of St Sophia built of oak by Vladimir's order immediately after his conversion in 988, and so contemporary with his masonry church of the Desyatinnaya in Kiev. Though the two buildings have long been destroyed (for St Sophia burned in the great fire of 1045), together they illustrate the two tendencies which were for centuries paramount in Russian ecclesiastical architecture: the southern Byzantine tradition of masonry construction, closely linked spiritually and culturally with Kiev and later with Vladimir-Suzdal and Moscow; and on the other hand the northern,

timber tradition, remote alike from prince and metropolitan, which came to represent the popular religious life, particularly after the tragic schism between patriarch and people in the seventeenth century (see below, page 216). By that time the different forms evolved from masonry and timber techniques could be taken as symbols of the separatist tendencies within the Russian Church.

Vladimir's church, probably because it was the first in the north on such a scale, immediately attracted much attention. It is described as having thirteen 'tops', but whether these were roofs, gables, or spires is not known. This first church was built under the direction of Bishop Joachim, who had been sent by Vladimir to convert the people of Novgorod. Since he must have been a Greek, and so familiar with Byzantine ecclesiastical architecture, it is tempting but futile to conjecture the appearance of this remote adaptation of Byzantine liturgical requirements to local timber tradition. Perhaps because he was unsure of the success of such a project, Joachim also erected in the same year a stone church dedicated to SS. Joachim and Anna, which may have perished with the wooden St Sophia in the fire of 1045.

The new cathedral [12], built between 1045 and 1062 by Prince Vladimir, the son of Yaroslav the Wise, was again dedicated to the Holy Wisdom, apparently to recall the great church in Constantinople rather than its only slightly elder contemporary, the church of St Sophia in Kiev.[7] Since the plan of the Novgorod cathedral [13] is a simplified version of the church in Kiev, it is probable that the Greek masters whom Vladimir called to Novgorod were among those who had recently completed the Kievan St Sophia. Parts of the fabric, of local grey-yellow stone alternating with courses of brick, are more typically Byzantine than others where irregular stones project from the mortar, recalling the prismatic effect of medieval gem setting. Before the exterior was stuccoed in 1151 it must have had some of the polychromatic play of light and shade seen in

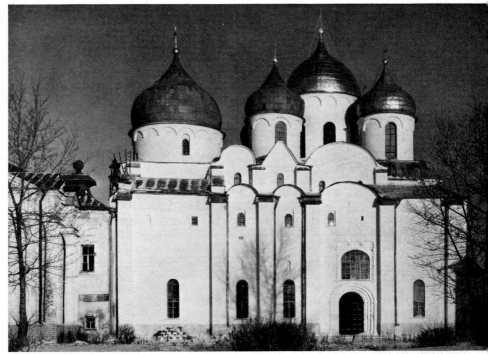

12 and 13. Novgorod, Cathedral of St Sophia,
1045–62, south façade and plan

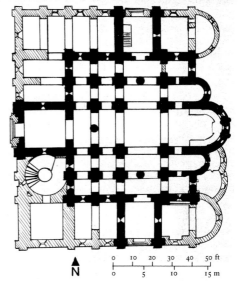

the Kievan churches. More important than the
general resemblance to St Sophia in Kiev are
the divergences from Byzantine practice which
prepare the way for the development of North
Russian architecture. The Novgorod church
has double aisles but only three apses, each
outer aisle ending in a straight wall.[8] Internally
the greater bulk of the stone piers, cross-
shaped in plan, divides the interior into even
smaller cells than in Kiev, and contributes to
the more insistent verticality which became
characteristic of Novgorod interiors. It is important to observe that there is still the broad
space beneath the central dome [14]; one bay
opens out in each direction to form an equilateral cross-shaped space separated now –
there had been two at Kiev and Chernigov –

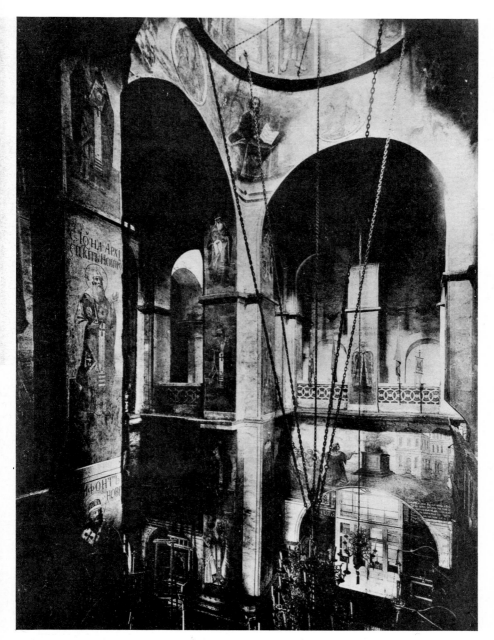

14. Novgorod, Cathedral of St Sophia, 1045-62, interior

by but one column from the adjacent bays of the nave and aisles. St Sophia in Novgorod still preserved, however far in the northern forest, something of the majestic Hellenic space of Byzantine architecture. The two-storeyed galleries to the north and south (including the south-west stair-tower) seem to have been added later in the eleventh or twelfth centuries to the original five-aisled structure, in emulation of the outer galleries which had risen beside the church in Kiev. Here, too, the result was the accentuation of the breadth of the church at the expense of its length. With the addition of the bishop's palace, Novgorod gained the nucleus of the court-church complex familiar at Kiev.

Externally the church differed most from its southern prototype. There were only five main domes with a sixth over the stair-tower, although in this city we might have expected some influence from its wooden predecessor's thirteen 'tops'. Throughout the structure the tendency towards multiplicity of parts to be seen in Kiev was replaced by a desire for unity, even uniformity. This led to the elimination of much ornament, including the shallow niches on the apses characteristic of Kiev. The equal height of the three apses which reach to the cornice, the smooth wall surfaces of the façades, and the shallow, flat pilasters contribute to this unity. Though the church retained the Byzantine rhythmical roof-line, since the roof was laid directly on the vaults, the height, the narrower windows, and the arched bands on the drums told of other than Greek influences. The latter details and the presence over the galleries above the outer aisles of quadrant vaults as buttresses for the pair of domes over each inner aisle, in the manner of French Romanesque architecture of the eleventh century, suggest that in Novgorod there were builders familiar with contemporary western European practice.[9] The greater verticality and the smaller windows, which affect the external appearance and distribute more concentrated light and shade within, may have been influenced by the existing tradition

of wood construction and the colder, damper climate.

To the climate may also be due the rapid development in northern Russia of the characteristic bulbous or onion dome. Whereas the cupolas of Kiev, and later of Vladimir-Suzdal, represented only a slight modification of the flat Byzantine dome towards the helmet-shaped type, in Novgorod as early as the mid twelfth century the dome had become higher, with apex drawn upward and slightly bulging sides. Since the presence of the bulbous dome in northern Russia antedates the Tartar occupation, its origin is not easily explained as an influence from Islamic architecture.[10] Indeed, the appearance in many widely separated regions, in the Near and Middle East, in Persia and India, of bulbous domes and of the sharply pointed ogee arch, which may be considered the section of such a dome, precludes the assumption that any single source was the model for the use of this particular form in eastern Europe. Since even masonry domes were probably evolved from earlier wooden prototypes, it is not impossible that the bulbous dome also developed more quickly in a carpentry culture, and the reasons for its appearance can be considered as much technological as aesthetic. Thus it has been suggested that the bulbous dome was an attempt to solve the problem of disposing of the heavy burden of winter snow and ice, and of rainwater during the spring thaws, which could quickly damage the external vaults. If this is so, the facility with which the design of the dome was solved in northern Russia may have been due to the carpentry tradition of Novgorod. While southern Russia clung to the masonry dome on a low drum, Novgorod worked more readily with a tall wooden superstructure. Although frequently restored, the central twelfth-century cupola of St Sophia represents an interesting intermediate stage between the flat Byzantine saucers which may have been used in Kiev and the later bulbous domes of the north. It is taller, and although the sides have not begun to bulge, the apex has been drawn out. The side domes, replaced at a later date, are typical fifteenth- and sixteenth-century bulbous domes.

Although St Sophia remained for long the largest and the only double-aisled church in this region, it had little influence on subsequent architecture in Novgorod. But its beauty was inseparably associated with the intransigent pride of the people. It became the symbol of civic power and independence, even as St Sophia of Kiev became symbolic of the spiritual authority of the early Russian church. 'Where St Sophia is, there is Novgorod,'

declared Prince Mstislav in 1215, when the Tartars had already threatened the independence of Russia.

The first churches to be built in Novgorod after the turn of the century resemble St Sophia in the general tendency towards simplicity, unity, and verticality. Three in particular exhibit these aspects: the Church of St Nicholas the Wonder-Worker (1113), erected by Mstislav I in the courtyard of his palace, the Nativity of the Virgin (1117) in the St Anthony Monastery, and St George (1119–30), founded by Prince Vsevolod in the Yuriev

15. Novgorod, Cathedral of St George in the Yuriev (George) Monastery, 1119–30

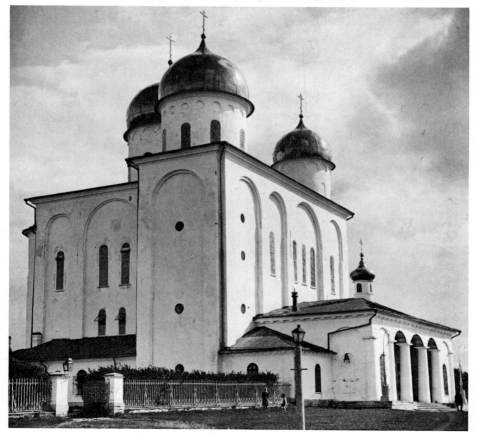

(George) Monastery, two miles south of the city on the left bank of the Volkhov [15] (the porch and all other subsidiary structures were removed in 1933–5). The plan of each church shows the swift contraction of the multiple naves of the two St Sophias into a simpler type, with nave and aisles, six piers, three apses, and a tall cupola over the crossing [16].

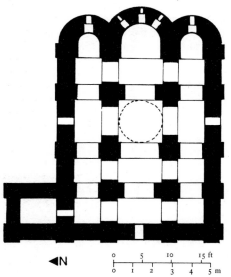

◀N   0 5 10 15 ft
     0 1 2 3 4 5 m

16. Novgorod, Cathedral of St George in the Yuriev (George) Monastery, 1119–30, plan

The impressive size and mass of St Nicholas have sometimes been traced to the continuing prestige, even in northern Russia, of the other great eleventh-century Kievan church, the Dormition in the Pecherskaya Lavra. It is noteworthy that St Nicholas originally had a full complement of five domes. Only the central one survives, but the bases of the others are preserved beneath the present pitched roof. In the latter two churches the addition of two smaller cupolas over the western façade creates an unusually picturesque asymmetrical composition. In each the three apses are carried the full height of the structure, the walls are divided into four panels by pilasters which

correspond to the position of the piers within the church, and the drums of the domes are decorated with an arched band.[11] The tendency at Novgorod towards unity and uniformity culminated at St George in the powerful massing of the apses, the clear articulation of the façades, vertically by arches supported on pilasters and horizontally by the division of the walls with alternate rows of windows and niches, and the emphasis given the north-western corner by the stair-tower treated externally as a continuation of the tall western façade.

The name of the builder of St George has been preserved. Since the chronicle mentions him simply as 'Master Peter', without further qualification, it would seem logical to think that in him we encounter the first truly native Russian architect.[12] And since the Nativity of the Virgin so closely resembles St George, it is tempting to think of it as an earlier work of Master Peter. Pushing conjecture one step further, the Byzantine apsidal treatment of St Nicholas, again only a few years earlier than the Church of the Nativity, hints that possibly as a pupil of the Greek masters working on St Sophia he may have built St Nicholas for Mstislav as his first work.

The insistent height of these three churches, in contrast to the still lingering traces of Byzantine breadth in St Sophia, gives them a cubical appearance. Here begins perhaps the most notable difference between Russian architecture and contemporary building in western Europe. Russian church architecture moved from elaboration towards simplification, from articulation of the separate elements, such as nave and aisles and choir, towards the gradual inclusion of these elements in a single mass until even the triple apses were almost submerged within the thick eastern wall. There was also a diminution in size, from St Sophia of Kiev to the smaller churches of the Kievan monasteries, and from St Sophia of Novgorod to the smaller churches of the Novgorod-Pskov region, until by the end of the fourteenth century the type was fixed. Again one observes as a constituent factor in Russian art the desire for conformity rather than diversity, the embracing symbol rather than the individual expression.

In the twelfth-century churches of Novgorod the growth of this type is seen in the gradual elimination of external decoration, in the broader wall spaces, unbroken save for a few small windows, and in the division of the north and south walls by shallow pilasters descending from arches which express on the external walls the internal division of the church by piers and vaults. Throughout the twelfth century the vaults, and consequently the arches of the external arcade, remained at the same or almost the same height, so that originally the churches of Novgorod resembled the smaller churches of Kiev and Vladimir-Suzdal. Apparently the roofs originally rested directly on the vaults, and so followed the arched curves of the cornice. The tendency of such a roof to collect snow and water caused the reconstruction of the roofs and frequently of the upper parts of the walls in later times, so that it is now difficult to judge their original appearance. Certainly the arched roofs would have mitigated the monotonous cubical appearance where the vaults have been replaced by a gabled roof unrelated to the structure as a whole (as in illustration 18).

An interesting attempt to recover the original appearance of these buildings was formerly to be seen in the restored Church of the Saviour at Nereditsa (Spas-Nereditsa) near Novgorod [17], erected by Yaroslav Vladimirovich in 1198 in the princely monastery not

17. Nereditsa, near Novgorod, Church of the Saviour, 1198, restored in 1904, destroyed 1941

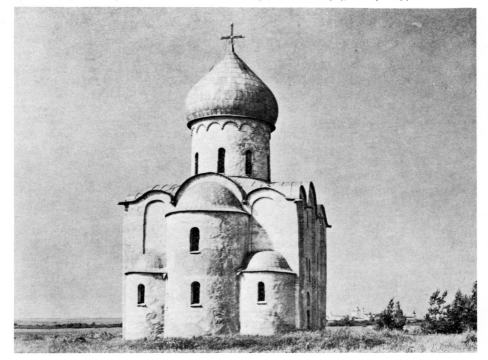

far from his new palace in the suburb of Gor-odischche, and indeed the last church founded by the princely family of Novgorod.

The restoration of 1904, which included the removal of later masonry and the substitution of an arched roof following the lines of the original walls, probably provided as authentic a picture as could be obtained of the earlier twelfth-century churches of Novgorod.[13] The total destruction of the little building in the Second World War is the more regrettable because of the loss of its complete and well-preserved painted interior (see below, pages 83–6).

Although the pre-eminence of the Byzantine manner was asserted as late as 1198 at Nereditsa, other parish churches of the twelfth century had already departed considerably from the tradition of St Sophia, still so much a part of such structures as St George in the Yuriev Monastery. These deviations from the Byzantine prototypes were perhaps in each instance minor, but taken together they make up a totality of change and experiment which led to the formation of the distinctive Novgorod type in the fourteenth century. The progressive simplification of the plan and the use of four piers instead of six affected the façades. The division of the walls by pilasters tended to follow the actual distribution of the space internally, so that the wall was divided into three unequal panels. The central one, which corresponded to the crossing, was the widest; the eastern, with the gradual reduction of the depth of the apse so that much of the altar-space was included within the church, the narrowest. The apses were also diminished in number and size. Although there were still three as at Nereditsa, the side apses were more often but half the height of the central one.

Most important of all, in terms of structure and appearance, was the discovery of a new roof treatment. The flat exposed vaults of St Sophia and at Nereditsa were impractical when for long months of the year ice and snow accumulated on the roof. A sharper pitch was required to dispose of such a load as quickly as possible. The solution finally obtained, and then on the basis of the four-piered plan expressed externally by a triple division of the façades, was to decrease the width and height of the side aisles. In this way on each façade the central bay was flanked by two lower ones which could be included within a single triangular gable. The roof then consisted of four equal gables surmounted by the central drum and dome. The date and place of origin of this eminently logical system are unknown, but it was undoubtedly assisted by the discovery of the quadrant arch, a western European buttressing device, which had been used above the upper chambers at the end of the aisles in St Sophia, both as vaults and as buttresses for the central dome.

The oldest Novgorod church with a gabled roof is the Annunciation of 1179 on Lake Myachin. It is tempting to think that the gabled system was invented on that occasion, when the church was built in seventy days, but the later reconstruction of the vaults and roof prevents absolute certainty on this point. By 1292, the date of St Nicholas na Lipne, near Novgorod, the system was completely developed, although again the upper part of the church was spoiled by the substitution of a hipped roof for the original gables. Nevertheless, the design of St Nicholas, with a single apse, gabled roof, and severe walls relieved only by a blind arcade running immediately below the peak of the gables, indicates that throughout the thirteenth century the architects of Novgorod had constantly refined their forms. St Nicholas was severely damaged in World War II, but has been rebuilt.

The proportional relationships between the cubical body of the church and the cylindrical forms of apse and drum are so skilfully managed in Novgorod architecture that we must assume a considerable period of development, culminating in the fourteenth century in two important churches in the Commercial Quarter. These churches were in a sense the merchants' cathedrals, and rose in visible opposition to the older princely and episcopal St Sophia within the fortified Kremlin on the other side of the river. They are St Theodore Stratilates, erected in 1360–1 by a certain Natalya, the widow of a wealthy merchant Simon Andreevich, and her son, and the Transfiguration of 1374 [18].[14] As had become customary in Novgorod, each church had one apse and a single dome above a tall, gracefully proportioned drum. The Transfiguration has a modern roof, too steeply pitched but substantially following the original lines. St Theodore has been restored since 1945, the new roof following the lines of the trefoil-shaped gables. The division of the walls follows the same pattern whereby four pilasters divide the wall into three panels, topped by a trefoil arch in the centre and a trefoil halved for the side panels. Internally a certain coarsening of the structure is evident in St Theodore. The piers, which rest upon very squat columns in the manner of the churches

18. Novgorod, Cathedral of the Transfiguration, 1374

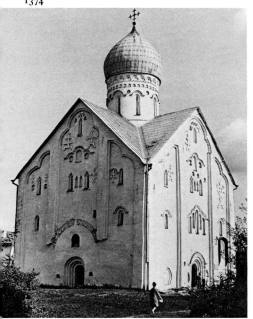

of Pskov, are joined to the lateral walls for the whole height of the building, so that the internal space develops in breadth rather than in depth, especially since a tall iconostasis was added in the sixteenth century. The Transfiguration shows greater verticality, both within and without. Except for the later cupola and small bulbous dome, it has considerably more refined proportions. In both churches the decoration of the apse by a double blind arcade, the upper containing two arches for each one in the lower, may be due to German influence, particularly strong in Novgorod in the fourteenth century. On the Transfiguration the applied ornament of devotional crosses, in addition to the customary Novgorod brickwork on the drum, speaks of the material affluence of the Novgorod merchant-patrons. This series of substantial, massive structures includes the church of SS. Peter and Paul (1367), also in the Commercial Quarter, but less majestic in its proportions.

Pskov, the 'younger brother of Novgorod', was also a free city during the earlier Middle Ages and just as jealous of its liberties, but it was less wealthy and its activities were more restricted by the pressure of its enemies, the Lithuanians to the west. Consequently Pskov failed to achieve as independent a style as did Novgorod. For all that, the technical devices of the Pskov builders were to prove of great advantage in later times, and the very conservatism of the city where much older traditions were maintained than in Novgorod led to an unexpected career for its architects at the end of the fifteenth century. By 1400 they had made practicable their most important structural invention. Instead of following the developed Byzantine system of pendentives for the support of the dome, which required a very nice knowledge of stone cutting, the Pskov architects placed arches at the corners of the crossing, above and slightly in front of the barrel vaults over the nave and transept, and upon these corbelled arches, which were sometimes doubled, they placed the drum of the dome. In this way proper height was obtained for the dome, without raising the vaulted arms of the church. The external expression of such interior corbelling may be documented as early as 1365–7, when the Cathedral of the Trinity in Pskov was rebuilt after the vaults supporting the base of the central drum and dome had collapsed. The exceptionally lively massing of the upper storeys, where an octagon buttressed by peaked and

By the fifteenth century the Pskov architects were able to place a drum and dome over a church without internal piers by throwing corbelled arches laterally across the nave. When such superimposed arches were expressed externally an elaborate and intricate decorative effect was the result. This became so popular after its appearance in the later fifteenth century that often multiple rows of arches were

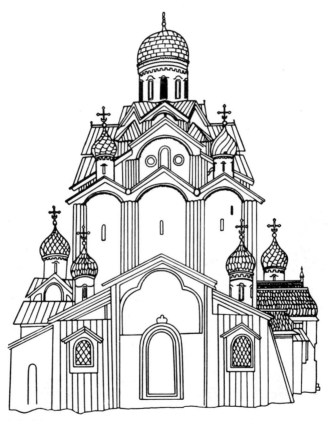

19. Pskov, Cathedral of the Trinity, 1365–7 (from a seventeenth-century drawing)

semicircular gables supports the drum, may be seen in a seventeenth-century drawing [19].[15] Although the Trinity has disappeared, the drawing clearly illustrates the derivation of these masonry forms from wooden precedents.

added for effect when they were not required for support.[16]

One of the oldest and most characteristic churches of Pskov is the Transfiguration in the Mirozhsky Monastery (1156). A four-piered church in plan, the nave and crossing were carried a storey above the adjacent bays of the aisle so that the cross was clearly expressed externally. Subsequent constructions above the western bays and at the east destroyed the original appearance which, Greek as it must have seemed, may have been due to the initiative of the founder, Bishop Nifont of Novgorod, a Greek by birth and education. From St Sophia in Novgorod may have come the suggestion for the broad arches on the façades and the low dome and drum with its blind arcade. The fundamentally conservative character of the builders of Pskov can still be seen in the Cathedral of the Nativity of the Virgin in the Snetogorsky Monastery, erected in 1310–11 as an almost identical copy of the

important capital to an active but much smaller trading centre, the forms became more primitive. Generally the proportions were stumpier, the walls thicker, the detail more rude. The typical Pskov system of corbelled arches, which came into frequent use in the fifteenth century, may be considered part of this system of grosser simplification. Yet in the simplicity and conservatism of such architecture there was much charm and a considerable future. A characteristic feature was the free and effective composition of the belfries, those several-storeyed constructions, pierced with arched openings, in which the bronze bells were fixed. With the simple directness of primitive art, they contribute much to the picturesque mass of the church [20].

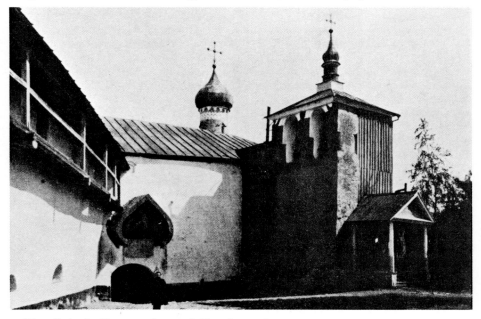

20. Pskov, Pechersky Monastery, fourteenth-fifteenth centuries

Mirozhsky church, and again more than a century later in the Church of the Holy Spirit of 1476 in the Trinity-Sergius Monastery in Zagorsk [138].

In passing from one city to another, from an

Conservatism and the remoteness of Pskov from Moscow were two valuable assets in its later history. Not until 1510 was the city obliged to recognize the suzerainty of Moscow, when Vasily III incorporated it in his dominions; and it escaped the terrible destruction Ivan IV visited upon Novgorod. Meanwhile the ingenuity of the architects of Pskov had come to the attention of Ivan III, who summoned them to Moscow in 1480 to undertake the reconstruction of the Annunciation in the Kremlin. One may think that it was not alone their cleverness which recommended them to the Great Prince, but quite as much their knowledge of the older traditions. Because Ivan III, like his predecessors before him, was intent on asserting the continuity of the princely line and the right of Moscow to take precedence over older cities, the fact that the architects of Pskov built churches very much in the old manner worked in their favour.

CHAPTER 4

THE ARCHITECTURE OF VLADIMIR-SUZDAL

1100–1240

Towards the middle of the twelfth century a third centre of architectural activity came into prominence. Derived from Kiev and not unrelated to Novgorod, and so to western influences, the constructions of the princes of Vladimir-Suzdal were a further refinement of the earlier Byzantine style leading towards the characteristic definition at Moscow in the fifteenth century. Once again, as first at Kiev and Chernigov and later at Novgorod and Pskov, local, particular, and national factors were working upon international currents to create a peculiarly Russian style.[1] The forest lands, lying between the Volga and Oka rivers, had been settled very early by Slavs from the waterways to the west who mingled with the indigenous Finnish tribes. The region, which was held as an appanage by the prince of Kiev, quickly prospered. Its cities commanded the headwaters of the Volga and so controlled the trade routes from Asia, from the Caucasus and beyond, and from Europe because Novgorod was but a short journey by portage to the west. Throughout the eleventh century the cities of Vladimir, Suzdal, and Rostov which was the seat of a bishop, increased in size and affluence.

The rapid emergence of Suzdalia as an important political and cultural centre is, like the contemporary history of Novgorod, linked to the steady economic and dynastic disintegration of the Kievan realm. Continuous nomad incursions in the south, and the consequent isolation of Russia from Constantinople, wreaked hardship on the peoples around Kiev. Seeking safety from attack, as well as security for the pursuit of a livelihood, numbers of Russians turned from trade to agriculture and ascending the river Desna from Kiev penetrated north-eastwards into the forest lands

until they reached the headwaters of the Volga. In the forest clearings they could begin farming, and the dense network of rivers and streams enabled them to maintain trade relations with both West and East. On these foundations of agriculture and commerce were laid the wealth of the cities of Suzdalia, of Suzdal itself and Rostov, the earliest settlements of pioneers from Kievan Russia in the tenth century, and of Vladimir, which became the capital after the middle of the twelfth century. South-westward from these cities, at a bend in the river Moskva, a tributary of the Oka, lay a small outpost established for the defence of the trade route. In the twelfth century it was scarcely more than a few cabins huddled upon a hill behind wooden ramparts. This was the site of the future city of Moscow.

The princes who ruled Suzdalia for a century and a quarter, from Vladimir Monomakh to the last ruling prince, Yury II, who with his army was defeated by the Tartars in 1238, were men of unusual energy, intelligence, and artistic interests. Their buildings are destroyed or too rigorously restored, barren now but once magnificent with frescoes and marbles, painted and gilded within and without, and adorned with countless gold and silver vessels, and with icons set with precious stones. Before the Mongol invasion Suzdalia rivalled Kiev in the number and splendour of its masonry structures. Only rulers of deep artistic sensibility could have created such an environment, for each church was in its own way a special foundation of the prince. They were also men of far wider culture than their heroic half-Scandinavian ancestors. Monomakh had won the reverence of all Russia for his wisdom and understanding. His grandson, Vsevolod III

Bolshoe Gnezdo (Big Nest, so-called because of his large family), probably knew more of the world than any Russian prince of his generation or of that immediately before him; as the son of a Byzantine princess, he had been educated in Tsargrad. Of his children Mikhail spoke both Latin and Greek, and Constantine founded in Vladimir a school for Greek and Latin monks which had a library of one thousand Greek texts. Suzdalia in this period of the decline of Kiev might well have surpassed the older city in the richness of its culture, had time been granted.

The churches of Suzdalia established a new direction in ancient Russian architecture. Just as the structures of the first period were dominated by the Cathedral of St Sophia, which, when transplanted to Novgorod, became the generating force there for St Nicholas, St George, and the Nativity of the Virgin, so those of Suzdalia derived from the type-church of the second Kievan building campaign, the Dormition in the Pechersky Monastery. The reasons are not hard to find. Not only was the Lavra church a newer, and consequently more immediately interesting building, but for Vladimir Monomakh, who was a boy when it was under construction, it must have stood in somewhat the same paternal relation as the Desyatinnaya had stood towards Yaroslav. And as the latter in his St Sophia realized the aspirations of his father Vladimir, so Monomakh in his churches in Suzdal and Vladimir perfected the type established during the preceding reigns by his uncle Svyatoslav and his father Vsevolod I in the Kievan Lavra.

Although nothing now remains of the buildings founded by Vladimir Monomakh, descriptions in the chronicles and a few traces uncovered in recent excavations prove their importance for the subsequent architectural history of this region. Before Monomakh here, as elsewhere in Russia, most building was in wood, and so has almost completely disappeared. Fragments of poorly preserved domestic dwellings of the eleventh and twelfth centuries seem to show that conical wooden roofs were placed over half-excavated earth foundations. Later, the artisans of Suzdal, like those of Novgorod, had a considerable reputation as wood-workers. As in Kiev, so here, in contrast to this wooden architecture, derived from older pagan practice, the Christian prince asserted the power of the new spiritual order, confirmed in his political tenure, by building new churches of fine masonry. But where the first churches of Kiev and Novgorod followed the familiar Byzantine technique of brick, cement, and tile construction, in Suzdalia there were quantities of white limestone, available locally or brought by boat up the Klyazma river to the very walls of the cities.

The close connexion between Kiev and the younger principality is explicitly recorded in the Kievan Paterik, according to which the 'God-fearing Vladimir [Monomakh] took the measurements of the Pechersky church [and] created a church exactly like it in height, breadth, and length in the city of Rostov. He also recorded on parchment [the place of] each picture of a feast-day, and repeated all this in the order and likeness of the example of the great church.'[2] The church in Rostov was thus erected after the plan and proportions of the Pechersky Dormition, and its mural paintings followed the scheme customary in Kiev. The chronicle adds that Vladimir's son, Yury I Dolgoruky (George 'Longarm'), had heard from his father of the splendid Pechersky church and in his reign built a similar church in the city of Suzdal. Although Yury at the time of the construction of the Suzdal cathedral was but a boy, and consequently the erection of both churches may be attributed to Vladimir, the chronicler's account of their relation to the Kievan model has been confirmed by recent excavations. Beneath the foundations of the present Suzdal Cathedral (1222–5) have been found the remains of the walls of Monomakh's building. It was monumental, with six internal piers, a western narthex, and gallery. The thick walls were divided by pilasters and, as the chronicle states, it was richly painted;

fragments of fresco have been found on the interior walls.[3] The technique of thin slab-shaped bricks and layers of local stone was still close to the Kievan Byzantine practice.

After Monomakh's death in 1125 there seems to have been little building activity until late in the reign of his son and successor, Yury Dolgoruky. Not until the year 1152 do the chronicles mention his church-building, which then became fairly intensive.[4] Before his death in 1157 Yury had founded at least five stone churches, of which the most important was that of SS. Boris and Gleb, in the village of Kideksha, on the river Nerl below Suzdal. In addition to the churches mentioned in the chronicles, he completed and restored the Suzdal cathedral, broadening it on the north side by the construction of the Chapel of the Redeemer, and built the Cathedral of the Trans-figuration beside the ramparts of Pereyaslavl-Zalessky, later to be finished by his son Andrey. Finally, in 1157, the Church of St George rose in his new palace in Vladimir. Of these many buildings there only survived, and then much altered, the Boris and Gleb Church in Kideksha and the Transfiguration in Pereyaslavl-Zalessky. St George in Vladimir is known only from its foundations, and St George in Yuriev-Polsky, as will be seen, was reconstructed at a later date.

To a degree the constructions of Yury, and of his son and successor Andrey, are a re-flexion in stone of the struggle between prince and boyar for control of the principality. The Church of SS. Boris and Gleb was built in the village of Kideksha, some three miles from Suzdal, within a fortified palace on the banks of the Nerl, where Yury could remain apart from the recalcitrant nobility and people of Suzdal. The Church of St George in Vladimir represented the next stage when Yury trans-ferred the seat of government from Suzdal to the smaller and less dependent city of Vladi-mir. His other churches, in Yuriev-Polsky and Pereyaslavl, were 'garrison churches' in new and strongly fortified border towns.

All these buildings were small and of the type of palace church, of which the first im-portant example was the Transfiguration na Berestovo, near Kiev, built by Vladimir Monomakh. Suzdal and its dependent towns had neither the need nor the means for structures so large or costly as the cathedrals of Kiev and Novgorod. And since the future history of Russia was in a dynastic sense to proceed rather from Vladimir than from those older cities, this type of small palace church, con-tinuing through the twelfth century in other princely centres, and ultimately receiving its final form in the churches of the Kremlin in Moscow, may be considered the culmination of the masonry church in ancient Russia.

Another element of the new Suzdalian style is the more precise definition on the exterior of the partitioning of the internal space. Al-though the architects of Russia would never attain, and apparently never desired, the rational articulation, or at least the appearance of a rational articulation, of internal and ex-ternal space so characteristic of medieval archi-tecture in the West, the important steps to-wards it taken in the buildings of Suzdal and Vladimir may indicate the presence in these regions of western builders, possibly from Galicia, where the princely churches and palaces exhibit many western details.

The two extant buildings erected by Yury demonstrate the origin of the Suzdalian type and the first step in its change from the Kievan original. In plan the partially ruined church of SS. Boris and Gleb at Kideksha (1152) was a four-piered structure with one dome and three apses. The internal piers were connected by arches to pilasters on the walls, and the divisions so created were expressed externally by the device of arches resting on pilasters, familiar from the churches in Nov-gorod. On the exterior the church suffered severely through the destruction of the original roof, dome, and upper part of the eastern bay, and the consequent reduction in size of the apses to half their original height.[5]

Yury's other extant church, the Cathedral of the Transfiguration at Pereyaslavl-Zalessky, finished by his son Andrey in 1158, is in a better state of preservation, having suffered only the replacement of the dome in the sixteenth century and the loss of the corbel table supported by colonnettes, which was visible until 1848 [21]. In plan it follows the four-piered, single-domed, three-apsed type of Kideksha. Again the internal piers are connected by arches with pilasters on the inner walls which are expressed similarly on the exterior.

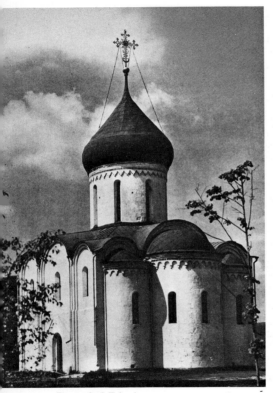

21. Pereyaslavl-Zalessky,
Cathedral of the Transfiguration, 1152–8

The apses rise the full height of the church, and with the original roof resting directly on the vaults, create a rhythmical composition of arches and semicircles which may owe its origin to Kiev but here has found a distinct

and harmonious expression. The fine white stone undoubtedly contributes to the aesthetic character of this, as of later Suzdalian churches. The different effect, in contrast to the churches of Novgorod and Pskov, may be noticed. In the latter regions the use of crude stone aggregate and brick permitted, as it encouraged, a wider variety of proportions, greater picturesqueness, and lack of standardization. The technique of stone construction whereby the nature of the material imposed a fundamental need and consequent desire for regularity gives the churches of Vladimir-Suzdal a powerful and authoritative coherence.

If the churches of Vladimir represent the transplantation to north-eastern Russia of the Kievan style of the second period, that is to say of the later eleventh century, and the churches of Yury, in so far as they have survived, stand for the first stage in the adaptation of the Kievan style to a new material and a new expressive need, that of an aristocratic ruler seeking to suppress the oligarchical and popular tendencies represented by the boyars and the veche, so the constructions of Andrey and of his younger brother Vsevolod III were the final realization of this particular combination of circumstances. Andrey, a man of violent impulse and determination, was more faithful to his Suzdalian inheritance than his father Yury, who was preternaturally disposed to look towards Kiev, where his own father had ruled. Andrey remained in Suzdalia even after his capture and sack of Kiev in 1169, appointing a deputy to rule in his stead. At home Andrey fixed his capital at Vladimir, still relatively insignificant, although fortified by Monomakh in the early twelfth century. Its secure position on the heights above the Klyazma recalled Kiev, and the resemblance was further developed by Andrey and his successors with their constructions.

Monomakh had already built one church in Vladimir, long ago destroyed, but it was the third church in stone after the cathedrals of Rostov and Suzdal to be built in this region. It was apparently a small four-piered structure, again resembling the Berestovo church, to which he owed a special devotion as the burial church of his family. In 1158, the year after his accession, Andrey commenced his time to be known as Andrey Bogoliubsky (Theophilus, 'God-fearing'). Although none of these monuments has been preserved intact, taken together they account for a noteworthy

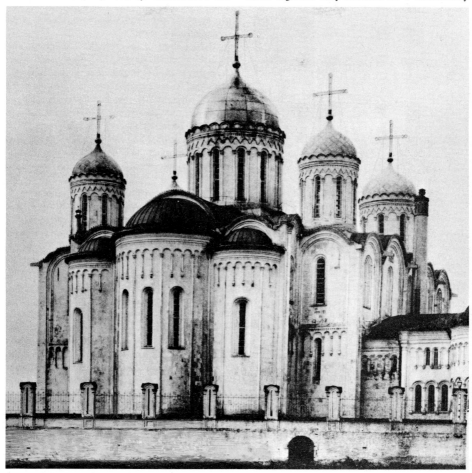

22. Vladimir, Cathedral of the Dormition, 1158–61, rebuilt 1185–9, view from the north-east

building programme with the construction of the Golden and Silver Gates and a new Cathedral of the Dormition in Vladimir and a new church and palace ten miles from Vladimir in the village of Bogoliubovo, whence he came in medieval building campaign, and in their time went far to define the Suzdalian style.

In Vladimir itself Andrey's new Cathedral of the Dormition of 1158–61 [22, 23] originally may have been closer to the tradition of Vladi-

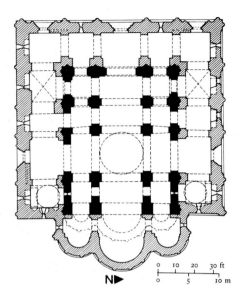

N▶ 0 10 20 30 ft
    0   5   10 m

23. Vladimir, Cathedral of the Dormition, 1158–61, rebuilt 1185–9, plan

mir Monomakh's cathedrals of Rostov and Suzdal. Like them, the plan derived from the Pechersky Dormition, with its six piers, three apses, and single dome, but in 1183 it was so seriously damaged by fire that an extensive reconstruction (1185–9) was undertaken by Andrey's brother, Vsevolod III.[6] This so changed the appearance of the building that externally and internally it must now be considered an example of late-twelfth-century architecture.[7] Fragments of the original walls indicate that it originally carried a corbel table at half the height of the walls, which were thicker below than above. Such windows as have been preserved were in the second storey and were deeply splayed. There were apparently galleries over the aisles and western bay. The exterior was adorned with reliefs, some of which were later transferred to the walls of Vsevolod's structure. Fragments of frescoes on the inner walls of the present outer aisles justify the chronicler's statement, written after Andrey's assassination in 1174, that

'just as in Bogoliubovo, so in the city of Vladimir, he had the domes gilded, and also the arches, and the corbel table, and he brightened it with stones, and the columns outside the church he also had gilded, and the arches, and round about the church gilded birds and other ornaments were set'.[8]

Before the fire of 1183 the Dormition and Andrey's palace church at Bogoliubovo must have been among the most magnificent buildings in Russia, recreating in the northern woodlands the sumptuous decorative splendour, if not the monumental scale, of the Kievan churches. Andrey certainly had some such intention, for he bestowed upon the Dormition much property, including 'a tithe of the income from trade'. It was to be his Desyatinnaya.

The only one of Andrey's buildings of which the present condition affords some conception of its original appearance is the Church of the Protection and Intercession of the Virgin (Pokrov Bogoroditsy) in the meadows above the river Nerl, near its confluence with the Klyazma [24]. It was erected in 1166, in memory of Andrey's son Izyaslav Andreevich, who had died the year before and been buried in the Dormition, but also in commemoration of a vision of the Virgin extending her veil (pokrov) over the congregation which Andrey, like his name-saint, Andrew the Fool, had experienced.[9] Like the churches at Kideksha and Pereyaslavl, it is a four-piered, three-apsed structure with a single dome. Here, however, the small size and the thickness of the exterior walls led to a progressive unification of the structural system, so that the apses appear in plan almost as if contained within the enveloping quadrilateral mass of the walls [25].

Of all the churches of ancient Russia, the Pokrov is distinguished by its fine state of preservation, and by the harmony of its proportions. In it the low Byzantine cube acquired not only height but grace, and an exquisite relationship was established between the various decorative elements, between column,

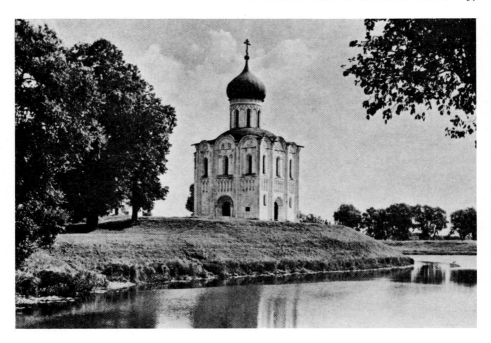

24 and 25. The Pokrov Bogoroditsy (Church of the Protection and Intercession of the Virgin) on the Nerl, near Vladimir, 1166, exterior and plan

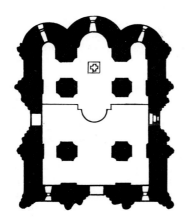

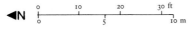

pilaster, and corbel table, between door and window, between the arches surmounting the façades and the drum and dome, between the wall surface and the carved decoration which is the oldest preserved sculptural ornament in Suzdalia.

The plan with the sharply projecting engaged columns and splayed doors and windows inserted within the thickness of the walls suggests something of the articulation of Romanesque architecture of the twelfth century, but the entrances on the north and west façades resemble such Eastern Byzantine churches as the cathedral at Ani in Armenia.[10] The Pokrov thus raises once more the issue of the relative significance at this place and time of western and eastern influences in the development of Russian architecture. Again it is important to avoid a dogmatic answer which would eliminate either influence, and so commit the history of Russian art to a one-sided development. Far as Suzdal and Vladimir may seem from present-day centres of European culture, it is well to remember that men and ideas in the Middle Ages travelled with greater ease and frequency than we are often ready to admit. Evidence of this constant interchange is provided by the statement in the chronicles that God brought to Andrey masters 'from all countries'. There was even a tradition in a chronicle now lost that Frederick Barbarossa had sent architects from Germany to Andrey in Suzdalia.[11] It is not surprising, therefore, that the doorways of the Pokrov should resemble contemporary Romanesque or Norman work in France or England. And from the West also may have come the taste for carved decoration which, like the corbel tables, is characteristic of German Romanesque architecture, familiar to the Russian princes and their builders through workmen from Galicia.

Yet the character of the carved ornament on the Vladimir-Suzdal churches, as well as the peculiarities of the plan of the Pokrov, have such close analogies with the tenth- and eleventh-century churches of the Caucasus and Armenia that one must accept the possibility that Andrey's architects, or the artisans collaborating on these structures, were familiar with the plan and distribution of relief sculpture on the Armenian cathedrals. In this connexion it is important to recall that the trade relations of Vladimir-Suzdal with the East and with the Caucasus were close, and, perhaps even more significant for this period, three successive princes – Yury I and his sons Andrey and Vsevolod III – married eastern princesses. Moreover, in 1184, Queen Tamara of Georgia married Yury, the youngest son of Andrey Bogoliubsky.[12]

More important than the weight of influence accorded either the Romanesque West or the Armenian East in the development of Suzdalian architecture must be the recognition that the builders of Suzdal and Vladimir were no mere copyists, but succeeded in creating a style inimitably their own. The delicate proportions of the Pokrov, and of the other extant churches, indicate the existence of a charac-teristic aesthetic. The churches, although generally cubical, are not precisely square. The plans are slightly lengthened along the east–west axis, and though the height is approximately equal to the total length, the slight reduction in height of the apses lends them an additional sense of slender verticality. On the south and north façades the external arches corresponding to the internal vaults have multiple profiles and are brought to the ground on pilasters faced with engaged columns running the full height of the building. The adjustment of the width of these divisions to the internal distribution of space, whereby the central arch which corresponds to the crossing below the dome is the widest, while the western is slightly and the eastern considerably narrower, gives the structure a continual proportional variety from any point of view. If the wealth of decoration is new in Russian architecture, surpassing not only the churches of the first Suzdalian period but those of Novgorod and Kiev as well, the principles of organizing that decoration according to a two-dimensional system were characteristically Russian.

By the end of the twelfth century the architects of Vladimir, more even than those of Novgorod and Kiev, had disengaged their taste from lingering Byzantine memories and, absorbing types and techniques reaching them from East and West, had created an unmistakably Russian architecture. Merely to reflect that such progress had been achieved in the two centuries separating the foundation of the Desyatinnaya from the reconstruction of the Vladimir cathedral, is to wonder what further developments might have occurred had not the political and spiritual history of the Russian people been so frequently and so violently diverted from a coherent course of formal evolution.

Of Andrey's palace and church at Bogoliubovo (1158–65), which, to judge from contemporary accounts in the chronicles, must have been one of the most magnificent palace complexes in eastern Europe, nothing now remains but a fragment of the north stair-tower leading to the gallery within the church [26]. Here Andrey used to take visiting notables, especially foreigners and unbelievers, that they might be amazed by the splendour of this shrine of the true faith. From the ex-

26. Bogoliubovo,
Prince Andrey Bogoliubsky's Palace,
remains of the tower, 1158–65

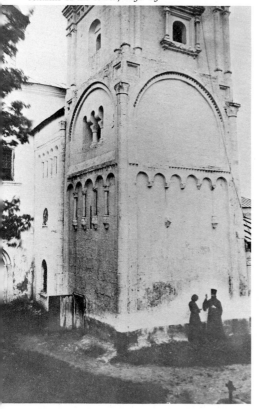

cavated foundations of the church the plan, of the usual four-pier type, may be deduced.[13] Within the tower groined vaults supported on columns with carved capitals suggest the work of foreign masters, as well as certain decorative details such as the two-storeyed blind arcades on the western façade of the tower, which are close to German Romanesque and Lombard

work. In these the presence of Barbarossa's master-builders becomes more than a suspicion. The most notable aspect of Andrey's palace church was the lavish decoration. The exterior and interior were faced with jasper, and certain details were gilded. On the interior, parts of the piers, doors, and walls were gilded, and the floor of the choir was laid with gilded copper plates. When to these and the frescoes were added the icons in gold frames, it is not hard to understand why the chronicler should have remarked that 'it was hard to look at all the gold'.

When Andrey, the victim of the jealousy of the aristocracy, was assassinated in 1174, his younger brother, Vsevolod III, continued his building activities. His first important work was the rebuilding of the Dormition in Vladimir after the disastrous fire of 1183 [22]. Apparently the fabric was largely intact but so badly calcined that Vsevolod was obliged to encase it in new walls. This he did by building two-storeyed galleries on the west, south, and north. Openings were pierced in the old outer walls which now became piers between the inner and outer aisles of the new church. New and larger apses were added on the east in scale with the new building, which required some not wholly satisfactory readjustments of the eastern bays of the earlier church. In plan the new structure was surprisingly like the many-piered, multiple-celled churches of St Sophia in Kiev and Novgorod, perhaps an intentional device to create for Vladimir a church reminiscent of those of the earlier Russian princely cities. The resemblance to St Sophia was further accentuated by the four domes which Vsevolod placed over the corners. The resulting five-domed, double-aisled church was the largest in north-eastern Russia at this period. Internally the central dome over a broad crossing was supported by eight small pendentives, achieving the transition from square to circle, more like the squinches common in Armenia and Asia Minor than the usual broad Byzantine pendentives. When it was rededicated in 1194, the new Dormition, with its frescoes, majolica floor tiles, gold and silver candelabra, and icons in gold frames, must have surpassed even Andrey's famous church at Bogoliubovo. Truly, as the chronicle says, 'it was like new, and great was the joy in Vladimir'.[14]

On the left of the iconostasis hung the most sacred object in the church, indeed in all Russia, the Byzantine icon of the Virgin 'of Vladimir' [54] (see below, pages 107–8), brought from Kiev by Andrey and so confirming the Dormition as the centre of Russian spiritual authority. Later it was only appropriate that this particular icon should be removed, with the transfer of political and spiritual authority to Moscow, to the Dormition in the Kremlin which in the late fifteenth century was rebuilt on the model of this church in Vladimir.

Externally the Dormition continued the tradition of the Nerl, if somewhat more elaborately, since the wall divisions now corresponded to the quintuple division of the interior. Here the corbel table on colonnettes was sunk within the thickness of the wall, but it may be that this peculiarity was due to a reworking of the exterior in the fourteenth century after damage sustained during the Mongol sack of the city. The multiple divisions of the walls, the judicious spacing of window and corbel table within each arched panel, and the fact that Vsevolod's galleries and apses were on each side somewhat lower than the walls of Andrey's church, so that the picturesque effect was obtained of a central mass rising above the peripheral constructions – all this contributes to make of the Dormition a structure elegant and refined today, even as it was splendid and majestic and unique in Vladimir in the twelfth century.

Vsevolod's second church, and one built wholly by him, is the Church of St Dmitry [27], which stood in the now vanished courtyard of the palace. It was begun either in 1193, soon after a fire had ravaged the palace, or in 1194, in honour of his patron saint and of his son Dmitry born that year. It was apparently finished in 1197, when Vsevolod installed in the church relics of St Dmitry brought from Salonika. Since the chronicle specifically states that Vsevolod did not summon masters from abroad, and the style of the church follows so closely that of the Pokrov, it would seem logi-

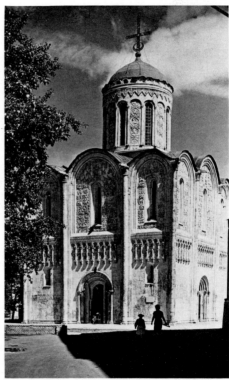

27 and 28. Vladimir, St Dmitry, west front, *c.* 1194–7, with (*right*) the relief sculptures. The figures and colonnettes at the bottom are eighteenth-century restorations

cal to assume that the same masters, or those trained by them, were still working in Vladimir throughout the later twelfth century. Like the Pokrov, this was a four-piered church with a single dome, and with an entrance on each side on axis in the Armenian manner.

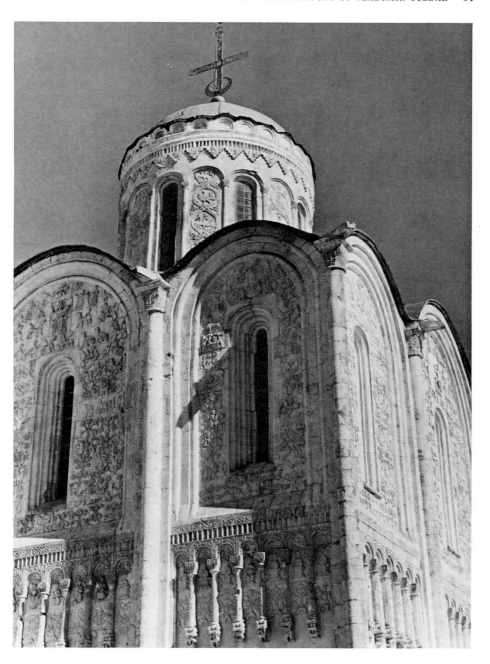

If the plan and general distribution recall the Pokrov, the difference in proportions creates quite another effect, broader and more massive, suggesting that within the strictest limitations of their style the Suzdalian architects could achieve considerable variety. The most striking contrast between St Dmitry and other churches of this group appears in the lavish distribution of carved stone reliefs over the upper walls and on the drum of the dome [28]. The character of these carvings will be examined in the general discussion of sculpture, but here again it may be noted that in their arrangement and two-dimensional character these reliefs resemble those of Armenian churches. In 1847 the church was drastically restored, losing in the process a two-storeyed construction at the north-west angle which may have contained remnants of one of the two stair-towers originally connecting the church with Vsevolod's palace.[15] The restorers were also unusually meddlesome with the carved decoration; much of it was severely cleaned and recut, some new reliefs were added, and others removed and transferred from one place to another.

Vsevolod was succeeded upon his death in 1212 by a younger son, Yury II, whose reign was disturbed by family quarrels and by the increasing threat of the Tartars. He was able, however, to accomplish one important building campaign, the reconstruction of Suzdal Cathedral (1222–5). This church, begun by Monomakh and thus scarcely a century old, had been repaired as recently as 1192, but according to the chronicles it had 'begun to collapse from its antiquity and the dome had fallen in'.[16] Unhappily even the new church has not been preserved intact. In 1445 the roof and domes were destroyed, and in 1528 the walls were demolished to the corbel table and rebuilt in brick. Consequently only the lower half of the building was preserved, but from this, the plan, and contemporary descriptions it is apparent that the new cathedral was a noble addition to Suzdalian architecture. In 1233 it was frescoed and decorated with 'beautiful coloured marbles'.

The most remarkable feature of the church was the wealth of decorative carving and the enriched architectural details. In this respect it may have stemmed from the plastic ornament of St Dmitry in Vladimir, yet such deductions as can be made from the surviving parts seem to indicate that the carvings were applied without regard to the structural logic maintained in the Vladimir churches by the disposition of the exterior arches and pilasters. Here at Suzdal the arches and pilasters did not correspond to the internal spatial divisions, and were in turn interrupted or broken through by the bands of decorative carving. It is apparent that by the beginning of the thirteenth century the brief period when the exterior and interior of the building were conceived as interrelated designs had passed. Possibly under the influence of the East, two-dimensional conceptions responsible for the carpeting of St Dmitry with sculpture had now grown stronger, and the façade of the church became a field for the display of virtuosity in decorative sculpture.

Such conclusions can be pronounced only hesitantly; for the succeeding monuments which might have demonstrated them are either destroyed or so radically altered as to

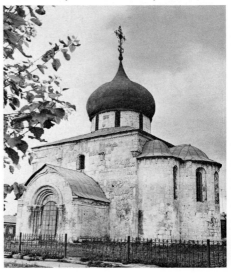

make certainty difficult. This is the more regrettable in that the last and in some ways most remarkable monument of Suzdalian architecture presents an almost inextricable problem in reconstruction. This is the Church of St George (1229–34), built by Yury II's brother, Svyatoslav Vsevolodovich, in the capital of his appanage, Yuriev-Polsky, on the site of Yury Dolgoruky's church of 1152 [29]. In 1471 the church collapsed, but was re-erected at the command of Ivan III by the Moscow architect V. D. Ermolin.[17] Un-

29 (*left*) and 30. Yuriev-Polsky, St George, 1229–34, view from the south-east and south porch

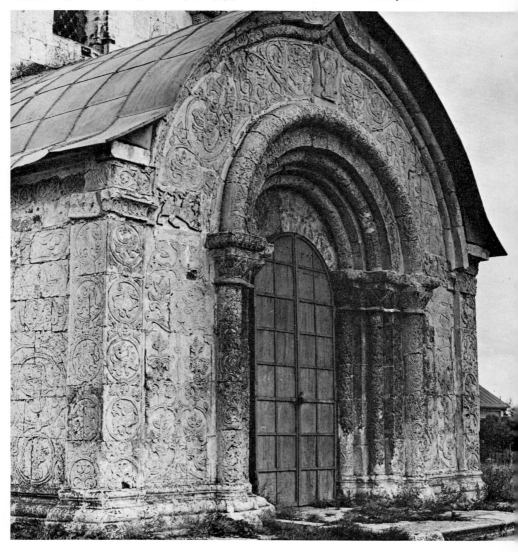

fortunately no care was taken to replace the stones in their original positions, so that at present the sculptural sequence is inextricably confused. The church must once have been much taller, if the remains of the engaged columns properly indicate half the height. In plan it had the traditional four piers, and at the sides were three porches, a now familiar feature in Suzdalian architecture. The most unusual aspect of the church was its wealth of carved detail completely covering all available wall surfaces, a sculptural treatment hitherto unknown in Russia [30].

Meanwhile the end of architectural activity in Suzdal had been reached. In 1228 the Tartars had inflicted their first defeat on the Russians at the battle of the river Kalka. Nine years later, in the winter of 1237, they attacked Suzdalia. Vladimir was besieged, taken, and burned. The independence and power of the principality were for ever eclipsed, and an extraordinarily vital and creative architecture was untimely interrupted. These churches had been the wonder of the age. In contrast to the chronicles of Novgorod, wherein are recorded the bare facts of the date and place of the church and the name of the founder, the chronicles of Suzdal abound in expressions of enthusiasm and surprise. The eloquent descriptions of Andrey's churches have been quoted. Elsewhere the churches of Vsevolod and his successors are described as 'wonderful, astonishing, of unusual beauty'. The pride which the clergy, princes, and people took in their churches was to prove in the end an imperishable legacy. Although the continuity of Russia economically and politically would be carried on at first by Novgorod and then imperceptibly by Moscow through two centuries of Tartar domination, the churches of Vladimir-Suzdal preserved in their fabric the traditions of princely Russia, until the day when the new rulers of Muscovy looked to them for the inspiration and forms wherewith to embody their conceptions of dynastic power.

CHAPTER 5

MOSAICS AND FRESCOES IN KIEV

Our knowledge of pre-Christian painting in Russia, like that of the earliest architecture, is handicapped by the absence of monuments and the scarcity of reliable documentary information. Probably the earlier Slavic worship of natural forces did not reach the stage of personifying the gods in human form until anthropomorphic images were introduced by the Varangians in the eighth and ninth centuries. The later idols were certainly colourful, as we learn from the description of those erected by Vladimir at Kiev before his conversion: 'On the hill outside the castle with the hall: one of Perun, made of wood with a head of silver, and a mouth [beard?] of gold.'[1] But the chronicles contain few details, since their priestly and monastic authors scrupulously avoided any extended description of pagan artifacts. Philological evidence suggests the polychromatic character of earlier Russian art. From the earliest times the Slavic language contained words for such specific colours as bright blue, dark blue, red, white, whitish, black, yellow, and green.[2] Among these the trinity of white, red, and green became the characteristic and conspicuous colour scheme of Novgorodian icon-painting. Again, the Russian language has the words krasota (beauty), krasivyi (beautiful), and kraska (colour), all three related to the root of the word for 'red', krasnyi, which is also synonymous with 'beautiful'.[3] This may be taken to mean that the Slavic, pre-Christian contribution to later Russian painting lay more in a traditional attitude towards brilliant primary colours, especially red, than in any inheritance of form or technical procedure. The colour schemes of medieval painting and architectural decoration, and even much later of the folk arts of embroidery and wood-carving, demonstrate this love of brilliant hues, among which red continued for centuries to play a dominant part.

Even when allowance is made for the possible though improbable existence in pagan times of an extensive and highly developed pictorial art, the speed with which Russia embraced a new religion and within less than two centuries achieved a complete, consistent, and technically accomplished art remains remarkable. It has been truly said that in ancient Russia there were no primitives; in the pictorial arts, as in architecture, the first works were complete.[4]

A situation so unusual as this is primarily to be explained by the transference of a body of highly skilled craftsmen to a new environment. Not only the technical controls evident in the earliest pictorial works on Russian soil, but the elaborate iconographical and liturgical schemes within which they occur imply that the first artists were probably Greeks, brought from Constantinople or from one of the important regional centres of Byzantine art. Greek inscriptions in the earliest mosaics must certainly mean that the first artists were closely supervised by the Greek clergy, whether or not they themselves had come directly from Constantinople.

Just as the architectural history of Kiev is compromised by the disappearance of the Desyatinnaya, so the destruction of its interior decoration obscures the origins of Kievan painting. It is known from the chronicles that the church was richly decorated. It was even called the 'Marble Church', because of the sumptuous interior panelling in marble; externally the structure was of brick. Fragments of panels, of a marble floor inlaid with geometrical patterns of an oriental character, of mosaics, and a few precious scraps of fresco confirm the chroniclers' admiration and suggest that the Desyatinnaya first demonstrated several aspects of pictorial decoration which soon became typical for Kievan Russia. A fragment of fresco depicting the nose and right eye of a human face is typical of Byzantine art of the second Golden Age; the green underpainting is overlaid with ochre for the flesh tones, with white highlights and touches of red on the lips and cheeks.[5] The combination of mosaic and fresco is rare in Byzantium itself, but frequent in the Caucasus. This eastern source for some of the decoration of the Desyatinnaya is further substantiated by the patterns of the inlaid flooring, and is historically probable in the light of the account of Vladimir's having brought to Kiev from Kherson not only priests to establish the Christian ritual, but images, vessels, and crosses with which to adorn the new church.[6]

On the other hand, the preservation of St Sophia, however partial and problematic as a result of the incessant repair and repainting of both the fabric and decoration, permits a more careful analysis of the early appearance on Russian soil of the pictorial arts. Here is to be found not only the oldest existing but in many ways the most important scheme of religious painting in ancient Russia and one of the most interesting in the entire Byzantine world. Here were established iconographic formulas which for the next millennium bound the religious art of Russia to its Greek sources, and hence proceeded the stages, however slight, for the iconographical and stylistic departures from these Byzantine models which in time became peculiarly Russian characteristics.

Chronologically the earliest mosaics and frescoes of St Sophia, which were executed between the foundation of the church, presumably in 1018, and its first consecration in 1046, take their place between the early-eleventh-century mosaics of the Katholikon at Hosios Lukas in Greece and those towards the close of the same century at Daphni. This sequence of eleventh-century Byzantine decorative schemes was derived from the now vanished ninth-century mosaics of the Nea Ekklesia and the modifications of a similar programme in the early-tenth-century Church of the Holy Apostles in Constantinople. All are saturated with the nobly hieratic and profoundly religious conception of painting of the middle Byzantine period, even though a progression may be traced from the austerity at Hosios Lukas to the milder benignity and lively anecdote at Daphni, which in turn prepared the way for the Byzantine Renaissance of the thirteenth and fourteenth centuries.[7]

The iconographical order inaugurated at St Sophia became customary for subsequent Russian mural painting.[8] Over the centre of this church-world, above the crossing at the juncture of the nave, apse, and side bays, was spread the great central dome, like the sky stretched spherically over the earth, and on its inner surface appeared in mosaic the representation of Christ the All-Ruler, the Pantokrator [31]. His swarthy, gaunt face is not that of the human historical Christ of the Gospels familiar in western art, but a specifically eastern conception of the divine Christ uniting in Himself the first and second persons of the Trinity, the apocalyptic Judge who on the Last Day will open the book held in His right hand. If the image, as seems reasonable, was made towards the middle of the eleventh century, it is one of the earliest surviving representations on a monumental scale of Christ as the Supreme Judge. The fearsome Hebraic God of Daphni is some fifty years later; those at Cefalù and Monreale were created about 1148 and 1190. Yet, although executed by Greek mosaicists, it is not wholly Greek. The drawing is neither deft nor elegant, and the expression is quite other than courtly or autocratic. This Christ, whose eyes reach through and beyond the spectator, is undisturbed by the doubts which those in Sicily have overcome. His authority is like that of one but lately come, like all of Kievan Russia, to total commitment to the Light and the Truth that He knows.

This bust-length medallion on a gold ground was originally surrounded by a rainbow

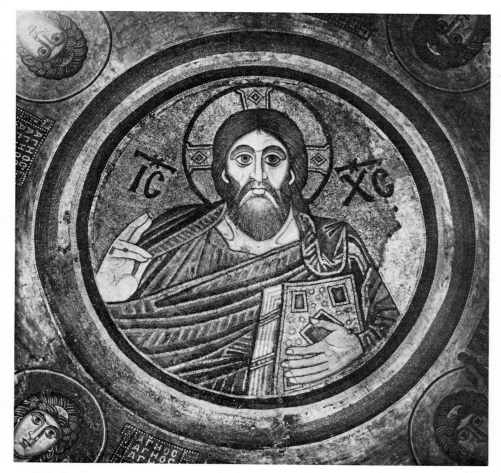

31. Christ Pantokrator, mosaic in the dome of the Cathedral of St Sophia, Kiev, 1043–6

supported by four Archangels, only one of whom survives, whose widespread wings filled the remaining spaces on the inner surface of the dome. These awesome leaders of the heavenly host were clad in the pearl- and jewel-studded imperial Court costume of the Byzantine sovereigns, in whose likeness they held in either hand a sphere and standard, the first emblazoned with the cross, the latter with the word Hagios (Holy), thrice repeated.

Below the Archangels the third zone embraces the drum of the dome, where between the windows stood the Apostles, of whom only half of one, St Paul, is still intact, and immediately below them, in the four pendentives supporting the dome, sat the four Evangelists, among whom only St Mark remains. The iconographical scheme symbolized the omniscient character of God and the means by which the divine law was made known to man through the acts of the Apostles and the writings of the Evangelists. Immediately below these figures, and on either side of the arch separating the apse from the central crossing, stand the Archangel Gabriel and the Virgin Mary of the Annunciation, signifying the mystery of the Incarnation whereby the Word was made flesh and dwelt among men.

In the semi-dome of the apse, isolated against a radiant gold background, appears the standing figure of the Virgin Orans, raising her arms in the antique gesture of prayer [7].

This image represents neither the Queen of Heaven nor the mortal Mother of God as she was more popularly known in the later Middle Ages, both in the East and West, but rather the Virgin as the symbol of the earthly Church interceding with her prayers for the salvation of mankind.[9] This image was venerated as the 'unbroken or indestructible wall', an allusion to the twelfth ikos of the Akathist Hymn, which commemorates the Virgin's protection of Constantinople against the siege of 626. From this association grew the legend that during the construction of St Sophia the walls collapsed, except for the central apse.

On the curved wall of the apse below the

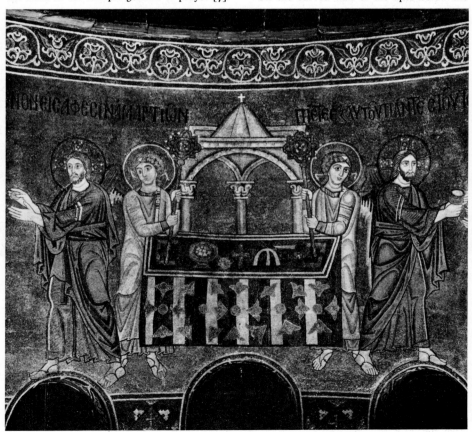

32. The Liturgical Eucharist, mosaic in the apse of the Cathedral of St Sophia, Kiev, 1043–6

Virgin are the agents and institutions whereby the Word was made known to man; the symbols of the dome have become effective on earth through action and ritual. Of the two zones in which this wall is horizontally divided, the upper [32] represents the Liturgical Eucharist or Communion of the Apostles, commemorating the institution of the sacrament of the Lord's Supper. Following ancient eastern precedent, Christ is represented twice, once on either side of an altar crowned with a canopy and flanked by two angels performing the office of deacon. Each Christ extends the chalice and wafer to six Apostles approaching from left and right in single file. In the lower row full-length figures, now much damaged, of the Church Fathers, bishops, deacons, and martyrs particularly honoured in the Eastern Church complete the programme. The remaining spaces in St Sophia are filled in the northern and southern aisles with scenes in fresco from the lives of Christ and the Virgin. On the western walls and vaults, opposite the Liturgical Eucharist, are episodes from the Old and New Testaments taken as prototypes or symbols of the Passion, such as the Children in the Fiery Furnace, the Sacrifice of Abraham, the Old Testament Trinity or Appearance of the Three Angels to Abraham,[10] Christ at Emmaus, the Marriage at Cana, and the Last Supper. The size of the church required an enlargement of the iconographical scheme which was ordinarily restricted in the middle Byzantine period to the twelve great Feasts: the Annunciation, Nativity, Presentation of Christ or the Purification of the Virgin, Baptism, Resurrection of Lazarus, Transfiguration, Entry into Jerusalem, Crucifixion, Resurrection, Ascension, Pentecost, and Dormition of the Virgin. The scheme at St Sophia departs in another particular from custom, since the Last Judgement usually depicted on the west wall was replaced by a representation of the enthroned Christ approached from the left by Yaroslav holding a model of the church, with his eldest son, and from the right by the Great Princess Irene

with her eldest daughter. The princely procession was continued on the adjoining south and north walls of the nave with full-length portraits of the remaining children, three sons and four daughters. Unfortunately this historically interesting, and for Russia unique, series of eleventh-century portraits is most grievously damaged. Numerous full- and half-length figures of saints and decorative medallions on the arches and piers completed the iconographical scheme.

The arrangement is coherent and systematic. From the presence of God in the heights of heaven to the ultimate salvation of his people through their knowledge of his earthly appearance and their repeated participation in the Sacraments, each part of the church received its logical expression. It is interesting to observe how this progression moves upward from the concrete, historical episodes of Christ's earthly life, painted on the flatter, uncomplicated parts of the fabric, to the tremendous pictorial demonstrations of Christian dogma on just those architectural elements which are themselves powerful, structural abstractions; the Virgin Orans on the apse, the Evangelists on the pendentives, the Pantokrator with the Archangels on the dome. As the structural system becomes more difficult or complex, so do the doctrines represented become more abstract and profound.

The poor preservation of the mosaics and frescoes of St Sophia handicaps stylistic analysis. Of the Archangels, Apostles, and Evangelists on the dome and pendentives, but one of each is intact, while the saints in the apse are preserved only above the shoulders or waist. The frescoes have suffered even more than the mosaics, and after frequent repainting are now only of iconographical interest, save for some few fragments preserved under whitewash throughout the drastic nineteenth-century restorations.

In execution, as in arrangement, these mosaics and frescoes are predominantly Byzantine, executed by Greek masters working under the direction of Greek priests, or in the less important parts by Russians working from Greek models. Yet among these Greek workmen there must have been some who, whether of eastern origin or merely acquainted with eastern style and iconography, introduced certain elements which differ from the Court style of the eleventh century. Thus, while such figures as the Virgin of the Annunciation or the standing saints in the apse have the slender proportions and delicate outlines of Byzantine painting, and the Virgin's head is of the purest classic type in proportion and drawing, the swarthy, bearded double Christ of the Liturgical Eucharist and the vigorously realistic yet rhythmically symmetrical expressions and gestures of the Apostles show some familiarity with the recurrent trends of Eastern ascetic realism which reached Byzantine art from Syria and Anatolia. The same influence appears in the severely formal figures of the standing Fathers, whose enlarged eyes have lost the play of expression seen in antique art.[11] This important contributory source of

Byzantine style is present in the pictorial decoration of St Sophia in much the same degree as the eastern elements in the plan, which, for all that it displays of the closest parallels with the conjectural plan of the Nea Ekklesia, is yet not without puzzling references to such a Caucasian church as Mokvi.

Stylistically the mosaics of St Sophia are among the great monuments of the second period of Byzantine painting, and in their own way, in the majestic expression of the Pantokrator or the linear grace of the Virgin Annunciate, they are not inferior to contemporary Greek work. More than any other aspect of Kievan art they witness the close ties, spiritual, cultural, and artistic, which bound the principality to Tsargrad.

Perhaps nowhere is this political and cultural affiliation more dramatically expressed than in the curious frescoes on the walls of the stair-tower leading to the galleries [33]. Here in 1843 was found a sequence of secular scenes such as had long been known from text-

33. Hunting and circus scenes, fresco from the staircase in the Cathedral of St Sophia, Kiev, late eleventh century

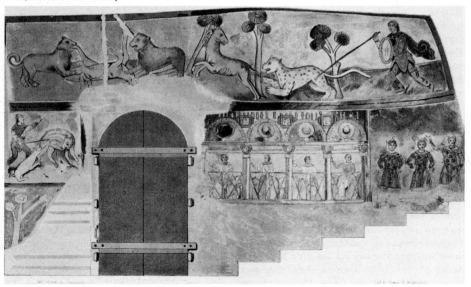

ual descriptions to have existed in Byzantine art.[12] These paintings, containing more than a hundred and thirty naturalistic figures, represent the life of the Byzantine Court, its ceremonies and festivals, such as the games enacted in the Hippodrome at Christmas time, including acrobats, gladiators, and wild animal hunts. Yaroslav and his nobles descending to the cathedral might fancy themselves very much like the Emperor and his courtiers as they glanced at these depictions of imperial festivities. The liveliness as well as the authenticity of those Constantinopolitan scenes, which include, in the south-west tower, a view of the façade of the Kathisma Palace which faced the Hippodrome, with spectators crowding the galleries and the Emperor with his retinue in the imperial box, may be traced to Vladimir's attachment to Greece, and perhaps to his desire to enhance his princely prestige by such associations with the Eastern Roman Empire. In spite of repeated and drastic restorations, certain parts of the frescoes show the same oriental types and realistic expression already observed in the Eucharist, here executed in a typically eastern technique, linear and with boldly opposed values.

If the date 1018–37 be accepted for the construction of St Sophia, one may think that the Greek masters who decorated it were the immediate successors of those who had earlier been active at the Desyatinnaya, or that they may even have been responsible for the conjectured redecoration of the Desyatinnaya immediately before the second consecration of that church in 1039. Be this so or not, the mosaics and frescoes of St Sophia differ to such a degree from later work at Kiev that the masters may be said to belong to the first Kievan generation. Not until after the turn of the century is comparable work again found, and in the lapse of time between St Sophia and the decoration of St Michael (after 1108), another group of masters must have come from Constantinople, bringing the later development of the Byzantine style.

Unfortunately what may have been the most important sequence of mosaics of this second generation long ago disappeared from the walls of the now destroyed Cathedral of the Dormition in the Pecherskaya Lavra (1075–89). In 1240 the upper half of the eastern apse was wrecked by the Tartars, yet enough remained into the seventeenth century to warrant an enthusiastic description by Paul of Aleppo, Archdeacon of Antioch. That it followed the traditional scheme, already examined in St Sophia, is known from the Pechersky Paterik, the monastery's own hagiographical collection. Paul added that the mosaics were: 'inlaid with gold like those in St Sophia and the church in Bethlehem. A beautiful mosaic decorates the

34. SS. Thomas, James, Simon, and Luke, from the Liturgical Eucharist, mosaic from the Church of St Michael with the Golden Roofs, *c.* 1100, now in St Sophia, Kiev

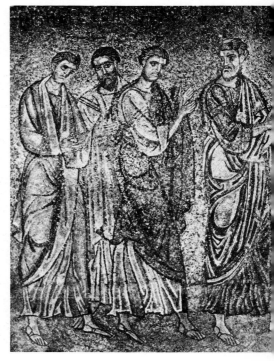

floor of the chancel.'[13] From his description it is apparent that the Pechersky church continued the scheme and splendour of the Desyatinnaya and St Sophia.

The decorative scheme of the late-eleventh- or early-twelfth-century mosaics and paintings in the St Michael church in Kiev followed so closely those in the Pechersky church that it is tempting to think that the Greek mosaicists who had worked in the Lavra, among whom were twelve who remained as monks, may have been responsible for the principal elements in the decorative scheme which, according to Paul of Aleppo's description, resembled those in St Sophia.[14] After St Michael was demolished in 1935 the surviving mosaics and frescoes were placed in an upper chapel at St Sophia; the splendid Greek mosaic of St Demetrius was removed to the State Tretyakov Gallery in Moscow.

Of the mosaics the Liturgical Eucharist [34] is certainly the work of Constantinopolitan

35. St Cyril instructing the Emperor, fresco in St Cyril, Kiev, twelfth century

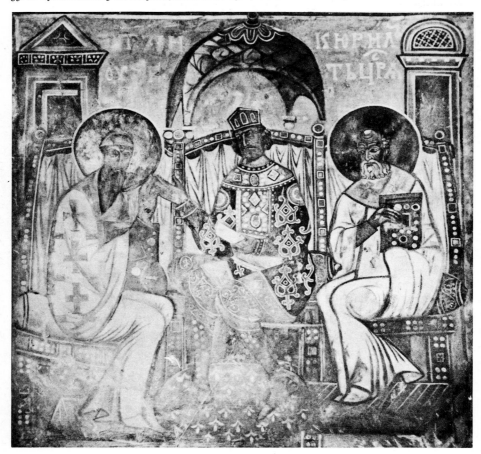

masters. In contrast to the agitated yet stereo-typed oriental Apostles in the earlier St Sophia Eucharist, these are tall, slender figures whose draperies are composed of intricate folds with broken silhouettes, very different from the continuous contours of the earlier figures. The former pattern of arms, hands, and feet repeating identical gestures is replaced by a complex rhythmical sequence, more intri-cate and yet calmer, more imbued with an inner contemplative spirit than that at St Sophia. The individual heads are more varied and their expressions, like the facial types, more antique and less drastically ascetic. A comparable change has taken place in the colours, which are more harmonious than the bright opposed hues in St Sophia. It is clear that the masters of St Michael not only belonged to a later generation, but stood in some respects closer to the Court style in By-zantium itself. The delicate drawing and colour, the variety and subtlety of expression, are eloquent testimony to the perfection of later-eleventh-century painting in Constantinople, resembling if not in detail at least in expression the slightly earlier mosaics at Daphni.[15]

With the deterioration of the frescoes of St Sophia, and the loss of those elsewhere, a per-haps excessive historical interest attaches to the remains of a frescoed interior preserved in the Church of the Holy Trinity in the St Cyril Monastery in Kiev, founded in 1140 by Prince Vsevolod. Unhappily these also have been ex-tensively restored, but enough remains to in-dicate that the powerful single figures in St Sophia continued to exert an influence over similar painting a century later. A departure from the familiar iconographical schemes appears in the frescoes illustrating the life of St Cyril of Alexandria [35]. If in a certain sense the broad areas of pattern and almost oppressive frontality recall mosaic technique, this indicates that after the first magnificent period of Kievan art, frescoes inevitably replaced mosaics, for they provided a less expensive substitute. The simplified linear rhythms and embracing outlines, as well as the presence of Balkan saints and Slavonic inscrip-tions, suggest that the Russian painters were working from more provincial models than had their predecessors at St Sophia and St Michael.[16]

CHAPTER 6

THE FIRST RUSSIAN SCULPTURE

Geographical and historical conditions are no less significant for the development of Russian sculpture than for the other arts. At the outset, the development of sculpture was compromised by the prohibition of the Greek Church, which forbade the use of 'graven images', taken to mean carved rather than painted likenesses of the holy personages. Thus from the end of the Iconoclastic Controversy in the ninth century, and consequently at the very beginning of Christian Russia, opportunities for monumental sculpture were closed to Russian artisans by the most affluent patrons of art. Yet if Russian churches lacked large figural sculpture, as it was known in western Europe, the will to create three-dimensional forms found expression in other ways. The elaborate liturgical vessels, the intricate metal frames which were fitted over icons, and the richly carved iconostases, as well as the continuous production of peasant crafts, show that throughout their history Russians have experienced an instinctive pleasure in making and using three-dimensional forms.[1]

Three factors of particular importance determined the character of Russian sculpture. There was a sculptural tradition among the Russian people even in pre-Christian times. In the century before Vladimir's conversion a mingling of the personifications of Slavic nature-worship with the deities introduced by the Varangians seems to have taken place. The Slavic god Perun, for instance, was apparently the counterpart of the Norse Thor, and probably the images of each were not unlike. The pagan idols were of wood or stone, standing freely in space, and carved in the full round as images of human figures. The Arabian traveller Ahmed ibn Fadlan, who was in Russia in 922, described the religious practices of the merchants on the lower Volga who worshipped upright pieces of wood surmounted by likenesses of human faces.[2] Slightly later European accounts contain tantalizing but inconclusive glimpses of the sculpture in the last pagan sanctuaries among the western Slavs. Dietmar of Merseburg (976–1018) described a 'skilfully fashioned wooden shrine, adorned on the outside with figures of various gods and goddesses'.[3] Helmold of Bosan (c. 1200) said that the Slavs carved 'many gods with two, three, or more heads'.[4] Such deities cast their reflexions far into Christian times. Their names were perpetuated in folk-songs, even in such a sophisticated work as the late-twelfth-century *Tale of the Armament of Igor*, the greatest of all ancient Russian poems. In this account of the defeat of one of the younger princes of Kievan Russia in an expedition against the Polovtsy, the anonymous poet invoked Dazhbog, Velos, Khors, and Div, a bird of ill-omen.[5]

Since wood perished and the idols which might have survived were conscientiously destroyed by the Church, we can only estimate the character of these figures from certain stone images, such as the granite block crudely worked as a man's head which was found near Novgorod in 1893.[6] A stone post discovered in 1848 near Gusyatin in the Ukraine is possibly more like those described in the chronicles. Each of the four sides had been carved in the likeness of a standing male figure (hence a god with 'three or more heads'), with other figures and animals below.[7] Vladimir's idols in Novgorod and Kiev may have been elaborate versions of such a stone image, incrusted with precious metals. The spirited silhouette of a horse and the crouching figure of a man at the bottom of the post are not unlike similar figures on the most enigmatic of these rare pagan sculptures. On the walls of a cave at Bush in Podolia on the river Murakhva, a tributary of the Dniester, a carving in low relief depicts a man kneeling before a tree where a cock perches on one of the branches.[8] In his raised hands he holds a now unidentifiable object; behind him a deer stands on a small hillock. Between the cock and the deer a now illegible inscription had been cut on a small square title. The scene probably represents an act of worship, since the cock is known to have been an object of adoration in pre-Christian Russia.

Although we may consider such subjects monumental in size alone, the will to create three-dimensional forms, whether carved or modelled, may take other directions, and here the history of wooden architecture in Russia must not be neglected. The builders of the earliest cities and towns were familiar with a superb sculptural material. No wooden buildings earlier than the seventeenth century are now in existence, but even in the late churches the skilful manipulation of wood and the amount of carved ornament, at the ends of beams and roofing planks, on the door- and window-frames, and in the shingles on the bulbous domes, suggest an ancient craft tradition.

The condition of the Kievan churches prohibits any adequate appraisal of the earliest Russian sculpture, but such as there was must from the first have been influenced by large and important examples of antique sculpture. On his return from Kherson in 989 Vladimir I brought to Kiev 'two bronze statues and four bronze horses' which were set up behind the Desyatinnaya and, as the chronicler somewhat patronizingly added, 'the ignorant think [they] are made of wood'.[9] Fragments of stone sarcophagi discovered in the ruins of the Desyatinnaya and a sarcophagus still preserved in St Sophia as the tomb of Yaroslav are so thoroughly Byzantine as to lead one to think that for the princely entombments such stone work may have been imported from Greece.[10]

The one truly flourishing and individual school in ancient Russia developed towards the middle of the twelfth century in Suzdalia.[11] In both quantity and quality this sculpture is unique in the history of Byzantine and Russian art. Its quite exceptional character is a consequence of the vigorous political and cultural policy of the princes of Vladimir, which made the region one of the most cosmopolitan artistic centres in either the European or eastern world during the twelfth century. The elaborate decoration of the churches of Vladimir may be due to the fact that Suzdalia was remote from Kiev, and so beyond the immediate supervision of the Metropolitan.

The work of the Suzdalian school first appeared in the carved decorations which are known to have existed on the Cathedral of the Dormition built by Andrey in Vladimir and on his palace church at Bogoliubovo. But since the latter has disappeared and the reliefs on the Dormition were destroyed or severely damaged in the fire of 1183, and in subsequent restorations, it is to the Pokrov on the Nerl that we must look for the first conspicuous evidence. On this church the upper parts of the triple divisions on three façades are lined with figures in relief, and the columns of the corbel tables on all four façades rest upon sculptured corbels composed of animal, plant, and purely decorative forms [36]. The reliefs on the south, west, and north façades are arranged in an identical fashion. High in the centre of each central arch is a male figure, inscribed 'Tsar David', seated between confronted pairs of doves and lions. He holds a stringed instrument and raises his right hand in blessing. Below is a range of three female heads, and on either side of the window two lions recline beneath stylized trees. The side panels contain a griffin attacking an animal, perhaps a wolf, and there are two female heads below. The capitals and voussoirs of the deeply splayed portals are covered with floral designs. The triple repetition of this enthroned King David may mean that he appears as the ancestral prefiguration of Christ. The confronted lions and doves would then symbolize

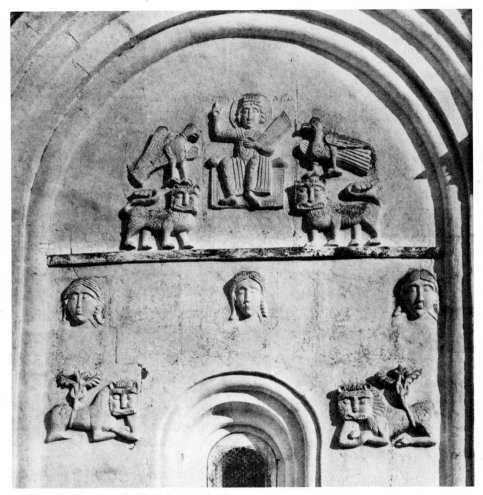

36. King David enthroned with birds and animals,
centre panel of the south façade of the Pokrov on the Nerl, c. 1170

aspects of the soul which David charmed with his music and Christ conquered with His sacrifice.

The second important sculptural ensemble is found on the exterior of St Dmitry at Vladimir, where, in addition to the treatment of portals and corbel tables resembling the Pokrov, the wall surfaces between the columns, within the triple panels on each façade, and between the windows of the drum are filled with low relief carvings [28]. Much of the present sculpture has been restored or reworked, first after a severe fire in 1719, and again in the nineteenth century in the course of a drastic restoration. Although the work of both campaigns can be distinguished from the original twelfth-century sculpture, it is more difficult to be certain that the original figures were not removed and rearranged when the windows were enlarged. As at the Pokrov, the central panel on each façade contains the figure of King David enthroned. He is surrounded by a multitude of animal and plant forms and occasional human figures arranged in confronted rows extending below him on either side of the window. There is a similar disposition in the side panels, but they seem to have suffered considerably. Among them may be found evidence of other compositions, such as two confronted flying angels (perhaps the remains of an Ascension), seated Apostles, standing saints, and groups representing the Baptism of Christ, the Sacrifice of Isaac, and the Ascension of Alexander. An enigmatic composition of a seated man holding a child on his lap and two pairs of kneeling men approaching towards him resembles the usual Adoration of the Shepherds or Magi, but the unmistakably male character of the seated figure has led to the suggestion that this is a portrait of Vsevolod III, the founder of the church, with his son Dmitry in his arms.[12]

In comparison with the figures on St Dmitry the sculpture on the Pokrov seems relatively crude and simplified, and so may represent an earlier, more tentative stage leading towards the elaborate treatment of the later church. Similarly the iconographical programme has been considerably enriched; to the simpler prophecy of Christ's coming has been added further confirmation of His divine mission in the prophetic enactment of the Sacrifice of Isaac, and of His Ascension in the pagan parallel of the Ascension of Alexander. Likewise the floral and animal decoration has been enlarged to such a point that the whole scheme has been considered an illustration of Psalm 148, with the exhortations 'Praise ye the Lord . . . Beasts, and all cattle; creeping things, and flying fowl: Kings of the earth, and all people; princes, and all judges of the earth: . . . Praise ye the Lord'. It has also been suggested that the source for many of the reliefs can be found in the old Russian popular poem, *The Book of the Holy Ghost* (*Golubinaya Kniga*), containing a theological world history in the form of questions and answers, as symmetrically posed as the confronted pairs of men and animals on St Dmitry.[13]

Application of decorative reliefs to church walls is known in the West, in such churches as Notre Dame la Grande at Poitiers, and in the East, in the church at Achtamar on Lake Van in Armenia. The latter perhaps most nearly resembles St Dmitry, although neither in East nor West were the iconographical programme and the formal arrangement so skilfully related to the structure of the church as here in Vladimir. The style of the human figures which are treated almost in the full round also resembles Romanesque sculpture, particularly in the greater projection of the heads, hands, and feet. Behind them lay a long tradition of three-dimensional carving, extending back to classical antiquity and reaching both West and East through the medium of portable Byzantine ivories. On the other hand, the floral and animal forms are distinctly oriental, especially the pairs of animals, the peacocks whose long necks cross in opposite directions, and the lions whose confronted heads merge into one. All these are familiar in eastern metalwork and textiles, and may have been copied from the textiles which are known to have been in Vladimir in considerable size and quantity. The chronicle, recording the great fire of 1183, mentions the loss of 'two wonderful series of fabrics which on feast days used to be hung on two cords from the Golden Gate to the Cathedràl of the Dormition and from the Dormition to the archbishop's palace'.[14]

The presence of eastern and western elements in the sculptural programme at the Nerl and St Dmitry is substantiated by the chronicles and by the history of Suzdalia. Since the chronicle specifically says of Prince Andrey that 'for his piety and great zeal for the Virgin, architects from all countries were brought to him by God',[15] we may presume that the

princely workshops in Suzdalia included architects and craftsmen from the West as well as
the East. The arrival in Suzdalia of such artisans can be postulated on the basis of dynastic
and trade relations. Vsevolod's marriage to a
Caucasian princess was symptomatic of the
continuous trade which flourished between
Suzdalia and the East along the Volga.
Through the intermediation of the Bulgars of
Kazan, who were settled along the middle
reaches of the river and who had embraced
Islam in the tenth century, articles of Persian
and Turkish origin easily reached Vladimir.

The constant movement of artisans in the
medieval world is not uncommon; in 1246 the
Franciscan emissary from the Pope to the
Mongols, Giovanni de Plano Carpini, met at
the Court of the Khan a Russian goldsmith
'who was greatly in the Emperor's favour'.[16]

The third and last of the important programmes in Suzdalia, if we omit the damaged
carvings in the Cathedral of Suzdal, which are
like the work at St Dmitry, is the sculpture
which covers the exterior surface of the
Church of St George in Yuriev-Polsky, the
summer residence of the Vladimir princes [30,
37].[17] The church collapsed in the fifteenth

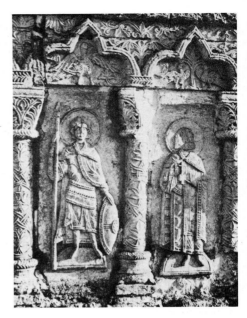

37 and 38. Yuriev-Polsky, St George, 1229–34,
relief sculpture and the Crucifixion

century, and was reconstructed at the command of the Great Prince of Moscow, Ivan
III, by the Moscow architect V. D. Ermolin.
Unfortunately Ermolin reduced the height of
the whole structure, and with complete disregard for the sense of the sculptures replaced
the stones in any order, possibly even including materials from an adjacent ruined church.
The original arrangement is now inextricably
confused, and only on an iconographical basis
can certain portions be studied in proper
sequence. Nevertheless it is apparent that once,
as now, the church at Yuriev-Polsky was completely covered with carved decorations; the
chronicles remark that Svyatoslav 'ornamented
it more than all other churches, for on the
exterior of the whole church wonderful saints
in carved stone were placed'.[18] This arrangement is unique in the history of western archi-

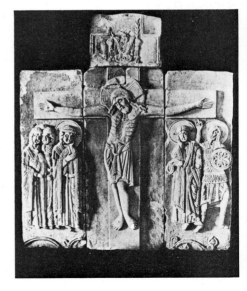

tecture, and recalls such ancient Syrian systems as the fifth-century carved reliefs at Mschatta. An eastern origin for the work at Yuriev-Polsky seems plausible, and would account for the pointed arches which occur above the portals on each porch and above the heads of the standing saints.

In contrast to St Dmitry, where the human figures were submerged in a welter of plant and animal forms, the saints standing between the columns of the arcades and the figures in such scenes as the Transfiguration and deesis, which can be reconstructed from isolated fragments, are considerably more monumental. Not only are they large in comparison with the rest of the decoration, but they tend to dominate rather than to be subordinated to their architectural surroundings. Within the frames provided by columns and carved bands they show by the slightest gesture, the turn of a head or the expression of an eye, a more pronounced humanism than the stilted marionettes of St Dmitry. The difference is perhaps due to the sources from which the artists drew their iconography. Where the craftsmen of St Dmitry may have used the small illustrations in illuminated manuscripts, the sculptors of St George were thinking of the spacious frescoes of St Dmitry itself, executed probably towards the close of the 1190s. Also, the connections with Byzantium were still close. The Crucifixion [38] is traditional, in composition, postures, and clothing.

Indeed, it is almost identical with an eleventh- or twelfth-century steatite carving now in the Hermitage.[19] Even the Centurion, with the same gesture, blesses the Christ in the Orthodox manner. What is Russian is the change from an aristocratic to a popular expression. The large-headed figures of the Virgin and St John are more ordinary people, crushed by grief, quite as much as they are the Queen of Heaven and the Beloved Disciple.

Three years after St George was completed the Tartars were at the gates of Vladimir and the brief period of its artistic pre-eminence was over. In the confusion of the occupation the artisans were probably dispersed. Perhaps one of them was the man whom Plano Carpini saw at the court of the Khan in 1246. Others may have gone westward to Galicia, where in 1259 Prince Daniel built a church of which the description in so many respects resembles the churches of Suzdalia that it is tempting to think that his architect may once have worked for Vsevolod or his successors. Certainly Daniel was aware of the value of articles of Russian workmanship for 'he ornamented the church with icons which had been brought from Kiev'. What interests us here is that 'the two entrance doors were carved of white Galician and green Cholm stone, and the designs were executed by a certain artist Avdey'. Perhaps Avdey was a fugitive from Vladimir, in which case he was the only Suzdalian sculptor whom we know by name.[20]

CHAPTER 7

FRESCOES IN VLADIMIR AND NOVGOROD

After the middle of the twelfth century Kiev was no longer a dominant power politically or artistically. Successive raids by the younger princes, culminating in Andrey Bogoliubsky's siege of the ·city in 1169, merely confirmed the fact that it would no longer be considered an effective centre, either for resistance against the nomads, whose incursions grew yearly more dangerous, or as a dynastic and cultural rallying point for the Russian people. In the north-east the princes of Suzdal were rapidly developing an almost independent state, its wealth derived from agriculture and international trade; for it lay athwart the great east–west trade route which now led down the Volga to the Caspian or by portage to the Don and thence to the Black Sea. Inevitably the pretensions of the princes of Suzdal incurred the hostility of Novgorod. As early as 1169 the Suzdalians attacked Novgorod, and were only prevented by a miracle from taking it [84]. Which city would have been pre-eminent in the future must remain in doubt, for the Mongol advance in 1237 devastated Suzdalia. Novgorod alone maintained the consistent development of Russian painting after the deterioration of Kiev and the collapse of Vladimir and Suzdal.

The earliest mural painting in Novgorod was related immediately to the Byzantine monuments of Kiev. The oldest and most important church, the Cathedral of St Sophia (1045–57), although almost contemporary with St Sophia in Kiev, apparently was decorated only after 1108, and then in fresco rather than in costly mosaic. Very little of the earliest painting survived damage and restoration in the nineteenth century,[1] and still less the burning of the cathedral during the Second World War. Only the now destroyed Pantokrator and the badly damaged Apostles in the

dome and drum showed how closely the masters – here, too, probably Greeks – followed the Kievan types. If, indeed, they were those who had worked in the south, their presence in Novgorod and consequent absence from Kiev might account for the fact that the builders of the Dormition in the Pecherskaya Lavra were obliged to send to Constantinople for artisans. In this way the masters of the later generation who worked in the Lavra and who may have created the mosaics at St Michael reached Russia.

It is recorded that the decoration of St Sophia was not finished until 1144, but the monumental, although fragmentary, figures in the southern gallery depicting SS. Constantine and Helena full-length on either side of the ever-blooming cross may possibly have been painted in the late eleventh century. The remaining frescoes which survived the drastic restorations of 1893 would seem to be notable, if not unusual, examples of early-twelfth-century Byzantine painting. The delicate colouring, the finely drawn outlines, and the tender gestures suggest that the independent spirit of Novgorod was already at work adapting the classic proportions and imperial dignity of such figures as the archangels at Kiev to a more naturalistic presentation.[2] The less skilful figures of seven prophets which survive in the drum are bold but provincial, and therefore probably by Russian painters.

During this period of the spread of Byzantine art in Russia, Greek masters were active not only in the north, in Novgorod, but also in the north-east, in the principality of Vladimir-Suzdal. The fire of 1183 severely damaged not only the fabric of Andrey Bogoliubsky's Cathedral of the Dormition in Vladimir, but also the frescoes of 1161. Fragments remaining after Vsevolod III's extensive reconstruction of the church included figures of prophets and two peacocks in an ornamental style which were recovered by the State Restoration Commission in 1918–20.[3] The position of these frescoes is particularly significant. They were found on the north exterior wall of Andrey's church (now the south or inner wall of the north aisle), and by their position indicate that Andrey's building followed the Kievan taste for exterior polychromatic decoration. Of Vsevolod's reconstruction of 1185–9 a few figures of prophets and Fathers with some traces of ornamental decoration remain. Greek inscriptions suggest the presence of Byzantine masters, which is borne out by the chronicler's pious statement that because of Andrey's great love for the Virgin, 'God sent him masters from many lands'. The Last Judgement on the west wall was repainted in 1408 by Andrey Rublev and the icon painter Daniil Cherny (Daniel 'the Black'), and will be considered in the account of their activity. From the fact that such a painting occupied this place and from the fragments of saints and prophets it can be assumed that Andrey's painters followed the usual mid-Byzantine scheme observed in the churches of Kiev.

It is almost miraculous that any frescoes in St Dmitry, painted in the last years of the twelfth century, survived until the present day.[4] In addition to the normal ravages of time, the successive 'restorations' of the nineteenth century spoiled the little that was left. Fortunately the State Restoration Commission in 1918–20 recovered fragments of a Last Judgement on the vault above the west entrance, with accompanying figures and scenes on adjacent vaults and arches which had escaped repainting in the late nineteenth century. What was left can be seen to have been executed by artists comparable in ability, in the best parts, to the mosaicists of Kiev. Considering the size of the church and the extent of the paintings which originally covered it, probably the co-operation of several masters and their assistants was required, and among the latter there may well have been Russian

pupils, since several different hands can be seen at work. The procession of righteous women led into Paradise by St Peter is painted in a lively and rhythmical style not unlike the Eucharist figures in the Kievan St Sophia, while the Apostles seated on high thrones have a hieratic and aristocratic dignity comparable to those in St Michael [39]. Several heads, such as those of St Matthew and St Paul, are among the most accomplished and spiritual achievements of Byzantine painting [40]. The classic regularity of the features is in the finest tradition of Byzantine Hellenism, and the play of spiritual emotion exemplifies that mystical disturbance of classic serenity which in a later age found expression in the last great master of the Byzantine tradition, El Greco. The bodies of the seated Apostles should also be noted. The varieties of posture, especially in the positions of their legs, are treated with an easy mastery of figures foreshortened and in three dimensions.

Behind the Apostles the rows of angel heads, some partially obscured by the lively play of intersecting haloes, can be counted one of the most gracious examples of Byzantine painting [41]. The refined Greek features, with the wide classic eyes, the long, curved nose, and small mouth, are so lightly painted that line and shade almost impalpably create the form. The painter achieved the most delicate balance between supernatural and human attributes. The spectator may be reminded of Duccio's and Simone Martini's angels in their Maestàs, and yet surprised to recall that the heavenly hosts of St Dmitry were painted more than a century before Simone spread his flower-like figures on the walls of the Palazzo Pubblico in Siena. The frescoes of St Dmitry indicate how the Byzantine artist could create a convincing three-dimensional style without recourse to what in the West became the direct observation of Nature. Byzantine art in its noblest examples preserved from its classic heritage that subtle equilibrium between the real and ideal, between the observed and the imagined, between abstraction and naturalistic

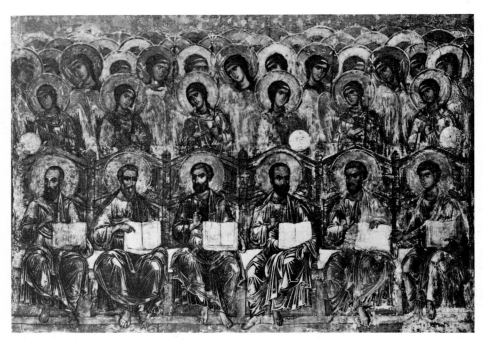

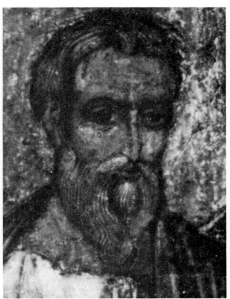
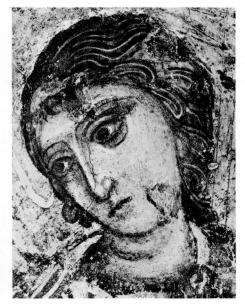

39–41. The Last Judgement, fresco in St Dmitry, Vladimir, late twelfth century, with details of the head of an apostle (*bottom left*) and of an angel (*bottom right*)

detail. This is perhaps its greatest and most characteristic achievement. The Apostles and angels of St Dmitry are proof, if proof were needed, that the best Byzantine artists would have found completely unintelligible the accusation that they were for ever immured within unchangeable abstractions.

The paintings are not all of the same quality. The Apostles and angels on the north side of the vault are due to the best of the artists, but even here the heads are superior to the garments. The colours, too, are more delicate than those on the south side; blues and blue-greens against gold predominate, while on the other side are murkier red, brown, and olive hues. It may be correct to say that the less technically accomplished parts were executed by Russian pupils of the Greek masters, but such apparent national distinctions may also be partly due to the poor preservation of the paintings.

Although Suzdalia may have claimed the best talents among the itinerant Greek masters of the later twelfth century, the very perfection of the frescoes of St Dmitry may have been felt as a challenge as much to be avoided as to be imitated. The course which Russian painting was to take in the following centuries was directed not by the infrequent masterpieces in Vladimir, but by the incessant activity which continued in Novgorod. Here, during the latter half of the twelfth century, no fewer than twenty stone churches were built and decorated, and in the succeeding centuries the chronicles almost annually record the construction of new churches or the rebuilding and redecoration of others destroyed by fire. Whereas Kiev disappeared for centuries from the Russian political and cultural sphere, and the cities of Suzdalia languished under Mongol vassalage, Novgorod maintained its independence and was able to continue its commercial and ecclesiastical relations with Constantinople. It is true that the confusions attending the Mongol invasion led inevitably to a decline of artistic creation during the later thirteenth century, and from this period few icons and no wall-paintings have been preserved. The more interest, therefore, attaches to the last great mural ensemble of the twelfth century, since in it may be seen the position of Novgorod painting at the end of the pre-Mongol period and some of the incipient influences which were later to become dominant.

Until the Second World War, when it was almost totally destroyed, the Church of the Saviour at Nereditsa, in the fields some two miles from Novgorod, contained the earliest complete ensemble of wall-paintings.[5] This church was but one of many which from the twelfth to the end of the fifteenth centuries rose in the suburbs and outlying villages of Novgorod. It had been built by a prince of Novgorod, Yaroslav Vladimirovich, in 1198 and painted the following year (see above, page 45). Abandoned in the later Middle Ages, its villagers gone, and its conventual structures destroyed, the little church had the good fortune to be ignored during the various restoration campaigns of the eighteenth and nineteenth centuries, until it was finally and carefully restored in 1904. The unusually extensive cycle of paintings covering the vaults and walls above a simulated marble dado quite reasonably attracted a degree of attention because of its completeness, but it also exhibited so many important aspects of the cultural conditions prevailing at the end of the twelfth century that its provincial character has perhaps been unduly ignored. The very fact that the frescoes represent a local variant of the dominant Byzantine trends makes them more significant for the history of Russian painting than the perfection found in St Dmitry in Vladimir.

The paintings reached from the dome almost to the floor of the church, and followed in the main the traditional mid-Byzantine scheme, except that in the dome itself the

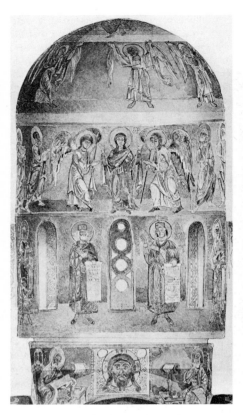

42. Scheme of the frescoes within the dome
of the Church of the Saviour, Nereditsa, 1199

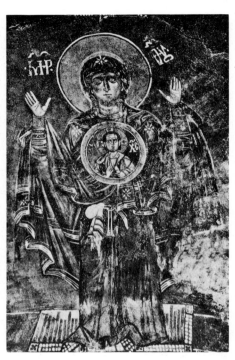

43. Virgin Orans, in the Church of the Saviour,
Nereditsa, 1199

Apostles and the Virgin accompanied by two angles. These figures, like the Archangels above them, stood upon a ground, so that they

Ascension replaced the Pantokrator [42]. Although this subject in that position was not unknown in earlier Byzantine art – it occurs in Venice, Salonica, and in the Caucasus at Ani – it is worth observing that the substitution of an historical episode for the abstraction of the Pantocratic image tended to humanize the religious history much as the Apocalyptic Christ of western Romanesque art was transformed into the Saviour of the Last Judgement in Gothic sculpture. At Nereditsa Christ rose in a rainbow aureole upheld by six winged angels. In the drum of the dome the dramatic movement continued in the agitated figures of the

seemed to move in a definite space. The Apostles were less doctrinal intermediaries between heaven and earth than companions of the corporeal, historical Saviour. In the zone below the story recovered its traditional symbolic character with the range of eight Old Testament prophets and with the Evangelists in the pendentives. These majestic, solitary figures were reminiscent of the traditional figures of the Kievan school, and indicated that the painters were still influenced by mosaic art.

In the apse stood the Virgin Blacherniotissa, a variant of the Virgin Orans, wearing on her

breast a medallion portrait of Christ Emmanuel, again the last of the great line descending from Kiev [43]. In contrast, however,

Last Judgement prepared with the Instruments of the Passion for Christ's second
coming, and of Christ as the Ancient of Days

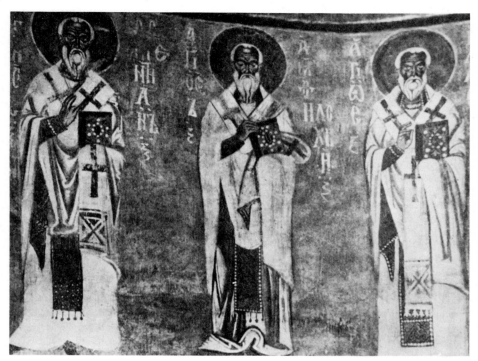

44. Fresco in the apse of the Church of the Saviour,
Nereditsa, 1199

to earlier apsidal figures, which were attended
only by Archangels, here there approached
from either side a procession of male and
female saints led by the first Russian martyrs,
SS. Boris and Gleb.[6] Below the traditional
Liturgical Eucharist were three rows of
figures, the upper two containing the customary Fathers and other dignitaries [44], and the
lower forming an unusual deesis wherein the
standing figure of the tonsured Christ as High
Priest was flanked by medallions of the Virgin
and the Baptist. The dogmatic symbols were
completed by representations on the chancel
vault of the Hetimasia or empty throne of the

flanked by the Archangels Gabriel and
Michael. On the whole, the frescoes of the
chief sacramental spaces of the church, the
dome, apse, and chancel, complied with traditional Byzantine formulas. On the west wall
was an extended depiction of the Last Judgement in two zones, with many separate and
traditional scenes. The similarity of the range
of seated Apostles to those in St Dmitry in
Vladimir permits a conjectural restoration of
the lost portions of the latter frescoes.

If the iconographical plan at Nereditsa exhibited no startling departures, except in matters of detail, or in the historical interest of

such scenes as the Ascension, in just those details and in the technical execution these frescoes provided most revealing evidence of the complex sources of Russian painting in the later Middle Ages. The presence here of several different hands could easily be noted.[7] That some of them may have been Greeks, or that the scheme was certainly devised by a priest of Greek origin or Greek training, can be assumed from the programme, but other factors indicate that among these masters, of whom some must have been Russians since many of the inscriptions are in the local Novgorod dialect, there were many who had come from the East or who had been trained elsewhere than in Constantinople. To the Constantinopolitan tradition we may ascribe the general iconographical plan, especially such representations as the Virgin Orans, the Hetimasia, the Archangels, and the deesis, all familiar from Kiev. The stocky figure of the Virgin was a provincial variant of the heavily proportioned Virgin in St Sophia.

On the other hand, although the painting of the dome, pendentives, and apse retained the clear articulation between symbolism and structure typical of the best Byzantine work in the capital, the remainder of the church was completely covered from vault to pavement with scenes enclosed in square frames on a blue ground, which were more suggestive of the paintings in the cave churches of Cappadocia. This eastern aspect was further substantiated in iconography and execution. Many details were closer to oriental, even Caucasian, precedent than to Constantinopolitan procedure. This was particularly evident in the Baptism of Christ, where the opportunity to portray the nude figure in a spirit evocative of classical antiquity was ignored in favour of a more matter-of-fact image [45]. More conspicuous were the anecdotal character and the realistic touches in the attendant neophytes, one of whom was removing his coat, while another swam out from the bank towards the centre of the river. Again the lack of spatial consistency whereby the figures were painted

in three sizes according to their hieratic importance, the attendants smallest, the angels of middle size, the Christ and the Baptist largest of all, followed Syrian precedent.

Also, in the heads of the various saints and Apostles not only different hands but different artistic traditions might be observed. The heads of such saints as Basil the Great, John Chrysostom, Gregory the Wonder-Worker, and Nicholas the Wonder-Worker were almost transcriptions in fresco of the heads of the Fathers in Kiev. In the head of St Peter in the Ascension light and dark lines and areas created an almost sculptural effect. Other heads of a more eastern type and, as noted, often those of a specifically eastern tradition, such as the ascetics and eastern saints, were treated as severely frontal linear patterns, now approaching a summary, even sketchy impressionism, elsewhere based on an arabesque of decorative motifs which symbolized rather than visually suggested the three-dimensional character of the forms, yet without sacrificing the vivid realism of eastern Byzantine art [46].[8] In addition St Rhipsime, particularly venerated as the proto-martyr of the Armenian Church, was depicted in the diaconicon. Her presence in the sanctuary leads one to wonder whether the clerical staff may not have included some eastern priest, come to Novgorod in the train of Yaroslav's Ossetian wife. In the heads of the first group the broad rhythmical divisions of light and shade in mosaic had been translated into a similar broadly plastic style resembling late antique illusionism [47].

With the loss of Nereditsa, an irreparable calamity for the study of European as well as Russian art, the extensive frescoes of 1156 or slightly earlier in the Cathedral of the Transfiguration in the Mirozhsky Monastery at Pskov have acquired a new importance as a precious example of a completely painted mid-twelfth-century interior. Although the work must have been directed by a Greek master, given the Greek inscriptions and the traditional Byzantine iconography, his less accomplished

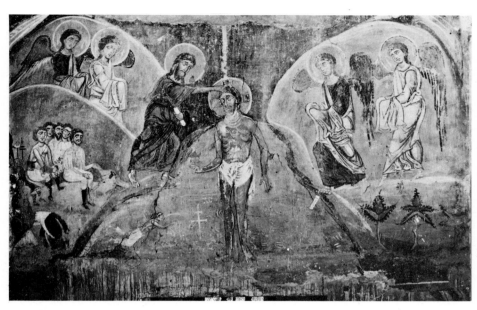

45–7. The Baptism, head of St Phocas, and head of St Peter,
frescoes in the Church of the Saviour, Nereditsa, 1199

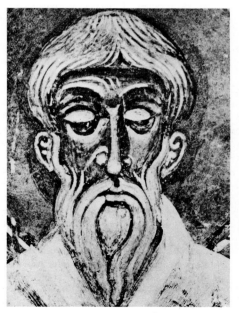

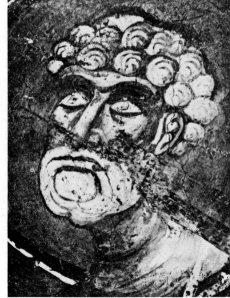

Russian assistants can be recognized by their dependence more upon line than upon modelling for the construction of their figures. More provincial than the work at Nereditsa, the Mirozhsky paintings nonetheless prove the vitality of the pictorial tradition at Novgorod and Pskov before the Tartar invasion.[9] After 1240 more than a century elapsed before monumental painting again appeared in northern Russia. This hiatus was in large part due to the disturbed times there and abroad. From 1240 the rest of Russia, with the exception of Novgorod and Pskov, was too seriously concerned with discovering a way to live under Tartar rule to undertake important schemes of public decoration, while to the south the Greek Empire itself lay for sixty years in bondage to the western crusaders who held Constantinople from 1204 until 1261. After the recapture of Constantinople by Michael VIII in 1261, the last and one of the most brilliant periods of Byzantine art was inaugurated under the Palaeologos dynasty. By 1303 new confidence in a revived political order had achieved remarkable artistic expression in the mosaics in the Church of the Chora Monastery in Constantinople, better known by its Turkish title as the Mosque of Kariye-Djami. The style which culminated in these mosaics prevailed not only in the capital itself, but throughout the Balkan peninsula, especially in Macedonia and Serbia. Hence it has come to be considered of Macedonian origin so far as it reached northern Russia, where iconographical similarities may be observed between Serbian and Macedonian scenes and their counterparts in Novgorod. Yet the fact that the late-fourteenth-century frescoes at Mistra in the Peloponnesus are in the same manner suggests that the Russian examples must have been related to Constantinople directly, as well as by the transmission of influences by itinerant masters coming north from the Balkans.

Direct connexions between Novgorod and Constantinople are in other activities historically so well attested that it would seem idle to predicate a roundabout route. The appearance of a flourishing school of fresco-painting in Novgorod and its environs soon after the middle of the fourteenth century cannot be entirely unconnected with the continuous and close relations between the clergy in Novgorod and the Patriarch in Constantinople. In 1353 emissaries sent by Bishop Moses to the Emperor John Cantacuzene and the Patriarch Philotheos returned from Constantinople and 'brought with them vestments ornamented with crosses and documents, with bestowal of great favour from the Emperor and from the Patriarch and a gold seal'.[10] From the middle years of the century there are several references to the activity of Greek painters whose influence, through their own works and the instruction they gave to their Russian pupils, may be held responsible for the revival of Russian painting after the Tartar interlude.

The impulse for much of this work can be traced to the presence of a learned and sensitive Greek, Theognostus, Metropolitan of Moscow from 1328 to 1353.[11] He had come of age in Constantinople during the first bright years of the Palaeologos Renaissance, and during his residence in Russia he continued to patronize Greek artists and to encourage their Russian pupils. Through his influence the Great Prince of Moscow, Simon Ivanovich, and his wife Anastasia also commissioned mural work. In 1344 two stone churches were decorated; the Cathedral Church of the Virgin in the Metropolitan's palace by 'Greek masters', and the palace church of the Archangel Michael by the Russian artists 'Zacharias, Denis, Joseph, and Nicholas', commissioned by Simon Ivanovich. The following year paintings in the church of the Monastery of the Saviour were ordered by Anastasia. They were executed by 'Goitan, Simon, and Ivan, of Russian birth but pupils of the Greeks'. In 1346 the Church of St John is mentioned, making a total of four masonry churches frescoed in three years by Greek and Russian painters.

Of all this work in Moscow unfortunately no trace remains, but a group of churches in

Novgorod and the vicinity preserved into the twentieth century enough of their original decoration to make possible some understanding of the character of late-fourteenth-century fresco-painting in Russia. The Church of the Dormition at Volotovo was built in 1352 and frescoed first in 1363 and again in the 1380s. Although the church was severely damaged by the Swedes in the seventeenth century the frescoes, almost alone among medieval Russian wall-paintings, had never been whitewashed or overpainted. The destruction of the church in the Second World War was therefore all the more unfortunate. In the main the decorative scheme followed the typical mid-Byzantine formula. The Pantokrator brooded in the dome; beneath him were the ranks of Archangels, Prophets, and Patriarchs, the Evangelists in the pendentives, and in the apse the Virgin, here enthroned with the Child, and below her the Divine Liturgy and the Church Fathers.[12] The narrative scenes, however, included several specifically Novgorodian and Russian incidents.

Familiar as this scheme may be, certain iconographical and stylistic innovations hinted that the classic serenity of the eleventh-century Byzantine concept was yielding to a more dramatic, emotional attitude towards dogma and history. The Pantokrator had lost his stern and serious expression and seemed to lean forward blessing rather than judging his people. The enthroned Virgin no longer reigned in lonely majesty in the apse, but was the focus of a double procession which included angels, prophets, and Joachim and Anna, as well as the usual saints who had appeared at Nereditsa. Taken as a whole the entire apse from dome to floor was organized as a triple series of concentric movements, from the angels and prophets moving towards the enthroned Virgin and Child, and the Apostles advancing to receive the bread and wine from the hands of Christ, to the Church Fathers contemplating the elements symbolized in the cross and chalice on the throne. The climax, of course, was daily re-enacted in the liturgical ceremonies. In this way later Byzantine iconography enriched the dogmatic programme and accomplished that instantaneous and mystical transition from the symbolic performance to the demonstration of doctrine on the walls.

This dramatic tendency was further elaborated in the scenes from the lives of Christ and the Virgin, where there were slight but telling indications that this growing interest in what may be called the human element of the story was affected by influences reaching Novgorod through her constant commercial relations with the West. The *Noli Me Tangere*, wherein Christ appears only to Mary Magdalene, the representation of the dead Christ standing in an open tomb, and the substitution of the Vernicle (Veronica's Veil) for the Mandilion portrait are three instances of western influence.[13]

Stylistically the frescoes were remarkable for the new manner which they announced for northern Russia, and which is best understood as the transmission of the finest type of Palaeologos art of the last Byzantine Renaissance. Like the authors of the mosaics of the Kariye-Djami, these Byzantine painters had almost abandoned their taste for the isolated single figure. Even in Constantinople this was in part due to the gradual replacement of mosaic by fresco, in which complex scenes could more easily be depicted. There was a preference for narrative with small figures placed in front of landscapes or architectural settings. Unlike the earlier backgrounds, which were often merely symbols of place and time, these atmospheric landscapes and buildings in reasonably accurate perspective suggested actual situations. The use of architecture was perhaps less conspicuous at Volotovo than the treatment of landscape, but the interior of a monastic refectory included a table in correct rather than oblique perspective, and in the background a most persuasive depiction of the exterior of a building with a dome on a drum and pendentives.[14]

Even more remarkable was the treatment of landscape as a play of sharp zigzags streaking

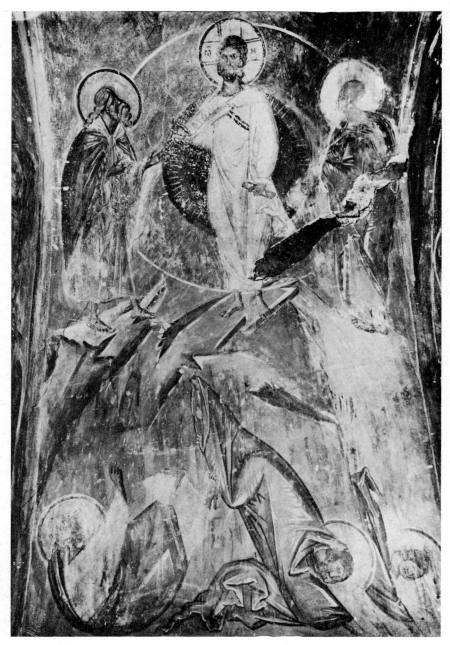

48. The Transfiguration, fresco in the Church of the Dormition,
Volotovo, 1380s

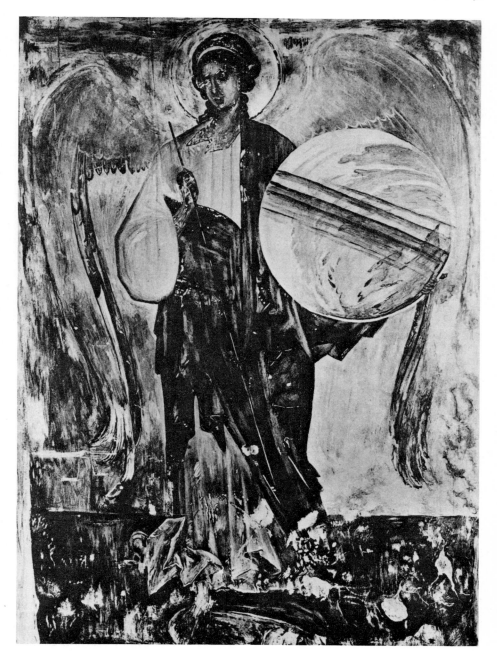

49. An Archangel fresco in the Church of the Dormition,
Volotovo, 1380s

above and behind the figures in such scenes as the Nativity, the Annunciation to the Shepherds, and the Transfiguration [48]. Only along the edges were there vestiges in the form of short white dots of the earlier terraces which had stood for mountains in the eleventh and twelfth centuries. It was as if the artist, hurrying to record his visual impression of moving figures, had only glanced at the landscape beyond them and set it down as a summary contrast of light and dark.

The painter lavished his peculiar and very personal skill on his figures. Even to a standing Archangel he imparted overwhelming energy in his spacious design of the great arcs of wings and globe punctured by the broken contours of the garments [49]. This search for a more complex yet unified action continued in the narrative scenes as an impressionist shorthand of extraordinary effect. The figures were quickly and slightly sketched by means of dark masses and light lines which succinctly conveyed their agitation. Gone for ever was the static equilibrium of the frescoes of St Dmitry, where tone and line are of equal value in rendering form and movement. Here the function of line was to urge the darker masses into violent movement. Only in this manner could the artist render the figure in so many positions hitherto unattempted in Byzantine painting. Paleologos realism dictated the attitude of Mary in the Ascension twisting her head to follow the rising Christ. The shepherd standing beside the sleeping Joachim turned his back to the spectators [50], and in the Journey of the Magi the youth seated on the brow of a hill, like the personification of landscape in classical art, turned half round to point out the star in the sky. The substitution of a visual for a conceptual aesthetic was complete.

The figures mentioned above were among the best at Volotovo, the work of an unusually gifted personality who could capture the peculiar quality of an image seen instantly and as swiftly recorded. The remaining scenes appear to have been executed by other hands and, although less competent, were treated

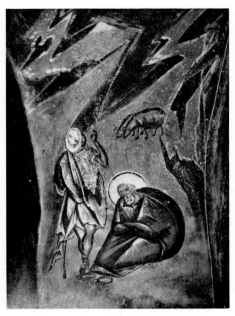

50. Joachim's Dream, fresco in the church of the Dormition, Volotovo, 1380s

within the same aesthetic conceptions, so that we may predicate the existence at Volotovo of a group of painters, of whom one at least must have been well acquainted with the latest developments at Constantinople.

It is tempting but imprudent to think that the leader of this atelier was the famous master, Theophanes 'the Greek' (Feofan Grek), who was working in Novgorod in 1378 in the Church of the Transfiguration.[15] If little is known of his activity in Russia, and less of his origin and early training, that little is still more than we know of his predecessors, including even the monk Alimpi of Kiev (see below, page 113). After the frescoes of 1378 there is no reference to him until 1395, when he painted the Church of the Nativity of the Virgin in Moscow with Semen Cherny (Simon 'the Black') and their pupils. In 1399 he was working with his assistants in the Cathedral of

St Michael in the Kremlin, and in 1405 with Prokhor of Gorodets and Andrey Rublev in the Cathedral of the Annunciation. All these frescoes disappeared when the Kremlin churches were rebuilt in the late fifteenth century, so that only the frescoes in the Transfiguration in Novgorod survived to show us what his style was like.

From other sources there are precious scraps of information about the man and his career. The most extensive account is found in a letter of 1414 or 1415 from Epiphanius the Wise, the biographer of St Sergius, to another disciple of the same saint, Cyril of Tver, wherein Theophanes is described as the 'very excellent zoomorph, book illuminator, and painter'. Epiphanius further says that Theophanes had a special gift for architectural drawing, that he had drawn a city in a fresco in St Michael, and that he had painted a panoramic view of Moscow on a stone wall in the palace of Prince Vladimir Andreevich. Theophanes had also made for Epiphanius a schematic drawing of Hagia Sophia in Constantinople. Cyril had seen this several years before, and wrote to Epiphanius asking for a copy.[16] From this letter two important facts emerge: Theophanes worked in Constantinople, and he surpassed his fellow artists and attracted the admiration of his contemporaries by his ability to draw living beings. Apparently he worked swiftly, without patterns, and in full view of spectators, thereby exciting much wonder. He must have possessed an admirably sure technique, an authoritative memory, and an imaginative faculty of the highest order. With these gifts he must also have been a painter thoroughly familiar with the pictorial impressionism of the Palaeologos Renaissance. Finally, if the chronological indications are to be trusted, if he was in Novgorod in 1378, if his last work was performed in Moscow in 1405, and if he died sometime before the date of Epiphanius's letter, his birth may be placed in the decade 1330–40.

Compared with Theophanes, the painters of Volotovo seem erratic and uncertain of the success of the effects for which they strive, or perhaps of the means by which they should achieve them. Theophanes's impressionism continued the same visual appreciation of forms in light, but based upon a more intimate understanding of the human body, as well as of the principles of Byzantine style. One might

51. Theophanes the Greek: The Patriarch Noah, fresco in the Church of the Transfiguration, Novgorod, 1378

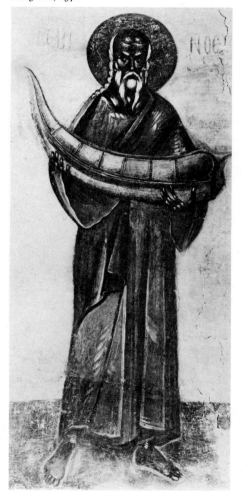

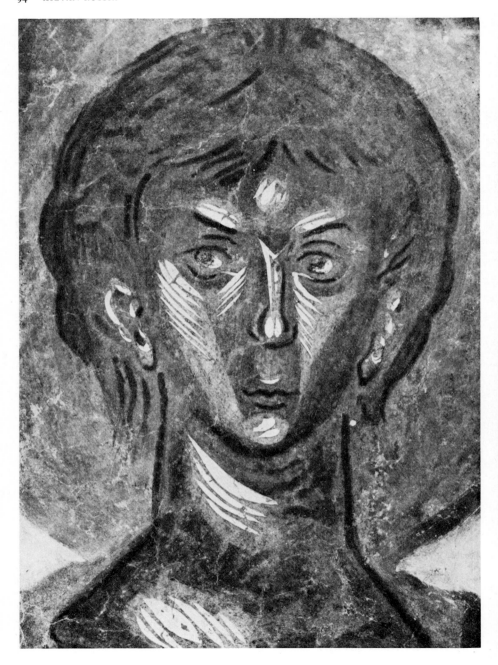

52 and 53. Theophanes the Greek: Head of the Patriarch Abel (*opposite*) and head of St Macarius (*right*), frescoes in the church of the Transfiguration, Novgorod, 1378

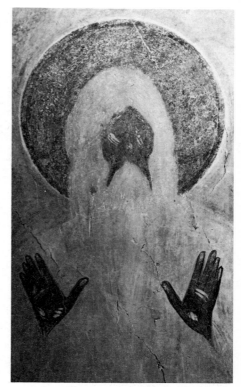

think Theophanes had studied ancient sculpture, so strong is the feeling that his Old Testament prophets are spiritual descendants of the late Hellenistic philosophers. The most conspicuous technical divergence from the Volotovo frescoes is the substitution of a curved for a straight line in the highlights. Although it is true that the slashing accents at Volotovo were frequently charged with dramatic and tragic sentiment, they often suggested to the eye more the flutter of drapery in the wind than the movement of substantial forms through space.

In the absence of any extensive narrative scenes we can only imagine how Theophanes would have painted movement, but his prophets show with how much care he observed the play of light over objects and distributed his highlights so that the fundamental rhythms of forms in space are suggested [51]. His technique is pictorial; the masters of Volotovo were graphic artists intent on seizing with lightning speed the combination of lines which would best suit their purpose. Theophanes's colour scheme seems to revive the earth palette of antique painting. In contrast to the intense, pure colour at Volotovo, his grounds and darker areas are a flat red, upon which the modelling in a lighter red, with black outlines and white highlights, suggests the same kind of colour simplification that was appearing contemporaneously in icons. In Theophanes's work there is that perceptible echo of antiquity inseparable from the best Byzantine painting [52].

Yet Theophanes was not only an artist in the classic tradition. The intenser experience of the religious life which the East brought to Byzantium found expression in his remarkable image of St Macarius, the ascetic who claimed that he lived in the Egyptian desert for thirty years without ever eating, drinking, or sleeping

as much as Nature required [53]. This figure is so like a fresco of St Anthemius in the Kariye-Djami, that it has been suggested that Theophanes may have executed his first work in that church.[17] But the Anthemius is too assured to be the work of a beginner. The temperament which produced it, mature and spacious, could scarcely have developed the nervous energy of Theophanes. Yet he may have known this fresco, for his peculiarities are divergences rather than differences.

From Epiphanius's letter we gather that before coming to Russia Theophanes had painted the interiors of more than forty stone churches, not only in Constantinople, but also in Chalcedon, Galata, and Kaffa (Theodosia) in the Crimea, and, after leaving Novgorod, in Nizhny-Novgorod (now Gorky) and Gorodets, as well as in Moscow. But nothing remains of his work except the frescoes in the Transfiguration, and a few icons which have been attributed to him.

Elsewhere in Novgorod, in the Churches of St Theodore Stratilates and of the Nativity of Christ in the Cemetery (na Kladbishche) and in the Church of Kovalevo near the city, are late-fourteenth-century frescoes which continue the impressionist tendencies of Volotovo and Theophanes's work in the Transfiguration, but with declining technical distinction and expressive power. Apparently early in the 1380s Theophanes left Novgorod on his way to Moscow, and without his presence the Russian painters were unable to maintain the high level of his achievement. But their work, though more timid and pedestrian, at least sufficed to fill the churches of Novgorod with so many frescoes that it rivalled any western European city of the later Middle Ages in the wealth of its pictorial embellishment.

PART TWO

ICON-PAINTING

All Angel-kind marvelled at thy great work of flesh-taking; they saw the inaccessible God accessible to all as a man, dwelling with us and hearing from all: Alleluia.
    The Akathist Hymn

CHAPTER 8

ICON-PAINTING: CRITICISM,

ICONOGRAPHY, AND TECHNIQUE

Of all the varieties of pictorial art, the religious subject on a painted panel, the icon, has become most completely identified with the conception of a specifically Russian art. The word has even seemed at times to have lost its original Greek significance and come to mean Russian, rather than generally Byzantine, panel-painting. The reason for this assimilation of the word to Russian art is that far more Russian than Greek icons have been preserved and that in Russia and elsewhere in eastern Europe the use and practice of icon-painting continued into the twentieth century, although, as the dominant manifestation of Russian pictorial expression, icon-painting was gravely compromised by the westernization of Russian art after the seventeenth century.

Familiar though the fact may be that quantities of Russian icons are still in existence, and some are even found in western museums and private collections, the understanding of the artistic qualities of icon-painting and its historical analysis present considerable difficulties for the western observer. Even in Russia systematic study had to wait until the beginning of the present century.[1] In the course of the nineteenth century the revival of interest in the Russian past on the part of the Slavophiles inevitably drew attention to the large numbers of icons preserved in churches, and in the houses of the Old Believers who had throughout the centuries continued to cherish the ancient religious pictures. Although icons at first were valued principally as examples of a historic and traditional way of life, they soon attracted the attention of connoisseurs who collected them for their rarity, technical perfection, and artistic quality. By 1914 the major historical and critical principles had been established by the study and publication of the important collections in St Petersburg and Moscow, especially those formed by N. P. Likhachev (now in the Russian Museum, Leningrad) and in Moscow by I. S. Ostroukhov (now in the Tretyakov Gallery and Historical Museum).[2] This preliminary work was reduced in value by the poor condition of almost all the icons, which were covered with layers of dirt and repaint accumulated through long years of use in churches. Although some cleaning and restoration had been done before 1917, only after the October Revolution were the true splendours of medieval Russian painting uncovered by the activity of the State Restoration Workshops in Moscow.[3] Of special interest was the recovery of a dozen icons of the twelfth and thirteenth centuries. For the first time it was possible to gain some conception of the character of icon-painting in Kievan Russia, until then merely a matter of tradition, since the oldest painted surfaces had been totally concealed beneath layers of repaint. In recent years a more coherent picture of the development of icon-painting in Russia has gradually emerged, although for the Western student the absence from Europe and America of any extensive collections of first-rate examples in public museums and the scarcity of private collections make the study of icon-painting at first hand almost impossible. In the circumstances we have to rely on the publications of the eminent Russian scholars who have devoted themselves to this work.[4]

As in the history of architecture and mural painting, the study of icons is handicapped by the difficulties caused by the successive destruction of Russian cities and the rebuilding of churches, with the usual dispersal or damage to the old furnishings. Such icons as were preserved have suffered seriously. The more revered the icon, the more frequently it was repainted or repaired if it showed signs of deterioration – a not unlikely situation in a humid climate with extreme contrasts of temperature. And each repainting, often executed with little regard for preserving more than the most casual indication of the original colours and forms, was followed by frequent re-varnishing, so that by the end of the nineteenth century the most famous icons venerated in the Russian sanctuaries presented a darkened surface bearing little or no relation to the original design, often buried under five or six layers of later paint.[5] And the general anonymity of medieval art meant that few icons were signed, and almost none dated. Moreover, in most cases the provenance is unclear or confused. Only by painstaking analytical comparison, constantly subject to modifications, as further icons are cleaned and unsuspected ones brought to light, can even a tentative identification of schools and manners

be made. Yet even at the present stage it is possible to grasp the general outlines of a historical process.

There is, finally, one more difficulty in studying Russian icon-painting of which the western student must be aware. His familiarity with the historical chronology and technical progression of European painting from the later Middle Ages to modern times prepares him for a similar development in Russian painting based on a gradual and continuous conquest, technically and expressively, of the world of sense impressions. In Russian and Byzantine art no such evolution occurs, and the infrequent evidences of intensive observation of the visual world are too slight to deflect painting from its inexorable pursuit of a very different kind of 'reality'. To the western observer Russian painting often appears static, hieratic, and repetitive, whereas actually its very lack of 'progress' is only proof that its methods as well as its aims were not only different but self-sufficient.

Icon-painting, and indeed almost all Russian painting up to the end of the seventeenth century, was religious in origin and use. The secular standards of western criticism, perceptible in European literature as early as the sixteenth century, whereby even a religious painting is examined as a work of art with definable aesthetic implications, were unknown in Russian art before the eighteenth century. The criterion of artistic beauty had nothing to do with the efficacy of the image as an aid to religious experience, although the more effective the image the more it would contain those qualities of technical perfection, formal order, tonal harmony, and expressive power upon which artistic quality may be said to be based. However, the search for these elements, so conspicuous a preoccupation of the western artist since the end of the fifteenth century, seems to have been only a secondary concern of the Russian painter. His image was intended for a specific place in a church or chapel, or alcove reserved for devotions in a private house. Until recently an icon was never studied as a historical document, or criticized as a work of art. Russian painting, in contrast to European painting, had been for centuries concerned, not with the conquest of space or of movement, but with the discovery of the mystical world which lies beyond sense experience. In its own terms it had its own schools, masters, and masterpieces, but they are impossible to assess on the basis of contemporary western work, just as they are difficult to understand on the basis of Latin religious experience.

To comprehend the particular character of Russian religious painting it is necessary to consider for a moment the Byzantine art from which it originated. Early in the history of the Eastern Church the popularity of pictorial images, encouraged in large measure by enthusiastic Syrian elements, aroused the concern of more conservative Greek churchmen in Constantinople who eventually, by the end of the seventh century, considered the making and veneration of images heretical and finally succeeded in establishing this view officially. From 754 until the end of this so-called Iconoclastic Controversy in 843 an effective prohibition was in force against the manufacture and use of any painting or sculpture. The loss of art objects, of those destroyed as well as those forbidden to come into existence, was incalculable, and the effects, even after the prohibition against painting was relaxed, were enduring.

Nevertheless, with the end of the Iconoclastic Controversy and the re-establishment of images within the churches, an important position had been gained. Henceforth the icon was considered worthy of veneration as a mystical counterpart of the doctrine or person represented. In this way it had a 'reality' different from and considerably more important than any actual sensory experience on the part of those who contemplated it. The intention of the painter could never be limited merely to the depiction of objects and situations in the world about him. His obligation was to portray as best as he could events and personages whose actual presence may have been remote in space and time, but whose spiritual reality could be invoked by his skill. An icon was neither a literal representation nor an abstract symbol. The painter needed some knowledge of the world, since the persons and places he was to portray were all considered historically true, but their mystical significance prevented any too precise identification with the living world around him. The Russian painter's task, like that of his Greek predecessors and masters, was to preserve an infinitely subtle balance between nature and the supernatural, between what is known through the senses and what is apprehended through the mind and the emotions. For ever forbidden to the Russian painter was the religious and artistic reasoning which led western worshippers and artists from the Greek abstractions of Cimabue and Duccio to the realism of Caravaggio. Consequently the western student must always, in considering any particular icon, ask whether or not the artist, granted his means and intention, successfully complied with the demands of his craft. A history of icon-painting based on the gradual conquest of the visual world would only demonstrate spasmodic and usually unsuccessful attempts to assimilate European techniques. It could not consider some of the greatest masterpieces as anything other than 'primitive', much as the Italian painters of the thirteenth and fourteenth centuries seemed tentative to the nineteenth-century critic.

Thus to distinguish eastern from western European painting does not mean that we have to do with a school having no resemblance to European art. Russian painting, like later medieval European painting, had its source in Byzantine art, and he who is familiar with Duccio and Giotto will be in a better position to assess the qualities of Theophanes and Andrey Rublev. To say that Russian painting is different is not to say that it is unconcerned with the fundamental problems of position in space, which in turn require consideration of time, action, and sentiment. It is just that the accent, the degree of intensity, is different. Space and time are not the place here and the moment now, but taken together create an imprecise mode of duration and extension. Action and sentiment do not derive from individual caprice or intention, but are related to the divine law that determined the creation of the world and its salvation by the Son of God. Feeling derives from the intimate communion between the observer and the object of his contemplation.

Under such conditions this painting may appear to western eyes stationary rather than evolutionary. But to charge the Russian icon-painter with an endless repetition of stereotyped models is not only to overlook the technological improbability that any two works made by hand are ever exactly identical, but also to disregard the fact that repetition also may imply constancy and permanence, qualities little valued in western art. What was sought was not an ever new or original interpretation, but rather the refinement of the familiar in the hope that thereby one approached more closely the ultimate authority of the divine prototype. Such painting will have its exalted moments, austere and uncompromising, perhaps revealed only after long and intimate communion, perhaps accessible in their fullest meaning only to those who share the same religious convictions.

Russian icon-painting shares with medieval European painting the subjects and images common to both the Orthodox and Catholic Churches, but the long independent history of the Eastern Church, as well as its close connexions with the ancient sources of Christianity, early led to a different emphasis on certain subjects, and even to the use of themes unfamiliar or unusual in the West. To the traditional sources in the Old and New Testaments and in the lives of the founders of Christianity the Russians added their own local saints and interpretations of their own religious history.[6] The chief distinction is the relatively longer life of old traditions and the lack of thematic variety. In Russian painting this appears in the omission of many anecdotal or genre details which as early as the thirteenth century became conspicuous factors in religious pictures in the West.

The formal and dogmatic scheme for the interior decoration of a church, inherited from Byzantine art of the post-iconoclastic period, best serves as an indication of the fundamental character of Russian religious art. Such a scheme appeared, as we have seen, in the first great church of St Sophia and was used, with only slight modifications, for such churches as received elaborate internal painting until the end of the fourteenth century.

In the usual mid-Byzantine and early Russian scheme a medallion of Christ Pantokrator was placed in the centre of the dome [31]. Two other images of Christ are related to this. Versions of a medallion head, slightly younger but still showing traces of ascetic experience, are known in Greek as the Mandilion (because it had been imprinted on a veil) or in Russian as the Nerukotvorny [59], the 'Image Not Made with Hands', referring to a legendary contemporary portrait of Christ supposed to have been miraculously painted for Abgar IV, King of Osrhoene. It had been found at Edessa in Mesopotamia in 544 and taken in 944 to Constantinople.[7] Since the Mandilion was presumably a portrait from life, it is easily distinguished from the western image of Veronica's Veil by the absence of the crown of thorns and marks of suffering. Another popular image of Christ Emmanuel in the form of a child, somewhat aged to western eyes, usually appears in the medallion worn by the Virgin Blacherniotissa or Znamenie ('of the Sign').

Similarly the Russian representation of the Virgin begins with the majestic images of the mid-Byzantine period, and while variations and adaptations of the major types communicate an increasing feeling of maternal love for the holy infant, even the most intimate portrayals maintain a dignity and aloofness which the West neglected or lost in the later Middle Ages. The earliest image of the Virgin, the Byzantine Hodegetria ('She who shows the Way'), was derived from an icon said to have been painted by St Luke and blessed by the

Virgin herself.[8] It had been sent by the Empress Eudocia from Palestine to Constantinople in 438 and placed in the church of the Hodegoi (the Pointers of the Way) within the imperial palace, where it became the palladium of the city and Empire. The ancient painting may have been destroyed during the Iconoclastic Controversy or when the Turks conquered Constantinople, but its form is preserved in many replicas and may easily be recognized. The Virgin is represented standing (although occasionally only the half-length figure is shown), and holds the Child on her left arm while she blesses him with her right hand. Christ is dressed in the antique tunic and mantle of an adult, holds a scroll in His left hand, and blesses the spectator with His right. Between the Mother and Son there is no play of sentiment. This austere and autocratic image is rarely encountered in Russian art. There is no extant example of it from the pre-Mongol period, but it appears occasionally in later examples, such as the fourteenth-century type of the Virgin of Tikhvin, copied from an earlier Greek original.[9] The familiar Russian variants, known by the names of the localities where particularly venerated wonder-working icons were preserved, such as the Virgins of Smolensk and of Murom, are seen to be later in date by the more sentimental relationship established between the Mother and Child. After the Hodegetria the Virgin Blacherniotissa enjoyed great popularity both in Constantinople and in Russia. This is the type of the Virgin Orans; she stands in a frontal position facing the spectator, her arms raised in the antique gesture of prayer, and on her breast she wears a medallion portrait of Christ as Emmanuel. The original of this version was the image of the Virgin in mosaic in the apse of the Church of the Blachernae in Constantinople, where the Virgin's veil was preserved. From this image and the circumstances of its veneration developed the specifically Russian scene of the Pokrov, or Miracle of the Virgin's Veil (see page 146).

The third most important image was the Virgin Platytera, enthroned as Queen of Heaven and holding the Christ Child on her knees. Although this image of the enthroned Virgin is found in western iconography, the easterners treated it with a difference, avoiding the use of royal garments in order not to compromise the supernatural character of the manifestation. In the course of time the Platytera became associated with the complex iconographical schemes of the Virgin's Assembly, and the Virgin as Queen of Angels, derived from stanzas in the ancient Akathist hymn (see page 126).

From the half-length representation of the Virgin Hodegetria there developed the images of mother-love known as the Eleusa (in Greek, pity or tenderness) or Umilenie in Russian. The most venerated icon of all the Russias up to modern times, the Virgin of Vladimir [54], was an early example of this type, a Constantinopolitan production of the early twelfth century. Yet, in spite of several variations in gesture, as in the manner in which the Virgin holds the Child and He embraces His Mother, the Russian artist never reached the degree of intimate human tenderness common to the western representations of the fourteenth and fifteenth centuries. Even the Virgin of the Umilenie maintains her autocratic reserve. Only in the sixteenth and seventeenth centuries did the image of the Virgin nursing the Child, the Bogoroditsa Mlekopitatelnitsa, enjoy much popularity, and then as the result of western influence.

Contrary to western practice certain Old Testament scenes frequently occur in Russian painting, chief among them those which prefigure the Incarnation and Passion of Christ, such as the Three Children in the Fiery Furnace or Elijah fed by the Ravens. Particular importance was attached to the appearance of the Trinity to Abraham and Sarah in the form of Three Angels [83]. The patriarchs and prophets of the Old Testament often accompany the image of the Pantokrator in the dome, or appear later on the iconostasis, and some were even admitted to the canon of saints, as St Elias (Elijah), to whom one of the first Christian churches in Kiev was dedicated.

Of the New Testament gospel accounts, the greatest attention was paid to the major episodes in the lives of Christ and the Virgin, particularly those illustrating the twelve principal feasts of the Christian year. These usually resembled the western counterparts, except for the Resurrection and Assumption. The former was always depicted in the Byzantine manner as the Anastasis, known in the West as the Descent into Limbo or Harrowing of Hell, where Christ appears as the victorious conqueror of the powers of evil, having broken down the gates of Hell and entered to retrieve the souls of the just who died before the establishment of the New Law. The Assumption was always represented in the Greek form of the Dormition, with the body of the Virgin stretched on a bier and attended by the sorrowing disciples. Behind the bier stands the invisible form of Christ, holding in his arms a small image of the Virgin's soul [76].

In the first period of Russian painting, from the end of the tenth to the end of the thirteenth century, these twelve feasts were usually painted in fresco on the walls of the church, illustrating the enactment of the doctrine of the Redemption through its historical incidents, in contrast to and in fulfilment of the more abstract portrayal of the dogma in the images on the dome and apse. Towards the end of the fourteenth century the peculiarly Russian development in ecclesiastical decoration known as the iconostasis, or wall of pictures, came into existence. In Byzantine churches the altar-space had been separated from the rest of the church by a low barrier, at first of slabs of marble, but later treated more architecturally as an arcade.[10] The earlier form of simple stone barrier can be seen in the mosaic of the Divine Liturgy from St Michael in Kiev. In the course of time to this barrier, or to the columns of the arcade, various icons were attached, sometimes only temporarily, sometimes permanently in the form of local icons (mestnye ikony), depicting the saint or feast to which the church was dedicated or which was particularly honoured in

that region. These local icons were often large, and as their number increased and it became more difficult to move them, a permanent barrier between the altar-space and the rest of the church gradually developed.

In the churches of the northern forest regions, which were almost invariably of wood, the representation of the twelve feasts on the walls was impractical in any other form than that of panel paintings, and it would appear that in the course of time icons of the twelve feasts were added to the barrier, directly above the local icons [120]. A two-fold tendency next developed. Not only did the wooden construction of the northern churches prevent the affixing to the upper parts of the building, in most cases only a flat ceiling, of the complex iconography of the Redemption which was easily portrayed in the dome, drum, and apse frescoes of masonry structures, but even in the latter the gradual increase in height of the double range of icons hid the frescoes in the apse from the view of the congregation [129].

Upon the central doors through which only the priest and sovereign might enter the sanctuary, whence they were called Royal Doors, were painted the figures from the pendentives and apse – namely, the four Evangelists, the Annunciation, and the Divine Liturgy. Immediately above the Royal Doors and the row of local icons was set the deesis range, containing the subjects formerly painted on the dome and drum. Here Christ appeared enthroned in the centre, accompanied by the Virgin on his right and St John the Baptist on his left. Strictly speaking, these three figures account for the deesis, but to them may be joined, according to the size of the iconostasis, St Michael and St Peter on the left, St Gabriel and St Paul on the right. On either side of them could be added the Church Fathers, who had formerly appeared in a row beneath the Divine Liturgy on the apse. Above the deesis came the icons of the Twelve Feasts, and sometimes other scenes, if space were available.

The image of the Virgin which had usually occupied the central apse appeared in the third row, usually as the Blacherniotissa, flanked on either hand by Old Testament prophets, headed by David and Solomon. If the iconostasis were unusually large or elaborate, a fifth range contained the figure of the Lord God of Sabaoth, the Ancient of Days, in the form of the Trinity, with the Crucified Christ and Dove of the Holy Spirit, accompanied by cherubim and seraphim and flanked by figures of the Old Testament patriarchs. In this way the complex three-dimensional demonstration of dogma which had formerly covered the walls of the church was accommodated to a two-dimensional surface in a strictly rational and coherent order, rising from the revelation of the Word through the Evangelists and the spectacle of the Risen Christ, accompanied by the scenes of His earthly life, to the mysteries of the Incarnation and the final Origin of the Law in the apparition of the Ancient of Days half lost in the darkness overhead.[11]

The community of Byzantine and Russian saints included several who may not be familiar to the western student. In addition to the Apostles and Evangelists, the Eastern Church honours the early Fathers, St Basil the Great, St John Chrysostom, St John of Damascus, St Gregory, St Cyril, and St Athanasius. A group of warrior saints was very popular with the laity; St George and St Dmitry, and the two Byzantine military saints, St Theodore Stratilates and St Theodore Tiron. Two female saints are interesting examples of the tendency towards abstraction which in the Greek Church is the counterpart of the Latin Church's search for a literal, naturalistic, identification of holiness with human personality. These are St Anastasia and St Paraskeva or Pyatnitsa. The former is a personification of the Resurrection or Anastasis; the latter a personification of Good Friday, Pyatnitsa being the Russian word for Friday, the fifth (pyatyi) day of the week.

To the saintly hierarchy the Russians added their own holy men and women.[12] First among them came St Vladimir, the God-Lover, and his mother St Olga, who first introduced Christianity into Russia. Then Vladimir's two younger sons, Boris and Gleb, innocent victims of the fierce family quarrels of the Rurikovichi for the succession to Kiev. Neither of these two princes, nor Vladimir himself for that matter, would appear to have been conspicuously virtuous, but the Russian people at once took to their hearts the pathetic stories of the defenceless Boris and Gleb, who, knowing that their elder brother Izyaslav was determined to remove them from the scene, willingly accepted death.

Subsequently the energetic founders of notable monastic establishments were canonized, including such remarkable men as St Sergius of Radonezh, St Cyril of Belo-ozersk, and SS. Zosima and Savva of the Solovetsky Monastery in the White Sea. The Russians also held in affectionate esteem such fanatical 'enthusiasts' as Andrew the Fool, whose vision prompted the development of the icon of the Pokrov, and St Basil the Blessed, an early-sixteenth-century anchorite much admired by Ivan IV.

For the painting of religious episodes and personages it is often charged that the Eastern Church restrained the invention of the artist and hampered the development of pictorial art by insisting on the strictest adherence to established iconographic principles. The existence of pattern books for the guidance of the icon-painter has been taken to mean that the medieval artists had little or no opportunity for freedom of expression. But as it can be shown that such freedom was unnecessary, even inimical, to the process of creating icons, so the pattern books appear only when, under western influences, the painter had begun to diverge from tradition. None are extant from the earliest period, and the later eighteenth-century examples, which are best known, are redactions of originals no earlier than the fifteenth century, if indeed as old as that.[13] Since the Greek painter Theophanes was admired in Moscow in the early fifteenth century for his ability to work from memory (that is, without a model), the later pattern books and painters' treatises were necessary disciplinary instruments in use at a time when for various reasons the artist no longer could or would follow traditional methods.

The technique of Greek and Russian icon-painting does not notably differ from that of western medieval tempera painting. The support was always wood, of lime or imported cypress for the best and earlier Greek works, more usually of pine for the later icons of the Russian north.[14] The wood was skilfully smoothed with an adze, and in earlier panels was much thinner than in later ones. The frame was not attached separately, but consisted of a flat raised border which was left when the centre portion of the panel had been cut back. These natural frames were at first very narrow, but gradually became so broad that in the seventeenth century they occupied half or more of the total area of small icons.

When the panel was thoroughly seasoned, it was often covered with a linen cloth upon which was laid a fine gesso ground. The design was drawn on this, often with the aid of a stencil by those painters who could not, like the celebrated Theophanes, work from memory.[15] The pigments, earth colours and mineral derivatives, were tempered with egg or wax. The latter medium resembling the ancient encaustic process produced a surface which could be smoothed and polished, and became very popular in the later elaborate works of the Moscow school.

With the systematization and even commercialization of painting in the seventeenth century, a division of labour was introduced. In the icon workshops there were masters, such as Simon Ushakov, who specialized in 'face-painting' after their assistants had completed the figures and landscape. The best works of the earlier periods however are indisputably by a single individual, just as the designs are personal, rather than servile copies of prescribed compositions. Only in the last period, when icon-painting had become susceptible to western influences, was an attempt made to enforce the use of stencilled patterns.

The background of the earlier icons was gold or silver, in accordance with Greek practice, but as early as the twelfth century a ground of white or yellow ochre was substituted, which gave the icon a characteristic brightness. Later, red, rose, even green and blue grounds were used, especially in Novgorod. Flesh tones were modelled in a mixture of ochre and white lead on a dark greenish-brown ground, which was allowed to stand for the shadows. Purple and violet, ultramarine, terra verde, light green, and red completed the palette. Effective colour harmonies were created by the contrast of complementaries in the modelling of garments, such as red or reddish-brown against green, set off by white highlights. In the finest icons the highlights were put in with gold leaf, mixed with lye and wax, which could be applied with a brush and then burnished. The effect was often like gold inlay. When the painting was finished it was covered with a layer of flax-seed or olive oil which temporarily brightened the colours, but after a few decades grew very dark. This dim surface, further disfigured by layers of candle soot, was continuously repainted until only the subjects remained. But so highly perfected was the icon-painter's technique that the original pigments endured unchanged, and with care can still be recovered from beneath numerous layers of repaint.

The considerable darkening of the originally brilliant primary hues affected the colour schemes of icon-painting in the sixteenth and seventeenth centuries, when the Church invoked the older icons as patterns to be scrupulously imitated. The contemporary condition of the colours was also taken as sacrosanct, so that in the later icons schemes of dark olive-green and black are frequent. The more thoughtful painters of the seventeenth century objected to such unnatural colours, as we see in the complaint of Joseph Vladimirov: 'Thou demandest that in our days the painter paint lugubrious and ungainly images and thus teachest us that we should be false to the ancient Scriptures. . . . Where and who found the instructions about painting the faces of the saints in dark, swarthy shades? Were all the saints dark and gaunt?'[16]

The custom of attaching metal decorations such as crowns and collars to the heads of the Virgin and Christ, which started in the fourteenth century, was gradually expanded to include stamped metal shields placed over the landscape backgrounds. Finally in the seventeenth century the metal frame (riza or oklad) became so elaborate that it covered all but the faces and hands of the figures. The bodies and other parts of the scene were represented in repoussé. In the last stage of icon-painting, undertaken during the eighteenth and nineteenth centuries, painters often executed only those parts which were not concealed by the frame.

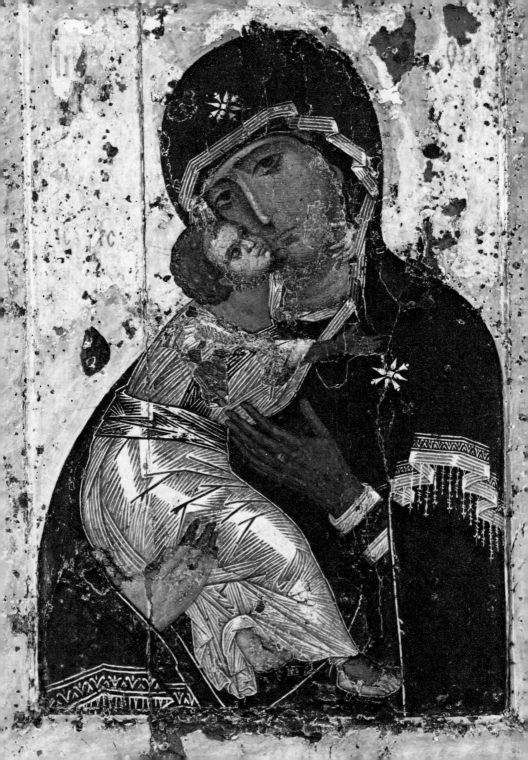

CHAPTER 9

THE EARLIEST ICONS

990–1250

The historical conditions of icon-painting in Russia are similar to those which determined the development of Russian architecture and mural painting. Upon the Christianization of the land at the end of the tenth century the immediate need for religious objects was satisfied by the importation of articles of Greek manufacture, and presumably by the arrival of Greek artisans. The prestige of Kiev as the centre of religious authority understandably led to the predominant influence exerted by Greek culture over the early schools of icon-painting elsewhere, whether immediately at Novgorod or shortly afterwards in Vladimir-Suzdal.[1] Legendarily the first icons were brought from Kherson to Kiev by Vladimir. Later in the eleventh century icons were imported for the Pecherskaya Lavra, and between 1131 and 1136 two icons of the Virgin were brought from Constantinople. One of these may have been the painting of the Virgin and Child [54] which in 1155 Andrey Bogoliubsky took from the Kievan suburb of Vishgorod to Suzdalia, where he subsequently placed it in his Cathedral of the Dormition in Vladimir.[2] As the miraculous Virgin of Vladimir, it had become by the late fourteenth century the most venerated of all the ancient Russian icons. In 1395 it was transferred to Moscow, ultimately to be seen on the iconostasis to the right of the Royal Doors in the later fifteenth-century Cathedral of the Dormition in the Kremlin. Its close and continuous identification with major events in Russian history, which gave it the distinction of a

national palladium, began with the legendary account that the horses bearing the icon to Rostov refused to move past Vladimir, thereby sanctioning Andrey's desire to establish his centre of government in the new city of Vladimir, where he would be immune from the pressure of the powerful boyars of Rostov.[3] Through the years the icon was frequently damaged, and just as often energetically repaired. In 1176, during the disturbances following the assassination of Andrey, and again in 1237 during the Tartar sack of Vladimir, the icon was stripped of its golden jewel-studded frame. At these times it may have lost the larger portion of its original surface. The extensive cleaning performed by the State Restoration Workshops in 1919 revealed that only the face and neck of the Virgin, the face of the Child, and inconsiderable portions of the background can be considered original.[4] Yet from these fragments and the general type of composition it is clear that what remains is a precious example of the finest Constantinopolitan painting of the early twelfth century, one of the earliest and most important examples of the Umilenie type of Virgin and Child.

The craftsmanship and conception are of the utmost certainty and elegance. In the faces the transition from contour line to modelled surface is accomplished with the greatest discretion. While the Virgin already displays such typical high Byzantine features as the narrow, pointed eyes, long nose, and small mouth and chin, there is no such insistence on either line or modelling as later led to strictly schematic renderings of the face. Over the whole a light veil of illusionism suggests rather than represents the soft play of living forms. In the

54. Greek: The Virgin of Vladimir, early twelfth century. *Moscow, Tretyakov Gallery*

Child the artist even attempted an infantile expression, very different from the aged baby who poses as Emmanuel in the usual Hodegetria. His snub-nosed, full-lipped countenance hints at the influence of classic sculpture, a suggestion borne out in the relatively lighter greenish-pink coloration of the Child in contrast to the swarthier flesh tones of the Virgin. A further illusion of living forms is seen in the interplay of glances; the Child eagerly reaches towards His mother, while the Virgin mournfully gazes at the spectator, and beyond him. The pervading gentleness of this image not only accounts for the unreserved affection in which it was held for centuries by the Russian people, but may also be considered as in some measure responsible for the quality of affectionate tenderness which constantly reappears in later Russian religious painting.

From earliest times the fame of the icons of Kiev was so great that neighbouring princes did not hesitate to make off with important ones whenever the occasion warranted. Just as the Virgin of Vladimir was taken by Andrey Bogoliubsky, so as late as the fifteenth century there are reports of the plundering of the Kievan churches. In this way, too, the style of the Kievan icons spread beyond the immediate vicinity of the older city to the provinces of the north and east. The fact that almost all the extant icons which can in one way or another be related to the earliest period of Russian icon-painting, and so to the regions of Kiev, Novgorod, and Suzdal before the Mongol invasion, were in modern times discovered in the cathedrals of the Moscow Kremlin or in towns in the neighbourhood of Moscow, may be considered as much the result of their artistic as of their dynastic prestige. They were later gathered from other parts of Russia to reinforce the pretensions of the Great Princes of Moscow as Tsars of All the Russias, and of the Metropolitans of Moscow as successors to the Greek Metropolitans of Kiev.

A large icon of the Annunciation [55], formerly in the Cathedral of the Dormition in

55. Russian under Greek influence: The Annunciation, early twelfth century. *Moscow, Tretyakov Gallery*

the Moscow Kremlin, and said to have been brought by Ivan the Terrible either from Veliky Ustiug in the far north-east or from the Yuriev (George) Monastery in Novgorod, may be an example of early-twelfth-century painting in Novgorod executed by Russian masters under Greek supervision.[5] The presence of a miniature figure of the Christ Child on the Virgin's breast (as if miraculously manifested in her womb) indicates an eastern iconographical source for this, the earliest surviving Russian representation of the Virgin of the Incarnation (Bogomater Voploshchenie) which was to recur for almost another millennium in the icon-painting of the Eastern Orthodox Churches. The majestic life-sized figures of the Archangel and the Virgin recall the mosaic of the Annunciation on the triumphal arch in the Kievan St Sophia, although the active gestures of the latter have somewhat subsided in the icon. In spite of much damage, including the loss of large portions of paint in the lower half of the panel and the tips of the Angel's wings, enough of the drawing survives to indicate that the artist was familiar with the finest pictorial canons of the middle Byzantine period. Although, in contrast to the author of the Vladimir Virgin, he depends more on line for the description of his forms, the relation of these to later Hellenistic sculpture indicates the continuity of the Greek tradition in early Russian painting. The Russian inscriptions, as well as several uncertainties in the draughtsmanship, such as the tendency of curves to become straight lines, as in the outstretched hand of the Angel, suggest that the painter was Russian rather than Greek. An important difference may be noticed between the heads of the two figures. The Virgin's face, with the large, heavy-lidded eyes of the Kievan Annunciate, resembles the Virgin of Vladimir's not only in its tenderness but also in the Greek

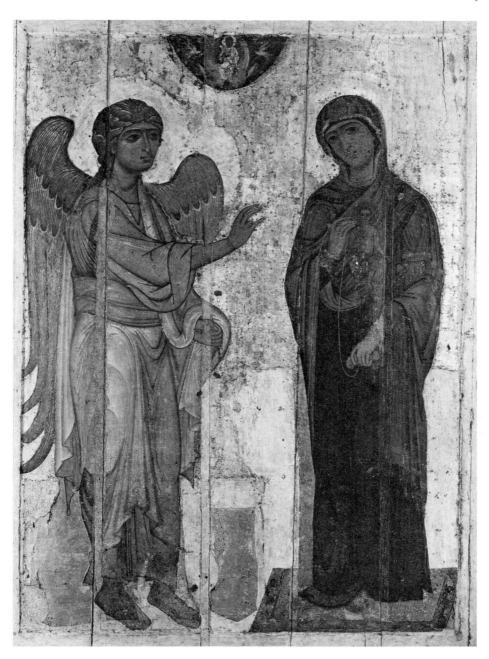

equilibrium between line and form, where the modelling of the contours of the cheek takes precedence over the linear outline. On the contrary, line is more insistent in the Angel's head, especially in the intricate plaiting of the gold-streaked hair and in the crisp folds of the garments. This difference accentuates the contrast between the serene expression of the Virgin gazing at the spectator, and the sober countenance of the Archangel. One may also observe the difference between the vestiges of pictorial illusionism in the Virgin's head and the more emphatic modelling of Gabriel's broad face and heavy features. If the Virgin may be thought to be looking backwards to the sunnier climate of Byzantium with its memories of Hellas, Gabriel anticipates the solemn definition of the Russian religious experience. There is a contrast too in the colours, between the Virgin's conventional red mantle over a blue gown and the clearer harmonies of the Archangel's red, white, and golden-yellow draperies, the latter colour being delicately built up in layers of ochre progressively mixed with more white. With the Ustiug Annunciation may be associated the noble head of an Archangel [56] from the Dormition in Moscow, and probably once part of a deesis. The almost identical arrangement of the gold-threaded hair is even more linear, a tendency carried further in the drawing of the eyes and nose. This head, however, is more Greek. Its large-eyed heavy-lidded ancestors with their plaited hair are the sixth-century korai on the Acropolis. Its collateral descendants can be found in the paintings of Poussin, and in our time in Picasso's nude figures of 1921–3. These agreements are not just stylistic imitations; they are moments when artists have sought, and found, that order of things and beings which we call 'classic'. However, this angel's gentler, more mystical expression, enhanced by the emphatic eyes which see beyond this world, endows the classic form with psychological, Christian expression.[6]

The Virgin Orans or the Great Panagiya (All-Holy) [57], discovered in 1919 in the

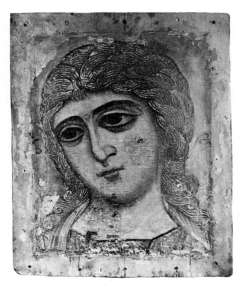

56. Kiev(?): Head of an Archangel, c. 1150. *Leningrad, Russian Museum*

Monastery of the Transfiguration in Yaroslavl, may also have come from Kiev. This is the earliest extant Russian example of the type of the Byzantine Blacherniotissa, familiar from the apse mosaic in St Sophia, although here she wears the medallion of Christ Emmanuel on her breast. The size suggests a princely source and further indications of a Kievan origin may be seen in the classical, even if increasingly linear, regularity of the faces of the Virgin and Child, in her attenuated figure which resembles the Apostles in mosaic from St Michael, and in the treatment of the busts of two Archangels in the upper corners. In the latter the play of a few broadly brushed planes in an embracing light seems like a distant reflection of ancient fresco-painting. The icon may be placed early in the twelfth century, and an attribution to a Russian rather

57 (*opposite*). Kiev: The Virgin Orans (the Great Panagiya), early twelfth century. *Moscow, Tretyakov Gallery*

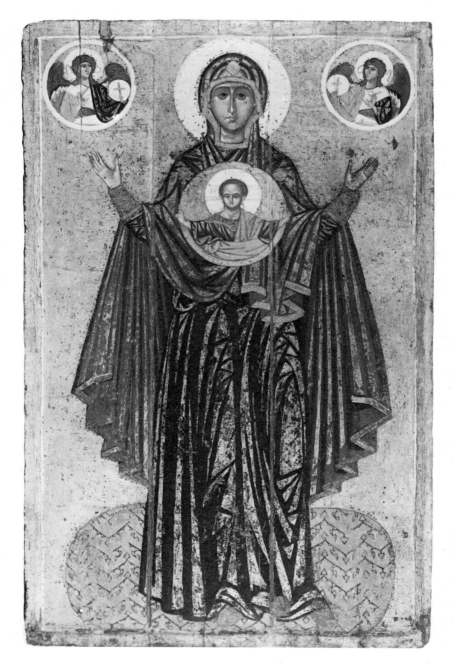

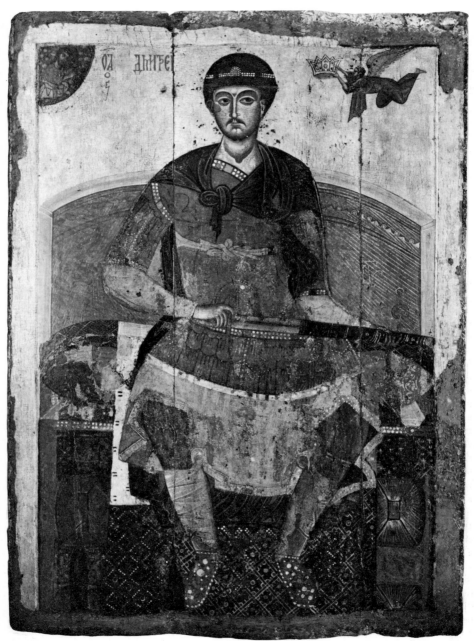

58. Kiev: St Dmitry of Salonica from Dmitrov, after 1150. *Moscow, Tretyakov Gallery*

than to a Greek artist seems probable given the uncertain anatomical structure. The position of the Virgin's figure beneath her heavy garment is incoherent and unrelated to her feet. The colour scheme also is distinctive. The creamy white background – an economical substitute for the silver or gold leaf of the finest Greek work – acts as a foil for the massive brown and dark blue robes, heavily patterned and edged with gold, and the crimson cushion. The colours are Greek, but the range and stress are Russian, a forecast of that mastery in handling a few brilliant primary and complementary hues which became characteristic of Russian painting.

The scarcity of twelfth-century icons makes all the more tantalizing the reputation of a monk of the Pecherskaya Lavra, Alimpi, known from an extensive account of his life in the Pechersky chronicle.[7] Since he is said to have died in 1114, it is possible that he was instructed by the second group of Greek artists who came to Kiev to decorate the Pechersky Dormition soon after 1073. Alimpi is said to have been a mosaicist as well, and so may have worked after 1108 on the mosaics in St Michael. Vladimir Monomakh so admired a large icon of the Virgin by Alimpi that he sent it from Kiev to the new church he was building in Rostov as an exact replica of the Pechersky Dormition. According to Polycarp, the author of the life of Alimpi, his icons were very large, and the Yaroslavl Panagiya is almost six feet high. Can the legend preserved in the chronicle indeed be true, and this is the very painting which Monomakh sent from Kiev to Rostov? Definite proof may never be found, but it is interesting to recall that in 1728 the more important icons in the Rostov church were removed to the Monastery of the Transfiguration in Yaroslavl.[8]

Another painting which may be attributed to the Kievan school later in the twelfth century is the large icon of St Dmitry of Salun (Salonika), one of the earliest warrior saints to be adopted by the Russian church [58]. This was found in the Uspensky Sobor in Dmitrov near Moscow. The town had been founded in 1154 as a princely fortress by Yury Dolgoruky, in honour of the birth of his son Vsevolod-Dmitry who later ruled Suzdalia as Vsevolod III. It is tempting to think that the oral traditions which linked this icon with the personality of Vsevolod, and which are in part confirmed by the symbols of princely ownership on the back of the throne (repainted, it is true, in the sixteenth century), may support a princely Kievan origin for this impressive painting. Although sadly damaged – only the head, torso, and right hand unsheathing a regal sword are original – the seated figure of the saint-protector of Rus is the embodiment of secular as well as of religious authority.[9] When the icon is compared with the mosaic of the standing St Dmitry from the Michael Monastery in Kiev (now in the Tretyakov Gallery, Moscow) the independence of the Russian masters from their Greek teachers is indisputable. The tendency towards a frontal, two-dimensional design is underscored by a schematic but powerful linearism. To be sure, the seated posture recalls the ancient likenesses of consuls and emperors on Byzantine ivory diptychs, but this would not have been the first occasion when the Kievan princes stressed their dynastic relations with Tsargrad.

An indication that the Russian religious experience not only derived from the doctrines brought from Constantinople but was also not without its share of eastern enthusiasm is found in another icon, tentatively attributed to the twelfth century, and once preserved in the Dormition in Moscow. The panel is worked on both sides, indicating that it was once a processional icon. On the front appears the Mandilion portrait of Christ [59], the 'Saviour not made with Hands' (Spas Nerukotvorny). The hair, drawn in symmetrical gold lines, and the precise contours of the features carry further the tendency noted in the heads of the Archangels, yet with certain expressive additions, such as the exaggerated eyes. Although we might trace this drawing back through the Archangels to the Virgin

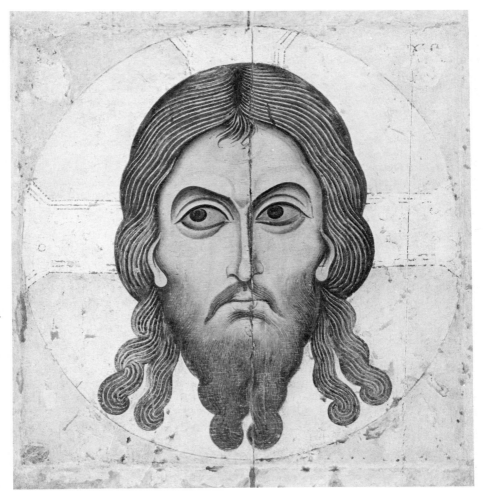

59. Vladimir-Suzdal (or Greek?): Mandilion portrait of Christ, the 'Saviour not made with Hands',
c. 1150–1200. *Moscow, Tretyakov Gallery*

Orans, and so to the heavy-lidded figures of late antique sculpture, we should not yet have accounted for the mystical expression which supplants the late antique illusionism still apparent in the bland countenance of the Moscow Archangel. On the reverse, however, the representation of two Archangels adoring the jewel-studded cross is clearly of eastern

origin [60]. The iconographical scheme derives from an early Palestinian tradition, related to the veneration of the monumental cross set up on Golgotha in the post-Constantine era. The spiritual energy of eastern, Syrian religiosity was to find its parallels in Russia, where some of the feats of endurance by the early monks rivalled the accomplishments of the desert

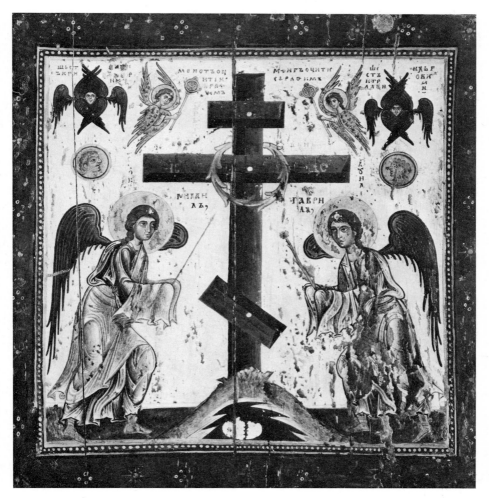

60. Novgorod: The Archangels Michael and Gabriel adoring the Cross,
reverse of the Mandilion, *c.* 1150. *Moscow, Tretyakov Gallery*

ascetics. That mystical energy, entering Russia through its many contacts with the East, continued to lend a particular colour to Russian religious life, and so helped to transform the aristocratic reserve of the Byzantine formulas into images of wide popular appeal.

The inscription on the drawing of the angels is in the Novgorodian dialect and must be taken as a sign of northern origin. Also the similarity in the drawing of the angels' robes to those of the angels in the frescoes at Nereditsa emphasizes the late-twelfth- and early-thirteenth-century date and the predominant influence exercised by monumental mural art over icon-painting during this period. The Mandilion Christ is an early and important instance of the transmission of the classic style of the Kievan mosaics to northern Russia and its transformation under the eastern agents at Nereditsa into a more linear mode, so simplified in colour that the multiple harmonies of Greek painting were replaced by a broader treatment of the surface in a few tonally unvaried colours.[10]

This tendency can be studied in another way, through the evolution of the typical Russian figure of the standing saint. Here again the mosaics in St Sophia and St Michael provided Russian artists with a useful pattern for the image of the individual saint. Such an icon as the half-length St Nicholas [61], from the Novodevichi Convent in Moscow, is so

61. Kiev(?): St Nicholas, from the Novodevichi Convent, Moscow, c. 1200 (the saints on the border were probably painted in Novgorod later in the thirteenth century). *Moscow, Tretyakov Gallery*

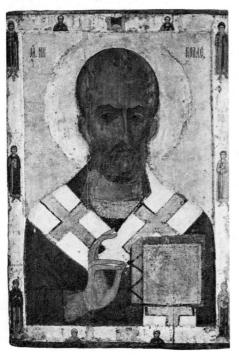

Greek in the refinement of the drawing, the careful modelling of the ascetic features, and the subdued colour scheme, that it might almost be Byzantine, but that the distortion of the face through the emphatic brow, diminished mouth and chin, and the uncertain drawing of the eyes betrays the hand of a Russian pupil of the Greeks. The small figures of saints on the frame are characteristic of Novgorod and perhaps indicate that the border of a Kievan original was repainted in the north.

The Novodevichi St Nicholas marks an interesting transitional point in the history of Russian painting which is also seen in the icon of Christ with the Golden Hair [62] in the Dormition in Moscow.[11] Here the same tenuous balance was established between the waning Byzantine illusionism of the Vladimir Virgin and the increasing concern of the Russian painters to transform shapes into linear patterns. In the Christ with the Golden Hair the modelling of the cheeks has become more schematic, the line of the eyebrows simpler, and the distortions of the shrunken mouth and chin even more marked than in St Nicholas. Simultaneously there is an insistence on flat pattern in the decorative treatment of the hair and the insertion of coin-like spots of gold on the garment and background. Indeed, this might in some respects be considered the continuous inherent formal proposition of medieval Russian painting. Line, with its symbolic function, its ability to suggest rather than to describe, and its power to induce through abstraction a mood of contemplation rather than observation, remained one of the basic elements of icon-painting. But simultaneously the artist was always obliged to refer his image back into the world of nature, since he had to deal not only with the reality of the spiritual life, but with the actuality which the prototype had had during its earthly existence. Again and again Russian painters would be recalled from their ecstatic meditations upon linear rhythms to the consideration of natural forms, here in the twelfth and thirteenth centuries by the

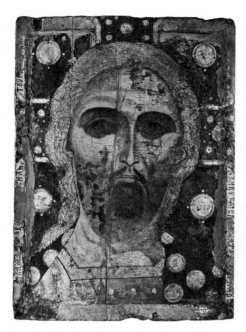

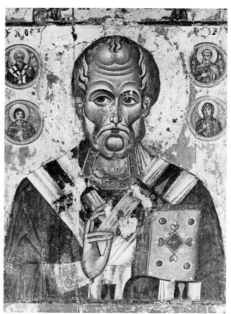

62. Yaroslavl(?): Christ with the Golden Hair,
thirteenth century.
Moscow, Cathedral of the Dormition

63. St Nicholas, from the Monastery of the Holy
Ghost, Novgorod, *c.* 1250.
Leningrad, Russian Museum

authority of the Kievan mosaics, in the fourteenth and fifteenth by the charms of late
Byzantine impressionism, and in the sixteenth
and seventeenth centuries by sporadic but
unsettling influences from western Europe.

The exact course of this tendency through
the thirteenth century is difficult to follow
among the few surviving examples, but an icon
of St Nicholas [63] from the Monastery of
the Holy Ghost, Novgorod, represents a more
consistent development of this ornamental
tendency. The ease with which the contours
and planes of Greek painting, still apparent in
the Novodevichi St Nicholas,[12] have been
reduced to a two-dimensional formula marks
the emergence of a Russian separatist tendency
in Byzantine painting towards the close of the
thirteenth century. But the insistent linear
pattern has transformed the aloof, intellectual

spirituality of Greek iconography, still much a
part of the Novodevichi St Nicholas, into a
more popular pietism. Although the icon is
badly damaged, enough of the bright contrasts
of black, white, and brown against ochre
remain to prove that already a distinctive Russian colour sense was at work. When in the
fourteenth century further waves of influence
from Constantinople reached Russia, the stylistic character of late Byzantine impressionism
would necessarily have to be fitted into the
already well-established Russian style.

The remarkable icon of St John Climacus
[64], with almost miniature accompanying
figures of SS. George and Blaise, continues
the process of decorative simplification, yet is
not without reminiscences of the great mosaic
schemes.[13] The unusual discrepancy in size
between St John and his diminutive com-

panions suggests the same proportional relationships which prevailed in the apses of Kiev between the standing Virgin Orans and the row of Church Fathers beneath her. In this possible formal echo of an ancient mosaic scheme we may have a replica of a Kievan product of the early twelfth century, possibly emanating from the studio of Alimpi, whom we know to have been a mosaic artist as well as an icon-painter.

64. Novgorod: St John Climacus, with SS. George and Blaise, after 1250. *Leningrad, Russian Museum*

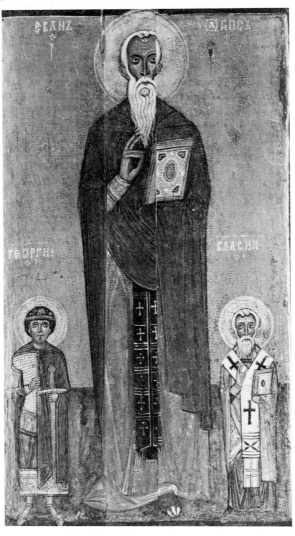

CHAPTER 10

PROVINCIAL SCHOOLS OF THE THIRTEENTH
AND FOURTEENTH CENTURIES

These earliest icons, which may have been painted in Russia, whether by Greek or Russian artists, reveal a fundamentally pictorial attitude towards the projection of three-dimensional forms on a two-dimensional surface. Where the contour line is most prominent, as in the drawing of the eyelids of the Ustiug Virgin or in the features of St Nicholas from Novgorod, the line carefully follows the edge of the living form, and is immediately adjoined by an area of shadow, which, although simplified and in the later thirteenth century even schematic to a degree, yet in conjunction with the line acts as a modelled plane. With the relatively sober colour schemes such a system is painterly rather than graphic. The position of planes meeting at an angle in three dimensions is still held in account, and the line is not yet free to describe decorative arabesques independently of the actual position of the planes in space.

The expression of the eyes also proves the close connexion between the earliest icons and the Hellenistic traditions still alive at Constantinople. Many faces stare directly at the spectator (the Virgins of Vladimir and of Ustiug), others look towards another character in the scene (the Christ Child and Gabriel in the Annunciation at Moscow). Or, if their glance is directed neither towards the spectator nor towards another figure, the sideways glance seems to observe some presence or situation beyond the frame of the icon. This is telling evidence of a strain of Hellenistic illusionism, and the gradual elimination of this expression will be a constant factor in four-teenth- and fifteenth-century painting. In the course of time the eyes, even when turned towards the spectator, will lose the intensity of a direct look; their gaze, as if slightly out of focus, will seem directed beyond him, beyond even the circumstances of actual life, or as if turned inwards upon some private reverie. It may be taken, then, as a rough rule of thumb that the presence of a speaking glance, embracing the spectator in an immediate visual relationship, is a mark, when it occurs in later painting, of a renewal of Greek influence through the presence on Russian soil of a Greek master or of an authoritative example of Greek painting.

In the next group of icons – those which with some degree of probability may be considered fourteenth-century – the effect of vast historical disturbances can be traced. The subjugation of southern and eastern Russia during the first century of Tartar rule and the interruption of relations with Constantinople, found their artistic parallels in the disruption of the Greek influence present in the icons of the twelfth and early thirteenth centuries. Again and again it appears as if the native Russian painters had been thrown on their own resources in copying or interpreting Greek originals, without the presence of Greek masters, until some time after the middle of the fourteenth century, when, with the revival of trade between Byzantium and northern Russia, masters from Greece and the Balkan peninsula brought to Novgorod and the north the latest innovations of Palaeologos style at the capital.

Since there are only the scantiest remains of painting in Russia during the later decades of the thirteenth and the early fourteenth century, the Novgorod icon of the Legend of St George [65] is of the greatest importance. The central episode representing St George victorious over the dragon was possibly derived from

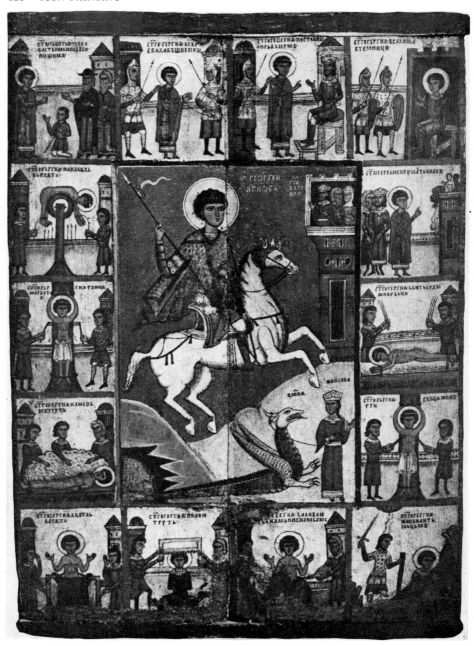

65. Novgorod: St George and the Dragon, with scenes from the saint's life, early fourteenth century.
Leningrad, Russian Museum

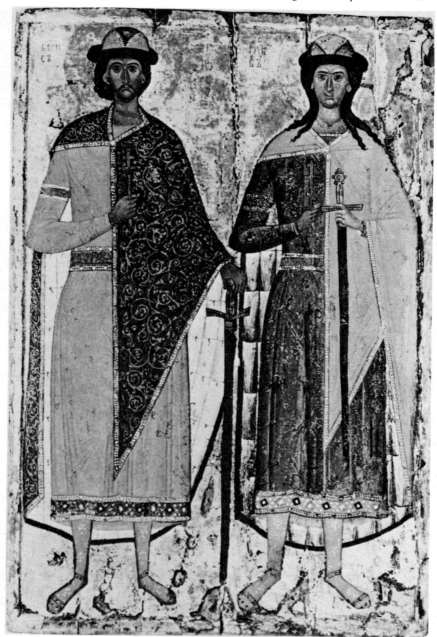

66. Moscow: SS. Boris and Gleb, *c.* 1290–1310.
Leningrad, Russian Museum

a fresco of about 1167 of the same subject in the Church of St George in Staraya Ladoga, but the resemblances between the two aristocratic horsemen are only iconographical.[1] The icon painter worked from a different point of view, treating his surface as a two-dimensional area upon which his figures are placed in a decorative pattern, more in the style of a manuscript illustration than of a fresco on a mural scale. The size of the figures follows a hierarchical rather than naturalistic canon. Naturalism is further destroyed by the cut-out design of the figures which avoids any overlapping. Yet enough of the earlier three-dimensional feeling survives in the faces of the Saint and Princess to remind us that the artist had known the Byzantine models at some remove. Around the border of the icon are fourteen scenes from the life of St George. The simplified drawing, the lack of spatial indications, and the insistent bilateral symmetry in most of the scenes accentuate the tendencies observed in the central panel. And since these characteristics, even if allowance is made for the use of a manuscript model, are common to folk art in many other times and places, we may conclude that the painter of the St George icon to some extent continued a much earlier tradition of popular painting in northern Russia. The icon was probably painted either in Novgorod or one of the subsidiary towns, since the inscriptions are in Novgorod dialect, and in the scene in the upper left corner, where St George distributes his wealth to the poor, he gives the cripple and beggar a handful of silver rods – the form of Novgorod currency in the fourteenth century.

A different expression appears in the important icon of SS. Boris and Gleb [66]. This is one of the oldest extant panels representing the first Russian martyrs, and perhaps may be related to an icon of the same Saints which was placed near the high altar of Hagia Sophia in Constantinople, where it was seen in 1202 by Anthony, Archbishop of Novgorod: 'In Hagia Sophia, at the right . . . [is] the very place where the Blessed Virgin prayed to her Son and our Lord for all Christians. On the same side there is also the large icon of SS. Boris and Gleb, which painters use as a model.'[2] Anthony's description is an eloquent testimony to the esteem in which the Greek Church held its Russian adherents, as well as to the fact that numbers of Russian pilgrims must have visited Constantinople to warrant such an organized industry. The present icon, which may have been painted soon after 1300, may be a copy of such a replica, for while the workmanship is certainly not Greek, the full-length standing figures have much of the monumentality of twelfth-century Byzantine painting.

In this icon there is a conflict between two modes of representation. On the one hand the painter sought to give some individual character to the two brothers, distinguishing them by the difference in age between the vigorous moustached Boris and the gentler beardless Gleb, by varying the colour-pattern of the garments from the blue brocaded cloak over a red caftan worn by Boris to the red cloak over a purplish caftan worn by Gleb, and by changing the position of their left forearms.[3] But such attempts at individuality and variety are overborne by the equilateral symmetry in the identical headdresses, position of the limbs, and garments. This oriental feeling, in such contrast to the vestiges of Greek illusionism in the previous Kievan and Novgorod schools, with the two-dimensional patterning such as we saw in the St George icon, indicates a provincial or at least non-Kievan provenance. On the other hand, the princely character of the painting, so different from the rustic crudity of the George icon, urges a source near a princely Court where something of the old Byzantine ceremonial was still preserved. Such a centre might have been the Court of Vladimir-Suzdal, which, as we know from its architecture and the presence there of some of the most celebrated icons of the Kievan school, prided itself on its Kievan heritage. But at Vladimir oriental influences were also pronounced. The decorative motifs on the garments – fleurs-de-lis, palmettes, griffons, and eagles – are almost identical with the reliefs on the Church of St Dmitry in Vladimir, and suggest that we have here an icon which so far as the general type is concerned originated in the Suzdalian region.

An icon of St Dmitry drawing his sword (State Russian Museum, Leningrad) has much of the same chivalric charm, that somewhat melancholy, doomed atmosphere of late Kievan knighthood which pervades the *Tale of the Armament of Igor* and seems to hover over the exploits of the Russian princes just before the Tartar invasion. Perhaps more than any other icons which have been recovered from Kievan Russia, these display a national, even if aristocratic, spirit. Although the personages depicted are saintly and the icons intentionally religious, the profounder spirit which they breathe is that of an ancient princely age.

The drawing of the faces of both icons demonstrates a stage midway between the plastic modelling of the earlier Kievan school and the emergence of a graphic Russian style in Novgorod in the course of the later fourteenth and fifteenth centuries. Over a prevailing dark-brown ground the highlights are placed in a symmetrical and highly simplified pattern. Where necessary the features are reinforced by lines which tend to substitute angles for curves. In this way line ceases to follow the curvature of a three-dimensional form and assumes an almost independent existence. As the forms flatten out on the surface, the eyes lose their expression. The typically Russian other-worldly, abstract relationship between the icon and the spectator, who no longer observes but rather contemplates the forms, grows more pronounced. In the icon of St Dmitry the highlights have lost even more of their plastic character, and have become streaks and scratches creating a design often at variance with the underlying shapes. The development of a two-dimensional graphic, linear style is understandable when we recall that Russian painters knew little sculpture and

no ancient Hellenistic painting: the two sources from which the Byzantine artist drew his continuous understanding of illusionistic form.

If we postulate at Novgorod in the first half of the fourteenth century a manner of painting which, while not without its Byzantine and Hellenistic references and its memories of the princely character of ancient Kiev, was dominated by a desire to render forms in a two-dimensional, semi-oriental manner, we shall the better assess the tremendous importance of the appearance of Greek artists in northern Russia soon after the middle of the fourteenth century. Whether they came directly from Constantinople or indirectly through Bulgaria and Serbia, they revealed to Russian eyes the Palaeologos style of the last Byzantine Renaissance. Two aspects of this style, as we know it from the early-fourteenth-century mosaics in the Kariye-Djami and from the later paintings in the churches at Mistra, were to be of overwhelming importance for Russian icon-painting. The first was an interest in movement and scenes of dramatic action occurring in a specific place; the second, the new technique of a visual impressionism, the inevitable concomitant of the search for movement in space and placement in time. After 1350 the Russian version of Palaeologos impressionism completely transformed the earlier two-dimensional linearism into a technique capable of communicating a much wider range of spatial experience.

The relatively few icons which can with any certainty be attributed to the fourteenth century, and in which there appears some attempt to undertake the new and difficult problems of spatial composition in scenes involving several figures, also contain iconographical details which show their relationship to Greek painting. One of the most impressive as well as one of the largest and most brilliantly coloured of the early icons is a Nativity of the Virgin [67]. The Russian artist in several instances failed to understand the complexities of his original models, if indeed the pattern which he used was not already itself defective. Although the

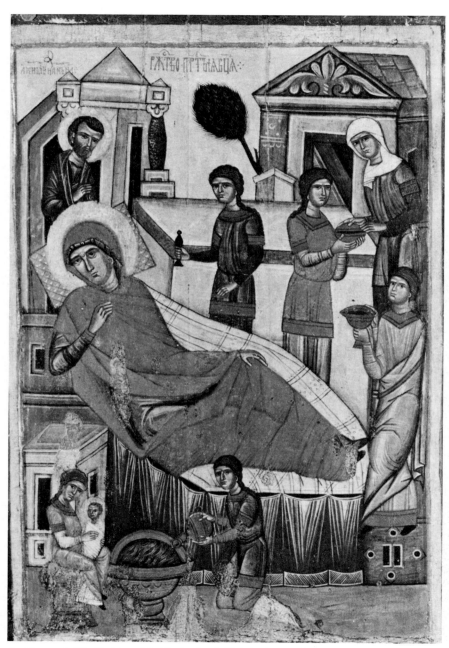

67. Novgorod: The Nativity of the Virgin, first half of the fourteenth century.
Moscow, Tretyakov Gallery

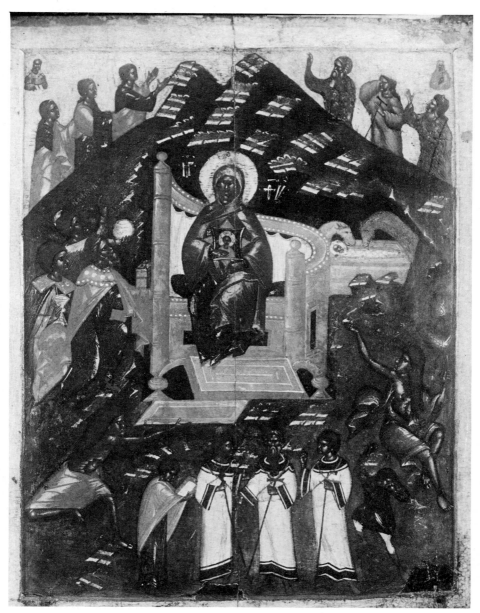

68. Pskov: The Virgin's Assembly, 'What Shall We Offer You, O Christ?' *c.* 1350–1400.
Moscow, Tretyakov Gallery

perspective construction contains several para-
doxes, and St Anne lacks any support for her
right elbow, the model, probably more than
once removed, must have been a fourteenth-
century Byzantine painting or manuscript
illustration related to the mosaic scenes of the
Kariye-Djami, which this icon resembles in the
character of the architectural background
which includes a portico in the upper left and
a temple-like structure with a pediment to the
right. The intricate posture of the servant girl
entering at the right has an even closer analogy
with similar figures in the Byzantine mosaics.
That an almost identical figure has also been
found in a fourteenth-century fresco at
Zarzma in the Caucasus perhaps speaks less
for a direct eastern influence than for the
common source of both images in the fourteenth-century Constantinopolitan painting.[4]
In other ways the artist betrays his provincial
origin. His conception is more blunt than gracious, and he exaggerates the illusionistic play
of facial expression by making his characters
glare at the spectator.

In other icons the Russian painter's attempt
to reproduce the illusionism of Palaeologos
painting led him to replace curves with straight
lines. This may be seen in the highlights on
garments which as sharp streaks are prolonged
beyond their place of origin until they destroy
the curvature of the drapery itself. Such a
tendency may be considered one of the essential characteristics of later Russian icon-painting just as that of straightening all curves.
Even the most gracious curves of the innumerable angels' wings or the droop of the
Virgins' heads will acquire much of their expressive effect from the presence or immediate
juxtaposition of a straight line. Throughout
the fourteenth century curves were never
intended to describe the rounded plane of a
form moving backward and out of sight, but
were rather the reduction of that form to two
dimensions through the association of curve
and straight line.

An icon [68] which illustrates this fusion of
the ancient traditions of classic painting with
Palaeologan innovations in terms of a peculiarly Russian unity is the icon of the Virgin's
Assembly (Sobor Bogomateri), painted in
Pskov in the second half of the fourteenth
century. The subject comes from the Christmas anthem of praise to the new-born
Saviour:

What shall we offer you, O Christ,
    you who for us appeared on earth
    as a man?
Each of your creatures offers you gratitude,
    angels bring you hymns;
    the heavens, stars; the Magi, gifts;
    the shepherds, adoration;
Earth, the tomb; the Desert, the cradle;
    and we, the Virgin Mother.[5]

In several respects the subject suggests a
fusion of the western versions of the Nativity
and the subsequent Adorations of the Shepherds and the Magi, but the formal and dogmatic rather than narrative intention is made
clear by the fact that the Virgin, enthroned at
the entrance of a cave (where the swaddled
Christ Child is attended by the ox and ass),
holds on her lap not her actual Son but an
icon of His image in an eight-pointed red and
green frame suggesting a star.

The iconographic sources are multiple.
From antiquity come the personifications of
Earth and the Desert; from Byzantium the
processional entrances of the Magi, angels, and
shepherds; from the architectural backgrounds
of such Palaeologos painting as the mosaics of
the Kariye-Djami the construction of the
throne; and from the East the decorative
character of the dispersed objects, the regular
terracing of the mountains, and the varieties
of perspective which create the angular ten-
sions between the footstool and crib. The
colouring is Russian in its reduction of many
tints within the generally uniform and sober
harmony characteristic of Greek painting to a
major scale of red and dark green against black
and white. Even more localized is the particular green, which can be attributed to the
school of Pskov or to painting which seems to
have originated in that city.[6]

Throughout the icon there is a stylistic compulsion to oppose curves with straight lines; the curve of the throne is so persuasive because of the vertical posts to which it is attached. The composition is a complete and unified expression with its own inner harmony and rhythms of curve, angle, and line. Sudden curves and sharp angles are counterpoints to the harsh colour accents, and the stylistic and technical elements are the equivalents of the expressive content of the painting, which with its weird association of images removes us from the comfortable domesticity of St Luke's narrative to the harsh wastes of a remote, almost hostile region.

This accent of earnest severity can be found in many icons of the later fourteenth century, perhaps a reflexion of the life of the people during those difficult times and of the consciousness of the Church that it was a bulwark against the ever-threatening waves of barbarism on the eastern frontiers. The large icon of SS. Paraskeva, Gregory the Theologian, John Chrysostom, and Basil the Great [69] illus-

69. Pskov: The Four Saints Icon, *c.* 1350–1400. *Moscow, Tretyakov Gallery*

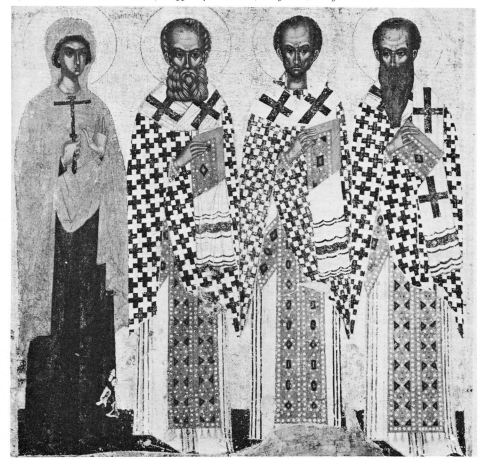

trates the independence won by Russian artists in these years. Content and technique combine lingering vestiges of tutelage to Greek painting with still stronger native characterizations. The individual personalities of the gaunt St Paraskeva, the full-bearded benign St Gregory, the more youthful and intense St John, and the placid patriarchal St Basil, are set against the decorative unification of the vestments of the three male saints in a repeated pattern of black, brown, and white, enlivened by the scarlet orphreys of their vestments and the sacred books they hold. The limited but harmonious colour scheme is completed by the red-and-green garment of St Paraskeva, and the green ground on which the figures stand. The background in this case is a creamy white.[7] The heads are slightly but delicately modelled in three dimensions in the best style of the Palaeologos Renaissance; the bodies are reduced to two dimensions and treated as decorative patterns. When this is compared with the best Greek work of the Palaeologos period it is clear how the Russian painter sought to counteract the plastic three-dimensional movement of the Greek figures by a more decorative effect.[8] The trace of Greek modelling in the heads of the four saints shows that this was deliberate. He also created an entirely new expressive content. Where the Greek artist through his command of formal and spatial representations desired and achieved a community of feeling, the Russian painter isolated each of the saints from his fellows. Their glances are directed neither towards each other, nor towards the spectator or some other point in common. Absorbed in their own speculations, their eyes tend to lose their focus and turn inwards. The work is unmistakably Russian, and in its strong accents of black and white clearly of northern origin, probably of the school of Pskov which favoured such monochrome schemes.

The Pskov icon of the Four Saints indicates that by the middle of the fourteenth century the Russian artist had reached a critical point in the development of a national style. On the one hand he was constantly tempted to treat his panel as a two-dimensional design; on the other he was under the obligation to produce reasonably life-like scenes and personages. The stage reached in the Four Saints icon is too perilously balanced between two and three dimensions to be of much value for scenes in complex perspective. Nor is it conceivable that from it anything could develop which would not require the sacrifice of one or the other mode. What would seem to have been needed was the invention of some system of linear description which would yet permit the introduction of slightly modelled surfaces. If this was the historical necessity, the appearance in Russia during the last two decades of the fourteenth century of an outstanding master of Palaeologos impressionism provided the solution to the dilemma.

As we have seen, the impressionism practised by Theophanes the Greek in his frescoes in the Church of the Transfiguration at Novgorod was essentially more graphic than pictorial. His method of suggesting three-dimensional forms was to reduce highlights and accents to lines rather than planes, setting them against broader areas of ground colour. This differed from the earlier system of the eleventh and twelfth centuries, where the form was modelled in tones and where line, following the curve of the plane, was inseparable, visually and conceptually, from the curved surface. This can be seen, even in a black and white reproduction, in the curving edges, which are not simply outlines, of such a painting as the head of an Archangel [56]. Within such a system the painter of the Novgorod St Nicholas devised his compact linear structure; on its periphery the painter of the Boris and Gleb icon was still trying to suggest three-dimensional form by broadened highlights slightly curved in plane. And continuing such a system the Pskov master of the Four Saints icon created the round heads of his figures.

A minor technical device helps, on the whole, to distinguish between the plastic, illusionistic constructions of the middle Byzantine and early Russian periods and the graphic, abstract designs of later-fourteenth- and fifteenth-century painting. In the earlier provincial variants lines are the counterparts of the shadowed or darkened areas; lines describe eyebrows, eyelids, edges of the nose. And the dark line is associated with the dark plane of a recessed area. In later painting line, and if not line then the edge of the adjacent plane, appears as a light, as a highlight, or as a convex area, the darker ground serving as the plane upon which the convexities are projected. This is of course not a complete reversal of the two roles, but a different, perhaps more subtle counterbalance between light and dark, dictated by an attitude towards nature which sees in terms of colour more than of plastic shape, for it is the only conceivable system whereby the brilliant juxtapositions of colour in later icon-painting could still suggest form. It represents the transition from Greek vision, based upon the appreciation of plastic values trained by the apprehension of three-dimensional sculptural forms, to Russian vision, closer to oriental art in its understanding of the infinite complexities and possibilities of two-dimensional pattern, yet keeping the late antique play of light over the surface of coloured forms as the principal although not the sole modelling agent. In the activity of Theophanes the Greek, so far as it can be deduced from extant paintings attributed to him or from works of his school, this transition was accomplished and the energies of Russian painters released for another and even more remarkable period of painting.

CHAPTER 11

FIFTEENTH-CENTURY PAINTING: MOSCOW

Since the first attempts in the later nineteenth century to establish a historical sequence of icon-painting, the so-called School of Novgorod has enjoyed an exceptional prestige, owing to the quite accidental circumstance that most of the surviving icons were found in the vicinity of Novgorod or in the northern territories once tributary to that city. Thus the assignment to Novgorod of every icon of good quality and the assumption that its painters enjoyed a superior mastery of technique and expression inevitably followed. But such a simplification omitted too many historical factors, and also certain necessary deductions. To accept the existence at Novgorod of an extensive icon industry it is not necessary to deny that elsewhere other shops may have been active. Moscow, while certainly inferior in size and wealth until late in the fifteenth century, was no more remote than Novgorod from those sources of Greek art which also nourished Novgorod's fresco- and icon-painters. There is abundant evidence that Greek artists and Greek works of art were well known in Moscow. In 1381 Bishop Dionysius of Suzdal ordered from Constantinople two copies of the Virgin Hodegetria, which he installed in Suzdal Cathedral and in the Church of the Redeemer in Nizhny-Novgorod. Six years later Archbishop Athanasius imported from Constantinople seven large icons for the Vysotsky Monastery in Serpukhov, six of which are now in the State Tretyakov Gallery, Moscow. These must have formed part of a deesis and constitute an early example of a large iconostasis.[1] Moscow also acquired a number of the earlier iconic treasures of ancient Russia. In 1395 the Virgin of Vladimir was brought from Vladimir to the Cathedral of the Dormition in the Kremlin, which in course of time received many ancient icons, including several discussed in an earlier chapter.[2]

In the face of the evidence it seems idle to assume that Moscow either possessed no painters at all, and so had to import all her icons from Novgorod, or that her painters were obliged to go to Novgorod to learn their trade. Nor need the fact that no important thirteenth- or fourteenth-century paintings can be attributed with absolute certainty to Moscow be taken as conclusive proof that no local school existed. Between 1380 and 1547 Moscow was several times ravaged by fire, with the loss of innumerable objects of art. As late as 1547 the damage was so extensive that the Metropolitan Macarius brought icons and painters from Novgorod, but the immediate restitutions might only have supplied the slowly reviving industry with certain stylistic elements which are found in the so-called 'mixed' style of the sixteenth century.

The presence of a famous master of icon-painting in Moscow and its environs shortly after 1400 renders untenable the hypothetical dependence of Moscow upon Novgorod. The achievements of Andrey Rublev will shortly be considered in detail; it suffices to observe here that the evidence of his influence upon fifteenth-century painting, gradually merging with the nascent personality of Master Dionisy, who was active in the last half of the century, guarantees to the Moscow school a character and kind of painting unlike that practised at Novgorod.

There are other deductions to be made from the historical contrast between the two cities. For centuries Novgorod had been active as a trading centre; her political institutions and her social customs were based upon an independent, commercial, and reasonably democratic form of life. Moscow, on the other hand, from its beginnings as a frontier post facing the Tartars to the east, had of necessity been dominated by the exigencies of a military situation which demanded an autocratic, centralized form of government. When in the course of time both the ecclesiastical hierarchy and the princely authority were transferred to Moscow, this closely knit economic and military organization received the support of religious and dynastic concepts. Under these conditions it is not difficult to understand that the art of Novgorod reflected the active, intransigent, almost republican sentiments of its inhabitants, while the art of Moscow was increasingly directed towards the expression of religious authority and political power.

Three icons of the same subject may demonstrate the relative position of the two centres towards the middle of the fifteenth century. In the Dormition in the Moscow Kremlin there is preserved an image known as the 'Saviour of the Fiery Eye', painted in the mid fourteenth century for the first Dormition, begun in 1326 [70]. The stern, almost disagreeable expression recalls the earlier Byzantine conception of the Pantokrator of the type of Daphni, which had been known in Russia since the execution of the mosaics in St Sophia in Kiev in the eleventh century, although this later image descends from the early-fourteenth-century mosaic in the Kariye-Djami in Constantinople.[3] Another Christ [71], from a deesis discovered in a storeroom at Zvenigorod (see below, page 139), is related to the Constantinopolitan figure or to one very like it. But there are deviations whereby the painter, most probably Andrey Rublev, transformed the severe majesty of the earlier image into a gentler Russian concept. The traces of an individual hand can be seen in the contraction of the mouth and chin, which emphasizes the slender proportions of the head, the elimination of the wrinkles on the brow, and the simplified treatment of the highlights. The total expression reveals such

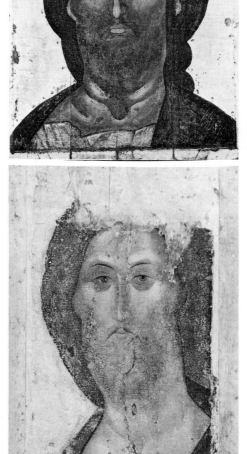

70. Moscow: The Saviour of the Fiery Eye, 1340. *Moscow, Cathedral of the Dormition*

71. (*right*) Andrey Rublev: Head of Christ, from a deesis, *c.* 1410–20. *Moscow, Tretyakov Gallery*

sensitivity to plastic values that one must recognize that at the beginning of the fifteenth
century Moscow possessed an artist of the first
quality. Far more than in the Saviour of the
Fiery Eye the corporeal elements have become
an almost material setting for intense spiritual
experience.

A later icon [72], severely and schematically
linear in its construction, also derives from the
Moscow image, and illustrates the continuance at Novgorod of the graphic traditions of

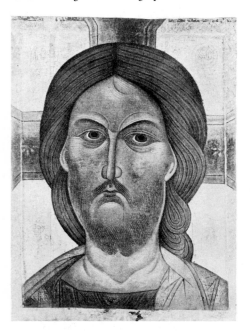

72. Novgorod: Head of Christ,
early fifteenth century.
Leningrad, Russian Museum

the fourteenth century. Where the Zvenigorod
work is all curve and turning plane, the Novgorod icon is strictly edge. Where the one
seems to move in a confined but perceptible
space, the other is scored on an unyielding
surface. Where the Moscow painter understood the consequences of the Greek example,
the Novgorod master remained faithful to the
traditional linearism.

In the face of the prevailing anonymity of
most medieval painting and the scarcity of
documentary evidence for the activity of individual masters, a fortunate and important
source of information for defining the separatist tendencies of the schools of Novgorod
and Moscow is provided by the work of the
painter Theophanes the Greek. Since he is
known to have worked in both cities, and
paintings from his hand can with some certainty be allocated to each region, the differing
use made of his methods suggests that the
separate characters of Novgorod and Moscow
painting were already effective. The circumstance that only frescoes by Theophanes are
preserved at Novgorod and only panel-paint-
ings can be attributed to him in Moscow is a
historical accident. His icons must have been
known in Novgorod, and the painters of
Moscow had had sufficient opportunity to
study his frescoes in that city before their
subsequent loss through fire and restoration
in the course of the fifteenth and sixteenth
centuries.

We do not know when or why Theophanes
left Novgorod for Moscow, but according to
the chronicle he painted the interior of the
Church of the Nativity of the Virgin in
Moscow with Semen Cherny and his pupils in
1395, and four years later was working, again
with his pupils, in the Cathedral of St Michael
in the Kremlin. None of this work has
survived, but the fact that he had by this time
gathered around him a group of younger
artists means that he was in a position to exert
considerable influence on painting in Moscow
at the turn of the century. Some proof of this
is supplied by the study of the iconostasis

which, according to the chronicle, he executed in 1405 for the Cathedral of the Annunciation in the Kremlin. On this occasion he was assisted by the painter Prokhor from Gorodets and by Andrey Rublev, who appears here for the first time in a historical document. In 1482 the fourteenth-century Annunciation was replaced by a new structure erected by masters from Pskov, but the old iconostasis was transferred to the new building. In 1547, during the great fire in the Kremlin, the panels were

severely damaged, but as they were promptly repaired, the older portions were preserved intact under the oil over-paint, which was removed in the 1920s. To Theophanes himself may be ascribed the large central part of the deesis range, the enthroned Christ with the Virgin and Baptist, and the figures of St Paul [73, 74], St Basil the Great, St John Chrysostom, and the Archangel Gabriel. Less authoritative but still close to the master are the figures of St Peter and the Archangel

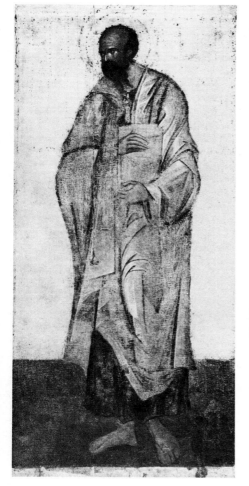

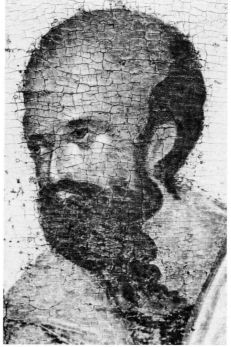

73 (*left*) and 74. Theophanes the Greek: St Paul, with detail, from the iconostasis in the Cathedral of the Annunciation, Moscow, 1405

Michael.[4] Yet even in their present damaged condition something of the Greek spirit of Theophanes emerges. The small heads with delicate features and subtle tonal modelling justify the contemporary praise of Theophanes as a 'zoographer', that is to say one who excelled in drawing living beings.

By analogy with these panels, and especially by comparison with the Novgorod frescoes of 1378, it is possible to attribute to Theophanes,

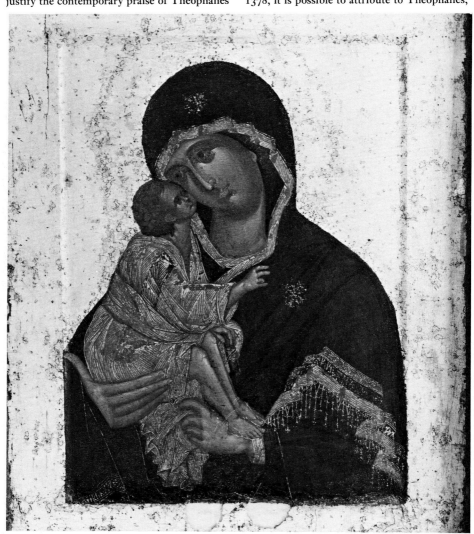

75. Novgorod, possibly by a follower of Theophanes the Greek: The Virgin of the Don, late fourteenth century. *Moscow, Tretyakov Gallery*

or to a member of his workshop, the painting of the Dormition of the Virgin [76] on the reverse of the famous Novgorod icon of the Virgin of the Don [75]. This was traditionally said to have been carried by the Prince of Moscow, Dmitry Donskoy, at the first Russian victory over the Tartars on the field of Kulikovo (1380), and was long preserved in the Cathedral of the Dormition. Here is a composition which, while following Byzantine

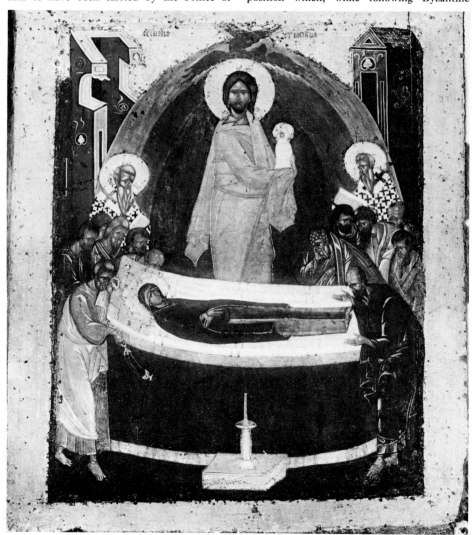

76. Theophanes the Greek, or a close follower: The Dormition of the Virgin, reverse of the Virgin of the Don, late fourteenth century. *Moscow, Tretyakov Gallery*

prototypes, shows in the skilful design the greatest artistic taste, as in the pathos of the group of Apostles bending over the Virgin's bier. Their bodies form the supports of an arch carried above in the mandorla surrounding the figure of Christ. The discretion with which the architectural elements, the bier, and the candle have been arranged is admirable. The tall ghostly figure of Christ emerges from the darkness like the materialization of a mystical experience. Theophanes's hand or influence is perhaps best seen in the painting of the Apostles' heads. Here is the same careful depiction of individual facial and physical types and the quick but accurate spotting of highlights against a darker ground to achieve the maximum relief which so distinguished his Novgorod frescoes.[5]

If the Dormition can probably be attributed to Theophanes's school on the excellent grounds of close technical resemblances to his Novgorod work, could he be considered the author of the Virgin and Child on the front of the icon? At first glance the extraordinary quality of this image would seem necessarily due to the hand of a master as accomplished and renowned as Theophanes, but closer examination shows that the execution has little if anything to do with his method. The modelling of the face as continuous curving surfaces and the rounded slow sweep of the contours, within which occurs the lace-like golden development of the child's garment and the border of the Virgin's mantle, resemble much earlier Greek work.[6] However that may be, this icon of the Virgin of the Don was to be as important for later Russian painting as the activity of Theophanes himself, for here was not only a more modern version of the Virgin Umilenie, which Russians had known since the twelfth century in the Virgin of Vladimir, but the intimate relationship established between the more naturalistic Christ Child and His mother, who appears to be looking into His eyes, was soon taken over in fifteenth-century paintings of the theme. In this connexion the bare legs of the child are a particularly charm-

ing detail. The modelling of the legs and of the Virgin's hands, as well as of the faces, shows a concern for three-dimensional illusionism which has led to the suspicion of western influence, possibly Italian. But if it is true that the Virgin's face with the long curved nose and almond eyes is close to those by Duccio and Simone Martini, in all probability the resemblance is best explained by the similar relation of Sienese painting to Byzantine art throughout the late thirteenth and early fourteenth century.

After his work of 1405 in the Annunciation in Moscow no further paintings by Theophanes are recorded. His position and reputation were quickly assumed by Andrey Rublev (c. 1370–1430),[7] the documentary sources for whose life are also infrequent and fragmentary. He was a monk in the Trinity-St Sergius Monastery, but he first appears as a painter at the Annunciation in 1405, working beside Theophanes and another monk, Prokhor of Gorodets, who may have been his teacher. From this fact it would seem that he was already an accomplished master at work on an equal footing with the most famous painter of the day. It has also been argued that Rublev underwent his early training outside Moscow and hence beyond Theophanes's immediate influence, but since the latter is known to have been Moscow from 1395 and may even have been there before then, it would seem reasonable to assume that Rublev was aware of the monumental character of Theophanes's art, although his own would always be less urgent and less tragic, if no less spiritually expressive.

In 1408 Rublev, with the icon painter Daniil Cherny, executed frescoes in the Dormition in Vladimir to replace the earlier twelfth-century paintings which had fallen into disrepair. They also painted the iconostasis in the same church. Finally, in 1425 occurs the last mention of Rublev's activity. In that year he was working with Cherny in the Trinity-Sergius Monastery near Moscow.

Since Rublev died in 1430, and was presumably a man of late middle age at that time, his schooling must have occurred during the latter part of the fourteenth century, in just those years when Theophanes and other Greek artists had brought to Russia the latest innovations of Palaeologan painting. The principal figures from the deesis on the iconostasis in the Cathedral of the Annunciation in the Moscow Kremlin, where Theophanes and Rublev are known to have worked together in 1405, still show a sensitive understanding of late Byzantine painting, particularly in the delicate impressionism combined with a personal draughtsmanship which suggests that Theophanes's powerful style has been reinterpreted by a younger hand and mind. The highlights are applied with less violence and the expression is gentler and subtler, but, like Theophanes, the painter of these figures understood late Palaeologan painting, with its revival of the spirit of antiquity.

The most extensive work which can be attributed to Rublev is the remains of the frescoes in the Dormition in Vladimir, the repainting of which in the early fifteenth century is an indication of the reawakening of Moscow and Suzdalia after long subjection to Tartar domination.[8] In ordering Andrey Rublev and Daniil Cherny to refresh the walls of the venerable church the Great Prince of Moscow, Vasily I, called attention to the new nationalism. The fragments which emerged after the extensive restorations of 1920 consisted of portions of a Last Judgement on the west wall and adjacent vaults. Rublev's line in Vladimir seems as certain and accurate as Theophanes's in Novgorod, although treated with more lyrical expression. Indeed, Rublev's substitution of a continuous contour for the impressionist broken outlines of Novgorod was his signal contribution to Moscow painting. In the representation of the Angel and the Prophet Daniel the inclusive outlines of the Angel's figure and the ethereal floating wing have all the individuality which only an accomplished master can give.[9]

The drawing of the angels in Vladimir is the most convincing stylistic evidence to support the assignment to Rublev of the icon of the Trinity from the Trinity-Sergius Monastery [77]. Although Rublev and Cherny are known to have been at work there in 1425, the attribution of this most famous of all Russian icons must rest on the superior quality of the painting as well as on the later-fifteenth-century tradition that it was Rublev's work.[10] In spite of severe and irreparable damage enough remains of the composition and colouring to indicate the traditional and progressive aspects of Rublev's art. In contrast to earlier representations where the hieratic position of the angels was opposed by the genre-like figures of Abraham and Sarah, Rublev retained only the three angels, the table with the dish containing the lamb's head, and the slightest semi-symbolic indications of place in the building, mountain, and oak of Mamre in the background. This tactful elimination of inessentials enabled the artist to concentrate on the design of the three figures. Through subtle variations on the theme of three – three figures within a triangular area, three heads, three haloes, three slender staves – Rublev achieved an intense rhythmical movement which never exceeds the boundaries of the whole design. Again and again the eye returns to pass from one figure to another without any sense of fatigue. Even when the design is reduced to its simplest geometrical intervals it is apparent that Rublev marvellously mastered the expressive content of his theme, of the unity of three elements in one, indivisible and yet separate. In this way he succeeded in distinguishing the three persons of the Trinity. The central angel symbolizes God the Father, who turns to the second person to indicate that he is prepared to send him as Messiah into the world. In accord with this he extends his hand over the dish containing the lamb's head, the symbolic sacrifice, while the angel to the left raises his hand in acceptance of the mission. Through the exercise of an instinctive pictorial imagination Rublev transformed one of the most ancient Byzantine iconographical themes, the

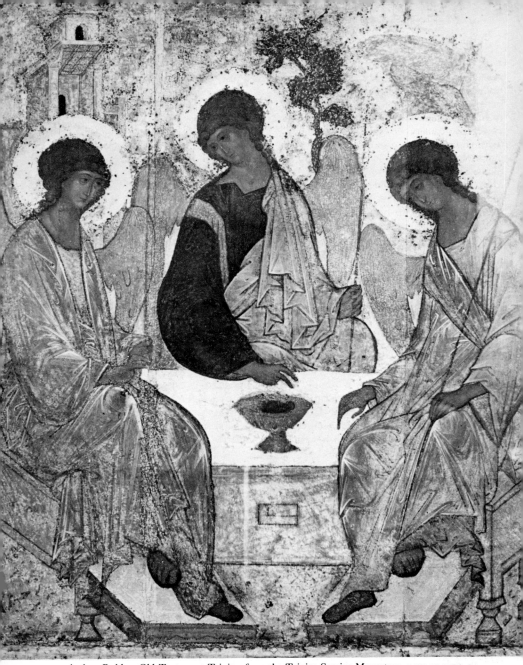

77. Andrey Rublev: Old Testament Trinity, from the Trinity-Sergius Monastery, 1411 or 1422–7. *Moscow, Tretyakov Gallery*

Deliberation of the Trinity, into a new and influential image for modern times.

Among the most important extant fragments of Rublev's art are three panels (State Tretyakov Gallery, Moscow) which were discovered in 1918 in a storeroom near the Cathedral of the Dormition in Zvenigorod.[11] The noble St Michael [78], with the coral robe and dark orange wings made resonant by the blue of the hair band and inner feathers of the left wing, resembles the angel to the left in Rublev's Trinity, especially in the arrangement of the hair, the slight inclination of the head, the facial type, and the withdrawn, contemplative expression. The adjustment of the highlights to the modelling of the receding planes of the St Paul [79] are more 'modern' – weightier and more three-dimensional – than the full-length St Paul from Rublev's iconostasis of 1408 from the Cathedral of the Dormition in Vladimir (State Russian Museum,

Leningrad) where the linear draperies and rhythmic contours suggest that Rublev was still influenced by Theophanes's iconostasis in the Cathedral of the Dormition in Moscow. But the Zvenigorod figure, which has more the mystical solemnity so conspicuous in the Christ from the same deesis, is still related to the Byzantine past. Rublev, as some scholars maintain, may have remembered the St Paul which was among the Greek paintings ordered from Constantinople in 1387 by Archbishop Athanasius for the Vysotsky Monastery in Serpukhov (see above, page 130). The damaged and incomplete icon of Christ [71], which has already been discussed, is possibly the most convincing proof of the new spirit which Rublev introduced into Russian painting. The combination of intense aristocratic dignity with an air of gentleness and compassion is peculiarly and characteristically Russian. It is as if the spirit which had inspired the anony-

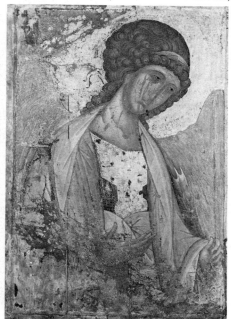

78. Andrey Rublev: St Michael, from a deesis, c. 1410–20. Moscow, Tretyakov Gallery

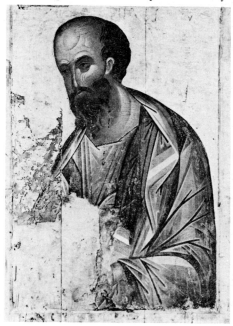

79. Andrey Rublev: St Paul, from a deesis, c. 1410–20. Moscow, Tretyakov Gallery

mous master of the Boris and Gleb icon to try to impart a feeling of the meekness with which the princes accepted death had here found fulfilment in the technically more sensitive and profoundly expressive image of the Risen Christ. Traces of the same quality may be seen in the seated figure of St Mark [80], probably painted in Moscow towards the end of the fifteenth century. Even if the composition falters under the burden of conventional architecture and accessories, the gracious drawing

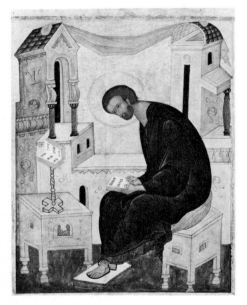

80. Moscow: St Mark, fragment from a royal door, late fifteenth century. *Moscow, Tretyakov Gallery*

of the saint's figure, and his poignant expression, prove that Rublev was still revered by a later generation.

Rublev's art, like that of any authoritative and successful artistic expression, depended not only upon the technical mastery of an individual craftsman, but upon contemporary social and spiritual conditions. At the beginning of the fifteenth century the Russian Church could look back upon a strenuous past from the time, almost half a millennium before, when Christianity was first introduced to Kiev by travellers returned from Tsargrad, through the hundred and fifty years when the Church, far more than any other Russian institution, had stood for the continuance of a national spirit during the Tartar domination, to the present, when the Metropolitan of Moscow, the spiritual successor of Kiev and Vladimir, could dream of attaining to the rank of Patriarch. The monastic establishments of the fourteenth century, in which Rublev had studied and worked, enjoyed a prosperity and stability which were soon to attract the envious attention of the Tsars. In addition to their material wealth they could number among their members, both past and present, many holy men whose lives were an inspiration to their fellow citizens. The atmosphere of piety and confidence in the Church is also that of Rublev's art. His security in the possession of his technical means is paralleled by the security of the Church in its knowledge of the means of salvation. Ahead lay the troubles between Tsar and Metropolitan in the sixteenth century which would ultimately lead to the restriction of the monasteries, the humiliation of the clergy, and the final seventeenth-century subjection of the life of the Church to a codification so severe that it provoked the great schism. The serenity and harmony of Rublev's art are not without resemblances to the similar qualities in Raphael's on the threshold of the sixteenth-century religious troubles in the West.

CHAPTER 12

FIFTEENTH-CENTURY PAINTING: NOVGOROD

To turn now to Novgorod and the use made there of the work of Theophanes is to move to an entirely different artistic environment. The way in which that art was understood in Novgorod can best be seen in the late-fourteenth-century icon of St Elias [81].[1] The

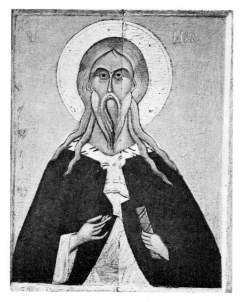

81. Novgorod: St Elias, *c.* 1400.
Moscow, Tretyakov Gallery

resemblance to the prophets of Theophanes in the long, braid-like strands of hair and beard suggests the influence of the frescoes in the Church of the Transfiguration. Technically the construction of the head in terms of an overall design of linear interlaces, marked with patterned highlights which have lost the spontaneous illusionistic quality of the frescoes, as well as the colour scheme of white, ochre, and

brown against a brilliant red ground, is typical of Novgorod painting for the next century. And the total character of a forbidding, unearthly, superhuman manifestation of prophetic wisdom, present in Theophanes's prophets, has here, through the distortions and the small eyes, set narrowly together, from which radiate the wider circles of the head, hair, and halo, been changed to a rather peevish expression.

The style of painting in Novgorod is further discovered in the large Four-Part Icon [82], with scenes representing the Resurrection of Lazarus, the Angels of the Trinity, the Presentation, and St John the Evangelist dictating his Gospel to Prokhor. Since the icon comes from the Church of St George in Novgorod, and a palaeographic examination of the inscriptions indicates a late-fourteenth- or early-fifteenth-century date, so well-documented a work is unusually important for the study of the Novgorod school. The representation of the Trinity [83] permits comparison with the style of the Moscow school as seen in Rublev's only slightly later Trinity. The Novgorod painter shows himself at once conservative by clinging to traditional iconography and yet aware of Theophanes's work, since the position of the central angel corresponds to the similar figure in the fresco of the Transfiguration. Nor is he so concerned as Rublev with endowing the subsidiary details with some degree of reality. His tree of Mamre is little more than a branch, and as it is placed directly above the head of the central figure it contributes to the symbolic rather than to the naturalistic character of the whole. Yet while the painter avoids enlarging his conception in terms of specific time and place, he retains the figures of Abraham and Sarah offering food and drink to their heavenly visitors, and

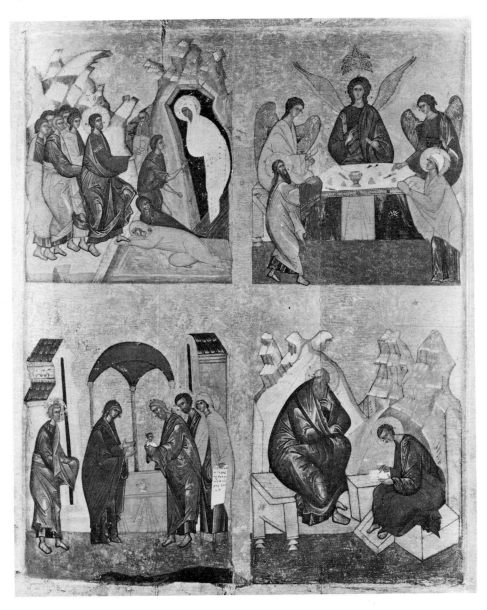

82 (*above*) and 83 (*opposite*). Novgorod: Four-Part Icon, with detail of the Old Testament Trinity, early fifteenth century. *Leningrad, Russian Museum*

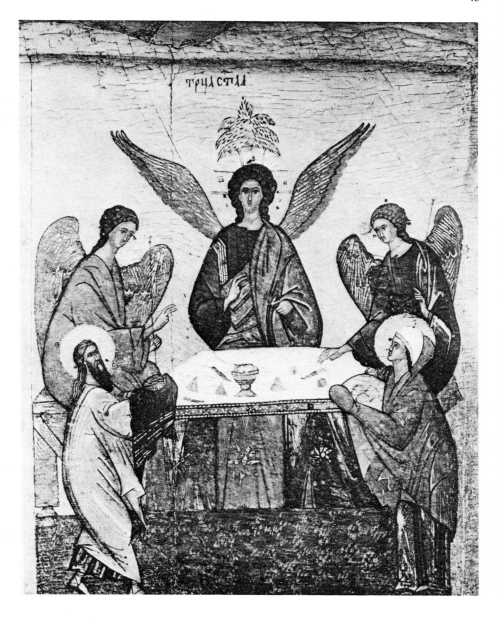

thus gives his conception a genre character. The conflict between the arbitrary, almost heraldic, representation of the angels and the anecdotal treatment of the earthly figures remains unresolved in spite of the strict symmetry of the composition. The suggestion of the swing and movement of forms turning in to the third dimension which had been Rublev's supreme accomplishment, is impossible where movement is principally reduced to the left-to-right passage of forms across the picture plane. The other scenes on this icon clearly demonstrate this. In both the Resurrection of Lazarus and the Presentation movement reads from left to right, and at the right side of the picture there is not that sense of a return backward and inward which is so irresistible in Rublev's Trinity. Iconographically the master of the Four-Part Icon preserves the traditional Early Christian and Byzantine formulas. Although they offered less promise for the future, they served Novgorod admirably in the present; for here, more than in any other centre and far more than in Moscow, may be localized the development of the narrative scene, specifically for the Twelve Feasts on the iconostasis. Not only are the oldest extant examples of the fifteenth and sixteenth centuries found in Novgorod, again probably the result of historical chance, but from its earliest independent beginnings Novgorod was an important source for the narrative icon. It suffices to recall the thirteenth-century icon of St George with the subsidiary scenes from the Saint's life, or the large local icon of the Nativity of the Virgin from northern Russia, which is such a remarkable essay in narrative painting.

It is thus no accident that two of the most famous icons which treat a historical or contemporary situation can be assigned to the Novgorod School. The first is perhaps the most typically Novgorodian, and may be less a religious symbol than the conjectured representation of an historical episode. The Battle between Novgorod and Suzdal [84] is the earliest known icon to deal with an incident in strictly Russian history. In three zones it recounts the miraculous events which occurred when Novgorod was besieged by the armies of Suzdal in 1169.[2] In the course of the siege the people of Novgorod invoked the protection of their special palladium, the icon of the Virgin of the Sign (Znamenie), which in the top zone is seen being removed from its church in the commercial quarter and carried in procession over the bridge across the Volkhov to the Cathedral of St Sophia within the Kremlin. At the entrance to the Kremlin it is received and honoured by the entire population. The second zone shows the negotiations between three men from Novgorod and three from Suzdal. But the negotiations were abruptly broken off when the Suzdalians interrupted the armistice by shooting arrows at the Virgin's icon, here seen suspended above the walls of Novgorod, behind which the army awaits the outcome of the interview. After such provocation the men of Novgorod could wait no longer. They emerged through the city gates, in the lowest zone, and, with the miraculous intervention of Russia's favourite warrior saints, George, Boris, Gleb, and Alexander Nevsky,[3] led by a warrior angel who appeared in the sky, they successfully vanquished the blasphemous Suzdalians.

Although the episode recounted had occurred some three hundred years before the presumptive date of this icon, no representations earlier than the fifteenth century are known, which has led to the conclusion that this icon is to be dated towards the close of that century, at a time when the people of Novgorod, hard pressed by Moscow and already threatened with the loss of their independence, recalled the glorious past when they had been able to overcome the ancestors of their present enemies. Style and technique support these conclusions, since they indicate that it could not have been executed before 1450. Although much is traditional, such as the conventional representation of the city walls and churches in variously oblique perspectives, much also speaks of a newer interest

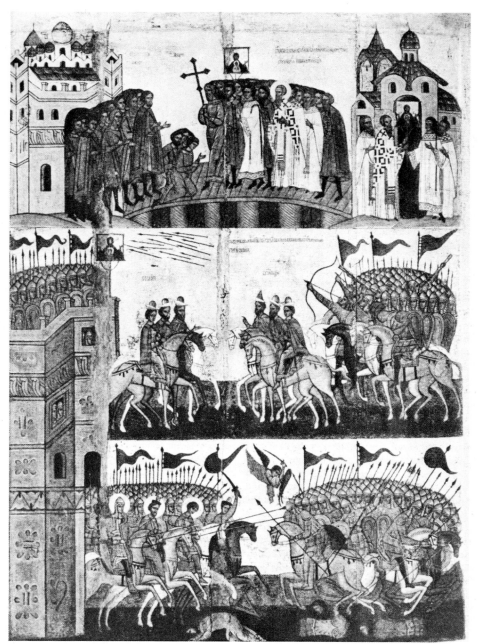

84. Novgorod: The Battle between Novgorod and Suzdal, *c.* 1450–75.
Novgorod, Museum of History and Architecture

in actuality. The details of the processional passage of the Znamenie from its own church to St Sophia have a most life-like character, more so than the battle scenes below, where the opposing hosts are treated as a repetitive pattern of massed helmets and spears. No attempt was made to distinguish the armies or the groups of deputies one from the other, while the pattern of the horses' legs supplies a delicate arabesque accompaniment to the supposedly violent action. As in the battle scenes of Paolo Uccello, tradition and innovation are inextricably combined, so that what at one place appears accurate observation of the immediately actual becomes at another part of an inherited decorative pattern. Indeed, the pattern is so thoroughly imposed upon all three zones that movement is reduced to the passage of men and horses across rather than through the space. Yet the tempo of each zone has been carefully rendered, the slow processional pace of the upper zone changes in the centre of the second to a brisker walk as the deputies confront each other and the shower of arrows passes overhead. At the bottom the violent charge of one army upon another is signalled by wildly flapping flags and the movement of spears which turn down and towards the enemy, like grain before a wind.

The subject of the Intercession of the Virgin (Pokrov), which corresponds to the Virgin of the Misericord in western iconography, is for all artistic purposes the depiction of a historical episode. In the Church of the Blachernae in Constantinople there had been preserved from early times the maphorion (pokrov) or veil of the Virgin, honoured as the palladium of the city and empire, whence arose the conception that as her veil had sheltered her body in life, so now she spiritually sheltered her followers.[4] In the eighth century Blessed Andrew the Fool while standing near the chancel had seen a miraculous apparition of the Virgin accompanied by Apostles and the Church Fathers. Her veil, which she spread over her people, remained suspended and shining in the air some time after the Virgin herself had disappeared.

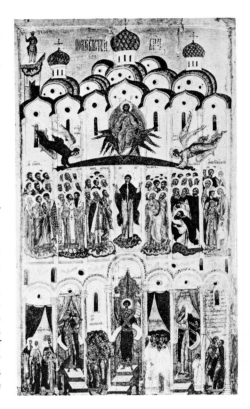

85 (*above*) and 86 (*opposite*). Novgorod or Moscow: The Miracle of the Intercession of the Virgin (Pokrov), with detail of an angel, early sixteenth century.
Leningrad, Russian Museum

The painter of a late-fifteenth- or early-sixteenth-century icon of the Pokrov [85] took pains to give his image the accent of historical authenticity.[5] For his architectural setting he chose the Cathedral of St Sophia in Novgorod, itself derived from the Constantinopolitan type of St Sophia in Kiev. Although the Novgorod church has only double aisles, the later additions of side galleries would easily have suggested his many-aisled basilica, shown below in an interior cross-section and above in an external elevation. This elevation is remarkably close to St Sophia in

Novgorod; here are the same exposed vaults, the high drums, and the swelling cupolas. Yet there is a startling indication that the painter had not mistaken the Novgorod church for its Constantinopolitan prototype; he carefully supplied the right touch of local colour by including, in the upper left corner, the colossal equestrian bronze statue of the Emperor Justinian which was one of the most conspicuous sculptures in Byzantium, and was in place as late as the fifteenth century. Lest there be any doubt in the spectator's mind as to whom the statue represented, it is carefully labelled 'Ustin'.[6]

With the stage set, the painter could proceed with his drama. In the lowest of the three tiers into which he divided his panel, he presented the interior of the church with groups of earthly personages who might actually have been present at the original miracle, or who might be thought to have attended the weekly apparition of the Virgin's image. In the centre the Cantor Romanus intones the evening service. To the left and right are seen the Emperor and the Patriarch upon their thrones. In the far right corner Andrew points out the mystic apparition to his companion, Epiphanius. In the corresponding position to the left appears the Empress with attendants. In the remaining two bays are groups of choir and clergy. The variations in gesture, pose, and number of the groups, as well as the asymmetrical distribution of closed and open bays, the latter partially shielded with drawn curtains, lend additional liveliness and veracity to the scene. Perhaps nowhere else in medieval Russian painting does one come so immediately into the presence of an actual courtly or religious ceremony. What is portrayed has been seen and recorded with the most careful attention to just those details and movements which shall pass for life. And in this connexion it is worth observing that while the perspective drawing of the stairs leading up to the three thrones is oblique, corresponding to the point of view of the personages within the scene, the approximation of a one-point perspective in the drawing of the exterior

roof of the church is a further indication of a desire for accuracy.[7]

The author's taste in the distribution of his elements appears again in the second zone,

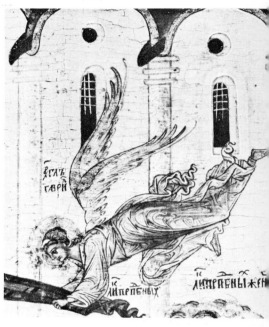

where the heavenly apparition of the Virgin, accompanied by saints and Fathers, is placed against the high white walls of the exterior of the church. The apparent discrepancy which a modern mind may feel in such an abrupt transition from the interior below to the exterior above may partially be resolved by considering the association in the painter's mind between the apparition and the actual mural treatment of the interior of such a church. Here the position of the Virgin corresponds to that of the fresco of the Virgin Orans in the apse of St Sophia in Novgorod. In both cases the image is situated directly below (or behind) the central dome over the crossing. And while the painter followed standard Byzantine custom for the representation of crowds of witnesses by arranging them in serried ranks, he has again and again subtly varied the other-

wise monotonous repetition of identical elements in the movement of the heads as the
saints and Fathers turn towards each other, as
St John the Baptist on the left reaches towards
the Intercessor or as the monastic saint to the
right falls on his knees in adoration. Even the
overlapping of the haloes adds to this effect
without distracting from the contemplative,
unearthly character of the apparition.

Above these figures the angels supporting
the Virgin's Veil and the image of Christ appearing within a mandorla carried by cherubim
are drawn in two dimensions and with a care
for linear arabesque which separates the
supernatural appearance from the lively spatial
three-dimensionality of the figures on the
earthly range below. The wave-like decorative
pattern of the clouds beneath the Virgin's feet
and the design of the angel's wings are unrivalled in fifteenth-century Russian painting
[86], and hint of the possibility of some
knowledge of Chinese art having reached
Novgorod through objects brought overland
across Asia.

Although it is probably a historical accident
that the earliest extant iconostases are found
in Novgorod, certainly here during the fifteenth century the workshops must have been
active in formulating the systematic character
of these important church furnishings. That
the Novgorod painters achieved almost a
monopoly in the production of large icons for
the iconostasis, particularly for the chin (the
range of saints and Church Fathers approaching the central deesis), is seen in two facts.
In 1547, after the burning of Moscow, the
Metropolitan Macarius decided to summon
icon-painters from Novgorod to restore the
damaged icons and in 1570, after the capitula-
tion of Novgorod, Ivan IV brought to Moscow
two large deeses which he placed in the Chapels
of the Entry into Jerusalem and of the Synaxis
of the Virgin in the Annunciation Cathedral.[8]
Until they are cleaned it will be impossible to
determine their quality, but apparently they
do not greatly differ in style from fragments
of other iconostases of the fifteenth and early

sixteenth centuries. Such are the Enthroned
Christ with the Virgin and the Baptist [87],
and the figures of Gabriel and St Paul from a
deesis.[9] In contrast to the icons of action and

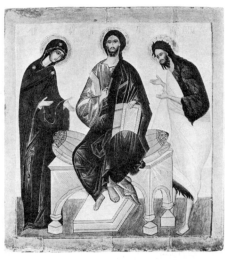

87. Novgorod: Enthroned Christ with the Virgin
and St John the Baptist, central panel from a deesis,
late fifteenth century.
Moscow, Tretyakov Gallery

event which we have just examined, these large
figures seem strangely inert. The opportunity
which Rublev might have found in the Enthroned Christ to create a three-dimensional
pattern of delicately balanced forms has been
neglected, and the lumpish shape of the
figures betrays another aspect of Novgorodian
art: the inability to articulate the body with
the draperies which cover it. This same trait
appeared in an exaggerated form in the seated
St John of the Four-Part Icon [82] and it
recurs constantly throughout the history of the
school. In the Gabriel and Paul the dangers of
drastic linear simplification are readily apparent. Figures of this type were produced in such
quantities in Novgorod that one can presume
the existence of large workshops organized on
a commercial basis.

On the other hand, for the painting of the Twelve Feasts and accompanying scenes which were placed in the row above the chin the painters of Novgorod lavished all their talents in the invention of narrative or the recreation of historical episode. Towards the middle of the century may be placed the masterly icon of the Entry into Jerusalem [88].[10] If at

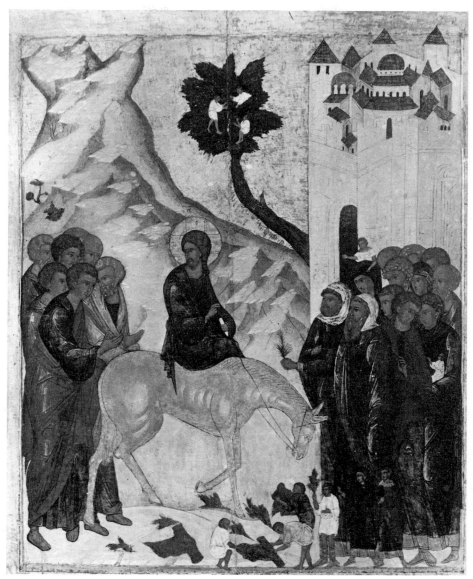

88. Mixed Style: The Entry into Jerusalem, *c.* 1450. *Moscow, Tretyakov Gallery*

moments it appears almost too close to the spirit of Rublev in the placing of the tree and the complex inner rhythms obtained by the two lateral groups of Apostles and Jews looking inward towards Christ, who himself turns to look back towards the Apostles, still there are unmistakable Novgorod accents. The high-piled white walls and towers are Novgorod, not Moscow, and only the masters of Novgorod could have created the busy activity of the children strewing garments before the triumphant Christ. Elsewhere, as in the drawing of the figures, the tree, and especially the mountain, the technical competence of the fifteenth century can be seen. The easy linear rhythms, the counterpoint of pattern among mountain, tree, and town, and the deft play of light and shade upon the rocky terraces were beyond the powers and experience of the painter of the Four-Part Icon.

When an icon such as the Entry into Jerusalem is described as in a 'Mixed Style', it can be taken to mean not merely that the painter, of Novgorod or Moscow, was familiar with the art of the other city, but that by the end of the century a national style was coming to the fore. That in the sixteenth century this style became localized in Moscow and acquired the special character of a hieratic and courtly art was historically inevitable. That the older manner of Novgorod was not easily forgotten is apparent in the many icons of the sixteenth century which show the continuation of the earlier manner in outlying regions. Such are the several icons from a large iconostasis illustrating the Crucifixion, Deposition, and Lamentation, which have all the marks of a provincial variant of Novgorod painting. Here is the immediate apprehension of a human situation, the direct and effectively uncomplicated design, the same attention to the emotional power of rhythmical repetition which we have found in Novgorod painting. Only in the summary and monotonous treatment of the landscape are we aware that the painter worked rather by rote than by invention, and that the model which he used was already hoary with

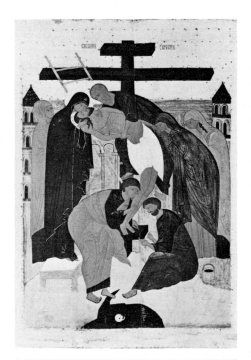

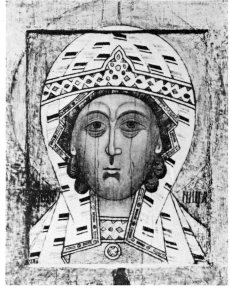

tradition. The Deposition icon [89] is perhaps the most successful. The continuous curves of the bodies of Christ, Nicodemus, and St Mary Magdalene are effectively arranged against the broad beam of the cross and the foil of the ladder, but even as pattern it remains so strictly two-dimensional that the forms seem fastened against a surface rather than moving through space.

When the spiritual demands were less insistent the Novgorod master could create an image often of great formal power, if not of remarkable insight. The head or bust-length icon of a single saint, of the type already noted in the late-fourteenth-century St Elias, occurs again in an icon such as that of St Paraskeva (Pyatnitsa) [90]. The broad, even noble, decorative pattern is in the favourite Novgorod scheme of black against white. If ever the term icon has accurately meant a symbolic, unearthly image it is here, where the Novgorod fondness for anecdote yields to a symmetrical design of hieratic power appropriate for an image of a truly unearthly being (St Holy Friday, as we might term her in English, is as much a theological abstraction as the Western SS. Faith, Hope, and Charity).

Anecdote and symbolic pattern are, however, equably and skilfully combined in an icon of SS. Florus and Laurus [91]. They were among the most popular saints in the Orthodox calendar, spiritual veterinarians so to speak, because, as physicians who accepted no fees,

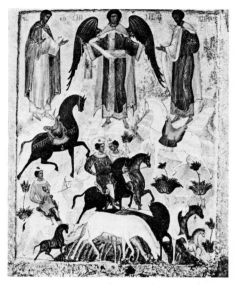

91. Novgorod: SS. Florus and Laurus, late fifteenth century. *Moscow Tretyakov Gallery*

they had been charged by St Michael with the protection of horses. At the top of the panel Florus and Laurus stand on either side of the Archangel, as they might in heaven. In the middle zone a pair of symbolic horses are confronted as in an eastern textile, while beneath them horses and riders appear in livelier, less formal postures typical of Novgorod's interest in the practical matters of this earthly life.

89 (*top left*). Novgorod: The Deposition, from a range of the Twelve Feasts, late fifteenth century.
Moscow, Tretyakov Gallery

90 (*left*). Novgorod: St Paraskeva (Pyatnitsa; Good Friday), *c.* 1500. *Leningrad, Russian Museum*

CHAPTER 13

PAINTING IN MOSCOW IN THE LATER FIFTEENTH

AND SIXTEENTH CENTURIES

While the Novgorod painters were developing a lively, anecdotal style, related to the dramatic narrative manner of the Palaeologos Renaissance yet coloured by the popular traditions of northern Russia and their own taste for positive facts, the painters of Moscow were working towards another end. In Novgorod the frescoes of Theophanes furnished suggestions for a more realistic technique. In Moscow the work of the same painter increased the desire for spiritual expression. However it may be, certainly the expressive gifts of Theophanes were understood and developed by Andrey Rublev, whose works left a pervading influence on later Moscow art. In such an icon as the Entry into Jerusalem the constant interplay of forms recalls clearly the similar changes rung in his Trinity.

From this principle of the rhythmic counterbalance of forms ceaselessly moving within a restricted space and so creating an effect of much greater depth than is actually present, were to come the greatest triumphs of Moscow painting. A mid-fifteenth-century Ascension [92], perhaps contemporary with the work of Rublev or only slightly later, shows how even while adhering to conventional iconography the Moscow painter was aware of the possibility of movement. The strictest symmetry has been observed throughout the panel. This necessarily imposes an almost irresistible tendency towards two-dimensional design which, joined with the traditional division of the scene into heavenly and earthly zones, might easily have caused the painter to divide his panel into four more or less equal parts. Yet he treated his composition as a contrapuntal exercise. By imposing an ellipse upon a circle he suggested the spatial inter-relations which might occur when such forms are projected in three

dimensions. The wider sphere formed by the apostolic congregation surrounds the elliptical central core composed of the Virgin's figure surmounted by Christ's in a mandorla borne by angels. Between the earthly and heavenly zones the angelic apparitions in the centre of the composition supply the necessary transition. Meanwhile, the contrast between the straight lines of the Virgin's figure and the circular design of the Christ above prevents the whole from degenerating into an exercise in academic design. In colour, too, the play of various olives and dark greens with red and maroon against the light ochre ground, and the contrast between the Virgin's purple maphorion and the white robes of the angels have a

92. Moscow,
after an icon by Andrey Rublev and Daniil Cherny:
The Ascension, *c*. 1450.
Moscow, Tretyakov Gallery

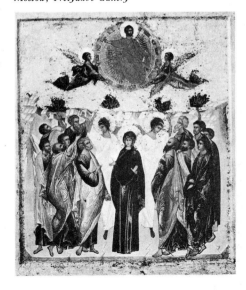

constant interplay analogous to the rhythmical development of the design.

This tendency is further demonstrated in a sixteenth-century icon depicting St Varlaam of Khutyn [93] with scenes from his life. Throughout the whole panel, from the large central scene to the smaller ones along the sides, there is an ease and assurance, not only in the drawing and colour, but more significantly in the massing of the figures, landscape, and architecture within the prescribed space. In a sense such work as this can be taken to represent the fulfilment of the promises of earlier Russian painting in terms of a classic moment in that art. Within the traditional conventions of iconography and technique the artist has achieved complete technical certainty and powerful expressive control. When an enlargement of one of the smaller scenes is compared with the earlier Novgorod Resurrection of Lazarus it can be seen how the Moscow painter thought in terms of space, no matter how shallow the actual space he described. Although there are no direct references to Rublev, the lessons of that master are observed in the overall unity of each smaller composition.

The classic moment in the development of any style, within any art, is necessarily brief; for the concept of the classic as well as its formal application imply an equilibrium between form and content, between technique and style, between material and expression which is subject to disturbance when any one of the component elements, for whatever reason, becomes more insistent than another. Evidence of such a change occurs towards the beginning of the sixteenth century in the radical re-definition of subject-matter. To the older types of icon, the narrative subjects of the Twelve Feasts, the single figures for the deesis and other ranges of the iconostasis, and the solitary devotional images of the Virgin and various saints, was added a new subject requiring not only the development of a new iconography, but also a new consideration of technique and formal properties. This is the kind of icon which presents, whether under the guise of narrative action or a devotional figure, new religious concepts of a didactic and mystical character.

The reasons for the appearance of new subjects and a new attitude towards more traditional scenes are to be found in the changed conditions prevailing both within and without the Russian Church in the course of the fifteenth century. After the fall of Constantinople in 1453 the Russian Church felt itself not only independent of, but, indeed, the successor to, the Greek Church, which was thought to have fallen to the enemy as a result of its lapse from orthodoxy. This feeling found expression in the theory that Moscow was 'the third Rome' (the first two, Rome and Constantinople, having failed to keep the faith).[1] The religious painting of fifteenth-century Russia was subjected to still another influence; the presence in Moscow after 1470 of Italian architects and craftsmen must inevitably have led to some familiarity on the part of the more intelligent native artists with the different iconography and means of expression of western painting. The result of these contacts will be unquestionable in the sixteenth century. Meanwhile, the character of later-fifteenth-century painting in the Moscow region is best seen by examining the work of the artist known as Master Dionisy (Dionysius, Denis).

Often in the history of Russian art the appearance of a new style, or a development within an existing style, depends upon the correct reading of evidence which, however complete in itself, is but a fragment of a much wider whole. As the activity and influence of Theophanes and Rublev must be deduced from mere portions of their original work, so with Dionisy no more survives of his activity than a few damaged frescoes in the Dormition in Moscow of about 1479–81, and the completely painted interior of the Church of the Nativity of the Virgin in the Ferapont Monastery.[2] The latter is signed and dated 1500–2, but it appears from documents that Dionisy must have executed these frescoes with the help of assistants well towards the end of his career, since he is first mentioned

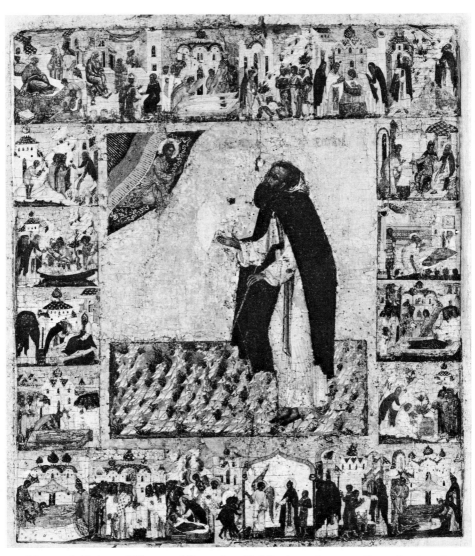

93. Moscow: St Varlaam of Khutyn and Scenes from his Life, sixteenth century. *Present location unknown*

in 1476 at work in the Monastery of St Paphnutius in Boroskovo, apparently as the assistant of an older master. In 1481 with three other painters he executed a 'deesis with Festivals and Prophets', that is to say an iconostasis, for

the Cathedral of the Dormition in Moscow, just completed by Aristotele Fioravanti. In the same year he repaired an icon of the Virgin Hodegetria which had been damaged by fire, and painted an iconostasis for the cathedral in

Rostov. Between 1480 and 1490 he painted a deesis for a monastery on Lake Koubensky. In 1484, with the Venerable Paissi and his own sons Feodosy (Theodosius) and Vladimir, he painted an extensive series of icons for the monastery of Volokolamsk. In an inventory of 1545 more than a hundred icons were attributed to Dionisy and his sons. Unhappily of all this work nothing has survived which can be assigned to their hands with absolute certainty. The esteem in which his work was held as late as 1545 reflected the reputation he enjoyed in his lifetime. Bishop Vassian of Rostov, in his life of St Paphnutius Borovsky, stated that Dionisy was 'the most famous of all painters of this time'. And the chronicler declared that his icons for Rostov were 'very beautiful'. In 1508 his son Feodosy is mentioned as the head of the workshop. The father was either dead or too old to continue working. From this evidence Dionisy was presumably born about 1440 and died shortly after 1500. The period of his greatest activity occurred two generations and more after the work of Rublev and his followers, and in this respect presents a further distinct stage in the development of Moscow painting.

Although no single icon can definitely be attributed to Dionisy, the amount of work he accomplished and the high regard in which he was held could not have failed to affect later-fifteenth-century panel-painting. Attributions must be based on the most extensive documented work, the fresoces at the Ferapontov (Therapont) Monastery on the White Lake. The fact that the monastery was situated in the far north-eastern part of the territory of Novgorod has led to the identification of Dionisy and his school with the painters of Novgorod. But it would seem that in spite of its territorial allegiance the Ferapontov Monastery was more closely associated with Moscow. Its founder, St Ferapont, came from Moscow, and his successors, notably the Abbot Martinian, were in frequent intercourse with the Great Princes and Tsars. Indeed, even were the documents less persuasive, the evidence of

the paintings is visually conclusive. In more than one respect they are typical of the intense spirituality and delicate coloristic grace of the Moscow school as it had developed after the time of Theophanes and Rublev.

Although the plan and structure of the Ferapont church follow the traditional orthodox formula, the iconography departs in many respects from the schemes already seen in the earlier Novgorod churches. In place of the customary exegesis of the main tenets of Christian dogma, the painted scenes are pre-eminently illustrations of the Akathist Hymn in honour of the Virgin.[3] High in the dome the Pantokrator still reigns, but no longer as the stern and brooding Ancient of Days; he is a gentle, aristocratic Saviour, very close to the Rublev type of the deesis of Zvenigorod. Below the Pantokrator, Archangels and Patriarchs in the drum and Evangelists on the spandrels continue the familiar disposition. An intensification of the worship of the Virgin is witnessed in the apse and chancel, where, in addition to the enthroned Virigin and Child represented above the Liturgy of the Fathers (instead of the Divine Eucharist), the Virgin appears in the types of the Sign (Znamenie) and Intercessor (Pokrov). On the walls of the nave are scenes from the Akathist Hymn illustrating the versicles 'Rejoice' and 'Praise of the Virgin'. A further departure from traditional iconography appears in the treatment of the life of Christ and in the representations of dogmatic and doctrinal subjects. In place of the customary scenes are representations of the parables and miracles of Christ, which very rarely appear even on icons. The choice of such incidents as the Parables of the Prodigal Son, of the Widow's Mite [94], or of the Faithless Servant, for which there were few if any iconographical precedents and which therefore required the invention of new types of movement and action, indicates the growing independence of the Russian Church from traditional Greek models, as well as the painter's willingness to enlarge the restricted repertory of his art.

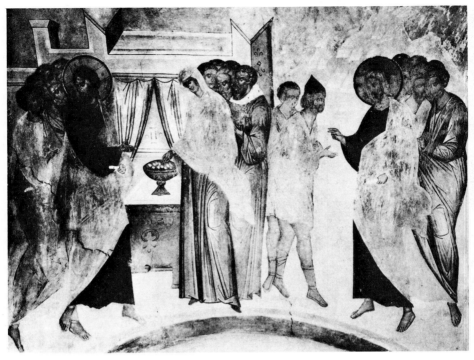

94. Dionisy and his sons: The Parable of the Widow's Mite,
fresco in the Church of the Nativity of the Virgin, Ferapontov Monastery, 1500–2

But what might in some respects be considered a tendency towards greater naturalism of type and action in these unfamiliar events is contradicted by another set of scenes: the representation of the Councils of the Church as conventionally composed groups of Patriarchs and Fathers symmetrically arranged on either side of the enthroned Emperor. In a certain sense the iconography of the Ferapont church summarizes the dialectical dilemma of later Russian painting, and introduces the drama which would develop in the course of the sixteenth century. The painter was interested in new naturalistic inventions; the Church preferred traditional representations of abstract dogma. Dionisy succeeded in achieving a harmonious compromise, but from

thesis and antithesis emerged no synthesis which was ever effective for long. Between abstract expression and naturalistic execution the gap was too wide to be bridged by less than a very great artist, perhaps by a Raphael or Michelangelo in the West, by a Rublev or Dionisy in the East. And Dionisy had no successors in this respect.

In the formal elements of technique and expression his art was a luminous and peerless solution of the programme proposed. For the sequence of scenes intended to illustrate various aspects of dogma, adoration, and exaltation he utilized a harmonious counterbalance of turquoise, pale green, and rose against darker blues and purples, the whole set off with gold in the haloes and accessories. For these har-

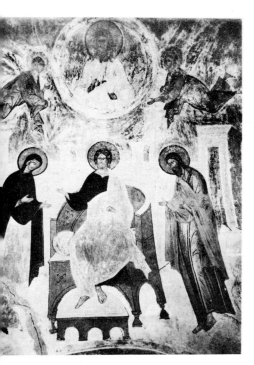

95. Dionisy and his sons:
Christ Enthroned with the Virgin
and St John the Baptist, from the Last Judgement
fresco in the Church of the Nativity of the Virgin,
Ferapontov Monastery, 1500–2

Rublev introduced a more delicate balance between the desire for slender grace and the need for expressing underlying physical structure. Although the angels of his Trinity would appear much taller were they standing figures, there is no doubt about the articulation of their bodies. In his deesis figures, even when only preserved half-length, the draperies are so disposed as to reveal more of the fundamental physical structure than in any previous Russian painting.

With Dionisy a new tendency was at work. Actually his figures are proportionally little, if at all, taller than some of those of his predecessors and contemporaries, but they communicate a sense of almost dematerialized buoyancy, achieved in two ways: by drastic simplifications of drawing, so thorough as to reduce the figures in many cases to flat silhouettes in colour against a lighter background, and by a new kind of composition. Since the character of the drawing prohibits any indications of depth, the figures tend, in spite of frequent overlapping, to be spread out across the picture surface, which enhances the effect of the silhouette. Indeed, it might be said that in contrast to Rublev's and earlier Novgorod compositions, which led towards a tighter inter-relationship of all the parts, the Ferapont designs are discursive and disparate. The compelling need to stress the spiritual content of the parables from the gospel or the mystical enthusiasm of the Akathist subjects required and received just such a treatment. Dionisy and his sons communicated not the narrative episodes so much as the spiritual overtones of their religious content. There was never again in Russia to be painting which so perfectly established an interchange between observed nature and exalted emotion as we find in Rublev. As Russian art approached the strident troubles of the sixteenth and seventeenth centuries, the aerial spaces of Dionisy's frescoes were to be for ever left behind.[4]

The reputation and activity of Dionisy and his sons had considerable influence on subsequent icon-painting, but panels can be attri-

monies his authority was Rublev and earlier-fifteenth-century painting in Moscow, rather than the brilliant primary oppositions of the Novgorod tradition. The figure style of Dionisy and his sons is also both personal and characteristic of the period [95]. Although in earlier Russian painting the figure had usually tended to be tall rather than broad, the masters of Novgorod had often conveyed a sense of massive physique beneath the heavy draperies. Often this effect was achieved by drawing the garments close about the body so as to emphasize the anatomy of the back and thighs.

buted to them only on the grounds of stylistic
affinity with the Ferapont frescoes and the
five large icons from the Ferapont deesis
which are now preserved in the Tretyakov
Gallery in Moscow.[5] Although Dionisy's sons
may have painted the panels, the figural style
is their father's. The billowing robes confer a
degree of movement which the attenuated
figures, conceivably scarcely more than skele-
tal supports, could not generate by themselves.
Nonetheless, they are all infused with the
special spiritual poignancy which was Dionisy's greatest gift, his ability to make flat
planes and simple contours express the most
mystical and immaterial situations. This may
be seen in a small panel, The Incredulity of
St Thomas [96], painted towards 1500 late in
his own life or by a close follower. Many
western artists have found it difficult to
convey, visually and formally, the fact that the
Christ is indeed 'risen'; Dionisy's skill permits
a willing suspension of disbelief, for St
Thomas as for ourselves.

The legacy of Dionisy was at once too personal and too refined to serve as the basis for
a new school, even had the political and religious history of the sixteenth century permitted
an uninterrupted succession of artistic tradition. The progressive and inescapable unification of Russia under the hegemony of the
Great Prince of Moscow entailed a concentration of artistic effort at the capital, a process
assisted by a curious combination of circumstances. After the fire of 1547 so great was
the need for new paintings to replace those
destroyed that the Metropolitan Macarius,
who had previously been Archbishop of Novgorod, not only brought to Moscow large
quantities of icons, but forcibly transferred
the icon-painters of Novgorod with their
workshops. Thus ceased the independent

96 (*above right*). Dionisy or a close follower:
The Incredulity of St Thomas, *c.* 1500.
Moscow, Tretyakov Gallery

97 (*right*). Moscow: The Vision of St Eulogius,
c. 1530–40. *Leningrad, Russian Museum*

character of the school of Novgorod. The presence of the Novgorod painters soon affected the character of Moscow painting, and regarding the whole sixteenth century it is difficult, if not futile, to attempt to distinguish the two manners. The term 'Mixed Style', invented to explain those icons which combine elements of technique or expression from both schools, is particularly appropriate for such sixteenth-century productions as the Vision of St Eulogius [97].

The further developments of the Moscow manner may be seen in the late-sixteenth-century icon of the Entry into Jerusalem [98].[6] When compared with the older icon of the same subject it can be seen how much of the spirituality of Rublev and Dionisy 'has been lost. Not only has the exquisite adjustment of the various shapes, which communicated a sense of space and processional movement, disappeared in the more vertical design, but an interest in decorative repetitions and a certain sentimental naturalism has destroyed the solemn mood of the earlier painting. The older icon was tragic with a sense of foreknowledge, the younger seems capricious and trivial. Yet there is a fine sense of decorative elegance in the chiselled terraces of the mountain and the high-piled architecture of the city gate. And in this period for the first time a specifically Russian facial type appears. The vivacious expressions of the round-headed Apostles and Jews are very different from the classic Greek types of the earlier icon. The high priest with the white headdress in the centre of the group on the right appears so oriental that one might be persuaded that the Tartars had left descendants in Russia.

Of the many factors which had gone into the production of sixteenth-century painting, the elegance of Rublev, the pragmatic naturalism of Novgorod, or the spirituality of Dionisy, none was to prove as important an element for later painting as the kind of decorative design which is clearly of eastern origin. So far all such tendencies towards equilateral symmetry as we have observed had been dictated either by traditional Greek iconography or by the nature of the subject, and more often than not the Russian painter had avoided absolute symmetry even in subjects which provided it. Such painting for the most part antedated the overthrow and expulsion of the Tartars, accomplished between 1480 and 1552. Possibly to the degree that the Tartars were no longer a constant threat to the security and independence of Russia, the vast reservoir of eastern art became less distasteful and more easily assimilable. Certainly throughout the sixteenth century the presence of a taste for oriental arabesques, for the decorative effect of line divorced from form, for the repetition of identical forms, became more insistent in painting as well as in architecture. The icon of

98. Moscow: The Entry into Jerusalem, late sixteenth century. *Leningrad, Russian Museum*

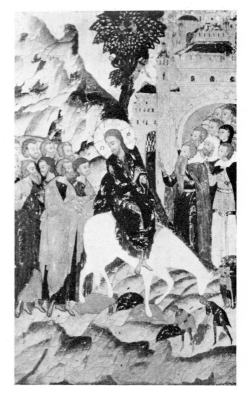

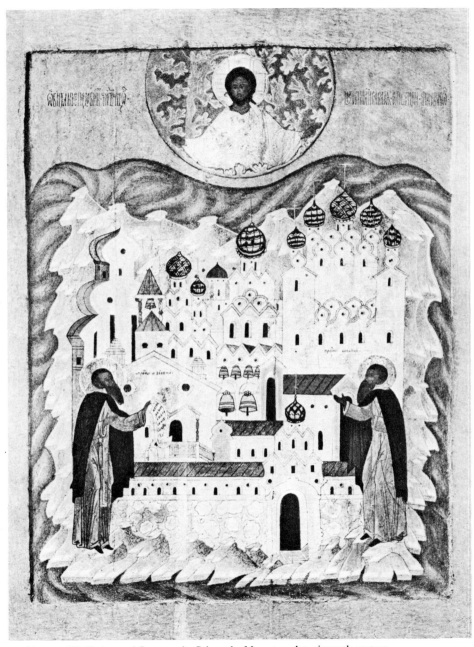

99. Moscow: SS. Zosima and Savva at the Solovetsky Monastery, late sixteenth century.
Moscow, Tretyakov Gallery

SS. Zosima and Savva [99], the founders of the Solovetsky Monastery in the White Sea, standing beside the monastic building, suggests the gradual dominance exercised by decorative aspects of design over the expressive end. It is worth noting that the icon shows a close observation of nature. The monastery was certainly familiar to the painter, if indeed he were not resident within it, and he went to some pains to deploy a consistent perspective in his drawing of the various windows. But the desire to recreate the exact appearance of a known locality was subordinated to the decorative aspect of the whole design, for it is impossible not to feel that the architectural elements have been multiplied in order to harmonize with the flat, two-dimensional description of the island floating upright, on end as it were, surrounded by the waves of the sea.

Throughout the sixteenth century, in addition to the use of the decorative aspects of line and colour for the visual enrichment of the icon, there was a comparable development of the mystical and doctrinal elements observed in the Ferapont frescoes. Such subjects had not been unknown in Greek painting, but they were comparatively rare.[7] Their appearance in numbers in Moscow was a result of the increased independence of the Russian Church, and also of the development of a technical mastery sufficient to represent the intricate symbolism such subjects required. In contrast to earlier representations of single figures or single scenes from religious history, these icons dealt with the subtleties of dogma, and the greatest ingenuity was required to find appropriate visual symbols for them. Frequently traditional and even western iconographical themes were so combined that considerable theological knowledge is required to interpret them. Such an icon was the popular Only-Begotten Son, the Word of God, in which were combined images and symbols representing the concepts of the Creation, Redemption, and Last Judgement, including even the western image of the Pietà.[8]

Such subjects were not introduced without difficulty. In 1551, four years after the appearance in Moscow of a large number of icons from Novgorod and Pskov, the important ecclesiastical assembly of Ivan IV's reign, the so-called Council of the Hundred Chapters (Stoglav), was convened in Moscow to consider problems of Church reform, including conditions prevailing in icon production. The Council took its name from the fact that the Tsar's queries and the Council's replies were presented in one hundred sections.[9] The Tsar's third 'question' dealt with icons and icon-painters.

The holy and venerable icons, conformable to divine rules, must reproduce the image of God, his likeness, and be faithful to the consecrated type. [According to the rules] one will paint the image of God, of the Most Pure Mother of God and that of all the intercessor saints. On this subject you have a witness in Holy Scripture. You must watch with the greatest care that the icon-painters have irreproachable sentiments and practise virtue, that they instruct pupils and teach them to paint the divine images, with skill and according to the consecrated type.

In reply the Council decreed that each priest should supervise with the greatest care the icons and sacred vessels in his church. Furthermore, it was stated that 'if certain icons have suffered from the injuries of time, [the priests] will have them repaired by the painters; those which are insufficiently coated with oil must be oiled'. (The disastrous effect of this practice has already been noted.) To the question as to how the Trinity was to be indicated – whether by haloes behind the heads of the three angels or by an inscription – the answer was that 'the painters will reproduce the ancient models, those of the Greek icon-painters, of Andrey Rublev and other famous painters. They will write below: The Holy Trinity. In nothing will the painters follow their own fancy.' The Council also undertook to regulate the production of icons by urging upon the bishops and priests a closer supervision of the actual process of manufacture. Not only were they to ascertain that the painter himself led a virtuous life and applied himself assiduously to his task, 'with his eyes fixed on older painters, taking for models the best icons', but they were to discourage mediocre work and punish able painters who misused their talents.

Whether or not the decisions of the Stoglav were ever operable, it is certain that the appeal to traditional types was ineffective against the newer mystical and didactic icons. At this time a celebrated controversy arose when the State Secretary Viskovaty, an able and intelligent man, took exception to certain idiosyncrasies he detected in a four-part icon in the Cathedral of the Annunciation. The separate scenes represented God Resting on the Seventh Day; The Only-Begotten Son; Come, Men, and Honour the Triune God; and In the Grave is the Flesh. It is possible that these complaints were intended to annoy the priest Sylvester of the Cathedral of the Annunciation, who was Ivan IV's favourite adviser. Viskovaty objected to artists painting 'according to their own understanding and not according to sacred tradition: the same subject was treated in various ways, so that although the subjects of several icons might be identical each was painted differently: they no longer abode by the ancient custom of putting an inscription on the icon, and introduced into the painting besides sacred subjects some profane images'.[10] He condemned such visual materializations as representations of 'the invisible and fleshless Godhead' and such realistic details as the crooked fingers of the crucified Christ.

Viskovaty's criticisms were presented to a Church Council in 1554, which upheld the authenticity of the icons. Viskovaty observed that in the icon Come, Men, and Honour the Triune God, 'tsars, princes, prelates, and people of the lower classes were represented as if they were alive'. The Council replied that an examination of icons of the Exaltation of the Venerable and Life-Giving Cross and of the Intercession of the Virgin showed that many people of all conditions were customarily depicted, as well as in representations of the Last Judgement. Viskovaty's objections were declared heretical and he was obliged to retract.

The decision had a paradoxical effect. The departures from traditional iconography which Viskovaty had noticed were indeed novelties, often due to western influences accepted by the masters of the Pskov school, as in the figure of God the Father as an elder, or Christ surrounded by cherubim. But the rejection of his criticism by an appeal to past authority really worked for rather than against the new. Succeeding years of the century saw a further attempt to codify and regularize traditions through the preparation of manuals of iconography. The so-called 'Illuminated Original', a collection of copies in outline of established and certified patterns, scarcely served its purpose of preventing any deviation from authoritative models. It offered the painters too many choices, since there was still room for the inclusion of variants, and only the most servile copyists could be constrained to follow exactly the patterns set for them.[11]

PART THREE

THE ART OF MUSCOVY

And now that they have come into stone-built Moscow,
They have not entered the royal palace,
They have gone into the sacred cathedral,
To sing the appointed Mass.
He has blessed his beloved Son:
'God grant that the Orthodox Tsar be well,
The mighty Prince Mikhail Feodorovich,
And that he may rule the realm of Moscow,
And all the holy Russian land!'

The Entry of the Patriarch Philaret into Moscow, 1619

CHAPTER 14

WOODEN CHURCH ARCHITECTURE

Up to now our architectural history has been principally concerned with the transmutation of foreign masonry forms and techniques. From the conversion in 988 to the establishment of the Russian Patriarchate in 1589 the most constant factors had been the continued presence of the Greek clergy, and the implicit presence in all liturgical and ecclesiastical events of the Greek heritage of the Russian Church. Despite the many modifications which prevented St Sophia in Kiev from being a slavish copy of Hagia Sophia in Constantinople, or the many differences which separate the Cathedral of the Annunciation in the Kremlin from earlier Byzantine churches, the affiliation of the Russian churches is clear. From Greece there had been brought and preserved the simple logical clarity of an interior space covered with at least one central dome-shape, directly stated on the exterior by the fundamental geometrical relation of cubical nave to semi-cylindrical apse to hemispherical dome.

Russia had, however, another building tradition, one of immemorial antiquity, whose origins can only be conjectured and whose relation to the imported systems of construction still remains enigmatic. This was the method of building in wood, the material originally found in abundance throughout central and northern Russia north of the steppe country. Within this area grew cities, villages, and monastic establishments which were to be brought together as the first truly national Russian state, the Muscovy of the period between the Tartar invasion in the early thirteenth century and the new Europeanized Russia of Peter the Great after 1700. Here were formulated many of the artistic and philosophical conceptions which most distinguish the Russia of the post-invasion period from all that had gone before. If the buildings of Kiev certainly, and even of Novgorod partially, still preserved for the modern eye something of the serenity and geometrical clarity we tend to associate with concepts of the classical age and the masonry architecture of the antique South, later Russian architecture of the fourteenth and fifteenth centuries, developing in the depths of the forests, was indelibly marked by the forms of wooden construction. To the static geometry of the cube of brick or worked stone succeeded the organic growth of the fir tree.

The successive stages in the history of wooden architecture present difficult, often insuperable obstacles to the historian who wishes to prove a neat and chronologically consecutive development.[1] It is incontestable that the peoples who inhabited the Russian land from ancient times had used wood in some form or other, and, as we have seen, the men of Novgorod upon almost their first appearance in history were derided by the Kievans as carpenters. Although wooden structures are among those first mentioned in the chronicles, the material was too perishable to allow any but the most hesitant conjectures about the appearance and construction of the earliest wooden buildings. When the Varangians arrived they must have found a thriving culture of wooden construction to which they probably added certain details of their own which are now undiscoverable.[2] Since there are, however, numerous wooden buildings, principally churches, still standing from the seventeenth and eighteenth centuries, and since from the chronicles and from the location of these structures we can deduce that a profoundly conservative attitude underlay their construction, it is not improbable that even the latest are often essentially older structures rebuilt. Thus churches of the eighteenth and even nineteenth centuries may be thought to perpetuate much earlier buildings. The location of most of the existing wooden churches points to a similarly conservative attitude. They are most often found in the north-east, in the former provinces of Olonets, Vologda, and Archangel, along the reaches of the Northern Dvina and its tributaries, far from the settled areas of Moscow and Novgorod and so somewhat immune from innovation. These regions after the middle of the

seventeenth century were the principal refuge of the Old Believers, who clung in spite of vicious persecution to traditional religious forms.

Under these circumstances the historian is obliged to propose a formal development of wooden architecture based not upon the succession of documented and dated examples, but upon a progression from simpler to more complicated forms. Yet even this may falsify or distort certain important factors, especially technique. Despite the fact that the most complex extant wooden church dates from the early eighteenth century [124], and so follows by only a few years the somewhat similar decorative elaboration of the Baroque churches of Moscow, the actual technical methods employed are not notably intricate, and must be assumed to have been in existence from a remote period. If we may predicate gradual complication and multiplication of the parts of the church structure, we must also assume that upon the introduction of Christianity into Russia there already existed a technique of working in wood which permitted the most complex effects.

To the difficulty of ascertaining the probable course of formal evolution is added that of determining the precise interaction exercised upon each method by the separate development of wood and masonry construction. The striking similarity between certain sixteenth-century stone and some seventeenth-century wooden buildings has been used to assert the influence upon masonry architecture of the widely prevalent wooden forms, although this is to overlook a chronological discrepancy which can only be explained by the assumption that the late wooden forms perpetuate certain earlier prototypes. On the other hand, it can be argued that the prestige of the masonry structures in the great cities, Moscow particularly, inevitably fascinated the simpler builders of the country regions, and the later wooden buildings are then described as imitations of the forms of Court architecture.[3] Either view may be unnecessarily exclusive.

Probably a certain give and take prevailed, at times preponderantly in favour of wood construction, at others of stone. Since the paradigm of religious architecture remained the Greek cubical church, the carpenters were constantly seeking to interpret that simple static form within the dynamic of their wooden technique, while in turn the variety and fancy achieved in wooden buildings were carried over by the masons into the decorative treatment of the non-structural parts of their edifices, particularly in the design of the roof and cupolas.

The use of wood implies, then, not only possibilities for experiment and invention due to the flexible nature of the material, but also, from the circumstances under which it was used, a certain traditionalism in the repetition of familiar forms. Ease of execution and speed of construction permitted more readily than in masonry the duplication of perished shapes, and at the same time afforded a degree of experiment not always possible in brick and stone. To this paradoxical interaction of tradition upon invention we may add the further factor of the relative simplicity of structural systems in wood, again leading to the contrast

between the elementary methods of construction and the elaborate, even sophisticated forms evolved.

The basic element common to all Russian wooden structures was a frame of logs laid horizontally on a rectangular or polygonal plan and interlocked at the corners, either through semicircular notches placed a short distance from the ends of each log so that the overlapping ends projected, or by a mortise and tenon joint, particularly for logs intersecting at an oblique angle as in the polygonal apses, which allowed the juncture to be neatly finished. By successively reducing the length of the logs at the ends of a rectangular frame a gable was achieved. The roof was made of planks laid on beams running lengthwise between the gables. This is the system used in the simplest form of peasant house or izba, and from it in combination with polygonal plans and applied carved decoration were created the most complex forms. Two examples of wooden structures of the eighteenth century doubtless repeat forms long familiar to the Russian carpenters. The small storehouses [100] show the structural method in its basic simplicity. The large farmhouse

100. Wooden storehouses, northern Russia, eighteenth century

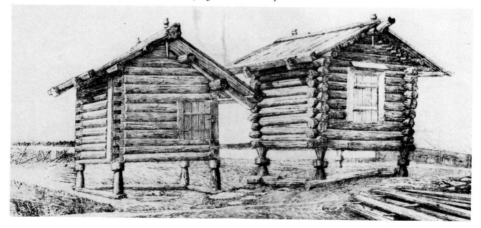

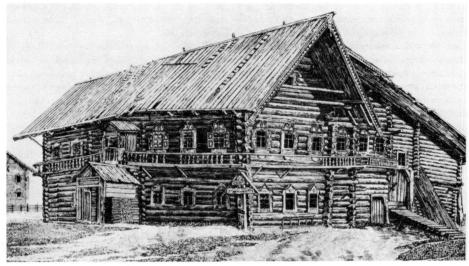

101. Terentiev house, northern Russia, eighteenth century

102. Tavern between Kostroma and Yaroslavl, eighteenth century.
Lithograph by André Durand, 1839

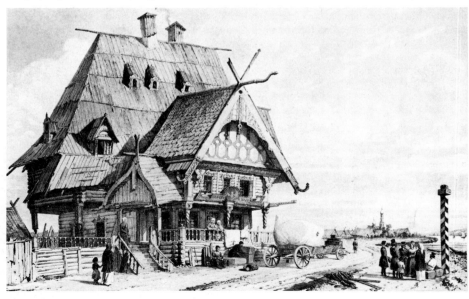

[101] differs from the storehouses only in size and in its decorative ornament. Throughout this structural system a certain modular standard prevailed, based on the average length of dressed logs. The introduction of interior partitions can be seen where the ends protrude as a vertical row of logs notched into the exterior wall, while the applied carved decoration, all of wood, can be seen on the edges of the roof, the window-frames, and the shaped slats of the exterior balcony. For even the most elaborate buildings this structural system remained the same, the greatest possible length of the beams serving as the basic element in the design [102].[4]

Another system can be seen in a wooden belfry of the seventeenth century [103]. Here by the use of a polygonal plan a greater interior space was obtained, although the actual length of the logs is not great. Towards the top of the structure longer logs are successively introduced, so that the slight flare of the upper part serves as a projecting cornice to throw rain-water and melting snow far enough from the base of the structure to prevent rot. The conical roof is covered with vertical planks, probably replacing the original shingles, of which a few rows can still be seen near the slender drum. The ends of the planks were usually cut in a decorative pattern, often in the form of a cross.

It should also be observed that construction remained throughout an additive system of horizontal parts. Few verticals were used except as interior supports for partitions or as slanting planks on conical roofs. The only tool was the axe or adze with which the carpenters cut, shaped, and smoothed the beams. On the exterior the logs were left intact once the bark had been removed, but the interior surfaces were worked quite flat. Even into the nineteenth century the axe remained the carpenter's only tool.[5]

Until the beginning of the nineteenth century with these tools and materials were constructed not only the spectacular wooden churches, which will be examined in more

detail, and the innumerable farmhouses of the peasantry scattered through the forests or clustered in tiny villages, but even whole towns and cities, including the greater part of Moscow itself. Few sights in Russia struck visiting foreigners more forcibly than their first glimpse of these wooden cities, so differ-

103. Tsivozero, bell tower, 1658

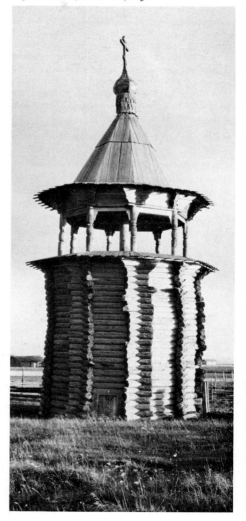

ent in appearance, if not in plan, from their own towns. Thus Giles Fletcher, the English emissary to Moscow in 1588, described this wooden world:

The streets of their cities and townes instead of paving are planked with fir trees, planed and layed even close the one to the other.[6] Their houses are of wood without any lime or stone, built very close and warme with firre trees plained and piled one upon another. They are fastened together with dents or notches at every corner, and so clasped fast together. Betwixt the trees or timber they thrust in mosse (whereof they gather plenty in their woods) to keep out the aire. . . . The greatest inconvenience of their wooden building is the aptness for firing, which happeneth very oft and in very fearful sort, by reason of the drinesse and fatness of the fir, that being once fired, burneth like a torch, and is hardly quenched till all be burnt up.[7]

Fletcher's description of the method of construction and of the perilous nature of the inflammable material is confirmed by many other travellers, who rarely failed to comment on the expendability of the Russian house. Guy Miege, who accompanied the Earl of Carlisle, Charles II's ambassador to Tsar Alexey Mikhailovich, wrote in 1669 that:

Their Streets are broad enough, and from place to place there are certain Intervals left to break off and cease the fury of the Fire, but the materials of

their Houses being so combustible, they have much ado to prevent its progress. All the remedy they have, is to pull down the Houses that are next, to the end that by taking away the matter, that should nourish it, they may give the flames more room to extinguish. But this not alwaies succeeding, especially if the wind be high, it happens sometimes, that they see a great part of the Town in ashes in a very short space. . . .[8]

Fortunately this material could be replaced almost as quickly as it perished. As Adam Olearius, secretary to the embassy from the Duke of Holstein to Tsar Mikhail Feodorovich in 1636, remarked: 'Those who have their houses burnt, have this comfort withal, that they may buy houses ready built, at a market for that purpose, without the white-Wall, at a very easy rate, and have them taken down, transported, and in a short time set up in the same place where the former stood.'[9] The Russians had perfected, by the sixteenth century if not earlier, a system of prefabrication far in advance of any in western Europe. In 1784 Archdeacon Coxe described the system in some detail:

Among the curiosities of Moscow, I must not omit the market for the sale of houses. It is held in a large open space, in one of the suburbs, and exhibits *ready-made houses*, strewed on the ground. The purchaser who wants a dwelling, repairs to this

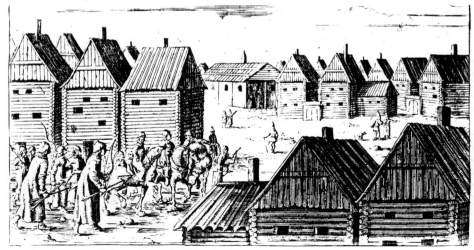

104. Tsaritsyn (now Volgograd), on the Volga, in the seventeenth century

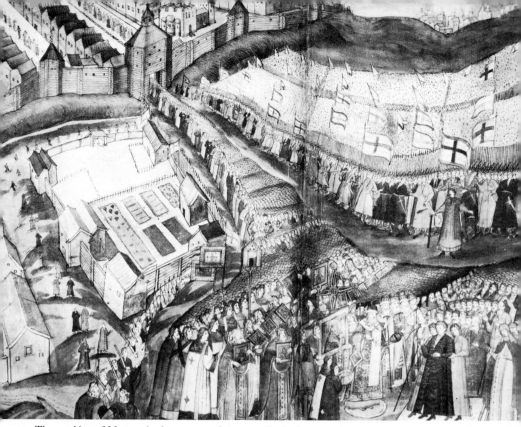

105. The outskirts of Moscow in the seventeenth century. In the foreground
a farm with wooden buildings enclosing the tilled area; above, in the distance,
the wooden walls of Moscow and behind them rows of wooden houses and
streets paved with logs. From 'The Book of the Election as Tsar of the Sovereign,
Tsar, and Great Prince Mikhail Romanov', Moscow, 1672

spot, mentions the number of rooms he requires, examines the different timbers, which are regularly numbered, and bargains for what suit his purpose. The house is sometimes paid for on the spot, and removed by the purchaser; or the vendor contracts to transport and erect it upon the place where it is designed to stand. It may seem incredible, that a dwelling may be thus bought, removed, raised and inhabited, within the space of a week; but it will appear easily practicable by considering that these *ready-made houses* are in general merely collections of trunks of trees, tenoned and mortised at each extremity, so that nothing more is required than the labour of transporting and adjusting them.[10]

Seventeenth-century views of Russian cities show the result of this system [104]. The houses are all the same size, a circumstance which doubtless led to their arrangement in parallel rows, so that the city of Moscow, so frequently burned and rebuilt, had a uniformity and regularity in certain quarters unlike that of any western European city[11] [105].

Not only houses and churches, with other civic buildings such as palaces for the prince or governor which served the purpose of a city hall, but even walls and other fortifications

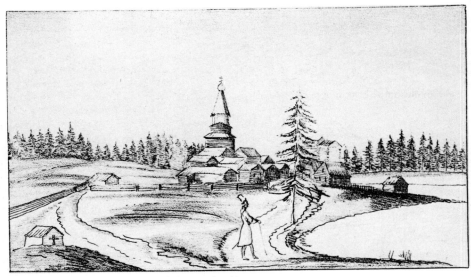

106. The village of Yadrovo, west of Moscow, in 1661–2

were of wood, which surprised many a travel-ler. As Olearius remarked of Novgorod: 'The number of its steeples promises yet somewhat more great and noble, than what may now be seen; since that coming to the Citie, we see onely Walls of Wood, and Houses built with Beams lay'd one upon the other.'[12] Moscow had wooden ramparts in the seventeenth cen-tury, and Tsaritsyn on the Volga, with the houses clustered behind wooden walls and

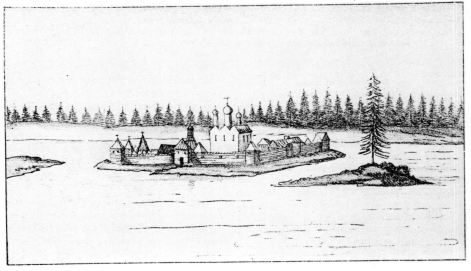

107. The Iversky Monastery, on an island in Lake Valdai, in 1661–2

towers as it appears in Olearius's view, must have been very like the usual Russian town.

Another seventeenth-century traveller, Augustin von Meyerberg, who was ambassador from the Emperor to the Court of Alexey Mikhailovich, had an album of drawings prepared to illustrate his account of his diplomatic mission in 1661.[13] Many of these are slight sketches of tiny villages deep in the forests. In the view of Yadrovo an elaborate wooden church rises above the wooden settlement [106], while the view of the Iversky Monastery on an island in Lake Valdai south-east of Novgorod [107] shows the unusual scale of the single masonry church towering above the lower conventual structures enclosed by a wooden wall with wooden towers. A closer view of such a monastery can be seen in one of the small scenes on the icon of the Virgin of Tikhvin of 1680 (Rublev Museum, Moscow) [108]. The borders illustrate twenty-four episodes in the history of the monastery of Tikhvin, including the erection of the stone cathedral of the Dormition after the destruction in 1395 of its wooden predecessor. The masonry churches and other buildings depicted are from the fifteenth and sixteenth centuries (compare the church in the upper right with the Descent of the Holy Spirit in Zagorsk [138]), but the wooden walls and towers are immemorial, in design and execution. Such must have been the original fortifications of Novgorod in the tenth century; such, as late as modern times, were the walls and towers of Yakutsk in farthest Siberia.[14] This was 'wooden Russia', a forest land where the people used the material for farm and city, for house and church, for street paving and eating utensils; a land where old traditions lingered centuries after they had been superseded in the metropolitan centres, where the greatest ingenuity in wood-working went hand in hand with the simplest structural methods.

That this virtuosity in the use of wood had prevailed from the earliest times is apparent in the chroniclers' account of the first church of St Sophia in Novgorod, which was built of

oak by Bishop Joachim and had thirteen 'upper parts' (vierkhy). Another oak church was in Rostov, then far in the interior of the forest land. It was erected in 992 by Bishop Hilarion, but burned in 1160, together with all the other churches in the city.[15] In the absence of all vestiges of these earliest wooden structures, and even of accurate descriptions, we are obliged to assume their gradual evolution from simpler to more complex forms; the first St Sophia in Novgorod itself succeeded a long tradition of temple and house construction in pagan Russia. The oldest surviving wooden church in Russia is thought to be the Resurrection of Lazarus, traditionally reputed to

108. Moscow:
Border scene from the icon of the Virgin of Tikhvin, 1680. *Moscow, Rublev Museum of Early Russian Art*

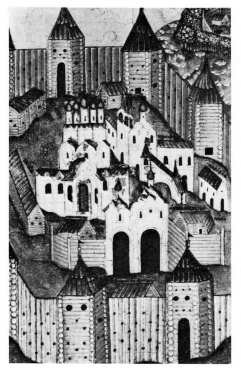

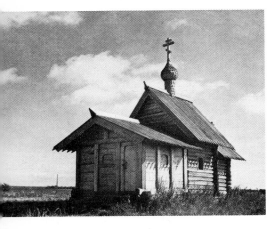

109 and 110. Olonets, St Lazarus, before 1391(?), exterior and plan

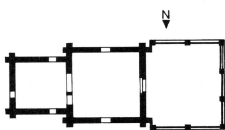

have been built in the Muromsky Monastery on Lake Onega during the lifetime of the monk Lasar, the monastery's founder, who died in 1391 [109]. The tiny church, which has been moved across the lake to the museum of historical wooden architecture at Kizhy, is a typical example of the klet (cell or chamber), or, as we might say, shed, church, from the fact that the interior space consisted of one or more separate rooms, each resembling the undifferentiated interior of a shed or of a peasant's izba [110]. In churches of this type the largest chamber served as the nave, with smaller rooms added to the east for the apse and to the west for the trapeza, an enclosed porch or vestibule where the congregation took their meals at intervals in the day-long services. In the Lazarus church the trapeza, unlike the other two chambers, seems to have been built of planks attached to upright posts (originally three to a side, as in the plan) rather than of logs. With its multiple roofs, often of different pitches, the shed church, although the simplest type of wooden religious architecture, quickly acquired a characteristic mass and silhouette, its angularity setting it apart from the compact geometrical mass of stone churches. Unfortunately the external appearance of almost all surviving wooden churches has been spoiled by the flat boarding applied in the nineteenth century as a protective meas-

ure. The resulting loss of the original texture, so intimately a part of the technique and visual effects of the earlier churches, is to be deplored; they suffer almost as much as do their masonry counterparts where a pitched tin roof often replaces the original vaulted covering.

The surrounding gallery, used as a vestibule in bad weather, gradually increased in size until it served as a community meeting-hall on Sundays and festivals, where the congregation, often assembled from great distances, might remain between services to take their meals if it were cold or wet. In time the galleries became so important that without them the church itself would have provided insufficient space for the congregation, as may be seen in the seventeenth-century brick churches at Yaroslavl [151].

The shed church, whatever may be the exact date of its appearance in Russia, was certainly the simplest solution to the problem of adapting the square Greek-cross plan to a different material and method of construction. The three fundamental spatial elements of nave, apse, and narthex were present, however much their proportional inter-relationships might differ. But the correspondence with Byzantine tradition was more internal than external, for the peaked roofs, which even in the earliest churches may have been quite steep, set the church apart from all other buildings in the town. A pitched timber roof is quite unlike a stone form, and when roofs were placed above polygonal forms, such coverings became even more conspicuous. The tall pyramidal shater or tent roofs above a central octagonal space are perhaps the most striking forms developed by the carpenters.

The origin of the octagonal church is still unclear. That it is of considerable antiquity is proved by the chroniclers' accounts of the fate of the Cathedral of the Dormition at Veliky Ustiug.[16] Originally constructed in 1290, this 'large wooden church' was first destroyed by fire in 1396, rebuilt immediately afterwards in the same style, burned again in 1398, and again rebuilt the following year by carpenters from Novgorod. After a third fire in 1490 Tikhon, Archbishop of Rostov, sent an architect, Alexey Vologshanin, who rebuilt the church but in a different style. The population complained to Tikhon with the result that Master Alexey and sixty carpenters from Rostov took down the new church and reconstructed it as a 'round church in the old style with twenty walls'. This building lasted until 1552, when, after a final fire, it was rebuilt in stone.

This record is doubly significant, not only in that it indicates the traditional attachment of the Russian villagers to the earliest wooden forms, thereby suggesting that large 'round' churches may have been built as early as the late thirteenth century, but also that early on rooms were added to the north and south sides of the octagon in addition to the apse and trapeza. When the interior walls of the whole structure were counted, including the eight walls of the octagon, the total came to twenty – hence the term twenty-walled churches for octagonal structures with four projecting rooms.

The interior space of these churches may have been an attempt on the carpenters' part to recreate the tall Byzantine crossing below a central dome, but when the interior was covered by a low ceiling [120], the usual custom in later times, the vertical effect was lost. Nor should we overlook the fact that the oval foundation of a large pagan temple has been uncovered in Kiev.[17] In the northern forest lands the population may have retained memories of sacred circular wooden structures far longer than in the south, and so have involuntarily willed that their new Christian temples should follow the same form. The technique of constructing a tent roof may have been evolved from roofing a polygonal, usually five-sided, chamber which was often added to a shed church in imitation of the semicircular stone apse, while the construction of such an apse may have led to the ability to enlarge the central space of the church by building it as an octagon, whereby a larger enclosed space could be obtained with logs no longer than those used for a rectangular frame. This development in the shed church can be seen in St Nicholas of 1766, originally in the village of Glotovo but now restored and moved to the historical museum in Suzdal [111]. During

111. Suzdal, St Nicholas from Glotovo, 1766

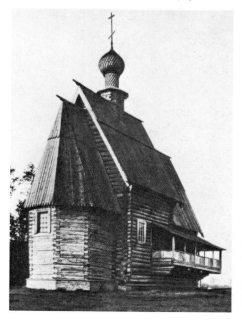

the centuries which had elapsed since the construction of St Lazarus at Olonets [109] the
three interior spaces had grown higher, and
through the juxtaposition of the acutely angled
roofs, gained in coherence as a more unified
whole. The five-sided apse where the liturgy
was celebrated is differentiated by sheathing
with logs planed flat, and crowned by a five-
sided roof whose height conformed to the
church's pronounced verticality. The shape
needed only three more sides to become the
familiar tent roof above a nave.

Until it burned in the 1920s, the best preserved surviving example of the earlier octagonal tent churches, as well as one of the most
nobly proportioned, was the Church of St
Nicholas at Panilovo, consecrated in 1600 and
probably erected the year before [112]. It was
the oldest of a group which includes the St
Nicholas Church at Lyavla (1589), the Church

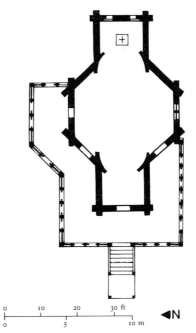

113. Nizhny Uftiug, Church of the Dormition, plan

112. Panilovo, St Nicholas, consecrated 1600

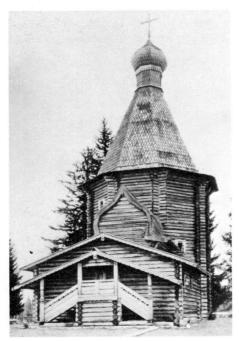

of the Virgin of Vladimir at Belaya Sluda
(1642), and St George at Vershino on the
Toima (1672). The plan of the church at
Nizhny Uftiug [113] is typical of this group
of tent churches. In each the octagon is
adjoined by a square apse and anteroom, the
latter surrounded by a low covered porch. The
main floor, being raised a few feet above the
ground for protection against dampness and
wet, was reached by a double covered stairway.
At Panilovo the porch had been extended to
form a gallery surrounding the trapeza. It will
be noted that although this plan is comparatively simple, since only the absence of
partitions and the substitution of the central
octagon for a rectangular volume differ-
entiates it from the plan of the shed churches,
the exterior has changed considerably. The
high octagon with an equally tall pyramidal
roof towers over the subsidiary rooms, which
are covered with curious arched roofs. These

bochki (singular, bochka) or barrels are really part of the structure itself rather than an applied covering, and furnish another unsolved architectural riddle. It may be that they represent the carpenters' attempt to imitate the profile of the bulbous dome, in this way associating the dome concept with the covering of the whole mass, or possibly they are the wooden counterparts of the masonry zakomars, the semicircular arches crowning the walls of the eleventh- and twelfth-century churches of Kiev and Novgorod [12, 17]. If this is indeed a transposition of masonry forms into wood, it was accomplished with that remarkable simplicity which distinguishes so much Russian wooden construction. All that was done was to change, progressively, the length of the logs on the end walls.

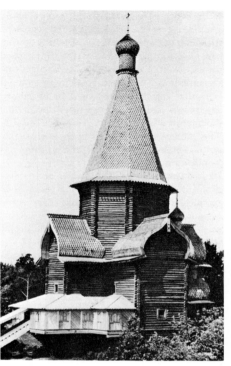

The Church of the Dormition from the Alexandro-Kushtsky Monastery, near the village of Ustye, now in the Spasso-Prilutsky Monastery in Vologda [114], built soon after 1519, is earlier than Panilovo but represents the next stage in the development of large wooden buildings. Square rooms, in size comparable to the trapeza and apse, have been added to the north and south of the central square, creating a cross in plan with an octagon rising from the centre. If the effect is less powerful than at Panilovo, the proportions are more elegant, with the lower bochki-roofed areas providing a firm base for the soaring roof over the octagon.

More complex forms appeared when chapels or apses were added on the east sides of the north and south additions to the octagon. Although the distribution of the spaces in plan was essentially simple, the three-dimensional mass became more elaborate, accounting for many of the most picturesque and typically 'Russian' effects in wooden architecture, as in the Church of SS. Florus and Laurus (1755) at Rostovskoe [115], where the

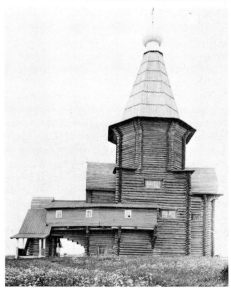

114 (*above right*). Vologda, Church of the Dormition from Ustye, after 1519

115 (*right*). Rostovskoe, SS. Florus and Laurus, 1755

main floor, now raised a full storey above ground, is reached by steep covered staircases. Although the square apses on the arms of what had now become a cross in plan emphasized the east–west axis on the exterior, the fact that the interiors of all three apses were shut off from the central space by carved and painted iconostases (see above, page 102), meant that the interior was in effect developed in breadth. This tendency can be seen in the early-eighteenth-century Church of the Trinity at Nenoksa on the White Sea (1727) [116, 117]. Its five tent roofs, built of planks laid on vertical rafters rather than of logs laid horizontally, rising not only above the central octagon but above each of the four projecting halls, testify to the affection which the people felt for these forms.

At Nenoksa it may be noted that the subsidiary octagons emerge from a lower cube. This combination of pyramid, octagon, and cube accounts for one of the most widespread types of wooden church in the seventeenth century. It would be tempting to think that the presence of the cubical substructure, recalling the mass of the Russo-Byzantine masonry churches, was the result of the reforms of Patriarch Nikon (see below, page 216), but such churches are known to have been built earlier in the century, and they may even have been influenced by similar combinations in masonry which apparently were constructed in the sixteenth century.

The conjunction of cube and octagon on a cross-shaped plan found exceptionally powerful expression in such churches as the Ascension at Konetsgore (1752) and St Clement at Una, west of Arkhangelsk, which burned in 1892. According to the parish register the latter church was erected in 1501, although a seventeenth-century date is more probable.[18] In each the plan was a simple cross, enlarged by additions to the eastern side of the north and south arms. At Una each arm was roofed with double bochki, the upper supporting a small cupola on a slender drum, and the huge tent

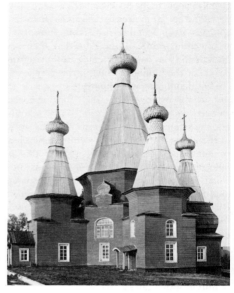

116 and 117. Nenoksa, Church of the Trinity, 1727, exterior and plan

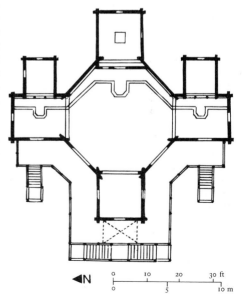

◄N   0   10   20   30 ft
      0   5   10 m

roof, constructed according to the usual method of a gradually reduced octagon of horizontal beams, was somewhat larger than the central square of the crossing. The octagon emerged from the cross arms only at its intersection with the bochki. At Konetsgore, on the other hand, the central interior square was expressed externally as a cube adjoined by the cross arms and apses. The circumstance that the whole mass of the building was raised a storey above the ground as a protection against dampness contributed to its commanding height. In both churches the composition of masses was worked out in what might well be called inverse perspective, since it progressed from the relatively near and small, the staircase and arched openings on the landing, to the remote and large, the huge central mass of the octagon. The effect overwhelms the spectator by the apparent discrepancy in scale.

Since so far the history of the tall wooden church seems to have followed a consistent formal development based upon the interaction of function and material on technique and to have achieved a form peculiar to a specific region, the question of possible influences from abroad can again be raised. Greater verticality could perhaps have been suggested by some acquaintance with European Gothic architecture. Certainly neither from the south, from Byzantium, nor from Italy, whose monuments became familiar to Russian architects only after the arrival of the Italian master-builders and craftsmen at the Court of Ivan III in Moscow in the later fifteenth century, could the Russians have derived such a taste for tall structures. Since ideas from Germany and Poland could enter Russia through Novgorod, it is interesting that most of these wooden churches have been discovered in the northern provinces which once belonged to that city. On the other hand, the gradual stabilization of relations between the Great Prince in Moscow and the Tartars which led to the opening of the Volga to Russian trade with the Near East and the Caucasus after the

middle of the sixteenth century, could have hastened the arrival of influences from those regions. Not less significant, and certainly very curious, is the frequent appearance in the Russian language of architectural terms of Tartar and Turkish origin. Such a word is shater, which described the tent form in wooden architecture.[19] Beyond the Tartars in the mountains of the Caucasus lay Georgia and Armenia, whence some three centuries earlier may have come the decorative motifs found in the churches of Vladimir-Suzdal. The Russians may well have had some knowledge of the medieval Georgian churches which frequently present, although in stone, just such a combination of tall masses subsidiary to a central cube whose pitched roofs lie just below the central polygonal or circular drum crowning the cube, which in turn is surmounted by a conical or pyramidal roof.[20] Yet, whatever may have been the influences which shaped the will of the Russian carpenters, their ultimate achievement is no deliberate imitation. The wooden church of the Russian forests, whether Gothic in its verticality or Georgian in the articulation of its parts, is, through the subtle disposition of its proportions and the brilliance of its technique, unmistakably Russian. Such is the Dormition at Varzug (1674) [118], to modern eyes one of the most skilful examples of the octagonal tent church on the cross plan. Again the arms surround a central cube, above which rises a low octagon supporting a powerful tent roof. The transition from each cross-arm through the cube to the octagon is managed by the introduction of a second, smaller bochka above the arched roof. A third row of diminutive bochki smooths the passage from the cube to the octagon. The proportions of this church have impressed Russian and foreign scholars alike as the most successful solution to the multiple problems presented by a structure, cross-shaped in plan, which must at one and the same time satisfy the ritual demand for a cube and the popular desire for an octagon, which could be seen as late as 1774

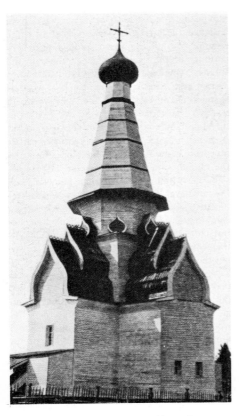

118. Varzug, Church of the Dormition, 1674

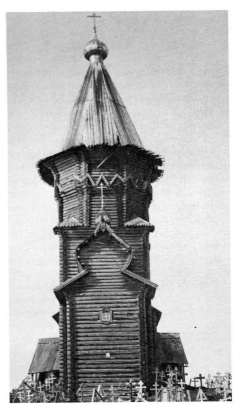

119. Kondopoga, Church of the Dormition, 1774

in the Church of the Dormition at Kondopoga [119, 120].

A type which came closer to the new ritual legality, while at the same time answering the Russian desire for height, appeared towards the close of the seventeenth century in the so-called storeyed churches (yarusnye tserkvy). In these structures the suggestion of placing a series of shallow cubes or octagons, or each alternately, upon a cubical mass came from the Ukraine, where such forms, in wood or masonry, had been influenced by Latin Baroque churches in Poland and Galicia.[21] There a type of wooden church, square in plan, cubical in mass, and with added cubical elements above the cornice line had been de-

veloped. Essentially the plan is not unlike those of the shed churches, the central square adjoined by a rectangular porch on the west and a pentagonal apse on the east. Upon the central portion there was then placed a smaller rectangle, surmounted by a low octagon in turn carrying the slender drum and bulbous cupola. The number of churches of this type which were erected throughout the seventeenth and eighteenth centuries in central Russia proves that this arrangement satisfied the church authorities. Farther north they were often more elaborate and combined with other more traditional elements. Thus the Church of St Nicholas at Berezovets [121], erected in the first third of the eighteenth century, is in plan

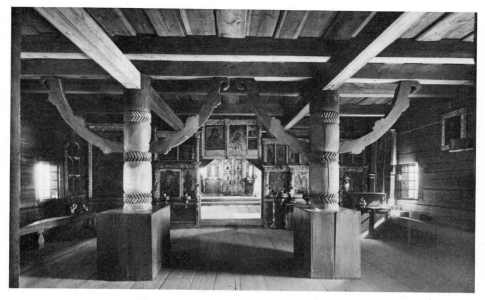

120. Kondopoga, Church of the Dormition, 1774

121. Berezovets, St Nicholas, early eighteenth century

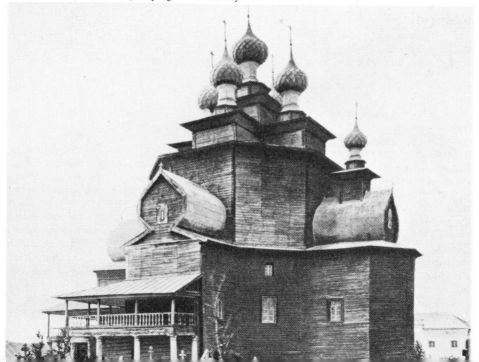

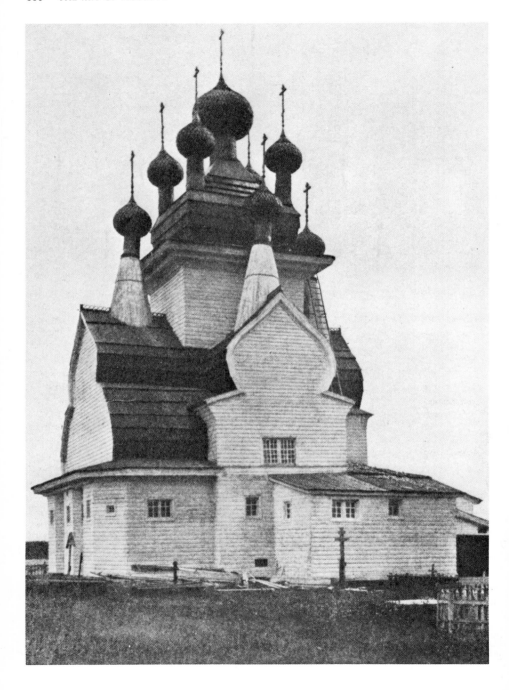

a cross composed of an octagon with equilateral arms roofed with large bochki. Above the octagon is a diminutive version of the church itself in the form of a central cube flanked by lower cross arms and crowned with small bulbous cupolas. Then comes a miniature octagon which carries the central cupola.

The reforms of Nikon are also reflected in the cube churches (kubovatye khramy), where the internal space is expressed externally through a large cubical mass. The roofing provides an ingenious solution to the desire to retain something, even if only the vaguest memory, of the silhouette of the tent roof. Hence upon the cubical mass rests what may perhaps be described as a square, flattened dome, not unlike a depressed version of the bulbous cupola which crowns the form itself. Often at the angles of this shape smaller cupolas were added to accommodate the whole to the liturgical requirements. The Church of the Virgin of Vladimir at Podporozhye (1741), north-east of Leningrad [122, 123], is an intricate example of the cube type. In plan the

122 and 123. Podporozhye (Lake Onega), Church of the Virgin of Vladimir, 1741, exterior and plan

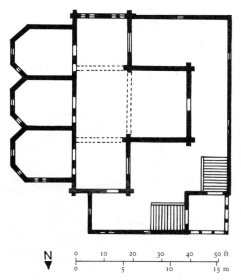

N

| 0 | 10 | 20 | 30 | 40 | 50 ft |
| 0 | | 5 | | 10 | 15 m |

cross is modified by the addition of three apses to the east. The bochki of the east and west arms are so large that they appear to be one axial mass, penetrated by the north and south arms and supporting the central cube. Although the clerical authorities may have been satisfied that the church fulfilled the letter of the law by wearing five domes above a cubical mass, from a distance the visual effect was much more in the spirit of the old tent churches, with their pyramidal silhouettes.

The famous Church of the Transfiguration at Kizhy on Lake Onega (1714) [124] shows how a carpenter could push his technique to its furthest limits. This church, which is to wooden what St Basil in Moscow [139] is to Russian masonry architecture, used to be cited as the most conspicuous example of the Russian architects' decorative extravagance and lack of control over materials and proportions. Yet perhaps both churches are more correctly interpreted as remarkable examples of a particular climax in the formal development of a style. At Kizhy the formal postulates are still apparent in the extraordinary contrast between the simplicity of plan and interior space and the startling three-dimensional external expression. The plan is the familiar central octagon with cross arms. Externally the arms are roofed by two superimposed bochki with domes which merge with eight at the top of the octagon and the four obligatory domes on the roof just below the larger central one. In this way the intricate cross-rhythms – vertical against horizontal, large against small – surpass the structural ingenuity of carpenters. Such an attitude towards form recalls the skill with which earlier goldsmiths had manipulated masonry forms in the church furnishings of the seventeenth century.[22] At Kizhy the central mass seems to consist of two diminishing octagonal tiers, an influence from the storeyed churches of the south. The astonishing effect of the church is due to the exceptional number of drums and cupolas placed over the bochki, to the total of twenty-two (the eastern arm has an additional cupola).

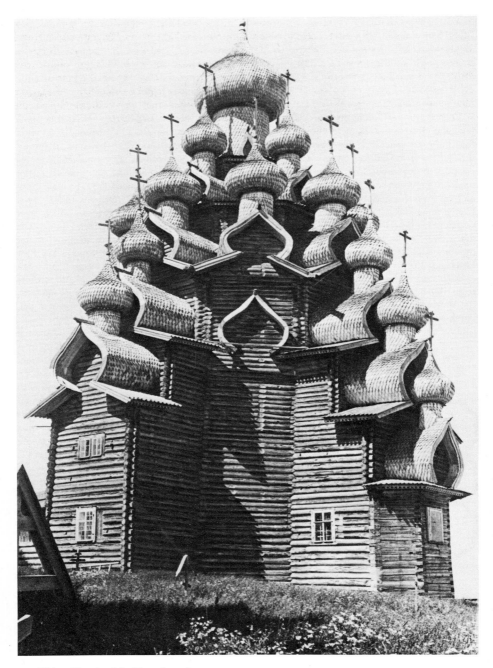

124. Kizhy, Church of the Transfiguration, 1714

With the church at Kizhy the traditions of ancient Russian wooden architecture were fulfilled. Beyond this it is difficult to see how a more harmonious balance among plan, structure, mass, and visual effects could be achieved. The bristling silhouette of the church, pyramidal in the tradition which can be traced back to St Sophia in Kiev, achieved the same kind of aesthetic contrast with the surrounding level landscape of lake and plain and forest that the conglomeration of masonry spires at St Basil accomplished for the urban landscape of red brick walls and low wooden houses. Nor could this have been realized without that age-long practice of wooden construction, that technical mastery of the resources and possibilities of a particular material.

CHAPTER 15

ARCHITECTURE IN MOSCOW

1400–1600

Towards the close of the fourteenth century the artistic and political recovery of Russia after a century and a half of Tartar domination became more perceptible. Just as the spectacular victories of Dmitry Donskoy in 1378 and 1380, even if they proved ephemeral, were a sign that the Tartars were not invincible and that better times might be ahead, so the activity of such painters as Theophanes and Andrey Rublev in Moscow after 1395 was a sign that Russia could once more create a monumental art.

The fifteenth century, which in western Europe saw the decline of many medieval concepts and the rise of new attitudes towards life and art, was an equally decisive period in Russia. But the word Renaissance cannot be used to describe the history of both western and eastern civilizations at that time. In the literal sense of a revival of ancient art and letters, it would be inadequate to include the new political, intellectual, and artistic developments of Russia, and it is moreover too intimately connected with the concept of humanism. The revival of ancient learning had to wait until the seventeenth century, when the influence of Polish and Catholic scholarship affected the schools of Kiev and Moscow.[1] Nor did the fifteenth- and sixteenth-century Russian architects entertain memories of antiquity. For want of a better term, therefore, it is customary to speak of the period between Russia's medieval Byzantine past and her later European future as Muscovite, because the energies which directed it and the accomplishments which remain are in large part the work of the Great Princes of Moscow.

The most decisive historical development in this period was the gradual concentration of

political, economic, and industrial power in the person of the princes of the Moscow line who, as cousins to the older families of Novgorod and Suzdal, descended from Ivan I, Kalita (Money Bags, Great Prince of Moscow 1328–40), a grandson of Alexander Nevsky (1220–63), Prince of Novgorod. Since Nevsky's grandfather, Vsevolod III, had been Prince of Suzdalia, and Vsevolod's grandfather, Vladimir Monomakh, Great Prince of Kiev, their descent was unimpeachable. Nevsky's policy of submitting to Tartar taxation in exchange for actual if not nominal independence was continued by the princes of Moscow, who became in the fourteenth century the principal tax-gatherers for the khans. In this way they learned such valuable lessons in the administrative organization and economic control of central Russia that, when the Tartar power disintegrated into a number of smaller khanates, they were in a position to assert their own independence with little difficulty. By the close of the sixteenth century the Russia of Kiev, distraught, magnanimous, and violent, had passed into history, and in its place had risen a new national power in the hands of the astute, patient, business-like, and violent Great Princes of Moscow.

The history of Russia during these three centuries, from 1300 to 1600, is the story of the gradual aggrandizement of Moscow. Slowly but inevitably the other Russian princes, whether sovereign or appanage, were obliged to acknowledge the suzerainty of the prince of Moscow, until, by the close of the sixteenth century, Muscovy embraced central Russia from the White Sea to the Caspian and eastward from Novgorod and Smolensk to the Urals. In this process the gradual weakening of the Tartar overlordship, largely through internal dissension, enabled Ivan III in 1480 to dispense with the payment of tribute, and his grandson, Ivan IV, to conquer the cities and territories of Kazan and Astrakhan by victories won in 1552 and 1554. The character of the new power appears in the development of the dynastic titles. In 1337, after several decades of strife among the younger princes of the Novgorod–Vladimir line, the dignity of Great Prince (Veliky Knyaz) was confirmed by the Khan to Ivan I Kalita and his heirs in recognition of his leadership of the other princes. The older order of succession through fraternal seniority, the cause of incessant conflict among the Kievan princes, was superseded by the relatively more stable principle of succession from father to son.[2] Towards the end of the fifteenth century Ivan III (1440–1505), through whose marriage to Sophia Palaeologa much Byzantine ceremony and protocol had been introduced at the Moscow Court, was accustomed to sign himself Tsar (a Slavonic corruption of the Latin Caesar) by virtue of Russia's theoretical assumption of the civil and ecclesiastical traditions of the Eastern Empire, and Autocrat (in Russian Samoderzhets, literally one ruling by himself or alone), signifying more his independence from Tartar overlordship than the absolutism of a later age. He also adopted the spelling 'Ioann' as more aristocratic than the familiar 'Ivan'. In 1547 his grandson, Ivan IV (1530–84), was the first Russian sovereign to have himself crowned as Tsar.[3] The title of autocrat was first used officially at the coronation of the first tsar of the house of Romanov, Mikhail Feodorovich, in 1613. The final formulation of the imperial style occurred in the early eighteenth century when Peter I assumed the western, Latinized title of Imperator.

The authority of Muscovy rested on the control of the sources of financial and industrial power in the hands of the Tsar and the ruling class. As independent principalities became subject to Moscow, their revenues as well as their rulers gravitated to the central court. The accumulation of financial and agricultural holdings was accompanied by the appearance around the person of the sovereign of a host of courtiers, variously princes of ancient lineage, and landed aristocrats or boyars, from whose ranks were drawn such talents as were needed to run the offices of government. The boyars were obliged to supply troops in time of war, and in return for these services were gradually guaranteed the peasant labour necessary to work their lands and to raise the required military strength. Gradually the obligations of the agricultural population to the landowners became codified and hardened into the institution of serfdom whereby the peasant was the absolute property of the master. Although this relationship was not legalized until the seventeenth and eighteenth centuries, the process was already at work in the sixteenth. The effect upon cultural expression is perhaps best seen in the considerable supply of cheap labour for large architectural enterprises which became available in the sixteenth and seventeenth centuries. The longer and more iniquitous effects lay concealed in the increasing separation between the peasants and the landowners. The former were reduced to the status of chattels as the latter were raised to a landed aristocracy, creatures of the sovereign, fearful of absenting themselves from his presence, and so taking and spending less and less time on their estates. Consequently the middle classes who were so important in western Europe as creators and consumers of works of art were eliminated. From the middle of the fifteenth century Russian art is increasingly two separate stories, of a Court art and of a folk art.

It will be recalled that although the artistic history of medieval art in Russia had centred round the Church, yet in its creation participated not only the aristocracy and the clergy who built the churches of Kiev and Suzdalia, but also the wealthy merchant class in the free cities of Novgorod and Pskov who commissioned frescoes and icons. Henceforth the

Church itself became gradually absorbed within the Court, both figuratively and literally. Such churchmen as Joseph of Volokolamsk (1439–1515), who energetically supported the tsar against the Tartars, maintained that it was proper for the Church to acknowledge the claims of the temporal power. Although Joseph probably had in mind the immediate end of securing to the Church control of the enormous monastic properties, the final result of such reasoning subordinated so thoroughly the spiritual to the temporal power that at the beginning of the eighteenth century Peter I could abolish the Patriarchate and assign the administration of church affairs to a government department.

With the consolidation of the national power of Moscow politically, economically, and spiritually went an increasing awareness that Russia would have to take notice of the rest of the European world. As the Tartar pressure decreased, the princes of Moscow more frequently turned to the west, at first in a long series of attempts to curb the power of Poland and Lithuania, and later of Sweden, and to recover for Great Russia of the central north-east the lands of White and Red Russia in the west and of Little Russia or the Ukraine in the south which had been ruled by Poland since the middle of the fourteenth century. Although the final unification of the Russian land had still to wait some time, the course of the wars and the diplomatic negotiations that they entailed brought the Court at Moscow more and more into relations with western Europe. It is true that no permanent embassies were established by foreign powers in Moscow until the close of the seventeenth century, but the succession of diplomatic visitors accompanied by their numerous attendants could not fail to arouse the curiosity of Russians, nor to acquaint the upper class, with whom these emissaries came most often in contact, with western manners, costumes, articles of luxury, and even works of art.

Two other important events may be noted. In 1553 the first English ships reached the White Sea, and made port near the later town of Arkhangelsk. From this date commenced Russian trade with western Europe, at first with England alone but later with France and Holland, leading in time to the establishment of merchant colonies in Moscow. Even though the tsar might later segregate the foreign merchants in a quarter by themselves, the so-called German District (Nemetskaya Sloboda), the presence of a large group of foreigners wearing western dress, worshipping in their own churches, and behaving with the relatively greater freedom of Europeans acted as a constant stimulus to turn the Russians' attention more and more to western matters. Concurrently the recovery in 1667 of the Ukraine, including all the Russian lands on the left (eastern) bank of the Dnieper with Kiev and its suburbs on the opposite bank, restored to Russia a large population which, although it had remained loyal and Orthodox through the long centuries of Polish and Lithuanian subjection, had been impregnated with western and Catholic, specifically Polish and Jesuit, ideas. However various may have been Russian reactions to these different events, ranging from the seclusion and even persecution of foreigners to the drastic reform of the Church in the seventeenth century, Russia could no longer maintain more than a pretence of being unconcerned with the affairs of the rest of the world. The reforms of Peter the Great made explicit what had already been implicit for some two centuries.

Yet the way towards the Europeanization of Russia, if the process whereby the country became less an outpost and more a participant in European affairs can be so called, was neither direct nor constant. The later conflicts in the nineteenth century between the Slavophiles and Westernizers were already foreshadowed by the alternations in political and artistic policy during the earlier period. An apparent sympathy with western concepts would suddenly be supplanted by a revival of older national or regional tastes. If the artistic history of Russia from 1400 to 1700 appears to be an inextricable stylistic jungle, the reason is that it represents the visual realization of this continual process of rejection and acceptance, a process in the course of which more than once, by adaptation and compromise, a specifically and characteristically Russian formal tendency can be detected. The same process can be stated in terms of whether the sovereign of Moscow conceived of himself as European prince or Russian tsar. The architectural history of the late fourteenth and fifteenth centuries reveals how the princely and spiritual authority still vested in the forms of Suzdalian architecture was combined with the structural variety and popular character of Novgorod and Pskov traditions. The merging of these two tendencies with traditional methods of wood construction and the appearance of a number of foreign architects created the conditions in which the new Muscovite style was formed. Whereas in Kievan Russia the separatist tendencies represented by the jealously independent princes had brought about the rise of such self-sufficient and characteristic centres as Chernigov, Novgorod, and Vladimir within the general Byzantine spirit of Kiev, the new architecture originating as the expression of a centralized government in Moscow was to be national and authoritative.

From its foundation, Moscow, like other Russian towns, had been built of wood, and a large proportion of its buildings were of that material until after the final disastrous fire of 1812, when new city ordinances made masonry construction obligatory. When the first stone churches were built in the thirteenth century they received special mention in the chronicles. During the reign of Ivan Kalita the cathedrals of the Dormition (1326–7), the Redeemer in the Wood (Spas na Boru, 1330), and St Michael, all of stone, rose on the fortified hill, the Kremlin, in the heart of the city. The Dormition and St Michael were later rebuilt, so that only of the Redeemer can one speak with any certainty; although it was lately pulled down, sufficient photographs and

drawings exist to show that at the time of its demolition the original walls stood to a height of some six feet. Although surrounded by many additions, it was clear that the church was a simple four-piered, single-domed building with three very slightly projecting apses.[4] It may be assumed from this plan, and from the subsequent history of Moscow, that these first churches followed the Vladimirian model, even if on a much smaller scale, and that the masons may have been brought from Suzdalia; although Moscow possessed a fine white stone in the neighbourhood, it had as yet produced no skilled or experienced builders.

In the absence of any precise knowledge of the appearance of the first churches of Moscow, some indication of late-fourteenth-century architectural practice is supplied by the existing monuments in Zvenigorod. The prince of this region, Yury, the second son of Dmitry Donskoy, contested for many years the succession of his brother to the Moscow throne, which he finally occupied for the last two years of his life, in 1432–4. His intention of rivalling the Prince of Moscow with a series of fine masonry buildings resulted in experiments important for subsequent architecture. Yury's first and still best-preserved structure was the Cathedral of the Dormition in Zvenigorod (1399–1400). It is so similar to the churches of Vladimir, especially to the palace church of St Dmitry, that we can see with our own eyes the dynastic and spiritual connexions between the two principalities. Here is the same cubical mass, the four-piered plan with three apses and three entrances on axis, the triple division of the walls, and a single dome. Even the decorative details are similar: the corbel-table on the apses, the recessed portals, and the decorative frieze running along at middle height. Yet the slighter projection of these elements and the substitution of a triple band of carved ornament for the arcaded frieze in St Dmitry create a two-dimensional orientalized design, more like the last church of the Vladimirian period, St George at Yuriev-Polsky. On the other hand, such details as the ogee arches over the portals and western windows, and the bases, capitals, and engaged columns of the façades and doorways, presuppose some familiarity with Gothic architecture. They may be the work of Russians who had travelled in the West; for the Zvenigorod churches demonstrate a more coherent treatment of the Russian tradition than is seen in the late-fifteenth-century churches of the Moscow Kremlin, where the presence of foreign architects is documented. The western elements at Zvenigorod may have come to Muscovy by way of Serbia, where certain fourteenth-century structures exhibit similar Gothic details and even bands of ornament very close to those at Zvenigorod. In this connexion it is significant that in 1404 a Serbian architect, Lazary, constructed a bell-tower in the Moscow Kremlin.[5] The ogee arches, moreover, could have come from Yuriev-Polsky. Finally, the Zvenigorod church differs from such Vladimir examples as the Pokrov on the Nerl by the absence of any clear integration of the internal and external structural systems. There are no pilasters on the interior walls, and the decorative divisions outside do not correspond to the interior bays. The roof of the Zvenigorod Dormition has been reconstructed, but there is a possibility that originally the walls terminated in ogee-arched gables between which additional arched gables above the vaults ran diagonally from the corners of the building to the drum of the dome. Such a system may be inferred from Paul of Aleppo's description of the Dormition at Kolumna which he visited in 1654. Erected between 1379 and 1382, this was larger and more lavishly decorated than any contemporary church in Moscow.

Other churches built by Yury in the next few years continued to modify the Suzdalian type with additional changes which prepared the way for the fuller development of the Moscow style at the end of the century. The Cathedral in the Monastery of St Savva in Zvenigorod (1404) shows the same treatment of the walls, with the dome slightly displaced towards the east. The roof originally consisted of a series of superimposed arches, or kokoshniki, the expression externally of the system of corbelling the arches above the interior crossing at the base of the drum.[6] This important structural device, first worked out in Pskov and Novgorod, was unknown in Vladimir until the end of the fifteenth century. Such a combination of the traditions of Pskov and Vladimir may have been effected through the influence of wooden architecture, for the resulting pyramidal roof resembles in a general way the cone-like silhouette of the tent church, and the rows of pointed arches are very like the horseshoe-arched bochki which were so popular in wooden architecture. But where in wood the bochki made for lightness and structural flexibility, the result in masonry was otherwise. Since the stepped arches of the roof were of stone, the weight of the vaults increased until the walls became thick, sloping buttresses. The grace of Vladimir was swallowed up in the more massive proportions.

Very close to the Savva church is the Trinity in the Trinity-Sergius Monastery (1422–3) at Zagorsk north-east of Moscow.[7] The same wide horizontal band, here interrupted by broad pilasters, gives the façade a rectangular, geometric character. Internally the iconostasis has now become a permanent partition wall separating the apse from the main body of the church. The result, when the church was four-piered in plan, reduced the remaining interior space to a rectangle, with the apparent effect of spreading the interior laterally.

In all these churches the arched divisions of the exterior no longer correspond to the position of the piers and vaults within. One may believe, therefore, that the tendency to consider the exterior a decorative scheme immediately related to the pyramidal treatment of the roof took precedence over the expression of the structural system. However illogical such an arrangement may seem when judged by the standards of western medieval architecture, for Russian architectural history it is of the greatest importance. Prevented as much by the relative scarcity of good building stone as encouraged by the ancient native tradition of

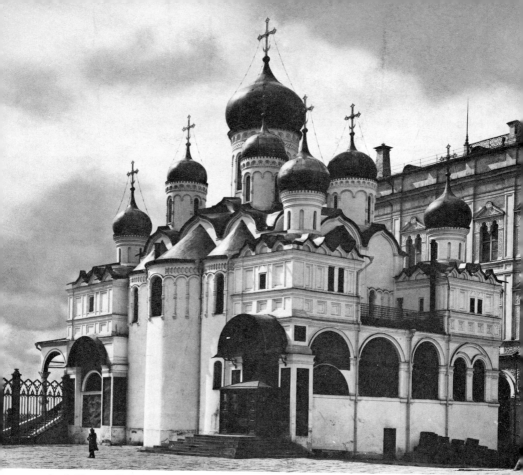

125 and 126. Moscow, Cathedral of the Annunciation
in the Kremlin, 1484–9, exterior and plan

wood construction where decorative effects
were achieved with the greatest facility, the
Russian architects of the sixteenth and seventeenth centuries reached their greatest triumphs through the combination of elementary
structural techniques with elaborate decorative
devices.

The culmination of this type of church
occurred in the Cathedral of the Annunciation
in the Kremlin [125, 126] and in the cathedral
of the Ferapont Monastery near the White
Lake. The Novgorodian origin of both structures is clear. The monastery was situated in

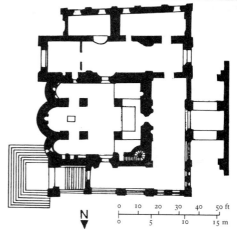

Novgorod territory, and the Annunciation was built by masters expressly summoned from Pskov. The upper part of the Ferapont church has been spoiled, but the Annunciation preserves much of its original character behind the sixteenth-century additions. This church, where the tsars were christened and married, was erected between 1484 and 1489 on the site of an earlier building, the old stone foundations of which were used. It was the second major work of reconstruction undertaken by Ivan III in the Kremlin, but it owes more to the architectural past of Russia than to the new structures which were built immediately before and after it.[8] Here again the Vladimir model prevailed in a four-piered, three-apsed plan with entrances on three sides. The treatment of the exterior, almost entirely concealed by later galleries with chapels above them, was close to St Dmitry, but the Vladimirian precedent is now visible only in the blind arcades on the apses. Ivan IV's additions of the two western domes with heavier drums than the three original ones, and of four more domes over the later chapels created a picturesque effect never intended by the fifteenth-century builders. The roof, with superimposed gables presumably much like those in Zvenigorod, was actually the work of masters from Pskov who would have been familiar with the multi-gabled roof of the Cathedral of the Trinity there (1365–7). The new type of roof, the tendency to consider the façades as separate problems in design unrelated to the internal structural system, and the enlargement of the iconostasis into a partition wall with a consequent reduction and alteration of the apparent internal volume of the church, were factors which prepared the way for the development of the national style in the new buildings erected in the Moscow Kremlin in the last quarter of the fifteenth century.

The personality of Ivan III, the Great (1440–1505), Great Prince of Moscow from 1462, was better suited to the role of European prince than of Russian tsar. While he resembled his forefathers and descendants, par-

ticularly Ivan Kalita and Ivan IV, the Terrible, in his ability to amass territory for Russia and in his deliberate delaying actions against the Tartars, in other respects his conduct and character seem more like those of the contemporary merchant princes of Italy and France. Through his marriage with the Greek princess Zoë Palaeologa, the niece of the last Byzantine emperor, Ivan III not only associated himself with the tradition of the Eastern Empire, assuming the title of tsar and the double-headed imperial eagle as his crest, but gained direct access to western, specifically Italian, culture. Zoë, who took the name of Sophia when she entered the Orthodox Church, had been educated in Rome as a ward of the Pope, and thus knew something of the developing art of the Italian Renaissance. Although she never renounced her imperial dignity, signing herself after twenty-six years' residence in Russia as Imperial Princess of Byzantium rather than as Grand Princess of Moscow, the persons and properties she brought with her were Italian as well as Greek. From her conversations and those of her retinue, from her books and plate, and from influences exerted during the many years of their marriage, her husband must have realized that if he truly aspired to the position of ruler of all Russia he had best make of his court something more fashionable in the western style.

Scarcely had Sophia reached Moscow in 1472 than Ivan sent emissaries to Italy to collect information about artists and craftsmen of all kinds, and to persuade the most promising to travel to Russia. Their services were required, not only for the erection of churches and palaces within the Kremlin, but also for the instruction of Russian workmen in the hitherto unfamiliar techniques of casting cannon, coining money, and similar crafts. The result of their activity was not only the Italianate appearance of the buildings erected during the reign of Ivan III, but also a lasting acquaintance with western architecture, which, even though known only partially and through details continually misunderstood and misapplied by local craftsmen, nevertheless through the next two centuries enabled the Russian masters to absorb more easily influences from the West.

In the later fifteenth century the buildings under construction in the Kremlin, and the number of foreign craftsmen working in Moscow gave the city an aspect not unlike that of some prosperous Italian or Flemish city. Ambrogio Contarini, the Venetian Ambassador to Persia, who was in Moscow in October 1476, saw the Italian architect Fioravanti at work on the Cathedral of the Dormition and a Master Trifoso, 'a goldsmith from Catharo, who had made, and was engaged in making, many beautiful vases and other articles for the Duke'.[9] Contarini also mentioned the many Greeks from Constantinople who had come with Sophia, and a 'great many merchants from Germany and Poland' who frequented Moscow in the winter 'for the sole purpose of buying peltries'. Although situated on the limits of the known world, on the farthest confines of Europe towards Asia, Moscow yielded to no other northern city in the cosmopolitan character of its population. Ivan himself in contemporary descriptions seems in his cordiality and informality more like a Medici than any of his successors. Contarini's description of the Great Prince communicates something of the ease and affability of his presence, for which the spacious churches he commanded to be built were the proper expression, and which was in marked contrast to the suspicious and introspective moods of his grandson Ivan IV, who similarly created a characteristic architecture.[10]

Ivan's building programme involved nothing less than the reconstruction of the Kremlin, a task largely accomplished in his reign and finished during the sixteenth century. When he came to the throne, the Kremlin hill was surrounded by a wooden palisade and covered with a mass of small structures, including the wooden residence of the prince and the churches which had gradually grown up around it. By the middle of the fifteenth

century the stone church erected in 1326 by Ivan Kalita was far too small to contain even the Court, let alone to serve as the cathedral for the whole city. Ivan began by building a new Cathedral of the Dormition. Within its walls a few fragments are preserved of the fourteenth-century church, and from these Soviet archaeologists have conjectured that it may have been influenced by the churches of Polotsk, notably in the single long projecting apse, and the lateral extension of the cross arms by porches which gave it somewhat the appearance of a western Romanesque structure with a transept before the choir.[11]

For the new construction two Moscow architects, Miskin and Krivtsov, were engaged and the foundations laid in 1471. But when part of the walls collapsed in the earthquake of 1474 it became apparent that more than the technical experience of the Moscow masters was needed. Even the masons of Pskov, who were called to the capital and who were known to have some acquaintance with western building techniques, proved unequal to the task, and as a last resort a foreign architect was summoned. Ivan's agents chose Aristotele Fioravanti of Bologna (*c.* 1415–*c.*1485–6), well known in northern Italy as an architect and engineer. In 1461 he had been appointed official engineer to the city of Bologna, and later he was briefly in the service of Galeazzo Maria Sforza in Milan. Somehow or other his popularity declined, and in 1467 he went to Hungary to build a bridge across the Danube for Matthias Corvinus. In 1475 he accepted the invitation of Prince Simyon Tolbuzin to go to Russia, where he spent the remaining years of his life. From a letter written in 1476 to Sforza it appears that he had travelled as far as the White Sea. It is said that he was invited to return to Bologna after finishing the Dormition but was prevented from leaving by Ivan.[12]

The new Cathedral of the Dormition [127, 128] is an unusual and provocative building.[13] It was intended as an affirmation of dynastic and spiritual traditions and as a demonstration

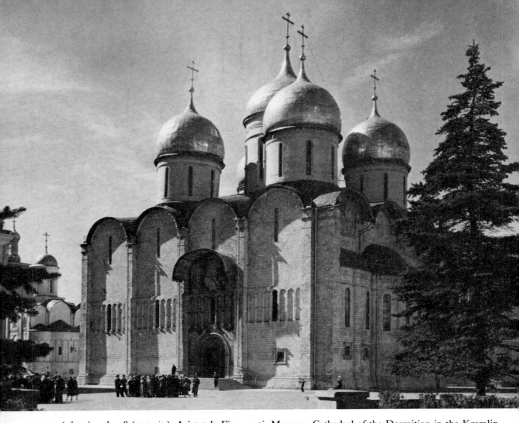

127 (*above*) and 128 (*opposite*). Aristotele Fioravanti: Moscow, Cathedral of the Dormition in the Kremlin, completed in 1479, exterior and plan

of progressive, for the Russians even experimental, structural techniques. For so we must interpret the programme presented to Fioravanti upon his arrival in Moscow. He was told that he was to repeat the general *ordonnance* of the Dormition in Vladimir [22], to which his church was to be considered the mightier successor. He was also to construct a building so sound, that there would be no repetition of the calamity of 1474.

Fioravanti fulfilled both obligations. The general design of the Moscow Dormition closely follows the Vladimirian prototype. Here is the same cubical mass with plain walls divided into arched bays and ornamented by an arcade at half the height. Even the position

of the windows is the same. The scheme of five domes is also retained. Fioravanti's church is so clearly based upon the Vladimir style that we have no difficulty in believing that he visited Suzdalia and carefully examined the churches there. The chronicle preserves a memory of this visit in its report that the architect, in his admiration for the churches, thought them built by his own countrymen. But Fioravanti travelled elsewhere in Russia too. The mass of the Dormition, especially the relation of the sturdy drums to the high white walls, suggests another Russian tradition – that of Novgorod. Since Fioravanti was renowned as an engineer, he probably accompanied Ivan on his campaigns against Novgorod in 1476 and 1477. The dates coincide with the slow growth of the Dormition; by the summer of 1476 the walls had risen only as far as the

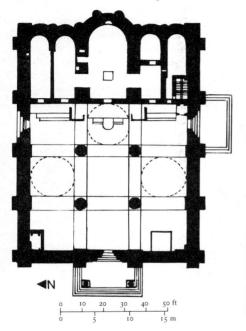

◀N

0 10 20 30 40 50 ft

0   5   10   15 m

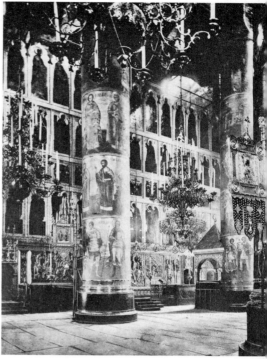

129. Aristotele Fioravanti: Moscow, Cathedral of the Dormition in the Kremlin, completed in 1479, interior

arcade, and the whole building was not finished until 1479. Fioravanti could thus have given them this pronounced Novgorodian character during the following summer. The plan, however, with six piers, including two concealed behind the iconostasis, and five apses resembles, but for the two additional apses, Andrey's original Dormition in Vladimir [23] rather than the present church with Vsevolod's additions. By abolishing the internal galleries Fioravanti established a new Russian type of unprecedented spaciousness. In other respects his plan was also novel for Russian architecture of the period. Through the position of the piers he divided the internal space into a series of compartments of equal

size, whether they were roofed with vaults or domes [129]. Disregarding the earlier Russian custom of making the aisles the same width as the apses, he widened the aisles and narrowed the apses so that a pair of apses could be placed at the end of each aisle. The logical precision of such a scheme speaks for his fifteenth-century Italian training and imposed a new sense of geometrical order upon Russian planning.

Fioravanti's experience as an engineer influenced his structural system. After removing the remains of the earlier walls, he enlarged and deepened the foundations, adding stumps of oak trees laid in pits. Upon these foundations rose the walls of white stone, cut in smaller blocks than had been customary in

Vladimir-Suzdal. For the vaults he used thin bricks, made in a kiln built to his own specifications. For further solidity and strength he bound his arches and walls with iron tie-rods in the Italian manner. There are also accounts of his having taught the Russian masters the use of hoists for lifting and moving materials. His workshops in the Kremlin were a true school of architectural construction, unequalled in Russia since the first Greek masters came to Kiev in the tenth and eleventh centuries.

A peculiarity of the Dormition was the fact that the main façade on the Palace Square had to be the southern rather than the western wall. Fioravanti's solution of this problem in design contained in essence many aspects of the subsequent as well as of the past history of Russian architecture. We have already seen that in the later churches of Novgorod and Suzdal it had become customary to arrange the decorative pilasters on the external façades so that they coincided in general with the internal disposition of the vaults and arches. As time went by the displacement of the dome towards the east, and so more nearly over the altar space below, resulted in a narrower eastern bay, although if the projection of the apse were included this bay with the apse might approximate the width of the western bay.

In the late-fourteenth- and early-fifteenth-century Moscow churches this tendency, for all that its asymmetry at least had a certain expressive freedom, had often ended in an inorganic, not to say illogical arrangement in which the projection of the apse added merely another uncoordinated element. Fioravanti's arrival at this juncture and his application to existing conditions of the logic of Italian Renaissance design may be seen on the south façade of his Dormition. In the first place, he masked the projection of the apses by reducing their depth, and by extending the south wall as a buttress some distance beyond its junction with the east wall. He then organized the remaining rectangular face by a system of proportional relationships as subtle and coordinated as in any Italian building of the period. In contrast to the jaunty and irregular vertical divisions of the Suzdalian churches, Fioravanti's four bays, corresponding to the internal distribution of the vaults, have a solemn processional rhythm. On the façade, up to the springing of the arches, the proportion of height to width is that of the golden section; the height of the upper windows from the ground equals the width of the two bays, etc.[14]

This complex interpenetration of old and new, of spiritual authority and modern technical practice, gives Fioravanti's measure as an architect. By his skilful combination of Suzdalian plan with Novgorod and Suzdalian massing, which reorganized the whole in terms of a modern intellectual aesthetic of abstract proportions, he created the first truly Renaissance building in Russia, new in its proportions, in its lofty yet lightly vaulted interior [129], and in the elegant rhythm of its bays and domes. Perhaps no less should have been expected of one who is said to have assisted Alberti in his excavations in the Roman Forum and in planning the rebuilding of Rome. However, to describe this church simply as an Italian building in Russian dress would be to minimize the coherent spirit which Fioravanti imparted to it. Its value becomes all the more apparent if it is compared with the next of the churches in the Kremlin to be built by a foreign architect.

Just before his death in 1505 Ivan III decided to rebuild the old Cathedral of St Michael the Archangel [130, 131]. Again an Italian was summoned, this time Aloisio or Alevisio Novi, 'the New', to distinguish him from an Alevisio who had worked in Russia from 1494.[15] Alevisio's commission was to build another monumental church, destined this time to serve as the burial-place of the tsars of the House of Rurik and of the earlier Romanovs. Again the authority of the Vladimir type determined mass and plan. But Alevisio was far less adventurous than his predecessor; his design, which resembles the

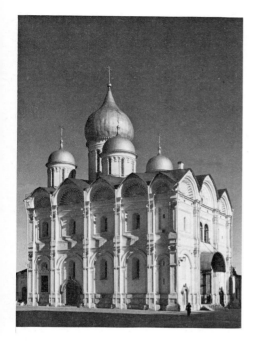

130 and 131. Alevisio Novi: Moscow, Cathedral of St Michael the Archangel in the Kremlin, 1505–9, exterior and plan

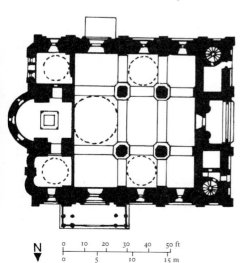

N
0   10   20   30   40   50 ft
0   5   10   15 m

Dormition in the displacement of the dome and the orientation of the side entrances further towards the east, is similarly six-piered and five-domed. Otherwise the general distribution of the interior space resembles more the Suzdalian type than the severer intellectual logic of the Dormition. Although Alevisio had to retain the entrance of the older church, which accounts for the small rooms to the north and south of his western entrance, expressed externally by a narrow extra bay on each side, he distributed his four free piers before the iconostasis so as to accentuate the breadth rather than the depth of the interior. His nave is thus wider than his aisles in the manner of earlier architecture. The thickness of the walls indicates that his structural technique was inferior to Fioravanti's. All in all St Michael, although completed in 1509, was in plan as well as construction retrogressive.

The exterior, however, was new and surprising. The walls are entirely covered with Renaissance details; arches, pilasters, recessed panels, and carved ornament give the church somewhat the appearance of a two-storey palace of the Italian High Renaissance. Alevisio was more a decorator than an architect, and his façades have little if any relation to interior volume or structural system, entirely unlike the fine proportions of Fioravanti's Dormition. Thus in his desire to relate the narrow windows of the Russian church to his broad wall-panels he introduced wider reveals which do not always disguise the fact that the window, an integral part of the structure, has little relation to the panel. The design of the pilasters with composite capitals and architraves, the whole carried on a high base, is as great a contradiction to the nature of the building as the scallop shells in the arches above the upper entablature which, unlike the earlier zakomars, deny the presence behind them of the internal vaults.

The building in its curiously composite and decorative character bears somewhat the same relation to Italian architecture as does an early-sixteenth-century French château such as

Blois. Each is the result of an attempt to apply an alien decorative pattern to a traditional structural system which had generated its own, although now rejected, decorative vocabulary. As in western Europe, it would be some time before the inevitable consequences of the experiment were fully understood: that the traditional style, in plan and massing as well as in technique, must be abandoned, or else a different decorative method more appropriate to the structure be discovered. Until the appearance of the Baroque churches in the later seventeenth century, where such secular splendour found a happier treatment, the higher clergy and their architects continued to think in terms of the old, familiar type of the Dormition.

Nevertheless, St Michael added much to the repertory of Russian decoration. The bold horizontal cornice beneath the scallop shells became a favourite device, as did the use of two materials in contrasting colours. Here white stone was used for the projecting parts, the cornices, capitals, arches, and shells, while the remainder, now plastered and painted white, was of red brick. Alevisio himself, before his summons to Russia, is said to have worked in Milan and Venice, which would account for the presence of such Venetian details as the group of four circular windows, one large and three small, over the main entrance. North Italian, also, is the treatment of this entrance as a two-storey loggia.

The cathedrals of the Kremlin, revered because of their close association with the dynasty, and as the chief metropolitan churches of the capital, cast shadows of differing lengths over subsequent religious architecture. Each of the three in its own way offered a different solution to the problem of the proper design of an Orthodox church, if not in plan and structure then in visual appearance. St Michael, in appearance the most novel, introduced a new repertory of decorative devices. The Cathedral of the Annunciation, especially in the treatment of the roof, was less an innovation, and so more congenial

to Russian taste. However one may choose to explain the origin of the stepped arches crowning the roof, whether as the external expression of the corbelled vaults at the base of the central dome or as a decorative device taken over from wooden architecture, the kokoshniki answered some strong formal desire and appeared with increasing frequency throughout the sixteenth and seventeenth centuries until the reforms of Nikon in 1650.

The Cathedral of the Dormition enjoyed a different authority. As the seat of the Metropolitan of Moscow, and so by inference the primary church in Russia, it was taken as a model for many later urban and monastic structures. Its compact mass crowned by five domes was frequently copied with such slight changes that it came in time to be considered the traditional, conservative, and basically orthodox pattern from which no deviations were permitted. Important sixteenth-century descendants, notable for a perceptible tendency to emphasize verticality through taller drums and swelling cupolas, are the Cathedrals of the Virgin of Smolensk in the Novodevichi Convent in Moscow (1524), of St Sophia in Vologda (1568–70), and of the Dormition in the Trinity-Sergius Monastery at Zagorsk (1559–85) [132]. After the middle of the seventeenth century Nikon, insisting on a strictly literal interpretation of the liturgy and church canons, condemned all but the most orthodox type of church. In this way the Moscow Dormition enjoyed a further prolongation of its authority into the later years of the century.

The churches of the type descending from the Dormition were usually monastic or cathedral structures, erected under the immediate supervision of powerful ecclesiastical leaders who were not unaware of the necessity of maintaining friendly relations with the authorities in Moscow. Another type of sixteenth-century church, startlingly different in appearance, arose under other conditions. These were the monumental churches built by members of the ruling house or by wealthy nobles, frequently

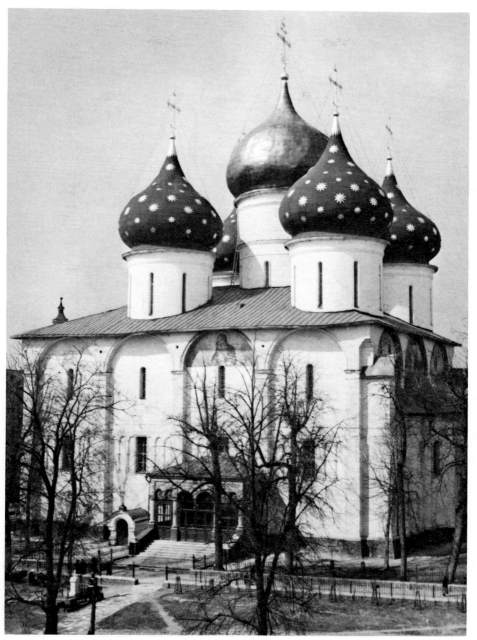

132. Zagorsk, Cathedral of the Dormition in the Trinity-Sergius Monastery, 1559–85

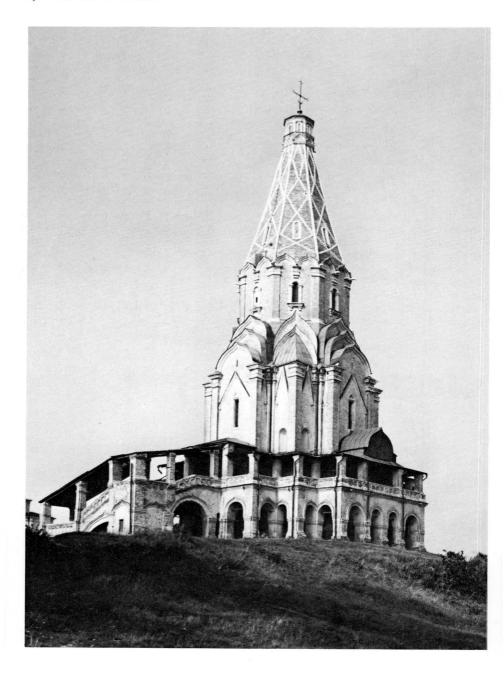

as thank-offerings or for votive purposes. In them the spiritual authority of the Church can be seen opposed by secular and personal taste, at variance with the hierarchy and possibly closer to popular tradition. As a group these monuments are characterized by their central plans, octagonal towers, and usually by their tent roofs.

Of the votive churches of this type the earliest and in many respects the finest is the Ascension at Kolomenskoe [133, 134], the Tsar's country residence near Moscow. Presumably built by Vasily III in 1530–2, as a thank-offering for the birth of his son Ivan, later the Terrible, the church is without precedent in Russian masonry architecture.[16] The tall, angular mass, enclosing the uncomplicated interior space, is composed of massive brick walls, reinforced along the sides and in the re-entrant angles, so that the effect is that of a powerfully buttressed support for the octagonal tower crowned with a tent roof surmounted by a lantern and cupola. Externally

the transition from the many-sided church to the octagon is managed by the corner buttresses and the rows of kokoshniki above each side. The church is placed on a high basement and is reached by a gallery, originally uncovered and approached by three flights of steps. It demonstrates once more that peculiarly Russian characteristic, a union of opposites, here as elsewhere typified in the superposition of extremely complicated forms upon an essentially simple and logical plan, and as well in the Russian taste for strong contrasts of colour, the brick walls having originally been painted red, the pilasters and other stone ornaments white. The inherent directness of the square plan internally had grown into a multi-faceted polygon in elevation. The transition to the octagon is both expressed and concealed by the buttresses and kokoshniki. The tower-like body of the church absorbs all the details in its vertical sweep, yet the whole is anchored to the ground by the broad gallery. The plan is axially symmetrical in both direc-

133 (*opposite*) and 134. Kolomenskoe, Church of the Ascension, probably 1530–2, exterior and plan

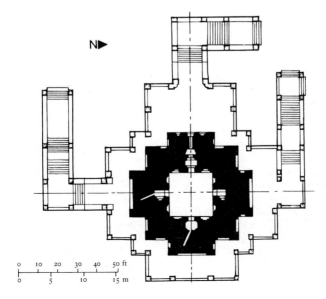

N▶

```
0    10   20   30   40   50 ft
0        5        10       15 m
```

tions, yet any appearance of too rigid a balance is avoided, both by the position of the church on a gently sloping hillside, and by the stairways to the galleries which are unequally placed on three sides.

The problem of the origin of this church is very intricate. It is idle to pretend that its impressive verticality can be explained by reference to the medieval architecture of western Europe. This had been familiar to Russian builders in one way or another since the appearance of German traders in the twelfth and thirteenth centuries in Novgorod, and, while it is true that Novgorod architects had tended to push their buildings upward rather than lengthwise, the whole cube had been made taller; no central element such as a cupola had dominated the whole building at the expense of others. Nor, despite the temptation to see in such a form some connexion, however devious and remote, with Persian and Indian architecture, such as Hindu stupas, is it really permissible to predicate an influence upon what may be only an accidental resemblance.[17] There remains the question whether the Kolomenskoe church is not an attempt to create in masonry the effect of the tall wooden churches of northern Russia in which an octagonal tower crowned with a tent roof rises over a central square. Since the earliest surviving example of such a church was that at Panilovo, built in 1599–1600 but destroyed by fire in the 1920s, and a closer resemblance to Kolomenskoe is not found until the church at Varzug of 1674 [112, 118], chronology does not support such an hypothesis. But since the central plan was known in Russia, and neither Panilovo nor Varzug need be or can be considered the primary example of such a church, it is probable that Kolomenskoe does represent an attempt to transfer to masonry wooden forms familiar at the time of its construction.[18] The argument may be supported by other deductions. The thick walls seem to betray some unfamiliarity with new problems of load and support. Had there been masonry precedents for Kolomenskoe,

probably some other solution than the sheer weight of so much brick would have been invented to carry the octagon and roof. Secondly, the massing of the superimposed kokoshniki seems much more an interpretation in brick of wooden forms than a decorative device evolved from the external corbels of such a church as the Kremlin Annunciation. And finally, the wide surrounding gallery is too familiar a wooden form, and too rare in preceding masonry architecture, not to have been taken over. To assert the almost instantaneous appearance of a new form of church, at best no more than hinted at in the relatively greater height of later-fourteenth- and fifteenth-century churches, and to assume that from 1532 the innumerable wooden churches in Russia were in turn derived from a few masonry buildings on the ground that the Court style would have had more prestige in the villages than would the village style in the tsar's country palace, is to mistake the fundamental nature of materials. The tent churches of the later sixteenth and seventeenth centuries are forms too coherently evolved to have been merely called into existence by the sudden appearance of a new type of church at Court. So far as ideology is concerned we must remember that the century covered by the reigns of Ivan III, Vasily III, and Ivan IV was coloured by an insistence on Russian nationality. That these tower-like churches appear first on dynastic estates and as assertions of princely prestige would seem sufficient warrant for the belief that the tsars themselves, in seeking a characteristic national expression, looked to the wooden tent churches of the popular cult. The disappearance of such churches by fire and reconstruction in Muscovy itself, and the preservation of many later examples in remote northern villages, have arbitrarily affected the interpretation of this aspect of Russian architectural history.

The votive churches, whatever their origin, were not without some relation to the churches of the Kremlin.[19] The lower part of the Transfiguration at Ostrov [135], which alone

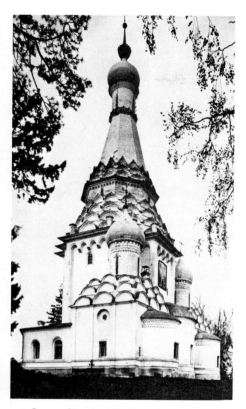

135. Ostrov, Church of the Transfiguration,
lower part sixteenth century,
octagon and roof 1646

by pilasters, in the main church they are framed by corner pilasters between which runs a blind arcade. Upon this profoundly simple and geometrical base the later kokoshniki – semicircular above the chapels, ogee-arched in four tiers around the massive octagon, and triangular at the base of the tent roof – create the effect of a prodigal expenditure of decorative forms. If less elegant in its profile, and less sensitive in its proportions than Kolomenskoe, the church at Ostrov nevertheless carries a step further the Russian fondness for lavish decoration. And once more it is worth observing that although in plan and structure the church is composed of few elements, and those rather rigidly placed, externally the composition is one of constantly varying dimensions, aided again by the position of the church on the gentle slope of a hill.

Another kind of tower is seen in the Decapitation of St John the Baptist at Dyakovo [136, 137], near Kolomenskoe. For long thought to have been erected in 1529 by Vasily III to secure the birth of a son, it has lately been established that the documents of 1529 referred to another church, and from the dedication of the chapels it can be deduced that it was built from 1555 by Ivan IV as a votive church for the birth of a son. His first-born, Dmitry, lived only a few months in 1552, but his unhappy and ill-fated son Ivan was born in 1555. Originally the church consisted of a central octagon flanked by four smaller octagonal chapels, the five elements standing upon a high square terrace.[20] At a later date the addition of an apse between the two eastern chapels and galleries on three sides with a belfry on the west spoiled the original composition where a livelier diversity had occurred in the relation between the large central element and the four smaller variants at its base.

If the builders of Kolomenskoe and Ostrov knew St Michael in Moscow, but were more familiar with nearby wooden towers and tent churches, the situation was reversed at Dyakovo. Here the majority of the decorative work is a Russian version of European motifs. The

is sixteenth-century, the octagon and tent roof having been added in 1646, is clearly from the hands of builders familiar with St Michael and the Annunciation, as well as with the Ascension at Kolomenskoe. From the Annunciation came the tiered kokoshniki over the side chapels and at the base of the central octagon; from St Michael certain details, such as the profiles of the pilasters and the circular windows in the side walls of the chapels. The cubic core of the main church and of the chapels is close to the Annunciation; in the chapels the walls are divided into three bays

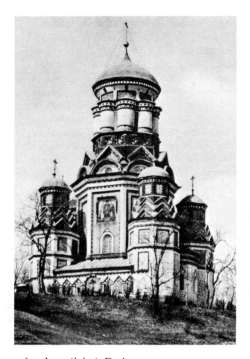

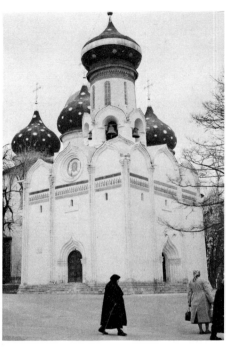

136 and 137 (*below*). Dyakovo,
Church of the Decapitation of St John the Baptist,
from 1555, exterior and plan

138. Zagorsk,
Church of the Descent of the Holy Spirit
in the Trinity-Sergius Monastery, 1476

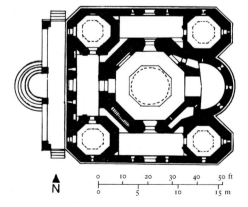

curious half-columns surrounding the upper
part of the tower, which look like a combination of Renaissance columns and Gothic but-

tresses, have a precedent in the squat columns
of the fifteenth-century belfries of Pskov and
in the belfry which replaced the drum of the
Church of the Descent of the Holy Spirit in
the Trinity-Sergius Monastery, built by a
Pskov master in 1476 [138].[21] Kolomenskoe is
basically a wooden form translated into brick;
Dyakovo is essentially and completely an expression of brickwork. Only in the considerable projection of the multiple cornices
crowning the central octagon is the existence
of wooden prototypes apparent. Even the
severe profiles of the kokoshniki are evidence
of this feeling for the material as the dominant
mode of expression, increased by the polychromatic effect of coloured tiles.

The churches at Kolomenskoe and Dyakovo
were the immediate prototypes for a third and

even more original building. With them in mind the votive church of Ivan IV in Moscow, dedicated to the Protection and Intercession of the Virgin, but popularly known as the Cathedral of St Basil the Blessed (Vasily Blazheny) [139–41], appears less as a monstrosity or inexplicable curiosity than as their logical if extravagant successor. The church was intended by Ivan IV as a national votive church commemorating his conquest of the khanates of Kazan and Astrakhan. It was erected between 1555 and 1560 by two Russian architects, Barma and Posnik. The tradition that it was built by an Italian who was then blinded by Ivan lest he create anything else like it is a later fantasy, popularized by travellers' tales in the eighteenth century as a way to account for its fantastic appearance. For the origin of the church it is perhaps of some importance that a series of separate wooden chapels commemorating the principal events of the siege of Kazan had first been erected. Then the central stone church was constructed and the adjacent chapels ultimately executed in masonry.[22]

Like its predecessors, St Basil enjoys a picturesque location, dominating the narrow southern side of the Red Square near the Saviour Gate of the Kremlin. Its site, like those of its prototypes, is uneven, slanting away from the square towards the river. The tall octagonal tower of the central church, in plan and structure a repetition of the Kolomenskoe Ascension, stands upon a high terrace or platform, but is concealed externally by the towers of the four large octagonal chapels placed on the main axes and by the four smaller polygonal chapels placed in the angles between them. Once again we observe the contrast between the simplicity of the plan and the complexity of its three-dimensional expression. The principle of unity is maintained by subordinating the eight smaller towers (nine, if the belfry is included) and their cupolas in two ranks, as it were, to the central tent roof of the main church, yet within this unity the greatest freedom allows each sub-

sidiary chapel a different height and surface treatment. The whole exhibits the widest variety of plastic expression, as can be seen by comparing any two photographs taken from different angles, and in this sense may be considered the most 'sculptural' achievement of Russian architecture. In one respect this variety is possibly more accentuated than the builders originally intended for in the seventeenth century a small chapel and a belfry were added on the north-east, and the polychromatic decoration of the cupolas was completed. Were the cupolas identical the effect would have been closer to Dyakovo. Later in the century the present extravagant onion-shaped cupolas replaced the original low helmet-shaped domes like those at Dyakovo, and in the seventeenth century the upper walls and kokoshniki were painted with polychromatic floral ornament [140]. The gallery, added later in the seventeenth century, conceals the articulation of the chapels so that their separation above the second storey seems unnecessarily capricious. A seventeenth-century engraving made from a drawing of the church before the gallery was enclosed proves how much more coherent the original design must have been [142].

Thus to describe St Basil as a logical outgrowth of the tendencies initiated at Kolomenskoe and Dyakovo is not to detract from its strangeness. Like the tsar who called it into being, the church exemplifies both the continuity of a tradition, perhaps in this case a dynastic rather than a national one, and the extreme divergences of character within that tradition. As Ivan IV was at all times most Russian, even as he was truly terrible, so St Basil is both a part of, and a departure from, old Russian architecture. Paradoxically, it is a most particular expression of the personality of one sovereign which could have been created at no other time or place, yet conversely it is rightly considered, even by the Russians themselves, one of the most typical examples of their national culture. As St Sophia was to Kiev the symbol of the mass

139. Barma and Posnik: Moscow, Cathedral of St Basil, 1555-60

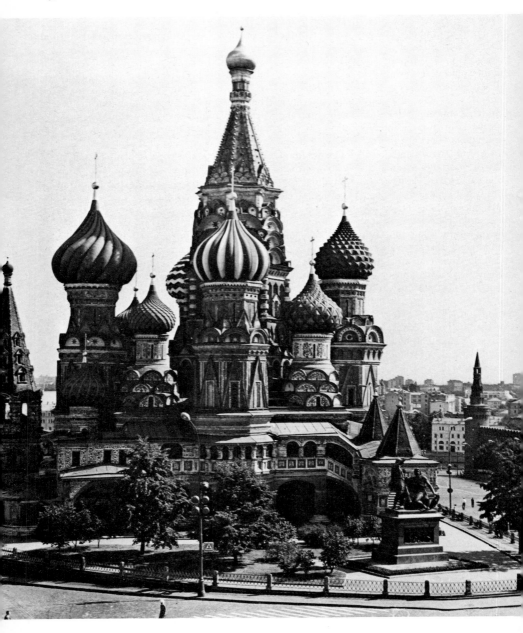

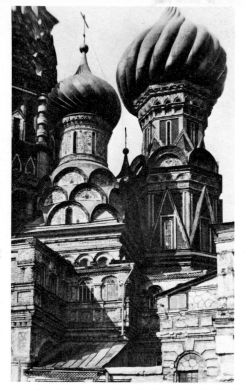

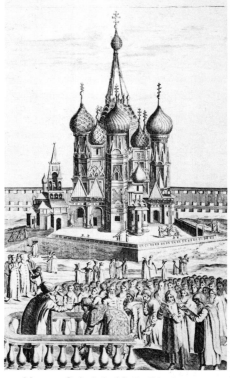

140 (*above left*) and 141 (*below*). Cathedral of St Basil, 1555–60, detail and plan

142. Moscow, Cathedral of St Basil in the seventeenth century, before the addition of the covered gallery

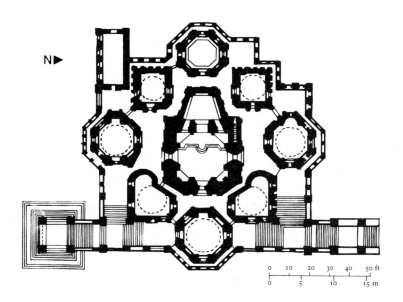

N▶

0 10 20 30 40 50 ft
0   5   10   15 m

acceptance of Greek Christianity, so St Basil came to mean that the Russia of Muscovy had attained its own special religious, political, and cultural expression. As we would associate St Sophia with the first Greek bishops and Metropolitans of Kiev, so with St Basil we may name those passionate and mighty builders of the Moscow Church: Joseph of Volokolamsk, who fought for the closest union between the Church and the Monarchy, and Philip the Metropolitan, who dared defy even Ivan himself.

For later generations, in Russia as well as in Europe, the church became a landmark and a stumbling-block. After the seventeenth-century reforms no churches again achieved such prodigality of colour and shape, until the revival of the national style in the nineteenth century. For the eighteenth-century European traveller the church 'offered little of interest'.[23] There have even been attempts to explain its peculiar design as an influence from the East, specifically from Tartary. But surviving Mongol architecture bears little relation to St Basil, and, as we have seen, the individual forms already pre-existed in traditional wood and masonry construction. If it owes anything to the Middle or Farther East, it is only the use of rich colour, although that had long been a factor in Russian art, and the complex, overall patterning of the surfaces somewhat in the manner of textiles. Indeed, it was in ornament rather than in structural methods that the Tartars, who left few permanent buildings, influenced Russian architecture.[24]

The tent roof, which is the dominant formal principle in the design of St Basil, served many purposes. At Alexandrov to the east of Moscow, which Basil III developed as a country residence, the bell tower of the Church of the Crucifixion (1570s) [143] has a serene elegance unexpected after the incoherence of Dyakovo or the turbulence of St Basil. The octagonal base is pierced by two storeys of recesses whose curved tops provide the transition to three rows of kokoshniki. Above the latter rises an octagonal base sur-

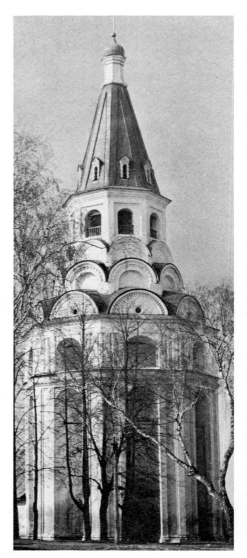

143. Alexandrov, near Moscow, Church of the Crucifixion, bell tower, 1570s

mounted by the tent roof. The builders must have been aware that suggestion can be as emphatic as emphasis. The narrow recessed panels on the lower storeys, framed by the slightest of mouldings, the single row of pointed bricks around the kokoshniki, the minuscule windows in the lowest row and their echo in the pedimented windows near the base of the roof, all are accents which reinforce

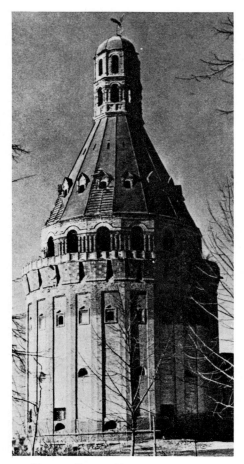

144. Moscow, Simonov Monastery, Dula Tower, 1640s

rather than disturb the simplicity of the whole.

To the south of Moscow the Simonov Monastery, heavily fortified in the late six-

teenth and early seventeenth centuries, was an important stronghold protecting Moscow's southern defences. It is now largely demolished, and the surviving remnants are engulfed in a car factory, but along the south wall are three towers of which the so-called Dula Tower [144] is among the most satisfactory as well as powerful examples of this kind of ecclesiastical architecture. The sixteen-sided base, with shallow panels like those at Alexandrov, is crowned with battlements and supports a tent roof resting on arches framed by paired columns which infer some knowledge of Italian architecture. The basic design, save for the absence of kokoshniki, is similar to the Alexandrov church, even to the pedimented windows in the roof, but the effect is totally different. Grace in one, impregnable authority in the other, yet both structures are entirely the product of the Russian genius.

The confusion and dislocation of the national political and economic life during the later years of Ivan's reign precluded any further elaborate building, nor was the short reign of his son Feodor (1584–98) any more propitious. Since this was followed by chaos and catastrophe during the ensuing Time of Troubles (1584–1613), there was in effect a suspension of monumental construction until the revival of prosperity under the tsars of the House of Romanov after 1613. Later-sixteenth-century churches are small, and in the provinces frequently echo the style of the capital. Among the smaller structures, however, there emerged towards the close of the period a type which proved influential for the first churches in Moscow built under the Romanovs in the following century. An example is the old cathedral in the Monastery of the Virgin of the Don in Moscow [145], built in 1593, which summarizes in miniature the architectural innovations of the sixteenth century. In spite of its small size, the plan contains many features which had grown common with the passing of time. To the central space, for instance, in this case without internal piers, were added not only the custom-

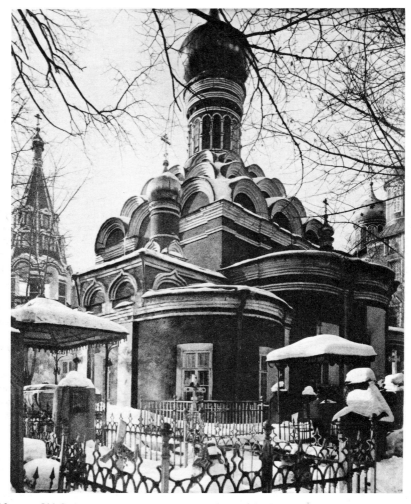

145. Moscow, Old Cathedral in the Monastery of the Virgin of the Don, 1593

ary three apses, but also side chapels, each with an apse, and a spacious gallery. Externally there is much that is familiar, however new the combination may at first appear; the cornices and lunettes of St Michael, the external massing of the side chapels at Ostrov, the pyramidal verticality of St Basil, as well as the full-blown cupola. The monastery, founded by Boris Godunov in 1591, was part of the southern line of Moscow's defences. The Michael Church has now been converted into a museum for monumental sculpture and architectural fragments from demolished buildings.

CHAPTER 16

SEVENTEENTH-CENTURY ARCHITECTURE:

THE 'MOSCOW BAROQUE'

The religious architecture of the seventeenth century reflects with unusual precision the multiple currents of thought and action present in the social and political history of the time. The slow revival of national energies after the Time of Troubles (1584–1613) following the death of Ivan IV and the Polish occupation of Moscow in 1611–12 necessarily delayed the construction of monumental buildings, although the first Romanov tsars, Mikhail Feodorovich (1613–45), and his son Alexey Mikhailovich (1645–76), felt obliged, like their predecessors in the sixteenth century, to make their contribution towards the formulation of a national Russian style. The expression of such a desire can be seen in the Church of the Nativity of the Virgin in Putinki (1649–52) [146, 147], built at the personal wish and with funds, some 800 roubles, an unusually large sum for the time, supplied by the Tsar. The church owes much to the picturesque, asymmetrical composition of Ostrov and St Basil, yet here three-dimensional variety is expressed in the plan as well as in the mass. The plan develops around a courtyard, later filled in by the low one-storey refectory in the foreground of the photograph. The church originally consisted of two separate chapels, each with an entrance from the courtyard. The first is a cube surmounted by triple rows of kokoshniki topped by a slender drum bearing a tent roof with cupola. The second chapel is again square in plan, but externally it emerges as a broad rectangle crowned with three tent roofs. The two chapels are joined by a rectangular belfry, which in itself is a more elaborate version of the four other pyramidal spires. The uneven alignment of the five spires, of unequal height and carrying onion-shaped cupolas of different sizes, and the various rows of kokoshniki contribute to the picturesque effect. The lack of correspondence between the external massing and the disposition of the plan, and the interpenetration of each element with its neighbour, introduces a new and more exclusively visual approach to architectural design. It is as if the architect of this, the last of the multiple tent-roofed churches of the seventeenth century, had attempted to re-create the apparent lack of unity of St Basil without considering the fundamental logic of structure and plan which underlay it.

This irregular plan and exceedingly intricate massing appear in other Moscow churches of the period, such as the Church of the Trinity and of the Georgian Virgin (1628–53) [148], built by Grigory Nikitnikov, a wealthy Yaroslavl merchant, with its load of crisply detailed kokoshniki whose profiles echo the pointed window frames set between coupled engaged columns beneath a crisply defined cornice of coloured tiles. It may be noted that such churches were often built on narrow city sites along already existing streets so that to secure proper orientation the architect had to arrange the entrance either off-axis or through a chapel or belfry. Here the western entrance is reached through a tent-roofed porch from which at the south-west corner a staircase ascends to a covered gallery along the western façade. Yet even churches standing in open grounds show the same multiple massing, uneven distribution of elements, and richness of surface decoration. Such is the Trinity at Ostankino (1678–83) [149], on the estate of Count Sheremetev near Moscow. Here accumulation and multiplication of parts reached a

146 (*below*) and 147 (*right*). Moscow, Church of the Nativity of the Virgin in Putinki, 1649–52, exterior and plan

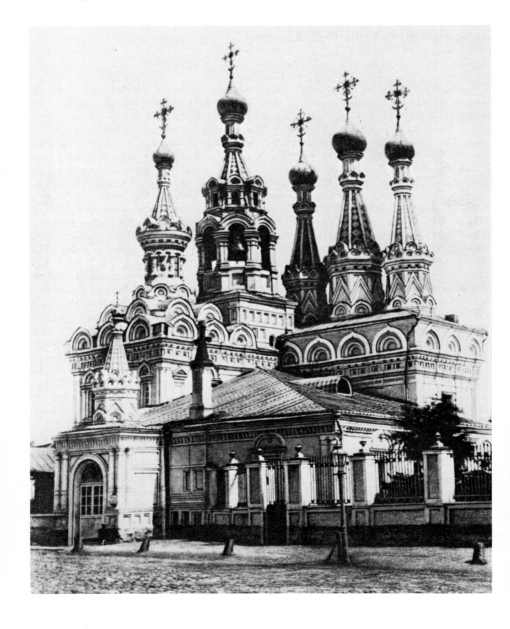

degree of pictorial richness unparalleled else-where. The principal cube is so enclosed by chapels, a two-storey gallery with adjacent vestibules and covered staircases, and an attached belfry that the total mass presents the same constant shifting of volumes in three dimensions as observed in St Basil, to which it bears some relation also in the imitation of the double flight of steps. Ostankino represents a curious moment of transition; the architect wished to retain the jagged silhouette and ver-

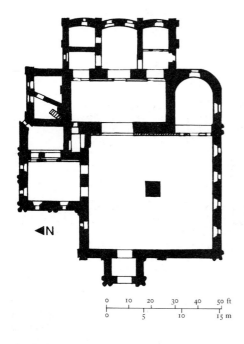

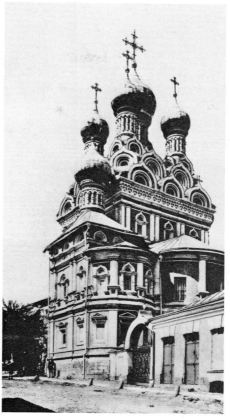

148. Moscow, Church of the Trinity and of the Georgian Virgin, 1628–53

ticality of St Basil, but also had to adhere to the now obligatory form of a cube with the canonical five domes. And, like St Basil, his church exhibits preoccupation with the character of brick as a decorative surface. It may be said to absorb and exude the qualities of moulded and coloured brick; bricks of vari-ous shapes, sizes, and colours, laid in numer-ous ways, lengthways, sideways, in zigzags, bricks cut or moulded for some particular course. The polychromatic walls topped with gilded and painted cupolas afforded that spec-tacle of abundant colour which so impressed foreign visitors to Russia.

This attitude towards brick intensively felt and worked to produce the utmost variety of colour, shape, and play of light and shade over the wall surfaces is characteristic of a large

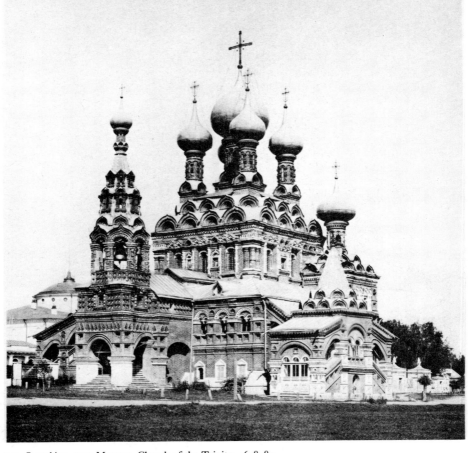

149. Ostankino, near Moscow, Church of the Trinity, 1678–83

group of seventeenth-century churches in Yaroslavl. This ancient city, founded in the eleventh century and long an outpost of the Russian land, had known the rise and fall of fortune through the years. Long ago it had been an important centre of religious culture, and it is not uninteresting that in the library of one of its monasteries was found the manuscript of the twelfth-century *Tale of the Armament of Igor*. The city had been sacked by the Tartars in 1238, and in 1463 accepted the overlordship of Moscow. In the course of the later sixteenth and seventeenth centuries its prosperity increased, for it not only com-

manded the Volga, which, when the Tartars had been overthrown, became a through-waterway to the East, but it also served as an important shipping point on the route between Arkhangelsk and Moscow. So long as the trade with western Europe reached Russia through the White Sea, Yaroslavl each year saw companies of English, French, and Dutch merchants on their way to the capital. Through Yaroslavl also may have passed some of the numerous western architects, stonemasons, and engineers, whose recorded presence in Russia throughout the seventeenth century is in itself sufficient explanation for the increas-

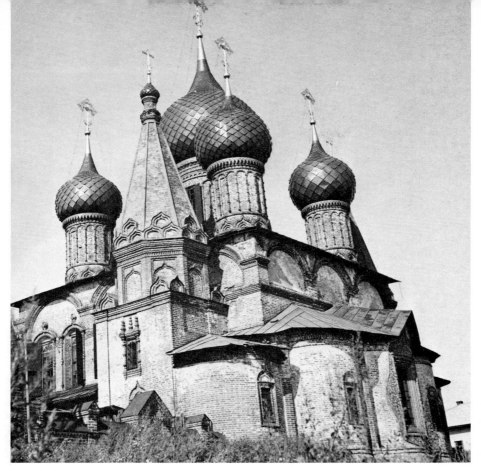

150. Yaroslavl, St John Chrysostom, 1649–54

ingly frequent appearance of western architectural details.[1] As if it had been a later and somewhat vulgar Novgorod the wealthy merchants and trading companies of Yaroslavl vied with each other to erect sumptuous churches. From 1620 more than forty stone churches were built, many of them larger than contemporary buildings in Moscow. Even a disastrous fire in 1658 failed to halt this building activity. Most of the extant churches were built between 1660 and 1690, after which, owing to the opening of the Gulf of Finland and the foundation of St Petersburg, the trade of Yaroslavl declined.

In accordance with most provincial architecture and, it may be, most architecture produced by mercantile societies, the churches of Yaroslavl, although large, magnificent, and ingeniously decorated, are conservative in plan and structure. They return to the earlier sixteenth-century disposition of a four- or six-piered, three-apsed plan, flanked by chapels and a wide gallery approached by porches on three sides. The Church of St John Chrysostom in the suburb of Korovniki (1649–54), repaired after the fire of 1658 [150], built by wealthy merchants, the brothers Nezhdanovsky, is a particularly lavish and happy fusion of eastern and western influences. The simple cubical mass of the church, supporting the canonical five domes, recalls the Kremlin type, perhaps most immediately St Sophia in Vologda. But the addition of the wide gallery at the base of the walls creates a two-storeyed effect which is further worked out in terms of the arcades resting below on squat engaged columns and above on wide pilasters, and at the corners on clusters of engaged colonnettes. In the distribution of arch and pilaster one can sense not only a distant echo of St Michael, but possibly even the presence in Yaroslavl of some more direct understanding of the European Renaissance reaching the city through foreign merchants. The elaborately framed windows in both storeys, wider below and taller above than in any Russian churches before, are hints of the new knowledge of the European Baroque which was entering Muscovy about this time from the Ukraine. The traffic of Dutch merchants in Yaroslavl may have contributed to the extensive use of coloured tiles. The window-frames and various mouldings throughout the building are worked in this material. The combination of tile and elaborately moulded brick was developed with even greater splendour, both inside and out, in the Church of St John the Baptist in Tolchkovo (1671–87) [151]. Here the eastern ends of the gallery were raised to the full height of the church and provided each with a dense cluster of five domes. The lavish effect of fifteen gilded cupolas rivals the multitudinous wooden domes of Kizhy [124].

The merchants and architects of Yaroslavl were obliged to accept Nikon's injunction against the use of more than three or five domes, but they were loath to forgo entirely the pyramidal tent roof of ancient memory. Such a roof appears in many of the Yaroslavl churches over the side chapels, as here in St John and in the powerfully proportioned chapel of the Deposition of Christ's Robe at the Church of St Elias (1647–50).[2] Tent roofs are also found above the noble bell towers which are a particular feature of Yaroslavl architecture. The bell tower near St John is

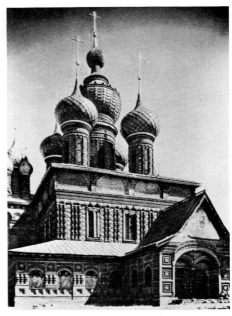

151. Yaroslavl, St John the Baptist in Tolchkovo, 1671–87

one of the finest of its type. The massive octagonal brick base is crowned with a delicately proportioned spire whose fine profile again suggests the probability of some eastern influence reaching the city from the lower Volga [152].

In contrast to the commercial splendours of Yaroslavl, such a city as Rostov-the-Great, on the Volga, offers the interesting picture of a fortified monastic establishment of the later seventeenth century. Rostov, too, had been founded in the eleventh century. It had been anciently the seat of the bishop serving Suzdalia. Like its neighbours it had been devastated by the Tartars, and like Yaroslavl it enjoyed a brief period of prosperity in the seventeenth century following the elevation in 1589 of the Bishop of Rostov as Metropolitan, equal to Novgorod and inferior only to Moscow. But Rostov fell into a rapid decline when Peter the Great deprived the Metropolitan of much of his revenue. The construction

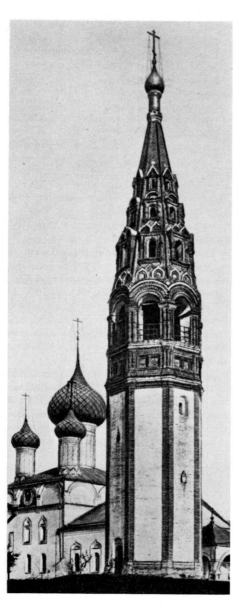

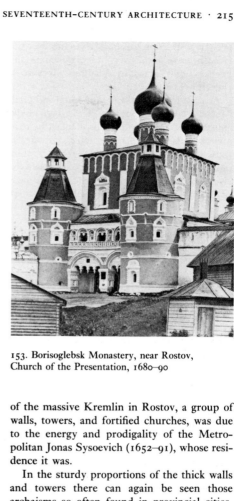

153. Borisoglebsk Monastery, near Rostov,
Church of the Presentation, 1680–90

152. Yaroslavl, St John Chrysostom, 1649–54,
bell tower

of the massive Kremlin in Rostov, a group of
walls, towers, and fortified churches, was due
to the energy and prodigality of the Metropolitan Jonas Sysoevich (1652–91), whose residence it was.

In the sturdy proportions of the thick walls
and towers there can again be seen those
archaisms so often found in provincial cities.
Although they are a century and a half later than
the towers and walls of the Moscow Kremlin,
those of Rostov show not the slightest trace of
that elegance which marked Italian design.
They seem intended to repel attacks of archers
rather than of riflemen. A peculiarity of the
churches of the fortified monasteries of the
later seventeenth century, not only here but in
the neighbouring forest-bound Monastery of
SS. Boris and Gleb (1680–90), also erected by
Jonas Sysoevich, is the construction of
churches above the entrances [153]. In a sense
this conforms to a most ancient Russian prac-

tice. In Kiev there had been churches over the Golden Gate, and over the entrance to the Pecherskaya Lavra; in Vladimir likewise a church over a Golden Gate.

At Rostov and in the nearby Boris and Gleb Monastery the composition of the mass of the churches high above the walls, flanked by twin towers with a lavishly decorated gateway, is most skilful. The Church of the Presentation in the Boris and Gleb Monastery surpasses the churches of Rostov in the delicate treatment of the portal and in the almost Rococo charm of the blind arcade below the roof. Whether this be considered an archaistic reminder of the arcades of Vladimir and Suzdal, or whether it be taken as a final degeneration of the early zakomars, it bridges the awkward juncture of wall and flat roof demanded by the canonical reforms after 1650.

While the churches of Yaroslavl and Rostov, although for the most part constructed after the middle of the century, continued to express certain long-standing tendencies in earlier Russian architecture, church-building at Moscow was affected by two significant developments. The first arose from the insistence of the Patriarch Nikon (elected 1652, deposed 1666) that all future church-builders renounce the pyramidal or tent roof and return to the ancient Byzantine form of a cube topped by three or five domes.[3] This arbitrary decision was only one aspect of Nikon's determination to reform the Russian Church by restoring original Greek practices. Once again paradox plays a peculiar role in Russian history. Nikon's intentions were in one sense progressive, since he wished to purge the Russian Church of errors which had gradually crept in, and so to place it on a theological footing sound enough to withstand criticism from the Roman Catholic countries to the west, but the results were on the whole reactionary. A large minority of clergy and laymen, who came to be called the Old Believers, refused to accept the so-called reforms and separated themselves from the official Church, insisting that they alone were the true heirs of Orthodoxy. The schism had enduring and unhappy effects. The official Church was for ever cut off from a large number of the most sincerely religious and intelligent churchmen, and it was so weakened that it could not hope for support from any quarter but the State. How uncertain that might be was soon seen, when Peter allowed the office of patriarch to lapse after the death of Adrian in 1700. Moreover, after the reunion of the Ukraine with Great Russia in 1667, a constant stream of clergy who had been educated in the more liberal, latinized academies in Kiev began to bring to Moscow innumerable western ideas, including firsthand knowledge of the European Baroque. Consequently in later-seventeenth-century architecture can be seen a pursuit of variety and picturesqueness. The heightened accent of surprise and caprice in the break of a wall, the turn of a pilaster, the penetration of one form into another, the obscuring of one shape by the passing of another across it, the play of painted colours against carved surfaces, and the irregular massing growing out of irregular plans give such architecture a truly Baroque character.

Yet, as every action breeds its counteraction, as in western Europe the Baroque of Bernini was countered by the classicism of Perrault and Wren, so the architecture emanating from the circle of Nikon may be taken as an academic reaction – academic in the sense that the designers looked to the past for rules for the present and, fearful of the play of emotion, sought to control their materials through plain surfaces, the suppression of detail, and the utmost sobriety of effect. Nikon's two most important constructions can stand as types of the academic reaction. In the Kremlin he built his own palace and patriarchal church beside the Terem or Palace of the Tsar as a visual affirmation of the political theory that Tsar and Patriarch were joint rulers of an indissoluble autocratic and theocratic monarchy. But the new Terem of Alexey Mikhailovich, with its small rooms, broken surfaces, bright colours, and European decoration, stood for the emergence of secular, personal luxury from under the shadow of Church authority. Thinking to restore the dignity of an older order by a close adherence to tradition, Nikon in his Church of the Twelve Apostles (1656) [154] imitated the bare cubical

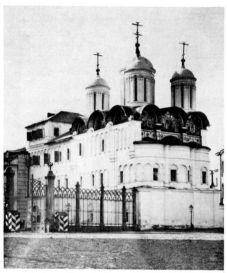

154. Moscow, Church of the Twelve Apostles and the Patriarchal Palace in the Kremlin, 1656

masses of the sixteenth-century descendants of the Moscow Dormition. The five domes on tall drums, the zakomars and engaged arcades, all witness his desire to separate his reformed Church from the extravagant tendencies of contemporary religious architecture and to return to the ancient lineage of Kiev, Vladimir, and Moscow. Nevertheless, the Twelve Apostles differs from its prototypes in Vladimir and Moscow in its modest dimensions, as well as in its richer details such as the double blind arcades on the sides, and in the fact that it was raised one storey above the ground in order that the interior, like that of the Annunciation, might be on the same level as the

main rooms of the palace. Paradoxically Nikon's insistence on simplicity was not matched in his palace, where the rooms were considerably larger than those in the Tsar's new Terem. They made a deep impression on foreign visitors, especially when Nikon received the Tsar himself in the great hall.[4]

Nikon's greatest church, in his Monastery of the New Jerusalem at Istra north-west of Moscow, was also a monument to his convictions [155]. This was intended as a demonstration of his restored architectural style, and as an assertion of the Russian Patriarch's position as actual if not titular leader of the entire Orthodox community. To prove this Nikon decided to rival the Patriarch of Jerusalem by building a replica of the most holy shrine of Christendom, the Church of the Holy Sepulchre in Jerusalem.[5] To this end he sent one of his monks, the cellarer Arseny Sukhanov, to Palestine to study the ancient structure. Arseny returned with plans and drawings from which a model was made, and in 1658 Nikon and his architects devised a large rotunda enclosing a replica of the Holy Sepulchre at the western end of a domed, cross-plan church [156].[6] The church itself was more 'Greek' than the churches of Kiev and Vladimir, for the cross was expressed externally as well as in plan, the arms projecting a full storey above the corner spaces. Upon Nikon's exile in 1666 the church had risen as far as the vaults. Work was then suspended, and the Tsar summoned the builders to Moscow to the government service. Not until 1681 was construction resumed by order of Tsar Feodor Alexeevich. The church was finished, with changes such as the belfry adjoining the south transept, and consecrated in 1685. Thus much of the decorative detail, including the elaborate window-frames of enamelled tiles, although planned by Nikon, was executed in a more exuberantly Baroque manner.

This church was Nikon's most successful attempt to revive the Greek spirit of the earliest Russian architecture. The space at the crossing rose three storeys to the drum of the

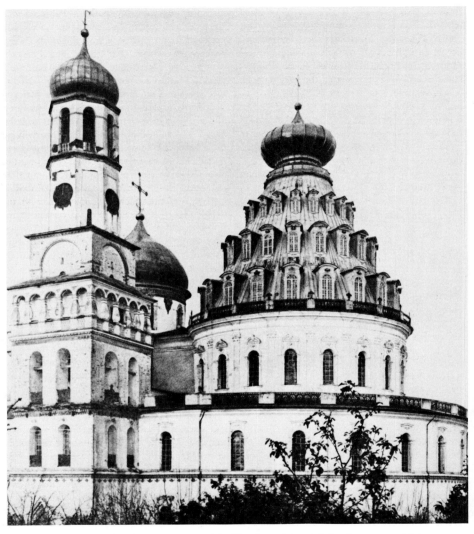

155 (*above*) and 156 (*right*). Istra, Monastery of the New Jerusalem, 1658–85, the oratory with its conical roof reconstructed by Rastrelli, 1747–60, with plan

dome, and the arcades and galleries were supported on columns in the manner of St Sophia at Kiev and the Transfiguration at Chernigov. Beside the church rose a tall bell tower of square and octagonal storeys; the base was supposed to resemble the campanile in Jerusalem, but the upper part looked more like the tower of Ivan Veliky in the Kremlin. The rotunda was originally covered with a stone tent roof, historically a paradoxical use of this earlier wooden form which Nikon himself had condemned, but which was the only structural means to cover such a large interior space. This stone tent collapsed in 1723. Thirty years later it was rebuilt, possibly by the Moscow architect K. I. Blank after designs by Bartolommeo Rastrelli (see below, Chapter 20). The new roof was of wood with three rows of dormer windows to lighten the walls and illuminate the interior. At this time the iconostasis, the replica of the Holy Sepulchre in the form of a small oratory, and the interior decoration of the rotunda were redone in the Rococo taste,

to the new age, not to the old. Nikon's artificial academic revival remained an episode rather than a decisive event in the history of seventeenth-century architecture.[7]

Yet that Nikon's restrictions were frequently more honoured in the letter than in the spirit we have already seen in northern Russia, where in the wooden churches various expedients were adopted to retain the familiar and beloved pyramidal silhouettes in the form of some combination of peaked roof and cupolas. In the capital, however, it was less easy to escape ecclesiastical censure, and on the whole the churches of the second half of the century in plan and mass conform to the

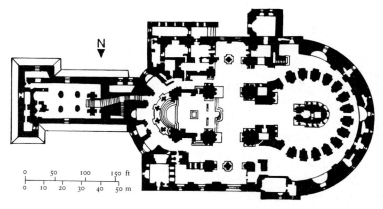

N
▼

0   50   100   150 ft
0 10 20 30 40 50 m

thereby concealing much of the sumptuous but restrained majolica decoration.

Nikon's building, for all his serious, even noble, purpose, remained, until its destruction in 1941, a unique architectural curiosity. Nothing is more difficult than for one age wholly to recapture the spirit of another. While Nikon might revile his enemies and boast that he alone had recovered the true spirit of the Russian Church in his return to the pure Greek sources, his buildings, like those influenced by his reforms, were not wholly without contemporary feeling. The powerful verticality of the Church of the Twelve Apostles and the picturesque grandeur of the Church of the New Jerusalem belong

requirements. Their appearance, however, was profoundly affected by waves of European influence after the middle of the century. This can be seen in the treatment of the façade of the church as a series of storeys, already observed in the 'storeyed' wooden churches, as well as in the frequent and more consistent use of decorative details from western European architecture. An example of this so-called Moscow Baroque is the late-seventeenth-century church of St Nicholas of the Great Cross (1680–8, now demolished) [157], which was founded by a family of wealthy merchants. The tall, five-storeyed cube was approached by a flight of steps to an elegant vestibule. Although the triple division of the façades,

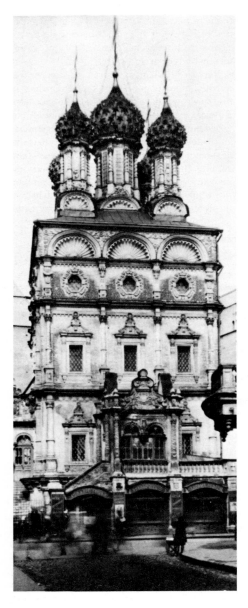

157. Moscow, Church of St Nicholas of the Great Cross (now demolished), 1680–8

crowned with arches, was a reminder of the traditional scheme, the treatment of the walls divided by engaged Corinthian columns supporting an entablature, the richly carved window-frames, and the scallop shells inserted in both zakomars and kokoshniki were evidence of the enthusiastic acceptance of the superficial innovations of the Baroque manner. Only the group of star-faceted cupolas on slender drums was left to remind the observer that this structure was not a secular building, but a church of the Orthodox rite.

The dynamic verticalism of the church to which the canonical cube opposed its static mass was not new in Russian architecture, but towards the close of the seventeenth century this verticality received a remarkable and characteristic expression in Moscow. No sooner had the canonical reform been accepted than it was ignored, for most characteristic of the 1680s and 90s and of the early years of the eighteenth century is a group of churches arranged either as a series of superimposed storeys of different shapes, or in the form of towers. It is of no little interest that these churches, which in so many ways represent the culmination of the Muscovite style, as it had developed from Kolomenskoe and St Basil, were also founded by the sovereign, his family, or his close friends.

A small urban example of this storeyed type was the Church of St Vladimir beside the Vladimir Gate of the Kitai-Gorod (the inner city to the east of the Kremlin in Moscow) [158], erected by Peter I in 1691–4 but since demolished. Upon a cubical base rested an octagonal upper storey covered with a dome-shaped roof, octagonal lantern, and cupola. The proportion of decoration to structure was admirable. The decorative elements, the window-frames, twisted colonnettes, even the spiky covering of the cupola and the spheres above the pediments, were placed with due regard for the contribution of each to the whole. The staccato silhouette would have been even livelier had not the outlines of the pediments been blurred by a protective tin

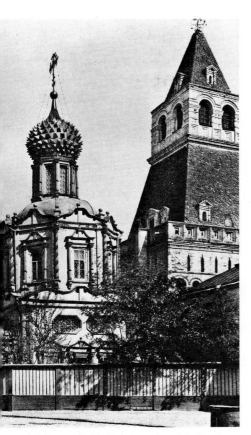

158. Moscow, St Vladimir (now demolished), 1691-4

covering. The author of this church was undoubtedly familiar with European Baroque design, but, like his predecessors long before in Kiev and Novgorod, he transformed alien ideas into something unmistakably his own. By 1690, when Baroque forms had been current in Moscow for several decades, this sense of design had become idiomatic. One can see this in the photograph where the Church of St Vladimir was completely in harmony with the huge medieval tower behind, itself a product of mixed Russian and Italian collaboration.

A most gracious as well as highly developed example of this type is the Intercession of the Virgin at Fili, formerly a village to the west of Moscow but now within the city limits [159, 160], built in 1690-3 by Prince Lev Kirillovich Naryshkin, Peter's uncle, whence the term 'Naryshkin Baroque' to describe the architecture of the last years of the century. The Intercession is perhaps the first Russian structure to realize on such a scale the three-dimensional spatial implications of the western European Baroque. Like so many of its predecessors, this church combines reminiscences from the past with the most recent innovations. Its general silhouette is not unlike the tower churches of the sixteenth century, especially Ostrov, where there occurs the same juxtaposition of lower subsidiary elements about a central tower. In another respect the wide gallery around the base recalls the gallery of the Ascension at Kolomenskoe, and the cupolas on the semicircular projections of the first storey are reminiscent of the clustered domes of St Basil. But the spirit, like the details, is new. An elegance and ease, a captivating gaiety in the play of white stone against dark red brick, foretell that lightening of the Baroque which would be present later in the work of Russia's most truly Rococo architect, Bartolommeo Rastrelli. Indeed, much of Rastrelli's best work can be thought of as closer in spirit to the more purely Russian church at Fili than to the European eighteenth-century styles by which he was also influenced.

Fili, like its predecessors, also illustrates the fundamental simplicity of much Russian church planning. A simple square is adjoined on four sides by semicircular ante-rooms. Externally the central cube rises one storey above the roofs of the circular projections. Upon it rests an octagon, above which a small open octagon serves as a belfry, and above that is a cupola on a slender octagonal drum. The window frames with their crested pediments, the carved ornament crowning each successive storey, and the crisp design of squares and points outlining the balustrades, are deftly related to the plain surfaces of the walls. Internally the space above the central nave

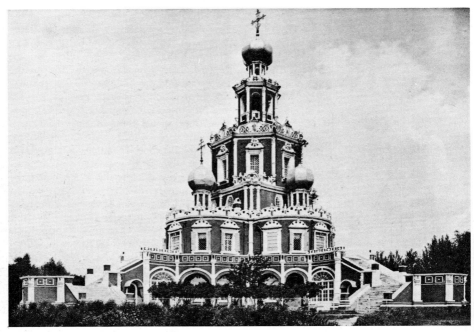

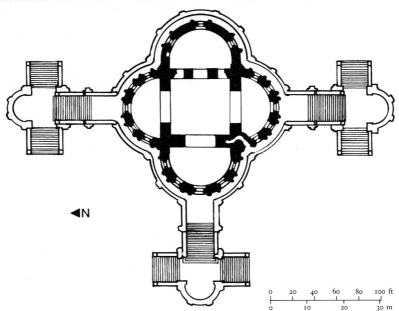

◄N

159 and 160 (*opposite page*). Fili, Church of the
Intercession of the Virgin, 1690–3, exterior and plan

161 and 162 (*right*). Dubrovitsy,
Church of the Virgin of the Sign (Znamenie),
1690–1704, exterior and interior

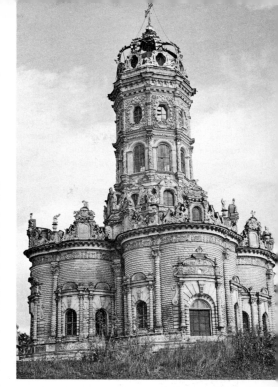

rises through the full height of the octagon, as
at Dyakovo and Kolomenskoe. As a true
Baroque building the church is situated in a
space through which the spectator must constantly move if he is to grasp the significance
of the whole, an effect due to the divided
staircases and to the tension set up at the
angles of the building by the opposition of the
protruding circular masses to the projecting
corners of the cube and the recessed sides of
the octagon.[8]

As an instance of the combination of European and older Russian forms the Intercession
at Fili is a singular example of success in a
field where Peter found himself beset by
difficulties. It is also interesting as evidence
that the world in which Peter came of age was
thoroughly impregnated with European ideas.
Peter's drastic 'reforms' were thus less self-
generated than fostered in him from boyhood
by the most advanced circles of Moscow
society. A further example of these tastes is
the contemporary Church of the Virgin of the
Sign at Dubrovitsy (1690–1704) [161, 162],
possibly built by a foreign architect for
Prince B. A. Golitsyn, Peter's tutor. Although
both descend from the same type of sixteenth-
century tower church, the contrast with Fili is
striking, and indicates how subtle was the balance attained there and how fraught with peril
was the problem for the Russian architect of
adapting western stylistic devices to older traditional forms. Dubrovitsy rather than Fili
may have persuaded Peter that only by breaking entirely with tradition could Russia move
forward into the future. Upon a plan much
like that of Fili, although with trefoil instead
of semicircular ante-rooms, rises a three-

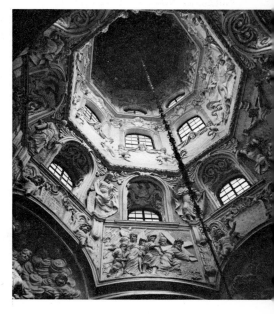

storeyed octagonal tower finished with an
open iron coronet. The church is so burdened
with carved ornament, including the sculptured
figures of saints, attributed to the German
sculptor Konrad Osner (1669–1747), that its
outlines are blurred; the separation of storeys
loses definition, and the eye is surfeited with
detail.

These Baroque tendencies did not disappear
from Moscow after Peter decided to turn his
people westward towards Europe, the sea, and
his new foundation of St Petersburg, although
with the growth of this city Moscow in the
course of the eighteenth century came to resemble a provincial capital living on the
memories of its past. The character of early-
eighteenth-century Moscow architecture can
be seen in the Church of the Archangel Gabriel (1701–7), known almost from the first as
the Menshikov Tower [163]. Prince Alexandr
Danilovich Menshikov (c. 1672–1729), Peter's
life-long friend and adviser, wanted to build a
church in the form of a tower which would
out-top all rivals, including the belfry of Ivan
Veliky in the Kremlin and the Sukharev
Tower erected by Peter himself (see below,
page 238). Menshikov entrusted the work to
the Ukrainian architect Ivan Petrovich Zarudny (died 1727) who constructed the church
as a tall tower composed of octagons rising
from superimposed cubes. Its resemblance both
to Fili and to Dubrovitsy, and to earlier sixteenth-century examples, was more one of
silhouette than of detail, for Zarudny embel-
lished his structure with more vigorous and
on the whole more correct Baroque elements. But the proportional discrepancy between the slender vertical elements and the
ponderous cornices, as well as the gigantic
scrolls flanking the west entrance, which resemble the carved and gilded wooden consoles
on contemporary iconostases, betray the book-
ish character of Zarudny's acquaintance with
European design. Unfortunately after 1711
Menshikov's attention was so taken up with
the construction of his new palace at Oranienbaum that he lost interest in his Moscow

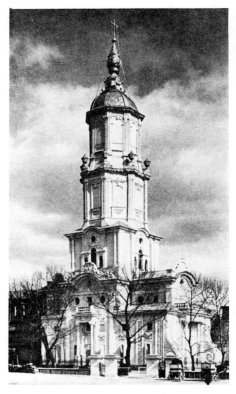

163. Ivan Petrovich Zarudny: Moscow,
Church of the Archangel Gabriel ('Menshikov
Tower'), 1701–7

'tower', even though he had raised it above all
its rivals. In 1723 the two upper octagons
burned with the loss of elaborate musical
clocks which Menshikov had imported from
England. Although the church was reconstructed in 1773 the upper storeys are apparently a meagre approximation of the original
ones.[9]

With the Menshikov Tower the last great
work of the Moscow Baroque had been
accomplished. Through the middle years of
the eighteenth century the Moscow architects
gradually evolved a compromise between their
own fanciful centralized tower churches and

the new Latin-cross plan which became fashionable in St Petersburg. For a time they still kept a storeyed tower over the crossing, but this gradually subsided into a single large dome shape which absorbed the octagon and rested directly on the crossing, itself the remnant of the earlier cube. Only the bell-tower at the western end of the church preserved the storeyed effect. It will be necessary later to return to Moscow to examine one or another exceptional structure, but the energies of Russia were so consumed in the creation of the splendid new city on the Neva that later Moscow architecture, like the architects themselves, is part of the currents set in motion in St Petersburg by Peter and his successors.[10]

CHAPTER 17

SECULAR ARCHITECTURE

The study of civil structures poses even more difficulties than that of religious architecture. Almost all domestic buildings earlier than the eighteenth century have been lost in the frequent fires which destroyed the older residential districts of most Russian towns and villages. From travellers' accounts we know that private houses were usually of wood, instantly burnt but quickly replaced from a supply of standardized materials kept in stock in the markets. The few surviving masonry structures indicate that secular buildings of the later Middle Ages, like those in western Europe, were essentially simple and functional and broken only by windows irregularly placed according to the interior arrangements and the need for light, a characteristic also of the Pskov churches of the period.[1] In plan the house consisted of a series of rooms, including large store-rooms, arranged en suite around a central courtyard, not unlike farms of the period. The most important group of surviving secular buildings are the fortifications and palaces of the Moscow Kremlin, which for political reasons were kept in better condition than the residences of even the wealthy boyars. But since repairs meant frequent rebuilding, especially after the fires of 1547 and 1571, and

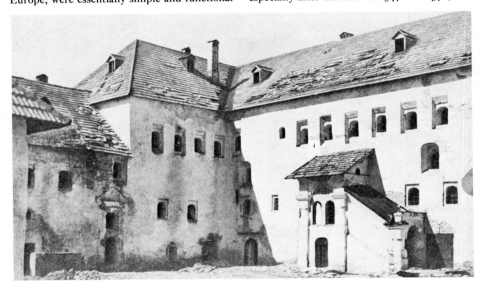

164. Pskov, Pogankin house, before restoration, late sixteenth or early seventeenth century

in plan. The Pogankin house in Pskov [164], a merchant's residence of the late sixteenth or early seventeenth century, shows severe stout walls unadorned with any architectural detail the Polish and French occupations of 1611 and 1812, the present Kremlin bears all the marks of the changing tastes of each successive age.[2]

Until 1367, when Dmitry Donskoy rebuilt

part of the walls in stone, the fortifications of the Kremlin, like those of most Russian cities, were of wood. Only Pskov and the Kremlin in Novgorod had masonry walls [165], and indeed the wooden walls around the city of Moscow can be seen as late as 1661 in the foreground of Meyerberg's drawing [166]. In 1451, during the Tartar attack, the enemy entered through the wooden sections, a fact which persuaded Ivan III to rebuild the walls of the Kremlin entirely in red brick. The work was commenced in 1485, under the direction of the Italian architect Pietro Antonio Solari, and was largely completed by 1516. Unfortunately no view of the Kremlin survives to show us the original appearance of the walls and towers, but since many visitors to Moscow commented on the Italian appearance of the fortress, we can perhaps assume that the Italian architects, with the help of Aristotele Fioravanti, created

and towers are remarkably Italianate. Solario devised an ingenious plan to bring order out of the existing confusion with a double, in part triple, system of walls and moats. These were excavated by a hydraulic engineer, Aloisio da Carcano, who also corrected the course of the stream which ran along the western side of the Kremlin.

During the Time of Troubles (1584–1613) the fortifications suffered severely, and in the course of the seventeenth century the upper parts of the towers were rebuilt in a variety of forms [167, 168]. In 1624–5 an English architect, Christopher Galloway, designed the upper part of the Gate of the Redeemer (Spasskiya Vorota) opposite St Basil on Red Square, and still the principal entrance to the Kremlin, in a fantastic style combining Gothic, Renaissance, and old Russian motifs. In an upper storey he inserted a clock, the largest piece of

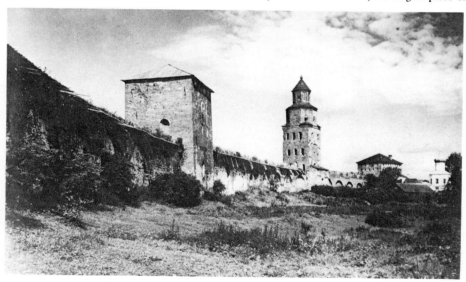

165. Novgorod, the fortifications of the Kremlin, fourteenth-sixteenth centuries

a system not unlike such contemporary fortresses of northern Italy as the castles of Milan and Ferrara. Certainly the robust, crenellated masses of the surviving portions of the walls

mechanical apparatus to be installed publicly in Russia. It was destroyed by fire in 1654, to the grief of the Tsar and the people. Other towers were crowned with peaked and tent-

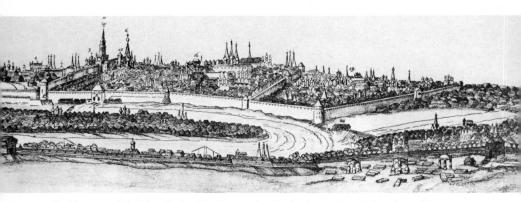

166. Moscow and the Kremlin in 1661. From a drawing by Augustin von Meyerberg. (The engraver neglected to reverse the drawing so that the view appears as a mirror image.
The Cathedral of St Basil, in Red Square near the Spassky Gate, the main entrance to the Kremlin, is indicated as no. 3)

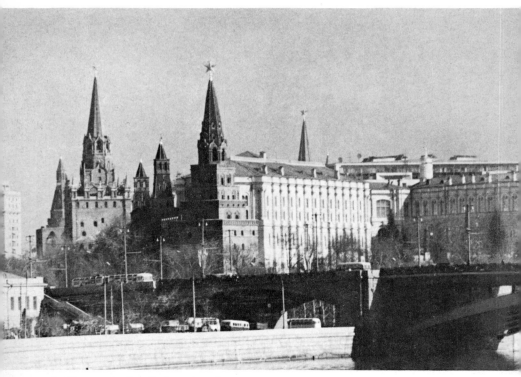

167. Moscow, the Kremlin in modern times

shaped roofs in the Russian manner, and at the end of the century the Borovitsky Tower was rebuilt as a series of diminishing square storeys in imitation of the Syumbeky Tower in Kazan, which, although ruined in 1552 and rebuilt in the seventeenth century, could be considered a rare surviving example of Tartar architecture.

After Ivan III had rebuilt the Cathedral of the Dormition, he turned to his own residence, which to his wife Sophia Palaeologa must have seemed far from adequate as a princely dwelling. At this time the palace was not a single building, but a group of small structures, principally of wood, although in some cases the foundations were of stone. The apartments of the Great Prince, his family, and the principal courtiers, were in the upper storeys. In

spite of subsequent rebuilding and much alteration, the present Kremlin palaces are still a group of buildings connected by terraces and staircases surrounding the site of the oldest church of the Kremlin, the Redeemer in the Wood. The replacement of wood by stone was gradually accomplished over a long period of time. Even in 1661 many log structures could still be seen within the walls.[3] Few of Ivan III's buildings remain, except the historic Faceted Palace (Granovitaya Palata), so called from its rusticated façade, which was built by Solari and Marco Ruffo between 1487 and 1491. This was a simple stone building, containing on the second storey a large rectangular hall, with a groined vault supported by a huge pier in the centre. The exterior walls were originally pierced by double-arched windows

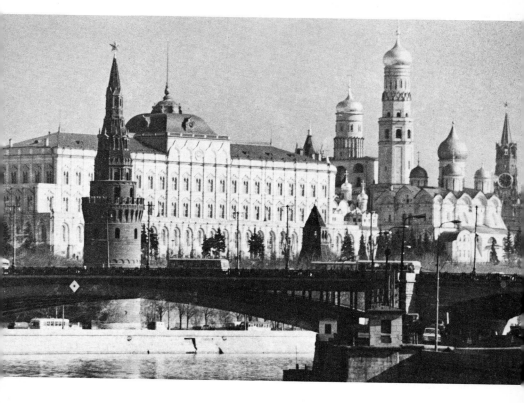

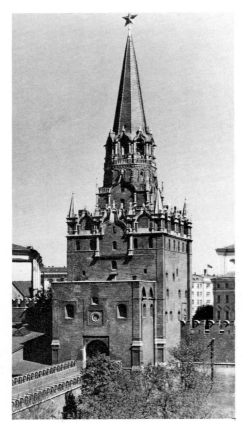

168. Moscow,
the Troitsky Tower of the Kremlin Wall,
1495–9. The stonework on the upper storeys
and tower was added in 1685

169 (*right*). The Palace Square in the Kremlin,
Moscow, 1672. The coronation procession of Mikhail
Romanov is represented entering the Cathedral of
the Dormition. In the background the rear of the
procession passes across the terrace from the
Granovitaya Palata through the Cathedral of the
Annunciation. Above the palace rise the peaked
roofs of the Terem. From the 'Book of the Election
. . . of Mikhail Romanov', 1672

Faceted Palace was due less to its architectural
character than to the fact that in the vaulted
hall the Tsar sat enthroned on state occasions
[170, 171]. Of all the rooms in the Kremlin it
was best known abroad through the reports of
the foreign ambassadors, who were here
granted an audience upon their arrival in
Moscow. It was also the scene of many notable
events in the nation's history, such as Ivan IV's
celebration of the capture of Kazan in 1552,
and Peter the Great's after the victory of Poltava in 1709.

The arrangement of the hall in the Granovitaya Palata as the throne-room of the Tsar
would seem to have been dictated by Sophia
Palaeologa, for certainly the protocol for the
reception of foreign ambassadors became increasingly Byzantine. The account by Augustin von Meyerberg, who was received by
Alexey Mikhailovich in 1661, is typical of such
a ceremony:

The hall was large enough, but in the centre was
a large column which supported the vault and
diminished its beauty very much. Old paintings were
on the walls, to which were attached silver plaques
between two windows. Around the room were
wooden benches built against the wall, covered with
carpets, and approached by four steps. Many boyars,
courtiers, and councillors and Dumni-Dorhanins

with smaller windows above, and two small
windows and doors opening into the store-
rooms on the ground floor [169]. The design
was very much like such early Renaissance
Italian palaces as the Palazzo Bevilacqua in
Bologna or the Palazzo dei Diamanti in Ferrara. The palace was altered in the seventeenth
century, when the arched windows were
replaced with square-headed openings in Renaissance frames. The importance of the

170 (*right*). The Vaulted Hall in the
Granovitaya Palata during an audience held by the
False Dmitry, early seventeenth century. From a
painting in the Budapest Museum. The floor is
covered with oriental rugs

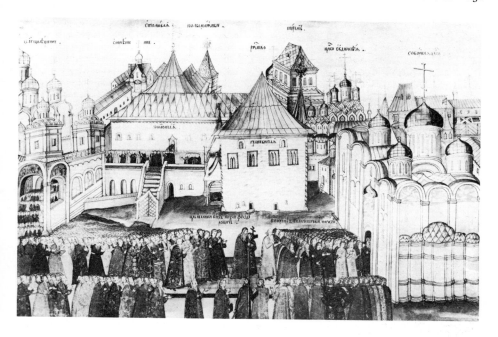

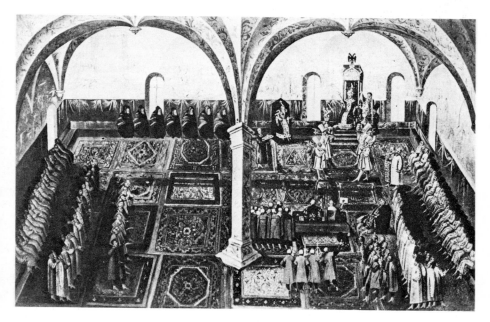

were seated on the right side of the Tsar, in all his state, and some of them on the left, everyone with his head uncovered. Not one deigned to honour us by a bow, neither on our entrance or departure. It was difficult to see the Tsar, seated on a silver-gilt throne, placed not in the centre but in the left corner of the hall between two windows. This throne was raised three steps above the steps of the councillors; but it was so narrow, and the obscurity of the room so diminished its splendour, that it did not look magnificent at all. In the centre and above the Tsar's head, hung an image of the Virgin Mother of God. Opposite, on the left, in the window was a clock in the shape of a tower, and in the other, which closed the corner of the wall, there was a silver pyramid supporting a golden orb. Higher, towards the vault,

profaned it with our lips when he presented it to us to kiss, since the Muscovites look upon us, and all who acknowledge the Roman Church as the Mother Church, as Pagans. He had on his head a sugar-loaf cap, edged with ermine, supporting a golden crown, ornamented with precious stones, which ended in a cross. He held his sceptre in his right hand.[4]

Burned and rebuilt after the fires of 1547 and 1571, the palace again suffered almost total devastation during the Polish occupation of the Kremlin. The palace or Terem,[5] which appears as a two-storey structure of Italianate design, resting on a base of earlier buildings, and crowned with a pavilion, the actual terem (chamber at the top of a house) [169, 172], was

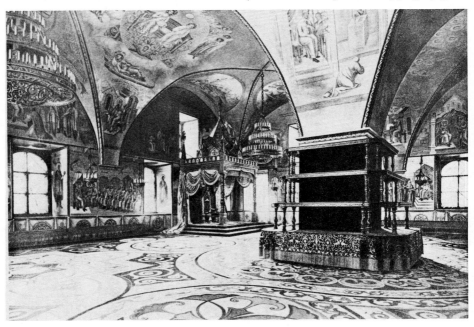

171. The Vaulted Hall in the Granovitaya Palata as restored in the nineteenth century. The throne and the shelves for displaying the imperial plate have since been removed

two images of saints were set out to be reverenced, hanging from the wall. And on a bench at the Tsar's right there was a basin, ewer, and towel, with which to wash and dry his right hand after we had

built by Tsars Mikhail Feodorovich and Alexey Mikhailovich, who had to reconstruct and redecorate the residential part of the palace. Under Alexey a host of craftsmen, principally from Poland, introduced a luxury hitherto unheard of in Russia. The walls were covered with gilded leather, the ceilings ornamented with precious metals, and new kinds of conveniences, doors and cupboards, bookcases and furniture from abroad, were installed [173]. In 1661 von Meyerberg noticed the Flemish and Persian tapestries which covered the walls of the state apartments so completely that neither the floor, walls, nor ceiling of the small rooms could be seen. The ceiling of the new dining room was decorated with a painting representing 'with astronomical accuracy the solar system and the fixed stars', an indication that modern science had pene-

Since his Majesty has been in Poland, and seen the Princes' houses there, and ghess'd at the mode of their Kings, his thoughts are advanced, and he begins to model his Court and Edifices more stately, to furnish his rooms with Tapestry, and contrive houses of pleasure abroad.[7]

The period of the greatest magnificence of the Kremlin Palace immediately preceded its almost complete decline. During the regency of Sophia, sister of Peter the Great (1682–9), it was redecorated by her favourite, Prince Golitsyn, following a fire in 1682. Inside and out the buildings were painted, the walls were hung with tapestries, and the rooms were filled with elaborate furniture and objects in silver

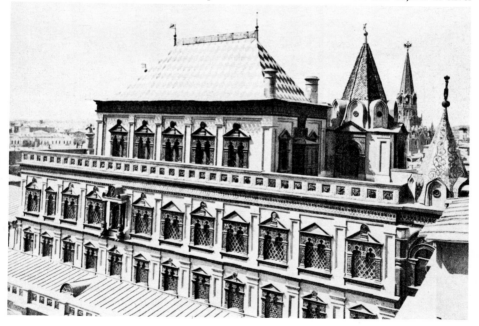

172. Moscow, the Terem Palace in the Kremlin, 1635–6

trated even the Tsar's private apartments.[6]

The English traveller Samuel Collins, who was in Russia in 1660–9, remarked on the Tsar's taste:

and gold. Much of this was of western manufacture, and had been obtained by Golitsyn from traders in the German suburb.

With the removal of the seat of government

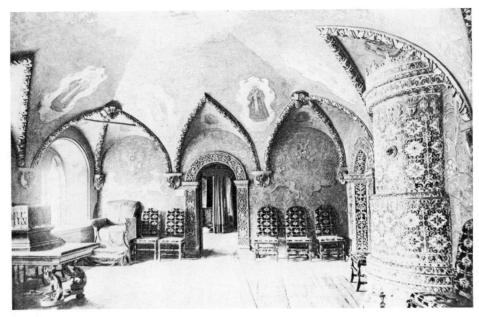

173. Moscow, the Terem Palace in the Kremlin, 1635–6

to St Petersburg, the palaces were allowed to deteriorate to a shocking degree. Frequent fires and neglect contributed to their ruin, and they were only patched up temporarily and in a most makeshift fashion, when the sovereign visited Moscow for his coronation or marriage.

Catherine II, who had a stronger sense of Russian tradition than any of the lineal heirs of Peter the Great, ordered the palace to be kept in better repair, and even proposed transforming the whole Kremlin into a national shrine by the construction of a new colossal palace enclosing the old buildings on all sides (see below, pages 297–9). Happily, this was never done, but the palace continued to suffer through several fires, the French occupation of 1812, the building of the new Great Palace by Ton (1838–49) for Nicholas I on the site of several of the older state apartments (the large building in the centre of illustration 167),

and the somewhat drastic methods of restoration practised in the nineteenth century. The latter spoiled the most conspicuous structure in the Kremlin, Ivan Veliky ('John the Great') [174], the tall belfry above the Church of St John, begun by Tsar Feodor Ivanovich and completed in 1600 by Boris Godunov. This and the tower and cupola above the adjacent Church of St Nicholas are noteworthy for their height, rising as they do from the highest point of ground in Moscow, but they are of little architectural interest. The upper storeys of both were destroyed in 1812 and rebuilt soon after in a flat approximation of their original appearance.

The Kremlin – the principal point of interest in Moscow – as a congeries of buildings built at various times, of different sizes and axial relationships, created a picturesque effect which could not fail to impress the foreign

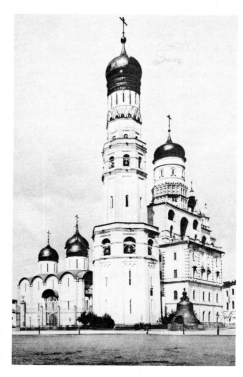

174. Moscow,
the Tower of Ivan Veliky in the Kremlin,
late sixteenth century

175. Model of the 1760s of the wooden palace at
Kolomenskoe, built in 1667–81

visitor [169]. Often he had no other word to describe this effect than 'eastern' or 'oriental'.[8] A view taken by the French draughtsman André Durand (1807–67), who visited Russia in 1839, proves how the Kremlin affected the romantic imagination [285]. Durand has impossibly exaggerated the height of the towers, and so accentuated the contrast of this group of buildings with anything in western Europe.

The most important evidence for the appearance of a Russian palace of the Muscovite period is the wooden model [175] made for Catherine II when she ordered the demolition of the dilapidated old timber palace at Kolomenskoe, on the outskirts of Moscow.[9] This had been at intervals a favourite country residence of the Great Princes and Tsars from the time of Ivan Kalita to the accession of Peter the Great. Between 1667 and 1681 it had been rebuilt by Tsar Alexey and his son Feodor Alexeevich, and had come to resemble a small village composed of many separate buildings [176]. Indeed, to judge by the model, it was like a gigantic dictionary of all the architectural terms invented by the Russian carpenters. Bochki, kokoshniki, tent roofs, bulbous domes, and all the variety of turned and carved woodwork have been preserved in the model. Only the original colour which lent the buildings an unworldly fairy-tale character has not been recorded, except in travellers' tales. Yet the accumulation and diversities did not produce any functional confusion. As each

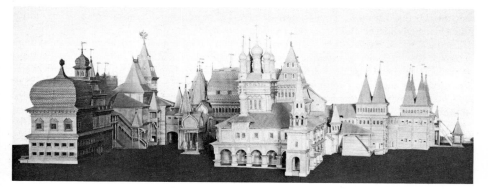

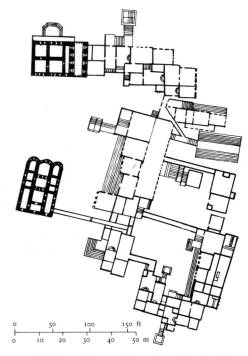

0   50   100   150 ft

0   10   20   30   40   50 m

176. Kolomenskoe, wooden palace, 1667–81, plan

part was added it took its place around a rectangular courtyard divided roughly in two by a bridge-like passage on the first-storey level. Various outbuildings, including the chapel, did not disturb this harmony, so characteristic of the Russian architects' ability to create variety from the simplest elements.

Externally the most picturesque dispersion prevailed, for the rectangular structures were so situated at angles one to another that the whole conglomeration presented a constantly shifting arrangement when seen from any point. To this effect the multitudinous roof-shapes and the uneven height of the different storeys contributed not a little. Since such an assemblage afforded the greatest contrast to the regularly aligned, box-like izbas in the vil-

lage streets, it is apparent that the effect achieved at Kolomenskoe was less accidental than intentional, and so may be related to the prevailing tendency to manipulate forms to achieve a play of masses moving in space, of light twisting and flickering over the agitated surfaces. The picturesque quality of the palace at Kolomenskoe was not the accidental result of a nostalgic vision of a vanished past, but a vital, creative contribution to Russian art. The palace was to have, however, quite another history in the art of Russia. Its physical destruction together with its sentimental preservation in the model and many drawings [177] is typical of an eighteenth-century rationalist attitude towards such clutter combined with the first stirrings of a romantic respect for the past.

By the end of Alexey's reign the Kolomenskoe Palace may have seemed old-fashioned, and more appropriate as a country house than as a truly palatial residence. It is even possible that the decision to reconstruct it may have been prompted by the desire of the first Romanov Tsars to assert the continuity of the new dynasty with their sixteenth-century predecessors. Certainly during the seventeenth century brick and stone palaces became more and more the custom. Olearius mentioned the 'very fair Palace of stone, according to the Italian architecture, for the young Prince', which he had seen in the Kremlin in 1634. But he added that 'the Great Duke [Tsar Mikhail] continues still in his wooden Palace, as being more healthy than stone structures'.[10]

Mikhail himself had been born in a 'stone structure' in Moscow, the so-called House of the Boyar Romanov, which was rediscovered and restored by order of Alexander II in 1858. Its condition was so ruinous and the restorations so drastic that it was more interesting as an example of the revival of Russian forms in the nineteenth century than as a source for the study of earlier architecture. Similar restorations have changed the character of the other few remaining seventeenth-century

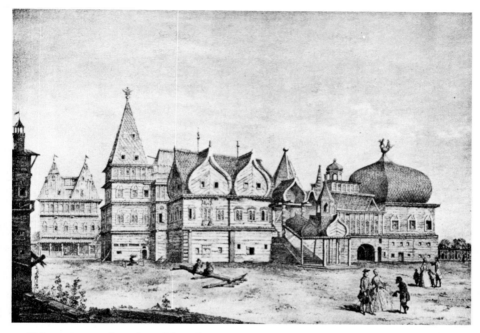

177. Kolomenskoe, wooden palace, eighteenth-century engraving

palaces and town houses such as the Yusupov Palace (formerly the Volkhov residence), and the library in the courtyard of the Synodal Printing Office (Sinodalnaya Tipografiya).[11] A more trustworthy source for the appearance of these structures is Augustin von Meyerberg's drawing of the palace set aside for the use of the foreign embassies in Moscow, as he saw it in 1661 [178].[12] What we can see beneath the superficial picturesqueness and the complicated mass is important for architectural history. Here, as at Kolomenskoe, the building had grown gradually through the years as rooms were added when they were needed. The additions were of two kinds. Some of wood, one or more storeys in height, were of traditional timber construction; others were stone buildings, more elaborately designed and often influenced by European architecture. Such is the windowed gallery

over an arcade in the square block beside the entrance, with quoins and a heavy cornice in the Renaissance taste. Meyerberg's attention was naturally attracted more by the unfamiliar than by the forms he knew at home, so that he exaggerated such typically Russian masonry forms as the stumpy columns and the staircases covered with tent roofs such as are known to have existed in the Kremlin at this time. Paul of Aleppo may have had some such building in mind when he wrote:

The palaces in this city are mostly new, of stone or brick; and built on the European plan, lately taught the Muscovites by the Nemtsas, or Germans. We gaped with astonishment at their beauty and the multitude of their windows, and of the sculptured pillars on every side of them; the height of their storeys, as though they were castles.[13]

The Ambassadors' Palace represents a critical period in the history of Russian architecture.

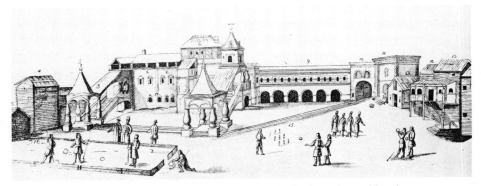

178. Moscow, the Ambassadors' Palace in 1661. From a drawing by Augustin von Meyerberg

In a sense we may say that in it the traditional elements, the wooden chambers and tent roofs, were gradually being relegated to the periphery, as the masonry core of the building more and more approached the European type. Many years before this Moscow had known a thoroughly European building, if we may trust the drawing of the Foreign Office (Posolsky Prikaz), erected in the Kremlin in 1591, made by Erik Palmquist, a Swedish engineer, in 1674. The ground-floor arcades, elaborately framed windows, and sculptured attic are so thoroughly in the Italian taste, reminding one of the sixteenth-century work of Sansovino in Venice, that the authorship of an Italian architect must be assumed. Beside it in Palmquist's drawing another building is under construction. The profiles of the bases of the tall pilasters also show considerable knowledge of European architecture.[14]

The Foreign Office was an early example of the direction which Russian architecture was to take. Towards the end of the seventeenth century the progress of western influence in Muscovy is demonstrated in the building of the State Pharmacy [179], later the County Office, in Moscow, on the site of the present Historical Museum.[15] This two-storey structure, in which the first Russian university was established in 1755, was a simple block-like mass broken only by a third storey over the central portion of the side façade. This in turn supported a typical late-seventeenth-century tower composed of two octagons on a cube. The architectural ornament was remarkably European, especially the windows provided with columns and curved pediment, the giant order of engaged columns on tall bases, and the entablature of triglyphs and metopes running around the entire structure. The Sukharev Gate and Tower (1692–5) was a similar construction, of three storeys surmounted by a taller tower, and with arched loggias in the Italian taste. This had been erected by the Moscow architect M. I. Tschoglokov for Peter I in commemoration of the loyalty of the Sukharev Regiment during the Streltsy uprising of 1682. Peter devoted the building to scientific purposes; here the first Russian school of navigation was held, the first Russian naval maps prepared, and important astronomical observations performed. In the nineteenth century the tower was used as a reservoir, but the whole building has since been demolished.[16]

More influential was the continuous building activity in the German Suburb (Nemetskaya Sloboda) on the eastern outskirts of Moscow. By the end of the century this region, populated entirely by foreign diplomats and merchants, was one-fifth the total size of the capital. In an early-eighteenth-century en-

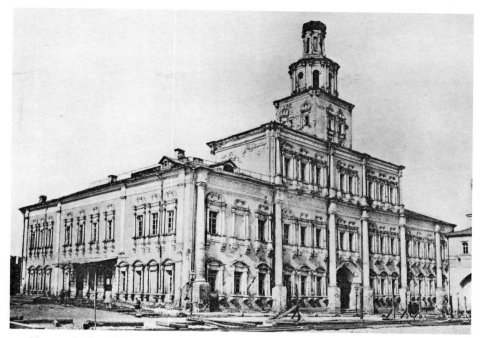

179. Moscow, the State Pharmacy (now demolished), late seventeenth century

graving by Hendrik de Witt [180] it looks more like a European town than a suburb of Moscow.[17] On one side of the river Yauza were the residences of the less affluent merchants, mostly two-storeyed brick or wooden houses standing neatly along the banks of the river. The steep gables and prim rows of trees tell of Dutch and German influence. On the opposite side of the river were the residences of the wealthier members of the community. In contrast to the crowded conditions in Moscow and the haphazard distribution of the palaces in the Kremlin, everything here was in order. The palaces and larger houses were in the European manner, two- and three-storeyed buildings, rectangular in plan, fitted with larger glass windows, and decorated with engaged columns, pilasters, and cornices. Even the grounds were arranged as European gar-

dens with avenues, pavilions, orchards, fountains, pools, and topiary work. Conspicuous among them was the palace Peter I built for his favourite, the Swiss adventurer François Lefort (1656–98).[18] The original building of 1697–9 seems to have been in the style of the Moscow Baroque, but in 1707, after Peter had given the palace to Menshikov, it was completely rebuilt by Giovanni Maria Fontana (in Russia 1703–8), in the late academic phase of the European Baroque. This was Peter's first large building in the modern style, and he used it for banquets and other state occasions. At the end of the eighteenth century it was again rebuilt by M. F. Kazakov. Of Fontana's work the entrance gate survives in the form of a triumphal arch with doubled pilasters beneath a low broad pediment. The building now houses the historical archives of the war department.

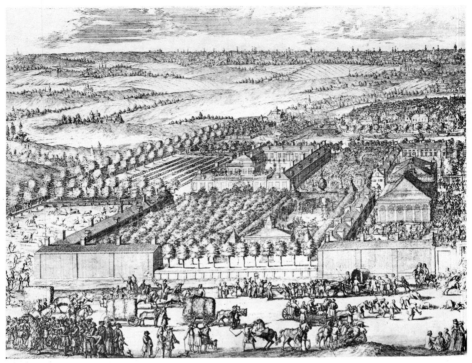

180. The German district on the outskirts of Moscow, *c.* 1700.
From an engraving by Hendrik de Witt (1671–1716)

The effect of the German Suburb on Russian culture turned out to be the very opposite of its purpose. The tsars had thought to relegate the dreaded foreigners to a quarter of their own, whence their improper customs and heretical ideas could not penetrate the citadel of orthodoxy. Actually the suburb proved so interesting to the higher nobility that it exercised an inescapable fascination over the younger generation. Here Peter learned his first lessons in European architecture; here he performed his first experiments in building; here he laid the plans for the new city he would later build by the sea.

CHAPTER 18

THE BEGINNING OF MODERN PAINTING: MOSCOW

1550–1700

The Viskovaty episode and the decisions of the Stoglav were not the only conspicuous incidents in the course of the long theological and political crisis which was to change the character of Russian art between 1550 and the end of the seventeenth century. So long as the State had needed the help of the Church against the Tartars, the Great Prince and the Metropolitan had shared the responsibility and authority of power. With the decline of the Tartar menace after 1450 and the fall of Constantinople the Prince considered himself an independent sovereign, while the Metropolitan of Moscow claimed his rights as head of the only independent Orthodox Church. If the State were to remain theocratic, the Tsar must submit to the decisions of the Metropolitan and Patriarch. But after 1589 the problem changed. If the State were to become an effective political and economic expression of the destinies of the Russian people, the Church must accept the political consequences. Three spectacular events marked the difficult adjustment of these problems. In 1568 the Metropolitan Philip, who had courageously denounced Ivan IV's savage cruelty, was deposed, imprisoned, and assassinated by the Tsar's orders. At the close of the Time of Troubles in 1613, however, a new working arrangement was reached, when Mikhail, son of the Metropolitan Philaret (Feodor Romanov), was elected Tsar (1613–45). In order that his father should not suffer any loss of prestige, Philaret was consecrated Patriarch in 1620 and honoured with the title of co-Tsar, so that theoretically if not actually the theocratic State was re-established. This harmonious relationship between Tsar and Patriarch persisted into the reign of Mikhail's son,

Alexey (Alexis) Mikhailovich (1645–76). As a young man Alexey deeply admired the Patriarch Nikon, but only so long as the priest recognized the authority of the Tsar.[1] When Nikon offended a large part of the faithful by his arrogance and stubborn insistence on correcting the church books, Alexey finally consented to the calling of the Assembly of 1666 which deposed Nikon and exiled him to a monastery. This was the last conflict between the Church and the temporal power. When Peter I allowed the office of patriarch to lapse after the death of Adrian in 1700, there was no one to protest.

Throughout this period the painters of Russia were obliged to work out a new iconography and new technique with which to express a theological system of the world wherein the conflicting claims of State and Church could be approximately resolved. They could no longer 'be faithful to the consecrated type'. The saints and scenes of the older icons had referred to the historical realities of the past; the mystical and doctrinal subjects of the sixteenth and seventeenth centuries were attempts to express the realities of the immediate present, among which was the fear of heresy in the western Russian lands, where Catholic and Lutheran ideas easily entered from Poland and Germany. The search for new means of expression was also complicated by the rise of a new class of patrons. In the earlier Middle Ages there had been only one kind of painting. To be sure, it had been executed under the supervision of the Church, but it had been intended for and had been used by the whole people. After the middle of the sixteenth century there emerged public painting, intended largely as propaganda for the State, and private painting made for individuals and reflecting their own special interests.

The opportunity for a revision of artistic production occurred accidentally early in Ivan IV's personal reign when the fire of 1547 devastated Moscow. The arrival of large numbers of craftsmen from Novgorod and Pskov, and the conditions of their work, led to the organization of the first government workshops for icon-painting, which in time became an important branch of the Treasury. They were established in the Armoury (Oruzheinaya Palata) in the Kremlin, and to the leaders were assigned the conservation and execution of all old and new painting in the churches and public buildings of Moscow. So great was the demand for icons, especially after the Time of Troubles, that numerous painters from the provinces were pressed into the government service. From the fact that the best of these painters worked exclusively for the Tsar and his family, came the terms 'Tsar's workshop' and 'Tsar's taste' for the superior icons of the earlier seventeenth century.[2]

The government workshops were in effect the first State art schools in Russia. Ancient icons and other materials were collected for the guidance of young painters who were instructed in their craft. Art became a function of government, and in this sense the decisions of the Stoglav and subsequent Church councils can be considered official attempts to regularize the production of art objects and bring it more and more under the control of the central power. The Stoglav's injunction to the painters to follow prescribed models was more forcibly restated in 1658: 'he who shall paint an icon out of his imagination shall suffer endless torment'.

A further definition of the relations between art and the State could perhaps be obtained from the important fresco cycles of the later sixteenth century, if more than verbal descriptions of them now remained. After rebuilding the Kremlin palace Ivan IV had the principal state apartment, the Golden Room,

painted with a series of frescoes wherein spiritual and secular symbols, spiritual and temporal powers, were strangely intermingled. The complicated cycle, probably prepared by the Priest Sylvester, commenced in an anteroom with a series of didactic pictures related to the preparation of the young Tsar for his duties (Ivan, born in 1530, had become Tsar at the age of three). Among the subjects were 'The Wise Son is the Mother's and Father's Joy', 'The Fear of God is the Beginning of Wisdom', and 'The Heart of the Tsar is in the Hand of God'. In the hall itself a sequence of Old Testament subjects – the first time such scenes had been painted on such a scale in Russia – included ten pictures of the battles and victories of Joshua, perhaps inspired by Ivan's conquest of Kazan in 1552. These were countered by scenes from Russian history, 'The Baptism of Vladimir', 'The Destruction of the Idols', 'The Deeds of Vladimir Monomakh', 'The Story of Boris and Gleb'. On the vaults and by the windows were presented the princes of the Rurik dynasty. Higher still a more religious symbolism prevailed in the painting of Christ as Emmanuel with symbols of the Evangelists and the gates of Heaven and Hell. But even here the intrusion of a secular concept of morality appeared in the allegorical figures of Virtues and Vices, an embracing cosmology of Sun, Moon, and Earth, with signs of the seasons and the elements.[3]

Such a programme, with its elaborate literary content, was not arrived at by accident; it was the expression of the Tsar's conviction that he was the head of both Church and State. Of special importance in this interpretation were the unusually extensive scenes from Russian history. No one, seeing them beside the Old Testament subjects, could doubt whence came the spiritual authority of the Russian Church. This identification of Church and State was worked out in another way in the Cathedral of the Dormition in Sviyazhsk, near Kazan, where frescoes of 1558, undoubtedly the work of Moscow painters, unfold the history of the Creation and Redemption with particular attention to scenes and characters on earth, including another lengthy series of Old Testament episodes. The association of the temporal power with the world order was made clear in life-size portraits of Ivan IV and the Metropolitan Macarius among the holy personages, the first time in Russian painting that historical and contemporary personalities had occupied such prominent positions.[4]

Another series of frescoes was executed in the principal chamber of the Faceted Palace for Boris Godunov, when he was regent for Ivan's feeble son, Feodor I. Here was the same combination of biblical episodes, moralizing parables, and allegorical figures, with even more emphasis on Russian history. Nor could the political aspect be overlooked; in the midst was the representation of the reigning 'Tsar, Feodor Ivanovich sitting on a golden throne. . . . At the right side of the throne stands the regent Boris Godunov . . . and beside him stand the boyars. . . . Above them the palace, and beside the palace the cathedral church'.[5]

While an art so expressive of centralized control was being defined in Moscow, elsewhere a new and entirely private art, likewise not immune from secular tendencies, was being developed by the so-called 'Stroganov Masters'. When Novgorod declined after 1470 many of the more energetic citizens migrated to the Novgorod territories in north-eastern Russia. Here in the course of the sixteenth century the members of the Stroganov family laid the foundations of a great fortune through the exploitation of salt-mines along the tributaries of the northern Dvina. They founded towns and villages, and through their efforts such remote villages as Perm, Veliky Ustiug, and Solvychegodsk became for a time important commercial and cultural centres. In the latter city, where the principal members of the Stroganov family made their home, churches and palaces arose comparable to those of Novgorod or Moscow.[6] So successful were the Stroganovs that they were among the principal

financiers supporting Ermak's conquest of Siberia in 1582, and during the Time of Troubles they were asked to lend money to Tsar Vasily Shuisky. Throughout the seventeenth century they bore the title of 'eminent personages' and until the end of the empire as the Counts Stroganov they maintained in their palaces in St Petersburg their reputation as connoisseurs and collectors of Russian art.

Two members of the family – the cousins Maxim Yakovlevich (c. 1550–1623) and Nikita Grigorievich (c. 1550–1619) – were unusually interested in art. They were themselves painters, and patronized the best artists they could find. Thus it is that a number of signed and dated icons from the last years of the sixteenth century and the first of the seventeenth, with inscriptions indicating that they were executed for the Stroganovs, have given rise to the supposition that there was a separate Stroganov school.[7] And since many of these icons are of the finest quality, superior to contemporary works of the Moscow school, many excellent icons of the earlier seventeenth century have without further justification been ascribed to the Stroganov painters. The fact, however, that several of the painters who worked for the Stroganovs are also known to have been active in Moscow, and even in the Tsar's workshops, indicates the danger of considering the so-called Stroganov school as much an entity as the school of Novgorod. Indeed, over a period so many different influences can be detected within the 'Stroganov' icons that the title may best be used to describe a kind of icon rather than a style of painting.

In the first place, the signed and dated icons painted for the Stroganovs themselves, and those which can be related to them, are the first examples of Russian icons executed in quantity for private persons. In their size, iconography, and technique they exemplify the tastes of wealthy and artistically sensitive individuals. These icons are small, to be held in the hand, of surpassing technical refinement, and were intended for private rather than public religious experience [181]. The

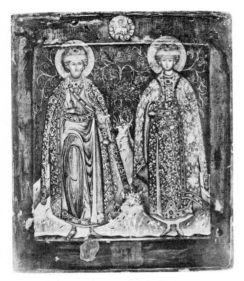

181. Follower of Prokopy Chirin (Stroganov School): SS. Boris and Gleb, seventeenth century. *Leningrad, Russian Museum*

brilliant colours, the lavish use of gold, and the exquisite draughtsmanship are such as would appeal to patrons who wanted to cherish them as works of art as well as venerate them as religious objects.

Like the Moscow painters, the Stroganov masters drew from the fund of expressive means common to the sixteenth-century followers of Dionisy, and to that extent are related to the history of painting in Moscow. The Novgorod origin of the Stroganovs themselves, and of the other families of merchants and industrialists who settled in northern Russia, perhaps accounts for the finer draughtsmanship and brighter colours. In this sense the Stroganov icons can be considered a last and brilliant product of the Novgorod schools of the Middle Ages. But since to such stylistic character they added a new interpretation of religious subjects, we must recognize that they also belong to the history of painting in central Russia in the later sixteenth

century, in this time of the struggle between Tsar and Patriarch, and that they supply a most important element which had so far been neglected in the controversy, namely painting for the private client rather than for public propaganda.

Nor was their influence strictly confined to northern Russia. With the disruptions of the Time of Troubles, during which not only Moscow but Solvychegodsk itself was plundered in 1613 by the Poles, the Stroganov painters were scattered, and many found their way south. After 1613, when Tsar Mikhail Feodorovich began to repair the devastated cultural pattern of Muscovite Russia, he, like Ivan IV in 1547, was obliged to summon icon-painters from other centres, this time the north and west, and in this way many of the Stroganov masters, voluntarily or against their will, arrived in Moscow and were incorporated in the Tsar's workshops, where they were gradually absorbed into the Moscow school.

It is ironic that from this period more signed and dated icons have survived, and more masters are known by name, than for any earlier period in Russian painting. Yet for all this wealth of factual information, this demonstration of the emergence of the individual from the anonymity of the Middle Ages, there is no corresponding variety of personal expression. In this there can perhaps be seen the result of the centralization of icon-painting as a government industry. Among these painters, one of the first to find a style of his own was Prokopy Chirin, to whom may be attributed the left wing of a small, portable deesis [182], of which the centre and right wing were painted by another well-known master, Nikifor Savin. The work of Chirin, who was active in Moscow from 1620 to about 1642, exemplifies some of the most characteristic traits of the transition period between the old styles of Novgorod and Moscow and the new painting of the Romanov period. The figure drawing is firm, the facial expression forceful, and there is clearly the intention of a devotional manner. Yet there is also a conscious aes-

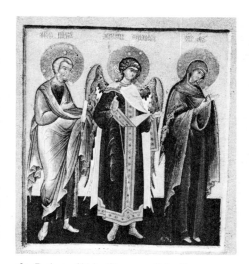

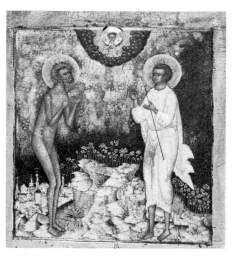

182. Prokopy Chirin (Stroganov School):
The Virgin, St Michael, and St Paul,
left wing of a small deesis, *c.* 1620.
Moscow, Tretyakov Gallery

183. Stroganov School:
SS. Vasily Blazhenny and Artemy Verkolsky,
c. 1620–30. *Moscow, Tretyakov Gallery*

theticism in the refinement of the drawing, in the svelte forms caressed by gold washes and in the gentleness, even gentility, of the faces. All these modifications of the older religious painting became more marked in one of the most familiar types of early-seventeenth-century icon, the one depicting a saint standing in an attitude of prayer. In the first place the three-quarter position of the saint immediately established a spatial relationship between the figure and its surroundings which was further developed in the landscape backgrounds. And to this interest in a specific place and time was added a new concern with the introspective psychological experience of the figure itself. This is seen even in the portrait-like faces. Each saint was no longer an impersonal means through which the worshipper gained access to divinity, but was himself actively engaged in worship, and subject to the same doubts and hesitations as the spectator. In this way a more humanistic spirit entered icon-painting, undoubtedly influenced by innumerable cur-

rents of western art and thought which reached Russia after the introduction of printing in 1552 and the importation and publication of religious books. It is also worth recalling that the region of the northern Dvina, where the first Stroganov icons were created and where many of the elements of this style were developed, lay along the main trade route between Moscow and Arkhangelsk on the White Sea, the port of entry for foreign traders.

The icon of SS. Vasily Blazhenny and Artemy Verkolsky [183] was painted for a member of the Stroganov family in the third decade of the century, and has the characteristically precious technique and refined expression. The saints themselves are also typical of a private attitude towards religion, for they were relatively new to iconography. Vasily Blazhenny, an 'enthusiast' and ascetic, spurned the comforts of civilization. His unclothed figure offered Russian artists one of their few opportunities to paint the nude.

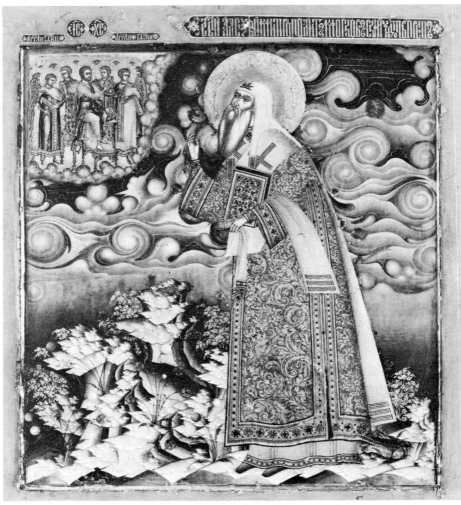

184. Moscow, the Tsar's workshop: St Alexey, Metropolitan of Moscow, *c.* 1640.
Moscow, Tretyakov Gallery

The landscape of this icon, with a distant view of a Russian city to the left, is another proof of the new naturalism growing up within the strictest observance of iconic rules. Although the mountains are still shelf-like terraces, the plants which grow along the ridges are drawn with considerable sympathy for nature and for the infinite variations in the shapes of living things. Yet there is also a feeling for their arrangement as a decorative pattern, seen for instance in the sky, where the clouds, themselves evidence of a new understanding of weather and time, are represented as tight little shell-like scrolls. The decorative element in these icons, taken together with the abundance of gold and the miniature technique, suggests that some new oriental influences entered Russian painting at this time. This would not have been unlikely. Although books and pictures were gradually filtering in from the West, from 1550 to 1667, the East was yet far more accessible. Poland and Lithuania still blocked Russian expansion to the West and were engaged in war with Moscow. An icon of St Alexey [184], the fourteenth-century Metropolitan of Moscow, by one of 'the Tsar's painters', illustrates how East and West met in Russian painting. The decorative pattern woven in the garments, the gold-washed mountains and the swirling clouds compel one to believe that the painter had some knowledge of Oriental art, that somehow a Chinese painting of the Sung Dynasty had reached Russia by the overland route from the East. Yet much about the icon tells of the westernizing tendencies of these years, the stooping figure of the aged Metropolitan, his expression so full of pathos and an intensity impossible to realize within the older canons of painting.

It should be noted that many of the so-called Stroganov icons, while small and square and executed with scrupulous attention to the smallest detail, are nevertheless not at all crowded. An appropriate balance between the infinitely small and the design as a whole was maintained until the middle of the century, when the concern of the Moscow school for complicated literary and doctrinal subjects overwhelmed the earlier and simpler compositions. The result was a kind of painting which fascinates by the multiplicity of its parts, as in the Christ Enthroned surrounded by twenty-eight miniature scenes from His life [185], but which nevertheless has lost much of the earlier power to persuade on other than purely technical grounds. The complicated iconography of such subjects as the Creed or the Lord's Prayer [186] supplied the skilled but more

pedestrian painters with unheard-of opportunities to demonstrate their virtuosity. Visitors to Russia have never failed to wonder at such icons. As early as the mid seventeenth century Archdeacon Paul declared that

The abilities of the painters who are found in [Moscow] are without parallel on the face of the earth, for their masterliness, the delicacy of their pencil, and their subtlety of art, in making small pictures, of every Saint or Angel, of the size of a pea . . . to the great astonishment of the beholder. We remarked, among the rest, a small picture, with three covers or lids . . .; the figures of the Angels in it were grouped as numerously as a swarm of flies, and with such precision and colouring as to make one grieve that the painter should ever die. . . . As to the paintings of the Nativity, the Resurrection, the Sufferings of Our Lord and his Miracles, and the Portrait of the Trinity, it is impossible for the intellect of man ever to comprehend all their devices, or to appreciate the excellence of their workmanship.[8]

This addiction to small detail was one solution to the dilemma confronting the Russian painter in the middle of the seventeenth century, the problem of how to express in terms of icons the enormous resources of the world of experience and imagination, which the enlarged iconographical programmes of the Church as well as the expanding intellectual horizons of Russia revealed to him. He might try to encompass this wealth of sensation and idea within his traditional technique, or, forgoing the attempt to express in one painting the whole world, he might concentrate on one aspect of it and exploit his visual impressions in the western manner. He stood to lose as much as he could hope to gain, for in the opposition of the irreconcilable elements of old forms and new content, of ancient themes and

185 (*left overleaf*). Yaroslavl: Christ Enthroned, with scenes from His life, later seventeenth century.
Yaroslavl, Museum

186. (*right overleaf*) Moscow: The Lord's Prayer, late seventeenth century.
Leningrad, Russian Museum

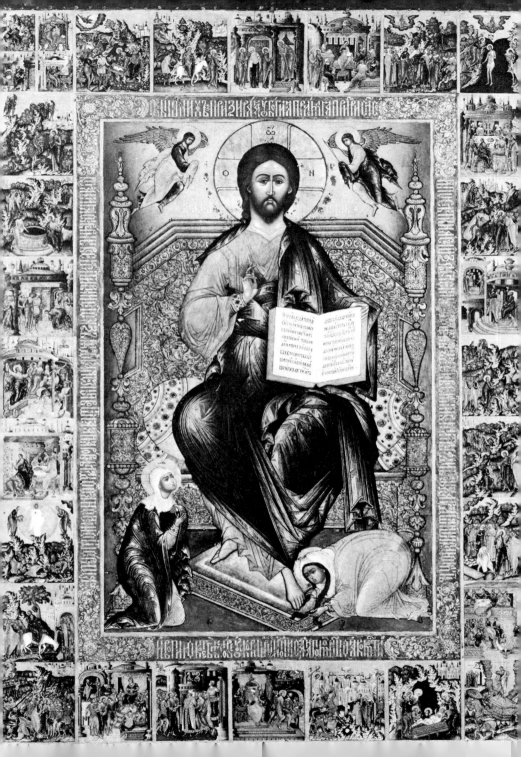

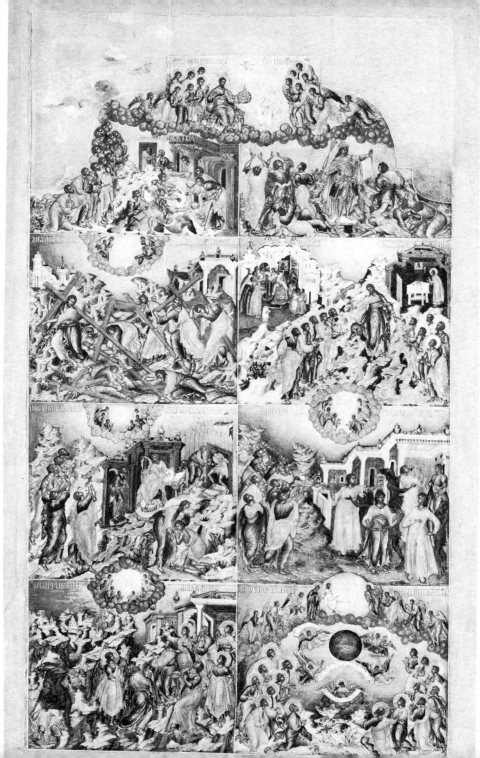

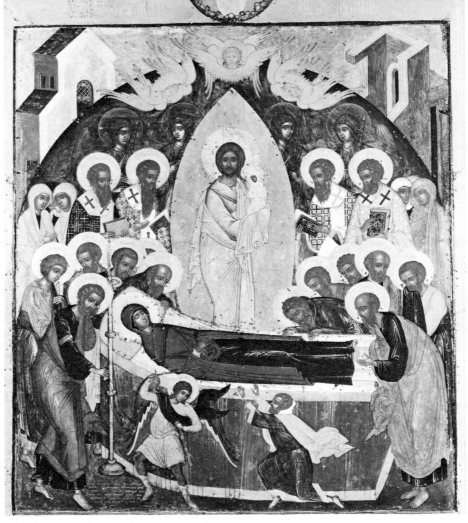

187. Simon Ushakov (Moscow): The Dormition of the Virgin, 1663.
Moscow, Tretyakov Gallery

new tastes, both the old religious conceptions and the traditional technique were destroyed [185, 186].

One master of considerable ability almost succeeded in making the new technical methods compatible with the older iconic subjects, but the narrow margin of his failure is only another indication that such reconciliation was impossible. Simon Ushakov (1626–86) at the age of twenty-two joined the Tsar's painters, and for sixteen years he worked for the Treasury, where he painted frescoes and banners as well as icons, drew maps and plans, and made designs for gold and silver instruments, coins, and rifles. His 'pictures on paper' are the earliest Russian prints which show an understanding of the western techniques of copper-plate engraving.[9] In his early work, even in so traditional a subject as the Dormition of the Virgin [187], dated 1663, he demonstrated his ability to compose with broader and more complexly interlocking rhythms (compare illustration 76). But he soon moved from the miniature-like technique and careful polish of the later Stroganov painters to work on a much larger scale in a notable icon of the Annunciation with Twelve Scenes from the Akathiṣt Hymn, which he and two other painters executed in 1659 for the Church of the Virgin of Georgia in Moscow (State Historical Museum, Moscow).[10] According to the inscription, 'the background and figures of this icon are painted by Yakov Kazanets, the details by Gavrilo Kondratev, but all the faces of the icon are painted by Simon Ushakov in 1659'. As one might expect from the collaboration of three artists, the work is eclectic, combining the detailed manner of the Stroganov school with an orientalizing, decorative feeling for pattern in the architectural silhouettes and landscape. Only the use of many European Renaissance architectural forms and the large scale of the central figures suggest that Ushakov was a man who had been seriously studying such western painting as might have come his way.

Ushakov's understanding of western painting appears to advantage in his celebrated images of the Vernicle [188; compare 59],[11] the form which the ancient icon of the Mandilion now usually received. Here is a reasonably successful interpretation of European painting, interestingly enough not of the contemporary Baroque art of Italy or France, but of the now archaic style of Flanders, Germany, and Holland in the early sixteenth century. Only the somewhat more lively play of light over the features might suggest that such icons were painted after the middle of the seventeenth century. But by the time Ushakov had mastered this style he was confronted with another obstacle; the contemporary direction of European painting was to a very great

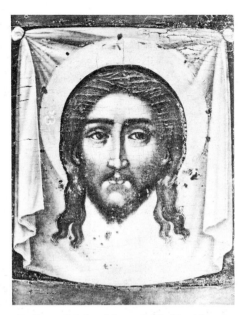

188. Simon Ushakov (Moscow): The Vernicle (Veronica's Veil), c. 1660. *Present location unknown*

degree determined by the implications of oil technique. In tempera Ushakov remained at a stage similar to that reached by Memling or Massys a century and a half before. How Ushakov came to study models already old in his own time, and why he was to all intents and purposes ignorant of contemporary oil practice, must remain a mystery. We can only conjecture that in the German Suburb of Moscow he must have seen some earlier religious paintings, treasured by the merchants and commercial agents who had come to Russia.

The relatively naturalistic image of Ushakov's Christ, much more a painting than an icon, is but the best known of many images which in their time met with the most vigorous objection from the higher clergy. In the polemical writing of the seventeenth century it is sometimes hard to tell whether the authors inveigh more against the content or the technique of icons in the new and foreign manner.

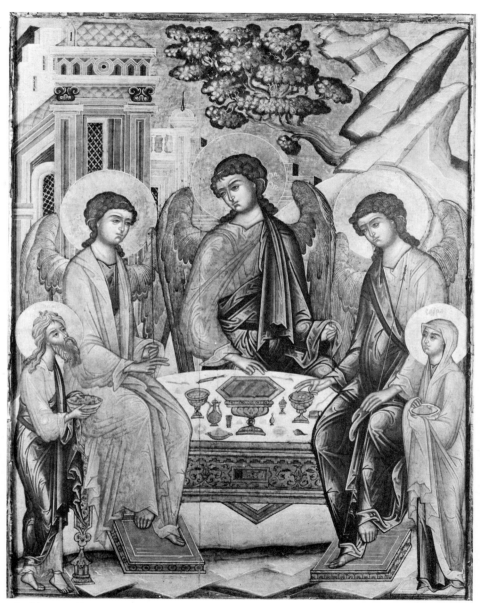

189. Moscow: Old Testament Trinity, seventeenth century.
Yaroslavl, Museum

In the mild and human features of Ushakov's Christ, however, we can feel something of that loss of earlier spiritual abstraction to which the Archpriest Avvakum took such violent exception when he attacked the westernizing painters:

By God's will much unseemly foreign painting has spread over our Russian land. They paint the image of Our Saviour Emmanuel with a puffy face, and red lips, curly hair, fat arms and muscles, and stout legs and thighs. And all this is done for carnal reasons, because the heretics love sensuality and do not care for higher things.[12]

Avvakum's objections may not seem quite so reactionary if the ethereal, two-dimensional, even disembodied personages in Rublev's Trinity [77] are compared with their corpulent descendants in a seventeenth-century icon of the same subject [189]. So much is the same, and had been for generations; the obligatory composition, the reverse perspective of the footstools, the folds of the garments exactly repeated even to the neckline of the angel in the centre. To be sure, some things have changed; the angels' wings now curve in space, and the background, although conventional at the right, shows at the left fragments of imaginary architecture which hint at the contemporary 'baroque' buildings in Moscow (compare illustration 146). What has been lost is the incomparable expressive dignity of the best of the earlier icons, the literally angelic character of Rublev's figures. If we compare the litter on the table with Rublev's single chalice, we know that less had once been more. These grumpy seventeenth-century angels can only look as baffled by the mystery of the Triune God as any later unbeliever.

On the other hand, the defence of modern technique and modes of expression was eloquently set forth by a friend of Ushakov's, one Joseph Vladimirov, a painter of the new persuasion. He protested in a letter to Ushakov against the attitude of a Serbian priest who had denounced as unacceptable one of Ushakov's icons of St Mary Magdalene:

Canst thou possibly say that only Russians are capable of painting icons, that only icons of Russian painting should be venerated, and that those of other lands should neither be accepted nor honoured? Ask thy father or the elders, and they will tell thee that in all our Christian Russian churches the church plate, chasubles, omophoria, altar cloths and palls, ornamental and gold cloths, precious stones and pearls – all these thou receivest from the foreigners and bringest them into church to adorn the altar and icons with no thought of their being good or bad.[13]

Avvakum's criticism could not stay the tide, nor could Nikon himself, who condemned such icons less for their technique than for their departure from standard iconography. Archdeacon Paul has left an interesting account of a service held by Nikon in the presence of the Tsar and the Patriarch Macarius at which Nikon formally denounced the icons in the new style and dashed them to the floor with such force that they were smashed to pieces.[14] On another occasion he commanded that the eyes of such icons should be gouged out and that after they had been carried in procession before the people they should be burned. At this point the Tsar, who on other occasions had cause to disagree with the intransigent Patriarch, is said to have taken Nikon by the arm and quietly urged that the icons be buried rather than burned.

Alexey's mild remonstrance was characteristic of the man, of his tastes, and of his times. Between his reign (1645–76) and his father's (1613–45) runs the borderline between medieval and modern Russia. In the earlier seventeenth century there were some who had been through the Time of Troubles and so had come into contact with western matters. But they were still few, and they could not by themselves combat the established way of life. This was the case with the Tsar's uncle, Nikita Ioannovich Romanov, who was 'very rich, and took a fancy to the French mode. He had a particular affection for Strangers [and went] in the French and Polish modes in his cloaths'.[15]

Mikhail Feodorovich himself, but recently seated on the throne, was aware that he must establish some continuity between his dynasty and the earlier Rurikvichi, to whom he was related only in a roundabout way by marriage.[16] More than his uncle or his son he was conscious of tradition, and the important works of his reign were designed to guarantee the historical continuity of Russian culture. Thus for the redecoration of the Dormition in the Kremlin (1642–4), five elderly icon masters supervised a team of a hundred painters in covering the walls and vaults with a thoroughly conventional decorative scheme.[17]

Alexey stood between the old and the new worlds, and accepted the best of both. The major political effort of his reign was devoted to finding a modus vivendi with the hereditary enemy, Poland, culminating in the recovery of Kiev in 1667. After that date a flood of contemporary western influence moved on Moscow, brought by the southern clergy, who had been educated in the liberal, latinized schools of Kiev. They introduced quantities of books and encouraged the development of printing. After those in Kiev, Moscow, and Chernigov, presses were established in Mogilev and Polotsk, the more Europeanized cities of western Russia. In addition to religious books, translations of Greek and Latin classics were published. In 1669 the brilliant statesman of the reign, Ordyn-Nashchokin, imported eighty-two Latin books. Artamon Matveev, the Tsar's friend and counsellor, read Latin and Greek and had the works of Homer, Aristotle, and Vergil in his library. The Tsar, and Nikon before this, had many Latin books. This interest in a learning far wider than the old church books had been able to provide culminated in 1689 in the foundation of the Slavonic–Greek–Latin Academy in Moscow, intended as its name indicates to acquaint Russian students with their twofold cultural heritage of eastern and western thought.

The Tsar and his friends pursued the same course in artistic matters. For the redecoration of the Kremlin Palace Alexey imported tapestries and paintings of secular subjects. Arch-

deacon Paul admired the colours of a marble pavement and the 'elegant and beautiful ornaments' which a wealthy merchant had brought from Germany for a church he had founded. Paul also had this to say about the houses of the richer citizens, giving us an interesting glimpse of a kind of decorative painting which could scarcely have been supplied by native painters:

We gaped with astonishment at the beauty of their decorations, their solidity and skilful management, their elegance . . . and the manifold variety of the painting, in oil colours, both of their interior and exterior walls, which you might suppose were covered with slabs of real variegated marble, or with minute mosaic.[18]

In western Europe the seventeenth century saw the rise of commanding masters of portraiture in Spain, Flanders, and Holland, so that it is not surprising that a similar concern for appearance and personality occurs in the earliest secular painting in Russia. Portraiture was not unknown before this time, but it had scarcely been divorced from the icon in such figures as the saintly founders of churches, or in the likenesses which were displayed above the tombs of the Tsars and Patriarchs in the Cathedral of the Archangel in the Kremlin. But between those and the icons of recently deceased personages such as the sainted Metropolitans of Moscow there was probably little to choose in the way of individual characterization. During the Time of Troubles foreign portraits and possibly even foreign portrait-painters appeared in Russia in some quantity, as can be seen from the numerous likenesses of the Pretender Dmitry and his Polish betrothed, Marina, which were circulated for political purposes.[19] Under the first Romanovs the taste for portraits increased; Tsars Mikhail and Alexey are the first Russian sovereigns whose likenesses, as they have come down in Russian and European engravings after lost originals, convince us that the artist had seen the living men. Indeed, we know that in 1671 Alexey sat for his portrait, and that other painters of this time worked from the living model.[20]

So far as the development of secular painting was concerned, portraiture was as important a branch of official activity as decorative painting, and the first foreign artists of Alexey's reign to be officially engaged in the government service were obliged to practise both kinds. One of the first was Hans Detterson, a Dutch painter who had entered Russian service in the last years of Tsar Mikhail's reign at the magnificent salary of twenty roubles a month, a considerable sum when many of the Tsar's artists were sending annual complaints to the Treasury about their niggardly wages. A condition of Detterson's employment was that he should teach Russian pupils, two of whom, Isaak Abramov and Flor Stepanov, helped him in painting ceilings and other decorative work. In 1650 Detterson declared to the Treasury that his pupils had learned enough and that if they studied with him only two years more they would be able to paint as well as he. Detterson died in 1655, and in the following year Stephen Loputsky, a Polish decorator, succeeded to the position of chief instructor in western technique. He, too, was a jack-of-many-trades, although he seems to have specialized in map-making. That he did not or could not offer a full curriculum in the western method is seen in the petition of two of his pupils that they be allowed to leave him and study with Daniel Vuchters, a Dutch painter who arrived in 1667. According to the latter's statement to the Treasury, he had been in the service of 'many monarchs and sovereigns' who had admired his work, and then had been for some time settled in Moscow, where he had married. In the absence of any documented work, it is hard to say whether any of these painters were men of particular ability, although a competent portrait of Nikon surrounded by the clergy of his Monastery of the New Jerusalem, which has been attributed to Vuchters, was painted with considerable knowledge of Dutch realism and communicated something of Nikon's almost unbearable arrogance.[21]

These men and several after them in the later years of the century seem to have reached Moscow by chance, rather than to have been specially selected for their abilities by the Tsar's agents, as were the Italian artists who worked for Ivan III. Russia may have meant for them a last opportunity to redeem a mediocre talent squandered in years of itinerant activity in Europe, where abler painters deprived them of a living. Certain it is that individually they left almost nothing behind them, and their influence upon younger Russian artists must have been more a matter of encouragement than of example. Until Russian painters could study abroad, or until a master of superior ability could be induced to come to them, they would remain in the trap which had snared Simon Ushakov.

The difficulties of their position and their last brilliant efforts to resolve the antagonism between medieval techniques and modern means of expression are found in the remarkable fresco cycles in the prosperous ecclesiastical and commercial centres east of Moscow. In the Volga cities of Rostov, Vologda, Kostroma, and Yaroslavl there flourished, in the period of political tension and partisan turmoil following the death of Alexey, groups of fresco-painters who wrote the final chapter in the history of old Russian painting.[22] Differences may be noted between different places; the frescoes of Rostov, for instance, are on the whole more conservative in subject and treatment than those of Yaroslavl. Rostov was dominated by its Metropolitan; Yaroslavl was the creation of wealthy merchants. Yet among them all there is a certain community of technical means and expressive intentions. Like the work of the contemporary painters in Moscow, these frescoes, which completely cover the walls of the churches and their surrounding galleries, shared the general seventeenth-century concern for overcrowding with scenes and figures, for bright colours, and fantastic architectural settings. To all this was added a lively curiosity about western costumes and accessories. For the latter the painters were deeply indebted to a handy compendium of iconographical information, the famous illustrated Bible of

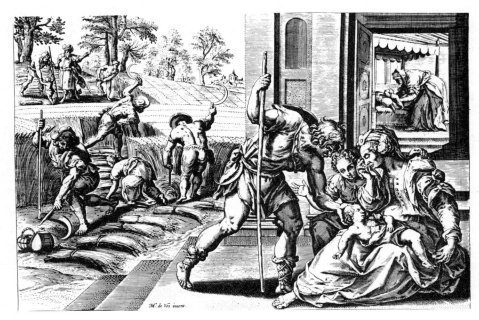

190. Martin de Vos: Elias and the Shunammite Woman,
engraving from Piscator's *Theatrum Biblicum*, 1674

Johannes Piscator (N. J. Visscher) [190], published in 1650.[23] This collection of almost three hundred engravings illustrating the Old Testament, the Gospels, the Lord's Prayer, and the Apocalypse was so popular that in 1674 a second edition was required. As early as 1673 the influence of Piscator's subjects can be seen in a fresco of Joseph and Potiphar's wife in the Church of St Nicholas at Yaroslavl. In the 1680s and 90s subjects from Piscator dominate the decoration of the Yaroslavl churches [191].

It might be thought that in some such way as this Russian painting would gradually be led towards a completer understanding of western art.[24] But this could not be. Beyond all questions of technical incompatibility – and these were almost insurmountable given the Russians' ignorance of oil-painting – the expressive ends were too divergent. Piscator's illustrators used, for the most part, the forms of northern European Mannerism, enlarged here and there by the broader energies of the early Baroque. Such an expression, stylistically mature, formally sophisticated, and inherently materialistic, bore no relation to the iconographical and formal requirements of Russian church painting. Yet even if the Russian painters of the later seventeenth century had been more familiar with contemporary European painting, one may still doubt whether

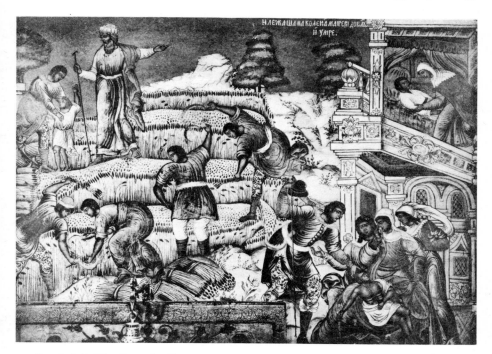

191. Yaroslavl, St Elias, frescoed wall,
late seventeenth century

they would have found it as useful as Piscator's compendium, by then quite out of
fashion in the West. The abrupt perspectives
of the high-piled architecture, the accumulation of elaborate decorative detail, and the
intricate contrapposto of the flattened figures
were just those elements in previous European
painting which responded to the visual habits
and emotional necessities of the iconic artists.
Not Rembrandt or Le Brun, the immediate
contemporaries of Ushakov and the Volga
artists, but rather the Flemish Mannerists at
second hand provided plausible if often in-
appropriate solutions to their specific spiritual
and technical problems. After the seventeenth

century religious and secular painting were
obliged to go their own ways. For the fashionable circles of Moscow and St Petersburg religious art adopted the western manner, until
its productions became indistinguishable from
the adulterated eighteenth-century Baroque
painting in the West. In out-of-the-way places,
where such were left, principally among the
Old Believers, it continued in the form of
traditional icon-painting in tempera. However, this was only a reprieve and led but to
the tired repetition of old themes, fatally
weakened by the withdrawal of support from
the wealthier and more influential parties of
Church and State.[25]

PART FOUR

ST PETERSBURG

I am at length going to give you some account of this new city, of this great window lately opened in the North, thro' which Russia looks into Europe.

COUNT FRANCESCO ALGAROTTI, 30 JUNE 1739

CHAPTER 19

PETER'S BAROQUE: 1703–1741

Peter the Great's return in 1697 from his first visit to western Europe marks the beginning of a spectacular change in Russian art. Although it is true that throughout the seventeenth century Russia had become better acquainted with Europe, Russian culture in general had remained profoundly traditional. The close ties between Tsar and Patriarch had strengthened the policy of closing the frontiers to all but a few travellers, and foreign merchants were confined upon their arrival in Moscow in a separate district, so that their Catholic and Protestant heresies, and their liberal political ideas, should not infect the Russian people. Yet in less than a century the point of view of the Russian upper classes had changed from terror lest they be mistaken for foreigners to fear that they might not be. Little more than a generation separated Nikita Ioannovich Romanov, the first of his family to wear western clothes, from Peter, who always dressed in the French fashion in a short coat, boots, and breeches, instead of the full-length Russian kaftan with long sleeves.

Peter's decision to open his country to western influence was based upon three considerations: the creation of a government which could negotiate on an equal basis with European powers, free and frequent trade with the West, and a social order capable of understanding western ideas and making them effective for the national life. In this sense Peter's reforms amounted to a revolution in Russian life, and it is understandable that his more conservative subjects should have looked upon him as the anti-Christ, or a false Tsar. The wonder is not so much that his intentions and actions met with resistance, nor that in encountering obstacles Peter grew violent and cruel, but rather that in the short space of a quarter of a century he accomplished so much. In spite of several attempts by his immediate followers to restore the old order, his work endured, and for the next two centuries imperial Russia was once again what it had been in the days of princely Kiev, a member of the European family of nations.

It may be convincingly argued that Peter merely brought to a head currents which were irresistible and which would inevitably have opened Russia to the West. Nevertheless, the city of St Petersburg, which he founded as a practical and symbolic demonstration of his political and social concepts, and which so dramatically summarized the Russia which he bequeathed to his successors, remains an unsurpassed achievement. No other eighteenth-century city grew so fast within so short a time. The barren marsh of 1703 was a world metropolis a century later. The measure of Russia's participation in European affairs can be taken by the fact that a hundred years after Peter's victory in 1709 over Charles XII at Poltava, which secured for Russia the Swedish-held coast of the Gulf of Finland, the armies of Alexander I were preparing for their titanic struggle against Napoleon. If it is true that Napoleon briefly occupied Moscow, exactly two centuries after a similar occupation by the Poles, in the end Poland had been destroyed and in 1814 the victorious Russians entered Paris.

St Petersburg was the principal focus for the artistic reforms undertaken by Peter and his successors. Here the innumerable small decisions which followed the great decision to build such a city resumed, as in a microcosm, the whole history of European art of the seventeenth and eighteenth centuries. In this sense the dynastic history of the period is of some importance. The eighteenth century in Russia was to an extraordinary extent a period of feminine rule, as seemed to befit a century in which women played such a prominent part. Another nation – Austria – also knew a great sovereign in Maria Theresa; but the succession of talented women on the Russian throne remains unique, especially since the strongest female personalities alternated with the weakest male remnants of Peter's line. The tradition of feminine rule had commenced in Peter's minority with the regency (1682–9) of his older half-sister Sophia. Peter (1682–1725) was succeeded by his second wife, Catherine I (1725–7), but her brief rule was merely a prelude to the political struggles which followed during the three-year reign of Peter's grandson, Peter II (1727–30), the child of the miserable Tsarevich Alexey Petrovich. During this time reactionary elements in Russian society almost succeeded in re-establishing the Court in Moscow. The next Empress, Anna Ioannovna (1730–40), Duchess of Courland, the daughter of Peter's older half-brother, Ivan V, had been brought up in Germany. She returned to St Petersburg, and for ten melancholy years the Court and country languished under her German favourites. Again a woman's reign was followed by a few months' occupancy of the throne by a male heir, Ivan VI, the infant son of Peter's great-niece Anna, wife of Anton Ulrich of Brunswick-Lüneburg. Since Ivan was only a baby, there was the prospect of a long regency under his mother, Anna Leopoldovna. The younger courtiers and army officers could not endure another German rule, and supported the *coup d'état* by which Peter's younger daughter Elizabeth ascended the throne (1741–62). She named as heir her nephew, Peter III (1762), Peter's grandson by his older daughter Anna. This Peter, too, had been born and reared in Germany. He hated Russia and was a devoted admirer of Frederick the Great. But if Elizabeth felt obliged to select this foolish young man, because he was her father's last legitimate male descendant, she was more fortunate in her choice of his bride. The German Princess, Sophia of Anhalt-Zerbst, was married to Peter in 1744. As the Grand Duchess Catherine,[1] she learned much in eighteen years about her husband, and even more about Russia. In June 1762, less than six months after Peter's accession, she swept him aside and began her long and brilliant reign as Catherine II (1762–96). To complete this bewildering succession of men and women her son, Paul I (1796–1801), was assassinated, after five years of insane cruelty, during a palace revolution.

The work initiated by Peter was carried on by two women who seem, in contrast to their funereal male relatives, essentially European, not only in terms of the works of art which they liked and the artists whom they employed, but also in their conception of themselves as empresses. Elizabeth's great good nature and spontaneous gaiety enlivened the simple, even dowdy city of her father and cousin Anna with the intricate graces of Italian Rococo architecture. Catherine II preferred a soberer style which became increasingly severe with time and prepared the final triumph of Russian Neo-Classicism in the reigns of her grandsons Alexander I (1801–25) and Nicholas I (1825–55). But, all the same, Elizabeth and Catherine were always conscious of their position as Tsaritsas of Russia, and the art which they sponsored, although impregnated with European influences and largely created by Europeans, is as Russian as the contemporary architectures of Germany, France, or England, likewise often created by artists of other countries within the general stylistic framework of the eighteenth century, are recognizably German, French, or English. Even when a building looks much like contemporary work elsewhere and the Russian accent seems less stressed, we must remember that in the eighteenth century the greater ease of communication, the wide distribution of printed works on architecture, and the more universal training of the architects enabled them to work in a more international style. The greatest monuments of Russian Classicism are distinctly Russian, for all that they are among the most significant achievements of that phase of European architecture in any country.

Analogies come to mind in other arts. In the nineteenth century the Russians did not invent the forms of narrative poem, novel, symphony, or opera; but Pushkin and Tolstoy, Tchaikovsky and Moussorgsky used the technical means common to European art to create works inimitably Russian which we number among the masterpieces of world literature and music. The task of the art historian is twofold: to relate Russian artistic expression to its sources in the general European cultural situation, and to indicate the specifically Russian contributions made by Russian artists, and by foreign artists employed by Russians.

It cannot be denied that these contributions were achieved at a heavy cost to Russian tradition. Henceforth the artistic energies of the nation were to be concentrated in St Petersburg, and in the nineteenth century, to a lesser extent, in Moscow, to the detriment of a living folk culture. In ancient Russia the arts had been the arts of all the people, only directed by the Church in the case of the more important monumental work, but even then by a Church to which the people subscribed. With rare exceptions the builders of Russian churches, the painters of icons, and the manufacturers who were also the designers of the works of industrial art – all these had come from the people. After the establishment of St Petersburg as the capital in 1712, the Russians were usually students of foreign artists. Such a state of affairs inevitably alienated the people from the arts of the Court, which they could neither create nor comprehend. The loss of cultural unity eventually reached the proportions of a national tragedy, until an embittered populace took a terrible revenge upon the upper classes for having deprived them of their right and proper place in the nation's economic, political, and cultural life.

The history of St Petersburg may be studied in three principal phases, comprising the time from its foundation in 1703 until almost a century and a quarter later, towards the close of the reign of Alexander I, when it had achieved its definitive form as a great capital and as one of the most remarkable expressions of eighteenth-century classicism in plan, form, and detail.[2] Of these the first (1703–40) covers the active participation of Peter and Prince Menshikov in the foundation and first constructions of the city, and continues through the reigns of Peter's immediate successors, his widow Catherine I, and his niece Anna Ioannovna. This period of the first thirty-seven years of the city's life is one of experiment, hesitation, and tentative search for the ultimate direction which the city would take. In the beginning there was not even a plan, and its eventual growth on the mainland was less a matter of choice than of necessity. By the 1730s it was apparent that the centre of population had shifted from the islands to the land side, and the main direction was fixed when Anna rebuilt the Winter Palace, thereby closing an era of utilitarian building. Elizabeth's reign marks the second period. For twenty years practical interests were submerged in her insatiable love of pleasure. All construction was in the hands of her favourite architect, the Italian-born Count Bartolommeo Rastrelli, and most of his buildings were palaces. St Petersburg added the attributes of an imperial residence to its maritime, military, and commercial establishments. During the third period, which includes the reigns of Catherine II and Alexander I (1762–1825), the city received its final classic definition, more as the centre of government than as a port, fortress, or residence. New palaces were chiefly in the suburbs; within the city rose government offices and ministries as demonstrations of autocratic power. Under Nicholas I (1825–55) the jealous watch which the sovereigns had kept over the development of their city was relaxed and, as with the loosing of the waters of the Neva each spring, a flood of eclecticism threatened to destroy St Petersburg's classic beauty. Only after 1900, through the work of such organizations as the Society of Artists-Architects, was antiquarian interest organized and an effort made to preserve what was left, if not to recapture what had disappeared.[3]

One of the most consistent aspects of this long architectural development was the gradual progression from the satisfaction of utilitarian towards the expression of symbolic values.[4] Because the architects were usually men of ability, sometimes of genius, and the sovereigns were by and large men and women of taste, it is remarkable how rarely, save perhaps for the Rococo extravagances of Elizabeth, architectural history departed from this course. The explanation must be sought in a number of historical and personal factors, not least of which was the extraordinary way successive strong rulers dispossessed weaker ones whose reigns, sanctioned in other countries by tradition or law, might have countenanced stylistic deviations. Thus Peter II's sojourn in Moscow, the prospect of a long German regency for the infant Ivan VI, the possibility of a lifetime of military subservience to Peter III, were quickly eliminated by the decisions

of Anna, Elizabeth, and Catherine. Even the unstable Paul, whose architectural excesses threatened for a time to wreck much of his mother's noblest work, was put out of the way after five years. Architectural continuity was thus assured, particularly as the reigns of the three empresses and of Alexander I covered ten, twenty, thirty-four, and twenty-four years respectively.

It might be thought that in thus emphasizing the dynastic succession one were neglecting more significant aspects of architectural history. But Russian architecture from 1703 to the middle of the nineteenth century is preeminently an account of the interest and participation of the rulers in the embellishment of their capital, somewhat to the neglect of other cities, which were reduced during this period to a provincial status. The dynastic succession is paralleled by the progression of style in the hands of a company of architects, of varying talents and different nationalities. Within each period both foreigners and Russians, the former predominantly Italian, German, and French, worked together to create a new and monumental Russian style. This remarkable homogeneity of expression was largely the result of the frequent participation of Russians in European affairs, artistic and social as well as political and economic. This was assisted by the educational system in Europe as well as in Russia during the eighteenth century. The growing power of the academies with their planned programmes, competitive examinations, and awards of prizes, and the numerous architectural publications tended to draw the different national traditions into a single body of theory and practice. The final seal of authority was conferred by the international prestige of antiquity. The excavations at Herculaneum and Pompeii, and the theoretical justification for the superiority of classical art which was spread throughout Europe by the doctrines of Winckelmann and other archaeologists, provided an international unanimity of artistic opinion the like of which the world had not seen since the Middle Ages.

How universal this attitude was can be seen by comparing late-eighteenth- and early-nineteenth-century architecture from widely scattered parts of the western world. The startling similarity between the Kamenny Ostrov Palace (1765, sometimes attributed to Bazhenov) and James Hoban's White House in Washington (1792), or between Decimus Burton's arch and screen at Hyde Park Corner (1825) and a street of early-nineteenth-century mansions in the city of Ekaterinburg on the further side of the Urals is due to this international acceptance of a supra-national point of view; for certainly the social, political, and cultural situations in Russian, English, and American life between 1750 and 1830 were as notable for their differences as for their similarities. Antiquity could serve a variety of purposes, so that superficial resemblances should not blind us to the fact that the same forms could be used as symbols of aristocratic romanticism in England, of democratic republicanism in the United States, and of authoritarian autocracy in Russia. Indeed, the latter interpretation of classical forms accounts both for their prevalence in imperial Russia and for their revival after 1930 by the Soviet state. Peter and his successors established the tradition of an autocratic architecture which found its most perfect expression, after a century's experiment, in the buildings of Alexander I.

Peter's choice of a site is intelligible only as part of a short-term programme of military and commercial expediency. The many islands in the estuary of the Neva where it enters the Gulf of Finland were marshy, the waters scarcely deep enough to float vessels of the lightest draught, and frequent floods made transportation dangerous. The climate of these fog-bound wastes was unpleasant and unhealthy; at sixty degrees of latitude the winters were long and dark, the summers brief and hot, spring and autumn fugitive at best. Apart from the water route by way of Lake Ladoga, St Petersburg could only be approached through dense and relatively unexplored forests, whereas the roads to Novgorod and

Moscow from other cities had been familiar for centuries. Wood was available in the neighbouring forests, but Peter wanted a fireproof city of brick and stone, which had to be manufactured in improvised kilns or transported at an inordinate cost in time and effort from other parts of Russia. Nor would such a situation seem congenial for the development of a typically national culture; St Petersburg lay on the periphery of Russia close to the Swedish and German enclaves in Finland and the Baltic lands to the west. Yet just this accessibility to other cultures may have appealed to Peter.

In 1702 he had taken the Swedish fortress of Noteburg on the point where the Neva issues from Lake Ladoga and had renamed it Schlüsselburg (now Petrokrepost), an indication that he considered it a 'key' to the lower Neva and the Gulf. The following year he and Menshikov on 7 May captured Nyenskantz, another Swedish fortress on the Neva a short distance from the estuary, and occupied the island of Kotlin in the Gulf, where he built the fortress of Kronslot, later Kronstadt. Finally, according to tradition, on 16 May 1703 ground was broken with a sword on one of the larger islands of the delta for a new maritime port and fortress where Peter established himself and which he renamed Sankt Pieter Burkh. Work started at once on two buildings which soon came to symbolize the political and dynastic as well as the military and cultural aspects of St Petersburg. These were the Fortress with its cathedral on the large Peter Island, and the shipyards, soon to be called the Admiralty, opposite on the mainland.

For the first few years construction of these and other utilitarian structures was the principal activity. Peter was still occupied with the Swedes and was also considering the possibility of another town, at the other end of Russia on the sea of Azov, as a warm-water port for trade with the countries of southern Europe and the Mediterranean. Only after his forced withdrawal from Azov and the overthrow of Charles XII of Sweden could he turn to his new city. From that year it consumed not only

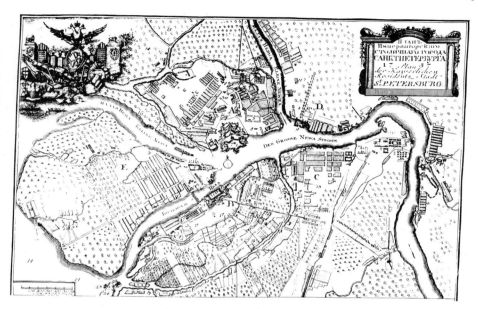

192. St Petersburg in 1737

Peter's energies, but also those of his favourite, Prince Menshikov, who was often quite as much master of St Petersburg as the Tsar himself. During these years construction proceeded very slowly because of the difficulties of the site, where all buildings had to be supported on piles sunk in the marshes, and the lack of sufficient labour and materials.[5] Although there were enough houses for Peter's immediate family and relatives, who had moved there in 1710, and for the most essential government services, much needed to be done even after the city was proclaimed the capital of the Empire in 1712. Forced measures were required, and through a series of ukases Peter conscripted labour, materials, tools, and even a population. Yet so scarce was the supply of stone that in 1714 masonry construction was prohibited elsewhere in Russia, while all vessels coming from Lake Ladoga were ordered to bring stone as ballast. Meanwhile the nobility and government officials were required

to build houses at once, the size, plan, and materials regulated according to each man's wealth and the number in his family. Even the design of each house had to conform to plans provided by the chief architect. The population consisted either of labourers – little better than slaves – who died by the thousand of overwork, poor food, and disease, or of the upper classes, who had been brutally wrenched from their ancestral homes. But for all that the city gradually took shape. By 1717 a panorama engraved for foreign circulation showed a series of substantial buildings lining both banks of the Neva.[6]

Peter had first thought that the island on which the fortress was constructed, later known as the Petersburg Side or Quarter, would become the administrative as well as the military centre of the city[7] (the fortress appears in the exact centre of illustration 192, and in the lower centre of illustration 193 where the points of the compass are reversed,

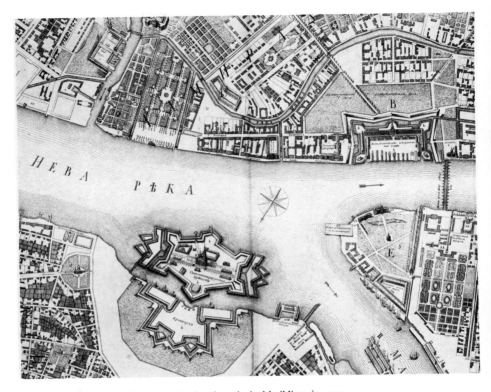

193. St Petersburg, central section, showing the principal buildings in 1753. From an engraving by M. I. Makhaev

north being at the bottom of the page). Here were first built, in addition to the fortifications, the two Cathedrals of SS. Peter and Paul and of the Trinity, the Twelve Colleges for use as government offices, and the markets. Later the colleges and customs were moved to the large Vasily Ostrov (Basil Island), so called from the Christian name of an officer of the public works. Neither of these locations was satisfactory in the long run, for the principal reason that transport to and from the mainland was always slow, usually difficult, and not infrequently dangerous, especially during the freezing and thawing of the Neva. Consequently the centre of the city gradually shifted to the mainland, where houses soon clustered around the Admiralty. Farther to the east a large park was laid out – the Summer Garden – where Peter had a small pavilion for his own use, while the palaces of the nobility stood along the embankment between the garden and the Admiralty. Somewhat to the south some small streams were widened and straightened into a concentric system of canals, providing transport by water through the city from the Neva and confirming the impression that St Petersburg was built around and upon the water in the manner of Venice, Amsterdam, and Stockholm.

Peter's admiration for Holland, which he had visited in 1697 and where he had been impressed by Dutch efficiency, was reflected in the name he gave his new city. He called it Sankt Pieter Burkh, pronouncing the words in the Dutch fashion. But despite his admiration for Holland, he employed few Dutch architects. When the work of the local builders – the most prominent of whom seems to have been Ivan Matveev (died 1707) who began the Tsar's residence in the Summer Garden – proved inadequate, Peter looked elsewhere for help. The first important architect he summoned seems to have known something of Dutch building. This was the Swiss–Italian Domenico Tressini or Trezzini (Andrey Petrovich Trezini, c. 1670–1734).[8] Soon after 1700 he had been in Copenhagen working on the palace of Frederick IV. The Russian ambassador, who had orders from Peter to recruit artists, offered him a contract on very generous terms. This was signed on 1 April 1703, several weeks before the founding of St Petersburg. Tressini, with ten other masterbuilders, engineers, and artists, reached Moscow in August by way of Arkhangelsk, since the approaches to Russia from the sea were still held by the Swedes.

Through his experience in Copenhagen, Tressini was familiar with the small-scale late Baroque architecture of northern Europe, which at this time bore many marks of Dutch influence. His ability to design small, practical dwellings, and to construct them in wood and brick, plastered and painted in imitation of stone, was just what Peter and his gentry required in these first years, when more monumental building was beset with difficulties. This sensible, utilitarian style appeared in his designs for houses for the various classes of citizens who were permitted or commanded to settle in the new city. For the nobility he provided a two-storey house with high-pitched roof, a dignified central doorway surmounted by an openwork balcony, and with the surface of the walls enlivened by quoins at the corners and panels between the windows. Well-to-do citizens had to be content with one-storey dwellings; artisans and labourers with timber or earthen huts. The earliest houses have long been demolished except for Peter's first residence (1703), a two-room log structure, indistinguishable from a peasant's izba although the interior was painted in imitation of Dutch tiles. Situated on the edge of the Neva near the Fortress, it has been reverently preserved, and frequently restored. Although almost all other traces of the earliest urban architecture on the mainland have disappeared, the character of Tressini's residential design can still be seen in his Summer Palace (1710–14), built for Peter at the edge of the Summer Garden. The palace was distinguished from the residences of the nobility less by its size than by Andreas Schlüter's terracotta reliefs, celebrating victories of the Russian fleet, in the panels between the first and second storeys.

Two aspects of this housing programme were in striking contrast to previous Russian domestic architecture. The imposition of a definite plan which everyone was obliged to follow according to his means at once gave St Petersburg a uniformity and homogeneity quite unlike the older cities where the decorative character of later medieval masonry and wooden architecture had encouraged the greatest variety of forms. Secondly, this homogeneity was achieved by a negation of the qualities and peculiarities of materials, an appreciation of which had been one of the most distinctive aspects of earlier Russian architecture. Peter wished his city to look like those he had visited in western Europe, which were almost entirely of brick and stone. As these were costly and unavailable in St Petersburg, recourse was had to substitutes. The first houses were of wood constructed according to traditional methods, but on the exterior the logs were smoothed and painted to resemble brick or stone; later on, brick buildings were covered with plaster and disguised in the same way. Thus both brick and wood, materials with an ancient and honourable history in Russia, where their special qualities had been evoked for the characteristic styles of the sixteenth and seventeenth centuries, were suppressed in favour of painted plaster imitations. But an older Russian tradition assumed new significance when these plaster surfaces were

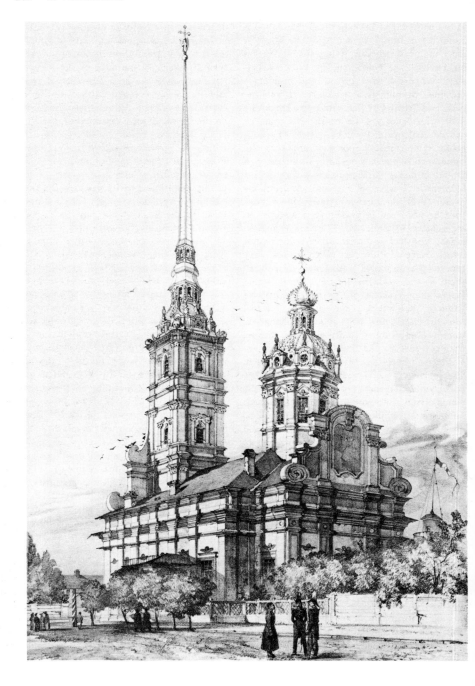

194. Domenico Tressini: St Petersburg,
Cathedral of SS. Peter and Paul in the fortress,
1712–33. From a lithograph by André Durand, 1839

painted various colours. Colour had been seen in the painted and gilded churches of Vladimir, in the painting of the interior surfaces of the wooden churches of the north, and in the coloured and gilded tiles which enlivened the stone and brick architecture of the later Muscovite period.

Very little of Tressini's work remains untouched. The early houses quickly deteriorated and were soon replaced, but his ability as a military engineer can be surmised from the Fortress of SS. Peter and Paul (Petropavlovskaya Krepost, 1706–40). This was of earth and wood, later faced with stone, on the pentagonal plan with projecting angular bastions popularized by Vauban. The principal entrance, the Petrovsky Gate (1717–18), is still a powerful archway of rusticated masonry surmounted by a pedimented attic containing a crude wooden relief by the German sculptor Konrad Osner (1669–1747, in Russia from 1702). The improbable subject, the Fall of Simon Magus, symbolizes Peter's victory over the Swedes, and the Tsar himself appears among the spectators to the Apostle's destruction of the magician. In the court of the Fortress Tressini raised the Cathedral of SS. Peter and Paul (1712–33) [194], the first ecclesiastical structure in St Petersburg and the burial church of Peter and his successors. This gaunt and awkward building does little for Tressini's reputation, but its present appearance is probably not very close to his original intention. When the wooden spire was struck by lightning in 1756, it fell and destroyed the roof and dome. For ten years the church lay in ruins, until it was restored by Catherine II. Although the architect then was the son of the Dutch engineer Harman van Boles (1683–after 1753), a 'master of spire and roof construction', who had built the tower for Tressini, a comparison of the present tower with that which appears in early engravings suggests that

it must once have been more gracious and more Baroque. Taste in Catherine's time had turned so far towards the soberer effects of Neo-Classicism that Tressini's church lost much of its original exuberance when its surfaces were flattened and peeled of their ornament. At present only the eastern façade preserves any vestiges of the once vigorous Corinthian pilasters, entablatures, and papery volutes.

At best, however, the cathedral was not a graceful building. The box-like mass and angular plan show that Tressini either had not familiarized himself with the Orthodox liturgy, or that he accepted Peter's determination to modernize the Russian church edifice as well as the ecclesiastical hierarchy. In contrast to earlier and even later Russian churches, the interior was more like a Protestant 'temple' than an Orthodox cathedral, for the wide windows admitted a flood of light.[9] Certainly the exceptionally tall spire – 394 feet high as against a total length of 210 feet – more in proportion to the city than to the church itself, was a visible assertion of Peter's wish that the horizon of St Petersburg should be the antithesis of Moscow's with its multitudinous painted and gilded cupolas. Such pointed spires were unknown in earlier Russian architecture and were certainly suggested to Peter during his travels abroad, possibly by the forest of spires above London. Within, the lengthy nave was interrupted midway by a sumptuously carved and gilded iconostasis, more Baroque than the church itself, by the Moscow architect Ivan Petrovich Zarudny (see above, page 224).

Tressini's usefulness to Peter lay in just that instinct for utility which militated against his success in the cathedral. To house the Senate, the Synod, and the government ministries he built the so-called Twelve Colleges on Vasily Ostrov (1722–33) [195]. This was a long row of twelve two-storey pavilions embraced within a colossal order of pilasters resting on a basement arcade. Each pavilion was marked out from its neighbours by a high hipped roof and projecting portico crowned by an attic with volutes. The material was red brick with

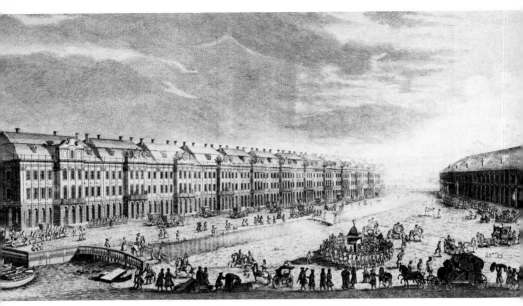

195. Domenico Tressini: St Petersburg, the Twelve Colleges on Vasily Ostrov, 1722–33. From an engraving by M. I. Makhaev, 1761

white stone facing for the simple pilasters. The whole effect was practical, reticent, and efficient. Peter had a building which was proof of his intention that his government was not to become so hopelessly enmeshed in confusion as had the old overlapping offices in the Kremlin. In 1819 the Twelve Colleges were assigned to the new University of St Petersburg, and with the levelling of the roofs their appearance was spoiled.

Tressini's position during his first years in St Petersburg had been that of Master of Building, Construction, and Fortification, in a sense the chief architect responsible for all building activity. But as Peter and his Court became more familiar with European architecture, Tressini's style seemed too plain. He was eventually superseded as chief architect by newer arrivals, although throughout his long career until his death in 1734 he was a respected and busy builder, principally re-

sponsible for such public works as hospitals, city gates, and powder magazines, and the barracks at Kronstadt and Schlüsselburg. His most ambitious design was a plan for the Alexander Nevsky Lavra (1715) but, because of his failure to orient the principal church towards the east, it was later reworked by other architects. It is regrettable that his first scheme was not executed, for it would certainly have been Tressini's masterpiece and one of the most notable monuments of early Petersburg architecture. He had designed the conventual buildings as a series of staggered blocks around three sides of a large rectangular court, joined by pavilions like those of the Twelve Colleges. The monastery cathedral, in the centre of the long side, would have resembled the Jesuit churches of the West, and was to have been crowned with another exceptionally tall tower and spire. To judge from contemporary engravings, the whole conception would have had a more energetic and Baroque spirit than can now be seen in the altered and damaged works by Tressini which have survived.[10]

When more sophisticated architects were sought to give the city the character of a palatial, governmental centre, it is possible that international reputation. He had fallen on evil days after the disastrous collapse of his Mint Tower for the Royal Palace in Berlin, and in 1713 was looking to repair his fortunes when he was offered a contract as Russian 'Oberbaudirektor'. Peter and Menshikov undoubt-

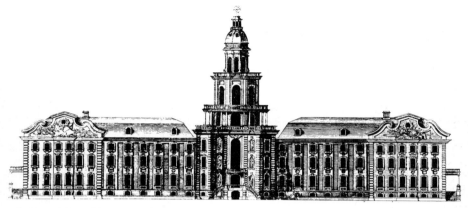

196. Georg Johann Mattarnovy: St Petersburg, Peter the Great's Kunstkamera (now the Museum of Anthropology and Ethnology), 1718–25

Menshikov's tastes were more decisive than Peter's. The Tsar himself liked plain buildings with small, low-ceilinged rooms, a curious preference considering his own great height. His Summer Palace in the Summer Garden and the wooden house he built for his wife Catherine in 1703 were not more pretentious than those of the wealthy merchants and higher officials.[11] When he required a large house for entertaining or the reception of important dignitaries, Peter borrowed one from Menshikov or another friend – a habit carried over from his younger days in Moscow, where Lefort's palace had stood ready for his use.

The second important architect to arrive in St Petersburg had been, like Tressini, summoned from the service of a European monarch. But Andreas Schlüter (1664–1714), the German sculptor and architect of the Royal Palace in Berlin, enjoyed a wider, even edly hoped that their new architect would produce buildings rivalling those of the European Courts they hoped to emulate, but unfortunately very little came of Schlüter's residence in Russia. His energy seems to have been vitiated by his misfortunes, he spent most of his time on a perpetual-motion machine, and in any case he died the next year. The most that can be given to him, apart from the bas-relief panels on the Summer Palace, are parts of the interior decoration of the building, and a drawing for a grotto which was subsequently erected in the Summer Garden by Le Blond. He may also have had something to do with the design of Peter's Cabinet of Curiosities (Kunstkamera, 1718–25) [196]. This was the first building in Russia designed specifically for scientific purposes, and the tower contained an observatory used by Russia's first great scientist, Mikhail Vasilievich Lomonosov (1708/15–65). Appropriately, the Kunstkamera later became the library of the Academy of Sciences and now houses Leningrad's Museum of Ethnography and Anthropology. It was begun by Georg Johann Mattarnovy (died 1719), a German architect who had been recommended by Schlüter as a specialist in grottoes and fountains and who seems to have stood in a close relation to the older man, possibly inheriting his plans and models.[12] The central octagonal section with concave faces divided into panels by rusticated pilasters and surmounted by a stepped tower resembles Schlüter's Tower in Berlin. As it stands now the building has suffered from the reconstruction of the tower and the loss of the ornate pediments on the end pavilions. Whether or not the original conception was Schlüter's, its utilitarian appearance, somewhat enlivened by the blue-painted walls and white ornament, was typical of Mattarnovy, who seems to have devoted most of his brief career to a customs house and dockyard. Little more can be said for his chunky design for the first Cathedral of St Isaac of Dalmatia of 1717 (illustration 197, in the distance to the

right of the Old Admiralty), finished after his death by Nikolaus Herbel (Gerbel, in Russia 1719, died 1724), another minor German architect, nor for the second Winter Palace (1721), a simple three-storeyed structure with a central projecting pediment supported on pilasters and with a rusticated basement; this replaced an earlier, more Dutch-looking residence of 1708–11. In 1726–7 Tressini remodelled Mattarnovy's palace, and then in 1732–4 rebuilt and enlarged Admiral Apraxin's house opposite the east wing of the Old Admiralty for Anna Ioannovna [197]. This, the third Winter Palace, was soon afterwards reconstructed by Rastrelli (see pages 283–6).

Menshikov's role in the development of St Petersburg was dramatically expressed by the two residences built for him by the German architect Gottfried Schädel (Shedel, died 1752), who arrived in St Petersburg the same year as Schlüter. On the Vasily Ostrov opposite the Admiralty Schädel, who may have been more a master builder than a professional architect, erected a palace which was the finest in St Petersburg at that time.[13] The general

197. Domenico Tressini and B. F. Rastrelli: St Petersburg, the third Winter Palace, 1732–6; and the Old Admiralty. From an engraving by M. I. Makhaev, 1761

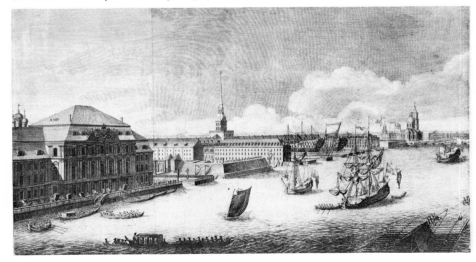

distribution of the plan and mass as a three-storeyed central block with projecting wings and pavilions, each with a separate high roof with each of the storeys carrying its own order of pilasters, may have lacked originality. It resembled a hundred late-seventeenth-century noblemen's houses elsewhere in Europe, and for these reasons was probably exactly what was wanted at that time. After Menshikov's fall it passed to the favourites of other sovereigns, until later in the century it was remodelled as the headquarters of the First Corps of Cadets. It then lost almost all its original character, especially when the pilasters on the upper two storeys of the main block were replaced with a single giant order, and the shapes of the windows were changed. Something of the early Petrovian style may still be seen in the interior, in the ceremonial staircase, and in a few rooms decorated with Dutch tiles. In spite of later alterations, Menshikov's country residence at Oranienbaum (now Lomonosov), of 1713–25 [198], on the southern shore of the Gulf to the west of the city, kept more of its original appearance. The

distribution of the various elements recalls the early engravings of the Vasily Ostrov Palace, and recaptures something of that unusual combination of ostentation and domesticity which was present in so many of the early buildings of the capital. The plan of a central block flanked by lower semicircular wings ending in octagonal two-storeyed pavilions was a bold attempt to embrace with some sense of spaciousness the wide panorama of land and water stretching below the house to the formal gardens and so down to the sea. As the first of the larger Petersburg country palaces, Oranienbaum had considerable influence on later estates, both imperial and noble.

The other German architects who are known to have worked in St Petersburg after 1715 left little to show for their activity, which may have been largely devoted to public works. The only one who approached the stature of Schädel was Theodor Schwertfeger (in Russia 1716–33), who worked for Menshikov at Oranienbaum and Kronstadt. Later he assisted Tressini in revising the plans for the Alexander Nevsky Lavra and himself built the cath-

198. Gottfried Schädel: Oranienbaum (Lomonosov), Prince Menshikov's Palace, 1713–25.
From an engraving by M. I. Makhaev, 1761

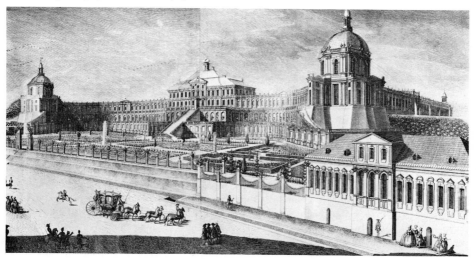

edral (1720–32, demolished 1755). From the wooden model [199] which has been preserved it can be seen that the rectangular plan was not unlike that of the Peter and Paul Cathedral. Schwertfeger reversed Tressini's proportions by designing a more powerful dome over a crossing which occupied half the length of the nave. At the west he placed two tall

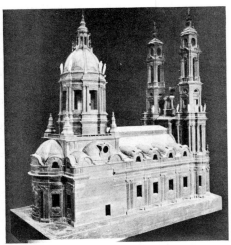

199. Wooden model for the Cathedral of the Trinity in the Alexander Nevsky Lavra, St Petersburg, by Domenico Tressini and Theodor Schwertfeger, built in 1720–32

five-storeyed towers. The vertical alternation of pilasters and engaged columns shows a lively instinct for the play of Baroque forms which one might almost think Italian, in the tradition of Borromini, were it not that the insistent verticality is closer to North German architecture.

From France came an architect as distinguished as Schlüter, Jean-Baptiste-Alexandre Le Blond (1679–1719). He was already well known in Paris when he was hired by the Tsar's agent in 1716 at the generous salary of 5000 roubles annually, on the condition that he would teach his art to young Russians.[14] Le Blond, whom Peter himself described as

an 'active and intelligent man', had built *hôtels* in Paris and had edited works on architecture and gardening. But, as with Schlüter, death unexpectedly interrupted a career which held the greatest promise for the future of Russian architecture. As it turned out, French influence, which might with Le Blond have proved a counter-attraction to German and Italian styles, was carried on by the painters, woodcarvers, and decorators who accompanied him to Russia. Immediately upon his arrival in his capacity as superintendent of all architectural work, he organized an Office of Construction, to which all designs were to be submitted. The following year he published his plan for St Petersburg, drawn up at Peter's request, which shows the dangers of theory unsupported by practical considerations. Le Blond followed Peter's thoughts in placing the centre of the city on one of the islands, in this case moving it from the Petersburg side to Vasily Ostrov, which he laid out as a series of straight streets intersecting at right angles between important squares which were also connected by diagonal avenues radiating from the imperial palace in the centre. An oval ring of fortifications with angular bastions tightly enclosed the city.[15] Rigid and arbitrary as the scheme was, it had its progressive aspects. Such public services as schools, prisons, and hospitals were to be situated on the periphery of the residential areas surrounding the central core of government buildings, while industries and commercial establishments were placed even further away. But the scheme failed to take account of certain practical and personal considerations. By planning the city on an island, Le Blond inhibited its natural and inevitable growth on the more accessible mainland south of the Neva, and he failed to understand the ambition of Menshikov whose palace was already well advanced and who had no intention of seeing his valuable properties on Vasily Ostrov turned into a municipal housing development. While Peter was abroad in 1717 the initial work was compromised by Menshikov; the canals were dug too narrow for shipping and so poorly that the earth fell back into them.

Le Blond's most important work was his design for the palace at Peterhof (now Petrodvorets), Peter's country residence on the Gulf on the road to Menshikov's Oranienbaum. Like the latter, this consisted of a central two-storey block flanked by low wings terminating in pavilions. But the whole was marked by French restraint and sobriety in contrast to Schädel's Baroque exuberance. The wings were straight instead of curved, and for the fanciful high-pitched roofs surmounted with princely crowns were substituted flat roofs over the main block and a square hipped roof over the central pavilion. Rastrelli later enlarged the palace for Elizabeth and destroyed its original coherence by adding an additional storey and formidably increasing the length in the manner of Tsarskoe Selo.[16] Peterhof, with its formal gardens, terraces, fountains, and cascades, must once have been more nearly what Peter seems to have wanted: a Russian equivalent of the palace and gardens of Versailles, which he had visited in 1717. The very names of the pavilions – Marly, Hermitage, Monplaisir – proclaimed that Peter, after having adopted Dutch and German names for his city and palace, was now moving in the wider orbit of French culture.

In addition to his general supervisory duties, Le Blond redesigned the Summer Garden, which he laid out as a series of ornamental and geometrical patterns like those in the separate parts of the park at Versailles. Despite the disappearance of all the buildings actually constructed or designed by Le Blond, the Summer Garden, even in its present mutilated condition, is a reminder of how successfully he had transported to the Neva the principles of French landscape architecture.

The premature deaths of Schlüter and Le Blond left Peter's remaining plans in competent if uninspired hands. The completion of Le Blond's second country residence for Peter, at Strelna near Peterhof, was carried forward

and the palace changed into an Italian villa by Nicolo Michetti (Miketti, in Russia 1718–23), who had worked with Carlo Fontana and in the papal service. Michetti would have turned Strelna into something more nearly resembling an Italian villa than anything Peter had yet achieved.[17] On either side of a monumental entrance in the style of a triumphal arch, a colossal order of pilasters, supported by an arcaded basement, rose through three storeys to an attic and flat Italian roof. But Strelna was rebuilt three times in the nineteenth century, so that it is of no interest for the Petrovian period. Michetti's principal occupation was the design and construction of fountains and arcades at Peterhof, at first only temporary structures of wood and plaster. The only surviving example of his architecture is the Ekaterinental Palace (1719–25) near Reval (now Tallinn). This country seat which Peter built for his wife was a modest, even confused essay in the late Baroque.

Among the last of Peter's architects was the first native-born Russian to work in the international style. Mikhail Grigorievich Zemtsov (1686–1743) was born in Moscow and educated in St Petersburg, where as a boy he learned Italian, Dutch, and German – necessary tools for communication with the foreigners in the capital. In 1710 he was apprenticed to Tressini, and later served as his assistant. He also worked with Le Blond and Michetti on the grotto for the Summer Garden. In June 1720 Michetti certified that Zemtsov was capable of undertaking architectural work independently, whereupon he went to Reval to finish Michetti's Ekaterinental Palace. Although he had never been abroad, his interior decorations, particularly the relief sculpture, are surprisingly elegant. When Michetti failed to return from a trip to Italy in 1723, Zemtsov took his place. In 1725 he designed a temporary 'Salon' in the Summer Garden for the wedding ceremonies of Peter's elder daughter, Anna Petrovna, with the Duke of Holstein-Gottorp. This was a single large hall appearing externally as a two-storeyed pavilion with a

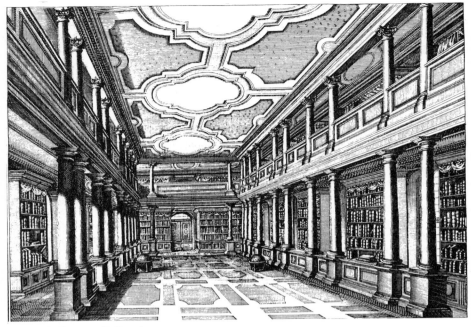

200. M. G. Zemtsov: St Petersburg,
Library of the Academy of Sciences in the Kunstkamera,
c. 1730

giant order of Corinthian pilasters and a low roof behind a balustrade. The taste was Italian, a consequence of his work with Michetti, but the gracious proportions suggest that Zemtsov had absorbed something of Le Blond's French manner. About 1730 he designed the library for Mattarnovy's Kunstkamera [200]. This solemn hall is an admirable expression of the serious side of Petrovian architecture. Practical arrangements for the shelving of books came first; the decorative adornments, the two orders of columns and the simple but effective design on the ceiling, second. For his two churches in St Petersburg, SS. Simeon and Anna (1729–34) and the Nativity of the Virgin on the Nevsky Prospekt (1733–7), the latter on the site of the present Cathedral of Kazan (see below, pages 317–20), he followed Tressini's scheme for the Peter-

Paul Cathedral, a long, rectangular nave with an eastern dome and western belfry and spire. However, he varied the proportions, reducing the height of the spire and increasing the size of the dome so that the three elements were more in harmony with each other. The plain surfaces and sober detail reflect Anna Ioannovna's economical attitude towards the expenditure of public funds. The 'Protestant' phase of Russian church architecture at no time was so pervasive as during the reign of this German princess. The interior of the Nativity of the Virgin, as it appears in an eighteenth-century painting, in its spacious lightness and lack of pictorial embellishment far more resembles Wren's City churches than any previous Russian building. If Zemtsov's architecture was not very original, and he was more an able eclectic than a creator of new forms, his career was important. It showed that a native-born architect could obtain some understanding and competence in the European manner, even without study abroad. Zemtsov maintained his position as the leading architect of the Court throughout Anna's reign and into the first years of Elizabeth's. Late in life he prepared a new plan for the reconstruction of the palace at Tsarskoe Selo (now Pushkin), a work which was ultimately carried out by Rastrelli.

With the accession of Elizabeth an old order ended and a new began. Peter and his immediate successors had been chiefly interested in the architecture, arts, and sciences of the north of Europe. Peter's enthusiasm for German science and for Dutch and English technology is seen in the choice of his first architects from among men working in Denmark, Germany, and Holland, although curiously the Dutch architects were the least numerous of all in early St Petersburg.[18] The presence and activity of Tressini, Schlüter, Schädel, and Schwertfeger gave to the first constructions a sober, utilitarian quality which was the visual expression of Peter's interest in military science and political economy. Only with the appearance of Le Blond and the French craftsmen who accompanied him was this sense of practicality relaxed to permit the building of pleasure palaces and the development of extensive gardens, which also had for Peter a practical interest as well as an artistic one.

At the time of his death Peter could have looked upon his city with a sense of accomplishment. Its monumental buildings – the Cathedral, the Fortress, the Twelve Colleges – were variations of a European style, to be sure, but they were also not quite like similar buildings in any other country.[19] As yet St Petersburg lacked a truly imperial residence and would have to wait until Elizabeth's Winter Palace, the fourth on the site (see pages 283–6), came into being. Meanwhile the future growth of the city, which could not have been contained within Le Blond's rigid scheme of 1716, had been foreseen in new plans drawn up by an imperial commission after disastrous fires in 1736 and 1737. From the Admiralty, rather than from the palace, three broad avenues, intersecting the concentric system of canals, were laid out in a goose-foot pattern, possibly suggested by the radial avenues leading from the palace at Versailles. The easternmost, the Nevsky Prospekt ending at the Alexander Nevsky Lavra on the Neva, was to become the principal thoroughfare of St Petersburg and one of the most famous avenues in Europe. If, by the end of Anna Ioannovna's reign in 1740, there were, between the fine palaces along the river and the encroaching forests, only clusters of wooden buildings, precariously supported on the treacherous marshes, still there was time to grow and space to grow in. The sporadic distribution of its buildings, on the low plains bordering the broad, swift waters of the Neva, gave the capital a wide, if somewhat empty, grandeur. Unloved and unlovable though the city may have been at first, it would acquire in time a strange and oppressive beauty.

CHAPTER 20

ELIZABETH'S ROCOCO:

1741–1762

The fourth of Peter the Great's successors was the closest to him in blood and most nearly resembled him in character. Elizaveta Petrovna was stubborn, sensual, hot-tempered, and wholeheartedly devoted to Russia. But she differed from her father in being blessed with great good nature, beauty, and an insatiable ability to enjoy herself. Elizabeth's attitude towards her inheritance can be seen in her affection for Moscow. She of course went there for her coronation in 1742, but she chose to stay a year, holding a gayer and more brilliant Court than the Muscovites had ever seen. And she continued to return to Moscow for lengthy visits throughout the twenty years of her reign, especially to worship at the holy shrines as a pilgrim during recurrent accesses of religious enthusiasm. In this way the old city recaptured some of the prestige which Peter had tried to destroy, and its new status is reflected in the considerable development of architecture in Moscow and its environs during the later eighteenth century.[1]

The combination of Elizabeth's love for her own country with her French tastes – she had once thought of marrying Louis XV, and all her life tried to maintain friendly relations with the French Court – proved extraordinarily beneficial for Russian culture. The influx of French diplomats, travellers who came to pay court to the fabulous Empress and to admire the sights – artists, adventurers, and odd-job men – stimulated an interest in international affairs on the part of the Russian upper classes which Peter had been unable to arouse with his peremptory reforms.[2] It is some measure of Elizabeth's accomplishment that although she may have been uninterested in political or territorial aggrandizement her

reign saw the emergence of the first great modern Russian intellectual, the renowned chemist and man of letters, Mikhail Vasilievich Lomonosov (1708/15–65), and the foundation in Moscow of the first Russian university (1755). The spectacular achievements of Catherine II were based, far more than she ever cared to admit, on the cultural and spiritual foundation laid by her predecessor.

The character of the sovereign and of the environment which she wished to create for herself and for Russia appeared immediately in the first works of her chief architect. Count Bartolommeo Francesco (Varfolomei Varfolomeevich) Rastrelli (1700–71) was the son of an Italian sculptor, Count Carlo Bartolommeo Rastrelli (the title was a papal one), who had come to Russia with Le Blond in 1716.[3] As a youth he entered at once into the activity of those first Petersburg years, and soon showed such a talent for architecture that on two occasions, in 1719–21 and again about 1725, he was sent abroad to study. The first time he went to Paris to work under Robert de Cotte; during the second trip, which may have lasted five years, he probably visited Saxony, Bohemia, Austria, and Italy. His talents were recognized by Anna Ioannovna, for whom he reconstructed Tressini's and Michetti's second Winter Palace in time for the Empress's return from Moscow in 1732. For Anna's favourite, Ernst Johann Biren of Courland, he began a palace at Mitau (now Yelgava). Neither of these works exhibits more than a competent handling of late Baroque forms, perhaps lighter in some respects than the architecture of Peter's time, but fundamentally simple, probably due to the German tastes of Anna and her courtiers. A more vigorous touch, hinting at things to come, possibly once distinguished the wooden palace that Rastrelli built for Anna in the Kremlin on the occasion of her coronation in 1730. The Empress was so pleased that the following year she had it re-erected in the German Quarter on the edge of the river Yauza. This 'Summer Annenhof' burned down in 1746, but was rebuilt for Elizabeth after new designs by Rastrelli.[4]

Rastrelli's real opportunities came with the accession of Elizabeth. For twenty years he

he was in turn the architect of Anna Ioannovna, of her German favourites Biren and Münnich, and of the Regent Anna Leopoldovna, for whom in 1740 he began the 'third' Summer Palace. This work involved only the enlargement of the little cottage Peter had built at the bottom of the Summer Garden for Catherine. The plans were revised and considerably enlarged for Elizabeth, so that in the end the new Summer Palace of 1741–4 [201] was the most magnificent building in St

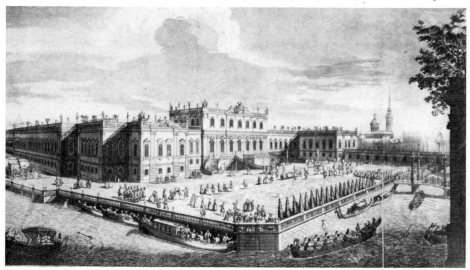

201. B. F. Rastrelli: St Petersburg, the Summer Palace on the Fontanka, 1741–4.
From an engraving by M. I. Makhaev, 1761

not only designed all the larger government buildings, but also supervised all other architectural activity in Russia. And since, as time passed, more and more of the younger generation became his pupils or followers, his genius is indelibly printed on Russian architecture of the middle years of the century. It was fortunate for Rastrelli that his imagination was matched by Elizabeth's taste. In this most autocratic of empires he survived what for a less talented man at the hands of a less generous sovereign would have meant exile and disgrace. It is little less than miraculous that

Petersburg and the Empress's favourite residence in town. It was built of wood, a material Rastrelli had already used for his vanished palaces in Moscow. Elizabeth's own spirit also began to work its spell; for the building, to judge from contemporary paintings and engravings, had a truly fairy-tale character. In plan it was French. From the street a central two-storey block which contained a single large ballroom somewhat in the manner of Zemtsov's pavilion of 1725 was flanked by one-storey service wings forming a courtyard not unlike that of a Parisian *hôtel*. The central

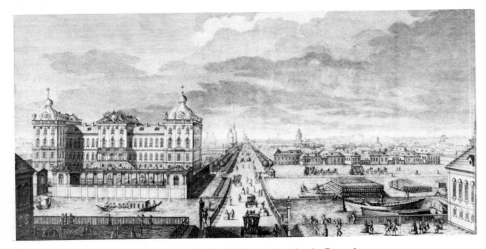

202. B. F. Rastrelli: St Petersburg, the Anichkov Palace on the Nevsky Prospekt,
looking north towards the Admiralty; begun by Zemtsov in 1742, finished by Rastrelli after 1744.
From an engraving by M. I. Makhaev, 1761

block carried two orders of pilasters, while the long expanse of the wings was broken only by pedimented windows and pilasters in the Italian manner. The flat roofs supported balustrades and a host of ornamental statuary. On the north the palace faced the Summer Garden across the Fontanka. Here, where the main storey stood upon a high basement and the gardens were reached by a double flight of curving steps, the effect was more Italian.

In this first building of the new reign the quality of Rastrelli's architecture was already evident. In the best sense of the word he was an eclectic, with that rare ability to combine elements from other styles into something not wholly derivative nor entirely untraditional. Elizabeth and her Court wanted neither. It was well that the palace resembled those of the Courts of western Europe, and yet that it was something which could only have been created in St Petersburg. The specifically Russian characteristics were undoubtedly due to scale and colour, two aspects which disappeared for ever when Paul I tore down the Summer Palace to make way for his Michael Castle.[5]

After the new Summer Palace, Rastrelli's next task was to finish the Anichkov Palace [202], on the Nevsky Prospekt by the Anichkov Bridge over the Fontanka. In 1742 Elizabeth had commissioned Zemtsov to design this residence for Alexey Razumovsky, but the Russian architect died the next year. After 1744 Rastrelli finished the palace as a five-part structure, with central and end pavilions separated by lower wings. As in the Summer Palace, the details were Italian, but the exuberant, dome-like roofs with onion-shaped cupolas over the pavilions were the first hints of Rastrelli's growing appreciation of the older Russian forms. The Anichkov Palace (now the Kirov Palace of Young Pioneers) has been several times rebuilt and so thoroughly altered that only early engravings show its original character. Makhaev's view of 1761 shows the contrast between the commanding height of the palace and the low one-storey housing after Tressini's designs. The view of the palace from the Fontanka Canal is now blocked by Quarenghi's Ionic colonnaded building, erected in 1803 as a shopping arcade and subsequently altered for Alexander I as administrative offices.

Within the next few years Rastrelli built many town residences for the nobility, but only two still preserved into the twentieth century their original exteriors. The Vorontsov Palace, later the Corps of Pages (1749–57), recalls the Summer Palace in the distribution of the pedimented windows and pilasters, but now the material was masonry and the individual elements, especially the paired columns flanking the main entrance, were more sober and assertive. If the relation to the Summer Palace could be considered a dynastic one – for Vice-Chancellor Vorontsov was related to the Empress by marriage – the building marks an important transitional stage between the caprice of the Summer Palace and the more august work Rastrelli would shortly create for Elizabeth.

The second of Rastrelli's preserved palaces, for Baron Stroganov on the Nevsky Prospekt at the Moika canal (1750–4), is closer to his imperial work. Here the earlier compartmented façade with two storeys of windows of equal size has been reorganized as a *piano nobile* on a basement with an attic above. The windows, differing in each storey in size and shape, are framed in the more playful style of the German or Austrian Rococo. The central element receives a more vigorous treatment, as the upper storeys are bound together by a giant order of Corinthian columns, the inner pair doubled in depth, supporting a curved, broken, and recessed pediment. The proportions of the whole have been somewhat spoiled by a rise in the level of the street, so that the windows in the rusticated basement have lost a third and more of their height. The Stroganov Palace, more than any of Rastrelli's work up to this time, shows his genius for combining the fancy of Rococo decorative devices with a powerful treatment of monumental Baroque forms.

Rastrelli's next task was the reconstruction of Peterhof. Elizabeth cherished this palace for its memories of her father, but his simple small rooms could no longer accommodate the crowd of pleasure-seekers who clustered around her. As early as 1741 she decided to enlarge the palace, but the revised plans were not accepted until 1747, and the palace was not finished until 1752. Elizabeth insisted that Rastrelli double the length yet retain the general *ordonnance* of the central block, to which he was obliged to add one storey in order to keep it the dominant element of his composition [203, 204]. Le Blond's original design can be seen on the south façade (towards the town), where the end pavilions of his building are still only two bays wide. On both north and south façades the outline of his high hipped roof can be identified against the new roof behind it. The central part of Peterhof is thus less Rastrellian, preserving as it does something of the early discretion of Le Blond. The interiors have been altered, but the Merchants' Staircase preserved much of the original brilliance of Rastrelli's inexhaustibly inventive decorations.

Rastrelli's flair appeared in the two square pavilions at the ends of the wings, one containing the palace chapel and the other known as the Pavilion of the Coat of Arms. They are flanked by low wings and bear the familiar giant order of pilasters on a high basement. The roofs, in the form of rectangular flattened domes crowned with lanterns and bulbous cupolas, are among his most ingenious improvisations on a theme from older Russian architecture. Elizabeth herself was interested in the late-seventeenth-century churches of Moscow, and in 1746 she unexpectedly ordered Rastrelli to change the original one-domed design for the palace chapel at Tsarskoe Selo to five domes. The next year she commissioned another five-domed church in St Petersburg after an 'approved model' based on drawings and measurements which had been made from the cathedrals in the Kremlin.[6]

The church at Peterhof was the first of a series wherein Rastrelli recovered for Russia the older Orthodox form after its brief eclipse

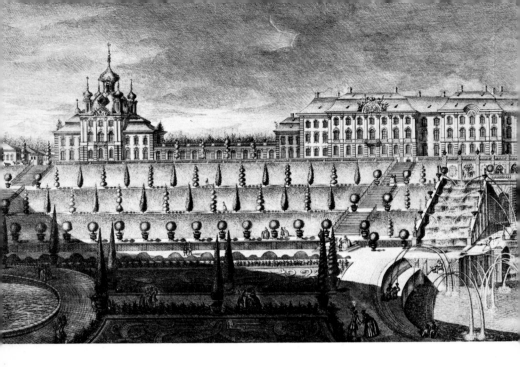

by the churches built for Peter the Great. In his Cathedrals of St Andrew in Kiev (1747–67), constructed from his designs by the Moscow architect I. F. Michurin, and of the Smolny Convent in St Petersburg (1748–57) [205] Rastrelli united the most spontaneous enthusiasm with a sensitive understanding of the harmonious relation and distribution of the parts. Both churches are Rococo in the fullest sense of the term, if by that we can understand that a very personal attitude towards Baroque forms has been imbued with a joyous, even secular feeling. Each was extravagant, not so much in the sense of the cost or value of the materials, as in the prodigal expenditure of architectural devices, yet each was at the same time unmistakably a religious building. In plan the Church of St Andrew is a Greek cross, lengthened along the east–west axis by the projecting apse and western bay. The four

subsidiary domes are placed on slender lanterns above buttresses extending diagonally from the angles of the cross. Additional importance is given to these projections by the paired engaged columns, in contrast to the paired pilasters which adorn the walls of the church itself. In the design of the central dome and subsidiary cupolas Rastrelli devised a variety of forms which in plan, section, and profile compose an intricate counterpoint upon the principal theme. Nowhere else could his genius show to better advantage than in the contrast of this blue, white, and gold invention with the lumpy Baroque details with which the legendary early churches of Kiev had been smothered.

For Elizabeth's Smolny Convent, which Catherine II converted in 1764 into a boarding school for daughters of the nobility modelled after Mme de Maintenon's seminary at St Cyr,

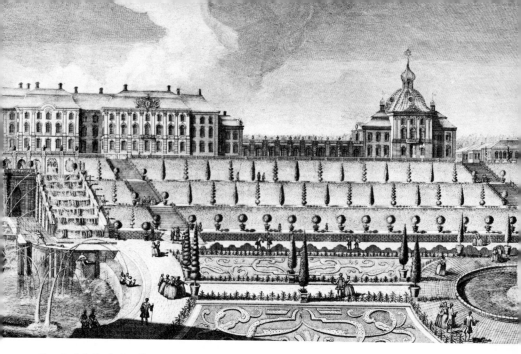

203. Peterhof, J.-B.-A. Le Blond's palace of 1716–17 as remodelled by Rastrelli in 1747–52. From an engraving by M. I. Makhaev, 1761

204. Peterhof. The centre of the palace in modern times

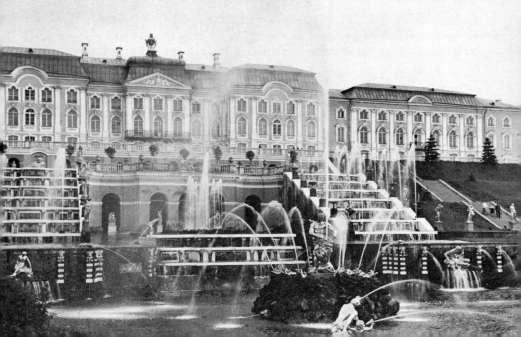

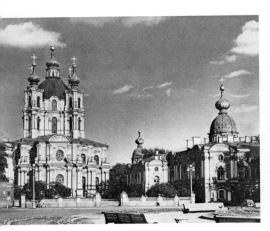

205. B. F. Rastrelli: St Petersburg, Smolny Cathedral, 1748–57

Rastrelli devised a vast plan of conventual structures arranged in a Greek cross with domed pavilions at the re-entrant angles repeating in diminished proportions the form of the cathedral in the centre. The model, which is still in existence, shows how carefully he intended the general silhouette to resemble the great monastic establishments of medieval Russia. The many domes and lanterns would have recreated the impression of churches rising behind their fortified walls. Over the main entrance Rastrelli intended to place an exceptionally tall tower, even loftier than the belfries of the older monasteries. Here again he combined the old and the new, for if the lower portions were treated as a rather ponderous version of the typical Baroque many-storeyed tower complete with columns, pediments, and brackets, the upper part was planned as a vertiginously elongated version of the tower of Ivan Veliky in Moscow. The unusual height may have been due, however, quite as much to Rastrelli's desire to create a monument which would dominate both the city and the convent, as to the Russian taste for sheer size [206].[7]

The magnificent blue and white cathedral [205] was only begun by Rastrelli, and the lack

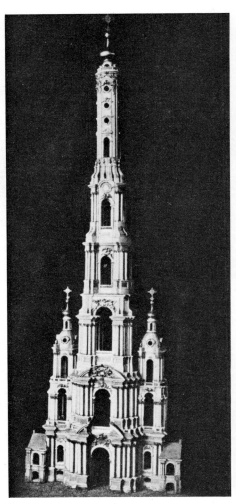

206. B. F. Rastrelli:
Wooden model of the proposed belfry
for the Smolny Convent, St Petersburg, c. 1750

of much of the ornament which would have enlivened the façades cannot be blamed on him. The wooden model, cut away to show the interior, proves that Rastrelli did not intend to place the subsidiary turrets so close to the central dome, and that the white-and-gold interior of the church would have been one of his most generous decorative schemes. As it happened the work dragged on and was finished only in 1835 by the architect Stasov, who replaced Rastrelli's original designs with a chastely severe Neo-Classical interior in white and gold, and grey marble.

Rastrelli's last large works for Elizabeth were the two most important imperial palaces. In the rebuilding of the Great Palace (also called the Catherine, or Old, Palace) at Tsarskoe Selo (now Pushkin) (1749-52),[8] and of the Winter Palace in St Petersburg (from 1752), Rastrelli again had to deal with unusually extended façades, as at Peterhof. The Great Palace [207] is 978 feet in length, and unlike Peterhof this tremendous range is unbroken by any significant projections or changes in height. Once again Elizabeth insisted on preserving as much as possible of the original palace, built for her mother, Catherine I. Rastrelli's problem was to find some way of adding larger state apartments to this relatively modest core which had already been reconstructed by Zemtsov and an enlargement planned by Kvasov.[9] The original element – a three-storey block with slightly projecting pavilions at the centre and ends separated by ranges of four windows' width – was in itself a more up-to-date version of Le Blond's central block at Peterhof. By enlarging the palace through the almost endless extension of the wings, Rastrelli could do little more than perform variations on the same theme. His effort was concerned with the parts rather than with the whole. For the long wings he adopted the powerful entrance motif of the Stroganov Palace: an exuberant arrangement of pilasters alternating with pairs of engaged Corinthian columns supporting broken pediments [208]. The original colours may have enlivened the endless expanse of columns and windows; for the walls were painted yellow (they are now light blue), the architectural ornament white, and the figural sculpture, caryatids, and garlands were gilded. The interior, in the style of the times, consisted of an immense succession

of state rooms extending from the only staircase at the south end to the chapel at the north, a thousand feet away. Cameron's later staircase, and his Fourth Apartment, were destroyed in the last war; the present central staircase or White Vestibule is an attractive Rococo confection of 1860 by Ipolit Antonovich Monigetti, who also built the Turkish Bath, an oriental folly, in the garden.

For the park at Tsarskoe Selo, Rastrelli designed three domed pavilions with one-storey wings ornamented with the familiar repertory of engaged columns and curved, angular, and broken pediments. The Hermitage (1748-52) and the Grotto (1755-7) were preserved to modern times, but suffered somewhat through the loss of much of their sculptural decoration. The finest of the three, Mon Bijou [209], familiarly called in Russian Monbezh, was allowed to deteriorate, and in the 1820s was demolished by Nicholas I to make way for a pseudo-Gothic 'Arsenal'. The disappearance of Monbezh is regrettable, if the eighteenth-century engravings have correctly preserved the Rococo brilliance of this little pavilion. The multiple flights of steps were among Rastrelli's finest studies in Baroque space, and the dome, with its tapered cupola, was yet another fantasy first evoked at Peterhof. Entirely of its time though it may have been, Monbezh could have evoked memories of an earlier Russia for those who knew the seventeenth-century churches of Moscow such as Fili and St Vladimir [158, 159]. Rastrelli's designs for the park and gardens closely followed the irresistible example of Versailles. Near the palace were small geometrical parterres, in the distance wooded groves bisected by broad avenues and rambling paths where the usual eighteenth-century architectural exotica could be found (see page 335).[10]

The fourth and final Winter Palace in St Petersburg presented once more the same problem of an interminable façade which had to be unified [210]. Rastrelli devised a five-part arrangement of no less than thirty-seven bays

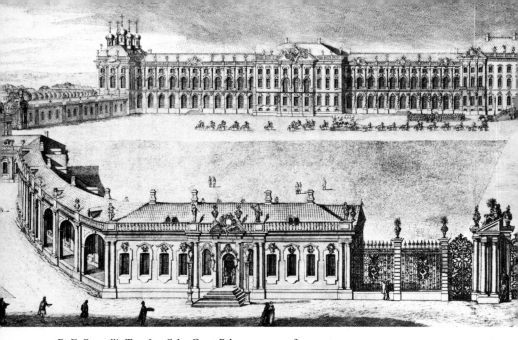

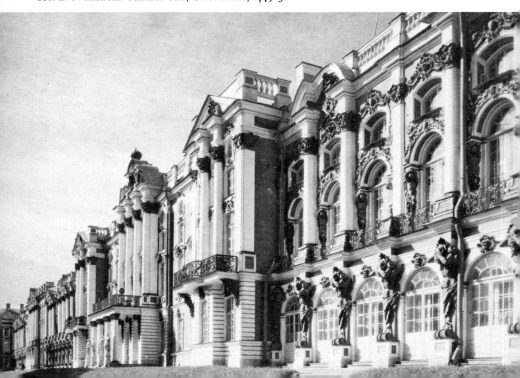

207. B. F. Rastrelli: Tsarskoe Selo, Great Palace, 1749–52, forecourt.
From an engraving by M. I. Makhaev, 1761

208. B. F. Rastrelli: Tsarskoe Selo, Great Palace, 1749–52

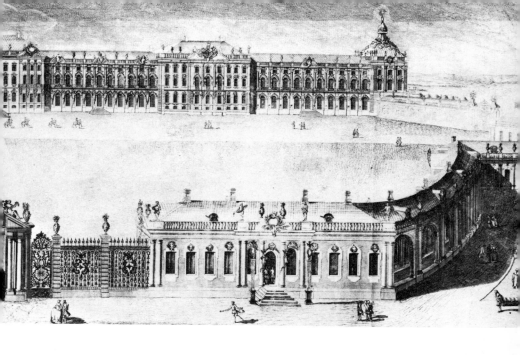

209. B. F. Rastrelli: Tsarskoe Selo, the pavilion of Monbezh ('Mon Bijou') in the park, *c.* 1750. From an engraving by M. I. Makhaev, 1761

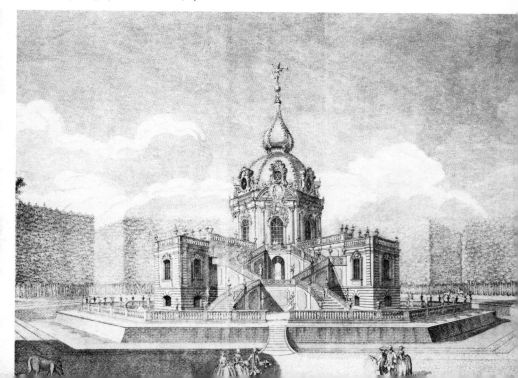

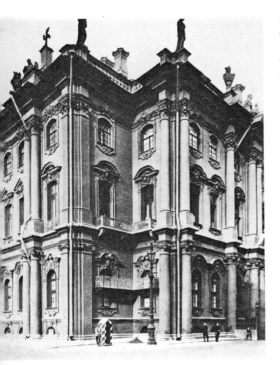

210. B. F. Rastrelli: St Petersburg,
the Winter Palace, 1754–62

which seems to crush the columns of the lower storey. This depressed effect has, however, been exaggerated on the Neva façade by the disappearance of the bases of the lower columns when the Neva quay was constructed in the 1770s. Since Elizabeth and Rastrelli preferred above all else the graces of the Rococo style, the pleasantest parts of the Winter Palace are the treatment of the windows and the host of statues and urns which once cavorted on the balustrade above the cornice [211]. When the palace was new and painted turquoise blue with white trim (it is now sea-green and white), it must have shimmered in the waters of the Neva, the last and most exuberant of Elizabeth's creations. In the nineteenth century a uniform coat of dark red paint extinguished its gaiety, and the interior suffered even more grievously. In 1837, after a fire which raged three days, it was completely rebuilt and renovated by a commission under V. P. Stasov (see below, pages 324–6). Fortunately Nicholas I's grandiose but heavy taste was kept under control by Stasov's impeccable Neo-Classicism. The Jordan Staircase [212], so called because the sovereign descended it for the annual Blessing of the Waters on the Feast of the Epiphany, was completely rebuilt without loss of its Rastrellian character.

A comparison of the three immense palaces – Peterhof, Tsarskoe Selo, and the Winter Palace – with the Smolny Cathedral and its belfry, St Andrew in Kiev, the pavilions of Monbezh and the Hermitage at Tsarskoe Selo, even with the oratory of the Holy Sepulchre in the New Jerusalem Monastery at Istra (1747–60) [155],[11] shows that Rastrelli was not really a monumental architect. He excelled when the programme required a small unified structure. Like all true artists of the Baroque inheritance, he saw shapes sculpturally. Perhaps that is why his smaller buildings are so complete. Rastrelli visualized them from all sides, as three-dimensional objects. The large palaces offered no such opportunity, and his imagination flagged when faced with the

on the Neva façade, thirty-nine on the west, and fifty on the Palace Square to the south. Each is too long for the height of the three-storey building, although the garden (west) side is perhaps more coherent. There the great length appears diminished by the handsome end pavilions projecting five bays beyond the central wall. On the Neva the end pavilions consist of no less than nine bays, and the effect is that of an endless succession of identical parts, however skilful the alternation of window and column may be within the separate groups. For the *ordonnance* Rastrelli returned to a more Italian arrangement than he had used since his first work. Upon a low basement he placed three storeys, the upper two embraced by a giant Corinthian order

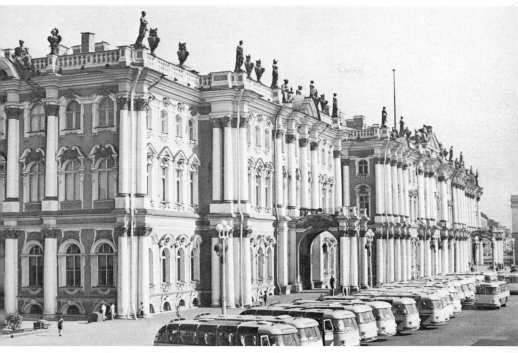

211. B. F. Rastrelli: St Petersburg, the Winter Palace, 1754–62

design of a long and flat façade. His use of columns at Tsarskoe Selo and of a two-storey *ordonnance* of engaged columns and pilasters at the Winter Palace was an ineffectual attempt to escape from what must have been the menace of formidable sterility.

The significance of Rastrelli's accomplishment for Russia lies in his creation of a consistent Russian version of the late Baroque, distinguished from its European counterparts by its scale, its plastic exuberance, and its colour. Had Smolny been completed as he designed it, the conventual city of towers and domes, painted blue and white with details picked out in silver, would have been one of the most sumptuous monuments of the style. Rastrelli's informed and tasteful eclecticism was undoubtedly drawn from many sources, a

circumstance common at the time. Yet though his work shows many resemblances to contemporary architecture elsewhere, especially in northern Italy and Austria, we may, in the absence of documentary information concerning his early life and travels, postulate his use of published sources.[12] The unmistakably theatrical quality of his architecture may even have a more direct relation to the theatre than has been suspected. The long façades of his palaces, the diagonal axes of his church towers and of the wings of his garden pavilions, the unexpected and inexplicable vertical elongation of his orders, are expressions of a visual rather than of a structural or functional aesthetic, such as he could have studied in the engravings of Piranesi and in the theatrical designs of the Bibiena.[13] If this be so, then

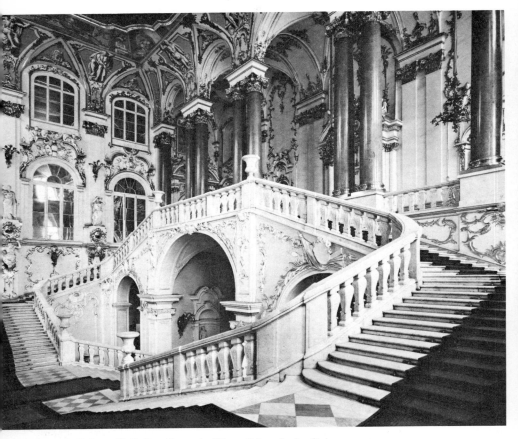

212. B. F. Rastrelli: St Petersburg, the Winter Palace, Jordan Staircase, 1757, reconstructed by V. P. Stasov after 1837

Rastrelli, perhaps more convincingly and certainly more grandiosely than any of his predecessors or contemporaries, made as imperceptible as possible the transition from the life of the stage to the life of the world. In this connexion we should not forget that his vivacious Empress was happiest in masquerade.

When Elizabeth died in January 1762 Ras- trelli's influence soon waned.[14] The new Emperor, Peter III, was more interested in drilling troops than in building palaces, and his wife, the Grand Duchess Catherine, had no more patience with his tastes than with those of her frivolous aunt. She was determined to alter matters drastically, and in a very short time she did.

CHAPTER 21

THE CLASSICISM OF CATHERINE II:

1762–1796

It is a paradox of Russian history that the greatest sovereign of the Romanov dynasty should have been neither a Romanov nor a Russian. The Princess Sophia of Anhalt-Zerbst was German by birth and education, but when she was married in 1744, at the age of fifteen, to the Grand Duke Peter, she entered the Orthodox Church, took the name of Catherine (Ekaterina), and settled down to make a career for herself in Russia. Six months after Elizabeth's death Catherine won the support of the guard regiments in St Petersburg, swept her weak and spiteful husband aside, imprisoned him, and probably countenanced his assassination a few days later. When she had secured the throne, she immediately demonstrated that singular combination of intelligence, energy, and taste which marked the thirty-four years of her reign. Her character was a compound of moral purpose, calculation, and instinct. Her sensuality surprised even her contemporaries; her opinions were respected by Voltaire, Grimm, and Helvétius. In her political actions she alternated between conservative liberalism and traditional Russian autocracy. She abolished torture as a legal instrument, yet condemned the Metropolitan of Rostov to perpetual solitary confinement for opposing the sequestration of Church property. She undertook, unsuccessfully to be sure, the revision of Russian law, in the hope of providing equal justice for all classes, yet she participated as greedily as Prussia and Austria in the three partitions of Poland. In these opposed though complementary aspects of her character she does not differ essentially from other sovereigns of the eighteenth century whose concepts of enlightened despotism combined a cruelty which

appals us with a theoretical liberalism we can still admire. For the history of Russian culture Catherine's enigmatic personality was of the greatest importance. She possessed an informed interest in European thought and taste as well as a sincere affection for and knowledge of her adopted country. No other ruler, with the exception of Peter the Great, travelled so widely throughout the country, and it is probable that no other had so comprehensive an understanding of the history and traditions of Russia.[1] During her reign the art of architecture lost the last vestiges of provincialism and became if not a decisive at least a fully valid contribution to the history of European art. The other arts – literature, painting, and sculpture – were slower to develop, but the foundations for their future were laid during Catherine's reign, largely through the institutions which she fostered and the climate of opinion which her lively intelligence induced. Those who consider a church by Rastrelli only a Russian variant of the European Rococo will be obliged to admit that Zakharov's Admiralty (1806–23) [235–7] and the poetry of Pushkin (1799–1837) are not only great works of Russian art but, in spite of all the difficulties of distance and translation, are important contributions to European classicism and romanticism. Neither is conceivable without the artistic preparation of Catherine's reign.

Catherine's taste was always a decisive factor.[2] Peter the Great and Elizabeth had both lived publicly, the father as a jack-of-all-trades and the daughter as the leader of a perpetual masquerade, and their buildings expressed their personalities. Catherine kept her public and private lives apart. For the first time in Russia the private and the official life of the sovereign were different in purpose and character. This situation, unimaginable in Muscovy, and unnecessary for Peter or Elizabeth, enabled Catherine to live as a European citizen, while outwardly maintaining the apparatus of an imperial state. Thus the buildings of her reign are of two different kinds: public buildings which surpassed in intention if not in execution anything hitherto proposed in Russia, and private buildings for her own use. Between the two a third class consisted of large palaces erected for her favourites, or by the wealthier gentry. They were less willing than Catherine to withdraw from the public eye and more anxious to attribute to themselves some of the magnificence which, as the owners of enormous estates and masters of thousands of serfs, they were able to afford.

The architecture of Catherine's reign represents not just one phase of later-eighteenth-century classicism, but includes several changes of direction and of emphasis. During the 1760s Catherine's first task was to establish a new point of departure by dispersing or dissolving the traces of the Rococo inherited from her aunt.[3] From the later 1760s and throughout the 1770s a more energetic attitude of innovation appeared in the work of three architects of different nationalities: Velten, a German, Rinaldi, an Italian, and Bazhenov, a Russian. Each created or conceived at least one important architectural complex which, though still Baroque in plan or elevation, was at least more demonstrably classic in massing and detail than any previous work. Bazhenov's designs were the culmination of the Russian Late Baroque in the hands of a master of plan and organization, but one whose very energy seems to have compromised him with the Empress. The third and last phase was marked by a thorough-going classicism based on the interaction of two influences: the study of antique architecture and the revival of Palladio. Again this was in the hands of an international triumvirate: the Scotsman Cameron, the Italian Quarenghi, and the Russian Starov.

Starov came last and committed the architectural future of Russia for two decades or more to that strict classicism known abroad as the Empire Style. For another half-century Paul I, Alexander I, and Nicholas I in a sense merely continued with modifications the fundamental elements of plan, structure, profile, and detail worked out by Catherine and her architects from 1780.

Catherine's preference for a simpler style than the Rococo was prompted as much by instinct as by her contempt for the antics of Elizabeth. Yet at the start she was obliged to look to the past for her first architectural projects. Even in the midst of Elizabeth's reign there had been agents at work ready to modify the Rococo. They would probably have done so even had Elizabeth herself lived longer. Such an agent was the young Count Ivan Ivanovich Shuvalov (1727–97), who of all his countrymen was probably the one most in sympathy with European civilization. He spoke several languages, had travelled extensively, and corresponded with several of the leading *philosophes*, including Voltaire and Helvétius. Under his patronage the young Russian architect Alexandr Filippovich Kokorinov (1726–72), who had been trained in Moscow in Prince Ukhtomsky's school, built a palace in St Petersburg (1753–4) where a precocious use of academic, even Neo-Classical, details was combined with a new sobriety in the plain walls relieved by the slightest of window-frames and panels. In the windows, too, he abandoned Rastrelli's aggressive plastic ornament for simple rectangular and oval shapes.[4]

Since it is unlikely that a Russian architect could have learned in Moscow, in a school saturated with Rastrellian influence, these decorative touches so thoroughly in the spirit of French classicism of the 1750s, it is probable that Shuvalov himself had discovered them in his travels. Shuvalov then commissioned the distinguished French architect, Jean-François Blondel, the Younger (1705–74), to design a building for the Academy of Fine Arts which he proposed to establish as a

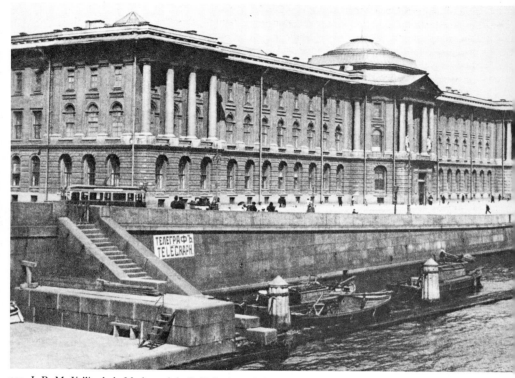

213. J.-B.-M. Vallin de la Mothe and A. F. Kokorinov: St Petersburg, Academy of Fine Arts, 1765–72

branch of the University of Moscow, founded through his initiative in 1755. The Senate, in response to Shuvalov's eloquent memorandum, issued a ukase in 1758 for the creation of an academy and the erection of a proper building in St Petersburg.

In 1759 Shuvalov summoned to Russia and appointed as a professor in the new Academy the French architect Jean-Baptiste-Michel Vallin de la Mothe (Vallen Delamot, 1729–1800, in Russia 1759–76).[5] Since there is a basic similarity between Blondel's design for the projected Academy in Moscow and the present building, as executed in St Petersburg, it may be that the younger architect was urged to make use of it, or perhaps even to enlarge

and make more monumental a structure commenced by Kokorinov from Blondel's designs before the arrival of Vallin de la Mothe. At all events through Kokorinov's long association with the Academy as professor, vice-rector, and rector, the building may have gained much of its character, and Levitsky's portrait [258] showing him pointing to the plan suggests that by his contemporaries he was considered largely responsible for the work, perhaps as a general superintendent.[6]

The French inclinations of Shuvalov and Kokorinov found a full and very beautiful expression in Vallin de la Mothe's design [213]. In plan it is a square with a large circular court flanked by four smaller rectangular courts. For the time this was a practical as well as palatial solution. From the principal entrance a double flight of stairs leads up to a circular ceremonial hall. To the left and right are long galleries for exhibitions culminating in octagonal halls at the far ends. Along the sides and around the circular courtyard are the drawing- and painting-rooms, and a chapel for the students and faculty. On the exterior Vallin de la Mothe retained Blondel's two storeys above a rusticated basement embraced by a giant order and the central pavilion, but he replaced an awkward roof over the principal entrance with a low dome. Although his design suffered in execution through the substitution of pilasters for columns except on the pavilions, changes in the roof, and the elimination of some delicate detail around the base of the dome, the Academy still holds a commanding position among the institutional buildings along the Neva. The increasing experience and sophistication of architect and patron alike could be seen by comparing Mattarnovy's strenuous but clumsy Kunstkamera, a few hundred yards to the east, with this dignified structure.

The Academy of Fine Arts must have made a deep impression on Catherine. Shortly after its completion she commissioned Vallin de la Mothe to build the first (the Small) Hermitage (1764–7), intended as a private residence whither she might withdraw from the draughty grandeur of the Winter Palace. The façade on the embankment shows Vallin de la Mothe working in a manner little removed from that of his Academy. Upon a high rusticated basement he placed two storeys embraced by a giant order of pilasters and accentuated by a projecting portico of six columns. The delicate details, such as the slight sculptural treatment of the keystones of the round-headed windows, with a carved Greek key above them, are in the best French tradition.

For the city of St Petersburg, Vallin de la Mothe built the Markets (Gostinny Dvor, now a large department store) on the Nevsky Prospekt as a huge two-storey arcade round a large open court.[7] In the nineteenth century the building was restored, and spoiled when the columns were shortened, but the stark forms still demonstrate a workman-like approach to the problem of conferring upon a humble building a certain civic dignity. This quality is even more apparent in the untouched portions of the brick-and-stone gateways and warehouses of New Holland (1765), an inner harbour and originally the main port of St Petersburg to the west of the Admiralty. The arrangement of coupled columns flanking an arch with round-headed windows at the corners is so close to the Markets that New Holland must be attributed to Vallin de la Mothe in the absence of documentary evidence. Only he could have invented this combination of heavy mass with delicate detail, still to be seen in the profiles of the arches and windows. Since this warehouse was never plastered or painted, the frankly exposed materials have a majestic dignity more like the masonry imagined by Piranesi or Hubert Robert than was usual in St Petersburg, where plaster and paint so often compromised the attempt to achieve an effect of antique solemnity.[8]

This ability to create a composition serene and dignified yet richly Baroque appears in the work of Catherine's second architect, who also had come to Russia during Elizabeth's reign. Antonio Rinaldi (c. 1710–94), who had studied with the famous Italian architect Luigi Vanvitelli, had been brought to Russia by Cyril Razumovsky, the younger brother of Elizabeth's morganatic husband, Alexey Razumovsky. In 1752–3 Rinaldi helped Cyril Razumovsky, now Grand Hetman of the Cossacks, to raise the village of Baturin to the position of a 'capital'. Little was built but the palace, subsequently entirely reconstructed. In 1755 Rinaldi was in St Petersburg, and the next year he was appointed Court architect to the Grand Duke Peter, who put him to work at Oranienbaum enlarging the pleasure pavilions of the old Menshikov Palace. His first works – a large hall for theatrical performances and the Chinese Pavilion and the Chinese Cottage – have

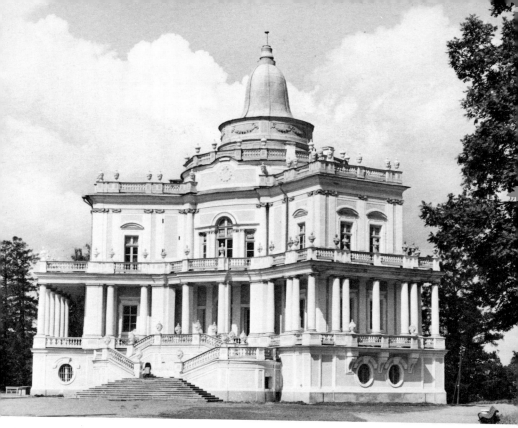

214. Antonio Rinaldi: Oranienbaum (Lomonosov), Katalnaya Gorka (Sliding Hill), 1760–8

not survived, but his later Chinese Palace (1762–8) revealed his knowledge of the more exotic aspects of the Rococo. Like many such structures elsewhere in Europe, the pink and white exterior was relatively sober: a low one-storeyed central portion with side pavilions connected by short wings. The decoration in the Chinese taste, which was limited to the interior, was dominated by frescoes executed by Italian decorators.[9] The Chinese Palace proved that the Russian Court was aware of the latest trends in European architecture. This style, so thoroughly unoriental, which by a curious inverted process reached Russia not directly from the East but by the long way round from China through Europe, enjoyed an international currency in the 1750s and 1760s. Although its exotic details are less conspicuous, the Oranienbaum pavilion is not far removed in spirit or date from Frederick the Great's tea-house at Potsdam (1754–6), or the similar structure at Drottningholm (1763), to mention only two of these eighteenth-century *chinoiseries.*

Rinaldi's own taste for simplicity had a better chance to appear in the two-storey pavilion which is all that is left of his Sliding Hill (Katalnaya Gorka, 1760–8) at Oranienbaum [214]. A Sliding Hill is a helter-skelter, or chute-the-chutes, that is, an artificial slope down which people coasted in winter on sledges or in summer on small wheeled carts. In a country so flat as northern Russia even such a slight elevation provoked a sensation of height and speed, and the hills were popular attractions at fairs and public parks. The

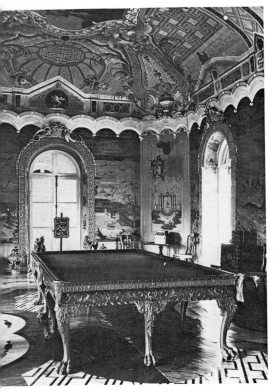

215. Antonio Rinaldi: Oranienbaum (Lomonosov), the Chinese Palace, 1762–8, the Large Chinese Room (the English billiard table is a later addition)

actual mechanical apparatus has long since disappeared, but Rinaldi's blue and white two-storey pavilion remains as an example of the sobriety of later-eighteenth-century pleasure architecture. The plan recalled the Baroque dispositions of an earlier age in the central circular hall with three square wings. Only the

crowning element – a slender tapering dome somewhat like a Chinese hat – was at all fantastic. Otherwise the walls with their severe pilasters and the surrounding verandah with paired and single columns were calm and dignified. Inside, Chinese effects were sporadic until the final Large Chinese Room [215].

As a Grand Duchess Catherine had enjoyed the Oranienbaum pavilions for their simplicity and intimacy; as Empress she called upon their architect for further and more important work. Rinaldi built two splendid private palaces for Catherine's favourite, Count Grigory Grigorievich Orlov. In the city the Marble Palace (1768–85, now the Lenin Museum), so called from the veneer of red granite, and grey and green Siberian marbles, which covers the exterior, was the first building to be faced with such costly materials [216]. The façade presents the familiar eighteenth-century *ordonnance* of two storeys framed by a giant order of pilasters resting upon a high basement.[10] The severe effect is lightened by the window niches inserted in the centre of each principal façade and by the interruption of the panelled attic by a large coat-of-arms in the centre of the roof over the niches. Above the main entrance, which was approached through an open court, Rinaldi placed a clock-tower with a broken pediment, a last Baroque intrusion in a design which was settling into the soberer mood of Neo-Classicism. The interior has been so extensively remodelled that little remains of Rinaldi's work except the marble staircase, the design of which complemented the exterior.

The second palace was at Gatchina (1766–81), in the country thirty miles south-west of St Petersburg.[11] This was more severe than the Marble Palace, with a central, three-storey block flanked by two octagonal towers. From the sides projected curving two-storey galleries, the upper floors of which were treated as open loggias. The arrangement of coupled Doric and Ionic pilasters was carried through the central block and the galleries on the entrance façade. Unhappily Gatchina was spoiled when the Grand Duke Paul received it from his mother in 1783 after Orlov's death. The open loggias were walled and glazed and two immense service buildings were put up on either side of the court, destroying the harmony of Rinaldi's original proportions. In the interior the marble staircase and White Hall alone recalled Rinaldi's mastery of a solemn ceremonial scheme.

Although Rinaldi's most important church, and one of his least Russian works, the new

tower supported a similar lantern with slight ornamental elements recalling Borromini's belfries in Rome. The treatment of the exterior as a single, monumental storey with an attic closely resembled St Peter's in Rome, and something of the majestic dignity of the Roman basilica might have been recalled by Rinaldi's lavish use of marble on the interior. But construction proceeded slowly, the costs were immense, and upon Paul's accession work was suspended. The marbles were carted off

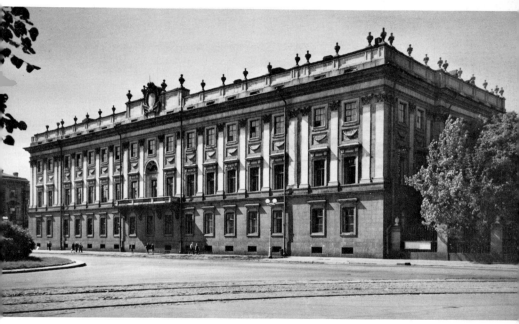

216. Antonio Rinaldi: St Petersburg, the Marble Palace, 1768–85

Cathedral of St Isaac, was never completed, from the model and drawings it would seem that it might have been an impressive structure. In plan it was a Greek cross with rounded apse and transepts extended by one bay to the west to form a Latin cross. The central crossing was to have been surmounted by five domes, a large dome surrounded by four lanterns with cupolas. To the west a stepped

to his new Michael Castle, and in 1801 the church was peremptorily finished by Brenna in brick.[12]

The third architect of the earlier years of Catherine's reign, and the only one of German origin whom the German-born Empress regularly employed, was Yury Matveevich Velten (Felten, 1730–1801), whose father, Johann Velten, had come from Danzig in 1703 as a 'master-cook' for Peter the Great. Velten was educated abroad; at the age of thirteen he had gone with a professor from the Academy of Sciences to study mathematics at Tübingen. Shortly afterwards he turned to architecture, and for a time worked on the castle at Stuttgart and in 1749 in Berlin. Upon his return to Russia he assisted Rastrelli at the Winter Palace in 1754, and by 1760 had attained the rank of an independent architect. Catherine valued Velten's engineering abilities, which were superior to his architectural imagination, and set him the task of facing the Neva quays with granite. These, with the exquisite iron grilles for the Summer Garden, were important contributions to the development of St Petersburg. The granite embankments, superbly severe and simply yet boldly adapted to the curving entrances of the canals, and intersected by flights of steps to the water-gates, supplied a magnificent base for the palaces, the most grandiose and coherent of any European city at that time. The same ability to work in the simplest forms is seen in Velten's grilles for the Summer Garden, where plain granite posts, in the form of Roman Doric columns, alternate with wrought-iron panels of a severe rectilinear design.[13] Velten's mastery of granite and iron was a result of his engineering and mathematical instincts, for his architectural works were less distinguished. From 1764 he worked for Catherine at the Winter Palace, adding a new pavilion on the southern or street side. By means of rounded corners, coupled columns on the ground storey, and a discreet use of pilasters and decorative swags above, he skilfully tied the new building to Rastrelli's florid palace which adjoins it to the west. He also connected Vallin de la Mothe's pavilion on the Neva with his own by long one-storey galleries, between and above which he constructed a 'hanging garden'. The garden and all the interiors were several times rebuilt, most drastically to serve as picture galleries, by Shtakenshneider (see below, page 390) in the nineteenth century.

Velten's most unusual work – a palace for Catherine in commemoration of the naval victory of the Russians over the Turks at Tchesme – was designed in a neo-medieval style, and will be considered later with other structures of the same character (page 335).

A similar interest in the stricter use of simple geometrical forms marked the work of two Russian architects, the first members of the younger generation to benefit by the new course of architectural training. The education of the elder, Vasily Ivanovich Bazhenov (1738–99), was in startling contrast to that which a Russian builder of pre-Petrine Russia would have received, and demonstrates how effective the systems devised by Peter and Elizabeth had become.[14] Bazhenov's father, a minor cleric from a country town near Yaroslavl on the Volga, had moved to Moscow, where he sent his son to the Slavonic-Greek-Latin Academy and, when he showed a talent for drawing, to Prince Ukhtomsky's architectural school. In 1755 the Prince enrolled him in the recently established Moscow University to study foreign languages, and in 1758 sent him to the new Academy in St Petersburg. Until the complete programme was ready Bazhenov was put to work with S. I. Chevakinsky (1713–83), Rastrelli's brilliant pupil, on the naval Cathedral of St Nicholas, then under construction.[15] When Vallin de la Mothe arrived, he quickly recognized Bazhenov's talent. In 1760 the young Russian was assigned to Rastrelli as his assistant, and a few months later was sent to Paris to study for two years with Charles de Wailly. He made such progress at the French Academy that he would have won the Prix de Rome in 1762 had he not been a foreigner. He then went to Italy, and in a short time became a member of both the Roman and Florentine Academies. When he returned to St Petersburg in 1765 his international reputation excited the jealousy of the members of the Academy, and it was some time before his talents were officially recognized. His first important commission, the new

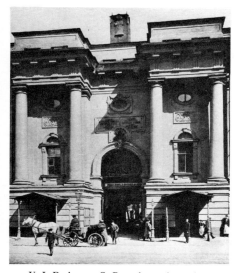

217. V. I. Bazhenov: St Petersburg, Arsenal
(demolished), 1769, principal entrance

Arsenal (1769, now demolished) [217], was
impregnated with French taste and is not far
removed from Vallin de la Mothe's work at
the Academy and the Hermitage. But close as
this design was to contemporary French work
a Russian taste for aggressive monumentality
appeared in the curious inverted proportions
of the entrance, the elements of which increased in size as they mounted upwards.

If the Kamenny Ostrov Palace, constructed
for Grand Duke Paul in 1776–81, can be attributed to him, Bazhenov by then had gone a
step further towards the definition of Russian
classicism in the unbroken walls, marked only
by a horizontal string course at the height of
the second storey and a plain six-columned
portico and pediment on the principal
façade.[16] This stern exterior, where the play
of abstract architectural elements was un-
relieved by any decoration, concealed a more
informal plan which included a private theatre
and a large oval salon across the garden front.
Here Bazhenov gave the measure of his ability.

Catherine soon appreciated his talent and
awarded him two tremendous commissions.
The first was for her Institute for Daughters
of the Nobility (1765–72), a school on the lines
of Mme de Maintenon's seminary at St Cyr,
which she proposed to add to Elizabeth's convent of Smolny. Bazhenov's designs were
never executed, but even in the drawings it is
apparent that this would have been one of the
masterpieces of Russian, indeed of European,
eighteenth-century architecture. The influence
of French academic practice, which he had
learned in Paris, can be seen in the plan, where
a great variety of square, round, and polygonal
rooms are disposed in rigid symmetry on either
side of a large central hall. On the court side
the building stretched in a great sweeping
curve. Yet for all the Baroque magnitude of
such a plan, on the façades variety would have
been subordinated to a massive unified *ordonnance*, the familiar scheme of a rusticated
basement, here of two storeys, supporting the
upper storeys with a giant order of coupled
columns at the principal entrance and on the
corner pavilions.

Bazhenov's second *magnum opus* was also
never carried out. It was nothing less than the
reconstruction of the Kremlin as a gigantic
triangular palace enclosing the most important
palaces and churches. Bazhenov's design of
1769–72 [218], known from drawings and a
large wooden model, would have altered the
character of the ancient Kremlin, and of
Moscow as well, so that the failure to erect it
can scarcely be regretted. But his genius can
be seen in the scope of the project and the
masterly control of an intricate plan with many
disparate elements brought together in a single
embracing unity. Russia was not yet economically or aesthetically prepared for works of
such comprehensive character, and it is even
possible that they might have eliminated too
thoroughly any sense of human scale. But the
plans must be included among the truly
monumental conceptions of eighteenth-century European architecture.

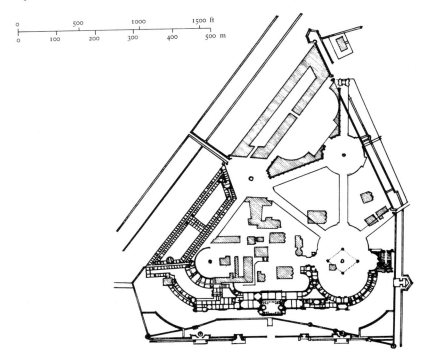

218 and 219. V. I. Bazhenov: Design for a new Kremlin Palace in Moscow, 1769–72, with detail of the wooden model

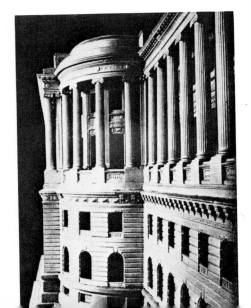

From the surviving fragments of the original wooden model [219] it can be seen that the palace had much in common with his designs for Smolny.[17] Upon the same basement, here in places unusually high because the scheme ignored the irregularities of the site, Bazhenov placed two storeys bound together by a giant order of Ionic columns. Much sculptural decoration and a freer treatment of the projections at the corner pavilions make the Kremlin design more classically academic than the Smolny project. Although the most important dynastic shrines were to be preserved, the construction of the palace would have required the demolition of a great deal within the Kremlin walls. Along the southern side, facing the river, work had already begun by the time the inaugural ceremonies were held in the

Empress's presence in 1772. But Catherine, who may have thought the project more important than its accomplishment, in the sense that it was a striking advertisement of the implied grandeur and stability of her reign,[18] lost interest, after thousands of roubles had been poured into the plans and models. She suddenly ordered the work to be suspended, and in 1776 commissioned Bazhenov to design the Neo-Gothic palace of Tsaritsyno. This she soon found too sombre, the half-finished palace was abandoned, and thus the third of Bazhenov's great undertakings came to nothing (see below, pages 323–4, 338). In the later years of Catherine's reign Bazhenov became one of Paul's favourite architects, and participated after 1796 in his fantastic project for the Michael Castle.

During his long residence in Moscow, Bazhenov exerted considerable influence over the younger generation of Russian architects, and from this period, the 1780s, date many of the late Baroque and early Neo-Classical country houses around Moscow. His spirit if not his hand may still be seen in the Pashkov Palace (1784–6), later the Rumyantsov Museum and now the old building of the Lenin Library, which occupies a commanding site opposite the Kremlin [220]. It has been attributed to the Moscow architect Kazakov, but the bold dis-

220. V. I. Bazhenov and M. F. Kazakov(?): Moscow, the Pashkov Palace (later the Rumyantsov Museum, now the old building of the Lenin Library), 1784–6

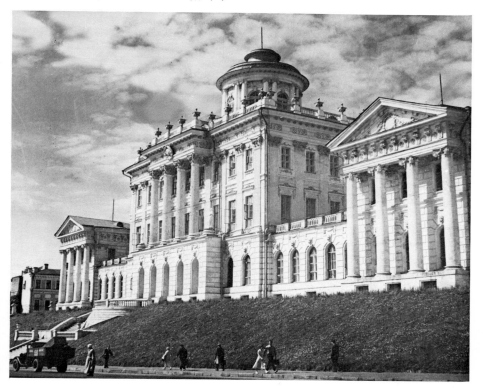

tribution of the parts is in Bazhenov's manner. If it is both less controlled and more delicate than the latter's usual work, it is also more powerful than other contemporary or later Moscow palaces.

The second Russian architect of the earlier years of the reign developed a style more in harmony with Catherine's own tastes. Ivan Egorovich Starov (1743–1808) was born in St Petersburg and, like Bazhenov, studied first at the University of Moscow and subsequently in St Petersburg at the Academy of Sciences, and in 1758 at the newly opened Academy of Fine Arts. In 1762 he was sent to Paris to study under de Wailly. After travelling in Italy and a second sojourn in Paris he returned to St Petersburg in 1768, where his talents were soon put to use designing country houses. His first work was in the restrained French manner of Vallin de la Mothe, who was head of the department of architecture in the Academy, where Starov was appointed an associate professor in 1770. The façades of his house for Catherine's and Gregory Orlov's son, A. G. Bobrinsky, at Bogoroditsa, near Tula (1771–6, since destroyed), resembled Velten's portion of the Hermitage, but in a country house for Prince Gagarin at Nikolskoe near Moscow (1773–6, now a rest home) Starov introduced a freer treatment of the familiar Neo-Classical elements, more in the manner of Bazhenov's use of late Baroque forms. Starov's invention of a circular terrace above the semicircular projection of the lower basement storey and a corresponding recession of the first storey is an ingenious manipulation of space. His niches, columns, and angular corner projections are slighter and more sensitive versions of Bazhenov's designs for Smolny.[19]

The delicacy and small scale of his forms seem to have appealed particularly to Catherine, for in the later 1770s she turned more and more from an extravagant to a purified, even demure conception of architecture. A possible connexion between the converging tastes of Catherine and Starov in these years may be found in the church, and more particularly in the belfry, at Nikolskoe (1773–6) [221]. Here all traces of the Baroque were banished in favour of a full and successful Neo-Classicism, based on the beauty of interrelated geometrical shapes. Starov's studies in

221. I. E. Starov: Nikolskoe, church and belfry, 1773–6

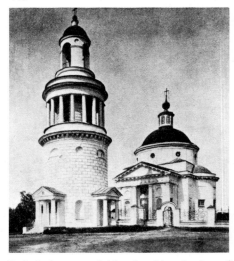

Paris had prepared him for this rejection of the Baroque. There is a feeling for French formal order in the lower cylindrical, rusticated mass, broken only by the circular and semicircular niches, and surmounted by a colonnade topped by a rhythmical series of mouldings diminishing in size. The small Roman Doric porticoes show even more clearly Starov's affection for classical architecture. This belfry was indeed precocious, the forms more suggestive of later Alexandrian classicism than of these still early decades of Catherine's reign.[20]

Because Catherine was in Moscow in 1775, and would probably have known Starov's work through the relationship between Gagarin and Bobrinsky, it is not unlikely that her opinion of Nikolskoe prompted the appointment of Starov as chief architect for the new cathedral

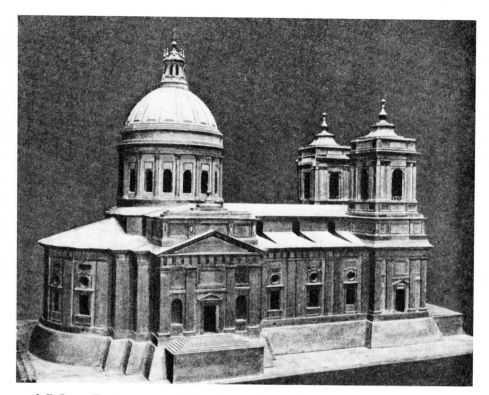

222. I. E. Starov: Wooden model of the Cathedral of the Trinity, Alexander Nevsky Lavra,
St Petersburg, 1776

of the Alexander Nevsky Lavra (1778–90). The earlier structure by Tressini and Schwertfeger had fallen into decay and threatened to collapse, but the competitive plans submitted by several architects failed to please the Empress, and she turned to Starov. His projects of 1776 are inscribed 'to be by himself', proving that he had obtained the exclusive right to construct the cathedral. The drawings and fine model [222] indicate that Starov's work, unlike Rastrelli's for Smolny, was built as designed except for minor details which had to be changed because of adjacent structures. The plan and mass of the cathedral have a noble simplicity characteristic of the full tide of Catherinian classicism. Starov continued

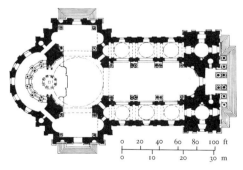

223. I. E. Starov: St Petersburg,
Cathedral of the Trinity, Alexander Nevsky Lavra,
1778–90, plan

the tradition of Tressini's Peter–Paul Cathedral, as modified by Tressini and Schwertfeger, retaining the Latin-cross plan, central
dome, and two western towers, but by reducing the verticality of Schwertfeger's design, he
achieved a more powerful composition. He also
suppressed the subsidiary turrets or lanterns
at the corners of the dome, whereby Rastrelli
and Schwertfeger, and even Rinaldi, had kept
up the pretence of a five-domed Orthodox
church. The plan [223] is the most remarkable
aspect of Starov's cathedral; it shows a greater
integration of the Orthodox central plan with
the Latin cross than any previous church in St
Petersburg. The relation of the nave and narrower aisles to the central space beneath the
dome, flanked by side spaces to the north and
south and a semicircular apse, is complete and
comprehensible as a single unity. For his
ornament Starov developed and carried
further the geometrical and planar harmony
of Nikolskoe. His surfaces are enlivened by
pairs of pilasters supporting a projecting entablature, and the main altar is a columnar
composition backed by six pairs of columns
turning the semicircular apse.

Catherine was so pleased with the cathedral
that she commissioned Starov to design a vast
town house for her lover, Grigory Potemkin,
ennobled as 'Prince of Tauris' after his conquest of the Crimea. The Tauride Palace
(1783–9) was occupied by Potemkin for little
more than a year. After he sold it to the Treasury it remained a favourite residence of
Catherine's. For this reason it was brutally
desecrated by Paul, who turned it into barracks and stables for the Horse Guards. When
Alexander I decided to restore the palace it
was so defaced that his architect practically
had to rebuild it. To counteract the dampness
which had developed, Luigi Rusca (1758–1822)
raised the floors two and a half feet, thus destroying the harmony and elegance of Starov's
Ionic order. Later in the nineteenth century
the splendid gardens between the main façade
and the Neva were sold, factories and water
tanks began to obstruct the river approach, and

after 1905 the building was again remodelled
for the Imperial Duma. All this is regrettable,
for the Tauride Palace, one of the earliest
Neo-Classical buildings in Russia, was once
one of the wonders of Europe.

Starov's design consisted of a central domed
and porticoed block connected by narrow galleries to large wings containing the private
living apartments, offices, and a theatre [224].

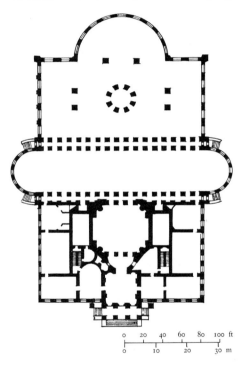

224 (above) and 225 (right). I. E. Starov: St Petersburg,
Tauride Palace, 1783–9, plan and Catherine Hall

The continuous low masses were broken only
by the flattened dome over the main entrance.
Nothing could more clearly exemplify the
change in Catherine's conception of architecture. Her new taste appears in the severely
plain walls, punctuated by very simple
windows and surmounted by the simplest of

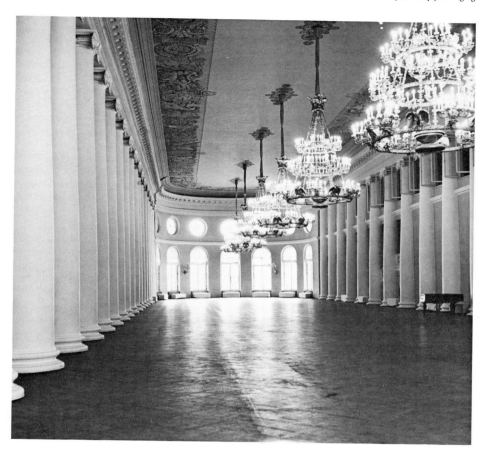

entablatures with a frieze of metopes and triglyphs. Although the columns of the porticoes on the main entrance and wings of the garden façade are still Tuscan, the effect was certainly more Greek than Roman. In the interior this impression was substantiated by the consistent use of a Greek Ionic order, closer to the Erechtheum than to any Roman version. And here Starov's instinctive sense for the 'poetry of columns' achieved its most successful expression. The central suite of reception rooms was entered from a square vestibule through which one passed to a high octagonal hall beneath the central dome. This hall, soon known to Potemkin's contemporaries as the 'Pantheon', resembled its antique prototype in the use of the dome, and to a certain extent in the treatment of the wall surfaces. Doors in the four long sides gave access to other parts of the palace, but the shorter sides were filled with tall blue-and-white tile stoves. Through the door opposite the entrance one passed into the Catherine Hall [225], a gallery with rounded ends longer than the main block itself, from which opened, through a range of eighteen pairs of columns, an immense enclosed Winter Garden, in the centre of which a small circular colonnade resembled the little rotundas then in fashion in the parks of country houses.

The scale of the Tauride Palace may owe much to Starov's training in Paris, but nowhere except in Russia could the grandeur of his designs have found fulfilment in actual execution. If only for this, the Tauride Palace could be considered a distinctly Russian work, but its influence was even more important. It became the ambition of many a nobleman and country gentleman to emulate the design of the central block with plain walls, simple six-column portico, and low dome. For forty years many smaller versions throughout the Russian countryside, in wood as well as in stuccoed masonry, showed how directly Starov's masterpiece appealed to the cultivated Russian taste of the period.

The dignity of the Lavra Cathedral and the Tauride Palace makes it all the more difficult to understand Catherine's often expressed dissatisfaction with her native architects. It is true that she was so discouraged by Bazhenov's extravagance and erratic behaviour that she exiled him to Moscow. But she had also been annoyed by the grandiose plans submitted from Paris by the French architect Charles-Louis Clérisseau (1722–1820), who had sent her a project for an enormous palace when she had asked for a small garden-house, apparently thinking that the Empress of Russia would stop at nothing.[21] The remaining architects in St Petersburg were either men of small matter, or were occupied with civil and utilitarian projects. Yet it is hard to understand why either Velten, at work on the Neva quays, or Starov, busy at the Lavra, deserved the reproach implied in Catherine's letter to Grimm of 16 April 1779. She asked him to direct her agent Reiffenstein to find her 'deux bons architectes, Italiens de nation et habiles de profession ... gens honnêtes et raisonnables, point de têtes de Falconet, marchant sur terre, point dans les airs', because, as she continued, 'tous les miens sont devenus ou trop vieux, ou trop aveugles, ou trop lents, ou trop paresseux, ou trop jeunes, ou trop fainéants, ou trop grands

seigneurs, ou trop riches, ou trop solides, ou trop éventés'.

Catherine exempted one architect. In a letter of 23 August 1779 she advised Grimm that 'à présent je me suis emparée de mister Cameron, Ecossais de nation, jacobite de profession, grand dessinateur nourri d'antiquités, connu par un livre sur les bains anciens'. And she added that she and Cameron were devising a terraced garden and gallery with baths below. The presence in Russia of a Scottish architect is not so surprising as it might seem. Catherine had for long turned to England almost as much as to France for her cultural and political ideas. On 21 June 1778 she wrote to Grimm: 'Le mois de mai m'a été très fatal; j'ai perdu deux hommes que je n'ai jamais vus, qui m'aimaient et que j'honorais: Voltaire et milord Chatham,' and she admired Charles James Fox so much that his was the only bust of a contemporary in the row of antique philosophers and statesmen to adorn the Cameron Gallery she was soon to build at Tsarskoe Selo. Even her dogs had English names, and as early as 16 July 1772 she had written to Voltaire: 'J'aime à la folie présentement les jardins à l'anglaise'.[22]

How exactly 'mister Cameron' turned up in Russia is still a mystery. Of the scraps of information about Charles Cameron (c. 1740–1812), Catherine's letters supply as much as any other source.[23] In addition to his Scottish birth, his presumed Jacobite sentiments, and his classical proclivities, we learn that he had lived at Rome in the house of the Pretender, and was an admirer of Clérisseau, whose drawings he used for his work in Russia. Besides this we know that in London in 1767 and 1772 he exhibited drawings of the Roman baths which he published in the latter year.[24] In addition to his admiration of antiquity, he was interested in the work of Palladio. Cameron seems not to have been much liked in England, and he may have realized that he would have to compete with the brothers Adam. Also, as a Jacobite he might stand a better chance of finding employment on the continent. Of all the European Courts only

Catherine's offered a fair field for a British subject. His estimate was correct and he spent the remainder of his life in Russia, except for a brief visit to England about 1800. During this time he was employed, not without interruptions and misunderstandings, by Catherine and her successors, and a proof of the esteem in which he was held is seen in the fact that in 1820 the Russian ambassador, Prince Lieven, acquired in England 114 of his drawings to be used by Stasov in restoring the apartments at Tsarskoe Selo which had been damaged by fire.

Cameron's first work for Catherine at Tsarskoe Selo, after a few additions to the Chinese Village, was a series of rooms where she could live in absolute privacy and on a scale befitting a noble lady rather than a monarch. These rooms, known as the First (1780–3), Fourth (1781–4), and Fifth (1782–4) Apartments (there were no Second and Third), consisted essentially of the rearrangement and redecoration of suites within Rastrelli's old palace. The Green Dining Room [226] in the First Apartment is among the most Pompeian of Cameron's decorative schemes.

226. Charles Cameron: Tsarskoe Selo, Green Dining Room, 1780–3

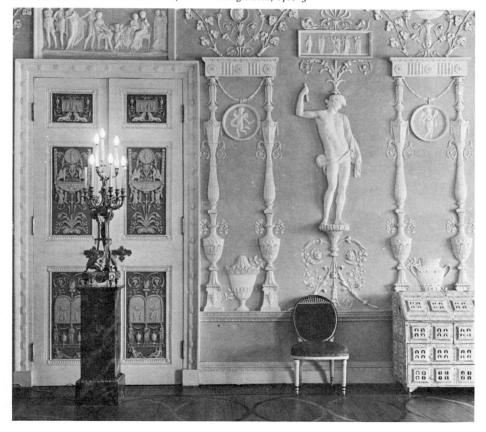

The Fifth Apartment contained one of the most spectacular examples of his mature manner, the richly three-dimensional decoration of the Empress's bedroom [227] with the walls inset with Wedgwood plaques and with gilded bronze embellishments mounted on glass panels. Effects of space and depth in a

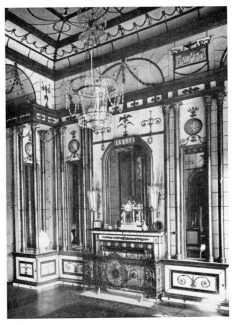

227. Charles Cameron: Tsarskoe Selo, Catherine II's bedroom, 1782–4

small room were further reinforced by an abundance of mirrored surfaces. The apartments, with the Agate Pavilion (1780–5) and the Cameron Gallery (1783–6), which were added to the south-west wing of Elizabeth's palace, constituted the most strictly classical interior environment achieved in Russia up to that time. Cameron's taste, shaped by Palladio and refined by Clérisseau, was Roman and Pompeian in the manner known in Europe and America as 'Adam'. Here was the same extensive knowledge of classical forms and

motifs, similarly manipulated to provide the utmost in comfort. Here was the same intimate, human scale, which could also rise to a more austere vision of antique dignity when the occasion required. Yet here was also a new and unexpected sumptuousness. Catherine boasted to Voltaire that the marbles available in Russia would not have displeased the Italians, and her feeling for materials, even in these small apartments, was in startling contrast to the St Petersburg tradition of architecture improvised in brick and plaster. Cameron not only used the customary materials of Neo-Classicism – moulded plaster reliefs, marble columns and revetments, wood panelling and parquet floors – but went much further in his search for the precious and exotic. The Agate Pavilion was perhaps the most conspicuous example of this, for the columns and walls of two rooms were made of small pieces of agate and malachite cunningly pieced together. He also used bronze for the capitals and bases of his columns and a whole repertoire of decorative forms in ceramic and glass. He inserted small Wedgwood plaques with figures after Flaxman's designs around his chimney-pieces. Cameron also used moulded glass for columns and ornaments, and flat panes of coloured or clear glass set on coloured felt, to create shimmering surfaces. Once again a Russian patron had called for the best a European artist had to offer and the product was a new contribution to European art. Cameron also brought to Russia a sense of colour which became an inherent part of the new classicism. The brilliant blues and golds, the strong clear hues which had characterized Tsarskoe Selo in the time of Elizabeth, went out of fashion. Primaries were replaced by complementaries or by muted tones, bronze for gold, lavender for blue, olive and pistachio for bright green, and grey-blue for Elizabeth's favourite azure.

Cameron's success at Tsarskoe Selo led to his retention by the Grand Duke Paul as architect for the rebuilding of his country house at Pavlovsk [228]. He worked there for four years (1782–6), although during this period he was

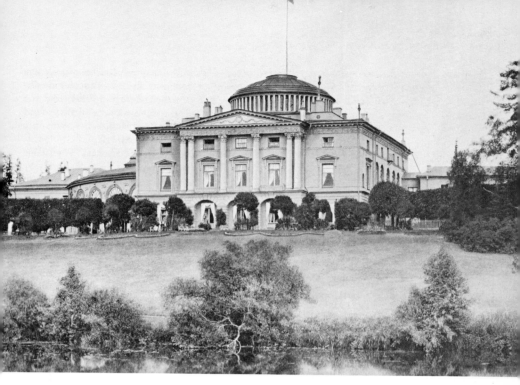

228. Charles Cameron: Pavlovsk, palace, 1782–6

handicapped by controversies with Paul's favourite architect, V. F. Brenna, who subsequently altered Pavlovsk in a less refined spirit. Cameron's first work for Paul, as the Chinese Village had been for Catherine, was a series of small pavilions in the park, of which the circular Temple of Friendship (1780) was the first in Russia in the Greek Doric order. The palace itself was designed as a square main block facing an elliptical court surrounded by service wings. It was Cameron's largest commission, but it must be said that the whole is too small in scale to be truly palatial, and, however exquisite the Palladian details, it is obviously the work of an inspired decorator rather than an architect. Brenna's additions after 1789 consisted of taller and more elaborate service wings which spoiled Cameron's main block by making it seem far too delicate

for the huge courtyard upon which it faces. Only within could one see his true genius at work in the Italian and Grecian Halls. In the first of these he combined motifs from the Pantheon and Roman baths in a circular hall beneath the central dome. The spacious Grecian Hall beyond is certainly his most successful palatial interior [229]. Here a richly ornamented stucco ceiling was supported on Corinthian columns of imitation marble which in turn framed niches in the walls in which were placed classical marbles. Catherine wrote to Grimm on 4 September 1794: 'J'ai tous les ouvrages des frères Adam', and Cameron may now have been obliged to use Adam engravings as he had earlier studied those of Clérisseau for inspiration for Tsarskoe Selo. The references to the work of Adam, especially in the Italian and Greek Halls to the Rotunda and

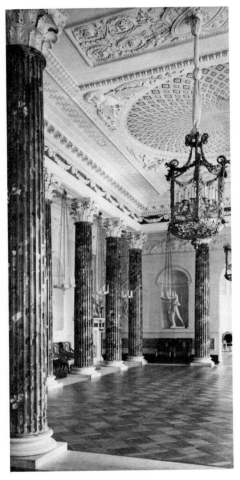

229. Charles Cameron: Pavlovsk, palace, 1782–6
Grecian Hall

Great Hall at Kedleston (1760), are unmistakable. But if Cameron was not the inventor of his Pompeian version of Neo-Classicism, and if his works differ more in degree than in kind from those of the brothers Adam, his *œuvre* was important for the preparation of the last phase of Russian Neo-Classicism, that style which can be called Alexandrian, and which flourished during the reign of Alexander I.

Cameron's immediate influence can be seen in Starov's 'Pantheon' in the Tauride Palace, where the painted and carved reliefs and the choice of ornaments against a plain ground owed much to the Scottish designer, especially to the Italian Hall at Pavlovsk.

Of his other work little remains. The palace at Baturin, commenced for Cyril Razumovsky (1799), has been attributed to him, but when the Hetman died in 1803 work was suspended and for more than a century it lay in ruins. The devastated Ionic portico along the garden front had something of the Piranesian majesty which Cameron had admired in Rome.[25] His church at Sofia, the village Catherine established near Tsarskoe Selo, and which she so named in 1780 in anticipation of her conquest of Constantinople and the establishment of a Greek Empire, is strictly classical, with flattened domes on squat drums, and belongs to the type of early-nineteenth-century church more profitably studied in the work of Stasov.[26] Cameron's first drawings show an attempt to suggest an eastern, oriental character. His contemporaries, however, thought that the church as it was built was an exact copy of Hagia Sophia in Constantinople. Upon Paul's accession Cameron was abruptly dismissed, only to be recalled in 1800. Alexander I appointed him chief architect to the Admiralty and he was set to work on buildings for Kronstadt, but was presently displaced by Zakharov. The sale of his library in St Petersburg in 1812 perhaps indicates that he had died, although the exact date of his death is unknown.

Giacomo Quarenghi (Dzhakomo Kvarengy or Gvarengy, 1744–1817), who arrived in Russia in 1780, was to prove not only the greatest architect of Catherine's reign but one of the most eminent European architects of the later eighteenth century. He had studied at the Academy in Bergamo, his birthplace, and later worked in Rome with Mengs. By 1779 his exquisite drawings had attracted the attention of collectors, and he was already in demand for architectural designs, although until then very few had actually been executed.

Possibly his connexion with Mengs stood him in good stead with Grimm. In the latter's reply of 17 July 1779 to Catherine's letter asking for two Italian architects, Grimm began by announcing Mengs's death, before he mentioned Trombara and Quarenghi, who, he said, would soon reach St Petersburg. Of Trombara little more has been heard; his talents were undistinguished and he left no mark in Russia. Quarenghi, on the other hand, immediately pleased Catherine, and she set him to work on the first of an endless series of projects, which increased in scope and expense until the end of her life. On 30 September 1782 she wrote to Grimm:

Je suis bien aise que cet habile architecte soit content; il ne manque pas d'exercice ici à son talent, car la bâtissomanie va un fort grand train. Il y a des endroits que vous ne reconnaîtriez pas si vous les revoyiez, comme par exemple les entours de la Fontanka, qu'on nettoie et dont les bords se bâtissent en pierre de quai.

Nor did her enthusiasm diminish; on 28 October 1785 she wrote:

Ce Quarenghi nous fait des choses charmantes: toute la ville est déjà farcie des ses bâtiments; il bâtit la Banque, la Bourse, des magasins en quantité, des boutiques et des maisons particulières, et ses bâtiments sont ce qu'il y a de mieux. Il m'a fait un théâtre à l'Hermitage, qui sera fini en quinze jours, qui intérieurement est charmant à l'œil; il peut y tenir deux à trois cents personnes, *ma* pas plus: c'est aussi le bout du monde pour l'Hermitage.

Catherine's constant use of the adjective 'charming' to describe Quarenghi's work seems scarcely consistent with her changing attitude towards classicism nor with Quarenghi's style. Catherine, like the century in which she lived, was passing from a sentimental, imaginative, and literary attitude towards antiquity to a more serious understanding of the character of ancient art and of its supposed relations to the private life of the individual and the public life of the state. The tempered, moderate classicism in the works of Vallin de la Mothe, Rinaldi, and Velten, had found a very personal expression in the monuments she erected in

her parks. The Egyptian pyramid near the graves of her favourite dogs is perhaps the most characteristic example of the sensitivity of this phase. Several years later she thought of a similar monument in a much more archaeological spirit. In the same letter of 1785 to Grimm she advised him that she had just had a long conference at the Hermitage with Quarenghi, who had been ordered to erect in the gardens at Pella, a country residence near Peterhof, 'les trois colonnes de marbre blanc, seul et remarquable reste du temple de Jupiter tonnant; voilà une fantaisie qui m'a prise depuis trois jours, ou j'ai comme une espèce de fièvre pour ces trois colonnes que je veux voir exécutées dans toute leur grandeur et beauté'. With his knowledge of Roman antiquity Quarenghi could quickly supply whatever she desired in the way of such reminiscences; for the gardens at Tsarskoe Selo he built an outdoor kitchen for the use of the Court on picnic days, cleverly disguised with bits of marble fragments and broken bricks as an antique ruin.

But there is much more to Quarenghi's work than the confection of artificial ruins like those in the paintings of Pannini and Hubert Robert. He was a great architect, a fact which Catherine realized. And he was the more remarkable in that he continued to create masterpieces in spite of the unending flood of commissions and projects with which Catherine overwhelmed him. His first important work, the English Palace, so called because it stood in the English Park at Peterhof, instantly gave the measure of the man and his taste. This uncompromisingly Palladian mansion demonstrated both the sources of Quarenghi's style and the use which he intended to make of them. His own words in this instance are important. In a communication addressed to a friend in Italy in 1785, enumerating the many commissions he had already received during his first five years in Russia, he confided his conception of architecture:

I tell you that the antique has been the fountain of all my observations. When I thought I had acquired a sufficient foundation of simplicity and antique grandeur, I studied the best things of the moderns and after having examined and drawn a little amidst the immensity of magnificent building at Rome, I twice undertook a tour of Italy to see, examine, and measure on the spot the best that our masters have left us. Florence, Vicenza, Verona, Mantua, and Venice were the places where I stopped longest; for there more than anywhere else abound the beautiful buildings of Palladio, the San Galli, Bramante, and others. I studied also the living masters, and I have pillaged the good wherever I could discover it, as I have sought as far as possible to make myself familiar with the distribution of rooms in the houses of the French, a skill which still appears to be entirely theirs, especially today when this nation can boast of a considerable number of artists in architecture.[27]

Such an eclectic programme could readily have led him to utter subjection to the past, whether of ancient Rome or of the Renaissance, but Quarenghi was aware of such dangers. He continued:

These studies and observations have made me adopt the principle that common sense and reason should not be the slaves of certain rules and examples, and in following servilely the theory and precepts of great masters, without studying their productions and without paying attention to their habits and the local circumstances, one will produce only mediocre things.

Here his programme emerges more clearly. On the basis of a searching and rigorous study of antiquity he conducted his analysis of great modern architecture which for him meant chiefly Palladio. After the first small churches he built in Russia, which suggest the influence of Bramante, his noble conception of antiquity was soon domesticated by general references to Palladio, and to contemporary French advances in residential planning. In this respect it is interesting to find that Catherine herself was less enthusiastic about French planning. In a letter of 23 August 1779 she explained to Grimm that she wanted Italians: 'Parce que nous avons des Français qui en savent trop et font de vilaines maisons intérieurement et extérieurement, parce qu'ils savent trop'. Quarenghi's architecture, more than that of any other contemporary master in Russia, was antique without being archaeological, grandiose yet human in scale. Not otherwise could he so easily and for so long have caught the enthusiasm of the Empress, or have persuaded her that these massive and stern buildings were 'charming'.

The English Palace (1781–9) [230] was the first and in many ways the paradigm of Quarenghi's work. This was the first successful

230. Giacomo Quarenghi: Peterhof, the English Palace (now destroyed), 1781–9

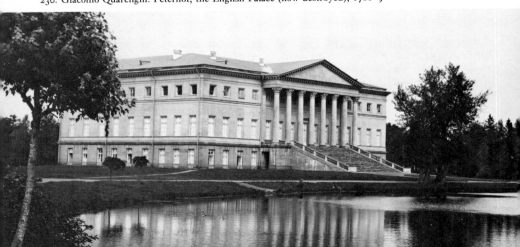

example of how he could adapt his eclectic programme to Russian conditions. The quality of the palace is antique, the *ordonnance* Palladian, the scale Russian. The simple, symmetrical plan, which included his favourite rotunda in the manner of the Pantheon for the entrance hall, and a circular staircase at either end of the vestibule opening upon a loggia, had a clarity and unity which Cameron never attained, for all that he, too, was en-

column, and mass were the figures with which he composed his geometrical equations. The degree to which he achieved a personal expression within the general system of late-eighteenth-century Palladianism can be seen by comparing his English Palace with Bazhenov's Kamenny Ostrov Palace of fifteen years before. Where Bazhenov hesitated, Quarenghi handled his forms with masterly confidence.

The formula of the English Palace, a cubical

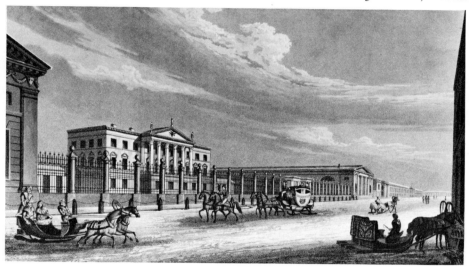

231. Giacomo Quarenghi: St Petersburg, State Bank, 1783–90

amoured of Palladian and Roman architecture. Not less interesting was the manner by which he reversed the rhythm of his two façades; the projecting eight-column portico at the head of the majestic flight of steps leading up from the garden became on the opposite façade a six-columned loggia set back between the two wings. No superfluous decoration appears on the plain walls, broken only by ranges of windows without decorative frames and by the horizontal string courses. This was the essence of antiquity rather than a copy of its details. Quarenghi excelled in architectural abstractions. For him the circle, triangle, cylinder, and cube in the form of arch, pediment,

mass enlivened by a central portico, was one which he used many times, notably for the Academy of Sciences (1783–9) on the Vasily Ostrov embankment between the Kunstkamera and the Twelve Colleges, and for the State Bank (1783–90), now the Leningrad Institute of Finance and Economics [231]. For the latter he placed his porticoed block in the centre of a two-storey semicircular gallery which served as warehouse and storerooms connecting the central administrative block with the two colonnaded wings. In plan and elevation the building was unequivocally an important governmental structure. Despite the rigour of the general scheme the street façades

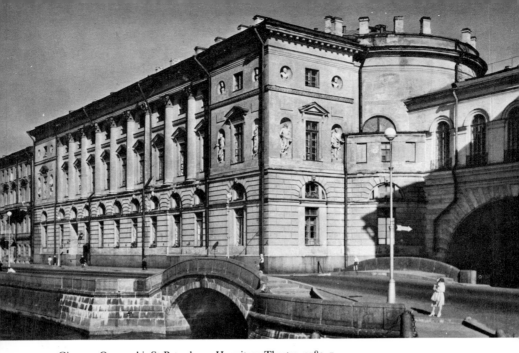

232. Giacomo Quarenghi: St Petersburg, Hermitage Theatre, 1783–7
(on the Neva Quay, by Y. M. Velten)

of the wings show Quarenghi's geometry enlivened by an unexpected play of ornament.

The Hermitage Theatre (1783–7) [232] was
another example of his success in adapting his
means to a specific end. On the exterior he
expressed the function of the building by
the high curved wall of the auditorium. For
the façade along the Neva the range of giant
Corinthian engaged columns upon a high rusticated basement, and the lively play of panels,
niches, and statuary created a ceremonial
atmosphere. Again his personal accent can be
seen in the insistent horizontal cornice and
string courses, and in the sharp accents of the
pediments above the windows.

The last important building Quarenghi
devised for the Empress was the Alexander
Palace at Tsarskoe Selo intended as a residence
for her favourite grandson, the future Emperor Alexander I. Here again he designed
a simple but low structure, tying the two

wings with a majestic colonnade of coupled
Corinthian columns. On the rear the rhythm of
his arched Palladian windows and the projecting central pavilion with its dome was exquis-
itely just. The size was modest, the scale large
yet restrained. A comparison with Cameron's
Agate Pavilion indicates the distance between
two temperaments working within the same
repertory of formal elements.

Cameron's Pavlovsk, too, serves as a useful
point of comparison with Quarenghi's magnificent country residence at Lyalichy near
Chernigov (1794–5) for Count Peter Zava-
dovsky, who had been for a short time one of
Catherine's favourites. Upon his retirement
from Court, the Count wished to surround
himself with mementoes of his earlier days in
St Petersburg. Quarenghi's design recaptured
much of the dignity of the later buildings in
the capital; the formula was essentially that of
the English Palace and the Academy of

Sciences. Again he used a Palladian central mass, with a projecting portico and a central rotunda on an arcaded basement, and then added two sweeping semicircular galleries connecting the palace with the service wings.[28] Although the building stood for half a century in ruins, it lost little of the powerful and majestic unity which had been frittered away at Pavlovsk by Brenna's additions, but which it is doubtful whether Cameron himself could ever have attained. This comparison is not intended solely to the disadvantage of Cameron. His interiors at Tsarskoe Selo and Pavlovsk are unsurpassed in the skilful management of classical elements. Quarenghi's are in quite a different spirit, more sumptuous in the use of sculpture and painting, but perhaps not so inspired nor so properly the accompaniment of the splendidly severe exteriors.

The buildings mentioned here are only a small part of Quarenghi's work, for not only was he the designer of many important structures, but he also served in an advisory capacity, so that the last two decades of the century belong more to him than to any other architect working in Russia. To a certain degree even his fellow-architects seem to have felt his influence, for there is a little of Quarenghi in Starov's Tauride Palace, just as there was a little of Cameron in the decorative treatment of Starov's central rotunda. Surprisingly enough, the Emperor Paul, who took such pains to wreck his mother's achievements, retained her chief architect in office. But during the five confused years of Paul's reign

Quarenghi's work was principally of a utilitarian character, such as the various designs for barracks and riding-halls. For the riding-stables of the Horse Guards (1800–4) his choice of a long rectangular mass ending in porticoes of eight Tuscan columns has the mark of his genius, but lacks the authority of his work for Catherine. Under Alexander I his fortunes declined. He endured his greatest chagrin when the Exchange, which he had begun for Catherine on the point of Vasily Ostrov looking towards the Fortress and the Winter Palace, was torn down to make way for a new design by the French architect, Thomas de Thomon (see below, page 320). Quarenghi's feelings could only partly be salved by the patronage of the Dowager Empress Maria Feodorovna, Paul's widow, who commissioned a huge new building at Smolny (1806–8) as a home for widowed noblewomen. The work was competent within his familiar Palladian formula of spare wings punctuated by porticoes of free-standing and engaged columns, but it added nothing to his prestige, which by this time had achieved international recognition.[29] Alexander's indifference to the greatest architect of the older generation is the more regrettable in that Quarenghi's design for a church in Moscow commemorating the war of 1812, in the form of an immense Pantheon with boldly projecting porticoes to the east and west, would have been a triumph of the Alexandrian style, at once the boldest and most monumental transposition to Imperial Russia of the spatial geometry of Imperial Rome.

CHAPTER 22

THE ALEXANDRIAN EMPIRE:

1796–1850

Since under the autocracy the selection of the chief architect and general superintendent of governmental building was in the hands of the sovereign, it was inevitable that even in a brief reign the Tsar's taste would affect the course of architectural history. The five years' rule of Paul I, the insane son of Catherine II, was a period of dread for his subjects which only ended with his assassination on 23 March 1801. Before this, Paul had had time to impose his capricious tastes on Russian architecture. As a boy and young man he had been neglected by his mother, who disliked him and made no secret of her preference for Paul's eldest son, the future Alexander I. The grandson was admitted to the councils of state, while his father was obliged to remain apart at the 'Little Court' which he maintained in the palaces of Gatchina and Pavlovsk. Although the choice of Rinaldi and Cameron as the architects of these palaces had been Catherine's, in the course of time the interiors were redecorated by Paul and his gifted wife, the Grand Duchess Maria Feodorovna, a princess of Württemberg. Her taste was better than his, and was further refined by the visit she and Paul paid to western Europe in 1782. Travelling as the Comte and Comtesse du Nord, they spent a month in Paris,[1] whence they shipped to Russia such enormous stores of furniture that their funds were depleted and Catherine herself not a little annoyed. Maria Feodorovna's affection for Pavlovsk appears in her detailed inventory, which lists the contents of the palace room by room.[2]

The young couple's favourite architect was an Italian, Vincenzo Brenna (Vikenty Frantsevich, c. 1750–1804), who had been working in Russia since 1780. That they admired his abilities as a decorator more than as an architect is seen from the fact that for the first five years or so after his arrival he was occupied with the completion of the interiors at Gatchina, and at Pavlovsk which Cameron had left unfinished. In Cameron's absence, Brenna was entrusted with architectural additions, so that in its final form Pavlovsk owed as much to Brenna as to Cameron.

The interiors of Pavlovsk preserve much of Brenna's style, which was more robust and massive than Cameron's. For the delicate subtleties of Cameron's relief decoration, Brenna substituted a more naturalistic treatment which can be seen in the vigorous caryatids which were executed by the sculptor Kozlovsky for the Throne Room [262]. The prevalence of military motifs in the sculptural decoration was due to the Emperor, who, like his father, Peter III, was devoted to his regiments. This martial aspect was a prominent feature of Brenna's most important undertaking, the Michael Castle (Mikhailovsky Zamok, 1797–1800), so called to distinguish it as a defensive fortress, surrounded by a moat, from the residential palaces of the previous sovereigns.[3] Paul had a constant fear of assassination, and wanted a palace where he could feel his life was safe. Upon his accession he commissioned Bazhenov, whom he had befriended when the elderly Russian architect had fallen out of favour with Catherine, to design one to take the place of Rastrelli's Summer Palace [201] on the strategic site, opposite the junction of the Moika and Fontanka canals opposite the southern end of the Summer Garden. Since less than four months later, when Paul went to Moscow for his coronation in February 1797, Brenna in a Court order was named responsible for the construction of the castle, Bazhenov may have had time only to work out the plan. This was in the form of a square enclosing an octagonal courtyard about which rooms of many different sizes and shapes opened out of loggia-like passages, recalling Bazhenov's designs for Smolny and the Kremlin. The two separate entrance pavilions, which are all that is left of the extensive group of subsidiary structures, are also closer to Smolny than to Brenna's work.

The castle itself looks more like the work of a decorator improvising as he went along than of an architect with as powerful an imagination as Bazhenov's. It has no unity of taste or style, within or without. The entrance façade is sombrely military, with heavy rustication and an abundance of trophies. Paul's haste is proved by the fact that much of the costlier material was pillaged from Catherine's still unfinished structures. The incongruous religious inscription above the entrance, for instance, came from Rinaldi's unfinished Cathedral of St Isaac. In the courtyard the ornamental rustication betrays Brenna's Italian descent in an order derived from the Palazzo Pitti in Florence; the façade opposite the Summer Garden resembles an Italian villa of the sixteenth century. The eclectic character of the building, so unlike the unified classicism of Catherine's architecture, probably pleased Paul, who desired nothing more than to eradicate his mother's memory. It is an architectural irony that this capricious and ineffective castle should have been under construction in the very years when the Tauride Palace was defiled by the cavalry regiments of the guard. Three weeks after he had moved into his castle, Paul was slain in his bedroom. In 1822 the structure, which was detestable to Alexander, who sincerely loved his father and deplored his murder, was transferred to the School of Engineers, and in the course of time the reconstruction of the interiors spoiled much of Brenna's decorative work.

Unlike his father, Alexander I (1801–25) had great good taste and a clear understanding of what his grandmother had accomplished for Russian architecture. And he had a profound affection for the city which his father had feared. During his long reign he continued to beautify St Petersburg with buildings in a consistent and harmonious style. To Alexander as much as to any of his predecessors was due the final classical homogeneity of the city as a whole. As a contemporary historian wrote:

He wanted to make Petersburg more beautiful than any of the European capitals he had visited. For that purpose he decided to set up a special architectural committee under the chairmanship of [General] Béthencourt. Neither the legality of private ownership, nor the structural durability of public or private buildings were the affair of this committee: it was to be concerned only with examining designs for new façades, to accept, reject, or alter them, and also to attend to the plan of streets and squares, projects for canals, bridges, and the better construction of the outlying parts of the city, in a word, to [bring about] its uniform exterior beauty.[4]

Alexander's building programme was consistent. At the lowest level of small private houses the designs published with the Emperor's approval called for structures of masonry or wood, wherein the minimum amount of classical motifs, plain wall, pediment, and portico, were handled with ease, if with no particular distinction.[5] Upon this foundation of private building Alexander's leading architects erected their monumental structures, buildings unmatched elsewhere in Europe.

The architectural activity of the reign can be divided into two parts, separated by the French invasion of 1812 and the burning of Moscow. The division, however, is due as much to accident as to the decline of Alexander's liberal idealism after the Napoleonic wars. It so happened that between 1811 and 1814 Voronikhin, Zakharov, and Thomas de Thomon, the three major architects of the first part of the reign, died. The three architects of the latter part, Stasov, Rossi, and Montferrand, lived on until the decade 1848–58, so that the principles of Alexandrian Classicism were continued, although with variations and modifications, until well towards the end of the reign of Alexander's successor, Nicholas I. There is in the architectural succession no growing bias towards native-born or foreign architects. During the earlier years two were Russian and one French; during the latter part one was Russian, one Italian, and one French.

Alexandrian Classicism can be interpreted as a Russian version of the Empire style so familiar in its original French decorative conceptions, and in the different national versions which spread throughout Europe. But it is only fair to say that nowhere, except possibly in the eastern United States during the 1820s and 30s, was the style used for so many public buildings. Even in France its proponents achieved only a limited success in the field of monumental architecture, and the few large buildings of the Napoleonic period – the Madeleine, the Bourse, and the Arc de Triomphe – are more Roman than Greek. Alexander's architects, on the other hand, thought more often in Greek forms, organized according to the rational and public conceptions of French planning. The reasons for the change in taste from Roman to Greek principles are many and well known, and are as consistent for Russian art as for European art in general.[6] Greater familiarity with the history of ancient art, promulgated by Winckelmann and supported by archaeological research, established the superiority of the Greek original to the Roman 'copy'. To this were added other conceptions, literary, sentimental, and picturesque, as the Near East was discovered by more and more travellers in the later years of the eighteenth century and the early nineteenth.

This interest in what Winckelmann called the 'noble simplicity and quiet calm' of Greek art appeared soon after 1750 in drawings by travellers and in competitive architectural designs, especially those produced by the students and prize-winners of the French Academy, which were executed in bold, geometrical masses with sharp contrasts of texture in smooth walls and rusticated masonry, and the opposition of strong, simple forms: cylinders,

obelisks, cubes, and domes. But in this as in much else theory outran practice. Not until 1769, and the acceptance of Gondouin's designs for the École de Médicine in Paris (1769–86), was a building actually undertaken which incorporated some of these elements.[7] Gradually the movement became saturated with Greek detail, as architects became more familiar with Greek art, at first in the temples of Paestum and Magna Graecia and later in Greece itself. Undoubtedly the most gifted French architect of the geometrical phase was Claude-Nicolas Ledoux (1736–1806).[8] His designs for municipal buildings, theatres, factories, etc., and especially his plan for a complete city for the salt-works at Chaux, were uncompromisingly antique, yet strangely inventive. His gatehouses of Paris – the so-called Barrières, consisting of variations of temple forms – had immense influence. From 1782 until well into the nineteenth century no visitor arriving in Paris could fail to be impressed by their classical and geometrical simplicity. Paul himself must have admired them, for after his return to Russia he purchased through an agent a collection of 273 drawings by Ledoux.[9] In 1804 Ledoux published a collection of his designs as *L'Architecture considérée sous le rapport de l'art, des mœurs, et de la législation*. The provocative title interested city planners and builders like Alexander who understood the larger purposes of architecture and were impressed by Ledoux's logical conception of the relation between architecture and ethics. Their taste for geometrical forms was confirmed when they read that such were the proper expressions of the new moral attitude towards architecture. It thus followed that, where Catherine's classicism had been instinctively sentimental and personal, and where the typical buildings of her reign had been palaces, Alexander moved more widely in the public domain. The greatest works of his best architects were almost without exception governmental structures or city-planning projects.

The first use of pure Greek forms can be attributed to Cameron. For all his Palladian and Pompeian predilections, he built at Pavlovsk in 1780 a circular Temple of Friendship, in which a correct Doric column and entablature appeared for the first time in Russia. In the same year Catherine approved a project for a church at Mogilev (1781–98), commemorating her friendship with Joseph II of Austria, by the self-taught architect and man of letters, Nikolay Alexandrovich Lvov (1751–1803), in which he used a six-column Greek Doric portico.[10] Somewhat earlier the Tuscan Doric entrances and geometrical forms of Starov's belfry at Nikolskoe had shown that he was familiar with the latest Parisian developments. But all these efforts were slight, scattered, and remained largely unknown. Quarenghi's Palladianism had no room for such Greek forms so long as he remained the Court architect. But the Italian and Palladian hold was broken, at first tentatively by the discursive Italianism of Brenna, and then completely by the moral conceptions of Alexander.

Apart from the Michael Castle there is but one other monument which illustrates the transition between the declining but still gallant classicism of Catherine's reign and the stricter geometrical style of the early nineteenth century – a style which in a sense corresponded curiously with the personality of Paul I. One of the most startling signs of his madness was his delusion that through his own efforts he could effect a union between Roman Catholicism and Eastern Orthodoxy. In this he was further persuaded by his unexpected election to the Grand Mastership of the Order of St John of Jerusalem, known as the Knights of Malta. This was the first time that a non-Catholic sovereign had ever occupied such a position, and to commemorate it Paul ordered Quarenghi to build a Catholic chapel dedicated to the Maltese Order of St John of Jerusalem in Rastrelli's Vorontzov Palace of 1756–8, which was then occupied by the Corps des Pages.[11] This was followed by his decision to revise the plans for the new cathedral in honour of the miraculous icon of the Virgin of Kazan, one of the most ancient Orthodox relics, which had been brought from Moscow to St Petersburg in 1710. It had first been placed in Zemtsov's Nativity of the Virgin, but towards the close of the century a new church was needed, for which Quarenghi prepared designs and selected massive columns of Finnish granite. When his star declined, Paul and his friend Count Alexandr Sergeevich Stroganov (1733–1811) decided that the new church should be an all-Russian creation. This arbitrary attitude towards the selection of architects, painters, and sculptors, contrary to Russian tradition, proved completely ineffectual as a nationalistic gesture; the Kazan Cathedral (1801–11, now the Museum of the History of Religion) was, if anything, the most thoroughly Catholic and Roman church in Russian classicism. This again was due to the Emperor's character; for after his elevation by the Knights of Malta Paul dreamed of being elected Pope.

Count Stroganov proposed and Paul accepted the appointment as architect of Andrey Nikiforovich Voronikhin (1760–1814), who had been born a serf on one of the Stroganov estates in Perm.[12] He showed such talent that his master sent him to Moscow to study painting, an art which he practised all his life. But his interest in architecture soon became paramount and attracted the attention of Bazhenov and Kazakov, who were working in Moscow in the mid 1770s. Count Stroganov responded by enrolling him in the St Petersburg Academy and then sending him as companion to his son, Count Pavel (Paul) Alexandrovich, on an extensive tour of Europe in 1784. Several years of study in Paris and Rome followed before Voronikhin returned to Russia in 1790. His first works in St Petersburg – the remodelling of a suite of state apartments in Stroganov's palace, originally built by Rastrelli, and the design of a dacha (country house) for Stroganov on the Neva – proved that the young architect was thoroughly conversant with the latest European versions of Neo-Classical design and decoration. The dacha particularly, where a light, open loggia floated above a rusticated lower storey, showed his ability to create that contrast of mass and void, of texture and colour, which would later become so prominent an aspect of Alexandrian Classicism.

the west façade, but unfortunately only the north colonnade was erected. In consequence the appearance of the church as the spectator views it from the Nevsky Prospekt is somewhat deceptive: the majestic transept, crowned by the dome and flanked by the arms of the

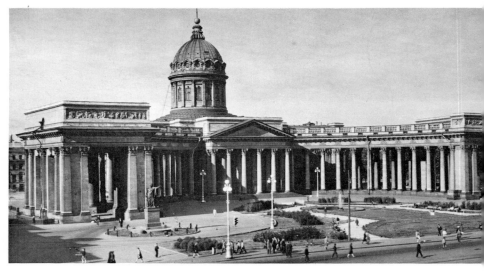

233. A. N. Voronikhin: St Petersburg,
Cathedral of the Virgin of Kazan on the Nevsky Prospekt, 1801–11, from the north

Voronikhin's design for the cathedral was influenced by St Peter's in Rome and the piazza before it, but it would be unfair to think the new church merely a reduced copy of the old [233]. Although the exterior order resembles Michelangelo's and Maderno's building as much as Rinaldi's Cathedral of St Isaac, which was still standing at that time, and the colonnade was obviously inspired by Bernini's, the heroic character of Voronikhin's conception was quite novel.[13] Since ritual orientation was obligatory he set his church, on a Latin-cross plan, parallel to the Nevsky Prospekt, and devised two semicircular colonnades to flank the north and south transept entrances. A third would have embraced a large square opposite

colonnade, appears to be the principal entrance.

Voronikhin, like Starov before him, understood the use of columns. In the interior double rows of granite shafts with gilt bronze bases and capitals support a powerful cornice upon which rests a richly coffered barrel vault. Without, the three porticoes and double colonnades would have created a majestic rhythm severely checked by the heavy attics above the portico and end pavilions, and by the balustrades between. The effect of the cathedral is complex, corresponding to the mixture of architectural currents which prevailed in Russia at this time. Although the order is Corinthian and the use of materials as luxurious as any in St Petersburg, the effect is austere and

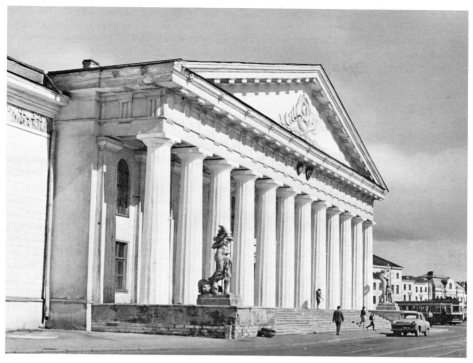

234. A. N. Voronikhin: St Petersburg, Academy of Mines, 1806-11

cold in the extreme. The exuberant panoply of the Baroque South seems caught and frozen in northern stone, granite, and bronze. The answer most probably is that Voronikhin's vision of Rome at the end of the eighteenth century had been tempered by his studies of Greek art and the Neo-Classical influences of the Paris Academy. His emotions were not capable of Baroque display, for all that the plan and order of the church were deliberately and intentionally Roman. Indeed, the influence of his studies in Paris can be seen in the fact that the general proportions and mass of the church, if the colonnades are removed, is far closer to Soufflot's Sainte-Geneviève (now the Panthéon), which was new when Voro-

nikhin was in Paris, than it is to St Peter's.

Although the Kazan Cathedral was begun and finished in the first decade of Alexander's reign, it had been planned for Paul, and his spirit pervades it, just as the great men it entombs and memorializes – Kutuzov and Barclay de Tolly – were as much the military heroes of Paul's reign as of his son's. Voronikhin's first important work for Alexander immediately showed the Greek turn of his thoughts. For the Academy of Mines (Gorny Institut, 1806-11) on Vasily Ostrov he chose as a model the Temple of Poseidon at Paestum, placing a twelve-column portico with a rather thinly drawn pediment against a plain wall [234].[14] This was also his last important building. The Cathedral of Kazan absorbed so much of his energies that before his premature death in 1814 he had time for little more than a few small country houses.

The full measure of the Greek contribution to the classical revival in St Petersburg was provided by the French architect Thomas de Thomon (Toma de Tomon, 1754–1813).[15] Born in Nancy and educated in Paris, he had travelled in Italy, where he admired the temples of Paestum and the engravings of Piranesi. Not wishing to return to France, since he was an ardent royalist, Thomon entered the service of the Comte d'Artois, later Charles X, and worked in Vienna for Prince Esterhazy before arriving in Russia in 1790. Alexander entrusted him with the reconstruction of two important public buildings – the Great Theatre (Bolshoi Teatr, 1802–5) and the Exchange. The theatre had been built by the German theatrical painter Ludwig Philipp Tischbein (1744–1806), and Quarenghi had begun the Exchange. Of the theatre, destroyed by fire in 1813, we can see from Thomon's drawings that it was derived from de Wailly's Odéon in Paris. A portico of eight Ionic columns adorned a two-storey block with Palladian windows, above which rose the pedimented roof of the stage. The plan also resembled French theatres of the later eighteenth century, a horseshoe-shaped auditorium surrounded by salons and offices to fill out an extended rectangle. Thomon's design for a theatre in Odessa, no longer preserved, is so much more antique that the Renaissance treatment of the façades may well have been due to the necessity of retaining part of the walls of Tischbein's first theatre.[16]

In Thomon's other municipal building, the Exchange of 1804–10 (now the Naval Museum), there was less compromise. On the plan of a peripteral temple he placed a large barrel-vaulted hall, painted blue and white, covered with a gabled roof and illuminated with large arched windows appearing above the colonnade. The columns, although unfluted, were based upon those of the Temple of Po-

seidon at Paestum, and are one of the earliest examples, on such a scale, of the revival of the early, almost archaic Doric order. Thomon, however, was more than just a slavish imitator of antiquity; he gave these columns his personal signature by introducing a wide neck just below the capital, and he added low bases, scarcely visible from a distance. In addition to the Exchange, Thomon planned the whole area at the end of Vasily Ostrov as a monumental setting for civic and commercial ceremonies with granite quays, ramps, and lighthouses in the form of rostral columns with seated figures of marine divinities at their feet. Although his plans were not completely carried out, the intention and even the partial realization were an indication that for St Petersburg the new century, under the direction of the new sovereign, would be a period of planning on an unprecedented scale. His other works, whether commercial buildings such as the warehouses on the Salny Embankment (1804–5) or the memorial chapel to Paul I erected by his widow in the park at Pavlovsk (1805–8), show him equally at home in the utilitarian as well as the monumental phases of Neo-Classicism, but there is about them, as in the Exchange, so much of the international character of the revival that they seem to belong to the general history of European architecture rather than to a specifically Russian version.

For a stronger Russian accent one can turn to the work of Andreyan (Adrian) Dmitrievich Zakharov (1761–1811).[17] He had entered the Academy at the age of six, was sent to Paris for four years (1782–6), where he worked under Chalgrin, and then travelled in Italy before returning to St Petersburg, where the remainder of his life was passed in the service of the Academy. Yet, stereotyped as the educational process had become by this time, and susceptible as Zakharov was to foreign influences, particularly those of the French Academy, his work was unmistakably and completely Russian. In it, and particularly in the one building on which his fame rests, the new Admiralty (1806–23), influences from the western past were combined with certain persistent Russian factors: the colossal scale, the ability to manage a tremendous plan, and the typically Russian materials, brick and painted plaster.

By 1800 the century-old Admiralty of Peter the Great was no longer an appropriate monument for the centre of a great city which it had more or less accidentally become. Its fortifications, moats, embankments, and drawbridges were outmoded as well as in disrepair. Zakharov's task was severely limited. Not only was he obliged to retain the plan and dimensions of the earlier group, for ship-building was still carried on, but he had to preserve something of the spirit of the old Admiralty, whose slender spire, the counterpart of the steeple of the Peter-Paul Cathedral across the Neva, had become a symbol of imperial St Petersburg. In the design of the new Admiralty, Zakharov kept the open plan of the earlier building as an extended rectangle, opening towards the river and enclosing the shipyards (later built up with blocks of flats). Yet his design is also a superior example of the way in which traditional elements can be shaped into something new. The building was an interminable series of storerooms and offices, arranged in a double row separated by a narrow court. The total length is more than a quarter of a mile. To control this gigantic plan Zakharov devised an alternating sequence of architectural forms, few in number and astonishingly simple, which nevertheless bind the whole into a single, integrated harmony. This is all the more remarkable since, so far as we can judge by his earlier drawings, Zakharov, like his contemporaries, had toyed with the fashionable archaeology of the day in all manner of fanciful projects. Thus his plan for a monument to Paul I took the form of a truncated pyramid with Doric porticoes flanked by crenellated Gothic pylons, the whole topped by a circular arcaded *aediculum* which might best be described as 'stripped Roman'. But for his executed work he eschewed the dangerous enticements of eclec-

ticism for a vocabulary of simplified antique and freely invented forms. He treated the central entrance of the Admiralty as a square pavilion, surmounted by a rectangular colonnade with statues supporting a square domed roof and slender spire. The gilded roof and spire echo the earlier building and are a subtle reminder of the primitive boisterousness of the Petrovian era. Although it is possible that the proportions and spacing of the sculpture and reliefs on the first storey of the pavilion were derived from French academic projects of the 1780s, Zakharov's fusion of medieval, Baroque, and classical elements is inimitably his own, and Russian into the bargain [235, 236].

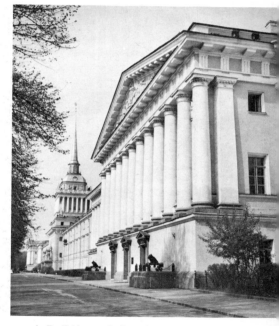

235. A. D. Zakharov: St Petersburg,
New Admiralty, 1806–23

The central pavilion could scarcely dominate the long façade were it not supported on either side by a wall of eleven bays treated with the utmost simplicity. The plain stuccoed walls on a rusticated base are relieved only by

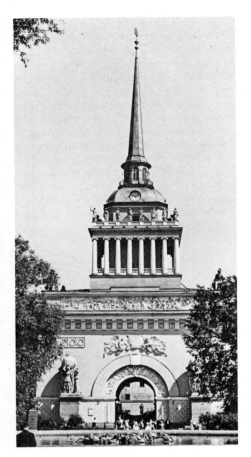

236. A. D. Zakharov: St Petersburg,
New Admiralty, 1806–23

the sharp profiles of the window-frames. The wings are treated as identical three-part compositions, with the middle portion enriched by pedimented porticoes of twelve columns on high bases, separated by six bays of wall from subsidiary pavilions with six columns. This treatment of the two ends of the main façade supplied the *ordonnance* for the narrow sides facing the Winter Palace to the east, and the Senate and Synod across the Decembrist Square to the west. Zakharov's most personal

touch is seen in the side façades towards the river. Here the ends of the building become cubical pavilions, flanked by colonnades and supporting low cylindrical drums above which masts rise from twisted gilt dolphins [237]. The combination of these simple cubes and cylinders of various sizes and proportions with the sparse sculptural embellishment, so knowingly placed and picked out in white against the bright yellow walls, created an effect which more than anything devised by Thomon or Voronikhin bore the accent of Alexandrian Classicism, related to, but not entirely like, similar designs elsewhere in Europe. In addition, Zakharov's genius in managing to achieve variety within the larger unity of his principal façade can be compared with other lengthy buildings, such as Rastrelli's Winter Palace and Tsarskoe Selo, where even the great Italian could not overcome the impression of restlessness and fragmentation.

In Zakharov's Admiralty, and other works, such as his designs for warehouses (1806–8) on the Neva and the executed Church of St Andrew at Kronstadt (1806–11), the high-water-mark of Alexandrian Classicism was reached. In these, and in Stasov's belfry at Gruzino (1822) [239], there is a distinction in the handling of geometrical forms which is unmistakably Russian. When this taste was applied to furniture, textiles, porcelain, and decorative objects of all kinds, an environment was created which is, like the architecture, similar to the French Empire or German Biedermeier styles and yet not identical with either.[18] The domestic application of the principles of the classical revival, and the creation of a peculiarly Russian environment, were perhaps best seen in and around Moscow, especially in the country houses of the nobility in the neighbourhood of the old capital. These houses were small and more intimate than their town houses in St Petersburg, which were often only reduced versions of the imperial palaces. Much of the most interesting Moscow architecture of the latter half of the eighteenth century was created by or under the influence

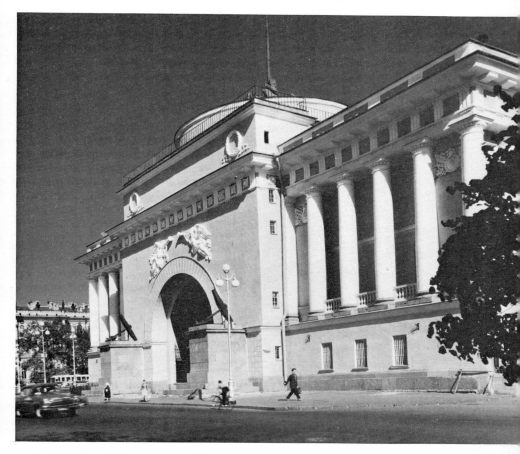

237. A. D. Zakharov: St Petersburg, New Admiralty,
1806–23, pavilion

of Matvey Feodorovich Kazakov (1738–
1812).[19] He had studied at Prince Ukhtomsky's unofficial academy with Bazhenov
and Kokorinov, where he at first absorbed the
Baroque manner of Elizabeth's reign, but later,
and largely on his own initiative, he passed
through all phases of the classical revival,
attaining in the end a style of remarkable
purity and serenity. In this he was perhaps
most encouraged by his work with Quarenghi,
for whom he supervised the construction of
Count Sheremetev's residence at Ostankino

(1792–9) to the north of Moscow, although
now within the city limits. This modest
wooden country house, extended by service
buildings for the large number of serfs who
constructed it and its remarkable private
theatre, may even owe something to Kazakov
himself; in comparison with Quarenghi's
palace at Lyalichy the Italian's aggressive Pal-
ladianisms have become more intimate and
personal. Kazakov was also more fortunate
than Bazhenov in his dealings with the Empress. Catherine commissioned him to build a

second palace at Tsaritsyno when she grew tired of Bazhenov's Gothic pile, and it was Kazakov, not Bazhenov, who in the end built a new palace in the Kremlin. His Senate of 1771–85 (later the Court of Justice and now the principal seat of the government) is the most systematically antique of all his buildings. A more personal statement, even if in the language of international Neo-Classicism, can be read in the Golitsyn Hospital in Moscow (now incorporated in the First City Hospital), of 1796–1801 [238]. The entrance

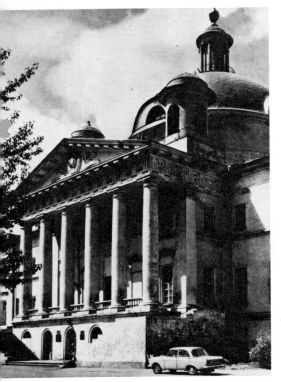

238. M. F. Kazakov: Moscow, Golitsyn Hospital, 1796–1801, entrance

pavilion, almost devoid of carved ornament and flanked by appropriately simple wings, is an adroitly managed fugue in four voices –

circle and square, column and cube. From the quiet statement in the doors and windows of the block supporting the colonnade the harmony increases in complexity to the spreading dome of the chapel behind. The architecture of Kazakov and his contemporaries created for Moscow a classical environment as coherent as Rastrelli's for Elizabeth's St Petersburg or Quarenghi's for Catherine's. Although many of Kazakov's finest buildings, such as the University, were damaged in the fire of 1812 and rebuilt after his death by others, through his copious work he had substantially made over Moscow in the image of his classical dream. Kazakov died in 1812, but he left a host of pupils and followers, who rebuilt the ruined portions of the city with fine residences and public buildings in his simplified classical style, so that his tradition was continued in and around Moscow until well towards the middle of the century.

The Patriotic War, with the burning of Moscow and the triumphal progress of Russian arms across Europe to Paris itself, marked a turning point in the history of Alexander's reign, in politics as well as in architecture. The Emperor's decreasing interest in liberal reform, and his feeling that the security of the throne and of the empire rested upon a stricter interpretation of the principles of absolutism, can be seen in the change in the architectural scene, although this again was accidentally hastened by the deaths of Voronikhin, Zakharov, and Thomon. After 1814 a new triumvirate appeared, composed of one Russian and two foreign architects, in this case an Italian and a Frenchman. The Russian, Vasily Petrovich Stasov (1769–1848), was born in Moscow, where he studied and first worked in the circles of Bazhenov and Kazakov.[20] Imperial recognition came in 1801, when Alexander admired his arrangements for the public festivities of the coronation, and in 1802 by imperial ukase Stasov was sent abroad to study. He spent six years in France, England, and Italy, where he was elected a member of the Roman Academy of St Luke. In 1808 he returned to Russia, entered the imperial service, and was entrusted with renovations at the palaces of Oranienbaum, Peterhof, and Tsarskoe Selo, where in 1811 he built the high school adjoining the Great Palace. In 1815 Arakcheev, Alexander's favourite adviser, commissioned Stasov to do some work for his

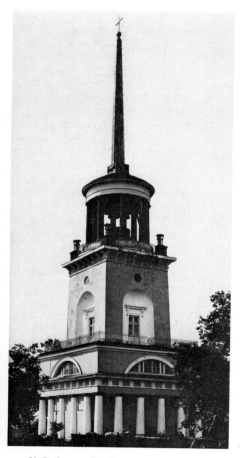

239. V. P. Stasov: Gruzino, near Novgorod, bell tower, 1822

country estate at Gruzino near Novgorod. The belfry he designed for the village church is perhaps his most famous creation [239]. Small

in scale, of delicate proportions and refined details, it demonstrates, like Zakharov's pavilions at the Admiralty, the ability of the greater masters of Russian classicism to achieve an unexpected harmony in the union of classical and traditional forms.

He also had another manner, more appropriate for official St Petersburg. In this he used whenever he could a simplified Doric system with large columns against severely plain walls, as in the Pavlovsky Barracks (1816–19) on the Marsovo Pole (Champ de Mars) west of the Summer Garden. Notwithstanding his clever handling of a few formal elements, the immense length and inevitable monotony of this military structure begin to suggest the implicit and eventually dominant conception of absolute power so characteristic of the later years of Alexander's reign. This sense of imperial authority received its fullest artistic expression in the Moscow Gate [240], a triumphal arch erected on the outskirts of St Petersburg (1834–8) for Nicholas I to commemorate the campaigns of 1826–31. The weighty entablature, bearing eight military trophies and resting on twelve columns arranged in a double row, pushed the classical revival in its Greek Doric mode as far as it could go, a memorial to Nicholas's barren victories, as cold as the cast-iron of which it was made. Yet even here Stasov's architectural ingenuity is seen in the use of this relatively novel material and in the substitution of armed and winged victories (by the sculptor Orlovsky) for the traditional triglyphs and metopes.

Stasov made a notable attempt to find for the early nineteenth century a solution to the problem of adapting the Orthodox church plan to modern architectural styles. Peter's first churches on the Latin-cross plan had been amplified by Rinaldi and Vallin de la Mothe, possibly under the influence of the Moscow Baroque, with larger apses and richer detail, but in every case a single large dome over the crossing, with or without subsidiary cupolas, had been preceded by one or two tall west

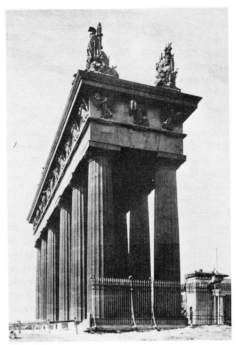

240. V. P. Stasov:
St Petersburg, Moscow Gate, 1834-8

towers. Neither Starov nor Voronikhin had much modified this type, although their churches – the Nevsky Lavra Cathedral and the Kazan Cathedral – carried farther the similarity of the plan and elevation with churches of the Western rite. Stasov returned to the central five-domed plan, most notably in two large churches, the Trinity Cathedral for the Izmailovsky Regiment on the Fontanka canal (1827–35), and the Transfiguration for the Preobrazhensky Regiment near the Tauride Palace (1827–9). For the latter he inscribed the cross in a square, and placed four small domes above the corners of a severely simple mass adorned with a four-column Ionic portico on the western façade. In the Izmailovsky Church his solution was more ingenious. Although the plain walls, relieved only by a heavy

frieze near the cornice, and the plan owe much to the Paris Panthéon, the plan is now quite literally a cross, emphasized externally by the projection of a six-column Corinthian portico on each façade. The smaller domes are placed over the arms of the cross, an arrangement which is more picturesque than the earlier disposition of the domes in the angles of a square and not as capricious as has been thought. At any rate, Stasov created a new silhouette for the traditional Orthodox elevation in the way the small domes, reductions of the greater one over the crossing, are related both to it and to the pediments below.[21]

Alexander's desire to make St Petersburg a city unrivalled in the world for its splendid public buildings found a perfect instrument in the personality and talents of an architect of Italian origin, Karl Ivanovich Rossi (1775–1849).[22] His imagination was as spacious as the Emperor's, and he was completely in sympathy with the exercise of authoritarian control over all new construction. Rossi was the son of an Italian ballerina, and as a child had lived with Brenna, who taught him the rudiments of architectural design. By 1796 he was accredited and was working as Brenna's assistant at Pavlovsk and Gatchina. This association with the older Italian, confirmed by a journey to Italy with Brenna (1804–6), after the latter retired from Russia in 1802, determined the character of Rossi's own style. By-passing the Academy, as it were, Rossi, more than any other architect since the arrival of Vallin de la Mothe, was uninfluenced by the style of Paris and directly inspired by ancient and modern Rome. In this respect he put an end to the Greek Revival and recovered for St Petersburg something of the earlier Roman grandeur it had known in the works of Rinaldi and Quarenghi. The scope of Rossi's imagination and his conception of his abilities were revealed in a memorandum to the Emperor describing his project for a granite quay in front of the Admiralty to provide continous access along the Neva without interrupting the passage of ships from the ways to the river. His plan

called for a new embankment pierced by twelve huge arches and ornamented with three rostral columns which, as Rossi boasted, would 'surpass those which the Romans considered sufficient for their monuments'.[23] After the Patriotic War such claims impressed Alexander, who felt it his duty to conduct the destinies of Europe. What better advertisement for the blessings of autocracy than that its architecture should surpass the moderns as well as the ancients? Rossi's assertions were not without foundation, for nowhere in Europe in the 1820s and 30s were projects on such a scale not only planned but also carried out.

Until 1816 Rossi had worked chiefly in Moscow, but after the disappearance of the earlier generation he was summoned to St Petersburg, where he joined Stasov on the Committee for Construction and Hydraulic Works under the chairmanship of a Spanish military engineer, General Béthencourt (Betankur).[24] Alexander had created this committee to supervise all private as well as public construction in St Petersburg. Soon the decisions of the Committee were effective for architecture throughout Russia. Alexander himself examined the projects submitted to the Committee, and this practice of personal intervention was continued by his brother Nicholas. Rossi eventually became the dominant member of the Committee, but in the beginning the character of his own work was affected by the severe classicism of Stasov.

In his first work for Alexander Rossi was not entirely a free agent. In the Yelagin Palace on the Yelaginsky Ostrov (1818–22) for the Emperor's mother he was handicapped by the proportions of an earlier building, and the result was somewhat heavy and old-fashioned.[25] Rossi's own taste prevailed only in the lavish interior decoration which, until the palace was damaged by fire in 1942, was reminiscent of Brenna. Alexander was pleased with the palace, and in 1819 commissioned an even larger residence for his youngest brother, the Grand Duke Mikhail Pavlovich. The New

Michael Palace (1819–23, later the Alexander III Museum and now the Russian Museum) was Rossi's most personal creation up to this time. Between two simple corner pavilions the central mass was faced with a noble Corinthian order and a prominent portico of eight Corinthian columns. The arrangement was clear, bold, and powerful. The palace rose above low service wings with a Doric order which framed a courtyard separated from the street by a fine iron grille. The group of buildings was only comparable to Brenna's Michael Castle, and, when its relation to the gardens beyond and to the square in front from which a street, on axis, leads to the Nevsky Prospekt is considered, it was unequalled by any residential ensemble in the city. Yet the plan is more impressive than the details, which have a feeling of repetition, of second-hand inspiration. Rossi, unlike Zakharov in his Admiralty or even Voronikhin in his Kazan Cathedral, could not re-work the familiar classical themes into a personal conception. Something of the heavy mediocrity of Brenna was present in this colonnade, the prototypes of which had been used for a century and a half in other countries. In the interior, only the splendid if somewhat pompous staircase was spared when the palace was converted into a museum late in the nineteenth century.

Fortunately Alexander and his successor appreciated Rossi's talents in city planning and gave him ample opportunity to demonstrate his genius in this field. The last of Alexander's projects – the design of the Winter Palace Square – was solved by Rossi with the construction of a huge triangular building for the General Staff with a concave curved façade embracing the south side of the square (1819–29) [241, 242]. The great sweep of this unadorned range throws into relief the fanciful agitation of the Winter Palace and provides an admirably taciturn setting for Rastrelli's loquacious Rococo. The General Staff is pierced in the centre by two large triumphal arches, the second behind and at an angle to the first, in order to accommodate the oblique

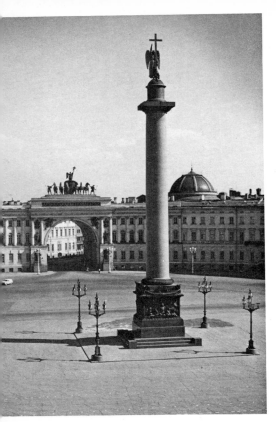

entrance of the Morskaya Ulitsa which connects the square with the Nevsky Prospekt [243]. The view from beneath these arches proves how successfully Rossi could create huge but strictly controlled spatial perspectives.

Before the Palace Square was finished Nicholas I commissioned Rossi to design a new theatre. The plan, upon which Rossi had actually been working since 1816, developed into a group of two new squares with a street between. The Alexandrinsky Theatre (now the Pushkin), between the Public Library and the Anichkov Palace, is at the head of one square [244]. Behind the theatre a new street (now Rossi Street) was cut through to the Fontanka canal, which it joined at Chernyshevsky Square (now Lomonosov). Rossi designed the façades

241 and 242. St Petersburg, Winter Palace Square, General Staff Arch, by K. I. Rossi, 1819–29 and Alexander Column, by R. de Montferrand, 1829; (below) military review at the inauguration of the column

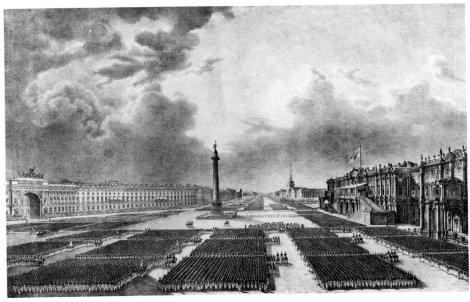

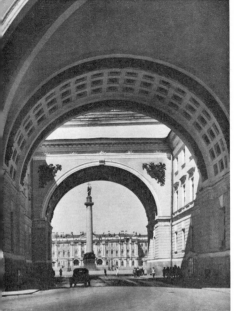

243. K. I. Rossi:
St Petersburg, General Staff Arches, 1819–29,
looking towards the Winter Palace Square

244. K. I. Rossi: St Petersburg, Alexandrinsky
(Pushkin) Theatre, 1827–32

of all the buildings on the squares and streets as parts of a single monumental ensemble. The yellow-and-white theatre is a rectangular structure with corner pavilions, lofty porticoes on the longer sides, a loggia behind a colonnade on the front, and a range of pilasters on the rear, all of the Corinthian order. The block-like character of Rossi's work was emphasized by the strong horizontal cornices behind which rises a high cubical attic, and the avoidance of pediments which he never used after the Michael Palace. But he knew how to make the best use of his few forms. Again the contrast between sober Doric and sumptuous Corinthian was reinforced by the paired columns between the bays of the continuous rows of houses facing Theatre Street which acted as a prelude to the monumental assertion of the theatre itself. But the day for such sober grandeur was passing. The inaugural performance in the great classic building, on 31 August 1832, of Krukovsky's tragedy *Prince Pozharsky*, could be taken to symbolize the approaching dispersal of such ideals by a Romantic interest in the Russian past.[26]

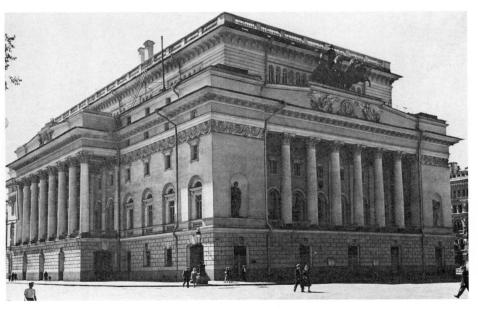

Rossi's fourth large municipal undertaking was his creation of buildings opposite the Admiralty and St Isaac for the Senate and Synod, the highest judicial and ecclesiastical bodies of the government. His solution for the difficult problem of designing a unified façade opposite Zakharov's Admiralty, and yet one which would include two separate buildings for two different government ministries, was a brilliant contribution to the classic environment of urban St Petersburg. The buildings, which had to be of different sizes because of the off-centre entrance of a street between them, are apparently identical, each with a central colonnade and end pavilions accented by paired free-standing columns, and are linked by a triumphal arch whose supporting pylons are the inner pavilions of the buildings on each side [245]. The greater

important work. Worn out by a lifetime of pleasure as well as labour, he retired in 1832, and executed nothing more before his death.

Although structures more or less classical in design continued to be built in St Petersburg and Moscow and elsewhere in Russia, especially in the provincial capitals, where all governmental buildings had to be approved by the Committee in St Petersburg, the works of Rossi in several respects were the final triumphs of Petersburg classicism. Already, as we have seen, a certain sterility and mediocrity had begun to appear in some aspects of his design. The finesse and precision, the fertile invention of new combinations of forms, which had been so characteristic of the work of his immediate predecessors, and which had been present in the architecture of St Petersburg from its foundation, had grown less ap-

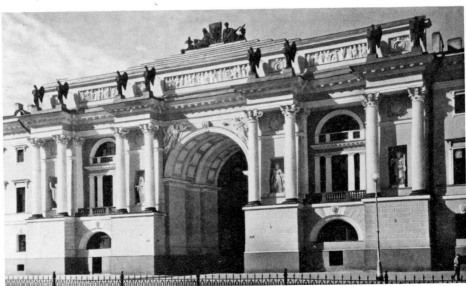

245. K. I. Rossi: St Petersburg, Senate and Synod
(now the State Archives of the Russian Soviet Republic), 1829–34

length of the Synod, to the right, was disguised as a curving colonnaded pavilion turning the corner towards the Neva. This was Rossi's last

parent. Other architects of the early years of Nicholas I's reign continued, with minor variations, the earlier solutions, so that, while the works of such men as Plavov, Briullov, and the Moscow architect Gigliardi are often noble and sometimes interesting, they added little to the development of Russian classicism.[27] But St Petersburg by then had become, and would remain, a city of truly imperial proportions, especially within the complex of buildings and squares which developed around and beyond the Winter Palace and Admiralty. In the far distance of illustration 242 Quarenghi's Horse Guards' Riding School (Konnogvardeiskiy Manezh) of 1804–7 closes the impressive sequence of open spaces stretching from the palace in the right foreground to the present Decembrists' Square (hidden by the Admiralty) which is dominated by Falconet's equestrian statue of Peter the Great and links St Isaac's Cathedral, still under construction to the left of the Riding School, with the Neva. The combined squares, over 1300 feet from east to west, are represented before the reconstruction of the area by the letters 'B' in illustrations 192 and 193.

Only in the activity of the last important Petersburg architect was a specifically Russian characteristic present, and then perhaps not the most commendable. This was a passion for size so obsessive that the more important considerations of scale and proportion were neglected to the disadvantage of the works concerned. In 1815 Alexander decided to rebuild the Cathedral of St Isaac, left in a mournful condition after Brenna's hasty patchwork. Three years later a competition was held but the results were unsatisfactory. Finally, in 1824 the commission was awarded to an obscure French draughtsman. Little is known of the early training of Auguste Ricard, who called himself Ricard de Montferrand (Avgust Avgustovich Monferran, 1786–1858),[28] but he seems to have worked as a youth on Vignon's church of the Madeleine in Paris before enlisting in the Imperial Guard. After the Battle of Leipzig he left the army and went to Russia, which he may already have known as a participant in the campaign of 1812. When he turned up in St Petersburg, he applied for a position as a draughtsman. In 1817 he submitted an album of sketches for the cathedral competitions, presenting designs in the Chinese, Indian, Gothic, and Byzantine styles. Such eclectic tastes may have influenced the Committee, quite as much as the chairman's preference for a westerner. Or may the choice of Montferrand have been due to the Committee's thought that an unknown architect with no reputation to lose might bring some order into the plans and use the best elements of the competitive designs?[29] Certainly Montferrand's design for the cathedral which passed through a number of stages through the years – the final drawings for the interior were not completed until 1842 – brought together many of the important features found in the drawings submitted earlier in a competition by Stasov, Mikhailov, Beretti, and others. In each the same solution was proposed: a huge church on a Greek-cross plan bearing a large central and four subsidiary domes.[30] Most of the competition drawings had placed the Greek cross in a square with identical porticoes on each side. Montferrand's plans of 1825, which seem to have been based on a project of 1820–2 by Mikhailov, transformed the square internally into an aisled rectangle of three central bays, with slightly smaller entrance and altar bays. Externally the proportions of the square, or cross, were retained by providing the porticoes on the long sides with a double row of columns. A sense of mathematical relationships prevailed in the elevation, which was designed as an almost equilateral triangle, or pyramid in three dimensions, evidence of Montferrand's interest in engineering [246].

From the extant plans and wooden model it is apparent that the cathedral would originally have been more gracious than it gradually became; for with the passing of the years, especially after the death of Alexander, successive changes were introduced, all in the direction of greater size and heavier detail, so that, as it stands, the building has the authoritarian character demanded by Nicholas I. The decline of classical standards of taste and

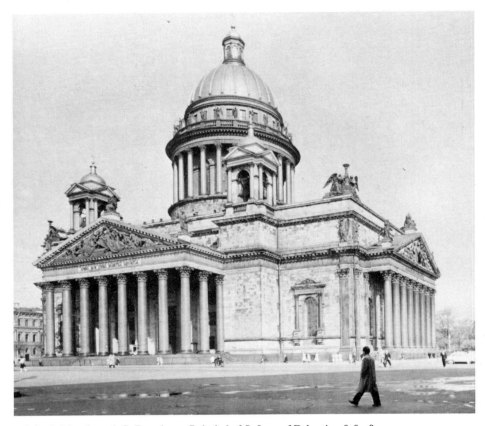

246. R. de Montferrand: St Petersburg, Cathedral of St Isaac of Dalmatia, 1818–58

the growth of eclecticism can be read between the lines of Montferrand's own description of the cathedral:

Sa majesté voulut bien permettre que les quatre campaniles fussent placés sur un plan carré autour de la coupole, et que les deux côtés de l'est et de l'ouest, qui avaient été jugés trop simples dans leur composition, fussent augmenté chacun du portique que l'on y voit aujourd'hui. Ces notables additions . . . augmentèrent de beaucoup l'importance de l'édifice, et devaient lui imprimer un caractère de grandeur et de noblesse bien supérieur à celui des premiers plans.[31]

Montferrand's solution of the problem of designing an Orthodox church in the classical style was related to a certain extent to Stasov's Transfiguration. The large central dome, resembling Soufflot's Panthéon and Wren's St Paul's, has little relation to the small lanterns with cupolas. Montferrand himself felt the lack of connexion between these elements, but was unable to bring them together. The cathedral creates its effect less through its rigid proportions than by the sheer size and unparalleled richness of the materials. The innumerable columns are monoliths of red

Finnish granite, with gilt bronze capitals and bases, dark against the tawny stone walls. Neither money nor effort was spared to create the most splendid interior, although this is slightly spoiled in its final form by the light which enters only feebly through the windows of the drum. Externally the wealth of realistically sculptured figures, the agitated groups of the pediments, and the kneeling angels at the corners of the attic holding great bronze candlesticks, lighted on Easter Eve, create a curious contrast to the static, even inert, classical forms of wall and column. A telling sign that the reign of classicism was over could be seen by those who ventured to inspect the interior of the great dome. The masonry shell was supported by a forest of cast-iron girders, the first use of this material in Russia on such a scale.

Two other undertakings of Montferrand remain to be mentioned: his successful raising of the enormous 'Tsar Bell' in the Moscow Kremlin, which had been damaged by fire shortly after it was cast (1735) and had remained buried in a deep pit, and his erection of the Alexander Column in the Winter Palace Square (1829), one of the primary visual foci of the classical centre of the city [242].[32] The granite monolith, the largest in the world, was intended to surpass all other memorial columns, whether in Paris or Rome, the two cities from which Russian architectural history had continuously drawn its inspiration. And surpass them it did, though in size only, not in beauty. Its transportation from the quarries on Lake Ladoga and its erection in the square were accounted among the engineering triumphs of the century, but the huge column, apart from its impressive height, is graceless in its proportions, another indication of Montferrand's fundamental lack of taste.

This confusion of scale and of artistic purpose is symptomatic of the imminent decline of all architectural standards in the following period of eclecticism which overwhelmed Russia as well as other European countries after the middle of the nineteenth century. St Isaac was the last great building erected under the supervision and control of Alexander's Committee. As time passed, such architectural censorship could no longer keep pace with the increasing exploitation of real estate by private capital. Even Nicholas himself, the most conscientious censor of all forms of popular expression, was obliged to yield, and in the 1840s Alexander's laws requiring all builders to conform to government designs were abrogated.

CHAPTER 23

THE MEDIEVAL REVIVAL:

EIGHTEENTH-CENTURY ROMANTIC ARCHITECTURE

Although the public buildings of St Petersburg are the most conspicuous monuments of eighteenth-century Russian art, they were not the only significant structures, and perhaps were not even the most influential. The cathedrals and palaces on the broad squares and avenues were conceived as symbols of power and public purpose. In unexpected corners of town gardens and country parks there were smaller buildings, manifestations of architecture as the expression of personal feeling. Such sentimental, frequently literary, architecture appeared towards the middle of the century in western Europe in the form of pleasure pavilions and monuments on the estates of the great landowners, and is familiar to us as part of the 'picturesque' and 'romantic' attitude towards nature.[1]

This attitude might not have reached Russia so quickly had Catherine II been less sensitive to changes of European taste. Not the least fascinating aspect of her personality is the way her passion for building encompassed an architecture of serious moral purpose as well as capricious schemes for the gratification of passing fancies. Towards the end of the first decade of her reign, when such dignified public buildings as Vallin de la Mothe's Market, Rinaldi's Marble Palace, Velten's quays, and Bazhenov's Arsenal were already under construction, her plans for the park at Tsarskoe Selo had developed in quite another manner. Catherine detested the stiff avenues and neat hedges of Elizabeth's gardens, patterned after Le Nôtre's at Versailles, and preferred the new attitude towards nature which had been introduced by the English gardeners of the early eighteenth century. On 25 June 1772 she wrote to Voltaire:

J'aime à la folie présentement les jardins à l'anglaise, les lignes courbes, les pentes douces, les étangs en forme de lacs, les archipels en terre ferme, et j'ai un profond mépris pour les lignes droites, les allées jumelles. Je hais les fontaines qui donnent la torture à l'eau pour lui faire prendre un cours contraire à sa nature; les statues sont reléguées dans les galeries, les vestibules, etc.; en un mot, l'anglomanie domine dans ma plantomanie.[2]

Beside Elizabeth's prim patterns, Catherine laid out the undulating ground around the ponds at Tsarskoe Selo as an English park, with wooded slopes traversed by irregular paths, along which the meditative stroller might catch unexpected glimpses of the monuments which were to take the place of the banished Elizabethan statuary.[3]

In another letter to Voltaire, written 14 August 1771, during the first Turkish war, Catherine described some of these monuments:

Si cette guerre continue, mon jardin de Czarskozélo [sic] ressemblera bientôt à un jeu de quilles, car à chaque action d'éclat j'y fais élever quelque monument. La bataille de Kogul, où dix-sept mille combattants en battirent cent cinquante mille, y a produit un obélisque, avec une inscription que ne contient que le fait et le nom du général: la bataille navale de Tchesme a fait naître, dans une très grande pièce d'eau, une colonne rostrale: la prise de la Crimée y sera perpétuée par une grosse colonne; la descente dans la Morée et la prise de Sparte, par une autre. Tout cela est fait des plus beaux marbres qu'on puisse voir, et que les Italiens même admirent. Ces marbres se trouvent les uns sur les bords du lac Ladoga, les autres à Caterinimbourg [sic] en Sibérie, et nous les employons comme vous voyez: il y en a presque de toutes couleurs. Outre cela, derrière mon jardin, dans un bois, j'ai imaginé de faire bâtir un temple de mémoire, auquel on arrivera par un arc de triomphe. Tous les faits importants de la guerre présente y seront gravés sur des médaillons, avec des inscriptions simples et courtes en langue du pays, avec la date et les noms de ceux qui les ont effectués. J'ai un excellent architecte italien, qui fait les plans de ce bâtiment, qui, j'espère, sera beau, de bon goût, et fera l'histoire de cette guerre.

These rostral columns, obelisks, and arches are typical of the first phase of romantic architecture in Russia, as elsewhere in Europe. The elements are antique forms familiar for several centuries to educated Europeans, but used now as decorative objects for the expression of private feeling. The monuments of the 1760s and early 70s were followed in the next few years by more exotic structures. The Egyptian pyramid beside the graves of Catherine's dogs is the first hint. In 1774 Velten added a ruin in the form of a colossal column, half buried in the earth and supporting on its capital a small Gothic pavilion.[4] Even the most devoted adherents of classicism were pressed into service. One of Cameron's first tasks was to design a Chinese village, a collection of small pagoda-like pavilions far more 'oriental' than the earlier chinoiserie decorations of Rinaldi's Italian villa at Oranienbaum. By 1790 the park also contained Neelov's Chinese theatre, Admiralty, and kitchen for the Hermitage, the latter two in the Gothic taste.[5] Quarenghi contributed the 'Great Caprice' [247], a pagoda on top of a huge artificial rock archway, a Turkish kiosk, and an outdoor kitchen for picnics disguised as an antique ruin. Tsarskoe Selo was not the only imperial park to be developed in this way. To the formal gardens at Peterhof was added an English Garden where stood Quarenghi's English Palace. At Pavlovsk the sloping banks of the meandering stream, the Slavyanka, were laid out as a wooded grove [248]. Even at Gatchina, where the terrain was less propitious, a series of pools was arranged, and at the head of one Paul built a little Gothic priory, theoretically an imitation of the headquarters of the Knights of St John in Malta. Throughout all these parks were distributed the usual obelisks, columns, arches, temples,

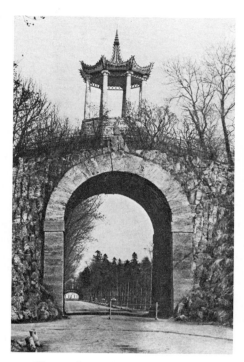

247. Giacomo Quarenghi and Ilya Neelov: Tsarskoe Selo, the Great Caprice in the park, c. 1785

Chinese bridges, and even, at Pavlovsk, an imitation rustic village like those Paul and his wife might have seen in France.[6]

Of all these, the Turkish and Gothic buildings provoke the most curiosity. Catherine's enthusiasm for Islamic architecture was a passing fad, prompted by Russian victories in the first Turkish war and unsupported by any serious study of Mohammedan art. The largest building in this style, Velten's Tchesme Palace outside St Petersburg (Chesmensky Dvorets, 1774–80), built to commemorate the naval victory that year at Tchesme in the Black Sea, was a very uncertain fantasy.[7] The rectangular block with circular corner pavilions was crowned with a series of flattened domes which were taken to be Turkish. The pink and

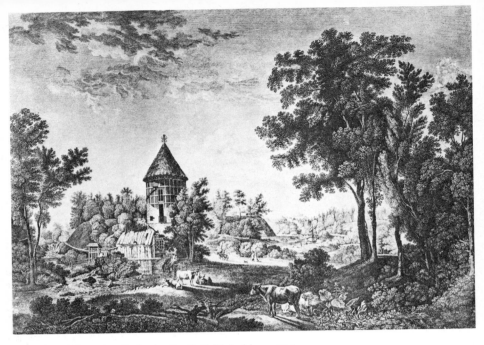

248. View of the park at Pavlovsk, after S. F. Shchedrin, c. 1795

249. Y. M. Velten: Tchesme Palace, church, 1777–80

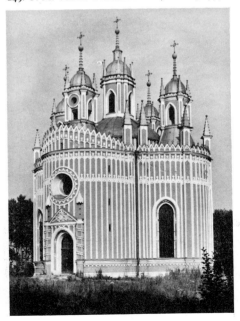

white palace church [249], on a quatrefoil plan, was striped and crested in a bizarre fashion and crowned with slender pinnacled lanterns. It was all imaginary old Russian combined with pastry 'Gothick'. Some years earlier a more serious attempt to recreate the forms of the past had been carried out by Bazhenov in the church at Cherkizov-Starak, near Moscow (1759). In this, his first independent production, he placed a storeyed cylindrical tower on a cubical mass reminiscent of the seventeenth-century churches of Moscow, and covered the surfaces with papery Baroque ornament. The slightly later church at Znamenki (1768–84), attributed to the same architect and usually considered the earliest strictly Neo-Gothic structure in Russia, developed further a decorative scheme of old Russian ornament combined with tall pointed spires, ogee and segmental arches.[8] The old Russian ornamental forms may have been demanded by Catherine, who was a serious student of Russian history. She knew that she had not the slightest legal claim to the throne and that, to maintain her position, she must identify herself as closely as possible with the past as well as the present of Russia. This had been brought home at her coronation in Moscow, when the people cheered more for her son, the legitimate heir, than for her. Catherine studied all the chronicles then known, using the actual documents and insisting on textual accuracy. As late as 1792 she declared: 'Je suis enterrée dans l'histoire ou plutôt dans les chroniques de la Russie que j'aime à la folie.' Her dynastic purpose can be read in her remark in 1784: 'Je crois qu'il est impossible de se délasser plus utilement pour l'empire qu'en débrouillant et arrangeant son histoire.'[9]

Her historical enthusiasm had immediate consequences for architecture. She had a genuine affection for Moscow, which she described to Voltaire as 'un monde, non une ville', and frequently visited. As early as 1762, when in Moscow for her coronation, she visited the old wooden palace at Kolomenskoe

[177] and regretfully conceded that it would have to be demolished. But she insisted that drawings be made and a wooden model prepared, which are still our best sources for the study of old Russian wooden secular construction. And since Catherine chose to appear in the rôle of sponsor of ancient Russian buildings, her favourite architect Quarenghi also paid his respects to them. His drawings of the Moscow Kremlin are among the most sensitive interpretations of the Russian past and of an architecture which to most people in the eighteenth century seemed exotic and meaningless.

Nor were Catherine's interests limited to archaeological research and preservation. She thought to make a visible link between her new Europeanized Russia and the old by building in a medieval Russian style, thus ideologically reversing the course Peter had taken a century before. For her Kazakov constructed another monument commemorating her victories over the Turks. The Petrovsky Palace [250], then on the outskirts of Moscow but now within

250. M. F. Kazakov: The Petrovsky Palace, near Moscow, 1775–82

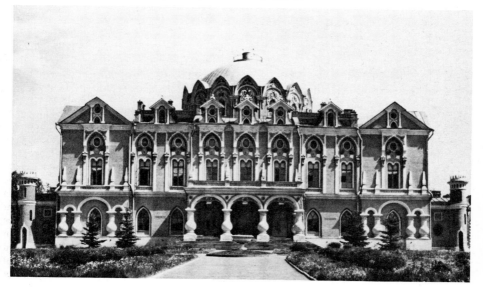

the city limits (1775–82), of red brick with white stone trim, was strictly Palladian in plan; indeed, reminiscent of Pavlovsk, with its central rotunda covered with a flat dome, and large semicircular forecourt.[10] But the exterior walls were adorned with details very much like Velten's, although Kazakov undoubtedly had a more intimate acquaintance with medieval Russian architecture through his work in the Kremlin. Unfortunately the palace was used by Napoleon and was wrecked when the French retreated. In the restoration of 1840 the proportions of the central block were slightly changed and more correct Neo-Russian detail was added which did not help its 'Gothic' aspect.

At the same time Catherine commissioned Bazhenov, whose work at the Kremlin had been suspended, to build another country palace at Tsaritsyno, a mile from Kolomenskoe. It is clear that her intention was to recapture something of the character of the vanished wooden palace, for Bazhenov was told to work in the medieval style. When Catherine visited Moscow in 1787 his grandiose palace of brick with limestone trim was almost ready to receive her. Unfortunately the Empress took an instant dislike to it; the rectangular palace with tall corner pavilions is said to have reminded her of a coffin surrounded with candles. She dismissed Bazhenov and ordered Kazakov to rebuild it (1787–93). Even this was never finished and remained in a half-ruined condition, vastly more picturesque in its dilapidation than it ever would have been if completed [251]. Meanwhile Kazakov produced a third design for a country house for Count Vorontsov at Koukov. This was in plan a pentagon with projecting turrets at the five corners and two circular bastion-like pavilions connected by wings to the main structure. It was never built, but the presence of these neo-medieval elements in the work of an architect noted for his mastery of the purest classical style is sufficient indication that architectural taste in the later eighteenth century was no longer the uniform body of doctrine it

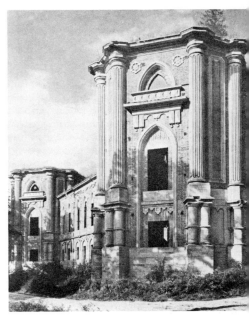

251. V. I. Bazhenov and M. F. Kazakov: Tsaritsyno, ruins of the unfinished palace, 1787–93

had been before. Petrovsky and Tsaritsyno, far more than the timid palace of Tchesme, may have seemed to Catherine valid contributions to Russian architecture. But neither she nor her architects were sufficiently versed in medieval techniques and forms to do more than use miscellaneous motifs plucked from seventeenth-century Russian architecture for the decoration of the surfaces of buildings planned and executed in a classical spirit.[11]

Catherine's interest in medieval architecture may have been encouraged, and certainly was authenticated, by the arrival in St Petersburg late in 1774 of one of the great monuments of eighteenth-century taste, the dinner and dessert services created for her by Josiah Wedgwood and Thomas Bentley. The 952 pieces of Queen's ware were painted in grisaille, as Wedgwood wrote, with 'perfectly picturesque' views of English scenery, country houses, churches and abbeys, and other well-known sites. The range, which extended from Stonehenge to Kew Gardens, provided Catherine with a repertory of ruined buildings, most of them Gothic. The service, which was intended for the Tchesme Palace, was used for state occasions, so it is unlikely to have been seen by other than Catherine's guests. Nevertheless, her medievalism, with that of her architects – Kazakov, Bazhenov, and Quarenghi – remained without immediate issue. It was a personal affair between the sovereign and her servants, and lacked any broad popular support, as well as any real understanding of medieval principles of design. Only later, when the Russian past began to have a political use, would such forms be revived with greater accuracy but without the same charm. Meanwhile the search for exotic styles continued, passing from garden structures to more serious buildings, and soon threatening the whole framework of Neo-Classical idealism. If this was preserved in Russia well into the 1840s and even beyond, it was due more to the insistence of imperial authority than to the taste of the architects themselves.

This collection of curiosities is more important in the sum than in the parts. If an architect of Quarenghi's Palladian persuasion could work in so many manners, then the stately columnar façades of public architecture were bound to lose the power to convince when the demand came for larger buildings in a variety of styles. Within the very heart of the classical revival the seeds of eclecticism had begun to germinate. The caprices of Quarenghi were the random thoughts of a great designer. Two decades later the eclectic spirit appeared more insidiously in the architectural conceptions of Luigi Rusca, who published in 1810 designs for the War College and a country villa in the Gothic manner, an Egyptian pavilion for a country house, and Moorish designs for Mohammedan mosques in St Petersburg.[12] In 1792 Andreyan Zakharov indulged in a hodge-podge of styles in his

project for a triumphal decoration, the sort of student work which a generation before would have been unmitigatedly classical. Now Zakharov's lighthouses in the form of monstrous Doric columns rested on crenellated medieval walls. In 1800 his designs for a monastery church at Gatchina showed a severely simple block, but with pointed windows and Gothic rib vaults.[13] Even Carlo Rossi, whose monuments and plans set the final classical seal on St Petersburg, had his romantic diversion. His two projects of before 1815 for a cathedral for the Nilus Hermitage on an island in Lake Seliger bristle with tent-roofed belfries rising above a trefoil plan with smaller radiating chapels.[14]

This curious interest, which was felt even by architects whose executed works were thoroughly classical, lived on into the reign of Nicholas I, under whom the gardens of Tsarskoe Selo received a complement of buildings marking the triumph of European Romanticism in its most eclectic aspect. Here in the late 1820s Adam Adamovich Menelas (1763–1831), an English architect resident in Russia from 1784, built a ruined 'chapel' (1827), a Turkish elephant house (1828), and several more habitable structures in a reasonably correct Gothic. Rastrelli's effervescent Monbezh was destroyed to make way for a Gothic Arsenal containing a collection of old arms and armour.[15] Menelas's most archaeological work was the Egyptian Gate at Peterhof (1827–32) [252], in the form of a double pylon, with bas-reliefs forming one of the largest groups of Neo-Egyptian sculpture ever executed.

Inevitably the medieval revival affected church architecture, and by the end of Alexander's reign two currents were at work. In the first, as at the Petrovsky Palace and Tsaritsyno, medieval forms were fastened to buildings of traditional, even Neo-Classical, plan and construction. Elsewhere another kind of design resulted from a study of western European Neo-Gothic design. Such are the façades of the Synodal Printing Office (before

252. A. A. Menelas:
Peterhof, Egyptian Gate, 1827–32

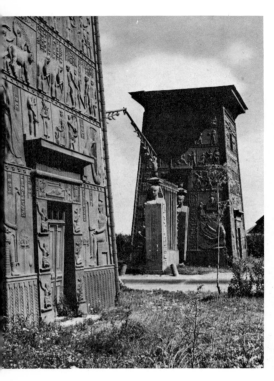

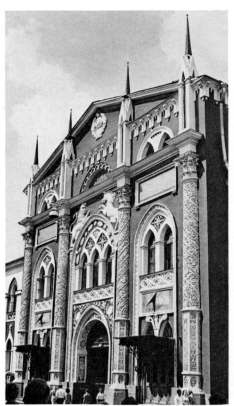

253. Moscow, Synodal Printing Office,
before 1770, rebuilt after 1812

1770, rebuilt after the fire of 1812) [253] and of the now demolished Church of St Catherine in the Convent of the Assumption in the Moscow Kremlin (1817) [254]. The western European sources for such a design were explicit in the small Church of St Alexander Nevsky at Peterhof by the German architect K. F. Schinkel (1832).

By 1842 Romanticism had become a passion for more than buildings. At a carnival held at Peterhof the ladies and gentlemen of the Court, dressed in costumes which passed for medieval, participated in hunts and tournaments in an environment made all the more real for them by the medieval architecture of

the Chapels and Arsenal in the park.[16] While the last classical monument, the Cathedral of St Isaac, was nearing completion, the Court of Nicholas I was thus unwittingly celebrating the end of a great architectural tradition. Henceforward nothing more was possible but an unconditional surrender to eclecticism.

Two of Nicholas's buildings, rather than St Isaac, which had been begun by his brother, may serve to represent this turning point. A church in Moscow commemorating the victorious conclusion of the wars of 1812–14 had long been contemplated. The ageing Qua-

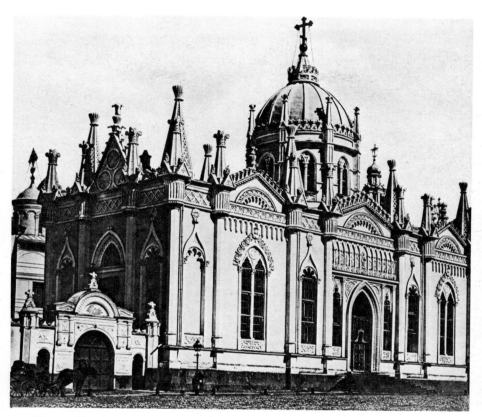

254. Moscow, Church of St Catherine in the Convent of the Assumption in the Kremlin, 1817

renghi had designed for it a majestic version of the Roman Pantheon. More symptomatic of the times was the project of a Swedish architect, Alexander Vitberg, who suggested a vast church on three levels, the lowest a rectangle, the second a cross, and the third a circle, symbolizing progression from imperfect matter to perfect immateriality.[17] But the Church of the Redeemer (1839–83) as it was finally built by the German-Russian architect, Konstantin Andreevich Ton (1794–1881), was an ineffectual attempt to graft Byzantine detail on a classical form (see also pages 391–2). Ton's inability to resolve an important architectural problem with any personal conviction was further demonstrated in the Great Kremlin Palace (1838–49) [167]. This part-Renaissance, part-classical, and (in the treatment of the upper windows) even part-Russian, mixture was a sorry successor to the Kremlin palaces of Rastrelli, Bazhenov, and Kazakov. The decline of the sovereign's taste is all the more dismaying when we are told that the Emperor took a keen interest in the designs and allowed nothing to pass without the stamp of his approval.

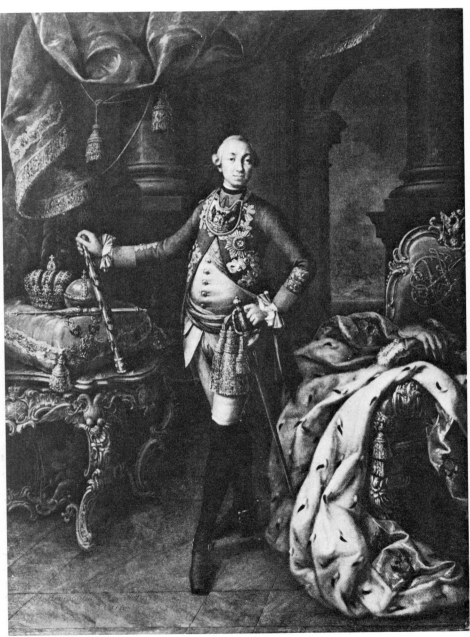

255. A. P. Antropov: Peter III, 1762. *Moscow, Tretyakov Gallery*

PART FIVE

MODERN RUSSIAN ART

'And dost thou not likewise rejoice in spirit? There lies our Russia, she is thine, Tsarevich!
There thy people's hearts are waiting for thee, there thy Moscow waits, thy Kremlin, thy dominion.'

Pushkin, 'Boris Godunov,' 1825

CHAPTER 24

EIGHTEENTH-CENTURY PAINTING AND SCULPTURE

An analysis of eighteenth-century painting in St Petersburg requires again a definition of the aims of criticism. To seek in it exclusively Russian values would be grossly to distort its purpose and the wishes of its patrons, while to compare it to its disfavour with contemporary painting in the West would be to disregard the peculiar historical conditions which determined its character. As with much colonial painting, its value is partly artistic and partly historical. Even when the degree of quality is lower than the average attained at the time elsewhere, such painting often has elements of rude vigour or unexpected psychological insight which have come to the surface in an environment where the social graces are a little thin. In the work of native-born artists trained abroad the same process of adapting a strange mode of expression to life at home can be full of surprise and charm.[1]

From the first not only new needs, as they were being supplied by the society of St Petersburg, but new educational methods were required. The Court had to be taught to want a new kind of art quite as much as artists had to be taught to produce it. From the first the demand was practical and secular. As in architecture, the useful took precedence over the decorative, and the first pictorial images were maps, topographical views, portraits of eminent men and women of the Court and upper classes, and prints of the victories by which Peter had won his empire.[2] The first group of itinerant painters resembled the first generation of architects, headed by Tressini. They were often from the northern European countries which Peter had visited on his first trip abroad, and on the whole they were not men of much talent. It may be that Peter admired those who had a considerable knowledge of Europe and so had more experience to impart to their Russian pupils. As Tressini, an Italian Swiss, had worked in Denmark and possibly in Holland, so Peter's first portraitist, Gottfried Danhauer (I. G. Tanauer, 1680–1737), had been born in Bavaria, studied in Venice, and was painting in Holland when Peter met him in 1697.[3] He arrived in St Petersburg in 1710, and remained there for the rest of his life. His portraits for instance of the Tsar and his wife and daughter are pedestrian and uninspired, at best adequate likenesses, and not above the standard for such painting elsewhere in Europe.

Peter was well aware that to promote Russian painting he must do two things: attract the best artists to Russia and send the most promising Russian pupils abroad. To this end he had issued in 1702 a manifesto inviting European artists to come to Russia and promising them special privileges. In 1711 the government icon workshops in the Moscow Armoury were transferred to the new capital, and in 1718 a proclamation urged the merchants to allow their children to become trained as artists and craftsmen. At the same time schools had to be created to provide such education. A class in engraving and drawing in the Petersburg Printing Office was at best only a makeshift until more thorough training could be had, and for this Peter projected an art department in his proposed Academy of Sciences of 1724. His death the next year cut short these plans, and when Catherine I established the Academy in 1726, instruction in the arts was limited to the practical crafts of drawing and engraving. The character of the topographical work is represented in the prints of Mikhail Ivanovich Makhaev (1716–70), whose maps of St Petersburg (1753) and various engraved views of the city and environs are invaluable for the study of Petrovian and Elizabethan architecture [193, 197, 198, 201–3, 207, 209].

The first group of Peter's 'artist-pensioners' which left Russia in 1716 included five painters, among them the brothers Nikitin, who went to Italy. The painter Andrey Matveev and the architects Ustinov and Korobov went to Holland. Only one was sent to France – the engraver Stepan (Stephan) Korovin. Peter's earlier enthusiasms for northern European architecture and Italian painting can be seen in this distribution. Of all these young Russians, only Matveev (1701–39) made any particular contribution. In the last ten years of his life he painted portraits of the nobility and icons for the Peter–Paul Cathedral (later repainted). His unfinished self-portrait with his wife (1729, State Russian Museum, Leningrad) hints that in Holland he had learned something of the contemporary Court style. The brothers Ivan (c. 1690–1740) and Roman

Nikitin painted with a bit more flair, but the famous portrait of Peter on his deathbed has also been attributed to Danhauer.[4]

Peter realized that these first efforts would be long in producing results; so in 1715 he ordered his agent in Paris to discover whether any of the French king's artists might be persuaded to come to Russia. When Peter himself reached Paris in 1717 he met some of the men selected by Konon Zotov, including the architect Le Blond, whose personality delighted him. When Le Blond left for Russia he was accompanied by a group of artists, of whom the most prominent was Louis Caravacque, a portrait-painter.[5] Caravacque's appointment was in the nature of a third choice. Nattier and Oudry, to whom Peter and his wife had sat for their portraits, had been approached, but both declined to enter the Russian service. Caravacque, born in Marseilles and educated in Paris, remained in St Petersburg until his death in 1754. He was a favourite of the Empress Anna, for whom he not only painted portraits and decorative ceilings in her Winter Palace, but also devised settings for Court ceremonies and theatrical performances. His talents were not above the ordinary, and his chief service to Russia was the instruction he offered in the art department of the Academy of Sciences. His portraits, especially the double portrait of Peter's daughters, indicate that he could handle the decorative French Rococo style, reminiscent of Largillierre, with modest competence.

Towards the middle of the century a brief revival of German influence, with the brothers Georg Christoph (1716–49) and Johann Friedrich Grooth (1717–1801), preceded a new influx of Frenchmen and Italians. From Italy in 1756 came Pietro Rotari (1707–62), who painted the Gallery of Graces at Peterhof with three hundred portraits of the loveliest ladies of Elizabeth's court, and in 1762 Stefano Torelli (1712–84), a decorative painter who, with Rotari, had studied under the Neapolitan master Francesco Solimena.[6] A third Italian, Giuseppe Valeriani (in Russia 1742–61), produced a quantity of theatrical decorations. The wave of French artists commenced with the arrival of Louis-Joseph Le Lorrain (1715–59), who came to St Petersburg in 1758 as director of the new Academy, but died the next year. He was succeeded by Louis-Jean-François Lagrenée, the Elder (1725–1806), who remained until 1765. Meanwhile Nicolas Gillet (1709–91), a sculptor, had arrived in 1758. He remained for twenty years, first as a professor and then as director from 1774 to 1777 when he retired and returned to Paris. In addition, the portraitist Louis Tocqué (1696–1772) had a lively success when he visited St Petersburg (1756–8).[7]

Against this shifting background of resident and itinerant foreigners of varying degrees of ability, the work of the first generation of Russian-born painters, following such pioneers as Nikitin and Matveev, is perhaps not very startling. Alexey Petrovich Antropov (1716–95), a pupil of Matveev and Caravacque, at the age of forty-one turned to Rotari and worked with the Italian at Peterhof and on the decoration of the Anichkov Palace and the Opera. The polished oval surfaces and scrupulous detail in his portraits demonstrate his ability to absorb a mixture of manners. In his state portrait of Peter III [255], for all the derivative pomp one's eye is immediately drawn to the mingled vanity and pathos in the tiny face. Antropov had studied icon-painting much earlier, but had so thoroughly absorbed the European style that his icons are indistinguishable from late Baroque Italian religious painting.[8]

Another portraitist, Ivan Petrovich Argunov (1727–1802), who had been born a serf of the Counts Sheremetev, profited by the interest his owner's family had long taken in art. The details of his education are unknown, but his 'Ivan Lazarev as Amor' [256] illustrates his superiority to Antropov in achieving movement. Where Antropov brought his figures close to the picture plane, as if to flatten them out, that he might the more easily examine all the details of face and costume, Argunov

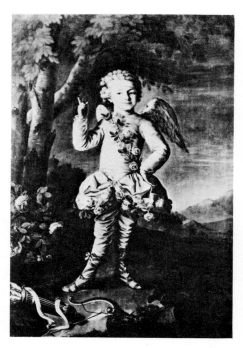

256. I. P. Argunov: Ivan Lazarev as Amor

mastered a convincing *chiaroscuro*. The design of his state portrait of Paul I may be insistently angular, but in comparison with Antropov's Peter III, he stands solidly in a three-dimensional setting.

The origins of Feodor Stepanovich Rokotov (*c.* 1735–*c.* 1808), the third of this triumvirate of early portraitists, are also obscure, but it seems that he had worked with the first professor of painting in the Petersburg Academy, where he acquired a more fluent manner and a greater compositional ability than his predecessors. For ten years or more, after 1765, Rokotov worked in Moscow. The distance from Court helped the development of a more intimate and personal style to be seen in his delicate colouring and more direct treatment of character with a preference for bust-length portraits against a neutral background, as in

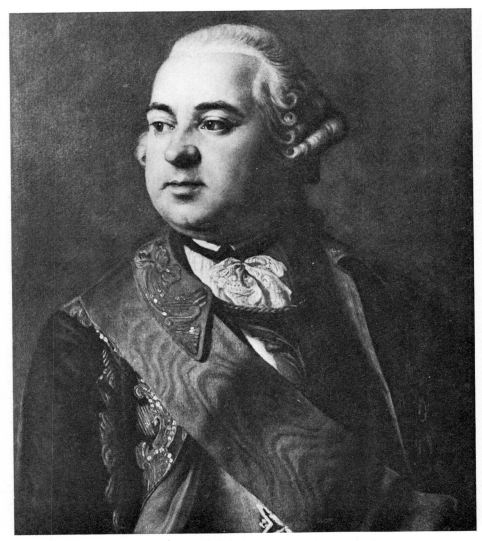

257. F. S. Rokotov: Count Peter Ivanovich Shuvalov

the likeness of Count Peter Ivanovich Shuvalov [257]. Something of Rotari is still there in the smooth, rounded surfaces, but the characterization appears both more candid and more truthful.

With the organization of the Academy of Fine Arts in St Petersburg instruction was put on a permanent basis. The project, which had hung fire since Peter's death, was revived by Count Ivan Ivanovich Shuvalov, the brilliant and enthusiastic favourite of Elizabeth, who in 1755 had inaugurated the first Russian university in Moscow. Elizabeth approved his plans, and in 1757 the Senate published a ukase establishing the Academy in St Petersburg, although it remained an administrative department of the University of Moscow until 1763. Meanwhile, as we have seen, Shuvalov had commissioned the French architect J.-F. Blondel to design the building which was finally erected by Vallin de la Mothe and Kokorinov. The Academy was not permanently organized until 1764, when Catherine II replaced Shuvalov as director with her own creature, the less imaginative and more disciplinarian Count Ivan Ivanovich Betskoy (c. 1703–95), who had lived in Paris during most of Elizabeth's reign. The regulations, like those for many academies elsewhere in Europe in the eighteenth century, were almost literally copied from the French Academy.[9] There was the same system of membership, rising through three grades from associate to academician and full professor. In the absence of any regular public schooling in Russia, there were added a secondary school which took pupils from the age of six, and trade schools which they might enter, if at the proper age they had failed to demonstrate sufficient aptitude for the fine arts. In contrast to France, where architecture, painting, sculpture, and the minor arts were taught in separate institutions, the Russian Academy brought all these under one roof. Provisions were also made to send the best students abroad in groups of twelve every three years. In 1760 the first two – the architect Bazhenov and the painter Losenko – went to Paris. Between 1760 and 1789, when the outbreak of the Revolution interrupted relations between France and Russia, more than forty young Russians studied in the French Academy and in the *ateliers* of Paris.[10]

The effects of this new institutional instruction soon appeared in the work of Anton Pavlovich Losenko (1731–73), one of the most gifted and neglected Russian painters of the early years of Catherine's reign. He had studied with Argunov and at the Academy under Le Lorrain before going to Paris as a pensioner for two years (1760–2). Whereas his predecessors had been pre-eminently portrait-painters, Losenko attempted historical subjects, in the grand manner. In Paris he worked with Restout, and his 'Sacrifice of Abraham' showed that he had acquired the accepted academic manner, mixing equal doses of Poussin and Raphael with a measure of the antique. His historical paintings were much admired by his contemporaries, yet they add nothing to the common repertory of late Baroque painting. With his 'St Vladimir and Rogneda' (1770, State Russian Museum, Leningrad), he became the first modern Russian painter to interpret a national historical subject on so large a scale, and on the strength of this was appointed professor of history-painting in the Academy.[11] In answer to the eloquent plea of Falconet, who recognized Losenko's talent in the beautiful drawing he had made of the sculptor's sketch for the monument to Peter the Great, Catherine acquired the 'St Vladimir' for the State, but imperial favour could not overcome the ill-will of the painter's colleagues. Losenko died three years later, a disappointed and discouraged man. Perhaps he had attempted too much, for certainly Russian history-painting had to wait at least two generations until a man appeared who was equal to its challenge and difficulties.

This first generation had come of age artistically during the reign of Elizabeth, and their works in one way or another were imbued with the Rococo and ceremonial character of Elizabeth's French and Italian tastes. If we cannot point to this or that Russian element in their paintings, we can at least surmise that they supplied the Russian Court with the sensation of being European which the Empress and her courtiers wanted. It is worth observing, too, that these artists were predominantly portraitists. They established the costumes and make-up for the characters who began to act their roles in the works of the next group of painters.

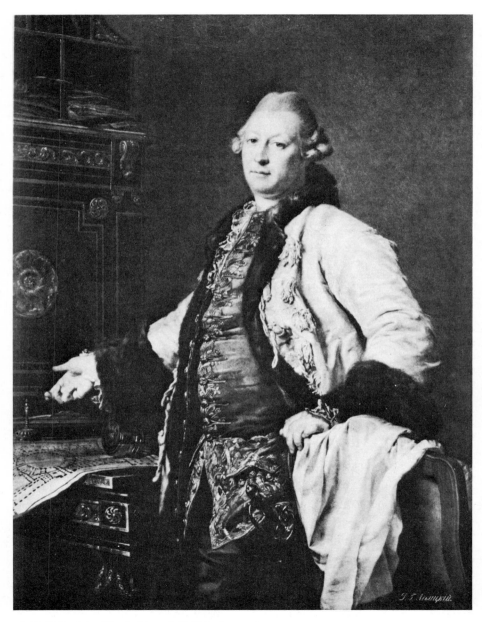

258. D. G. Levitsky: The Architect A. F. Kokorinov, 1769–70.
Leningrad, Russian Museum

Losenko, whose less formal works prove that he had a truly pictorial gift, was an Ukrainian, and also from Little Russia came the greatest portraitist Russia had yet known. Dmitry Grigorievich Levitsky (1735/7–1822)[12] was the son of a priest who worked as an engraver in the Printing Office of the Pecherskaya Lavra in Kiev. The elder Levitsky's prints show considerable familiarity with western art, especially with Italian painting and engraving of the sixteenth and seventeenth centuries.[13] in 1752 the boy's talents were recognized by Antropov, when he came to Kiev to paint the iconostasis in the Church of St Andrew. When he was recalled to St Petersburg in 1756, he took Levitsky with him. By 1762 he was a registered painter, and in 1769 became an associate of the Academy. Perhaps he was fundamentally an eclectic, but however much he absorbed from his contemporaries, the results were inimitably his own. It is not too much to say that Levitsky invented the character of St Petersburg society for some time to come, much as Van Dyck earlier in England had created an image of an aristocracy which the members were from that time onwards obliged to emulate. More than that, his susceptibility to different personalities far surpassed that of his predecessors. He found a proper type of portrait and style of interpretation for each class and kind of person.

At the first exhibition of the reorganized Academy in 1770, to which seven artists contributed twenty paintings, Levitsky became famous over-night with his five works. The spectators most admired his portrait of the architect A. F. Kokorinov [258]. For the inauguration of the Academy Kokorinov had ordered a splendid new suit of lilac satin and a voluminous white fur-trimmed coat, which gave Levitsky an opportunity to show his mastery of textiles. But his brilliant painting of materials was surpassed by the elegance of the three-quarter-length figure, turning easily towards the plans of the Academy spread out beside him on a fine French bureau. However

numerous the influences of European Court portraiture, Levitsky had absorbed them, made them his own, and was now prepared to offer his own contribution to European painting. This portrait of Kokorinov, for which Levitsky was made an academician, was the clearest proof of the distance Russian society had come in the little more than a lifetime which had elapsed since the foundation of St Petersburg.

The Rococo scheme of the Kokorinov portrait was more informally, and amusingly, developed on a large scale in the full-length portrait of P. A. Demidov (1773; State Tretyakov Gallery, Moscow), an eccentric philanthropist who had founded the School of Commerce. Demidov in informal dress stands by a table and points to two potted plants, symbols of institutions which he had nourished. In contrast to the *brio* and elegance of Kokorinov's lilac and white costume, the soberer hues of Demidov's clothing and the carefully distinguished textures of wood, fabric, and metal, show Levitsky's genius for creating a portrait in character.

The success of these paintings and his growing European reputation – his early portrait (1762) of Prince A. M. Golitsyn (State Tretyakov Gallery, Moscow) was engraved in Vienna in 1773 – attracted the attention of the Empress, who commissioned Levitsky to paint her favourite pupils in the Smolny Institute. Between 1773 and 1776 Levitsky painted seven portraits of these young ladies, including some of the most beguiling delineations of childhood and adolescence which the eighteenth century has left us. Perhaps the best known is the double portrait of Princess Khovanska and Mlle Khrushcheva (1773, State Russian Museum, Leningrad) acting their roles in a play given before the Empress. Levitsky's mastery of textures can be seen in the contrast between the man's taffeta coat, a bit too large for Mlle Khrushcheva, and the silks and sheer muslins worn by the young Princess. The coquetry of this school performance, where the youthful pupils mimic their elders, is belied by something ineffably tender in the lingering traces of adolescent awkwardness. The double portrait of Mlle Rzhevska and Princess Nastasya Davydova (1771–2) [259] combines technical brilliance, the grand manner, and an engaging pertness in the expressions of the little girls who are almost submerged by their elaborate costumes. In this

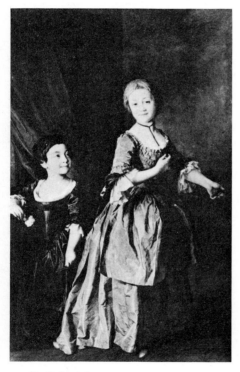

259. D. G. Levitsky:
Princess Davydova and Mlle Rzhevska, 1771–2.
Leningrad, Russian Museum

suite of seven paintings the greatest variety prevails: Mlles Levshina and Nelidova are dancing, Mlle Alymova plays the harp, and Mlle Molchanova seems to address the spectator. In the background of this last portrait there is a piece of electrical equipment, reminding us that this was the century when scientific experiment was the privilege of the upper classes.

Levitsky's success with the Smolny portraits prompted Catherine to commission a series of full-length portraits of herself, although it seems unlikely that she posed for any of them. They are among the most majestic state portraits of the eighteenth century, but individually they tell us very little about the woman. Levitsky dressed Catherine in flowing garments to conceal her increasing embonpoint and surrounded her with appropriate imperial symbols. The greatest contrast to these impressive but psychologically empty images is provided by his portraits of eminent men of letters. In 1773 he painted a bust portrait of Diderot, who was then visiting St Petersburg. The philosopher appears without a wig in a dressing-gown of green and white, Levitsky's favourite colours. Possibly here he penetrated further than in any portrait up to this time into the sensibilities of a distinguished sitter.[14]

Towards the mid 1780s Levitsky's style changed considerably. Inspiration from France, which had been so strong in design, even in costume, and certainly in the search for expressive gesture, was replaced by the influence of English painting. There were many ways by which this could have reached Levitsky: through Pierre-Étienne Falconet, the sculptor's son, who had studied in England under Reynolds, through the presence at Court of the English painter Richard Brompton, or through the numerous engravings after portraits by English masters which were circulated throughout Europe. The shift of interest from France to England is also understandable for other reasons at the close of this decade. Catherine had always liked English civilization, as we have seen in her enthusiasm for English landscape design, and when the French Revolution broke out, her fear of any threat to legitimacy caused her sympathies to turn towards England. Thus something of a simpler English manner appears in the late 1780s and

first years of the 90s in Levitsky's portraits of Catherine's grandchildren, the son and daughters of Paul I.[15]

These were the last evidence of Levitsky's favour at Court. Ostensibly for reasons of health he had retired in 1788 from the Academy, where he was professor of portraiture. During Paul's reign his work was slighted, and the Emperor almost refused to pay for a series of portraits of the Knights of St Vladimir commissioned by his mother. After 1795, when the French portraitist Mme Vigée-Lebrun was in St Petersburg for eight years, his work takes on something of her sentimental and slightly Neo-Classical manner. In 1808 he returned to the Academy, but his powers declined; after a few years he went blind, and died in 1822.

A last reflexion of eighteenth-century elegance persists through the reign of Alexander I in the work of Vladimir Lukich Borovikovsky (1757–1825).[16] Of noble Cossack origin, he came of a family of icon-painters in the Ukraine. Among his earlier works are the iconostasis for the church built for Catherine II by Lvov at Mogilev to commemorate her meeting with Joseph II of Austria. The cold and limpid style of these paintings is so thoroughly Italian that Borovikovsky's future reputation is all the more surprising. When Potemkin arranged Catherine's triumphal journey through the Crimea in 1787, Borovikovsky was summoned to decorate a temporary palace at Kremenchug on the Dnieper. Catherine was so pleased with his allegories that she sent him to St Petersburg, where he seems to have first worked under Levitsky and later as an assistant to the Austrian portraitist Johann Baptist Lampi (1751–1830; in Russia 1791–7). From the first he enjoyed the favour of the Court, even remaining in Paul's good graces after Catherine's death.

Borovikovsky's first works were generally small, often miniature reductions of portraits by better-known painters, but after his service with Lampi he graduated to a larger scale, usually the life-size portrait. In addition to state portraits of the imperial family, which are not more distinguished than others of their kind, his principal works were portraits of women and young girls. These are very English, often introducing the informal dress and summary park-like background familiar in Reynolds and Gainsborough, but through all this appears Borovikovsky's own personal sentiment, in the large eyes and languid postures which are a little reminiscent of Greuze. His women might be monotonous were it not for the fact that within this generalized *fin-de-*

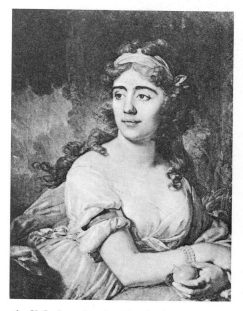

260. V. L. Borovikovsky: Mme Skoboeva, c. 1795

siècle mood of self-indulgent melancholy he was at heart a realist who never failed, so we feel, to create a likeness. His Russian women and young girls, for instance, seem really Slavic [260]. Somewhat apart from his usual production is a delightfully informal portrait of Catherine II in the last year of her life (1796). She is here not an empress but an elderly lady leaning on her stick in the park at

Tsarskoe Selo. Beside her is her favourite dog, and in the distance the rostral column she had raised so long ago to the glory of Count Orlov. Without Gainsborough the portrait could not be, and it is a precious document of late-eighteenth-century sensibility in the relation of human personality to nature. After 1800 a new indication of French influence can be seen in the sturdy portrait of Ekaterina Alexandrovna Arkharova [261]. The frontal pose, crisp drawing, and precise detail prove that French Neo-Classicism had reached Russia, but

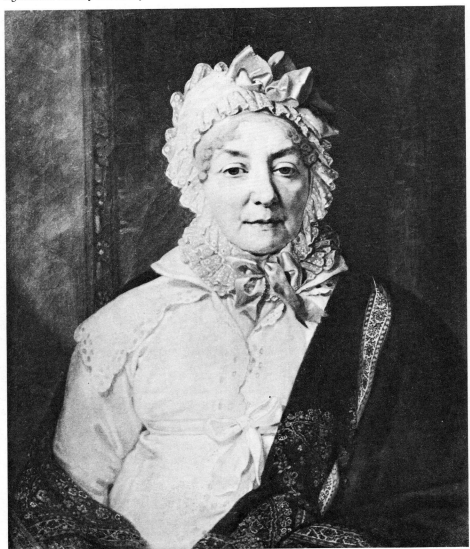

261. V. L. Borovikovsky: Ekaterina Arkharova, c. 1810

Borovikovsky leaves these David-like qualities behind in the sharp features and individual expression.

Although portraits and historical paintings occupied the major talents in eighteenth-century St Petersburg, other genres were not entirely neglected. In landscape the works of Russian masters, while not without charm and a certain historical interest, do not rise above the general European standard. Simon Feodorovich Shchedrin (1743–1804) and Mikhail Matveevich Ivanov (1748–1823) continued the topographical painting of Matveev, but enlarged it with a new feeling for the poetry of nature, for which the development of the imperial parks may be held responsible [248].[17] Feodor Mikhailovich Matveev (1758–1826) and Vasily Petrovich Petrov (1770–1811) represented the more cosmopolitan tendency. After his studies in Italy, Matveev's landscapes were usually classical subjects based on the Roman Campagna; Petrov used a similar manner for pictures of Russian scenery. There was very little genre-painting, the lowest class in the academic hierarchy. The evidence of only one canvas, long attributed to Losenko, until the signature of a little-known painter, Ivan Firsov, appeared when it was cleaned, need cause no regrets. The rendering of a young artist seated at his easel sketching his younger sister is thoroughly French in design and technique, a testimony to Firsov's schooling in Paris (1748–56).[18]

Of the major arts, sculpture offers even fewer surprises than painting. If in architecture Peter's task was to transform old traditions, in the case of sculpture he had practically to create a new art. The still effective prohibition by the Church limited the knowledge of three-dimensional forms to ecclesiastical furnishings, and such rare sculptural embellishment as that which decorates the church at Dubrovitsy was entirely western and without any specifically Russian characteristics. The scanty vestiges of folk sculpture are also to be explained by the influence of western traditions, whether from Germany

through Novgorod into the north-east, or through Poland and Lithuania to the Ukraine. In both regions from the middle of the sixteenth century there was a tradition of religious sculpture in wood, but the seated figures of Christ as the Man of Sorrows or the iconic images of the head of the Baptist are all in the manner of late medieval or Baroque European folk sculpture, and not essentially Russian.[19] Only rarely, as in some of the wooden standing figures of saints in the northern churches, where the flat, two-dimensional forms are derived from painted icons, or in the few Court sculptures such as the reliefs which decorate the so-called Throne of Ivan IV and which again are related to two-dimensional pictorial design, was there anything approaching the scale or character of western sculpture. The three-dimensional instinct of the Russian people found its outlet in the bronze and silver-gilt religious vessels, in some of which the figure may attain a considerable size, or in carved wooden pulpits.[20] Under these circumstances the activity of foreign sculptors in Muscovy in the later seventeenth century was a prelude to the course which Peter followed. For the Petrovsky Gate in the St Petersburg fortress the German sculptor Konrad Osner (1669–1747) carved a relief in wood representing the 'Fall of Simon Magus'. It is now so covered with paint that it is hard to judge its original condition, but it would certainly seem to have been much like, if no better than, the sculpture which may be attributed to him on the church at Dubrovitsy and which is thoroughly and unskilfully Baroque.

The first requirements for decorative sculpture were satisfied by the import of marbles from Europe, and casts of antique statues from Italy. Much of this was second-rate, like the allegorical figures in the Summer Garden ridiculed by Casanova. Soon recourse was had to artists summoned from abroad, such as Andreas Schlüter, the German architect and sculptor, to whom may be attributed the reliefs on Peter's diminutive Summer Palace, or Nicolas Pineau, who executed the ornamental woodwork for Peter's work rooms at Peterhof. A more monumental sculptor was Count Carlo Bartolommeo Rastrelli (c. 1675–1744, in Russia from 1716), the father of the great architect.[21] His bronze busts of Peter, from a vivid life mask (1723–9, Hermitage, Leningrad), and of Menshikov (1727; a marble reproduction of 1840 is now in the State Russian Museum, Leningrad), as well as portrait medallions of Peter and other members of his family, are competent if somewhat awkward exercises in the manner inaugurated three generations before by Bernini. Yet the confusion of his interpretation of the Baroque play of light and shade on costume and armour was made up by the strength of his likenesses. Rastrelli's major accomplishment was his equestrian portrait of Peter, finished after his death by Alexander Martelli, and erected much later by Paul I in front of his Michael Castle.[22] This chunky, ponderous group, dominated by a pop-eyed Peter in Roman dress, is in keeping with the practical character of Peter's art. A more commanding as well as more accomplished work was the bronze group of the Empress Anna Ioannovna and her little Negro page (State Russian Museum, Leningrad). Rastrelli's surfaces were still timid, more etched than modelled, but he introduced a little more light and shade, and thus lent the figure of the Empress a sense of movement and vitality lacking in his other sculpture.

Until the establishment of the Academy of Fine Arts in the later 1750s there was no further sculptural activity of much moment, except such trivial decorative schemes as the clumsy figures on the roof of the younger Rastrelli's Winter Palace.[23] The lack of any conspicuous talent obliged Catherine to summon the French sculptor, Étienne-Maurice Falconet (1716–91), when she decided to erect a monument to the memory of Peter the Great. Her choice was undoubtedly prompted by Diderot, who had an extravagant admiration for his work.[24] Falconet arrived in St Petersburg in 1767, and at once set to work on the equestrian statue which he envisaged as a figure of Peter in antique dress on a rearing horse, poised on a huge natural boulder. The lively action was intended to symbolize the Tsar's conquest of an unruly nation and his vision of the future. In 1770 the model was exhibited in the sculptor's studio, where a crowd of eager spectators studied it in silence, an indication that the sense of sculptural criticism was still undeveloped. Through the years the difficulty of finding properly trained workmen to do the casting and perennial squabbles with Count Betskoy over his salary embittered the sculptor, until he left Russia in 1778, before the work was finished. Meanwhile a colossal boulder was quarried in Finland and transported with enormous effort to St Petersburg, where the statue itself was finally cast and erected in 1782.[25] This first and last truly Baroque monument of French art in Russia became a symbol of Peter's city. The boulder was, as it were, a test of Russian ingenuity, a foretaste of the heroic exertion later undertaken to bring the columns for St Isaac and the monolith for the Alexander Column to St Petersburg. Upon the base the laconic inscription, 'Petro Primo Catharina Secunda' (and on the other side in Russian translation), summarized Catherine's attitude towards her predecessor and her conception of her place in the line of great Russian sovereigns.

At the Academy French influence was further confirmed by a succession of instructors, most notably by Nicolas-François Gillet (1709–91), professor of sculpture from 1757 until 1777. Although a mediocre sculptor, he was a good teacher, and through his encouragement a group of young Russians within a generation mastered the international style of the school of Paris.[26] The first and in some respects the ablest Russian sculptor was Fedot Ivanovich Shubin (1740–1805), whose work, like that of the best contemporary painters, was primarily in portraiture.[27] He had been born in the far north near Arkhangelsk, the son of a fisherman. In 1761 he entered the Academy, and by 1767 had won a scholarship to Paris, where he studied for six years with Pigalle. Later he visited Rome, Turin, and London, where he worked with Nollekens. Upon his return to Russia, Catherine and Potemkin commissioned their portraits, and his reputation was apparently secure. But his vivid and realistic busts failed to capture the interest of a nobility which did not yet understand sculpture as an art, and his career languished. His standing figure of 'Catherine, the Legislator', commissioned by Potemkin for the rotunda in the Tauride Palace, was completed in 1795 and may already have seemed old-fashioned.[28] The relaxed posture, tumbling draperies, and coquettish expression belong more to the waning Rococo than the nascent Neo-Classicism. To gratify Catherine's historical curiosity Shubin produced a series of forty-nine portrait reliefs of the sovereigns of Russia, from the Great Princes of Kiev through the Tsars and Emperors. Although these were executed in the realistic Baroque manner and have only the slightest pretensions to historical verisimilitude, they are interesting symptoms of the growing interest in the national past. In 1801 Shubin's studio was burned, with the loss of his life's work, and four years later he himself was dead. It is impossible to feel that his was a completely Russian talent. Without his training under Gillet and his experience in Paris, he perhaps could not have developed his gifts at all. The comparison frequently made between Shubin and Houdon works to his disadvantage, since, while he too possessed a gift for psychological characterization, his portraits lack the beauty and sensitivity of Houdon's.

A second pupil of Gillet, Mikhail Ivanovich Kozlovsky (1753–1802), also studied in Paris on two occasions (1772–9, and again in 1788–94). He liked ideal classical themes, and his 'Sleeping Cupid' (1792), 'Hymen' (1797), and 'Mounted Hercules' (1799) are competent essays in the familiar eighteenth-century manner, differing little from the earlier productions of Pigalle or Pajou. Slightly more energetic is the style of his caryatids in the

throne room at Pavlovsk (1798) [262]. It hints that the coming Alexandrian Classicism would be severely linear. For his monument to Gen-

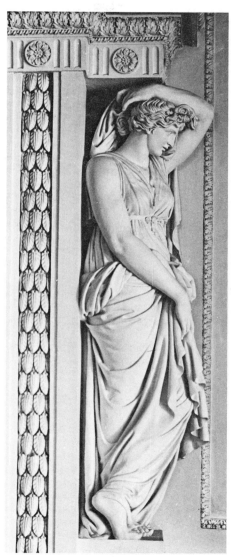

262. M. I. Kozlovsky: Caryatid in the throne room, Pavlovsk, 1798

eral Suvorov, whose rotund and common-place appearance was unmanageable in monu-mental sculpture, Kozlovsky awkwardly posed the hero as a youthful Mars. It is interesting that Suvorov is clad in a complete suit of plate armour and wears a plumed helmet – another indication that a more romantic and less real-istic attitude towards history was approaching.

The last sculptor of this generation to rise above the level of mere competence was Feodosy (Theodosius) Feodorovich Shchedrin (1751–1825). He studied in Rome, and from 1775 in Paris with Allegrain, where he de-veloped a vigorous yet not ungraceful decora-tive manner, at its best in his groups of female figures supporting spheres [263] before the

he went abroad in 1773, he set a precedent by remaining in Rome, which had already become an artistic Mecca for Russian architects in the 1770s and 80s.[29] There he studied with Anton Raphael Mengs, from whom he absorbed not only the doctrine but the manner of Neo-Classicism in a stricter sense than had yet been seen in Russia. Sentimental subjects requiring an emotional interpretation were executed on a broad scale in the coldest Neo-Classical technique. The result is of an intensity which sets Martos apart from the ruck of his con-temporaries. He excelled in funeral sculpture, which he executed in quantity for the tombs of the nobility in the fashionable cemeteries of the Alexander Nevsky Lavra in St Peters-burg and of the Monastery of the Virgin of

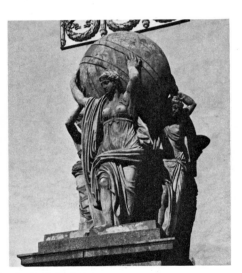

263. F. F. Shchedrin:
Caryatids in front of the principal entrance
of the New Admiralty, St Petersburg, 1812

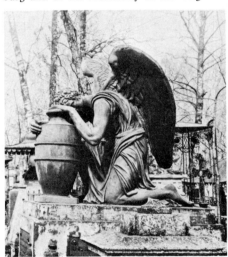

264. I. P. Martos:
Funerary Monument, Monastery of the Virgin
of the Don, Moscow, 1830

principal entrance of Zakharov's Admiralty. In their mingled elegance and coldness they stand as a sign of the transition between the last bloom of Shubin's Rococo and the fully de-veloped Neo-Classicism of Martos.

Ivan Petrovich Martos (1754–1835) studied like his predecessors under Gillet, but, when

the Don in Moscow.[30] In these he continued the tradition of Canova's and Thorvaldsen's mourning figures but with more personal ex-pression [264]. When his subject was other than classical, the result is less credible. At Odessa his standing figure of the Duc de Richelieu (1823–8) garbed as a Roman emperor lacks life, and in the famous group of 'Minin and Pozharsky' (1804–18) [265] he used antique garments for the prince and butcher who rallied the populace to the defence of the fatherland in 1611. The historical incongruity is all the more poignant since the monument was designed to be placed in the Red Square in Moscow opposite the walls of the Kremlin.[31]

After Martos, whose works have a certain irrational distinction, there is little more to be said for Russian sculpture of the nineteenth century than for that of any other academic national tradition. Boris Ivanovich Orlovsky (1793–1837) continued the forms of Neo-Classicism in his angel for the Alexander Column and in his statues of Kutuzov [266]

the century. After that the innumerable classical divinities and ideal figures, so popular in Europe through the 1830s and 40s, were gradually replaced by more naturalistic subjects and genre scenes. A last reminder of the earlier strength of the classical manner which had made St Petersburg an urban whole unique in the western world was supplied by the works of Baron Pyotr (Peter) Karlovich Klodt (1805–67).[32] His four horse-tamers on the Anichkov Bridge (1839) became one of the sculptural landmarks of the city, somewhat like the horses of Marly at the entrance to the Champs-Élysées in Paris. But the weak modelling and angular design prove that the classical vision of Martos had run out. Klodt's is a typical and pathetic instance of an artist

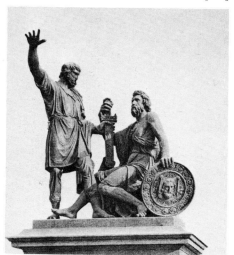

265. I. P. Martos: Minin and Pozharsky, 1804–18.
Moscow, Red Square

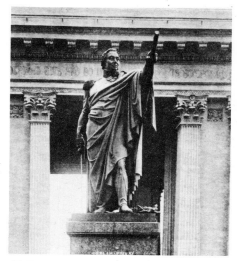

266. B. I. Orlovsky: Marshal Kutuzov, 1832.
St Petersburg, Kazan Cathedral

and Barclay de Tolly for the square in front of Kazan Cathedral. His iron manner is the perfect complement to Voronikhin's linear architecture. The long life of Count Feodor Petrovich Tolstoy (1783–1873) enabled him to continue a tenuous classicism in his coins and portrait medallions until almost the middle of

of real talent whose gifts were distorted by the fashions of the day and the official discipline of an Academy. His many studies from nature, especially his horses, show that he had a deep sympathy for animals and a not unselective eye for detail. At his best these small bronzes are not inferior to those of Barye. But the groups on the Anichkov Bridge are a disturbing blend of naturalism and idealism in technique and subject which required a consistent degree of abstraction. After this even the Academy was obliged to open its doors to naturalism. Probably this same unstable mixture of classicism and naturalism accounts for the peculiar effect of one of the most conspicuous sculptural ensembles in the centre of St Petersburg. This is the ten gigantic Atlantes of dark grey granite, each over nineteen feet high, by Alexandr Ivanovich Terebenev (1814–59) which support the lintels of the New Hermitage (1852) on the Winter Palace Square. This was intended by Nicholas I as the public entrance to the Hermitage collections, and was designed by Leo von Klenze, the German architect (see below, Chapter 27, page 390). But the building itself seems a timid echo of expiring classicism in contrast to the overwhelming size and scale of the sculpture.

CHAPTER 25

ROMANTICISM

Russia's isolation from western Europe at the close of the eighteenth century was a brief episode imposed by Paul's insane fear of revolution and his prohibition of foreign travel. In the following decade the Napoleonic Wars precipitated Russian intervention in European affairs to such an extent that henceforward Russian art history remained woven with the pattern of European expression as a whole. Therefore the examination of Russian art and architecture according to the standards of European criticism of comparable works during the same period does no violence to the intentions of Russian painters, sculptors, and architects during the middle years of the century. Just as they still continued to travel and study abroad, once their academic training had been completed, and visited the same cities as their western colleagues, so they competed for the same honours at international exhibitions, and were respected at home so much the more if their works resembled the types of European painting then in favour in St Petersburg and Moscow. And during the nineteenth century for the Russian, as for every artist, first Rome and then, after 1860, Paris were the centres of artistic research with Düsseldorf and Munich important for briefer periods, the first in the 1840s, the second towards the end of the 70s. With such an international scale of values we may also expect to find the same standards of technical competence which prevailed throughout Europe, the same selection and interpretation of academic and popular subjects, the same sequence of stylistic mannerisms from the polished Neo-Classicism of the early years through the romantic revival of the Baroque to the realist attitude to nature and then the development of naturalism culminating in the Impressionist movement of the 1870s.[1]

What, then, can we say is Russian in painting executed by Russians or in Russia during this period? If such qualities do not reside in technique, and after the disappearance of icon-painting Russia produced no notable technical discoveries, and was original only superficially in the choice of subject, where shall we seek it? It is perhaps to be found in what we may call the iconology of Russian painting – that is to say, in the meaning more than in the identification of the images which were used.[2] In this way we may hope to penetrate beneath the arbitrary distinctions of genre, portraiture, and history painting to discover what the Russian painter sought, and what all too occasionally he found, in the course of the artistic experience of the nineteenth century.

A step towards understanding this point of view may be taken by comparing the last of the eighteenth-century portraitists with the first of the truly nineteenth-century painters. In Borovikovsky's portraits sentiment is an additive element, something which colours or intensifies the forms, while the design remains eighteenth-century in the fullest sense of the word, derived from late Baroque spatial compositions, the individual shapes generalized or idealized, even when the details, as in much of Levitsky's work, were deceptively realistic. And with it all there was ever present that eighteenth-century attitude towards society which saw men and women first as types, as members of a class, and only secondarily as individuals. With the portraits of Orest Adamovich Kiprensky (1782–1836) much more than the accent was shifted.[3] The sentiment was now directed towards a particular person as one individual with special psychological responsibilities to society and himself. Such comment was no longer added to a composition essentially generic, but was part of a

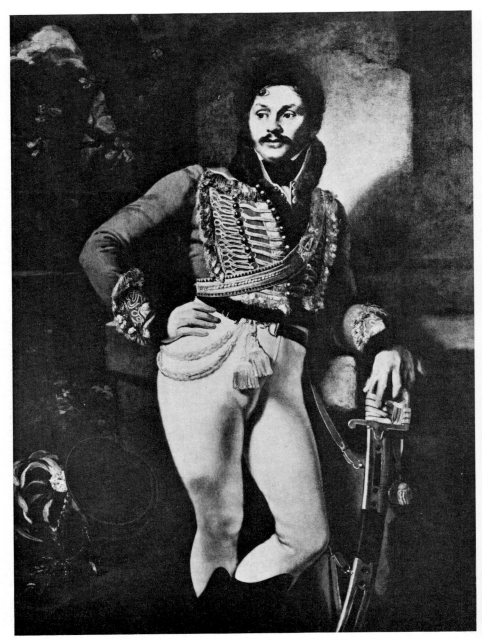

267. O. A. Kiprensky: E. V. Davydov, 1809. *Leningrad, Russian Museum*

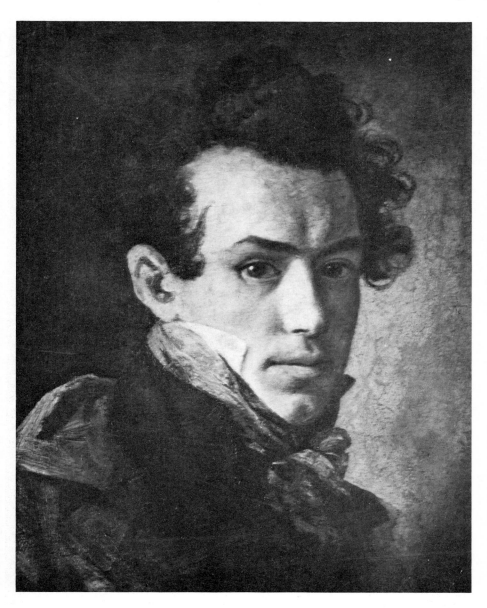

268. O. A. Kiprensky: Self-portrait.
Leningrad, Russian Museum

compositional arrangement dictated by particular circumstances. The difference in the formal result quite as much as in the motivation can be compared with that which exists between an eighteenth-century garden pavilion in the Gothic taste, and the recreation of a Gothic environment in much European religious architecture of the 1830s and 40s.

Not only the work but the life of Kiprensky exemplifies this distinction. In contrast to the more or less orderly career of an eighteenth-century painter whose reputation, once his talent had been recognized, was reasonably assured by an official position and adequate patronage, Kiprensky's life, however much it may have been disturbed by personal problems, suggests that already the close ties which had heretofore existed between painter, academy, and patron were loosening. Kiprensky had been born the illegitimate son of a nobleman, and brought up as a serf. His talent was acknowledged at an early age, and he was sent to the Petersburg Academy, where in 1805 he won the gold medal and a travelling scholarship for his thoroughly academic treatment of 'Dmitry Donskoy on the Field of Kulikovo'.[4] Some suggestion of a new and more introspective attitude towards a historical subject can be seen in the fact that the Prince is depicted reclining in an attitude of prayer rather than at the head of his victorious troops. But Kiprensky soon turned his back on academic instruction; as early as 1804 a portrait of his stepfather Adam Shvalb (State Russian Museum, Leningrad) reveals his study of the Baroque masters, especially Van Dyck, Rubens, and Rembrandt, whose works he saw in the Hermitage. While waiting for the end of the wars in Europe, he moved to Moscow, where his pencil and oil portraits were appreciated by the nobility. Among many portraits of distinguished sitters, his handsome three-quarter-length likeness of the poet and warrior Evgraf Vladimirovich Davydov (1809) [267] shows an early acquaintance with contemporary French painting. Even without presuming some as yet unexplained knowledge of Gros and Géricault, Kiprensky caught to the life the romantic yearning for heroic exploits which marked the generation absorbed in the Napoleonic Wars. Symptomatic, too, of romanticism were his many self-portraits [268], painted at short intervals throughout his life. In these he usually characterized himself as the artist he was, fixing his gaze irresistibly on the spectator and marking candidly the changing aspect of his countenance through the years.

After peace had been established, Kiprensky went to Italy, but this had a disastrous effect on his life and his art. He succumbed to the spell of the Italian Mannerists and Raphael, and produced a series of sentimental, ideal heads of beggar boys and peasant girls. From the romantic tragedy of Géricault he passed to the pathos of Léopold Robert. In 1825 he returned to St Petersburg for four years, and during this period painted a portrait of Pushkin, one of his best known and most typical works (State Tretyakov Gallery, Moscow). The mixed ingredients of early Romanticism, the searching details, and the classical reference of the statuette in the background, create that combination of the real and ideal which is found in Pushkin's poetry. The twist of the head and set of expression are romantic assertions of individual personality. After the accession of Nicholas I in 1825 even the limited Romanticism of such a portrait, like the poet's verses, was in disfavour. In 1827 Kiprensky returned to Italy for the remainder of his life, disturbed by ill health and an unhappy love affair, and achieved nothing which matched his earlier portraits.

Somewhat the same psychological dissatisfaction and artistic uncertainty mark the work of Karl Briullov (1799–1852), one of the most celebrated artists of his day, and the first Russian painter to enjoy an international reputation.[5] He had been born in Italy, and came to Russia as a child with his father, a sculptor of Huguenot descent named Briullo, whose name was later russified with imperial permission. By 1823 he had completed his

academic education, won the necessary prizes, and reached Rome. There his first works were on the popular classical and sentimental themes, although for a series of ideal heads of Italian girls representing the times of the day, he apparently did much painting out of doors, for it is known that he was obliged to leave his study of Evening unfinished because the sun set too soon. He would scarcely have distinguished himself from the host of painters from all countries working in Italy, had he not conceived the idea of a picture of the destruction of Pompeii. His imagination, fortified by a visit to the ruins, a performance of Giovanni Pacini's opera, *L'ultimo giorno di Pompei* (1825), and Pliny's description of the catastrophe, soared until the result was an enormous canvas which became the wonder of the age. When 'The Last Day of Pompeii' (1830–3) [269] was finished, the Italian press hailed it as a masterpiece, foreign visitors flocked to the studio, and Briullov himself at once became famous. Sir Walter Scott is said to have sat in front of the painting for an hour and then to have remarked that it was not a painting but an epic.[6] Public enthusiasm for this huge 'machine' is easy to understand. In a period when artistic intuition had been systematized in the formulas of eclecticism, Briullov offered something for every taste. The melodramatic, even morbid treatment of a classical subject with a wealth of realistic detail appealed to all manners of intelligence, and even today surprises by its intensity. Artistically Briullov's sources were irreproachable; reminiscences of Raphael, Poussin, and David were cunningly mixed with the histrionic effects of Vernet, and the lurid brilliance of the colours outdid the later Bolognese.[7] When Briullov returned to Russia in

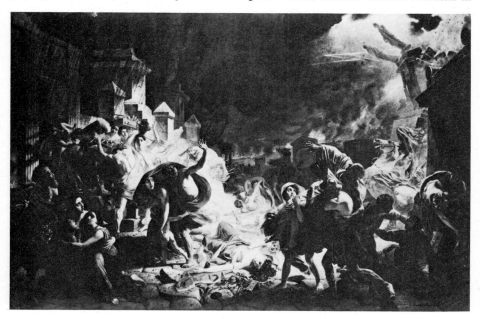

269. K. P. Briullov: The Last Day of Pompeii, 1830–3.
Leningrad, Russian Museum

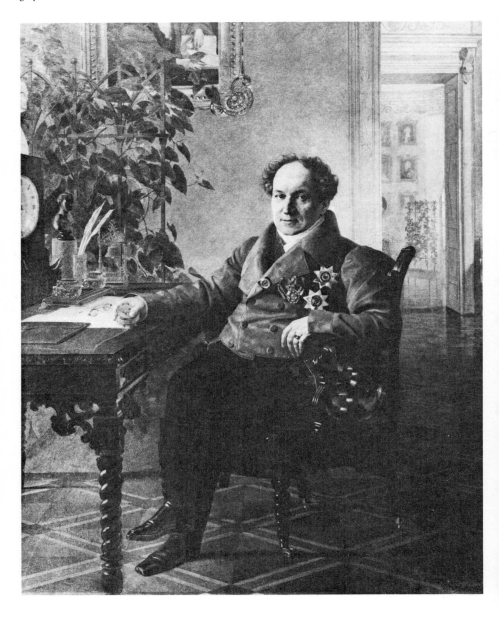

270. K. P. Briullov: Prince A. N. Golitsyn, 1838–40

1841 he was hailed as the greatest master of the day, and was expected to repeat or even surpass his first work. But 'The Siege of Pskov by Stefan Batory in 1581' (1839–43), so large that it was never finished, was a disappointment. Confused, crowded, lacking the violent *chiaroscuro* of 'The Last Day of Pompeii', it concerns us only because of Briullov's conscientious attempt to recreate the historical past through careful attention to costumes and furnishings.

More interesting are the many portraits which he painted throughout his life. His women are often represented in fancy dress, to intensify their sentimental postures, or in out-of-door settings, sometimes on horseback as in the familiar portrait of a young lady of the Samoilov family (1832), often called 'The Amazon' (State Tretyakov Gallery, Moscow). In many of these his attitudinizing cannot quite conceal his fondness for the poetry of nature. His portraits of men are usually simpler and more penetrating. In the fine seated portrait of Prince A. N. Golitsyn (1838–40) [270], Briullov recreated not only the man but his surroundings. The trellis with growing plants, repeated in the distant room, is evidence of his feeling for nature, and the distribution of light throughout the space is in the tradition of the painting of interiors in which so many Russians excelled.

Briullov's Pompeii became a mark to be emulated by others of his generation. Feodor Antonovich Bruni (1799–1875), born in Moscow but of Italian parentage, reached Italy at an early age. In 1818 he was in Rome, where his bacchantes and ideal nudes matched those of Briullov and Kiprensky. But the renown of Briullov's famous painting stirred his ambition, and he proceeded to emulate its size, complication, and historical melodrama. His 'Moses and the Brazen Serpent' of 1826–41 (State Russian Museum, Leningrad) merely transposed to the Old Testament the pseudo-classical repertoire of agonized nude figures which had swarmed through 'The Last Day of Pompeii'. How much he hoped that it would

become equally famous can be seen in the fact that he arranged his light to fall in a direction opposite that in Briullov's canvas. But public response was less enthusiastic, and Bruni's later works are scarcely distinguishable from the general run of academic art in these years. For much of his life he painted religious subjects for the Isaac Cathedral, but they are lost in the cold gloom of that church.

Neither of these enormous history-paintings would be worth mentioning at such length, were it not that they provide an illuminating contrast with a third large canvas on a similar 'historical' theme, one wherein even more clearly than in the work of Briullov and Bruni the counter-currents of Classicism, Romanticism, and Realism can be seen at work, while an intensely personal conception of nature prepared the way for the future. Alexandr Andreevich Ivanov (1806–58) was the son of a competent professor at the Academy, A. I. Ivanov, under whom he studied.[8] After winning the usual medals for exercises in the academic manner on classical and Old Testament themes, Ivanov went to Rome, where he remained for the next quarter of a century. His first painting in Italy after his student days, a composition of 'Apollo, Hyacinthus, and Zephyrus' (1831–4, State Russian Museum, Leningrad), demonstrated his ability to handle the standard classical subject, not without some sensitivity for the nude figure.[9] After 1830, when Briullov's masterpiece excited so much attention, Ivanov's thoughts turned towards the creation of a similarly large work. A deeply religious man, he was taken with the subject of the first appearance of Christ to the people announced by St John the Baptist [271]. The theme was peculiarly suited to his mystical faith, for it combined certain traditional motifs with the opportunity to interpret them in a new manner. It was Ivanov's intention that his painting should surpass in spiritual profundity and natural truth all previous religious painting in the West. So he undertook the most extensive studies, and consulted every artist whose

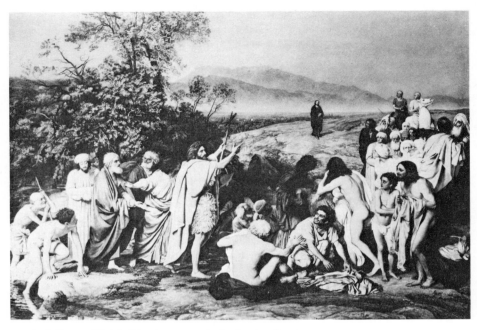

271. A. A. Ivanov: Christ's First Appearance to the People, 1837–57.
Leningrad, Russian Museum

opinion he respected, especially the Nazarenes Cornelius and Overbeck, who influenced him considerably. The inevitable result was that his work took indefinitely long and that again and again he had to change his composition. Not only did he pursue the usual studies of earlier religious painting and investigate the historical aspects of the New Testament scene, although to his great regret he was unable to travel to Palestine, but he ransacked the storehouses of classical sculpture for types and expressions which he felt would best reveal his message. To the modern eye much of this seems academic rubbish, such as the derivation from classical sculptures of centaurs and fauns of the expressions of the young men who cynically mock the teaching of the Baptist. Of more interest was his search for truth to nature, which took him into the country. His landscape-paintings, with their range of bright

fresh colours, anticipated the naturalistic vision of the French Impressionists. And in his studies for the figures climbing from the water Ivanov's naturalistic treatment of the classical nude [272] cannot fail to remind the western eye of Degas's early work.[10] When the painting was finally exhibited in St Petersburg in 1858, after twenty years of painful effort, it failed to arouse the enthusiasm which had greeted Briullov's and even Bruni's canvases. In the later 1840s Ivanov himself had begun to doubt the effectiveness of his undertaking, especially when his social and religious convictions were disturbed by the revolutions of 1848–9 and by the new biblical criticism in France and Germany. Yet he did not shun sources dangerous to his faith, and visited D. F. Strauss in Germany, whose positivist *Life of Christ* had almost convinced him that his work had been in vain.

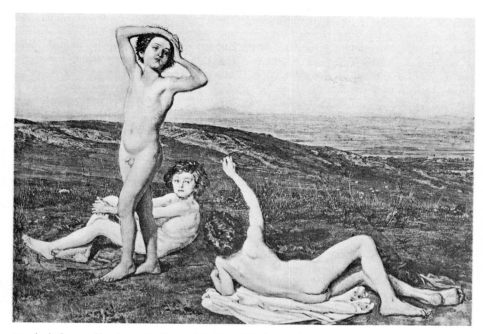

272. A. A. Ivanov: Youths on the Shore of the Bay of Naples, *c.* 1840.
Leningrad, Russian Museum

Ivanov's 'Appearance of the Messiah' must be called a noble failure. His figures are skilful, serious, and full of deep and varied feeling. The emotions of the listeners range from doubt and scepticism to sudden, overwhelmed conviction. But the contrast between the naturalistic background and the classically contrived groups is too abrupt to be bridged by spirituality alone. By the middle of the nineteenth century the conflicting claims of naturalism and idealism could no longer be reconciled; when the former took precedence it necessarily destroyed the latter. The reasons for Ivanov's failure are apparent in the curiously insignificant figure of Christ. There truth to naturalistic atmospheric and linear perspective vitiates the truth of spiritual experience.

Ivanov's message and legacy to Russian art were of another kind. His simpler studies of landscape, his sensitive nudes, and his provocative portraits of Roman women, in their casual design and brilliant effects of light and colour, opened the way for the understanding of Impressionism. In later years to allay his doubts he projected a series of religious scenes arranged according to a scheme which should reconcile ancient history and mythology with the Old and New Testaments.[11] At his death the series was incomplete, but he had already finished 257 drawings. Among them were many wherein his search for the purest revelation of the spirit took him into the then unexplored territory of Byzantine art. Already he had studied the Byzantine mosaics of Palermo and Monreale for the physical types and facial expressions of his Christ and St John. In these later drawings he often recovered, through the mysterious radiance which surrounded his allegorical figures signifying the great abstractions of the spiritual presence, the character of earlier icon-painting [273]. In this way his work, however much the more elaborate part of it failed to justify either his efforts or his intentions, ultimately was of great value. Under the impetus of the Slavophiles' enthusiasm for the recovery of the national artistic heritage, a younger generation found in these drawings justification for the Byzantine revival of the later nineteenth century.

possible and consistent patrons of painting, did not care to be reminded that their national customs and costume were so different from those of Europe. Consequently, for the painters who were striving under considerable difficulties to learn European techniques and modes of expression, the treatment of Russian manners offered no particular advantages. Only with the rise of a nationalist spirit in the nineteenth century could genre-painting of

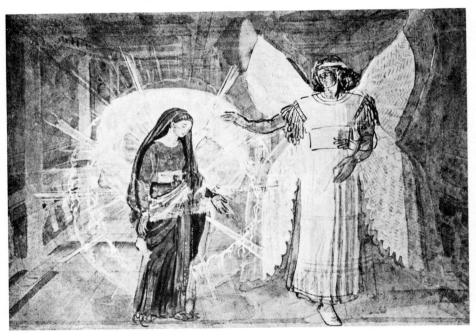

273. A. A. Ivanov: The Annunciation.
Moscow, Tretyakov Gallery

While the conflicting demands of idealism and naturalism vitiated the work of Briullov, Bruni, and Ivanov, a less spectacular but ultimately more conclusive victory for the painting of Russian life was won by the emerging genre-painters of the 1830s and 40s. Until then the painting of everyday life had occupied the least part of Russia's pictorial talents. The members of the upper class, who were the only

this sort come into its own. Meanwhile in a handful of works of the later eighteenth century the gradual intrusion of such painting can be traced.

From the first years of the Academy subjects from Russian history had been proposed for the annual prize competitions, but this was no guarantee that the young painters' treatment of such themes would in any way reflect

Russian customs.[12] The evidence of Losenko's 'Vladimir and Rogneda' shows that as late as 1770 a Russian painter could consider such a subject merely an excuse for devising a historical composition as a late Baroque allegory, with the figures draped and undraped in the modish Roman manner. This pseudo-historical tendency, which took no thought of archaeological discoveries or of existing folk arts and costumes, was continued by Grigory Ivanovich Ugryumov (1764–1823). He had studied under Levitsky and for three years in Rome (1787–90), and possessed a certain technical facility, but the totally unhistorical character of his works belies his success as a painter of truly Russian history. He first came to prominence with 'Yan Usmar's Feat of Strength' of 1796–7 (State Russian Museum, Leningrad), showing the mythical folk hero subduing a bull in the presence of Prince Vladimir of Kiev. The subject, more appropriate for one of the Labours of Hercules, the composition, costumes, and expression derive from Rubens and other Baroque masters with complete unconcern for historical accuracy. His later works, especially the two historical canvases for Paul's Michael Castle, 'The Capture of Kazan' and 'The Coronation of the First Romanov Tsar, Mikhail Feodorovich', are not only theatrical but insipid and sentimental. With the coming of Neo-Classicism a stricter regard for historical appearances accompanied the closer scrutiny of the past. Something of this can be felt in two paintings of the turn of the century, the 'Minin and Pozharsky' and the 'Meeting of Prince Igor and Olga' which have been attributed to a little-known painter, Vasily Kirillovich Malyshev (born 1782).[13] They show a more careful attempt to recreate the spirit of the past. The costumes bear some resemblance to traditional peasant dress, and in the background a wooden izba marks an improvement over the tents and draperies of Ugryumov's pictures.

The interest in native costume was a considerable step towards a more sympathetic understanding of the past. Even before Maly-shev, Argunov in 1784 had painted a portrait of a girl in peasant dress, and Levitsky's portrait of his daughter of 1785 (State Tretyakov Gallery, Moscow) presented her in a compromise between contemporary international fashion and traditional Russian clothing. Yet a decade earlier Mikhail Shibanov, a serf of Potemkin, had created the first purely Russian paintings of manners in his 'Betrothal' (1777) and 'Peasant Family at Table' (1774, State Tretyakov Gallery, Moscow).[14] In spite of certain crudities of design and technique, and the general resemblance to the peasant scenes of Greuze, such paintings provide an unexpected glimpse of the appearance and habits of the wealthier peasant families of the eighteenth century, and more than anything executed under the supervision or influence of the Academy prepared the way for the true painting of peasant life early in the nineteenth century.

After the turn of the century interest in Russian life increased, as is proved by the work of Alexey Gavrilovich Venetsianov (1780–1847).[15] Of Greek origin, he had been brought up in the provinces, and had gone through the Academy, where he made a particular study of Dutch genre-paintings in the Hermitage. Like many at this time, he was influenced also by French painting, especially the works of Granet. After 1820 he withdrew to his country property, where he devoted himself to the study of peasant life, and out of suggestions from Vermeer, Le Nain, Chardin, and De Hooch created the most original Russian painting of manners of his time. His talents were mild; his drawing was sometimes insecure; his perspective often askew or exaggerated, and his composition frequently a collection of parts rather than an integrated whole. But for all that he had certain qualities which were as yet unknown in Russia and which set him apart even from his contemporaries in western Europe. Above all else he understood the dignity of peasant life. His best pictures are devoid of that anecdotal preoccupation which distorts so much nineteenth-century genre-

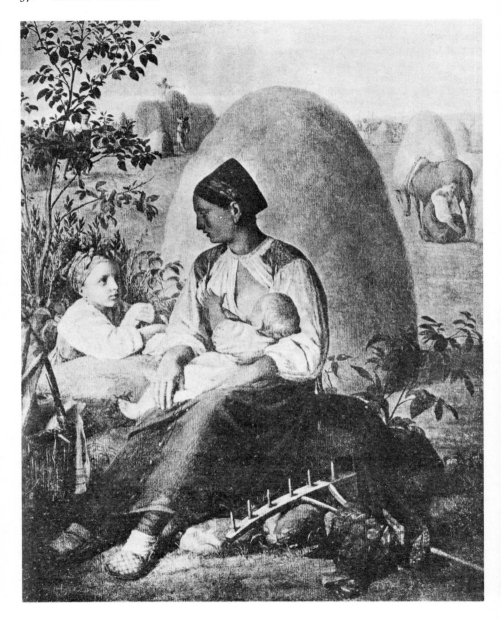

274. A. G. Venetsianov: Harvest, *c.* 1820–30.
Private Collection

painting [274]. They lack drama but not feeling, and in the best of them Venetsianov recaptures something of the grave serenity with which Louis Le Nain interpreted similar scenes in seventeenth-century France. We may add to this a very personal feeling for the quality of Russian light, for the long, low beams which fill the empty landscape.

The spiritual calm of Venetsianov's works distinguishes them from those of a young contemporary, Pavel Andreevich Fedotov (1815–53), who had been born on the outskirts of Moscow and grown up amid the busy activity of the provincial capital.[16] He studied briefly at the Academy, but more important for the formation of his talents were the Dutch paintings in the Hermitage. Where Venetsianov saw light and space in such works, Fedotov was fascinated by anecdote, costume, gesture,

and detail. It is even possible that he found the sources of his brisk little anecdotes in Hogarth's prints [275]. His works, small in dimensions and artistically unassuming, nevertheless are of some importance as indicating the emergence both of a new class, the wealthy urban bourgeoisie whose manners and tastes provided the source and demand for his paintings, and a new and more critical attitude towards Russian life. Fedotov's satire may seem to us bland enough, but in its time it risked official censure. His first popular success, 'A Newly Decorated Knight', showed the officer in dishevelled condition the morning after a hearty celebration. The government refused to permit the publication of a lithograph after the painting until the order had been removed and the title changed to 'The Morning After a Party'. It is typical that the

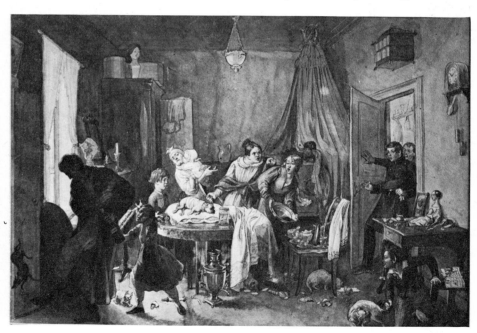

275. P. A. Fedotov: Fido's Last Illness, 1844.
Moscow, Tretyakov Gallery

zeal of Nicholas I to suppress criticism extended even to such good-natured raillery as
Fedotov's mockery of the inordinate worship of
the military caste. His most famous painting,
'The Major's Courtship', depicts the excite-
ment of a rich merchant's family when a
middle-aged and impecunious nobleman
comes courting the daughter. Although form
and technique are typical of much nineteenth-
century genre-painting, the description of the
pretty, distraught young girl, her coarse and
over-dressed mother, and the bewildered father
in his old Russian caftan amounts to a sly
criticism of the manners of the rising middle
class. As Russian society became more sophisticated and more class-conscious, such episodes
seemed more piquant, and suggested to young
rebellious minds the innumerable contrasts
between the appearances and the realities of
Russian life. In Fedotov's work there is more
than a touch of Gogol, who with more brilliance and effect drew pictures of similar social
conditions in *The Adventures of Chichikov*
(*Dead Souls*, 1842) and *The Inspector General*
(1836). In spite of the brevity of his career –
his paintings were first exhibited only four
years before his death – Fedotov's influence
was considerable at the time. The accidental
circumstance that he had come to art too late
to enter the Academy, had the salutary effect
of proving that an academic education was not
essential for the development of true talent,
and the restriction of his efforts to scenes
from contemporary life breached the ramparts
until then held by the idealists. Fedotov's
satire was so gentle that with the passing of
years it became almost imperceptible, and his
pictures appeal now more as the painting of
manners than as criticism of society. But in
the stifling atmosphere of the later years of
the reign of Nicholas I such subtleties were
not lost on a younger generation which hoped
to produce a new art for a new age.

Although Russia produced no unques-
tionably great master of Romanticism – for
even the indubitably earnest and prophetic
labours of Ivanov cannot be compared with
the production of a Delacroix or a Turner – in
the less majestic fields of portraiture and con-
versation pieces a number of inconspicuous
artists made their contributions in a style of
painting which we can call romantic realism.
In their painstaking but poetic interpretations
of upper-class and bourgeois life they left a
social record which is artistically and historically valid. The unfinished 'Portrait of Count
Ya. I. Rostovtsev and his Family' by Sergei
Konstantinovich Zaryanko (1818–70) [276] can
stand as an example. The study of detail is as
searching as the later literary realism of the
great Russian novelists, but the painting is not
yet naturalistic. The details are subordinated
to an affectionate concern for the persons
portrayed, even as the family acquires artistic
integrity by its enclosure within a receding
triangle.

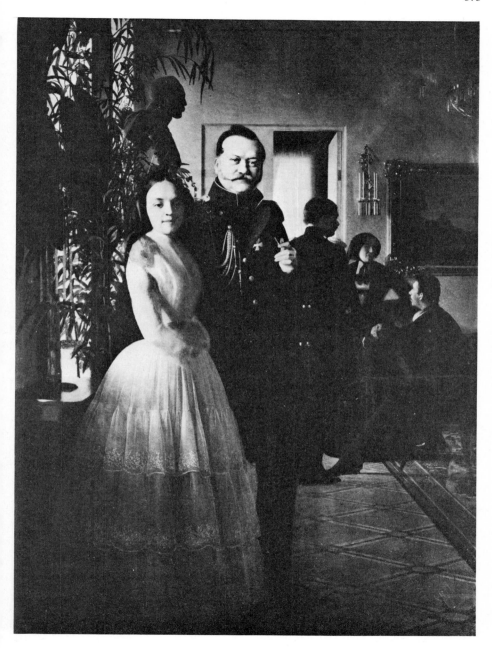

276. S. K. Zaryanko: Count Rostovtsev and his Family, *c.* 1850–5.
Leningrad, Russian Museum

CHAPTER 26

IDEOLOGICAL REALISM

With the accession of Alexander II (1855–81) a period of limited liberalism commenced in Russian political and artistic life which culminated in the proclamation of the abolition of serfdom on 3 March 1861. Now the discreet satire of Fedotov was succeeded by bolder social criticism. In the freer atmosphere of Moscow, where the art school was less riddled with bureaucracy than the Petersburg Academy, there developed a number of interesting painters, the first of importance being Vasily Grigorievich Perov (1834–82).[1] Even before

he received a travelling scholarship in 1861 and went to Paris, he had shown that, although his point of departure was the social satire of Fedotov, his own views were more critical of conditions in Russia. As early as 1857 he had caused a sensation with 'The Arrival of the Rural Police Inspector'. The edge of the moral was blunted by the slack and sentimental drawing of the peasant under interrogation, but the attack on the methods of the police was sharper than had been seen before. Four years later he exhibited two paintings critical

277. V. G. Perov: Easter Procession, 1861. *Moscow, Tretyakov Gallery*

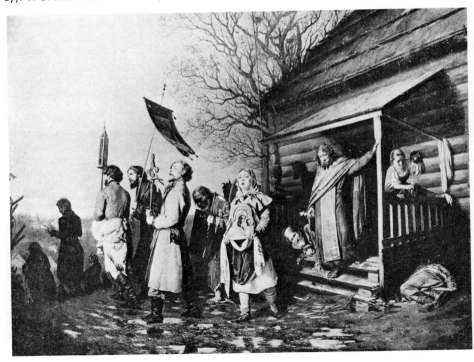

of the Church. 'The Village Sermon' is something of a Hogarthian fable, with the local landlord asleep before the pulpit, while his wife listens to the whispers of her lover and an obsequious lackey keeps the peasants at a distance.[2] In 'The Easter Procession' [277] he struck directly at the corruption and offensive manners of the rural clergy. This shows a group of priests in various stages of intoxication staggering out of a village tavern where they have been too well entertained in the course of their ceremonial visits. Such pictures were recognized for what they were, and even under the liberal regime, clerical authorities saw to it that they were withdrawn from exhibition.

Unfortunately the emergence of a new expressive point of view was not accompanied by a demand from artists or public for technical innovations. In this circumstance can be seen the persistent dilemma of much Russian nineteenth-century painting. To a large extent each of the radical artistic movements of the West had been based upon an examination of current technical resources and the invention of new means for new expressive purposes. In that way and in no other could a new kind of painting be created. One need only recall the technical discoveries of the Pre-Raphaelites or of the young naturalist painters in the circle of Courbet and Manet in Paris in the 1860s. In each case public disapproval was as much a matter of dismay at the unfamiliar appearance of a painting as at the new subject-matter.

The extent to which Russian painters of the middle years of the century were unaware of the necessity for such studies can be seen in the experience of Perov in Paris. He was there for only two years (1862–4), although his scholarship was for six, but after searching the boulevards for picturesque types and executing a few sentimental genre-paintings, he applied for permission to return home. He had been in Paris during the episode of the *Salon des refusés*, the first occasion since 1849 when the conflict between official approval and private investigation reached the proportions of a

public scandal, yet in his work there was never a hint that he was aware of the position taken by Courbet, Manet, or Whistler.

When he returned to Moscow, the first liberal decade of the reign had ended, and government was hardening into the slow reaction of the later years. Perov's paintings also lost their bite. His 'Arrival of the Governess' (1866) was a return to Fedotov's satirical descriptions of the middle class, with a touch more attention to the vulgarity of the newly rich. More sentimental still was his attitude towards the poor, whose hardships and sorrows he presented in 'The Village Burial' (1865), 'The Drowned Girl' (1867), and 'Aged Parents at their Son's Grave' (1874). Although the titles suggest his increasingly sentimental attitude towards the poor, the homeless, and the bereaved, Perov's concern with the lower classes also contained an implied criticism of the existing social order which set him apart from such an impassive observer as Venetsianov, or even from Fedotov, who had never descended below the bourgeoisie. The religious and historical paintings of his later years, to be sure, were less accomplished than those by his contemporaries, but Perov retained his importance for the younger generation as a painter seriously concerned with the social order, whose earlier realistic studies had been honestly conceived and strongly executed.

While Perov had been abroad, a notable event had occurred in St Petersburg. In 1863 growing discontent with the reactionary attitude of the Academy and its artificial distinctions between genre and historical painting burst into open revolt. A group of students competing for the annual gold medal objected to the attempt of the authorities to suppress the painting of contemporary life by imposing a specified subject for the competition. They demanded the right to choose their own; the Academy replied by stipulating 'The Banquet of the Gods in Valhalla'. Thirteen painters, joined by one sculptor, thereupon resigned from the Academy. This was a daring step in a place where, and at a time when, an artist's livelihood depended upon his successful completion of the academic programme. Yet it is interesting that their action was precipitated by the problem of freedom of expression more than of technique. The younger painters' insistence on their right to compose their own programmes can be seen as a result of the new criticism proclaimed by the social revolutionary N. G. Chernyshevsky in his doctoral thesis, 'The Aesthetic Relations of Art to Reality' (1855). On the threshold of the age of reform he declared the superiority of reality to its imitation in art. From this it followed that subject and expression were more important than form, and that in the interests of the social order the choice of subject was all important. Soon after their withdrawal from the Academy the 'Thirteen Contestants', as they were called, and their associates formed an Artists' Co-operative Society (Artel Khudozhnikov) for the exhibition of their work. The results were encouraging, and eventually led to the formation in 1870 of the Society for Travelling Art Exhibitions (Tovarishchestvo peredvizhnykh khudozhestvennykh vystavok), whence the term 'Peredvizhniki' ('travellers' or 'wanderers') for the members.[3] In the course of the next twenty years almost all the important contemporary painters contributed to the exhibitions, and many of the significant works of art created in Russia during the 1870s and 80s reached a wider audience than would have been the case had they been restricted to exhibitions in St Petersburg and Moscow. In their earlier struggles to obtain an audience the members of the Artel and the Peredvizhniki were given material assistance and encouragement by the Moscow collector P. M. Tretyakov (1832–98). The collection given by Tretyakov and his brother to the city of Moscow in 1892 contained important paintings by most of the more significant Russian artists of the nineteenth century, with special emphasis on the work of the realists and 'wanderers'. Not all the works shown in the travelling exhibitions were of the first quality – they varied from revolutionary realism through historical

painting to excessively sentimental genre – but in general the society can be credited with the propagation on a wide scale of a kind of art which we may describe as ideological realism.[4]

The leader of the Thirteen Contestants and one of the founders of the Society was the painter Ivan Nikolaevich Kramskoy (1837–87), whose sincere but limited artistic imagination exercised a profound influence over the character of the works sponsored by the Society. Kramskoy had started life as a painter of religious pictures and had worked as a retoucher in photographers' studios in Kharkov and St Petersburg before entering the Academy in 1856. He was well on the way to academic distinction, having won the small gold medal in the competition of 1863, when he joined the Thirteen Contestants and resigned from the Academy. Kramskoy's art was created out of the tension between a deeply personal mysticism and the most desperately acute photographic vision. The results of his early photographic training can be seen in his numerous portraits – he left over 400 of them – which are striking likenesses as well as psychologically intense. Again and again he caught his subjects in characteristic poses and painted them with minute attention to detail against backgrounds severely unadorned. His pedestrian colour sense increased the similarity to photographs. But having conquered the veracity of natural appearances, Kramskoy knew some deep spiritual dissatisfaction, and dreamed of a religious painting on the theme of man's perpetual and painful search for moral truth. For this purpose he selected the 'Temptation of Christ' or 'Christ in the Wilderness' (1872–4) [278] which he conceived as a figure crouched at daybreak in a stony waste. His desire was to portray not the outward man but the inner struggle between good and evil. The artist himself declared: 'This is no Christ, it is an image of the sorrows of humanity which are known to all of us.'[5] Certainly the painting has a strange and tragic fascination, although the conflict between the spiritual motivation and the accumulation of physical

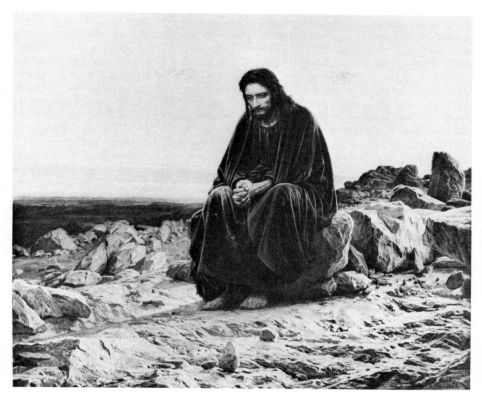

278. I. N. Kramskoy: The Temptation of Christ, 1872–4.
Moscow, Tretyakov Gallery

detail in the rocks, crumpled garments, and sombre figure invalidates the expression. The contrast between mysticism and accurate reporting suggests situations in the contemporary novels of Dostoevsky, whom Kramskoy admired and whose portrait he painted.

Except for the 'Temptation', an unfinished 'Christ Mocked', and some undistinguished work in the Cathedral of the Redeemer in Moscow, Kramskoy's work consisted almost entirely of portraits, although there are indications that he had a gift for genre and sentimental subjects. Of his 'Inconsolable Grief', showing a mother who has just lost her only child standing beside the funeral flowers, he

painted no less than three versions. The final one (1884) is another instance of the irreconcilable gulf between naturalism and symbolism, for certainly harrowing sorrow is more described than expressed in the figure, and strangely contradicted by the precise and exquisite flowers, the springtime freshness of the potted plants in the foreground, and the innumerable details of carpeting, furniture, and the like. As in so much narrative painting, the content fails to inform the design, and must be communicated through the title. The success or failure of such paintings – and success as well as failure must be considered apart from changes in taste – recalls the similar predicament of Ivanov, who hesitated between the real and the ideal. But there are in Kramskoy's work occasional revelations of higher imaginative faculties. In one of his rare genre-paintings – the unfinished 'Inspection of an Old House' (1884) – he treated a lighted, silent, shuttered room disturbed only by the passage of two figures in a mood so intense that it forecast the concluding moments of Chekhov's *Cherry Orchard*.

Kramskoy's 'Temptation', with its unresolved mixture of confidence in scientific truth and doubtful spiritual resolve, is an important turning-point in the history of nineteenth-century religious painting. It finds its parallel in the political and social disillusion of the 1870s and 80s. Ivanov had been confused by biblical criticism, and his Messiah, who had been much closer to the foreground of the composition before doubt entered the artist's mind, finally dwindled into insignificance in the distance. The faith of Kramskoy's generation had been so shattered by scientific discoveries that his man-Christ was powerless to act. Henceforward only two paths were open: to work out some compromise with official religion or to withdraw into oneself. The latter course was chosen by one of the most remarkable of Russian painters, Nikolay Nikolaevich Ge (or Gay, 1831–94), between whose early work of the 1860s and his last paintings there exists somewhat the same difference, and the same descent below the surface of literal description in the search for spiritual and psychic truth, which we can distinguish in the early realistic and the later symbolist novels of Dostoevsky.[6] Ge, who was of French descent, entered the Academy in 1850, and by 1857 had won the first gold medal and the travelling scholarship. After desultory travel and landscape painting in southern Italy, he settled in Florence, where he lived, except for one brief visit to Russia, until 1869. In Rome he had met Ivanov, and had been deeply impressed by the faith and research which had gone into the creation of 'Christ's First Appearance'. Ge, too, read Strauss and Renan, but salvaged his faith in the determination to discover the historical Christ of the Gospels. His first large religious painting, 'The Last Supper' (1863, State Russian Museum, Leningrad), seemed to the academic circles of St Petersburg a startling departure from iconographical traditions, whether Byzantine or Baroque, although in the naturalistic composition there was little which was artistically novel. The general plan was reminiscent of Caravaggio, and the dramatic *chiaroscuro* and commonplace physical types could have been found in Rembrandt. Upon his return to St Petersburg he was attracted for a time to historical painting. The results enjoyed much attention, although they reveal the weakest side of his talents. Even the more subtle colours of his 'Peter the Great Interrogating the Tsarevich Alexey' (1871) or of 'Catherine II at the Bier of Elizabeth' fail to conceal awkward, even amateurish composition. Until then Ge would have been considered a very minor member of the large group of religious and historical painters, but at this point he renounced the career of an academic professor and withdrew for a period of ten years to his estate in the Ukraine. There the study of religious texts led him to Tolstoy, whose disciple he became in 1882.[7] Ge joined Tolstoy in his attempt to apply the principles of primitive Christianity to the realities of contemporary life. The first active result appeared in 'What is Truth' (1890), depicting a gross, contemptuous Pilate flinging his question at the mute, motionless Christ. The clumsy composition and naïve lighting were now the perfect means with which to express the irreconcilable conflict between the two protagonists. Although the painting was instinct with genuine religious feeling, the unconventional portrayal and the haggard, unprepossessing Christ offended the Church, already outraged by Tolstoy's teaching, and the painting was removed from exhibition.

Ge soon pushed his search for spiritual and historical truth even farther. In his unfinished 'Golgotha' (1892) [279] a distraught, almost frantic Christ clutches his head in

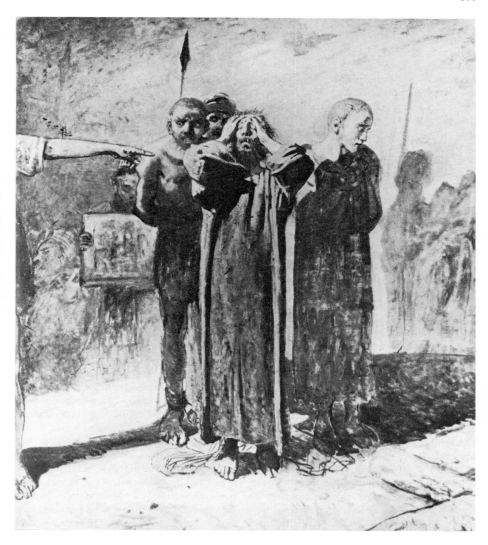

279. N. N. Ge: Golgotha, 1892.
Moscow, Tretyakov Gallery

horror as he waits for the dreadful preparations to be completed. The 'Crucifixion' (1892, present location unknown), set in a desolate, lunar landscape, which moved Tolstoy to tears, is an unforgettable demonstration of terror and agony. It is almost inconceivable that the imaginative reconstruction of historical actuality could be carried so far as this without loss of spirituality. Ge's paintings were more than simply exercises in shocking melodrama. The inexpressibly tragic figure of his wasted, wretched Christ forced the observer to reconsider the miraculous intervention in that pitiful being of the human and the divine, much as Tolstoy's intransigent insistence on the essentials of Christianity shocked a generation into a new examination of traditional Christian conduct.

In these last works Ge became the first important Russian painter to devise a new technique for his expressive needs. His crude compositions, simplified shapes, and abbreviated lines were virtues rather than handicaps in the communication of this strange and poignant experience. It is difficult to think of any other religious painting of this period, when biblical criticism had shattered the comfortable familiarity of traditional iconography, which is such a combination of vision and faith. It is as if the religious emotion of medieval art had been recreated in modern terms. In Ge's work we can see the reasons for the failure of Ivanov and Kramskoy. Ge rejected Ivanov's idealism, and at the same time, in choosing subjects which possessed an immediate communicative and dramatic content, avoided the weakness of Kramskoy's 'Christ', whose image was too deliberate to convey the conceptions with which he burdened it.

During the 1860s and 70s Russian painters, in company with their contemporaries throughout the western world, had mastered an increasingly realistic technique, and they were now faced with the problem of what to do with it. In France the attitude of Manet and the Impressionists to the painting of modern life without anecdote or comment was the expressive counterpart of their descriptive technique and objective vision. In Russia the lack of an audience so experienced, so critical, and so vocal prohibited the development of that kind of naturalistic painting, and we find instead, during the 1880s and the period of social and political reaction under Alexander III (1881–94), two more traditional types of pictures, the continuation of social criticism in a milder form in the works exhibited by the

Peredvizhniki, and on the other hand the development of an energetic if less aesthetically gratifying school of historical painting.

Certainly there was nothing particularly novel about history-painting as such. Nor was the specifically nationalist character of much of this painting new; the curious student will perhaps remember the political themes which inundated the Paris Salons in the years before the centennial celebration of the French Revolution in 1889. And certainly such objects were the stock in trade of academic exhibitions everywhere in the nineteenth century. Yet for all that the Russian paintings are not without interest. They have long been the most familiar and most popular works of Russian art, both at home and abroad; and in technique and composition, if not in the implied attitude towards history, they have inspired much history-painting under the Soviets.

In our present context they concern us for a new attitude towards the choice of subject which appeared soon after the middle of the century, when social criticism had become more dangerous. The works of a little-known painter, Valery (Valerian) Ivanovich Yakoby (1834–1902), are a case in point. In 1861 his competition painting showing the momentary halt of a long convoy of chained prisoners bound for Siberia (State Tretyakov Gallery, Moscow) won him the Academy's gold medal, and was so enthusiastically received by the public that it was in some small measure held responsible for the alleviation of the conditions of political imprisonment. A trip abroad at this point distracted Yakoby from contemporary life; upon his return he treated historical subjects in a manner diluted by the French Rococo masters. His 'Marriage in the Ice Palace in the Reign of Anna Ioannovna' recounted the humiliation of Prince Golitsyn, who was obliged to marry an aged Kalmuk and spend his wedding night in an elegant igloo constructed on the frozen Neva for the sin of having embraced Roman Catholicism.[8] Before this Konstantin Dmitrievich Flavitsy (1830–66) had painted 'The Last Moments of Princess Tarakanova' (1864, State Tretyakov Gallery, Moscow), showing the beautiful woman in the Peter Paul Fortress about to be drowned in her cell by the flooded Neva. Although neither of these pictures, in technique, design, or historical interpretation, differs to any extent from the standards for such sensational subjects elsewhere, taken together they could be understood as subtle attacks on the irresponsibility of autocratic power.[9]

In the work of Vasily Ivanovich Surikov (1848–1916) this tendency towards social criticism continued, although smothered in the trappings of nationalist pageantry.[10] His most famous works, 'The Morning of the Execution of the Streltsy' (1881, State Tretyakov Gallery, Moscow) and 'The Boyarin Morosova' (1887) [280], representing a fanatical Old Believer

the specific hues of old Muscovy, lulled the authorities into admiration. In addition, Surikov communicated a feeling for the Russian climate in the grey light of dawn which invests the Red Square as the implacable Peter watches his enemies being prepared for their terrible fate, and in the gloomy winter skies above the Boyarin Morosova. In such atmospheric painting there was a faint reflexion of the general contemporary interest in nature which found its most conspicuous development in French Impressionism, and which is present to somewhat the same degree in the music of Moussorgsky, whose prelude to *Khovanshchina* (1872–80) suggests the dawn breaking over the Red Square in Moscow only a few years after the event illustrated by Surikov.[11]

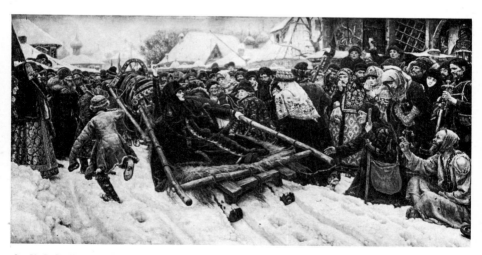

280. V. I. Surikov: The Boyarin Morosova, 1887.
Moscow, Tretyakov Gallery

dragged off in chains to prison and death, were on the theme of personal opposition to the established Church and State. Surikov's compositions, so knowingly designed to bring the spectator into the painted space through the arrangement of circumstances which, if not always accurate, at least were drenched with

A historical painter with a different purpose and very inferior ability, Vasily Vasilievich Vereshchagin (1842–1904) enjoyed during his life-time a wider international reputation than any Russian artist. This was largely the result of extensive self-advertisement and the appeal of his Tolstoian pacifism. He entered the Academy, but in 1863 forsook it to study in Paris with J.-L. Gérôme, who developed his taste for meticulous detail, but could not improve his undeveloped sense of design and harsh colouring. Vereshchagin was fond of travel, and in the next few years executed a series of pictorial reports on the landscape of the Caucasus and Turkestan. More than any other Russian painter of the age he maintained constant contacts with Europe, residing in Munich and Paris for extended periods, and arranging one-man exhibitions of his work throughout Europe and America. The success of these exhibitions was due to the startling, even gruesome, character of his military paintings. These dealt, not with the usual triumphs of Russian arms and the pleasure of military life, but with the horrors of war which he had seen for himself as an artist-correspondent at the front during the campaigns in Turkestan (1867–8) and the Russo-Turkish War (1877–8).[12] From his recollection of his first experiences he painted three canvases dealing with the plight of soldiers surrounded and annihilated by the enemy or left dying to be devoured by vultures. Vereshchagin added a touch of sadism to the contemporary taste for painted bloodshed, but he also showed a genuine hatred of war in his lectures and pamphlets. In the intervals between battles he travelled in India (1875–6) and Palestine (1884), and covered numerous canvases with what he saw there. He was at his best when he could display his startlingly photographic technique without at the same time trying to preach. At the beginning of the 90s, when there was a lull on the fighting fronts, Vereshchagin painted his famous series of the French invasion of Russia in 1812. For all his industrious research into military records he had no real gift as a history-painter; the compositions are clumsy, the colours crude, and the famous characters lack personality. As illustrations for Tolstoy's *War and Peace*, however, they are still the best-known Russian paintings of the period.

The course of late-nineteenth-century Russian realism was epitomized in the long career

of Ilya (Elias) Efimovich Repin (1844–1930).[13] Of humble stock, he had come from the southern provinces to the Academy in 1864, the year after the revolt of the Thirteen Contestants. In 1871 he was awarded the large gold medal and a six-year travelling scholarship for his 'Resurrection of the Daughter of Jairus' (1871, State Russian Museum, Leningrad), an exercise in the archaeologically realist manner of Ge's 'Last Supper' of 1863. Having satisfied the academic requirements, he immediately demonstrated his natural inclinations in a large group portrait representing an 'Assembly of Russian, Polish, and Czech Musicians' (1871–2), and in his 'Bargemen', or 'Haulers' (Burlaki), often known as 'The Volga Boatmen' (1870–3, State Russian Museum, Leningrad). The 'Musicians', a competent if undistinguished essay in managing a variety of postures within an interior space, disappeared into the halls of a Slavic society in Moscow, but when the 'Bargemen' was exhibited in Vienna in 1873, it brought the young artist immediate European recognition as a realist. Between the two extremes represented by official, upper-class portraits and the study of humbler social conditions Repin's long career developed, with occasional excursions into history-painting. As a portraitist he made his reputation in St Petersburg, where he painted most of the prominent artists, writers, scientists, and statesmen of his day, and memorialized important public events for the government. In a hundred portraits Repin satisfied his sitters and his public by his combination of a striking likeness with a traditional design, undisturbed by the psychological penetration of Kramskoy, and unalleviated by the elegance with which the young portraitist V. A. Serov (1865–1911) portrayed the fashionable men and women of the period.

At the other extreme his 'Bargemen' [281], a study of the unfortunate wretches who hauled the heavy boats against the Volga current by sheer physical exertion, was the result of a trip along the river in 1870. The pathos and implied criticism of social conditions

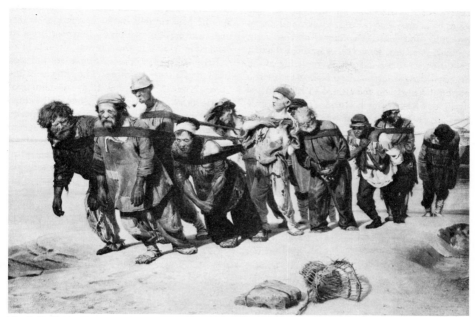

281. I. E. Repin: Bargemen (detail), 1870–3.
Leningrad, Russian Museum

which permitted this brutal exploitation of human labour linked him at once with the Peredvizhniki whom he had joined, while his sensationally realistic presentation of these degraded creatures surpassed anything which had yet been seen in the Travelling Exhibitions, and still can so impress the spectator that he overlooks the artificial and not entirely integrated composition.[14] The combination of photographic detail, sentiment, and brilliant colour – for Repin had caught the broad white light of the Volga region – proved unfailingly successful in other historical paintings.

When Repin reached Paris, he was already an accomplished realist, who could learn from the French naturalists only how to brighten his palette, and how to put forward a more objective, less anecdotal point of view. But he was slow to take advantage of these opportunities, and they were only realized in his work much later. Thus his studies of Parisian men and women for his 'Paris Café' (1875, private collection, Stockholm) rival the oblique detachment of Degas's modified realism of those years, while the finished canvas is merely another example of overcrowded sentimental genre. And the same slow maturing is true of his experience of Impressionist colour. Gradually, after his second visit to Paris in 1883, his brush-stroke loosened and his light became more intense, and in such informal studies as his daughter 'Vera in the Sunlight' (1885) one can say that he had tentatively adopted the Impressionist palette, although he never went in for the broken colour of Monet. Perhaps his most truly naturalistic painting, in colour, design, and expressive content, is the 'Surgeon E. V. Pavlov in the Operating Room' (1888), in which he grafted the noncommittal attitude of Monet to that interest in human experience so earnestly championed at this time by Zola. The subtle whites and greys reveal Repin's sense of colour at its best.

Such painting, however, was too detached to suit either the sentimental moralizing of the Peredvizhniki or the sensational tastes of the public, both of which he tried to reach in his 'Religious Procession in Kursk' (1880–3). This was an enormous canvas of a huge crowd shepherded by the clergy and police following a portable shrine down a country road on a hot day. It was a stupendous demonstration of his ability to amass innumerable details, but it lacked the directness and pathos of the 'Bargemen' of a decade before. Even such incidents as the cripple hastening to keep up with the procession, the mounted police lashing at an upraised arm, or the stout *bourgeoise* carrying an icon had neither Fedotov's humour nor Perov's point. The government censorship as

well as Alexander III's aggressive Orthodoxy may be held responsible for the failure of this uneasy attempt to combine a 'purpose' with an ostensible tribute to the Church.

Like so many others, Repin in the 80s turned to history painting. The subject of his 'Tsar Ivan IV with the Body of His Son' (1881–5) [282] was a favourite one at the time, and again can be taken as an implied criticism of autocratic rule. Repin had the courage to concentrate on the essential human tragedy of the situation. In the best tradition of historical horror painting he depicted Ivan's insane remorse as he slowly realizes the enormity of his crime and seeks to staunch the blood flowing from his son's shattered head. There is very little of the Muscovite bric-à-brac so dear to Surikov and other historical painters of the day. Something of the same directness is present in the broad humour of his seventeenth-

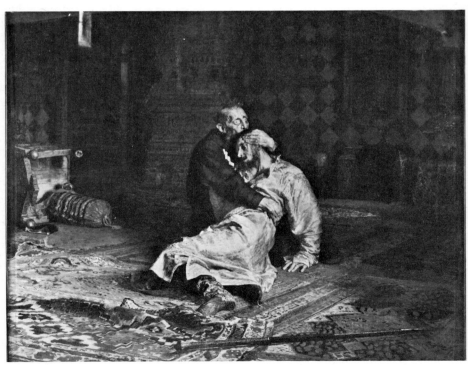

282. I. E. Repin: Tsar Ivan IV with the Body of his Son, 1881–5. *Moscow, Tretyakov Gallery*

century episode 'Zaporozh Cossacks Drafting a Reply to the Turkish Sultan' (1880–91), on which he spent years of ethnographical research until it became practically an anthology of the racial types of southern Russia. This, too, was critical of the regime; for the Cossacks, now the notorious bodyguard of the Emperor and whose name was synonymous with despotic brutality, had once been known throughout Russia as champions of the oppressed.

This interpretation of Repin's historical paintings might be thought fanciful were it not for the evidence that through the 1880s he was sincerely critical of tyranny and that his artistic sympathies were on the side of the social revolutionaries. In content, form, and expression these paintings provide a notable sequence in his artistic development. 'The Arrest of the Propagandist' was commenced in 1878, in the manner of Perov's anecdotal genre, but by the time the final version was finished in 1890 Repin had refined this portrayal of a young man in the hands of the police, who are ransacking his quarters for subversive literature, and given it the simplified dramatic quality of his 'Ivan IV'. In the 'Rejected Confession' (1879–85) and 'Revolutionary Awaiting Execution' (1880s) he entered the darkness of the prisons to paint the proud and horrible last moments of men and women condemned to death for political offences. His most sensitive, intuitive, and in many ways most tragic political painting is also his most completely realized work, and one which ranks with the finest narrative painting of the nineteenth century. The comparison between the first and final versions of 'They Did Not Expect Him' (Ne Zhdali, 1883–98) also proves that when Repin's emotions were stirred, his pictorial imagination became more acute [283]. In the first version a young woman revolutionary, unexpectedly returned from exile, has just entered the living-room of a house where her appearance evokes varying responses from three other figures, two girls and a boy. The tone of the whole is one of

sudden and dramatic surprise. In the second version Repin amplified the situation and endowed it with the overtones of tragedy. The political prisoner, now a man, uncertainly enters the room; the reactions of his family range from his mother's dawning recognition as she rises from her chair to the joy and fear on the faces of his three children, the youngest of whom is frightened by the appearance of this haggard and ragged figure.[15] What gives the picture true artistic quality is Repin's masterly balance of form and expression, especially in his oblique, asymmetrical composition. The right-to-left direction in space, opposed by the sharpened perspective drawing of the floorboards, is so suggestive of Degas that we can believe that the lessons learned in Paris ten years before had at last come to fruition. At the same time Repin also revived the sensitive painting of middle-class interiors which had been one of the triumphs of the romantics. In 'They Did Not Expect Him' tradition and innovation are marvellously combined. The picture must be regarded as the finest artistic achievement of the social point of view of the Peredvizhniki. With it Repin can be said to have crowned and closed the history of ideological realism in Russian painting.

In his later years Repin continued on the whole the vein of academic realism in which most of his work was composed. His history indicates the Russian painter's gradually growing awareness of contemporary developments in the West. In such works as 'They Did Not Expect Him' or the brilliant portrait of D. I. Mendeleev (1907) so reminiscent of Degas's portrait of Duranty, he could elevate the realist tendencies which had been such a fundamental part of Russian painting during the nineteenth century into something approaching the formal coherence of the European tradition. Repin's age – he was a contemporary of the major French Impressionists – undoubtedly prevented him from going further in the direction of Post-Impressionism, although in his eighties, after the

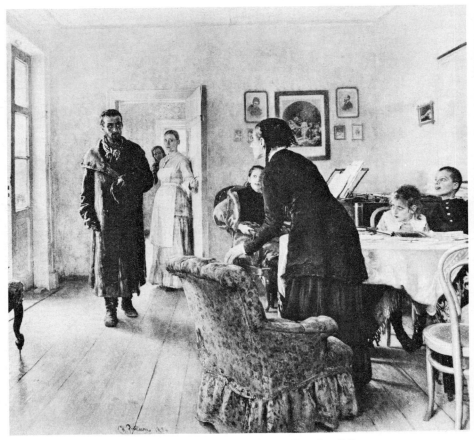

283. I. E. Repin: They Did Not Expect Him, 1883–98. *Moscow, Tretyakov Gallery*

October Revolution, when he had retired to his country house in Finland, a series of vivid Passion scenes proves his interest in the exacerbated expressionism of Munch and Nolde.[16] He had very considerable talent, an eye for character and situation, a sense of colour, and a gift for drama, all of which he spent perhaps too generously and too often in the service of the narrow aesthetic of the age.

During the nineteenth century Russia produced many able and several distinguished painters, but it is difficult to say that there was a 'Russian School' of painting comparable to those in music and literature. The reason

can be found in the absence of a traditional body of practice and opinion such as existed in western European countries. Two hundred years is too short a time to develop a tradition, especially if the supervision exercised by an academy and the State discourages nonconformist talent. Nineteenth-century French painting is another example. Its least significant aspect is the work produced for or under the supervision of the Academy and the State. And Russia lacked what we might call a private public which, though small in numbers, through its encouragement made possible the experimental art of the West. While France

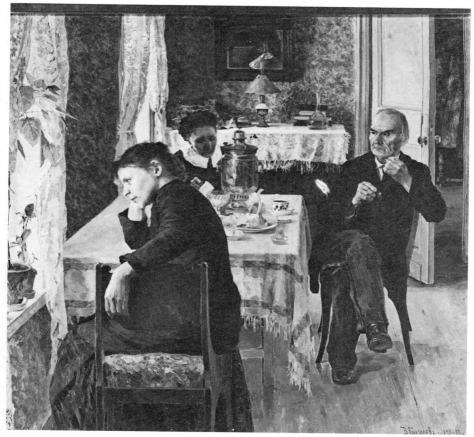

284. V. N. Baksheev: The Prose of Life, 1892–3. *Moscow, Tretyakov Gallery*

had more than one Bruyas, Caillebotte, or Pellerin, men like Tretyakov were rare in Russia, and he, for all his interest, did not often depart from the prevailing standards of naturalism. The difficulty of the Russian painter's situation can be seen in 'The Prose of Life' (Zhiteiskaya proza, 1892–3) [284], by Vasily Nikolaevich Baksheev (1862–1958).[17] The content resembles the situations in the contemporary dramas of Chekhov, who also expressed the dissatisfaction of the Russian intelligentsia with a way of life which no longer had any relation to political or economic reality. And as Chekhov was a creative master of the

dramatic form, so in this one painting Baksheev demonstrated his command of the resources of modern painting. The oblique right-to-left perspective and the subtle treatment of a lighted interior recall the works of the French Impressionists and prove that the Russians were aware of the formal qualities of modern art. Yet they could afford neither to renounce the advantages of subject-matter as the Impressionists had done, nor to wait for public approval. Their successful works were brilliant but isolated attempts to integrate the pictorial experience of modern times with the crumbling structure of their world.

CHAPTER 27

THE SLAVIC REVIVAL AND *MIR ISKUSSTVA*

During the last two decades of the nineteenth century the most progressive developments in Russian art were closely related to the antithetical concepts of nationalism and internationalism. These tendencies were the further development of the controversy between the Slavophiles and the Westernizers which had appeared in the 1840s under the reign of Nicholas I; and they continued in a modified form until the end of the Empire in the social and political programmes of Pan-Slavism and the system of western military alliances. As in the eighteenth century, so again, Moscow and St Petersburg were the centres from which emanated propaganda calling on the one hand for a return to the principles of ancient Russian life, summarized now in the formula of 'Orthodoxy, Autocracy, Nationality', and on the other urging that Russia's future lay in a closer political and cultural integration with the West. However antagonistic these systems might at first appear, the forms of their artistic expression had much in common.

The origins of the art of both programmes can be related to the aspirations of the Peredvizhniki. Although their intention during the 1870s and 80s had been the creation of a truly national art, and for that reason they had scorned too close associations with artistic movements abroad, their work had closer analogies with the technique and subject-matter of contemporary European genre and historical painting than with any specifically Russian tradition. But while the Peredvizhniki tried, as did Tolstoy and Dostoevsky, to find the soul of Russia in the conditions of contemporary life, there arose simultaneously a tendency to exploit 'Old Russian' sources which eventually affected even the historical paintings of the Peredvizhniki and the arts of architecture, sculpture, interior decoration, book illustration, and stage design as well.

But it would be a falsification of cultural history to attribute the Slavic Revival of the later nineteenth century exclusively to political and philosophical causes. Just as it may be considered a continuation of Muscovite objections to Peter's reforms, so it was also assisted by the scholarly investigation of the Russian past, comparable to the archaeological and scientific investigations which were occurring in other European nations.[1] Indeed, changing conceptions and deepening knowledge of Russian archaeology and art history were soon reflected in contemporary creative work.

In 1839, when Count Anatol Nikolaevich Demidov travelled through western Russia with the intention of compiling an illustrated account of Russian architecture, he was accompanied by a French draughtsman, André Durand (1807–67), whose hundred lithographs provided the most accurate visual account yet published of the more important Russian monuments [102, 194, 285].[2] While Durand was a man of his times and a westerner into the bargain, and his visual impressions of Russian buildings are romantically exaggerated in that he records what was strange to him rather than what was familiar to the Russians, on the whole he faithfully described the monuments as they appeared at the time. A significant advance towards determining the chronology and formal development of Russian architecture was made by A. A. Martynov (1820–95) and I. M. Snegirev (1793–1868), whose numerous publications in the 1850s and 60s contain much information still useful today.[3] Late in the reign of Nicholas I the government became interested in these investigations and sponsored several folio volumes illustrating Russian antiquities, principally works of decorative art reproduced in coloured lithography.[4] Serious attempts to put these scattered studies on a sound basis began

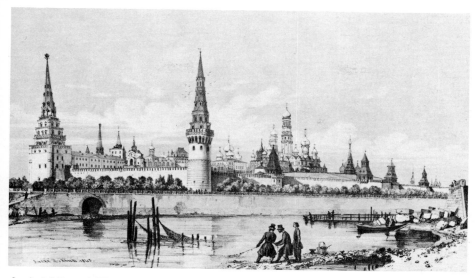

285. André Durand: The Kremlin, Moscow, lithograph, 1843

with the organization of the archaeological societies of St Petersburg (1846) and Moscow (1864). The latter, the Moskovskoe Arkhaeologicheskoe Obshchestvo, inaugurated in 1869 a series of triennial congresses in various Russian cities and towns. The publications of the papers and reports presented at these s'ezdy provide an invaluable store of information, not only for archaeological material (prehistoric and antique remains, principally in the south), but also for the earliest Russian architecture and painting in the Kievan and early Moscow periods.[5] In St Petersburg the Academy of Fine Arts also sponsored research, particularly the systematic examination of early Russian architecture by V. V. Suslov [122].[6] Meanwhile the study of painting kept pace with architectural research. As early as 1856 D. A. Rovinsky (1824–95) laid the foundations for a systematic study of icon-painting, based on iconographical research and the correlation of chronicle texts.[7] This work was carried on in a series of scholarly studies by N. P. Kondakov (1844–1925) and N. P. Likhachev (1862–1935).[8] The latter, with I. S. Ostrou-

khov and S. P. Ryabushinsky, established the principles of modern connoisseurship on the basis of their important collections of icons.

The western student will recognize in this account the general outline of similar studies of national traditions in the West, which also progressed from a romantic interest in the picturesque aspects of medieval art, through the 'scientific' examination of monuments in the spirit of the positivist principles of nineteenth-century science and philosophy, to the gradual realization of the necessity for a synthesis. Such an inclusive history, incorporating the most recent discoveries and opinions, was begun under the editorship of Igor Grabar (1871–1960) with the publication in 1909 of the first volume of a general history of Russian art, with contributions by the leading archaeologists and art historians of the day.[9] Unfortunately the progress of the work was interrupted by the outbreak of the First World War when only five volumes and a portion of a sixth had been published.

These studies also followed a pattern which had a parallel in western European research.

The gradual recovery of the past proceeded in reverse chronological order. The medieval revivals of the early nineteenth century in France and England started with the study of Late Gothic or Early Renaissance architecture, and slowly worked backwards, so that it was only towards the end of the century that the qualities of Early Gothic and Romanesque, and finally of Early Christian and Byzantine art, were fully understood. The same principle applies in Russia. Sixteenth- and seventeenth-century art was appreciated and utilized from the first; the earlier medieval periods were exhaustively explored only towards the end of the century.[10]

A preliminary but not altogether satisfactory attempt to discover the characteristics of a Russian national style was instigated by Nicholas I, under whom, as we have seen, the solid front of Petersburg classicism was first breached by the forces of eclecticism. His predecessors had moved easily and with authority in the contemporary stylistic movements of Europe, and to each may be attributed the patronage of some more than ordinary master. Schlüter, Rastrelli, Quarenghi, and Rossi were choices of which any ruler and any nation might be proud. With the Tsars of the nineteenth century the story changes. Throughout this period a succession of German alliances (the wives of the last six emperors, from Paul I, whose mother, Catherine II, had been a German princess, were German except for Alexander III's, Dagmar of Denmark, who was of German descent) strengthened German influence, which can be seen in the official domestic propriety and social dullness which pervaded the Russian Court. The result was an increasing separation between the sovereigns' artistic interests and those of the progressive artists of the day. At best they acquiesced in the popular bourgeois attitude towards art.[11]

Nicholas I's uncertain taste determined his choice of his favourite architects, A. I. Shtakenshneider (1802–65) and K. A. Ton (1794–1881), to create important palaces and churches of his reign. In addition the German architect Leo von Klenze (1784–1864), who built the Glyptothek and Alte Pinakothek in Munich, was called upon to design the New Hermitage Museum (1839–52). Shtakenshneider, perhaps the first self-consciously eclectic architect in St Petersburg, built large palaces for members of the imperial family, skilful but dull variations on the work of Rastrelli, Rossi, and Montferrand. His Mariinsky Palace on St Isaac's Square (1839–44) for Nicholas I's eldest daughter, the Grand Duchess Maria (later occupied by the Imperial Council and now by the Executive Committee of the Leningrad City Soviet), is typical of his ability to maintain at the least the city's reputation for massive dignity.[12] At Peterhof and Tsarskoe Selo, however, the Tsar and his architects indulged in a riot of eclecticism, the more surprising in that Nicholas was sincerely fond of Peterhof. For him the English architect Menelas, who had been successful as a landscape architect after adding his Egyptian

286. A. I. Shtakenshneider: Peterhof, The Nicholas Cottage, 1834

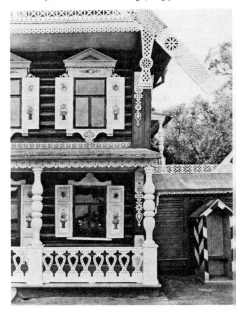

and Oriental fantasies to the park at Tsarskoe Selo, designed a Gothic 'kottedzh' which became Nicholas's favourite country house. N. L. Benois (1813–79), the son of a French émigré, built the huge imperial stables in an English Tudor style, and Shtakenshneider, in addition to several pavilions and a belvedere in the classical manner, designed the 'Nikolsky domik' (Nicholas Cottage) [286] as a surprise for the Empress in 1834, in a style truly a surprise for its date. In contrast to Bazhenov's

and Kazakov's fantasies on the theme of old Russian masonry architecture, this was a peasant farmhouse of horizontal timber construction with an unusual amount of appliqué ornament in the manner of peasant carving.[13]

But this first attempt remained without issue for some time to come. The task of creating a new national style was assumed by Ton on the occasion of the erection of the colossal Church of the Redeemer in Moscow [287], commemorating the victories of 1812–14

287. K. A. Ton: Moscow, Church of the Redeemer (demolished), 1839–83

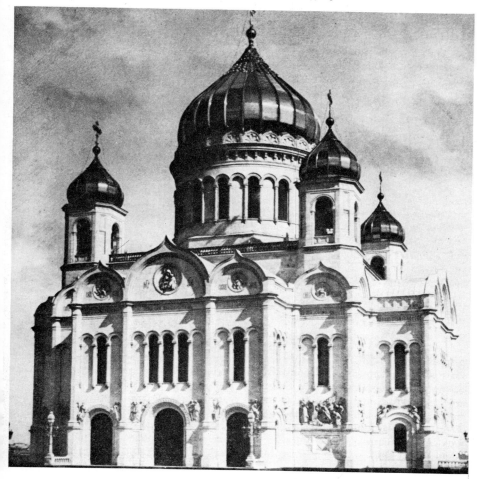

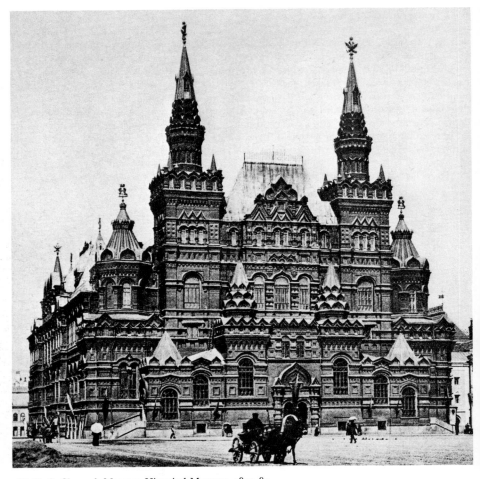

288. V. O. Shervud: Moscow, Historical Museum, 1874–83

(1839–83). Although this structure might seem at first to upset the canons we have established for the chronologically reverse recovery of the Russian past, a glance assures us that only the horizontal arcades in the manner of the twelfth-century churches of Suzdalia revealed any archaeological investigation; the elevational system was taken from Montferrand's St Isaac. This timid compromise between archaeology and the clarity of Petersburg classicism was as much as the age could accept, and Nicholas approved Ton's general plan for churches throughout the Empire.[14]

Such a solution did not long satisfy the energetic Slavophiles, nor could it resist serious archaeological criticism. A more acute appreciation of old Russian architecture was inaugurated in the reign of Alexander II with the construction of the Historical Museum (1874–83) [288] by an architect of English descent, Vladimir Osipovich Shervud (Sherwood). Here, no doubt, there was a certain justification for the revival of older national forms. The site lay beside the Kremlin walls and towers at the opposite end of Red Square from the Church of St Basil.[15] But Shervud's building obeyed more the letter than the spirit of sixteenth-century structures. Octagonal towers, tent roofs, kokoshniki, were piled one on top of the other, but without any understanding of the constant contrast of masses which had been the essential formal principle of old Russian architecture. Shervud's limitations can be seen in his symmetrical distribution of these elements on either side of a central axis. As a result the building is lifeless and flat. The same axial principles appeared in the design of the Trading Rows (Torgovye Ryadi, 1889–93, now GUM, the state retail stores), along the east side of the square, notable for the use of glass and iron in the interior galleries, by A. N. Pomerantsev (1848–98), and the Duma or City Hall (1890–2) partially filling the angle between the Trading Rows and the Historical Museum, and now the Central Lenin Museum, by D. N. Chichagov (1836–94).

In religious architecture the revival of sixteenth-century forms was exhibited in a more aggressive manner by the Church of the Ascension, or of the Saviour of the Blood (1883–1907), constructed in St Petersburg on the spot where Alexander II had been assassinated in 1881 [289]. The architect, Alfred A. Parland (1842–1920), arranged a cluster of nine gilded, tiled, and enamelled domes around a central tower in imitation of St Basil in Moscow, and filled the interior with lavish mosaic decorations. The brick and marble walls, reminiscent of Ostankino [149], and the bulbous domes breaking the horizontal skyline of St Petersburg, and so out of keeping with its classical serenity, composed an excep-

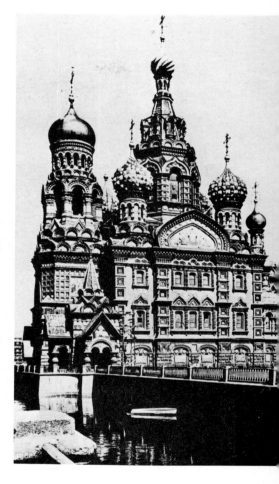

289. A. A. Parland:
St Petersburg, Church of the Ascension, 1883–1907

tionally conspicuous instance of Slavophilism.[16]

In domestic architecture an irresistible temptation was provided by the well-known model of the palace of Kolomenskoe [175]. In Moscow in the 1890s two large private houses – the Igumnov house (now the French Embassy) by N. I. Pozdeev and the private

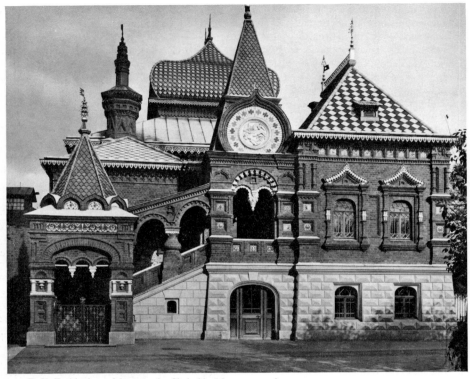

290. B. V. Freidenberg: Moscow, the Shchukin Museum, *c.* 1890

museum of P. I. Shchukin [290], designed by B. V. Freidenberg to house the owner's collection of old Russian decorative arts – were curious combinations of the rusticated foundations and canopied staircases of the Kremlin Palace with the elaborate wooden roof shapes of Kolomenskoe. This phase of the Slavic Revival, which had its pictorial counterpart in such historical scenes as Surikov's 'Boyarin Morosova' and Repin's 'Ivan IV', cannot be without some relation to the work of the historians of the period, especially I. E. Zabelin (1820–1909), whose monumental studies of Russian life in the Muscovite period provided a mine of information.[17] The revived wooden style, which had emerged in Moscow as early as the 1850s in the Pogodinsky house [291], a log izba with lace-like pierced panels around the eaves and windows, made a more elaborate appearance abroad in the Russian Pavilion at the Paris Exhibition of 1878 [292].[18]

Sculpture, too, knew its exponents of the realistic interpretation of Slavic themes. The sardonic crouched figure of 'Mephistopheles' (1882) by Mark Matveevich Antokolsky (1843–1902) may be his best-known work in the West, but Russian audiences admired 'Ivan IV' (1870), slumped on his throne remorsefully contemplating his crimes, or 'Peter the Great' (1872), boldly braving a gale.[19] Except for the subjects, nothing in Antokolsky's technique or interpretation was exceptionally

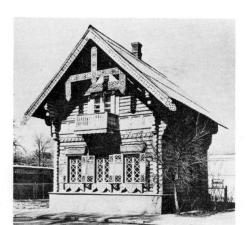

291. N. V. Nikitin:
Moscow, Pogodinsky house, 1850s

Russian. As with the work of so many of the ideological realists, the identification of their expressive content with the past and present history of Russia could not conceal their debt to European style and technique.

A second phase of the Slavic Revival can be identified with the programme of Pan-Slavism. This entailed lengthening the artistic and historical perspective to include the remote

292. The Russian Pavilion
at the Paris Exhibition of 1878

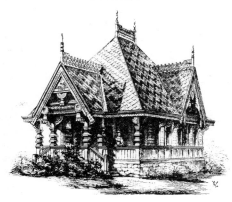

past of Kievan Russia, after the resources of Muscovy had been exploited. The most conspicuous monument of this period was the Cathedral of St Vladimir at Kiev, commenced in 1862 on the occasion of the millennial celebration of the Russian nation.[20] The foundations were defective, and a considerable lapse of time intervened before the present structure was completed (1876–82) from designs by A. V. Beretti, the municipal architect of Kiev.[21] The plan was a compromise between an aisled basilica and a central cross with two more cupolas over the western bays making seven in all. The interior decoration, planned by the medieval archaeologist A. V. Prakhov (1846–1916) and executed by Viktor Mikhailovich Vasnetsov (1848–1927), was an elaborate attempt to create a national orthodox religious art on the basis of Byzantine painting and mosaics.[22] Vasnetsov was of humble birth, the son of a country priest, and had studied in a seminary before entering the Petersburg Academy in 1868. There he absorbed the realistic methods of the 'purpose painters' which he utilized for genre-paintings in the manner of the Peredvizhniki. A short stay in Paris (1876–7) did little to change either his technique or his expression; his boulevard scenes are indistinguishable from those of his contemporaries.[23] When ideological realism declined in official favour, after the accession of Alexander III, he turned to history-painting, rejecting episodes from the political turmoil of the sixteenth and seventeenth centuries for scenes from the earlier 'heroic' history of Kievan Russia. His 'After Igor's Battle with the Polovtsy' (1880, State Tretyakov Gallery, Moscow) [293], where the field is strewn with corpses while vultures hover in the light of the rising moon, is an interesting contrast to Vereshchagin's battlefields of the same years inspired by the Russo-Turkish War. Where Vereshchagin's concern with actuality led to his aggressive pacifist statements, Vasnetsov's canvases evoked melancholy reveries of wars as remote as Charlemagne's.[24] Folk tales were another source of inspiration; his settings for

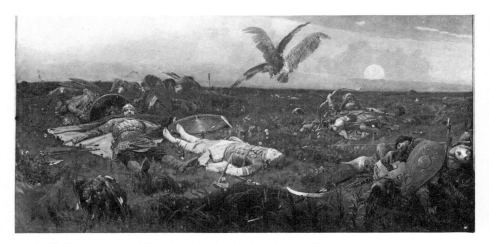

293. V. M. Vasnetsov: After Prince Igor's Battle with the Polovtsy, 1880.
Moscow, Tretyakov Gallery

Ostrovsky's drama *Snegurochka* ('Snow White') [294], produced by the wealthy Moscow art patron Savva Ivanovich Mamontov in his private theatre in 1885, were the most accurate evocations of the Russian past which the stage had yet seen.

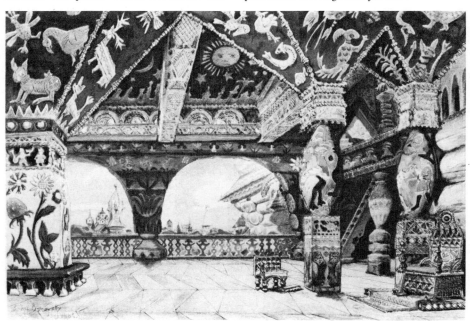

294. V. M. Vasnetsov: Setting for the third act of Ostrovsky's drama
Snegurochka, 1885. *Moscow, Tretyakov Gallery*

Through such work as this Vasnetsov's imagination was attuned to the programme for St Vladimir, and upon winning the competition he went to Italy and Sicily to study Byzantine painting at its source. His paintings in St Vladimir (1886–96) consist of fifteen large canvases, thirty single figures of saints, and numerous smaller portraits. His style is an uneasy combination of naturalism and symbolism, for although he appreciated the Byzantine two-dimensional treatment of the wall surface, he could not quite renounce the three-dimensional figural style he had learned in the Academy. In his larger compositions, such as the 'Baptism of St Vladimir' and the 'Conversion of the Kievans', he failed to subordinate his archaeological detail to spiritual abstraction. Even in the single figures of saints, where more of the two-dimensional effect of mosaic and icon-painting was present, the expressions of his figures are more mournful than majestic. Vasnetsov's younger brother, Apollinary (1856–1933), had first been a landscape-

painter, but in the 1880s he, too, began to investigate the Russian past. His scrupulous historical realism left no room for even the slight poetry which was present in his brother's work, but his reconstructions of medieval Russian life are at the least ingenious [295].

A more successful modern religious style was devised by Mikhail Vasilievich Nesterov (1862–1942). A deeply religious man, like Vasnetsov, he had learned a realistic technique under Perov in the Moscow Art School, and his first works were in the vein of sentimental realism. But by 1887 his 'Bride of Christ', a study of a young novice in a nunnery, called attention to his special talent when it was exhibited by the Peredvizhniki. Nesterov had an instinctive sympathy for the saints and hermits of medieval Russia, and more than any other religious painter of the age he knew the conditions of their life; for it was his custom to withdraw for long periods to the monasteries and hermitages in the remotest parts of Russia, even as far as the Solovetsky Monastery on

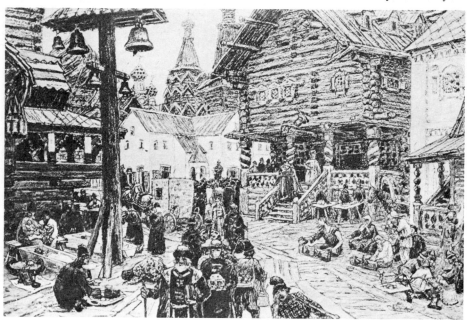

295. A. M. Vasnetsov: Old Moscow – the Crossroads on the way to Kitai-Gorod, 1902.
Moscow, Historical Museum

the White Sea.[25] In contrast to Vasnetsov's strained academism Nesterov's paintings were built of the simplest elements. His figures were placed singly or in a row in the foreground, and behind them stretched an idyllically placid Russian landscape, emphasized as a flat background plane [296]. The combination of simplified contours, flat patterns, and naturalistic detail recalls the murals of Puvis de Chavannes which he had seen in Páris, although his backgrounds were never so

from the new generation of the 90s. In Russia, as in France, the realist aesthetic fell into disrepute when it became apparent that as a social force it could not alleviate injustice and as an artistic programme it hardly ever led to the production of true works of art. Nesterov's design, like his taste, was unmistakably refined and – a parallel to the discoveries of Gauguin and the Symbolist painters after 1889 – led him to the conclusion that formal elements were as artistically important as the ends they

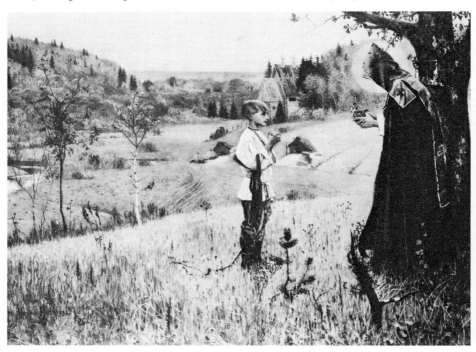

296. M. V. Nesterov: The Vision of St Bartholomew, 1889–90.
Moscow, Tretyakov Gallery

idealized. More than any other master of these years he succeeded, by his substitution of symbolic line and colour for historical fact, in creating a truly artistic interpretation of Russian pietism and medieval faith.

The contrast between the religious paintings of Nesterov and those of Ge shows the gulf which separated the realists of the 70s and 80s

served. Just as the Symbolists destroyed the aesthetic of Impressionism, so Nesterov was one of the principal agents to prepare the artistic movement known as Mir Iskusstva ('World of Art').

The transition from the mystical idealism of Nesterov's religious pictures to the evaluation of art as symbol was accomplished by

Mikhail Aleksandrovich Vrubel (1856–1911), a tragic yet typical exponent of the international Symbolist movement of the 1890s.[26] In a strange way his brief career seems symbolic of the impending doom of imperial Russia. It extended through the early part of the reign of Nicholas II and ended when in 1905, the year of the catastrophe of the Russo-Japanese War and the first fateful Revolution, Vrubel went mad. Yet from another point of view he also belonged to the international artistic generation of the *fin-de-siècle*, whose brilliant talents were so often allied with constitutional and psychological weaknesses, and whose artistic expression was permeated with a strange and melancholy sense of beauty. In his origin, too, Vrubel was an internationalist. To his mixed Polish and Danish ancestry he added a wide experience of Europe and of European art and literature. Before entering the Academy he had studied philosophy at the University of St Petersburg, and in 1876, and again in 1892 and 1894, he visited France and Italy. During his years at the Academy (1880–4) he subordinated academic proficiency to his interest in works of art which were then so esoteric as Greek vases and early Russian icons. His understanding of the artistic as well as archaeological significance of Russian art recommended him as a mural painter for the restoration of the ancient Church of St Cyril at Kiev. In preparation for this task he visited Venice, where he admired the brilliant colour of the mosaics of St Mark and of the Venetian painters. But his St Cyril frescoes show far more his profound sympathy for old Russian painting. Where Vasnetsov, who two years later won from Vrubel the competition for St Vladimir, only collected archaeological facts, Vrubel possessed an uncanny ability to imbue the old religious iconography with his own disturbing conceptions.

After his work in Kiev he settled in Moscow as one of a group of young artists patronized by Mamontov, for whom he designed mural paintings, an addition to Mamontov's house, and made drawings for sculpture and decorative objects to be manufactured at Mamontov's

art colony on his country estate of Abramtsevo.[27] In all his work intense personal expression took precedence over any non-aesthetic programme. Form, colour, line, texture, and subject-matter were not merely instruments for the communication of meaning, but were meaningful in themselves. In colour he explored the strange harmonies of Persian carpets and oriental glass in an effort to clear up the muddy mixture of local hues which so afflicted contemporary Russian painting. With Vrubel, for the first time in the history of Russian art, the spectator is aware of art created for an essentially aesthetic purpose, or to use the much misunderstood term, it is 'art for art's sake'.

In the many versions of his 'Demon', Vrubel not only expressed the crisis which was present in so much late-nineteenth-century art, its disgust with realism and the agonizing search to replace it with some truly artistic symbol, but he also made visible his tragic personal obsessions. He had treated the theme as early as 1890 as an exotic illustration to Lermontov's poem of a demon's love for a human being, but as time passed his vision changed, until his image of a Lucifer-like being, more than mortally beautiful, had become a half-female figure fallen to earth, the body contorted and crushed, its peacock-feather wings broken beneath it, and on its face an expression of unfathomable despair. The despair was Vrubel's, for during these years he was increasingly subject to the nervous attacks which culminated in his madness. The last five years of his life were spent in an asylum.

Vrubel's career has certain analogies with Van Gogh's. As was the case with the Dutch painter, to his constitutional nervous disorder was added the wracking difficulty of finding himself in an impossible situation between the old and the new. Contemporary taste was still shackled by conceptions of aesthetic meaning which demanded the externalization of experience at the price of sincerity, and the twentieth-century conviction that the aesthetic elements and their proper manipulation are what distinguish the work of art from any other form of expression had not yet been formulated. Unlike his French contemporaries, however, Vrubel was unable to find an entirely satisfying or successful technique for the expression of his ideas. The principles of Russian artistic life were too thoroughly saturated with the canons of academism, and Vrubel's work even at its best remained a decorative exercise on the meaning of colour and form rather than the creation of new colours and forms. The deeply personal and tragic spirit of Vrubel's art can be seen by comparing his unfinished water-colour of 'A Boyar' [297] with the historical paintings which can be related to the Slavophile programme. Where

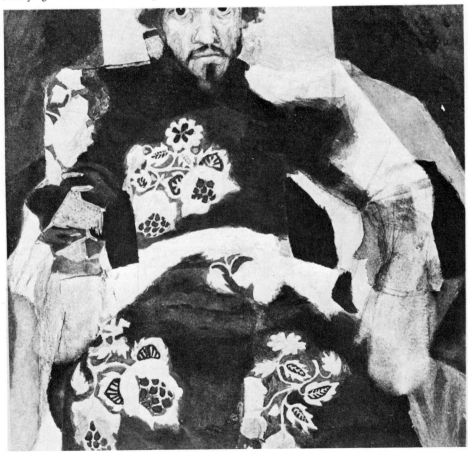

297. M. A. Vrubel: A Boyar, 1886. *Kiev, Museum of Russian Art*

Surikov or Apollinary Vasnetsov accumulated details like theatrical properties, Vrubel used a bold splash of colour in the costume to stress the tragic expression of the face. And though the abrupt margin at the top is a matter of accident, since the study was painted on the back of another composition, it serves to emphasize the expressive elements in the painting at the cost of the merely descriptive. In this respect Vrubel belongs to that group of masters who did so much, often with great pain and sacrifice, to create the conditions of much modern art, Munch in Norway, Klimt in Austria, Beardsley in England, Toorop in his early work in Holland, and Gauguin in France. How much Vrubel might have accomplished, had he lived longer to profit by the greatly expanded knowledge of European art which reached Russia after 1900, we can only conjecture, but the strange, unfinished decorative abstractions in his last portrait, of Valerian Briussov (1905) [298], suggest that in the discoveries of cubism he might have found formal satisfaction.

In cosmopolitan St Petersburg the search for modern expression led to a comparable revolution against academic traditions, but the forms which were discovered were very different from those favoured in Moscow. Once again Slavic Moscow and 'western' St Petersburg were artistically opposed, although the essential problems remained the same. And in spite of the authority of the Academy, the revolt, when it came, occurred outside its walls and showed no concern for its standards or traditions. Indeed, the new artistic expressions in St Petersburg were not primarily concerned with the major arts of painting, sculpture, or architecture, but were developed in theatre design, book illustration, and antiquarian research.[28]

In the early 1890s a group of university students interested in discussing art and music gradually formulated a programme and created the circumstances for a new direction in Russian art in the movement eventually known as Mir Iskusstva ('The World of Art', from the title of their principal publication). The educational and cultural advantages enjoyed by the members of this group, several of whom soon achieved an international reputation, were in contrast to those of the Moscow artists or of their predecessors among the Peredvizhniki. Some of them were only partly or not at all of

Russian blood, many of them belonged to the wealthier upper class; they had been educated at the University, and they travelled extensively abroad. Although their preferences were for French art and their greatest triumphs were to occur in Paris, it is well to remember that the leaders of the group – it is difficult to call it a movement – were not narrowly Francophile. It can be said of them more than of any comparable group of young artists of this period, that they had familiarized themselves with European culture as a whole. Situated geographically as they were on the eastern periphery of Europe, they saw its westernmost manifestations across the central European cultures. Consequently the flavour of their work is frequently eclectic, combining elements from various modern sources with reminiscences of the past, yet attaining an unmistakable quality of its own. Their style did not precipitate a final cleavage with the Peredvizhniki. When Serge Diaghilev (1872–1929) first began to collect pictures, he bought a quantity of sketches and drawings by Kramskoy; Alexander Benois (1870–1961) admired the work of Repin and Isaak Levitan (1861–1900), the painter of idyllic Russian landscapes. The first issues of *Mir Iskusstva* contained Repin's Memoirs and numerous illustrations of work by many of the painters who regularly exhibited with the 'Wanderers'. Benois, however, and his principal colleagues, Diaghilev, Léon Bakst (1868–1924), and V. A. Serov, realized that the artistic horizons of Russian cultural life had grown desperately restricted after so many years of social and political reaction. The museums of St Petersburg contained no examples of modern western art and exhibitions were few and inferior. In these circumstances it is all the more remarkable that these young men should have succeeded in familiarizing themselves with the most advanced currents in European art. In this they were assisted by the providential appearance in St Petersburg of a young French diplomatic official, Charles Birlé, who told them of Gauguin, Van Gogh, and Seurat, and

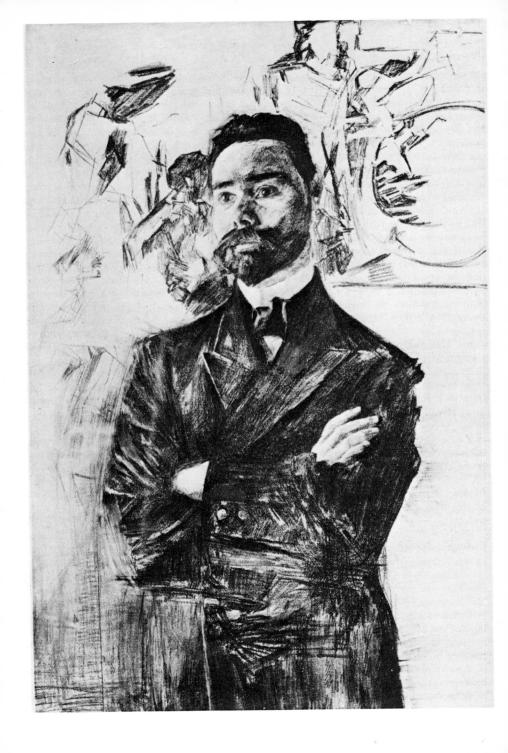

298 (*opposite*). M. A. Vrubel: Valerian Briussov (unfinished), 1905. *Moscow, Tretyakov Gallery*

helped them to read Baudelaire, Verlaine, and Mallarmé. Their enthusiasm for French culture became so great that by 1895 Bakst and Benois had settled in France, where they were frequently visited by Diaghilev and other friends from St Petersburg.

For Benois and Diaghilev French art and architecture were decisive factors. Their determination to awaken an appreciation for the former splendours of St Petersburg, a city they deeply loved, recalls the enthusiasm, a generation earlier, of the de Goncourts for the eighteenth century. Similarly their efforts were at first more antiquarian than creative. Nostalgia accounts for much of the charm in the scenes of eighteenth-century St Petersburg

their cultural resources.[30] In 1906 he arranged an exhibition of Russian art at the Salon d'Automne in Paris, the first occasion on which so many of the finest examples of Russian painting from the earliest times to the end of the nineteenth century were seen outside Russia.[31]

Meanwhile, in 1898, Diaghilev and his friends had founded the periodical *Mir Iskusstva*, which in its brief existence (1898–1904) became the organ for the most advanced artistic opinion in Russia. In its pages can be found a still exciting record of the enthusiasms of these young men. The early issues contained articles on Beardsley, the Pre-Raphaelites, and Whistler, and illustrations of works by Menzel, von Marées, and Böcklin whom they most admired. Before long these examples of weary realism and tarnished idealism were

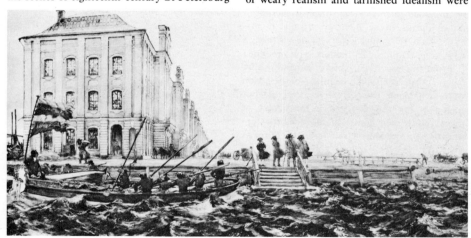

299. E. E. Lansere: St Petersburg in the Days of Peter the Great, 1906. *Leningrad, Russian Museum*

by Benois and by his nephew Eugène Lanceray (E. E. Lansere, 1875–1946) [299].[29] Diaghilev's enthusiasm for eighteenth-century painting led him to organize a huge exhibition of Russian portraiture, held in the Tauride Palace in 1905, which for the first time revealed to the Russian people the extent of

succeeded by accounts of important foreign exhibitions. French paintings began to appear in increasing quantity; works by Degas, Renoir, Gauguin, Vallotton. In architecture there were buildings by Olbrich and Mackintosh. They neglected little that was important or provocative in those years. This first of the important Russian art journals was soon followed by others. Benois, who had been absent in Paris when *Mir Iskusstva* was founded and who regretted not occupying a more prominent position among the editors, secured funds for a publication of his own, *Khudozhestvennyya sokrovishcha Rossii* (*Artistic Treasures of Russia*, 1901–7), a lavishly illustrated monthly composed of articles on public and private collections of Russian and European art, with special emphasis on aspects of St Petersburg and the imperial residences. This was followed by *Starye Gody* (*Past Years*, 1907–16), another monthly with a series of important articles on Russian art and on the work of European artists in Russia. When *Mir Iskusstva* ceased publication, its work was carried on by a comparable journal in Moscow, *Zolotoe Runo* (*The Golden Fleece*, 1906–9), and we may add to this extraordinary flowering of art publications the monthly *Apollon* (1909–17), which resembled *Starye Gody* although with more emphasis on modern developments.

From this record of editing and publishing one might think that the members of the group were dispersing their creative energies, but such was not the case. Since the talents of these young men consisted more in the formulation of a mood or tone in their approach to artistic problems than in the discovery of a new philosophy of art or the invention of a new technique, their greatest accomplishments appeared in the reorganization and renovation of an art which had grown shabby in recent years.[32] The enthusiasm of Benois and Diaghilev for the theatre, especially for the ballet, and their desire to rid the official productions of outworn conventions, and particularly to restore the tradition of pantomime combined with dance and to make the ballet once more an integrated whole, led to their experimenting with new ideas for librettos, music, and theatrical settings. The story of their relations with the imperial theatres is complicated, but in 1907 they scored a triumph with the performance of *Le Pavillon d'Armide* at the Mariinsky (now Kirov) Theatre in St Petersburg.

The book, stage-settings, and costumes were by Benois, the music by Nicholas Tcherepnin, and the choreography by Michel Fokine. Anna Pavlova was Armide, and the young Nijinsky danced the part of her slave. The following year Diaghilev presented Moussorgsky's *Boris Godunov* at the Paris Opéra.[33] The success of this brilliant production, with sets and costumes by Benois and the Moscow painter Alexandr Yakovlevich Golovin (1863–1930), persuaded him to arrange a season of ballet performances in Paris the following year.[34] The story of Diaghilev's *Ballets russes* is too well known to need recounting in detail, but it is worth observing that this first triumph of Russian art outside the boundaries of Russia

300. L. Bakst:
Costume study for the ballet *L'Oiseau de feu*, 1910

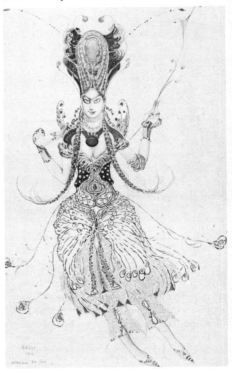

united certain elements of the Slavic Revival of Moscow with the ideals of the Mir Iskusstva group in St Petersburg. Among the productions of the first years, Benois's *Pavillon d'Armide* and *Sylphides*, evoking the atmosphere of eighteenth-century France and of the earlier nineteenth-century classical Russian ballet, demonstrated the nostalgic tendencies of Mir Iskusstva. In contrast, there were ballets where Russian themes, set to new or unfamiliar music, provoked the greatest enthusiasm and were thought to be more typical of modern Russian art.[35] Such were the *Polovtsian Dances* from Borodin's *Prince Igor*, with scenery by Nicholas Roerich (1909), Stravinsky's *L'Oiseau de feu*, with settings and costumes by Golovin and Bakst (1910) [300], and *Petrouchka*, with libretto, settings, and costumes by Benois (1911) [301]. In *Petrouchka* Benois recreated the atmosphere of carnival week in St Petersburg in the 1830s, remembered from his childhood only a few decades later. Bakst's designs for Debussy's *L'Après-midi d'un faune*, Ravel's *Daphnis et Chloë*, and Tcherepnin's *Narcisse* [302] recalled the earlier aestheticism of Mir Iskusstva, and especially his own predilection for classical themes; when he was a young man, one of his commissions had been the design of two classical tragedies for the theatre of the Hermitage.[36] But the more exclusively Russian elements reached a climax in the *Sacre*

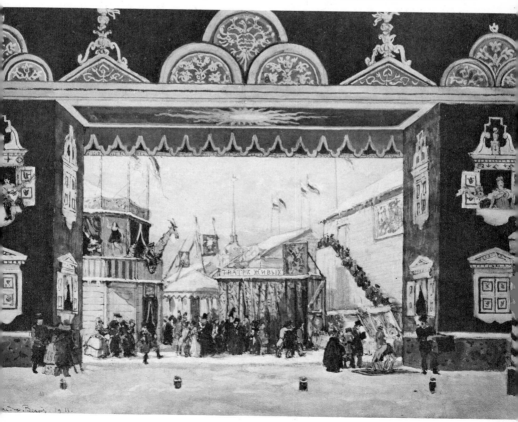

301. A. N. Benois: Design for the first act of the ballet *Petrouchka*, 1911. *Hartford, Conn., Wadsworth Atheneum*

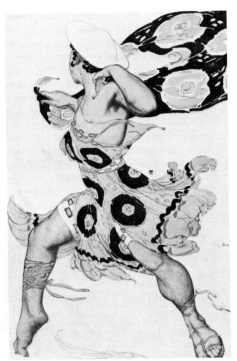

302. L. Bakst:
Costume study for the ballet *Narcisse*, 1911

du printemps (1913), with sets and costumes by Roerich. In this, the most complex and profound of all Stravinsky's ballets, a new chapter in the history of modern music was opened – paradoxically by a work described as 'Tableaux de la Russie païenne'.[37]

So far back into the past, to pagan Russia, the course of taste had reached. In this culmination of the Slavic Revival we encounter a number of artists from Moscow. Much of their work was done for the stage, and it is a sign of the times that the first production, and one of the most successful, by the Moscow Art Theatre (1898), was Count Alexey Tolstoy's tragedy on a sixteenth-century subject, *Tsar Feodor Ioannovich* (1868).[38] Although the

sets by V. A. Simov were not distinguished, the presence in the repertory of this and subsequent productions of Tolstoy's *Death of Ivan the Terrible* (1899) and Pushkin's *Boris Godunov* (1907) kept the old Russian scene in the famous naturalistic style of the Moscow Art Theatre continually before the eyes of the Moscow public.[39] Golovin and Nikolay Konstantinovich Roerich (1874–1947) represented what we may call the expressionist period of the Slavic Revival.[40] For his subject-matter Roerich, like Vasnetsov, frequently explored remote periods in Russian history, as in his *Idols* (1901–10), representing a group of idols in a sanctuary such as Ibn Fadlan had described in the tenth century. But he treated such scenes in broad areas of flat bright colour analogous to the work of the early Expressionist and Fauve painters in Germany and France. Golovin's interest in Old Russia led him to study mosaics and icons, from which he developed his intricately patterned stage designs. This Moscow style was also used by Natalya Goncharova in her sets and costumes for Rimsky-Korsakov's *Le Coq d'or* (1914), and in her designs for the 1926 revival of *L'Oiseau de feu*, where the backdrop for the last act was a colourful synthesis of architectural scenes in medieval icons.

Much of the work inspired by the theories of Mir Iskusstva recalls the contemporary manifestations of Art Nouveau, which was the most progressive artistic movement in Europe during the decade 1895 to 1905, but the more characteristic Russian examples should not be confused with them.[41] At times there is the same interest in restrained colour schemes and two-dimensional patterns, and even the same attenuation of plant forms and other natural motifs. But the essential character of early modern Russian art was different. The productions of St Petersburg were more Rococo, influenced by Benois's and Diaghilev's admiration for the period of Elizabeth's and Rastrelli's Tsarskoe Selo, while those of Moscow were affected by the desire to revive older

Russian traditions. In the Russian equivalent of the Arts and Crafts movement a connexion with certain aspects of the Art Nouveau episode can be found. Mamontov's colony at Abramtsevo was linked with the names of Vasnetsov and Vrubel, whose works were impregnated with Russian themes, although Vrubel in some of his designs, as for a series of jewelled combs, used natural forms in the manner of Art Nouveau. Closer to the ideals of the Moscow manner was Princess Tenisheva's self-supporting agricultural community at Talashkino, where instruction was offered not only in the popular crafts of the day, wood-carving, ceramics, weaving, and embroidery, but also in manuscript illumination and choral singing in an attempt to revive the ancient beauties of the Russian liturgical services.[42] Meanwhile a widespread movement to promote cottage industries and im-

303. M. V. Yakunchikova:
The Cemetery, coloured woodcut

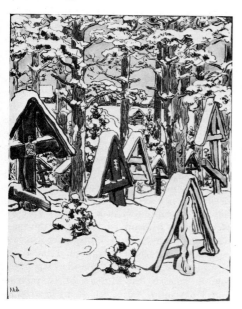

prove the standards of peasant arts and crafts, inaugurated by the zemstvo, the rural administrative body, enlisted the services of many prominent artists, among them Marya Vasilievna Yakunchikova (1870–1902), who produced a quantity of designs for textiles, embroideries, bookbindings, and the like. Pattern and line in her more independent productions, such as her coloured woodcuts [303], are thoroughly in the spirit of the Russian version of Art Nouveau.[43]

With the exception of Vrubel's rare terracotta and majolica compositions and K. A. Somov's witty figurines, the Mir Iskusstva movement included little that was notable in sculpture, although a curious example of pre-Christian iconography, expressed in terms of late-nineteenth-century Symbolist form and technique, is the six-foot wood and enamel figure of Stribog, an early Slavic divinity, by Sergei Timofeevich Konenkov (1874–1971) [304]. Konenkov's earlier work had been academically realistic; after 1917 he was to have a long and distinguished career as a Soviet sculptor working as a Socialist Realist. But for a few years before 1914, as his 'Stribog' indicates, he made a minor but significant contribution to the ideals of the Slavic Revival. At the end of the century Prince Pavel Petrovich Trubetskoy (1867–1938) achieved an international reputation with his contributions to the Paris Exposition of 1900 and the Mir Iskusstva exhibition in St Petersburg that year. Entirely self-taught, he had succumbed to the lure of Impressionist light and shade and sought in his small portraits the movement of Rodin, and something of the atmospheric effects achieved by the Italian sculptor Medardo Rosso [305]. His one large undertaking, the equestrian figure of Alexander III in St Petersburg, is a curious departure from his usual manner. While the composition is conceived more as an enlarged statuette than as a monumental design, the comparatively broad shapes indicate that Trubetskoy had studied the more narrowly national work of such men

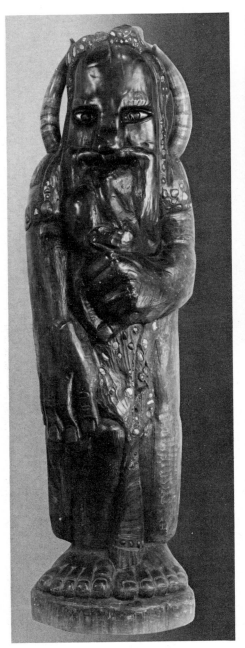

as Vasnetsov, with whose 'Bogatyri', depicting the warrior knights of Ancient Russia, the horse and rider have much in common.[44]

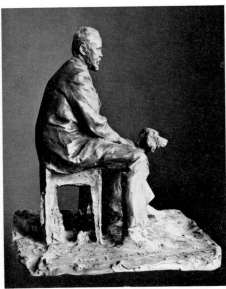

305. P. P. Trubetskoy: S. Yu. Vitte, 1901. Bronze. *Leningrad, Russian Museum*

In architecture, too, the counter-currents of the Slavic Revival and Mir Iskusstva curiously combined to create some of the most interesting, but still little-known work of the period. In St Petersburg, as we might expect, the earlier years of the century saw a revival of classicism, urged in large part by the activities of Mir Iskusstva, especially for banks and Government structures. At times the mass and detail were so resolutely derivative that it is difficult to realize that such buildings were so recent.[45] To Moscow we may trace the tendency to revive the forms of the older Russian past. This could have been seen at the Paris Exposition of 1900, where the Russian pavilion, designed by the Moscow artists Golovin and Konstantin Alexeevich Korovin (1861–1939), was a poetic yet accurate re-creation of

304. S. T. Konenkov: Stribog, before 1914. *Moscow, Tretyakov Gallery*

Russian wooden architecture.[46] A similar village, of great charm but little architectural novelty, was erected in Yaroslavl on the occasion of the tercentenary celebration of the Romanov dynasty. Masonry forms were also revived, often with startling fidelity. The Church of Our Saviour on the Waters (1910) in St Petersburg, commemorating the 12,000 sailors who perished in the Russo-Japanese War, was a replica of St Dmitry in Vladimir with the addition of Andrey Bogoliubsky's palace tower as a belfry. At Leipzig a memorial church commemorating the centenary of the allied victory over Napoleon closely followed the Ascension at Kolomenskoe (1913). Such scholarly inventions, like those elsewhere in the West, remained architectural curiosities without promise for the future.[47]

More interesting and potentially more influential were the attempts to rework old traditions in the spirit of a new age. At Abramtsevo and Talashkino there were churches in which older Russian forms were freely used to create an effect at once religious and new.[48]

Such religious architecture occasionally required decorative schemes of considerable character. Although in a memorial church at Abbas Tuman in the Caucasus Nesterov followed closely the style of medieval Caucasian frescoes, he was impelled to do so by the design of the church, which was an obvious imitation of medieval Armenian architecture. On the other hand, at Talashkino and Schlüsselburg, Roerich created murals and mosaics powerful in scale and bold in colour.[49] A further impetus towards such design was given in 1905 with the removal of restrictions against public worship for the Old Believers, who had suffered civil and religious disabilities from the middle of the seventeenth century. It was certainly not their intention to return to the Orthodox forms of the State religion, and for this reason their architects attempted to suggest in their churches not only the Orthodox character of the Old Believers' faith and its relation to Byzantine and Russian history, but also their long exile in the north. Thus an

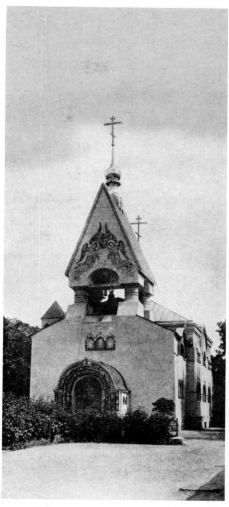

306. I. E. Bondarenko:
Moscow, Old Believers' Church, 1909

Old Believers' church in Moscow by I. E. Bondarenko (1909) [306] contains elements reminiscent of wooden architecture. The exaggerated proportional relations also are a sophisticated comment on older Russian forms.

More romantic still, and certainly less successful as a solution to the problem of adapting older Russian forms to modern uses, were certain structures where pictorial effects took precedence over the expression of function. Such are the design of the Tretyakov Art Gallery by Viktor Vasnetsov (1900–2) [307], based wards through the centuries as far as the sixteenth-century Tartar Syumbeky Tower in Kazan, perhaps to remind travellers of their destination. Only a few years later Shchusev, by then a prominent Soviet architect, designed the impressive granite tomb on Red Square for Lenin who had died in 1924.

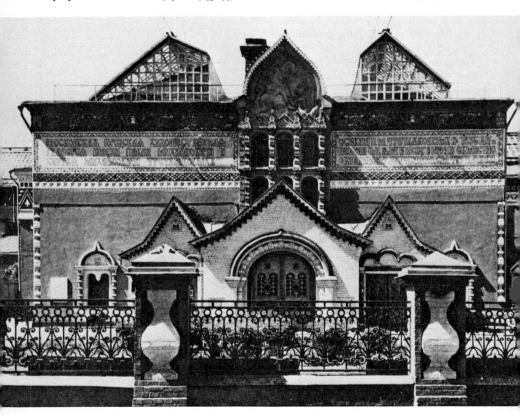

307. V. M. Vasnetsov: Moscow, Tretyakov Art Gallery, 1900–2

on his study of medieval manuscript illuminations, and the Kazan Station in Moscow (1913–26) [308] by Alexei Viktorovich Shchusev (1873–1949). The first is a painter's decorative reverie, the other a conglomeration of seven architectural souvenirs looking back- During the first two decades of the twentieth century Russia also looked westward, to Berlin, Brussels, Paris, and other capitals of Jugendstil and Art Nouveau. This style has been considered less successful in architecture than in the decorative arts and interior design.

But there is no denying that between 1890 and 1910 Horta, Guimard, Mackintosh, Frank Lloyd Wright, and others created significant structures, outside as well as within, which are among the basic monuments of twentieth-century culture. To their names should be added that of an architect little known in

materials and textures, the unexpected shapes of the curved openings, and the designs of the metal grilles on the windows and fence, as well as the floral mosaics, place this building in the mainstream of European modernism. On the other hand the proportional relationships of mass to plane, as in the heavy stone entrance

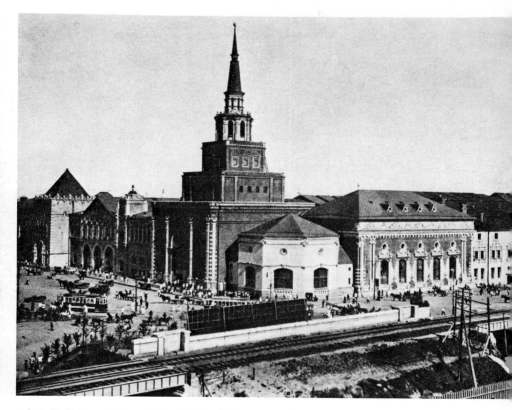

308. A. V. Shchusev: Moscow, Kazan Railway Station, 1913–26

western Europe, Feodor Osipovich Shekhtel (1859–1926). The quality of his talent can be seen in his house in Moscow for S. P. Rya-bushinsky, the early collector of icons, of 1900–2 (now the Gorky Museum) [309]. Such Western European elements as the contrast of

or the curved marble balustrade in the stair hall [310], are more powerful and therefore probably more Russian; but the assertive horizontality of the roof and the proportion of the frieze to the wall below recall Wright's exactly contemporary houses in Illinois.[50]

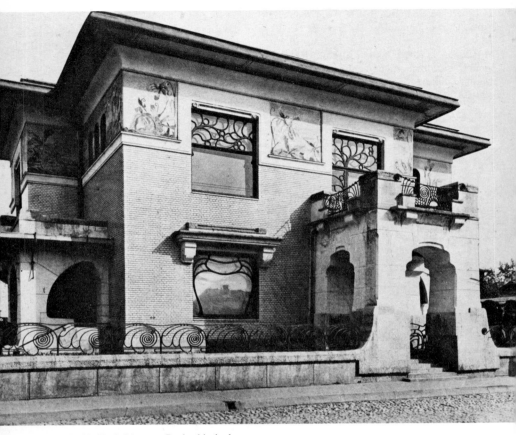

309. F. O. Shekhtel: Moscow, Ryabushinsky house, 1900–2

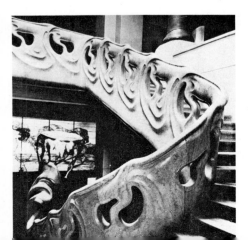

310. F. O. Shekhtel:
Moscow, Ryabushinsky house, 1900–2, staircase

Also in Moscow where most of his work was done, Shekhtel's Yaroslavl Station (1902–4) [311] includes, like Shchusev's building, reminiscences of the past as in the steepled tower at the left. But there is more originality in the free disposition of the parts and an imaginative fantasy in the over-sized entrance with its unexpected peaked and crested roof (compare illustrations 175 and 177 and illustration 292). The low relief decoration is

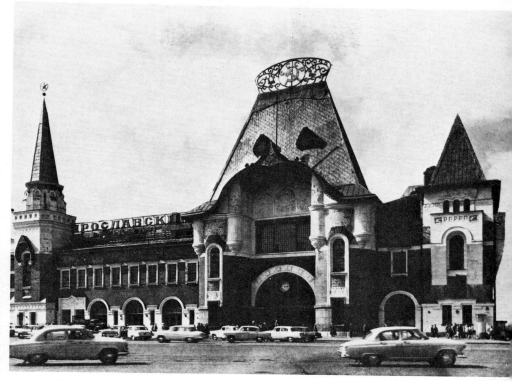

311. F. O. Shekhtel: Moscow, Yaroslavl Railway Station, 1902–4

composed of majolica tiles made from Shekhtel's designs by members of Mamontov's colony at Abramtsevo (page 399). Fantastic as the façades of both stations are, behind them extend eminently functional systems of waiting rooms and tracks.

A few years later Shekhtel created a truly twentieth-century building for the Utro Rossii (Russian Morning) Printing House (1907) [312]. Here he left tradition behind to handle glazed brick, metal, and glass without prejudice from the past. The directness and clarity of its utilitarian purpose is stated with an elegance – the rounded corners, for instance – as exact as, and perhaps even more styleless than, Peter Behrens' AEG Turbine Factory in Berlin (1909–10), so long the paradigm for modern industrial architecture.

That the future held the promise of Russia's increasing participation with western Europe in the formulation of modern art as we have come to know it and in the development of a particularly Russian revision of that art, there can be no doubt. In Moscow itself the promise of that future could be seen. The outstanding examples of contemporary European painting,

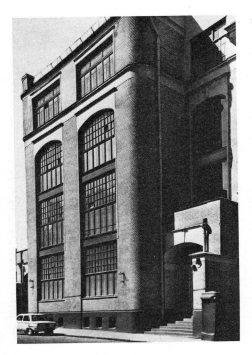

312. F. O. Shekhtel:
Moscow, Utro Rossii Printing House, 1907

collected by S. I. Shchukin and I. A. Morozov, had already inspired members of the younger generation.[51] Meanwhile the Russian artists stood at an important turning point. They might, like D. S. Stelletsky (187–1944) [313], attempt to adapt progressive techniques to older formal and iconographical programmes.[52] This was much like the position taken by Simon Ushakov in 1650, but, just as in the seventeenth century, it led all too easily to mannerisms. Even Vasily Kandinsky (1866–1944), after he had been living in western Europe for almost ten years, was still trying to evoke the Russian past, and his own memories of the gilded domes of Moscow flaming in the sunset, in such a painting as the 'Russian Woman in a Landscape' [314], where an imaginative evocation of Old Russia is executed with the squared, mosaic-like brushstrokes of late Neo-Impressionism. On the other hand the younger generation after 1900, and this was soon to include Kandinsky himself, might seek, like their eighteenth-century predecessors, for the springs of modern experience in the European centres of artistic research. This was the path chosen by Kandinsky, Gabo and Pevsner, Chagall, and their many colleagues who were at school in Europe between 1900 and the outbreak of the War.[53] After the brief but important triumph of the Constructivists in 1917–20, most of these distinguished artists went into exile. Their magnificent talents are indisputable proof of the continuity of Russia's artistic heritage in the twentieth century.

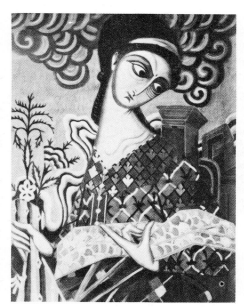

313. D. S. Stelletsky: Dawn, 1910

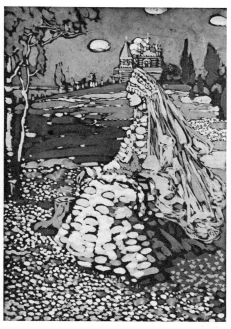

314. Vasily Kandinsky:
Russian Woman in a Landscape, *c.* 1905.
Munich, Städtische Galerie

ABBREVIATIONS

Ainalov, *Grossfürsten.*	D. V. Ainalov, *Geschichte der russischen Monumentalkunst zur Zeit des Grossfürstentums Moskau* (Berlin and Leipzig, 1933)
Ainalov, *Vormoskov.*	D. V. Ainalov, *Geschichte der russischen Monumentalkunst der vormoskovitischen Zeit* (Berlin and Leipzig, 1932)
Alpatov-Brunov	M. Alpatov and N. Brunov, *Geschichte der altrussischen Kunst* (Augsburg, 1932)
AN	*Akademiya Nauk* (Academy of Sciences)
Antonova and Mneva	V. I. Antonova and N. E. Mneva, *Katalog drevnerusskoi zhivopisi, XI-nachala XVIII V. V.* (Gosudarstvennaya Tretyakovskaya Gallereya, Moscow, 1963), 2 vols.
Aplaksin	A. P. Aplaksin, *Kazanskii Sobor* (St Petersburg, 1911)
Benois	A. Benois, *Russkaya shkola zhivopisi* (St Petersburg, 1904), 10 parts
Bobrinskoi	A. A. Bobrinskoi, *Reznoi Kamen v Rossii, Sobory Vladimiro-Suzdalskoi Oblasti, XII–XIII vv.* (Moscow, 1916)
Bondarenko	I. E. Bondarenko, *Arkhitekturnye pamyatniki Moskvy* (Moscow, 1904–5), 3 parts
Buxton	D. R. Buxton, *Russian Mediaeval Architecture* (Cambridge, 1934)
CSRW	Central State Restoration Workshops, Moscow
Demidov	A. de Demidov, *Album du voyage pittoresque et archéologique en Russie* (Paris, 184?)
Diaghilev	S. P. Diaghilev, *Russkaya zhivopis v XVIII Veke, D. G. Levitskii* (St Petersburg, 1902)
Drevnosti, trudy kom.	Moskovskoe Arkheologicheskoe Obshchestvo, *Drevnosti, trudy kommissii po sokhraneniiu drevnykh pamyatnikov,* I–VI (1907–15)
Grabar	I. Grabar, *Istoriya russkago iskusstva* (Moscow, from 1909), 6 vols.
Istor. panor.	A. I. Uspenskii, *et al.*, *Istoricheskaya panorama Sanktpeterburga i ego okrestnostei* (Moscow, 1911–14), 10 vols.
Istoriya-Geschichte	I. E. Grabar, V. N. Lazarev, and V. S. Kemenov, eds., *Istoriya russkogo iskusstva* (Moscow, 1953–68), 13 vols. in 16; the first six vols. in German translation as *Geschichte der russischen Kunst* (Dresden, 1957–76)
Khudozh. sokrov.	*Khudozhestvennyya sokrovishcha Rossii* (1901–7)
Kondakov	N. P. Kondakov, *Russkaya ikona* (Prague, 1928–33), 4 vols.
L'Art byzantin chez les slaves	G. Millet, ed., *L'Art byzantin chez les slaves* (Paris, 1930–2), 2 vols.
Lazarev	V. Lazarev, *Old Russian Murals and Mosaics from the XI to the XVI Centuries* (London, 1966)
Lukomski	G. Lukomski, *L'Architecture religieuse en Russie du XIe au XVIIIe siècle* (Paris, 1929)
MAO	Moskovskoe Arkheologicheskoe Obshchestvo
Meyerberg	F. Adelung, *Sammlung von Ansichten, Gebräuchen, Bildnissen, Trachten, u.s.w. welche . . . Augustin Freyherr von Meyerberg auf seinem Aufenthalt in Russland in den Jahren 1661 und 1662 hat entwerfen lassen* (St Petersburg, 1827)
MMA	Metropolitan Museum of Art, New York
Moskva	*Moskva v eya proshlom i nastoyashchem* (Moscow, 1910–?), 12 vols.
Moskva; sobory	*Moskva; sobory, monastyri, i tserkvi* (Moscow, 1882–3), 4 vols.
Myasoedov	V. Myasoedov, *Freski Spasa Nereditsy* (Leningrad, 1925); French ed. (Paris, 1928)
Naidenov	N. A. Naidenov, *Moskvy, snimki s vidov mestnosti* (Moscow, 1886)
Nekrasov, *Ocherki*	A. I. Nekrasov, *Ocherki po istorii drevnerusskogo zodchestva, XI–XVII veka* (Moscow, 1936)
Nicholas	Grand Duke Nicholas Mikhailovich, ed., *Russkie portrety XVIII i XIX stoletii* (St Petersburg, 1905–9), 6 vols.
Olearius	A. Olearius, *The Voyages and Travels of the Ambassador from the Duke of Holstein to the Great Duke of Muscovy, and the King of Persia . . . Rendered into English* (London, 1662)

Prokhorov   V. Prokhorov, *Pamyatniki drevne russkago iskusstva* (Moscow, 1873)
Rzyanin   M. I. Rzyanin, *Pamyatniki russkogo zodchestva* (Moscow, 1950)
Schweinfurth   P. Schweinfurth, *Geschichte der russischen Malerei im Mittelalter* (The Hague, 1930)
SCR   The Society for Cultural Relations with the U.S.S.R. (London)
Sem. Kond.   Seminarium Kondakovianum, Prague
Suslov   V. V. Suslov, *Pamyatniki drevnyago russkago zodchestva* (St Petersburg, 1895–1901), 7 parts
Thieme-Becker   U. Thieme and F. Becker, *Allgemeines Lexikon der bildenden Künstler* (Leipzig, 1907–47), 36 vols.
Travels of Macarius F. C. Belfour, tr., *The Travels of Macarius, Patriarch of Antioch; Written by his Attendant Archdeacon Paul of Aleppo, in Arabic* (London, 1829), 2 vols.
Voronin   N. N. Voronin, *Pamyatniki Vladimiro-Suzdalskogo zodchestva XI–XIII vekov* (Moscow, 1945)
Zabello   S. Ya. Zabello, *et al., Russkoe derevyannoe zodchestvo* (Moscow, 1942)

NOTES

CHAPTER I

15. 1. For the early history of Russia and of the Slavic people see G. Vernadsky, *Ancient Russia* (New Haven, 1943), and *Kievan Russia* (New Haven, 1948), *passim*. Some of Vernadsky's conclusions, as well as the interpretation of the *Primary Chronicle* (see below, Note 3), have been questioned by N. V. Riasanovsky, who has reviewed the conclusions of recent Soviet scholarship in his *A History of Russia* (New York, 1963), *passim*.

2. M. I. Rostovtsev, *Iranians and Greeks in South Russia* (Oxford, 1922).

16. 3. Under the presumptive date of 860–2 the *Russian Primary Chronicle* recorded the event. For the vexed question of the identity of the Varangians see G. Vernadsky, *Kievan Russia*, chapters vii–viii. Hereafter the texts of the chronicles will be cited for the appropriate year in the complete collection published by the Academy of Sciences (AN, Leningrad, 1843–1929), as *Polnoe sobranie russkikh letopisei* (PSRL), and in the English translations of the Laurentian Chronicle for the years 852–1116 by S. H. Cross as *The Russian Primary Chronicle* (Cambridge, Mass., 1930); and the First Novgorod Chronicle for the years 1016–1471 by R. Michell and N. Forbes, as *The Chronicle of Novgorod*, Royal Historical Society Camden Third Series, xxv (London, 1914). For a concise history of the various texts see N. de Baumgarten, 'Chronologie ecclésiastiquę des terres russes du Xᵉ au XIIIᵉ siècle', *Orientalia Christiana*, XVII (Rome, 1930), 17–21.

The important *Primary Chronicle* was not composed until the early twelfth century; hence the account of the earliest events in Russian history, especially the dynastic descent from the legendary Rurik, may be a later embellishment to support the pretensions of the Kievan princes. But even if the events recorded in the following paragraphs in this text may be partly mythical, they may also, like much myth, embody aspects of actual historical experience. For a recent interpretation of the political implications of the chronicle texts, see A. Poppe, 'The Political Background to the Baptism of Rus', *Dumbarton Oaks Papers*, XXX (1976), 195–245.

20. 4. For the dynastic genealogies of the descendants of Rurik see N. de Baumgarten, 'Généalogies et mariages occidentaux des Rurikides russes du Xᵉ au XIIIᵉ siècle', *Orientalia Christiana*, IX (1927); S. H. Cross, 'Medieval Russian Contacts with the West', *Speculum*, X (1935), 137–44. Riasanovsky has a useful genealogical table of Russian rulers from Rurik to Nicholas II (*op. cit.*, 644–7).

CHAPTER 2

21. 1. For the most searching documentary and archaeological analysis in English of the early Kievan churches, see S. H. Cross, H. V. Morgilevski, and K. J. Conant, 'The Earliest Mediaeval Churches of Kiev', *Speculum*, XI (1936), 477–99. The most important Russian monumental inventory is E. E. Golubinskii, *Istoriya russkoi tserkvi*, 2nd edition (Moscow, 1901–4), I, part 2, 1–161. For a summary incorporating the results of later Soviet archaeological excavations, see N. N. Voronin, *Istoriya*, I, 111–54: *Geschichte*, I, 67–94. See also A. L. Mongait, *Archaeology in the U.S.S.R.* (Harmondsworth, 1961; first published in Russian in 1955).

22. 2. In Russian usage a cathedral, sobor, was not necessarily the seat of a bishop but might be a more important or venerable church, tserkov. See A. Grabar, 'Cathédrales multiples et groupement d'églises en Russie', *Revue des études slaves*, XX (1942), 91–120.

3. These and remains of later Christian burials have been published by M. K. Karger in his 'Knyazheskoe pogrebenie xiv v. Desyatinnoi tserkvi', AN, Institut istorii materialnoi kultury, *Kratkie soobshcheniya*, V (1940), 1219.

4. See K. J. Conant, 'Novgorod, Constantinople, and Kiev in Old Russian Church Architecture', *Slavonic and East European Review*, XXII (1944), no. 59, for the plan of St Irene, 87, and for a conjectural restoration of the Desyatinnaya, 79.

23. 5. The curious construction of the foundations, laid upon a bed of cement placed over crossed timbers which would quickly decay and produce uneven settling, suggests that the workmen were local artisans more familiar with wood than with masonry construction. See Cross, Morgilevski, and Conant, *op. cit.*, 484, 488.

6. S. H. Cross, *The Russian Primary Chronicle*, for 1037. For an estimate of Yaroslav's reign, see S. H. Cross, 'Yaroslav the Wise in Norse Tradition', *Speculum*, IV (1929), 177–97; N. K. Chadwick, *The Beginnings of Russian History, an Enquiry into Sources* (Cambridge, 1946).

7. The extensive literature on St Sophia may be approached through the papers by Cross and Conant, and the bibliographies in D. Ainalov, *Geschichte der russischen Monumentalkunst der vormoskovitischen Zeit* (Berlin and Leipzig, 1932); and M. Alpatov and N. Brunov, *Geschichte der altrussischen Kunst* (Augsburg, 1932). See also G. G. Pavlutskii, 'Kievskie khramy domongolskago perioda', Moskovskoe Arkheologischeskoe Obshchestvo, *Trudy*, XIV S'ezd (Chernigov, 1908), II (1911), 29–36; N. Brunov, 'L'Église à croix à cinq nefs dans l'architecture byzantine', *Échos d'Orient*, XXVI (1927), 257–86. See also N. N. Voronin, *Istoriya*, I, 111–154; *Geschichte*, I, 67–94.

24. 8. Some leeway may be allowed the earlier dates in the chronicles. See Cross, *The Russian Primary Chronicle*, 109–15.

9. S. H. Cross, 'The Earliest Mediaeval Churches of Kiev', 491.

25. 10. For Professor Conant's conjectural restorations of St Sophia, see Cross, Morgilevski, and Conant, *op. cit.*, plates 2–7 (including our illustration 3); a model partly based on such drawings, and now exhibited in the church, is reproduced, *Istoriya*, I, 132; *Geschichte*, I, 82; W. F. Volbach and J. Lafontaine-Dosogne, *Byzanz und der christliche Osten* (Berlin, Propyläen Kunstgeschichte, III, 1968), plate 278.

11. Less expensive brick and mortar construction took the place of *opus mixtum* in the later eleventh century, in such buildings as the Golden Gate, St Irene, and the early-twelfth-century Church of the Redeemer at Berestovo. For views of the ruins of the first two in 1848, see the paintings by M. M. Sajin, reproduced by A. Simsen-Sytchevsky, 'Un Peintre de la ville de Kiev', M. Hrushevskii, ed., *Recueils d'histoire, d'archéologie, des mœurs, et des arts de Kiev*, I (1930), 364–76 (in Ukrainian).

27. 12. K. J. Conant in 'Novgorod, Constantinople, and Kiev in Old Russian Church Architecture', *op. cit.*, 79, has published a conjectural restoration of the wooden St Sophia with octagon and tent roof, but the possibility of a Caucasian origin for such forms at this date is problematical.

13. For the Nea Ekklesia and Fenari-Isa, see R. Krautheimer, *Early Christian and Byzantine Architecture*, 3rd ed. (Harmondsworth, 1979), *passim*.

28. 14. For plans of these churches see J. Strzygowski, *Die Baukunst der Armenier und Europa*, II (Vienna, 1918), 839, 848. N. Brunov has pointed out that Mokvi was not painted until 1089–1118 and may have been built only shortly before. His conclusions temper Strzygowski's enthusiasm for an Armenian origin for Kievan architecture: 'La croix inscrite à

cinq nefs est originaire de Constantinople. Salonique, Mayafarquin, Mokvi, la Russie, ont imposé à ce type constantinopolitain des modifications plus ou moins profondes sous l'influence du style local', *Échos d'Orient*, *op. cit.*, 286.

30. 15. *Sbornik materialov dlya istoricheskoi topografii Kieva* (Kiev, 1874), II, 23; Grabar, I, 148, n. 3.

31. 16. Abraham van Westerveldt (d. 1692) accompanied Prince Janusz Radziwill as military draughtsman in the campaign of 1650–1 against the Cossacks of the Ukraine. His drawings were first published as views of unidentified structures by Y. I. Smirnov, 'Risunki Kieva 1651 goda po kopiyam ikh kontsa XVIII veka', MAO, *Trudy*, XIII S'ezd (Yekaterinoslav, 1905), Moscow, 1908, 197–512 (with excellent reproductions). Certain drawings were identified as representations of St Sophia by I. (H.) V. Morgilevskii, 'La Ste Sophie de Kiev, recherches nouvelles', in M. Hrushevskii, ed., *Kiev et ses environs, histoire et monuments* (Kiev, 1926), 81–108 (in Ukrainian). Archdeacon Paul of Aleppo visited St Sophia between 24 June and 10 July 1654. His description of the interior as it appeared in the mid seventeenth century is the more interesting in that he had seen Hagia Sophia in Constantinople the previous November. See *Travels of Macarius*, I, 225, 230.

17. To this group may be added the rebuilt Cathedral of St Sophia (1044–66) in Polotsk. It had five aisles, the outer ones ending in straight walls as in St Sophia in Novgorod. The duplication of the three apses on the western façade may be due to German Romanesque influence in western (White) Russia. The technique of unstuccoed brick without admixture of stone speaks for the Kievan source of the builders. The church has been analysed by N. Brunov in Alpatov-Brunov, 49–50. See also Ainalov, *Vormoskov.*, 67–8, and A. I. Nekrasov, *Ocherki po istorii drevnerusskogo zodchestva* (Moscow, 1936), 36–8.

32. 18. *The Russian Primary Chronicle*, A.D. 1034–6.

19. R. Krautheimer, *op. cit.*, 299–301.

34. 20. Lavra, from the Greek *laure*, a passage, alley, avenue, or street, later a group of shops along a street, hence a bazaar. In ecclesiastical usage a lavra came to mean a series of hermitages around a monastery, and by association an important monastic foundation. Of the more than a thousand Russian monasteries (and convents) active before 1917, only four had the rank of lavra: the Kievan Pecherskaya, the Trinity-St Sergius near Moscow, the Alexander Nevsky in St Petersburg, and the Pochaevskaya in western Russia.

21. For the interior and exterior walls at Berestovo

after the removal in 1919 of later stucco, see *Istoriya*, I, 143, 145; *Geschichte*, I, 88–9.

22. Reproduced respectively in Nekrasov, *Ocherki*, figures 19–22; Grabar, I, 153.

23. *The Russian Primary Chronicle*, A.D. 945. N. K. Chadwick has analysed the documentary evidence in *The Beginnings of Russian History*, 81–2. For plans and illustrations of objects found in the excavations of the palace area see I. A. Khoinonskii, *Raskopki veliko-knyazheskago drevnago grada Kieva* (Kiev, 1893).

35. 24. The Latin description of Kiev as an exceptionally large and well-fortified city with almost 400 churches and eight markets, composed by Dietmar, or Thietmar (975–1018), Bishop of Merseburg and German historian, will be found in the *Monumenta Germaniae Historica*, III, 871.

CHAPTER 3

36. 1. G. Vernadsky, *Kievan Russia*, 121.

37. 2. V. N. Lazarev, *Iskusstvo Novgoroda* (Moscow, 1947), is a useful history of Novgorod art and architecture, with extensive bibliographies.

38. 3. A convenient summary of ecclesiastical extracts from the chronicles, including those relating to church building before the Tartar conquest, is provided by N. de Baumgarten's 'Chronologie ecclésiastique des terres russes du Xᵉ au XIIIᵉ siècle', *Orientalia Christiana*, XVII (1930). Among the private citizens who built churches were Irozhnet (1135), Sedko Sitinits (1167), Mikhail Stepanits and Moisei Domanezhits (1176), Radko and his brother (1183), and the Volodarevitsy and Noseovitsy families (1207). Sedko Sitinits may have been the historical personage whose activity gave rise to the legend of Sadko, the merchant of Novgorod.

4. *The Chronicle of Novgorod*, 1179.

39. 5. *The Chronicle of Novgorod*, 1015–16.

6. K. J. Conant, 'Novgorod, Constantinople, and Kiev in Old Russian Church Architecture', *Slavonic and East European Review*, XXII (1944), no. 59, 75–92, for a conjectural reconstruction of the wooden St Sophia.

7. See the bibliographies in Ainalov, *Vormoskov.*, and Alpatov-Brunov. In 1893 St Sophia was restored under the direction of V. V. Suslov. His report is described in 'Pervonachalnyi vid Sofii Novgorodskoi', MAO, *Trudy*, XI S'ezd (Kiev, 1899), II (Moscow), 82. See also Archbishop Arsenii, 'Nastoyashchee sostoyanie Sofiiskago sobora v Novgorode', MAO, *Trudy*, XV S'ezd (Novgorod, 1911), I (Moscow, 1914), 283–92. Suslov's work has been criticized by N. Brunov and N. Travin in their report of a thorough examination of the fabric in

1945, 'Sobor Sofii v Novgorode', *Soobshcheniya instituta i teorii arkhitektury* (Moscow, 1947), no. 7. They contend that Suslov concealed the picturesque quality of the building under too uniform a coat of plaster. In removing the subsidiary additions, however, Suslov disclosed for the first time the monumental mass of St Sophia. During the Second World War the upper part suffered considerable damage when the roof and cupolas burned, destroying the frescoes on the vaults within. For photographs of the damage, see V. Lazarev, *op. cit.*, and I. Grabar, ed., *Pamyatniki iskusstva razrushennye nemetskimi zakhvatchikami v SSSR* (Moscow, 1948).

40. 8. Brunov and Travin, *op. cit.*, 16, believe that towers originally rose at the eastern corners. Presumably they were a defensive measure, to protect the princely and episcopal edifice from the townspeople.

42. 9. For cross-sections of the cathedral see Imperatorskaya Arkheologicheskaya Kommissiya, *Materialy po arkheologii Rossii*, XXI (St Petersburg, 1897), 12, 17.

10. The origin of the bulbous dome and the means of its transmission to Russia must remain uncertain, but it seems probable that suggestions from oriental architecture, reaching Russia through innumerable contacts with the East, deserve equal consideration with the undeniable virtuosity of Russian carpenters. See the documented articles by A. P. Novitskii, 'Lukovichnaya forma russkikh tserkovnykh glav', MAO, *Drevnosti, Trudy kommissii po sokhraneniiu drevnikh pamyatnikov*, III (1909), 349–62; W. Born, 'The Origin and Distribution of the Bulbous Dome', *Journal of the American Society of Architectural Historians*, III, no. 4 (Oct., 1943), 32–48. Dr Born concluded: 'The bulbous dome originated in a stratum of wooden architecture which extended through India, the Near East, and Russia. Its evolution is based on two elements of Indian architecture: the bulging but unpointed stone cupola of the *stupa*, and the ridged horseshoe vault of the wooden *chaitya* halls. . . . Syria seems to have led the revolution. Russia followed probably in the thirteenth century.' The earliest representation of a bulbous Russian dome appears in an illuminated manuscript, the Dobrilov Gospel of 1164. Throughout the fourteenth century bulbous domes frequently occur in such illustrations.

44. 11. The churches in Novgorod and Pskov discussed in this chapter are reproduced, Grabar, I, 171–222; *Istoriya*, II, 16–62, 311–30; *Geschichte*, II, 13–51, 223–36.

12. A recently discovered fresco in the stair-tower of the Nativity in the Anthony Monastery, crudely

drawn and inscribed 'Peter' with an undecipherable date, may be a portrait of this early architect. See A. Vinner, 'Freski Novgoroda', *Arkhitektura SSSR* (1945), no. 10, 22–8; and M. Ilin, 'Master Petr', *ibid.* (1943), no. 2, 37–9; Grabar, I, 171.

46. 13. The restoration is illustrated with measured drawings in P. P. Pokryshin, 'Otchet o kapitalnom remont Spaso-Nereditskoi tserkvi v 1903 i 1904 godakh', *Materialy po arkheologii Rossii*, XXX (St Petersburg, 1906).

47. 14. For measured drawings of these two churches see V. V. Suslov, *Pamyatniki drevnerusskago iskusstva*, II (St Petersburg, 1909).

48. 15. The drawing is reproduced, *Istoriya*, II, 317; *Geschichte*, II, 228.

16. For the technique of these corbelled arches see P. P. Pokryshkin, 'Tserkvi pskovskogo tipa XV–XVI stol. po vostochnomy poberezhniiu Chudskago ozera i na r. Narove', *Izvestiya imperatorskoi arkheologicheskoi kommissii*, XXII (1907), 1–37; for theories of their origin see H. Weidhaas, *Formenwandlung in der russischen Baukunst* (Halle, 1935).

CHAPTER 4

51. 1. The architecture of Suzdalia has been studied on the basis of archaeological investigations by N. N. Voronin in several publications of which the most convenient is *Pamyatniki Vladimiro-Suzdalskogo zodchestva XI–XIII vekov* (Moscow, 1945). See also Nekrasov, *Ocherki*, chapter 5. For further illustrations see Grabar, I, 103–21; Buxton, plates 8–15; *Istoriya*, I, 340–95: *Geschichte*, I, 210–49.

52. 2. Laurentian Chronicle, A.D. 1222.

53. 3. A. D. Varganov, 'Freski XI–XII vv. v Suzdalskom sobore', AN, *Kratkie soobshcheniya*, v (1940), 38–40.

4. Tipografskaya Chronicle, A.D. 1152.

5. For the truncated condition of SS. Boris and Gleb towards the end of the nineteenth century, see the photograph reproduced in the first edition of this text (Harmondsworth, 1954), plate 11A.

56. 6. The contemporary account of this fire is a vivid description of the destruction caused by these periodic conflagrations. According to the Hypatian Chronicle, A.D. 1183: 'Almost the whole city and the great princely palace were burned down, and the churches to the number of thirty-two; and the Cathedral of the Virgin [of the Dormition] with the golden domes was burned down, and all its golden domes with which the devout Prince Andrey had adorned it. And so the fire burned from the top to the bottom. . . . And the silver censers and innumerable gold and silver objects and all the gold and

pearl embroidered vestments and cloths . . . were burned.'

7. Photographs showing the condition of the remaining portions of Andrey's church, including evidence of fire damage, were taken during the restoration of 1891. See V. K. Trumovskii, 'Kratkii otchet o restavratsii Vladimirskago Uspenskago Sobora v 1891', MAO, *Drevnosti*, XVI (1900), 1–41.

8. Hypatian Chronicle, A.D. 1175.

9. For the history and iconography of the image of the Pokrov, see p. 146.

57. 10. For the plan see J. Strzygowski, *Die Baukunst der Armenier und Europa*, I (Vienna, 1918), 185.

58. 11. The first modern Russian historian, V. N. Tatishchev (1686–1750), in his *Istoriya rossiiskaya*, III (Moscow, 1774), 487, n. 483, stated that in the absence of skilled architects in Vladimir, master builders were sent to Andrey by the Emperor Frederick Barbarossa 'with whom he was friendly'. Unfortunately Tatishchev failed to mention his source, which has never been discovered, but since he said that the texts he read were on parchment, he probably used an old and authentic manuscript.

12. Yury Dolgoruky married a Cuman princess, the daughter of Aëra II; his sons married Ossetian princesses. See N. de Baumgarten, 'Généalogies et mariages occidentaux des Rurikides russes du Xe au XIIIe siècle', *Orientalia Christiana*, IX (1927).

59. 13. For photographs and conjectural reconstructions of the Bogoliubovo church and palace see N. N. Voronin, *Pamyatniki*, figures 15–19; N. N. Voronin and M. K. Karger, eds., *Istoriya kultury drevnei Rusi* (Moscow, 1948), 227–9.

60. 14. Laurentian Chronicle, A.D. 1194.

62. 15. See Voronin, *Pamyatniki*, figure 27, for an old view before restoration.

16. Laurentian Chronicle, A.D. 1222.

63. 17. For this little-known architect and sculptor, who also worked on the walls of the Moscow Kremlin, see N. N. Sobolev, 'Russkii zodchii XV veka, V. D. Ermolin', *Staraya Moskva* (1914), no. 2, 16–23.

CHAPTER 5

65. 1. Laurentian Chronicle, A.D. 978–80. For the importance of ornament in pre-Christian times see A. Guscin, 'L'art indigène préchrétien de la Russie Kiévienne', *Revue des études slaves*, VIII (1928), 194–202.

2. L. Niederle, *Manuel de l'antiquité slave* (Paris, 1926), II, chapter 12. Brilliant primary colours remained for centuries characteristic of the Russian environment; see Chapter 10, Note 7.

3. Thus in Moscow the Krasnaya Ploshchad, 'Red' or 'Beautiful Square', and in the Kremlin the Krasnoe kryltso, 'Red' or 'Grand Staircase'.

4. P. Muratov, *L'Ancienne peinture russe* (Rome and Prague, 1925), 29.

66. 5. N. P. Sychev, 'Drevneishii fragment russkovizantiiskoi zhivopisi', *Seminarium Kondakovianum, Recueil d'études*, II (1928), 91–104, with colour plate and French summary.

6. For these patterns see D. V. Ainalov, 'Mramory i inkrustatsii Kievo-Sofiiskago sobora i Desyatinnoi tserkvi', MAO, *Trudy*, XII S'ezd (Kharkov, 1902), III (Moscow, 1905), 5–11.

7. For the relation of the St Sophia mosaics to other Byzantine systems see C. Diehl, *Manuel d'art byzantin*, 2nd ed., II (Paris, 1926), 513–18.

8. For mosaics and frescoes in St Sophia and other medieval churches see V. Lazarev, *Old Russian Murals and Mosaics* (London, 1966), with bibliography. Earlier publications are iconographically useful, such as the large lithographic plates in colour and line after drawings by F. G. Solntsev in *Drevnosti rossiiskago gosudarstva, Kievskii Sofiiskii sobor* (St Petersburg, 1871–87). See also V. Lazarev, 'Nouvelles découvertes dans la Cathédrale de Ste Sophie', *Arkhitektura SSSR* (1936), no. 5, 51–4 (in Russian).

68. 9. The iconography of the Virgin in Byzantine and Russian painting has been thoroughly examined by N. P. Kondakov in *Ikonografiya Bogomateri* (St Petersburg, 1914–15), 2 vols.

69. 10. See below, p. 137.

70. 11. See Alpatov-Brunov, plates 158–65, for comparative details of the St Sophia mosaics with other Russian and Greek examples.

71. 12. A. Grabar, 'Les Fresques des escaliers à Sainte-Sophie de Kiev et l'iconographie impériale byzantine', Sem. Kond., *Recueil d'études*, VII (1935), 103–18.

72. 13. Quoted by D. V. Ainalov, *Vormoskov.*, 26.

14. *Travels of Macarius*, I, 231.

73. 15. For the mosaics and frescoes from St Michael with the Golden Roofs, see V. N. Lazarev, *Istoriya*, I, 206–12; *Geschichte*, I, 118–23; his *Mikhailovskie Mosaiki* (Moscow, 1966), and, in English, his *Old Russian Murals*, 69–74; 243–4. The St Demetrius mosaic is discussed in detail in Antonova and Mneva, I, 49–51. See also the important earlier study by D. V. Ainalov, 'Die Mosaiken des Michael-Klosters in Kiev', *Belvedere*, IX–X (1926), 201–16.

16. A. V. Prakhov, 'Kievskie pamyatniki', MAO, *Drevnosti*, XI (1887), part 3, plates 4–5.

CHAPTER 6

74. 1. In the absence of any general or authoritative history of early Russian sculpture, see the summaries in L. Réau, *L'Art russe des origines à Pierre le Grand* (Paris, 1921); Ainalov, *Vormoskov.*; Alpatov-Brunov. For Perun and the other gods see L. Leger, *La Mythologie slave* (Paris, 1901); N. K. Chadwick, *The Beginnings of Russian History*, chapter 5. See also B. A. Rybakov, 'Iskusstvo drevnikh slavyan', *Istoriya*, I, 29–92; *Geschichte*, I, 23–58; G. K. Varner, 'Skulptura drevnei Rusi', in R. V. Timafeeva, ed., *Trista vekov iskusstva* (Moscow, 1974), 236–66.

2. A. S. Cook, 'Ibn Fadlan's Account of Scandinavian Merchants on the Volga in 922', *Journal of English and Germanic Philology*, XXII (1923), 58. A straight-sided wooden post with incised linear decoration and surmounted by a three-dimensional head of a wide-eyed bearded man with open mouth, discovered at Staraya Ladoga, has been thought to be from the seventh to ninth centuries, but its excellent preservation suggests that it may be a later pagan survival rather than a pre-Christian sculpture. It is reproduced opposite the title page in *Russkaya derevyannaya skulptura –Russian Wooden Sculpture* (Moscow, 1967, with text in English).

3. R. Holtzmann, *Die Chronik des Bischofs Thietmar von Merseburg* (Berlin, 1935), 302.

4. F. J. Tschan, *The Chronicle of the Slavs by Helmold* (New York, 1935), 219.

5. L. A. Magnus, ed. and tr., *The Tale of the Armament of Igor* (Oxford, 1915), 5, 6, 8.

6. Reproduced, Ainalov, *Vormoskov.*, plate 1b.

7. Now in the Academy, Cracow. See L. Niederle, *Manuel de l'antiquité slave*, II, 148, figure 48. Reproduced, *Istoriya*, I, 76–7; *Geschichte*, I, 46–8.

75. 8. V. B. Antonovich, 'O skalnykh peshcherakh na beregu Dnestra v podolskoi gubernii', MAO, *Trudy*, VI (Odessa, 1884), I (Moscow, 1886), 86–102. The relief was first dated to the ninth or tenth century; recent Soviet opinion places it as early as the first to third. Reproduced, *Istoriya*, I, 51; *Geschichte*, I, 40.

9. *The Russian Primary Chronicle*, A.D. 988.

10. Reproduced, Ainalov, *Vormoskov.*, plate 11. The Desyatinnaya fragments are published by M. K. Karger in 'Knyazheskoe pogrebenie XI veka v Desyatinnoi tserkvi', AN, *Kratkie soobshcheniya*, IV (1940), 12–20. For discussion and illustration of other fragments of early Kievan sculpture see N. Makarenko, 'La Statuaire et la sculpture de Kiev à l'époque prémongole', in M. Hrushevskii, ed., *Recueils d'histoire, d'archéologie, des mœurs, et des arts à Kiev*, I (1930), 27–96 (in Ukrainian). The reliefs from St Michael's are now in the Museum, Kiev. See also A. I. Nekrasov, *Drevnerusskoe izobrazitelnoe iskusstvo* (Moscow, 1937), 65–6.

11. For the history and reproduction of this sculpture see the illustrated work by F. W. Halle, *Die Bauplastik von Wladimir-Ssusdal* (Berlin, 1929); and

A. A. Bobrinskoi, *Reznoi kamen v Rossii, Sobory Vla-dimiro-Suzdalskoi Oblasti*, xii–xiii, xv (Moscow, 1916), an album of 41 plates; *Istoriya*, I, 396–442; *Geschichte*, I, 250–79.

77. 12. Halle, *op. cit.*, 62–3; Voronin, *Pamyatniki* (Moscow, 1945), 55, figure 26. V. N. Lazarev (*Propyläen*, III, 300) suggests that the Russian tradition of low-relief carving in wood tended to flatten the more three-dimensional character of twelfth-century (Romanesque) sculpture elsewhere.

13. Alpatov-Brunov, 265–6, with quotations in German; A. Luther, *Geschichte der russischen Literatur* (Leipzig, 1924), 25.

14. Hypatian Chronicle, A.D. 1183.

15. *The Russian Primary Chronicle*, A.D. 1160.

78. 16. C. R. Beazley, ed., *Texts and Versions of John de Plano Carpini and William de Rubruquis as Printed for the First Time by Hakluyt in 1598* (London, 1903), 141.

17. The sculptures have been carefully studied and put in a conjectural order by K. K. Romanov. Among his many publications are 'K voprosu o tekhnike vypolneniya reliefov sobora sv. Georgiya v g. Iurieve-Polskom', Sem. Kond., *Recueil d'études*, II (Prague, 1928), 149–60; and 'La Colonnade du pourtour de la cathédrale de Saint-Georges à Jurev-Polskij', in G. Millet, ed., *L'Art byzantin chez les slaves*, II (Paris, 1932), 54–67, with bibliography of his previous work.

18. Voskresensk Chronicle, A.D. 1234.

79. 19. Reproduced A. Bank, *Byzantine Art in the Collections of Soviet Museums* (New York, 1977), plate 148.

20. On the so-called 'Gates of Sigtuna' of the cathedral of Novgorod, a pair of bronze doors made in Magdeburg, Germany, towards the middle of the twelfth century, a small figure of a sculptor inscribed in Russian characters 'Master Avraham', may be a self-portrait of a Russian craftsman who helped to restore the doors when they were removed from Poland to Novgorod in the fourteenth century. See A. Goldschmidt, *Die Bronzetüren von Novgorod und Gnesen* (Marburg, 1922).

CHAPTER 7

80. 1. For the restoration of St Sophia see V. V. Suslov and others, 'Obsuzhdenie proekta stennoi rospisi Novgorodskago Sofiiskago sobora', *Materialy po arkheologii Rossii*, XXI (St Petersburg, 1897), 1–46.

2. V. Lazarev, *Old Russian Murals*, 94–6, 245; see also P. Schweinfurth, *Geschichte der russischen Malerei im Mittelalter* (The Hague, 1930), figure 29.

81. 3. I. Grabar, ed., *Voprosy restavratsii*, I (Moscow, 1926), 25–6.

4. I. Grabar, *Die Freskomalerei der Dimitrii Kathedrale in Wladimir* (Berlin, 1925); summary by L. Réau, 'Les Fresques de la Cathédrale Saint-Dmitri à Vladimir', *L'Art byzantin chez les slaves*, II, 68–76. Grabar dates the frescoes *c.* 1196; Lazarev, *Old Russian Murals*, 81–7.

83. 5. V. Myasoedov, *Freski Spasa-Nereditsy* (Leningrad, 1925); French edition, *Les Fresques byzantines de Spas-Nereditsa* (Paris, 1928). See also J. Ebersolt, 'Fresques byzantines de Nereditsa', Fondation Eugène Piot, *Monuments et mémoires*, XIII (1906), 35–55, plates 4–5; Lazarev, *Old Russian Murals*, 116–30. The few surviving fragments have been incorporated in the restoration of the church since 1945.

85. 6. The dynastic character of the Spas-Nereditsa as a princely foundation explains the presence of SS. Boris and Gleb, younger sons of St Vladimir, and of Anna, St Vladimir's wife, in this procession. See N. P. Sychev, 'Sur l'histoire de l'église du Sauveur à Nereditcy', *L'art byzantin chez les slaves*, II, 77–108.

86. 7. Myasoedov, II, identified no less than ten different manners, but despite the presence of as many painters considered the ensemble entirely characteristic of Novgorod. At least three, and possibly four, hands can be seen in Lazarev, *Old Russian Murals*, figures 55–6, 58–9, ranging from the Greek naturalism in Christ the Priest to the dramatic abstraction of the heads of St Phocas (our illustration 46) and St Luke.

8. For the Caucasian influences at Nereditsa see C. Amiranachvili, 'Quelques remarques sur l'origine des procédés dans les fresques de Neredicy', *L'Art byzantin chez les slaves*, II, 102–20, and especially the comparison between figures at Nereditsa and early-twelfth-century frescoes at Chio-Mghvime and Achtala.

88. 9. Lazarev, *Old Russian Murals*, 99–103. See also the surviving frescoes of 1167 in the Church of St George in Staraya Ladoga (Lazarev, *Freski Staroy Ladogi*, Moscow, 1960).

10. Novgorod Chronicle, A.D. 1338, 1353.

11. For the activity of Theognostus see G. V. Zhidkov, *Moskovskaya zhivopis sredinu XIV veka* (Moscow, 1928), an important study of the documentary and critical bibliography up to that date. The chronicle excerpts are from the Patriarchal Chronicle, 216–17.

89. 12. V. V. Suslov, 'Tserkov Uspeniya Presvyatoi Bogoroditsy v sele Volotove, bliz Novgoroda, postroennaya v 1352', Moskovskago predvaritelnago komiteta, *Trudy*, XV S'ezd (Novgorod, 1911); II (Moscow, 1911), 5–65. For similarities between Volotovo and Palaeologos art compare especially the mosaic of the *Massacre of the Innocents* in the

Kariye-Djami; reproduced, F. Schmidt, *Kakhrie-Dzhami* (Munich, 1906) (Albom, vol. XI, Izvestii russkago arkheologischeskago instituta v Konstantinople), plate 37.

13. For the iconographical significance of the Mandilion portrait see p. 100.

14. The Volotovo frescoes are extensively reproduced in Grabar, VI, 158–67; Lazarev, *Old Russian Murals*, 156–71.

92. 15. V. N. Lazarev's *Theophanes der Griece und seine Schule* (Vienna and Munich, 1968) is abundantly illustrated, and the best documented work on this important master. See also I. Grabar, *Feofan Grek* (Kazan, 1922). Summary by P. Schweinfurth in Thieme-Becker, XXIII (1939), 2–3. See also A. Anisimov, 'La Peinture russe du XIVe siècle (Théophane le grec)', *Gazette des beaux-arts*, 6e pér., III (1930), 158–77. Grabar and Anisimov give most of the Novgorod frescoes to Theophanes.

93. 16. The letter has been analysed by A. I. Nekrasov in 'Les Frontispices architecturaux dans les manuscrits russes avant l'époque de l'imprimerie', *L'Art byzantin chez les slaves*, II, 253–81.

95. 17. Reproduced, Alpatov-Brunov, plate 211. See also M. V. Alpatov, 'Feofan v Moskve', in his *Etiudy po istorii russkogo iskusstva* (Moscow, 1969), 88–98.

CHAPTER 8

97. 1. The pioneer nineteenth-century studies of icon-painting culminated in such works as M. I. and V. I. Uspenskii's *Materialy dlya istorii russkago ikonopisaniya* (St Petersburg, 1899), 101 plates; and N. P. Likhachev's *Materialy dlya istorii russkago ikonopisaniya* (Leipzig and St Petersburg, 1906), 2 vols., 419 plates (text never published). The earliest works were iconographical rather than critical or historical. This archaeological attitude is also found in N. P. Kondakov's studies such as his monumental *Russkaya ikona* (Prague, 1928–33), 4 vols., with excellent reproductions. His *The Russian Icon* (Oxford, 1927), translated by Sir Ellis Minns, is a preliminary sampling of the *Russkaya Ikona*. Kondakov's stylistic conclusions are subject to revision, since they were based on colour notes made before many of the icons were cleaned. For Russian icons in the context of Greek painting, see H. P. Gerhard, *The World of Icons* (London, 1971).

2. A more critical and historical attitude appeared in the first decade of the twentieth century. See especially the synopses of lectures by A. I. Uspenskii, *Ocherki po istorii russkago iskusstva* (Moscow, 1910); P. P. Muratov's catalogue of the Ostroukhov

collection, *Drevne-russkaya ikonopis v sobranii I. S. Ostroukhova* (Moscow, 1914). His sections on icon-painting in Grabar's *Istoriya russkago iskusstva*, VI, chapters I–II, have been translated as *L'Ancienne Peinture russe* (Rome and Prague, 1925). See also his *Les Icones russes* (Paris, 1927).

3. The first discoveries of the State Restoration Workshops (*Tsentralnye gosudarstvennye restavratsionnye masterskie*) were published as *Voprosy restavratsii*, ed. by I. Grabar and A. Anisimov, 2 vols. (Moscow, 1926–8). For summaries in French of this work see A. Anisimov, 'Les Anciennes Icones et leur contribution à l'histoire de la peinture russe', Fondation Eugène Piot, *Monuments et Mémoires*, XXX (1929), 151–65; and G. Millet, 'Les Ateliers de restauration', *L'Art byzantin chez les slaves*, II, 51–3. A collection of icons cleaned and restored by the Workshops was exhibited in western Europe and America in 1929–31. For the catalogue see M. Farbman, ed., *Masterpieces of Russian Painting* (London, 1930) with good colour reproductions; Metropolitan Museum of Art, New York, *A Catalogue of Russian Icons* (1931), with preface by I. Grabar. For an account of the travelling exhibition and a concise history of icon-painting see A. H. Barr, Jr, 'Russian Icons', *The Arts*, XVII (1931), 295–314 ff.

98. 4. The most useful *résumés* of icon-painting are those by A. I. Nekrasov, *Drevne-russkoe izobrazitelnoe iskusstvo srediny XIV veka* (Moscow, 1937), and V. N. Lazarev in his *Iskusstvo Novgoroda* (Moscow, 1947). See also O. Wulff and M. Alpatov, *Denkmäler der Ikonenmalerei* (Hellerau bei Dresden, 1925); reviewed by L. Bréhier, 'Les Icones dans l'histoire de l'art byzance et la Russie', *L'Art byzantin chez les slaves*, II, 150–73; W. Felicetti-Liebenfels, *Geschichte der russischen Ikonenmalerei* (Graz, 1972).

5. A curious example of the distorted appearance of an icon much repainted can be seen in the 'Annunciation' of the Anthony Monastery, Novgorod, reproduced, Kondakov, *Russkaya ikona*, III, 141 and figure 16. The twelfth-century subject is identical with the Ustiug 'Annunciation' [55], but the forms have become grotesque caricatures of the originals.

100. 6. For a detailed analysis and summary of the Byzantine prototypes of Russian iconography, see G. Millet, *Recherches sur l'iconographie de l'évangile aux XIVe, XVe et XVIe siècles* (Paris, 1916). Specific iconographical problems will be annotated as they appear below. A convenient summary of the principal iconographical themes appears in L. Réau, *L'Art russe des origines à Pierre le Grand* (Paris, 1921), 141–64; and Schweinfurth, 218–32. See also N. Scheffer, 'Symbolism of the Russian Icon',

Gazette des beaux-arts, 6e pér., xxv (1944), 77–94.

7. For these images see J. Beckwith, *Early Christian and Byzantine Art (Pelican History of Art)*, 2nd ed. (Harmondsworth, 1979), 86–8; S. Runciman, 'Some Remarks on the Images of Edessa', *Cambridge Historical Journal*, iii (1931), 238–52; L. Bréhier, 'Icones non faites de mains d'hommes', *Revue archéologique*, 5e sér., xxxv (1932), 68–77. An early Slavic (not identifiable as Russian) Mandilion is preserved in the cathedral at Laon; A. Grabar, *La Sainte Face de Laon, le Mandylion dans l'art orthodoxe* (Prague, 1931). Icons treating scenes from the legend occur as late as the seventeenth century; I. Myslivets, 'Skazanie o perepiske Khrista s Avgarom na russkoi ikone XVII veka', Sem., Kond., *Recueil d'études*, v (1932), 185–90, with German *résumé*.

101. 8. L. Réau, *op. cit.*, 153, publishes a convenient chart of the Russian examples and their Byzantine prototypes. For a more extensive iconographical index see B. Rothemund, *Handbuch der Ikonenkunst* (Munich, Slavisches Institut, 2nd corr. and enl. ed., 1966).

9. Copies of an icon of the Virgin miraculously discovered at Tikhvin in 1383 remained for several centuries the most purely Greek type of Russian painting. See N. Toll, 'Ikona tikhvinskoi Bozhiei Materi', Sem. Kond., *Recueil d'études*, v (1932), 181–4.

102. 10. Comparative examples, illustrating the development of the iconostasis from the Byzantine altar rail, will be found in E. E. Golubinskii, *Istoriya russkoi tserkvi*, Atlas (Moscow, 1906), plates 46–8, 50, and 51. Panels fixed on the chancel barrier appear in the frescoes at Assisi attributed to Giotto.

103. 11. A complete iconostasis of the sixteenth and seventeenth centuries is illustrated in detail in D. K. Trenev, *Ikonostas Smolenskago sobora Moskovskago Novodevichyago monastyrya* (Moscow, 1902).

12. In addition to standard hagiographies see E. E. Golubinskii, *Istoriya kanonizatsii svyatykh v russkoi tserkvi* (Moscow, 1903).

13. An eighteenth-century pattern book by Dionysius of Phourna was discovered on Mt Athos, translated, and published by A. Didron and P. Durand as *Manuel d'iconographie chrétienne grecque et latine* (Paris, 1845). The so-called Stroganov family pattern book (present location unknown) has been twice reproduced in facsimile: *Stroganovskoi ikonopisii litsevoi podlinnik* (Moscow, 1869); *Ikonen Malerhandbuch der Familie Stroganow* (Munich, Slavisches Institut, 1965). The outline drawings, mostly of individual saints for each day of the liturgical year, include a few schematic patterns for the principal feasts and other occasions.

104. 14. For the technique of icon-painting see N. P. Kondakov, *The Russian Icon*, chapter 3; Wulff and Alpatov, *Denkmäler der Ikonenmalerei*, 96–7; Schweinfurth, 209–16.

15. A late practice panel with heads of old and young men in various stages of completion, including one of each type in outline on the gesso ground, is reproduced, N. P. Likhachev, *Materialy*, plate 311, no. 594.

105. 16. P. Miliukov, *Outlines of Russian Culture*, iii (Philadelphia, 1942), 44.

CHAPTER 9

107. 1. Russian icons are part, perhaps the most important part, of a kind of painting, derived from ancient Greek and Hellenistic art, which can be traced at least from the fourth century A.D., and which developed in the eastern countries of the Orthodox faith until modern times. For the earliest Greek (Byzantine) icons see K. Weitzmann, *et al.*, *A Treasure of Icons, Sixth to Seventeenth Centuries, from the Sinai Peninsula, Greece, Bulgaria, and Yugoslavia* (New York, 1966). For collections and other schools see, as instances, *Les Icones dans les collections suisses* (Geneva, Musée Rath, 1968); *Ikonen-Museum* (Kunstsammlungen der Stadt Recklinghausen, 5th ed., 1976); K. Balabanov, *Icones de Macédonie* (Belgrade, 1969); *Icones Bulgares, IXe-XIXe siècle* (Paris, Musée du Petit Palais, 1976).

2. The Laurentian Chronicle, A.D. 1155: '. . . in the same year Andrey went from his father to Suzdal, whence he took the icon of the Blessed Virgin, which on the same ship had been brought from Tsargrad'.

3. A later and more influential tale had it that when on 26 August 1395 the Great Prince Vasily Dmitrievich entered Moscow with the icon, Tamerlane, chief of the Tartars, left Russia forever. A slit for a staff in the lower border of the frame indicates that the Vladimir Virgin was once carried in processions. For its presumptive history as recorded in the chronicles see Antonova and Mneva, i, 61.

4. For a detailed and illustrated analysis of the condition of the icon see A. Anisimov, *Our Lady of Vladimir* (Prague, 1928). For further studies see also the bibliographies in Antonova and Mneva, and K. Onasch, *Icons* (New York, 1963), 342. The latter author, an East German scholar, believes the Vladimir Virgin to be of Russian workmanship. V. N. Lazarev does not indicate its origin in *Istoriya*, i, 442–4; *Geschichte*, i, 280–1. W. Felicetti-Liebenfels in his *Geschichte der russischen Ikonenmalerei* (Graz, 1972), 18, suggests that the icon was in large part repainted after the fire which severely damaged

the Assumption in Vladimir in 1182. See above, page 60.

108. 5. For the documentary sources for both cities see Antonova and Mneva, I, 56–7. A Novgorodian origin is more persuasive, given the reference in the second Novgorod Chronicle under the year 1561 to Ivan the Terrible's having removed to Moscow 'an image of the Annunciation in the Yuriev Monastery'.

110. 6. The Byzantine prototypes are well represented by the Archangel Michael from the Homilies of St John Chrysostom of about 1078, now in Paris (Bibliothèque Nationale, Coislin 79). The full page, showing the Emperor Nicephorus III Botaneiates between St John and the Archangel, is reproduced in J. Beckwith, *Early Christian and Byzantine Art* (*Pelican History of Art*), 2nd ed. (Harmondsworth, 1979), illustration 205; also, with a full-page detail of the Archangel in colour, in D. T. Rice, *Kunst aus Byzanz* (Munich, 1959), plates 163 and XXII.

113. 7. Three icons have traditionally been attributed to Alimpi: the Virgin of Vladimir in the Dormition in Rostov, 'The Queen Did Stand' in the Moscow Dormition, and the Svensky Virgin from the Svensky Monastery near Briansk (now in the Tretyakov Gallery, Moscow). The first two are now recognized as much later paintings, but the third may be a late-thirteenth-century copy of a Kievan original from the Pechersky Lavra. For reproductions see M. and V. I. Uspenskii, *Zametki o drevne-russkom ikonopisanii* (St Petersburg, 1901), and for the Svensky icon, Antonova and Mneva, I, 76–7, plate 34.

8. Although the icon is now usually attributed to a workshop in Yaroslavl, the possibility of its derivation from a Kievan original cannot be entirely dismissed. It is worth noting that among a collection of Kievan manuscripts acquired in 1795 by A. I. Musin-Pushkin from the monastery in Yaroslavl was the only surviving copy of the late-twelfth-century *Lay of Prince Igor*, the masterpiece of ancient Kievan poetry.

9. A colour reproduction of St Dmitry showing various stages in the removal of layers of repaint will be found in M. Farbman, ed., *Masterpieces of Russian Painting*, 13. See also Antonova and Mneva, I, 71–3.

116. 10. The icon has usually been attributed to a late-twelfth- or early-thirteenth-century workshop in Novgorod on the basis of influences from Nereditsa where a similar mandilion portrait existed in fresco, by the suggestions of the Novgorod dialect and orthography in the inscriptions on the reverse, and by the existence of a Mandilion adored by angels

in a Novgorod manuscript of 1262 (reproduced, *Istoriya*, I, 115; *Geschichte*, II, 86). Antonova and Mneva (I, 66–7) attribute the icon to two masters working in Vladimir-Suzdal in the mid twelfth century, one painting the obverse from a Byzantine or Kievan model, the other possibly a Novgorodian artist.

11. Schweinfurth, 144, note 1, calls attention to the gilded hair on late antique imperial portrait statues.

117. 12. The Greek sources for the icons of St Nicholas [61, 63] will be apparent by comparing them with the twelfth-century icon of St Gregory the Thaumaturge Leningrad, Hermitage), reproduced in A. Bank, *Byzantine Art in the Collections of Soviet Museums* (New York and Leningrad, 1978), plates 237–8.

13. In rejoining the icon after it had been split, two narrow vertical sections were lost down the centre.

CHAPTER 10

122. 1. The fresco at Staraya Ladoga is reproduced in Lazarev, *Old Russian Murals and Mosaics*, 106 (figure 84).

2. Anthony of Novgorod's *Pilgrim's Book*, translated by B. de Khitrovo, *Itinéraires russes en Orient* (Geneva, 1889), 95.

3. For enlarged details see P. Neradovski, 'Boris i Gleb iz sobraniya N. P. Likhacheva', *Russkaya ikona*, I (St Petersburg, 1914), 62–78.

126. 4. L. Matsulevich, 'Dve ikony Rozhdestva Bogomateri iz sobraniya S. P. Ryabushinskago', *Russkaya ikona*, III (St Petersburg, 1914), 163–79.

5. N. Scheffer, 'Religious Chants and the Russian Icon', *Gazette des beaux-arts*, 6ᵉ pér., XXVII (1945), 129–42. The icon is reproduced in colour, M. Farbman, ed., *Masterpieces of Russian Painting*, 69.

6. I. Grabar, 'Ancient Russian Painting', *A Catalogue of Russian Icons* (Metropolitan Museum of Art, New York, 1931), xiii: 'The love of particular shades and combinations of colours which recur again and again in the icons produced in Novgorod, Pskov, or Ferapontov are borrowed from the landscape of those localities.... The rosy, lilac, and light blue shades of the fresco paintings by Dionysius at Ferapontov are still to be seen on. the shores of the neighbouring lake; but the marvellous green that predominates in the icons of Pskov was first discovered as recently as last summer on the banks of the river Velikaya.'

128. 7. This contrast of bright primary colours occurred even in the architectural landscape. An early-nineteenth-century English traveller, describing a monastic settlement in western Russia (the Iversky Monastery on Lake Valdai, see the seventeenth-century drawing [107]), wrote that: 'The whole scene around glows with that luxuriant interchange of white and red, and green and gold that enters so largely into the composition of a Russian view' (J. T. James, *Journal of a Tour in Germany, Sweden, Russia, Poland, During the Years 1813 and 1814* (London, 1816), 349).

8. The Four Saints icon may be compared with the admirable early fourteenth-century icon of the Assembly of the Apostles, formerly in the Moscow Historical Museum but now in the Pushkin Museum of Fine Arts, reproduced in colour in A. Bank, *Byzantine Art in the Collections of Soviet Museums* (New York and Leningrad, 1978), plate 270.

CHAPTER II

130. 1. Five of the six remaining panels from Serpukhov are described and illustrated by Antonova and Mneva, I, 375, plates 243–7.

2. For the claims of Moscow see the argument by M. Alpatov in Alpatov-Brunov, 302 ff. The historical documentation for early icon-painting in Moscow has been set forth by G. V. Zhidkov, *Moskovskaya zhivopis srediny XIV veka* (Moscow, 1928). See also V. N. Lazarev, *Iskusstvo Novgoroda* (Moscow, 1947), 65; Nekrasov, *Drevne-russkoe izobrazitelnoe iskusstvo*, 149–50 and 223–4.

131. 3. For the iconography of this image see H. (G.) Zhidkov, 'L'Icone du "Sauveur à l'œil courroucé" de la cathédrale de la Dormition à Moscou', *L'Art byzantin chez les slaves*, II, 174–94.

134. 4. The icons in the Annunciation are reproduced in V. N. Lazarev, *Theophanes der Grieche und seine Schule* (Vienna and Munich, 1968), plates 130–53. See also Grabar, *Voprosy restavratsii*, I, 83; summary in Schweinfurth, 303.

136. 5. Antonova and Mneva, I, 255, attribute both sides of the icon to Theophanes and date it to 1392, twelve years after the battle of Kulikovo. Lazarev retains a date in the 1380s but rejects the attribution to Theophanes in his *Theophanes der Grieche und seine Schule*, 63–7, plates 73–7. The most recent opinion (Felicetti-Liebenfels, 1972, 30–2) attributes the Virgin and Child to Theophanes as an exceptionally rare example of Palaeologan painting, and the reverse (the Dormition) to a follower of Theophanes. Undoubtedly two hands were at work, but the fact remains that the painter of the obverse was extraordinarily accomplished, and that the agitated and highlighted apostles in the Dormition closely resemble those in Theophanes's frescoes in Novgorod.

6. Although the type is Greek, the peculiarly Russian tenderness and the simplified treatment of the highlights preclude a Greek origin. Recent Soviet opinion considers the work Russian; V. N. Lazarev, *Iskusstvo Novgoroda* (Moscow, 1947), 84–5. For a good colour reproduction see Volbach and Lafontaine-Dosogne, plate XLIII.

7. A. I. Uspenskii, *Drevne-russkaya zhivopis XV–XVIII veka* (Moscow, 1906); N. P. Likhachev, *Manera Pisma A. Rubleva* (St Petersburg, 1907); I. Grabar, 'Andrei Rublev, ocherk tvorchestva khudozhnika po dannym restavratsionnykn rabot 1918–25 gg.', *Voprosy restavratsii*, I, 7–12; Schweinfurth, 301–18; V. N. Lazarev, *Andrey Rublev i ego shkola* (Moscow, 1966), 67–71. (A condensed version of Lazarev's Russian text, with fewer illustrations, is available as *Andrej Rublev* (Milan, 1966).)

137. 8. In 1774, on the occasion of the visit of Catherine II to Vladimir, the frescoes were repainted in oil and the iconostasis replaced with a new one in the Baroque style. The old panels were sent to the nearby village of Vasilievskoe where several were recovered by the Restoration Commission in 1919–22. Four icons from the Vladimir deesis painted by Rublev and Daniil Cherny in 1408 are now in the State Russian Museum, Leningrad; seven others are in the State Tretyakov Gallery, Moscow. See Antonova and Mneva, 267–72.

9. Reproduced, Lazarev, *Andrey Rublev . . .*, figure 87.

10. V. N. Lazarev, 'La Trinité d' André Roublev', *Gazette des beaux-arts*, 6ᵉ pér., LIV (1959), 289–300. Lazarev believes the icon was painted in 1411 for the original wooden church in the monastery where St Sergius was buried. Antonova and Mneva (I, 287) prefer a date between 1422, when the Abbot Nikon commissioned a painting of the Trinity in honour of St Sergius, and Nikon's death on 17 November 1427.

139. 11. The origin of the Zvenigorod panels is obscure. They may have been painted in Moscow about 1410–20 and removed in the seventeenth century to the Savva-Storozhevsky Monastery in Zvenigorod (Antonova and Mneva, I, 283; Lazarev, *Andrey Rublev . . .*, 132–3). On the other hand, since Rublev's hand has been recognized in fragmentary frescoes preserved in two churches in Zvenigorod

built by Prince Yury Dmitrievich, the son of Dmitry Donskoy, which may be attributed to the workshop of the Trinity-Sergius Monastery of which Rublev had been a member, it is possible that the deesis was originally executed for Yury's monastery of St Savva in Zvenigorod (see W. Felicetti-Liebenfels, *op. cit.*, 85).

CHAPTER 12

141. 1. Reproduced in colour, Kondakov, I, plate 2.

144. 2. A. Frolov, 'Le *Znamenie* de Novgorod, l'évolution de la légende', *Revue des études slaves*, XXIV (1948), 67–81; XXV (1949), 45–72; A. Anisimov, 'Etiudy o novgorodskoi ikonopisi', part 2, *Sofiya* (1914), no. 5, 5–21; N. Scheffer, 'Historic Battles on Russian Icons', *Gazette des beaux-arts*, 6e pér., XXIX (1946), 193–206. The venerable *Znamenie* is reproduced, Kondakov, *Russkaya ikona*, II, plate 8.

3. The identity of the fourth saint is obscure. Alexander Nevsky's appearance would be chronologically impossible but spiritually appropriate. N. Scheffer, *loc. cit.*, has suggested the legendary Kievan hero, Ilya Muromets.

146. 4. P. D. Lathoud, 'Le Thème iconographique du "Pokrov" de la Vierge', *L'Art byzantin chez les slaves*, II, 302–14.

5. Detail of central section reproduced in colour, *Russkaya ikona* (1914), 39.

147. 6. This equestrian figure was one of the sights of Constantinople, especially for Russian travellers who had seen nothing like it since the bronze horses brought by Vladimir to Kiev from Kherson had disappeared during the Tartar invasion. See the descriptions by Stephen of Novgorod, who visited Byzantium about 1350, and by other Russian travellers, translated by B. de Khitrovo as *Itinéraires russes en Orient* (Geneva, 1889), 155 ff. The icon, when exhibited in Paris in 1967 (*L'Art russe des Scythes à nos jours, Trésors des Musées Soviétiques*, Grand Palais, no. 280), was given to the school of Moscow. The lively even if hieratic disposition of the figures, as can be observed by the formal and structural similarities between illustrations 84 and 85, at the least resembles the typically Novgorodian interest in narrative and dramatic action.

7. The inverted perspective of old Russian painting has been studied by A. I. Nekrasov, 'O yavleniyahk rakkursa v drevne-russkoi zhivopisi', Institut arkheologii i iskusstvoznianiya, *Trudy*, I (1926), 7–22.

148. 8. Reproduced, Grabar, VI, 301–11.

9. Reproduced in colour, Grabar, VI, facing 241.

149. 10. Reproduced in colour, *Russkaya ikona*, III (St Petersburg, 1914), 183.

CHAPTER 13

153. 1. This concept first found literary expression in an epistle from the monk Philotheus to the Great Prince Vasily III (1505–33); N. Zernov, *Moscow the Third Rome* (London, 1937), 36. A pictorial expression of this concept can possibly be read in a curious sixteenth-century horizontal icon, now in the Tretyakov Gallery, which has variously been interpreted as the Church Militant, or as a commemoration of the victory of Ivan IV over the Tartars at Kazan. It represents the Russian armies, led by holy tsars and saints and accompanied by a cloud of angels, approaching the Celestial City where the Virgin and Child are enthroned. See P. P. Muratov, 'Dva otkrytiya', *Sofiya* (1914), no. 2, 5–17; Ainalov, *Grossfürsten.*, 104–5, and figure 57; Antonova and Mneva, II, 128–34, with extensive bibliography; W. Felicetti–Liebenfels, *Geschichte der russischen Ikonenmalerei* (Graz, 1972), 156–7.

2. Dionisy's frescoes in the Ferapont Monastery are reproduced in V. Lazarev, *Old Russian Murals and Mosaics . . .* (London, 1966), 195–211. See also V. T. Georgievskii, *Freski Ferapontova Monastyrya* (St Petersburg, 1911).

155. 3. E. Georgievskij-Druzinin, 'Les Fresques du monastère de Thérapon, étude de deux thèmes iconographiques', *L'Art byzantin chez les slaves*, II, 121–34. For the iconography of the Akathist see J. Myslivec, 'Ikonografie akathistu Panny Marie', Sem. Kond., *Recueil d'études*, V (1932), 97–131, with French *résumé*; N. Scheffer, 'Akathistos of the Holy Virgin in Russian Art', *Gazette des beaux-arts*, 6e pér., XXIX (1946), 5–16.

157. 4. The hand of Dionisy's son Feodosy, who is known to have worked in the Kremlin Annunciation in 1508, might possibly have been seen in the frescoes discovered in 1882 by V. D. Fartusov in the vestibule of the cathedral. The unmistakably Italian Renaissance character of the figures and the astonishingly lifelike portrait heads might have been due to the influence of some Italian painter arrived in Moscow in the wake of his architectural colleagues. Unfortunately, the style of these frescoes was so little in accord with prevailing official conceptions of old Russian painting that Fartusov was accused of having too drastically restored them. A conservative icon-painter who was hired to 'restore' them succeeded in destroying them by repaint. Fartusov's photographs, the only remaining record of these important and problematic works, seem to have been retouched, but the style as a whole was too remarkable a combination of Renaissance realism and Moscow idealism to have been entirely invented in 1882. For reproductions, A. I. Uspenskii, *Drevne-*

russkaya zhivopis (Moscow, 1906) (reprinted from *Zolotoe runo* (1906), nos. 7–9); A. I. Uspenskii, 'Stenopis Blagoveshchenskago sobora v Moskve', MAO, *Drevnosti Trudy kom.*, III (1909), 153–77.

158. 5. For the icons from the deesis at Ferapont, see Antonova and Mneva, no. 278, reproduced plates 212, 216–23.

159. 6. Reproduced in colour, Grabar, VI, facing 336. The naturalistic atmosphere of such a scene as this may be related to actual ceremonial drama to somewhat the same extent that western European painting derived from the mystery plays. In the Russian church the ritual on Palm Sunday became very elaborate, especially in Moscow where the Tsar and the Metropolitan (later the Patriarch) took part in a solemn procession between the Kremlin and the Church of the Pokrov (St Basil's) on Red Square. Olearius's description of the ceremony he witnessed in 1636 is substantiated by Meyerberg's illustration of 1662. In each case a prominent place is given to 'a very large chariot, made of boards nailed together, but low, drawing after it a Tree, on which were hung abundance of Apples, Figs, and Grapes'. In it were 'four Boys with surplisses who sung the Hosanna', Antonova and Mneva (I, no. 599), with some hesitation but no discussion, assign the icon to Yaroslavl towards the end of the century.

161. 7. Such a subject was the representation of St Sophia, the personification of Divine Wisdom. For this type of icon the most useful source is Kondakov, *The Russian Icon*, chapter 6.

8. Reproduced and described, Kondakov, *The Russian Icon*, 107.

9. E. Duchesne, *Le Stoglav ou les cent chapitres* (Paris, 1920); G. Ostrogorskij, 'Les Décisions du "Stoglav" concernant la peinture d'images et les principes de l'iconographie byzantine', *L'Art byzantin chez les slaves*, I (1930), 393–411.

162. 10. P. Miliukov, *Outlines of Russian Culture*, III, 37; N. E. Andreev, 'O "Dele dyaka Viskovatago"', Sem. Kond., *Recueil d'études*, V (1932), 191–242, with résumé in German.

11. Miliukov, *loc. cit.*, 39.

CHAPTER 14

164. 1. For the structural principles of wooden architecture until the end of the sixteenth century, see *Istoriya*, III, 177–99. The construction of a wooden church is graphically illustrated in a late-seventeenth-century icon of the Virgin of Tikhvin, now in the Rublev Museum of Early Russian Art in Moscow; reproduced in colour in *Muzei drevnerusskogo iskusstva imeni Andreya Rubleva* (Moscow, 1968), plates 91–9 (captions in English). See also S. Ya. Zabello, *et al.*, *Russkoe derevyannoe zodchestvo* (Moscow, 1942). Three important pioneer studies are A. S. Uvarov, 'Ob arkhitekture pervykh derevyannykh tserkvei na Rusi', MAO, *Trudy*, II S'ezd (St Petersburg, 1872), I (Moscow, 1876), 1–24; V. V. Suslov, *Ocherki po istorii drevnerusskago zodchestva* (St Petersburg, 1889), 19–54, 85–108; B. Dunaev, 'Derevyannoe zodchestvo severo-vostoka Kostromskoi gubernii', MAO, *Drevnosti, Trudy, Kom.*, VI (1915), 313–32, with many illustrations.

Many important surviving examples of early wooden architecture, from various regions in Russia, are now preserved in three outdoor museums: at the State History Museum in Kolomenskoe near Moscow, at the Vladimir-Suzdal Museum of History, Art, and Architecture, and in the north at Kizhy on Lake Onega. Many buildings are reproduced in G. I. Mekhova and V. I. Baldin, eds., *Russkoe derevyannoe zodchestvo* (Moscow, 1965).

2. The Hypatian Chronicle, A.D. 842, mentions two 'chambered' churches, but a stone building does not occur in the Laurentian Chronicle until A.D. 945. A tenth-century Arab traveller reported that the Russian traders 'come from their own country, anchor their ships in the Volga, which is a great river, and build large wooden houses on its banks'. See A. S. Cook, 'Ibn Fadlan's Account of Scandinavian Merchants on the Volga in 922', *Journal of English and Germanic Philology*, XXII (1923), 57.

3. M. Alpatov, in Alpatov-Brunov, 117, 183, emphatically rejects the theory that wooden forms influenced the sixteenth-century stone churches. But telling evidence for the contrary opinion is provided by the Church of the Resurrection (1578–9) in the village of Gorodin, near Kolomna. There the stone of the tent roof is unmistakably copied from a wooden original. See M. Krasovskii, *Kurs istorii russkoi arkhitektury* (Petrograd, 1916), 145, figure 72; *Istoriya*, III, 445; *Geschichte*, III, 315.

167. 4. Wooden buildings were notoriously unstable. When Catherine was still a young grand duchess she had a narrow escape from death when a wooden house in which she was sleeping suddenly slid down a hill. Wooden supports had been removed during the winter; when the ground thawed in the spring the whole building slipped from its foundations. See *Memoirs of Catherine the Great*, translated by K. Anthony (New York and London, 1927), 138–41.

5. For the use of the axe in the eighteenth century see Archdeacon Coxe, *Travels in Poland, Russia, Sweden, and Denmark* (London, 1784), 270.

168. 6. The importance of wood as the primary structural material in northern Russia during the early Middle Ages has been abundantly de-

monstrated by archaeological excavations in the central area of Novgorod conducted between 1951 and 1962. The High (main) Street was relaid with heavy oak planks no less than twenty-eight times between 953 and 1462. For a view of Level 13, at the intersection of High and Serf Streets, laid in 1275–8, see M. W. Thompson, *Novgorod the Great, Excavations at the Medieval City Conducted by A. V. Artsikhovsky and B. A. Kolchin* (New York and Washington, 1967), figures 16–17.

7. G. Fletcher, *Of the Russe Common Wealth* (London, 1591), in R. Hakluyt, *Collection of . . . Voyages . . . A new edition* (London, 1809), 542. Fletcher's assumption of the use of the plane by the Russians was erroneous.

8. G. Miege, *A Relation of Three Embassies from His Sacred Majestie Charles II to the Great Duke of Muscovie . . . in the Years 1663 and 1664* (London, 1669), 135, 301.

9. A. Olearius, *The Voyages and Travels of the Ambassador from the Duke of Holstein, to the Great Duke of Muscovy, and the King of Persia, Begun in the Year m.dc.xxxiii and finish'd in m.dc.xxxix Rendred into English* (London, 1662), 57. The prefabricated houses were also observed by Miege, *op. cit.*, 301.

169. 10. W. Coxe, *op. cit.*, I, 348. Such logs in uniform lengths in orderly piles can be seen for example in the engraving of St Petersburg in the middle of the eighteenth century [202].

11. The regular alignment of houses along the curving streets of a radial plan was more real than apparent. In spite of the comments of foreign visitors who frequently remarked on the lack of order, the evidence of existing maps and views [105] proves the contrary. The necessity of leaving open spaces as fire-breaks, as well as the garden plots around each house, both made for and concealed the regular distribution of the houses. William Coxe, who found Moscow bewildering, nevertheless remarked that 'the streets are exceedingly long and broad', *op. cit.*, I, 265. For old maps and plans of Moscow, see Grabar, II, chapter 14.

170. 12. Olearius, *op. cit.*, 48.

171. 13. F. von Adelung, *Augustin Freiherr von Mayerburg und seine Reise nach Russland* (St Petersburg, 1827), 2 vols.; *Albom Meierberg* (St Petersburg, 1903).

14. Reproduced, Grabar, I, 498–500. See also N. V. Sultanov, 'Ostatki Yakutskago ostroga i nekotorye drugie pamyatniki derevyannago zodchestva v Sibirii', *Izvestiya, Imp. Arkh. Kom.*, XXIV (1907).

15. See N. de Baumgarten, 'Chronologie ecclésiastique' (*op. cit.*, Chapter 1, Note 3), 90.

173. 16. *Istoriya*, III, 264–6; *Geschichte*, III, 190.

17. The excavated plan of the temple is reproduced, L. Niederle, *Manuel de l'antiquité slave* (Paris, 1926), II, figure 47. See also *Istoriya*, I, 89; *Geschichte*, I, 53.

176. 18. Grabar, I, 380–1; Zabello, 93. V. V. Suslov, who examined and measured the church in the 1880s, believed it had been built in the seventeenth century. In 1871 it was sheathed with planks, and in 1892 was destroyed by fire. See also *Istoriya*, III, 271–3; *Geschichte*, III, 193–6.

177. 19. For this and other philological similarities see R. Wischnitzer, 'Orientalische Einflüsse in der russischen Architektur', *Osteuropa*, I (1925–6), 252–5.

20. For reproductions, Buxton, part II, 'Transcaucasia', and plates 92, 97, 100; N. V. Sultanov, 'Russkiya shatroviya tserkvi i ikh sootnoshenie k gruzino-armyanskim piramidalnym pokrytiyam', MAO, *Trudy*, V S'ezd (Tiflis, 1881) and *ibid.* (Moscow, 1887), 230–44.

178. 21. Grabar, I, chapter 21.

181. 22. See, as an example, the jewelled gold censer of 1616, designed as a single-domed church, from the Trinity-Sergius Monastery, now in the Moscow Kremlin. Reproduced in colour in the exhibition catalogue, *Treasures from the Kremlin* (New York and Paris, 1979–80), plate 66.

CHAPTER 15

184. 1. Despite the descent of the Russian Church from the Greek, the Christianization of Russia was not accompanied by any thorough study of ancient authors. The early translation of the Greek service books into Church Slavonic discouraged the spread of learning among the priests who, unlike the Latin clergy, were not obliged to know any language other than the spoken vernacular. See G. P. Fedotov, *The Russian Religious Mind* (Cambridge, Mass., 1946).

185. 2. Although succession from father to eldest son became customary, the crown was considered the property of the sovereign who might bequeath it at his pleasure. The order of succession based on primogeniture was not regularized until the accession of Paul I in 1796.

3. As early as 1054 Yaroslav of Kiev had been mentioned in a graffito as 'tsar'; Lazarev, *Old Russian Murals and Mosaics*, 48, 215, note 91.

187. 4. The Redeemer and other churches of Moscow and vicinity are carefully analysed and illustrated in M. V. Krasovskii, *Ocherk istorii Moskovskago perioda drevne-russkago tserkovnago zodchestva* (Moscow, 1911). For the buildings discussed in this chapter, see also *Istoriya*, III, 51–70 and 282–481; *Geschichte*, III, 34–46 and 200–338.

188. 5. Alpatov-Brunov, 83; Ainalov, *Grossfürsten.*, 1–4.

6. Reconstruction in Nekrasov, *Ocherki*, 197. The arches are called kokoshniki from their fancied resemblance to a kokoshnik, the arched headdress worn by Russian women in the Middle Ages. The cathedral is reproduced in colour in T. Talbot Rice, *A Concise History of Russian Art* (New York and Washington, 1963), figure 92.

7. Reproduced, *Istoriya*, III, 57–61; *Geschichte*, III, 41–3.

190. 8. The Annunciation has been carefully studied and published by V. V. Suslov, *Pamyatniki drevnerusskago iskusstva*, I (St Petersburg, 1908), 11–20; II (1909), 6–14; III (1910), 11–26.

191. 9. *The Travels of the Magnificent M. Ambrosio Contarini, Ambassador of the Illustrious Signory of Venice to the Great Lord Ussuncassan, King of Persia, in the Year 1473*, in *Travels to Tana and Persia by Barbaro and Contarini* (London, Hakluyt Society, 1873), 107–73. Examples of metal-work made by foreign artists in Russia are the orb and sceptre of Tsar Mikhail Feodorovich in the Moscow Armoury, reproduced, *Khudozh. sokrov.*, II (1902), nos. 9–10, plates 101–2.

10. The rigid ceremonial and disconcerting aloofness of later tsars and boyars are described by Herberstein, Olearius, Meyerberg, and other travellers.

11. Reconstruction of plan and section of the earlier Dormition in Nekrasov, *Ocherki*, 182–4, figures 117–18.

12. For Fioravanti's activity in Italy and Hungary see A. Venturi, *Storia dell'arte italiana* (Milan, 1924), III, 2, pp. 298 ff.; summary in *Istoriya*, III, 298, *Geschichte*, III, 209. See also the review of V. Snegirev, *Aristotel Fioravanti i perestroika Moskovskogo kremlya* (Moscow, 1935), by P. Schweinfurth, 'Die italienische Forschung und das Buch von V. Snegirev', *Jahrbücher für die Geschichte Osteuropas*, II (1937), 413–32. See also N. Brunov, 'Due cattedrali del Kremlino costruiti da italiani', *Architettura e arti decorative*, VI (1926), 97–110.

13. V. Dorofeev, *Bolshoi Uspenskii sobor v Moskve* (Moscow, 1896), with 105 photographs of the exterior and interior of the cathedral taken during the restoration of 1894–5. See also M. A. Ilin, 'O postroike moskovskogo uspenskogo sobora Aristotelem Fioravanti', in *Iz istorii russkogo i zapadnoevropeiskogo iskusstva, materialy i issledovaniya* (Moscow, 1960), 53–60.

194. 14. Alpatov-Brunov, 97–8. Such proportional relationships have sometimes eluded the most scru-

pulous observers. In the plan and section of the Trinity of 1422 in the Trinity-Sergius Monastery (*Istoriya*, III, 57–61; *Geschichte*, III, 41–3) the subtly unequal spacing of external pilasters and the eastern displacement of the dome have been regularized.

15. Nekrasov, *Ocherki*, 216. The articles in Thieme-Becker, I (1907), 331 and the *Enciclopedia italiana*, II (1929), 585, confuse him with the earlier Alevisio who had worked on the Kremlin Palace and fortifications from 1494.

199. 16. The church was dedicated in 1532, but in 1977, during restoration, the date '1553' was found on the capital of a pilaster. The arabic numerals, as well as the date (given according to the Western Christian era), were uncommon in Russia at that time. They suggest the presence of foreigners, among them architects, who were in Moscow at the time and may have worked at Kolomenskoe.

200. 17. See Alpatov-Brunov, 118, 229, and plates 61–3, 149, a–c, for comparisons of Russian tent churches with Persian and Indian architecture. See also R. Wischnitzer, 'Orientalische Einflüsse in der russischen Architektur', *Osteuropa*, I (1925–6), 252–5.

18. Soviet opinion, however, holds that the technology and aesthetic of the builders of Kolomenskoe were based on masonry, not wooden, considerations. See *Istoriya*, III, 432; *Geschichte*, III, 299.

19. From 1557 to 1807 there was even a tower church in the Moscow Kremlin, St Sergius in the Epiphany Monastery, with a tall tent roof. It can be seen in a drawing of 1672, reproduced, *Istoriya*, III, 443; *Geschichte*, III, 314.

201. 20. Nekrasov (*Ocherki*, 256–64) proposed Italian influence for the massing of the five elements at Dyakovo, by analogy with such High Renaissance Italian churches as Alessi's S. Maria di Carignano in Genoa. More remarkable, however, is the similarity between the plan of St Basil in Moscow (1555, see below), and such a typical Renaissance plan as Sebastiano Serlio's design for a square domed church with circular chapels projecting from the centre of each façade, which appeared in the fifth book of his treatise on architecture, published in Paris in 1547. Even the relation between the intermediate chapels at St Basil and the spaces in the corners of Serlio's square seems too close for coincidence. But if by some remarkable chance the architects of St Basil possessed a copy of Serlio's treatise, they scorned the Italian's elevation with dome and paired belfries.

202. 21. The Church of the Holy Spirit at Zagorsk is well illustrated in colour in V. Chernov and M. Girard, *Splendours of Moscow and its Surroundings* (Cleveland, 1967), plate 164. For the reconstruction *of the church, see Istoriya,* III, 291; *Geschichte,* III, 203. The columnar buttresses also occur in the tower of the seventeenth-century Boris and Gleb Cathedral in Chernigov, reproduced, G. K. Lukomski, *O proiskhozhdanii form drevne-russkago zodchestva Chernigova* (St Petersburg, 1912), opp. 26.

203. 22. V. V. Suslov, *Tserkov Vasiliya Blazhennago v Moskvie . . . istoriya, znachenie i sovremennoe sostoyanie pamyatnika* (St Petersburg, 1912). An interesting example of the technical primacy exercised by the sixteenth-century votive churches can be seen in the carved wooden altar canopy in the form of a cluster of tent roofs with kokoshniki, in imitation of St Basil, reproduced, MAO, *Drevnosti, Trudy kom.,* I (1907), plate 6. 8.

206. 23. J. Richard, *Tour from London to Petersburgh, and from thence to Moscow* (Dublin, 1781), 52.

24. The Tartars, being nomads, used temporary architectural forms such as tents and portable pavilions. Their chief contribution to Russian art was in the field of ornament. See A. I. Nekrasov, 'Tartarismen im russischen Ornament des XV.–XVI. Jahrhunderts', *Slavia,* IX (1930), 139–50.

CHAPTER 16

213. 1. N. N. Voronin in his *Ocherki po istorii russkago zodchestva XVI–XVII vv.,* 129–30, lists twenty-nine foreign architects active in the seventeenth century. Among them were Thomas Bailey, a Scottish engineer (1658–60), and Christopher Galloway, an Englishman, who installed the clock and built the upper part of the Spassky Tower of the Kremlin (1624–5). Others came from Holland, Germany, and Sweden. See also I. Lubimenko, 'Les Étrangers en Russie avant Pierre le Grand', *Revue des études slaves,* IV (1924), 264–81. The Yaroslavl churches have been published by N. G. Pervukhin, *Tserkov Ioanna predtechi* (Moscow, 1913); *Tserkov Ilii proroka* (Moscow, 1915); *Tserkov Bogoyavleniya* (Yaroslavl, 1916). See also *Istoriya,* IV, 200–12; *Geschichte,* IV, 137–48.

214. 2. The unusual title of this chapel commemorates the presentation in 1624 of a relic of Christ's robe, which had been stolen from a church in Georgia, to the Patriarch Philaret and Tsar Mikhail Feodorovich by the Persian Ambassador as a gift from the Shah. The relic was ceremoniously deposited in the Moscow Dormition. An icon of *c.* 1630 illustrating the event is reproduced, Grabar, VI, 389.

216. 3. 'In observance of the rules of the Holy Apostles and the Fathers the Lord's church should have five cupolas and not resemble a tent. . . . It

should be built conforming to regulative and statutory law as prescribed by the rules and statutes of the church, and should be a one-, or three-, or five-domed, but never a tent-shaped church . . . neither should the cupola have the shape of a tent', quoted by P. Miliukov, *Outlines of Russian Culture,* III, 13. See also M. Spinka, 'Patriarch Nikon and the Subjection of the Russian Church to the State', *Church History,* X (1941), 347–66.

217. 4. Paul of Aleppo, who was present at the first reception in the new palace, described its sumptuous interior, Nikon's taste for luxury, and the close relations between Patriarch and Tsar.

5. Russia, having come late to Christianity, possessed few actual relics of the early Church and had to make do with replicas. Foreigners were often surprised at the matter-of-fact way in which venerated objects, such as the Manger and the Pillar, were pointed out to them, when they knew for themselves that the originals were elsewhere.

6. Nikon and his builders certainly used contemporary illustrations of Jerusalem, especially those in Bernardino Amico da Gallipoli's *Trattato delle Piante e Immagini de Sacri Edifizi di Terra Santa disegnate in Ierusalemme* (Florence, 1620). Compare particularly plates 22 and 24 with Nikon's church and tower. See also M. A. Ilin, *Kamennaya Letopis Moskovskoi Rusi* (Moscow, 1966), chapter 4, and pp. 192, 194 for Amico's engravings.

219. 7. The Monastery of the New Jerusalem was mined and demolished on 10 December 1941. The roof of the rotunda was destroyed and the interior of the church reduced to ruins. With the collapse of the interior walls some remains of Nikon's majolica arcades, in a restrained Renaissance style, came to light. For the history and condition of the church, see I. Grabar and S. Toropov, 'Arkhitekturnye sokrovishcha Novogo Ierusalima', in I. Grabar, ed., *Pamyatniki iskusstva razrushennye nemetskimi zakhvatchikami v SSSR* (Moscow, 1948), 174–99. To explain the fact that Nikon condemned the tent roof after he had himself built the largest, Grabar advances the supposition that he was persuaded by the Latinized clergy from the Ukraine. A. I. Nekrasov has studied the origins of the church and has indicated its possible influence on the centralized plans of the Moscow Baroque churches of the second half of the century. See his 'Arkhitektura Istry i ee znachenie v obshchem razvitii russkogo zodchestva', *Ezhegodnik muzeya arkhitektury,* I (Moscow, 1937), 9–51.

223. 8. For a recent examination of the church at Fili see *Pamyatniki russkoi arkhitektury* (Moscow, 1945). For other examples of the Naryshkin storeyed churches see Bondarenko, parts II–III, plates 1, 3, 4, and 7. Stylistically similar to the church at Fili is the bell-tower in the Novodevichi Monastery of *c.* 1690, one of the most memorable sights of Moscow. Its elegant profile is composed of six octagonal balustraded storeys gradually reduced in size and crowned by a bulbous dome.

224. 9. A conjectural reconstruction of the upper storeys has been published by A. Akselrod, 'Menshikova Bashnya v ee pervonachalnom vide', *Arkhitektura SSSR* (1939), no. 10, 57–61. He adds a slender spire in the style of the Petrovian Baroque. The elaborate stucco reliefs on the interior are reproduced, MAO, *Drevnosti, trudy kom.*, v (1914), plate 1.

225. 10. Several hundred characteristic examples of Moscow church architecture from 1600 to *c.* 1850 are well reproduced in gravure in the publication *Moskva; sobory.*

CHAPTER 17

226. 1. The Pogankin house, restored in 1902, was severely damaged in 1941. For this and other secular buildings see the thoroughly documented study by A. Potapov, 'Ocherk drevnei russkoi grazhdanskoi arkhitektury', MAO, *Drevnosti*, XIX (1901–2), parts 1–3; XX (1904).

2. The standard work on the history and buildings of the Kremlin is S. P. Bartenev, *Moskovskii Kreml v starinu i teper* (Moscow, 1912–16), 2 vols. For more recent opinion, see A. I. Nekrasov, 'Le Kremlin de Moscou, les murailles et les tours', *Arkhitektura SSSR* (1935), nos. 10–11, 90–3 (in Russian). The early-sixteenth-century fortifications of Smolensk have been thoroughly examined by P. P. Pokryshkin, 'Smolenskaya krepostnaya stena', *Izvestiya imperatorskoi arkheologicheskoi kommissii*, XII (1904), 1–25.

229. 3. Temporary wooden structures of traditional horizontal log construction were erected within the Kremlin as late as 1896, for the coronation of Nicholas II. See the photograph of the procession in *Moskva*, X (1911), facing 66.

232. 4. A. von Meyerberg, *Relation d'un voyage en Moscovie*, I (Paris, 1858), 99.

5. *Terem*, from the Greek, meaning an attic, garret, or chamber at the top of a house; in ancient Russia the rooms where the women lived.

233. 6. S. Bartenev, *Le Grand Palais du Kremlin et ses neuf églises* (Moscow, 1912). But scientific knowledge made slow progress. Olearius reported that in 1643 he showed the Muscovites a *camera obscura*: 'All that was done in the street and men walking upon their heads, wrought such an effect in them, that they could never after be otherwise persuaded than that I held a correspondence with the devil.'

7. S. Collins, *The Present State of Russia, in a Letter to a Friend at London* (London, 1671), 64. A seventeenth-century upholstered armchair covered with a Persian fabric, which is said to have belonged to Alexey Mikhailovich, was preserved in the Storozhevsky Monastery near Zvenigorod, reproduced, MAO, *Drevnosti, Trudy kom.*, III (1909), plate G (IV), figure 1.

235. 8. W. Coxe, *Travels in Poland, Russia, Sweden, and Denmark*, I, 265, 'Moscow may be considered as a town built upon the Asiatic model, but gradually becoming more and more European; exhibiting a motley mixture of discordant architecture'.

9. Catherine visited Kolomenskoe on 4 October 1762. The historical sources have been published by I. E. Zabelin, *Domashnii byt russkikh tsarei v XVI i XVII st.* (Moscow, 1872), part I, *materialy*, 3–38. Another important residence was the Stroganov mansion at Solvychegodsk which was in existence until the early nineteenth century. Old drawings and the historical data for it have been published by Zabelin.

236. 10. Olearius, *op. cit.*, 57.

237. 11. For illustrations of these and other secular structures of the seventeenth century see Grabar, II, chapter 15.

12. A. von Meyerberg, *op. cit.*, 99: 'The building which was given us was large enough, and built of brick, which is rare in Moscow. For the houses of the Muscovites are ordinarily of wood. For some years a considerable number of brick buildings have been built in Moscow, either for vanity, or for greater security against the fires which are very frequent there.' G. Miege, in his *Relation of Three Embassies* (1669), wrote that: 'The House we were lodged in in this Town, was a large building of Stone, no great distance from the Castle, and one of the most commodious to be found. The Chambers were all arched, every window had its shutters of iron, and every passage-door was also of iron, which gave one occasion to say, we were certainly in the iron age, though otherwise it be a mettle rare enough in that Country.'

13. *Travels of Macarius*, I, 397.

238. 14. Reproduced, Grabar, II, 274.

15. I. Mashkov, 'Drevnee zdanie kitaiskoi Apteki, Moskovskago Universiteta i staroi Dumy', *Drevnosti, Trudy kom.*, III (1909), lvi–lviii.

16. See Bondarenko, 19–20, plate 9; *Istoriya*, IV, 232–4; *Geschichte*, IV, 163–4.

239. 17. The other half of this engraving is reproduced, Grabar, IV, 29. The whole plate is reproduced in facsimile by D. A. Rovinski, *Materialy dlya russkoi ikonografii*, VIII (St Petersburg, 1884–91), plate 308.

18. See A. A. Kiparisova, 'Lefortovskii dvorets v Moskve', *Arkhitekturnye pamyatniki Moskvy XVII–XVIII vekov*, Moscow, Akademiya Arkhitektury SSSR (1948), 45–54, with a reconstruction by N. N. Sobolev in a picturesque old Russian manner, 56.

CHAPTER 18

241. 1. For the problem of religious precedence between Tsar and Patriarch see G. Vernadsky, 'Notes sur les vêtements sacerdotaux du patriarche Nikon', *L'Art byzantin chez les slaves*, I, 412–15.

242. 2. A. I. Uspenskii, *Tsarskie ikonopistsy i zhivopistsy XVII veka* (Moscow, 1910–16), 4 vols.

3. These frescoes and the later cycle in the Faceted Palace were repainted in 1672 for Tsar Alexey by Simon Ushakov, whose written descriptions are the chief source of information for the subjects. Ushakov's restorations were destroyed in the fires of 1682 and 1812. See Grabar, VI, 320, 336; I. Ee. Zabelin, *Domashnii byt russkikh tsarei*, I (Moscow, 1895), 149, 151–78. Viskovaty was shocked by these frescoes. He complained: 'The parables are not painted according to the canonical rules. Near the figure of Our Saviour a woman is painted dancing nonchalantly, and the inscription on it is "lechery and jealousy" '; Grabar, VI, 320.

243. 4. D. Ainalov, 'Freskovaya rospis khrama Uspeniya Bogoroditsy v Sviyazhskom muzhskom Bogoroditskom monastyr', MAO, *Drevnosti*, XXI (1906); M. K. Karger, 'Les Portraits des fondateurs dans les peintures murales du monastère de Sviiazsk', *L'Art byzantin chez les slaves*, II, 135–49.

5. The last large frescoes of the sixteenth century were painted in 1598 in the Cathedral of the Virgin of Smolensk, in the Novodevichi Monastery in Moscow. They were commissioned by Boris Godunov, who had been crowned Tsar in the church that same year. Four rows of icons were also added to the iconostasis in 1598, but like the frescoes they are in poor condition. See Grabar, VI, 337–46; D. K. Trenev, *Ikonostas smolenskago sobora moskovskago novodevichyago monastyrya* (Moscow, 1902).

6. For views of the architecture and church furniture in this city, see N. Makarenko, *Iskusstvo drevnei Rusi v soli Vychegodskoi* (Petrograd, 1918).

7. For the 'Stroganov school' see Grabar, VI, chapter 10 (and the French translation in P. Muratov's *L'Ancienne Peinture russe*); N. P. Kondakov,

The Russian Icon, chapter 9; Schweinfurth, 328–53.

247. 8. *Travels of Macarius*, I, 401.

251. 9. A. I. Uspenskii, *Drevne-russkaya zhivopis* (Moscow, 1906); Grabar, VI, chapter 13; summary in Thieme-Becker, XXXIV, 5–6; *Istoriya*, IV, 370–86, 388–90; *Geschichte*, IV, 273–6, 290–3. Ushakov's etching of The Seven Deadly Sins is reproduced, *Istoriya*, IV, 499: *Geschichte*, IV, 373.

10. Reproduced, Kondakov, *The Russian Icon*, plate 59; *Istoriya*, IV, 375; *Geschichte*, IV, 277. For details of the small scenes, see Grabar, VI, 431–7.

11. The Vernicle illustrated [188] is but one of many variants of Ushakov's original icon. A slightly less forceful example, now in the State Tretyakov Gallery, Moscow, is signed and dated 1658 (Antonova and Mneva, II, no. 910 and plate 144). See also K. Onasch, *Icons* (New York, 1963), 398–9 and plate 132.

253. 12. Grabar, VI, 426; G. Lebedev, *Russkaya zhivopis pervoi poloviny XVIII veka* (Moscow, 1938).

13. P. Miliukov, *Outlines of Russian Culture*, III, 44.

14. *Travels of Macarius*, II, 49–50.

15. Olearius, *op. cit.*, 76.

254. 16. Mikhail's father, Feodor Romanov (Patriarch Philaret), was a nephew of Anastasia Romanova, first wife of Ivan IV.

17. For reproduction, V. Dorofeev, *Bolshoi Uspenskii Sobor v Moskve* (Moscow, 1896). Certain frescoes are reproduced after cleaning, MAO, *Drevnosti, Trudy, kom.*, IV (1912), xii ff.

18. *Travels of Macarius*, I, 397.

19. Paulus Giovius (1483–1522) mentions a portrait of Vasily III taken from Moscow to Rome by Dmitry Gerasimov. See G. Lebedev, *Russkaya zhivopis pervoi poloviny XVIII veka* (Moscow and Leningrad, 1938), 13–14. See also W. Troutowsky, 'Le Boyard Khitrowo à la tête de la Salle des armures à Moscou', *Starye gody* (July–Sept. 1909), 345–83; A. Novitsky, 'Le Portrait à la cour de Moscou', *ibid.*, 384–403; A. Mironoff, 'L'Authenticité des portraits du Tsar Michel', *Starye gody* (July–Sept. 1913), 7–24.

20. Lebedev, *op. cit.*, 15.

255. 21. The painting, now in the museum at Istra, was damaged in the destruction of the monastery during the Second World War. Reproduced, Grabar, VI, 417; *Istoriya*, IV, 455; *Geschichte*, IV, 338–9. See also N. Romanov, 'Parsuna izobraziaushchaya patriarkha Nikona proiznosyashchego pouchenie kliru', in I. Grabar, ed., *Pamyatniki iskusstva razrushennye nemetskimi zakhvatchikami v SSSR* (Moscow and Leningrad, 1948), 201–16.

22. The principal series are in Kostroma, Trinity Cathedral (1685); Rostov, St John (after 1683), the Resurrection (1680), the Redeemer (1680); Vologda, St Sophia (1668–88); for Yaroslavl, see the works of Pervukhin, above, Chapter 16, Note 1.

256. 23. For the influence of Piscator's Bible see E. P. Sachavets-Feodorovich, 'Yaroslavskie stenopisi i bibliya Piskatora', *Russkoe iskusstvo XVII veka, sbornik statei* (Leningrad, 1929), 85–108. See also Grabar, VI, chapter 17.

24. There is little iconographical, technical, or formal evidence to support P. Miliukov's contention: 'It seems that Russian art, living in the atmosphere of general religious exaltation, stood at that moment on the threshold of another revival of Christian painting, similar to the one experienced in the West during the fourteenth and fifteenth centuries. Had it been left to its own devices, Russian art perhaps would have followed the same path as that of western art, and three or four centuries later would have attained its classical epoch' (*Outlines of Russian Culture*, III, 47). The influence of Russian painting outside Russia, especially in the Balkan countries, has been suggested by A. Grabar in 'L'Expansion de la peinture russe aux XVIe et XVIIe siècles', Sem. Kond., *Recueil d'études*, XI (1940), 65–93.

257. 25. In the late nineteenth century the revival of interest in the Russian past led to a search for the few surviving workshops. See A. V. Bakushinskii, *Iskusstvo Palekha* (Moscow and Leningrad, 1934).

CHAPTER 19

259. 1. After 1700 the titles of Great Prince and Great Princess (*Veliky Knyaz, Velikaya Knyaginya*) are rendered as Grand Duke and Grand Duchess, according to European usage since the seventeenth century.

260. 2. For the illustrated architectural history of the city see L. Hautecœur, *L'Architecture classique à Saint-Pétersbourg à la fin du XVIIIe siècle* (Paris, 1912); L. Réau, *Saint-Pétersbourg* (Paris, 1913); V. Ya. Kurbatov, *Peterburg, khudozhestvenno-istoricheskii ocherk* (St Petersburg, 1913).

261. 3. The important research undertaken by the Petersburg Society of Artists-Architects culminated in a comprehensive architectural exhibition at the Academy of Fine Arts in 1911, with an illustrated catalogue by A. Benois and I. A. Fomin, *Istoricheskaya vystavka arkhitektury* (St Petersburg, 1911).

4. For the emergence of symbolic values in town planning, with special reference to the sequence of five interrelated squares beside and between the Winter Palace and the Admiralty, see I. A. Egorov,

The Architectural Planning of St Petersburg (Athens, Ohio, 1969), translated and with an introduction by E. Dluhosch.

263. 5. As early as 1739 Count Francesco Algarotti, an Italian adventurer visiting Russia, noticed the rapid deterioration of the jerry-built architecture: 'Their walls are all cracked, quite out of the perpendicular, and ready to fall. It has been wittily said, that ruins make themselves in other places, but that they are built at Petersburg. Accordingly, it is necessary every moment, in this new capital, to repair the foundations of the buildings, and its inhabitants build incessantly: as well for this reason, as on account of the instability of the ground and of the bad quality of the materials.' See *Letters from Count Algarotti to Lord Hervey* (London, 1769), I, 77. Luigi Rusca, an architect of the later eighteenth century, published detailed information on the construction of damp-proof foundations in Russia. For his own buildings he preferred vaulted stone basements. L. Rusca, *Recueil des dessins de differens batimens construits à Saint-Pétersbourg et dans l'intérieure de Russie* (St Petersburg, 1810), 4 ff.

6. For details of early panoramas and engraved views of St Petersburg, see Grabar, III, *passim*; *Istoriya*, V, 75–8.

7. *Peterburgskaya Chast*, hence the nickname 'Peter' for the city as a whole. In 1914 the city was renamed Petrograd (Peter's City), and in 1924, Leningrad.

265. 8. *Istoriya*, V, 85–90; M. Korolkov, 'Les Architectes Trezzini', *Starye Gody* (April, 1911), 17–36 (in Russian).

267. 9. The character of this church, for all that it was a dynastic sepulchre, is suggested by Baedeker's remark (1914): 'The interior is adorned with military trophies, flowers, and growing plants, and makes a very light and cheerful impression.'

269. 10. Engravings of the 1715 design and of the later revised plans by Tressini and Schwertfeger are reproduced, *Istoriya*, V, 102–3. Numerous wooden models for eighteenth-century buildings have been preserved and are invaluable for studying the architects' original conceptions; V. Linkovski, 'Les Modèles d'architecture en Russie', *Starye Gody* (Dec. 1910), 3–19.

11. The Catherine Palace (Ekaterinhof), of traditional horizontal timber construction with Corinthian pilasters and a balustrade, is reproduced, *Istoricheskaya panorama Sanktpeterburga i ego okrestnostei*, I (Moscow, 1911), plate 20.

270. 12. Grabar, III, 75–82. The Kunstkamera was damaged by fire in 1747, and all the decorative sculpture destroyed. The early engravings re-

produced as illustrations 196 and 200 are taken from *Palaty Sankt Peterburgskoi Akademii Nauk, Biblioteka i Kunstkamera* (St Petersburg, 1741), by the librarian J. D. Shumacher, brother of a German architect active at that time. In 1941 the building again suffered during the bombardment of Leningrad. See P. Kaplan-Ingel, 'Petrovskaya Kunstkamera k vosstanovleniiu zdaniya', *Arkhitektura SSSR* (1946), no. 13, 36–40.

13. Grabar, III, chapter 6; the first Menshikov Palace is reproduced, 98–9. Schädel later worked with Rastrelli in Moscow, and in Kiev, where he completed the seventeenth-century belfry at St Sophia (1744–8), and built the belfry at the Pecherskaya Lavra (1731–45).

272. 14. Grabar, III, chapter 8; the plan of 1716–17 is reproduced 123; *Istoriya*, V, 105. See also B. Lossky, *J.-B.-A. Le Blond, Architecte de Pierre le Grand, son œuvre en France* (Prague, 1936).

15. Le Blond's plan (Egorov, *op. cit.*, figure 4), which took little account of the three great waterways flowing through the future city, and would thus have hindered development beyond the Admiralty on the south bank, seems to have been influenced by Scamozzi's plan for an ideal city. See Vincenzo Scamozzi, *Dell' Idea della Architettura Universale . . . Parte Prima* (Venice, 1615), 165.

273. 16. For an early engraving of Le Blond's palace, see Grabar, III, 129; *Istoriya*, V, 80. The palaces at Peterhof were shelled and burned during the siege of Leningrad, but have since been reconstructed. The ruins of the main palace and the English Palace, and those of Tsarskoe Selo, Pavlovsk, Gatchina, and the Yelagin Palace, are described and illustrated in I. Grabar, ed., *Pamyatniki iskusstva razrushennye nemetskimi zakhvatchikami v SSSR* (Moscow and Leningrad, 1948).

17. *Istoriya*, V, 110–11, for the plan and elevation of the principal façade of Strelna.

275. 18. The 'Dutch' aspect of St Petersburg is more apparent in the decorated gables of a few houses in the early engravings than in any monumental structures. The few Dutch architects who came to Russia worked in the current international style. See Grabar, III, 19, and chapter 7. Algarotti's impression seems to have been based on the general effect of tree-lined streets and canals, more than on any specific buildings: '[Dutch architecture] is the most prevalent, and it is no wonder. The Czar's first studies were in Holland, and it was at Saardam that this new Prometheus took the fire with which he animated his nation. It seems likewise to have been solely in remembrance of Holland that he planted rows of trees along the streets, and intersected them

with canals, which certainly are not the same here as at Amsterdam and Utrecht' (*Letters from Count Algarotti to Lord Hervey*, I (London, 1769), 76, letter of 30 June 1739).

19. Algarotti, *op. cit.*, 76. A curious indication of that mixture of the most modern European fashions with Russian provincialism which prevailed in early St Petersburg can be found in the carved panelling in Peter's study at Peterhof, executed before 1721 by Nicolas Pineau (1684–1754), who had accompanied Le Blond to Russia. The modishly Rococo designs contain in the over-door panels asymmetrical motifs as advanced as any in France at that date. See Fiske Kimball, *The Creation of the Rococo* (Philadelphia, 1943), 132–4.

CHAPTER 20

276. 1. C. Marsden's *Palmyra of the North, the First Days of St Petersburg* (London, 1942), is an informed account of the social and artistic life of the Russian court, principally under Elizabeth.

2. See E. Haumant, *La Culture française en Russie (1700–1900)* (Paris, 1910).

3. There is as yet no monograph in a non-Russian language on this important architect. The Russian sources are summarized in Thieme-Becker, XXVIII (1934), 26–8. For reproductions, Grabar, III, chapter 13; *Istoriya*, V, 174–209; A. Matveev, *Rastrelli* (Leningrad, 1938), with bibliography.

277. 4. Contemporary engraved views of this palace are reproduced, Bondarenko, parts 2–3, plate 51. Foreign visitors were always astonished at the portability of wooden buildings. Archdeacon Coxe described the removal of a palace in Catherine II's time: 'Wooden structures of large dimensions and handsome appearance are occasionally formed in Russia, with an expedition almost inconceivable to the inhabitants of other countries. A remarkable instance of this dispatch was displayed during the last visit of the Empress to Moscow. Her Majesty proposed to reside in the mansion of Prince Galitzin, which is esteemed the completest edifice in this city; but as it was not sufficiently spacious for her reception, a temporary addition of wood, larger than the original house, and containing a magnificent suite of apartments, was finished within the space of six weeks. This meteor-like fabric was so handsome and commodious, that the materials were afterwards taken down and reconstructed upon an eminence near the city, as an imperial villa' (W. Coxe, *Travels in Poland*, etc., I, 348).

278. 5. The Summer Palace charmed visitors to the very end of the century, when Rastrelli's Winter

Palace already seemed old-fashioned and ungainly. Andrew Swinton, in his *Travels into Norway, Denmark, and Russia, in the years 1788*, etc. (Dublin, 1792), wrote that 'the Summer Palace [is] built of timber, and yet the most regular and elegant. It is placed in the Summer Gardens, upon the banks of the river, and is truly a delightful residence'.

279. 6. Grabar, III, 199–200. For the palace see also A. Benois and A. Uspenskii, 'Petergof v 18 veke', *Khudozh. sokrov.*, II (1902), nos. 7–8, with many illustrations.

282. 7. The Russian tradition of a tall belfry must be considered the factor determining the height of Rastrelli's tower, but it is interesting to compare his model with the design for a combination belfry and fountain published by Paul Decker in 1713 as plate 3 of the supplement to his *Fürstlicher Baumeister oder: Architectura Civilis* (Augsburg, 1711). Decker's tower corresponds in many respects to the first four storeys of Rastrelli's.

283. 8. The name of the original Finnish settlement on the site, *Saari mos* ('High Place'), was russianized as Sarskoe Selo ('Saari Village') and after Peter I offered it to his wife Catherine as a country estate soon became Tsarskoe Selo ('Tsarist, or Imperial Village').

9. Models and drawings for the successive alterations at Tsarskoe Selo are reproduced, A. Benois, *Tsarskoe Selo v tsarstvovanie imperatritsy Elisavety Petrovny* (St Petersburg, 1910).

10. The original drawing for the park is reproduced, Matveev, *op. cit.*, 35.

286. 11. Reproduced, Grabar, III, 215.

287. 12. There is scant evidence in Rastrelli's work for the tradition that he studied in Paris and travelled widely in central Europe. There are, however, indications that he may have known the architecture of northern Italy and Austria more intimately. To cite but two instances, at Smolny the relation between the dome and the subsidiary cupolas recalls Juvara's dome and belfry at the Superga near Turin (1706–20), and the diagonal axes of the towers at Smolny and St Andrew in Kiev resemble Lukás von Hildebrandt's treatment of the Peterskirche in Vienna. It is interesting to think that if Rastrelli visited Vienna before 1725 he could have seen the Bibienas' sets for the opera, and could have studied Hildebrandt's designs for the new Hofburg (unexecuted) as well as the recently finished Belvedere. Hildebrandt's palaces, more than any others in Europe, have points in common with Rastrelli's early work in St Petersburg, such as the Anichkov Palace.

13. This theatrical manner can be seen in the Cathedral of St Nicholas of the Sea in St Petersburg (1753–62) by Rastrelli's pupil and assistant, S. I. Chevakinsky (1713–83), reproduced, Grabar, III, 247–9; *Istoriya*, V, 216–17. The arrangement in each of the projecting angles of a cluster of Corinthian columns on high bases and supporting sections of a powerful entablature is virtually a translation of the familiar Bibiena programme of similar elements set on an axis diagonal to the proscenium. See the drawings by Ferdinando and Giuseppe Galli Bibiena in C. Ricci, *I Bibiena* (Milan, 1915); and A. H. Mayor, *The Bibiena Family* (New York, 1945), *passim*. Rastrelli's peculiar cupolas, especially those at Peterhof, resemble far less those of Pöppelmann's Zwinger at Dresden (1711–22), with which they are usually compared, than those in such typical Bibiena stage sets as Giuseppe's design of 1723 for *Costanza e Fortezza*, an opera presented that year in Prague, reproduced, G. G. Bibiena, *Theaterdecorationen . . ., Entwürfe . . . von G. G. Bibiena* (Berlin, n.d.), plate 19. Another provocative comparison may be made between Rastrelli's Hermitage at Tsarskoe Selo (1748–52), and Piranesi's *Gruppo di scala*, plate 11 of his *Prima parte de architettura* (1743), reproduced, Grabar, III, and A. M. Hind, *G. B. Piranesi* (London, 1922), plate 73. The arrangement of columns, bases, and curved pediments is almost identical, and Rastrelli's wings projecting diagonally from the central portion exemplify the principle of Ferdinando Bibiena's *scena veduta per angolo*. Rastrelli's energetic but inorganic decoration may have been suggested by the engravings in Ferdinando Bibiena's *L'Architettura civile* (Parma, 1711; enlarged edition, Bologna, 1731).

288. 14. Elizabeth died 25 December 1761, Old Style (5 January 1762, New Style), hence the date 1761–2 for the six-months reign (January–June) of Peter III.

CHAPTER 21

289. 1. Catherine's dual conception of Russia's position can be seen in the contrast between her interest in Russian history (see below, Chapter 23, pages 336–7 and Note 9), and the peremptory statement at the head of her *Instructions to the Commissioners for Composing a New Code of Laws* (1766), that the first 'natural situation' to be kept in mind was that 'Russia is a European State'. W. F. Reddaway, ed., *Documents of Catherine the Great* (Cambridge, 1931), 215.

2. A less favourable attitude towards Catherine's taste is presented by L. Réau and G. K. Lukomski in *Cathérine la grande, inspiratrice d'art et mécène* (Paris, 1930). They insist upon her lack of under-

standing of the arts and believe that she was merely lucky in her choice of men of genius. Réau even deprecates her passion for collecting, since it deprived France of so many fine objects. However that may be, the works of architecture and art commissioned and collected by Catherine constitute the most remarkable artistic achievement of any eighteenth-century sovereign.

290. 3. Her attitude towards Elizabeth's taste is summarized in Casanova's account of his meeting with her in the Summer Garden in 1764. The Italian adventurer had been examining the sculptures, 'all being made of the worst stone and executed in the worst possible taste', when the Empress appeared and asked 'smilingly' if he were interested in them. Casanova replied that he presumed 'they had been placed there to impose on fools or to excite the laughter of those acquainted with history'. Catherine replied: 'From what I can make out, the secret of the matter is that my worthy aunt was imposed on, and indeed she did not trouble herself much about such trifles. But I hope you have seen other things in Russia less ridiculous than these statues' (*The Memoirs of Jacques Casanova de Seingalt*, translated by A. Machen, x (n.p., n.d.), 183–4).

4. Grabar, III, chapter 16. Prince Shuvalov's residence is reproduced, 265. See also the even more sober Razumovsky Palace in St Petersburg of 1762–6 (*Istoriya*, VI, 53).

291. 5. L. Réau, 'Vallin de la Mothe, documents inédits', *L'Architecture*, XXXV (1922), 173–80. He was a cousin of J.-F. Blondel, who may have suggested his appointment to Shuvalov.

6. Blondel's design is reproduced, Grabar, III, 267.

292. 7. Rastrelli had prepared the first design for the Markets as a two-storey Rococo building with a central clock-tower. Vallin de la Mothe's plan followed Rastrelli's but stripped it of its ornament. See A. Matveev, *Rastrelli*, 20–1.

8. Grabar, III, 87; *Istoriya*, VI, opp. p. 68.

293. 9. The interiors are reproduced by A. Uspenskii and A. Benois, 'Kitaiskii dvorets v Oranienbaum', *Khudozh. sokrov.*, I (1901), 183–210. See also H. Honour, *Chinoiserie, the Vision of Cathay* (London, 1961), 117.

294. 10. The similarity between the *ordonnance* and that of Juvara's Palazzo d'Ormea in Turin (1730) suggests that Rinaldi, like Rastrelli, may have spent some time in northern Italy. See the comparative photographs in A. E. Brinckmann, *Die Baukunst des 17. und 18. Jahrhunderts in den romanischen Ländern* (Berlin, 1919), 124–5.

11. The palace, its interior, and furnishings, are extensively illustrated in a series of articles by N. Lanceray, P. P. Weiner, *et al.*, *Starye Gody* (July–Sept., 1914), 5 ff.

295. 12. Something of the character of the lost St Isaac can be seen in the cathedral at Yamburg, west of St Petersburg (1762–82). Here the belfry with its circular lantern and baluster finial is very Roman, and the lower storeys and rounded arms of the crossing are also derived from St Peter's. Reproduced, Grabar, III, 309.

296. 13. Velten's grilles were the first of many such characteristic adornments of St Petersburg. See G. N. Germont, *Reshetki Leningrada i ego okrestnostei* (Moscow, 1938).

14. Grabar, III, chapter 19; *Istoriya*, VI, 85–129; various essays on Bazhenov, *Arkhitektura SSSR* (1936), no. 2, 2–27; V. L. Snegirev, *Arkhitektor V. I. Bazhenov* (Moscow, 1937); 'Vassily Bazhenov', *Architectural Review*, XCVII (1945), 15–20.

15. Grabar, III, 247–9; *Istoriya*, V, 216–17.

297. 16. No drawings exist for the palace, which was built by Velten, but it has been attributed to Bazhenov on stylistic grounds. Reproduced, Grabar, III, 327; see also *Istoriya*, VI, 94–5.

298. 17. The model was much admired in the later eighteenth century by those fortunate enough to see it. In 1800 the English scientist Edward Daniel Clarke, Professor of Mineralogy at Cambridge, visited Moscow and wrote that having 'obtained the keys from the secretary's office we were admitted to see the famous Model of the Kremlin ... one of the most curious things in Moscow. ... Its fronts are ornamented with ranges of beautiful pillars, according to the different orders of architecture. Every part of it was finished in the most beautiful manner, even to the Fresco painting on the ceilings of the rooms, and the colouring of the various marble columns intended to decorate the interior. ... Had the work been completed, no edifice could ever have compared with it' (E. D. Clarke, *Travels in Russia, Tartary, and Turkey* (London, 1810; ed. of 1839), p. 32).

299. 18. At the head of her instructions to the Legislative Commission of 1766 Catherine declared that: 'The Intention and the End of Monarchy, is the Glory of the Citizens, of the State, and of the Sovereign' (W. F. Reddaway, ed., *Documents of Catherine the Great* (Cambridge, 1931), 217).

300. 19. Grabar, III, 341; *Istoriya*, VI, 169. See also N. Belekhov and A. Petrov, *Ivan Starov* (Moscow, 1950), where Starov's work is copiously, if indifferently, reproduced.

20. This belfry was totally destroyed on 20 December 1941. The ruins are reproduced, *Pamyatniki*

zodchestva razrushennye ili povrezhdennye nemetskimi zakhvatchikami, part II (1944), 57–9.

304. 21. The Clérisseau *contretemps* is discussed by Catherine and Grimm in letters exchanged on 17 December 1778, 2 February, 26 April, 7 November 1779. See L. Réau, 'Correspondance artistique de Grimm avec Catherine II', *Archives de l'art français*, nouv-pér., XVII (1932), 1–206. More quotations from this correspondence will be found under the corresponding dates.

22. *Documents of Catherine the Great*, 163, letter to Voltaire, 25 June 1772.

23. For Cameron, see Grabar, III, chapter 21; *Istoriya*, VI, 215–25; *Charles Cameron* ... (Edinburgh, Glasgow, London, 1967–8), an Arts Council exhibition of his architectural drawings; I. Rae, *Charles Cameron, Architect to the Court of Russia* (London, 1971).

24. C. Cameron, *The Baths of the Romans Explained and Illustrated, with the Restorations of Palladio Corrected and Improved* (London, 1772). Cameron's debt to Palladio can be seen by comparing the plans and elevations of the palace of Pavlovsk with Palladio's Villa Trissino at Meledo (best reproduced in the Hoepli facsimile text of the *Quattro Libri dell'Architettura* (Milan, 1945), 60).

308. 25. G. K. Lukomskii, *Baturinskii dvorets, ego istoriya, razrushenie, i restavratsiya* (St Petersburg, 1912); Grabar, III, 387.

26. Grabar, III, 386.

310. 27. Published by F. M. Tassi, *Vite de' pittori, scultori e architetti bergamaschi* (Bergamo, 1793), 150. In addition to the works here described, Quarenghi listed designs for two-storey shops, churches, hospitals, and other public works, and added: 'Ho fatto moltissimi altri Progetti per S.M., che forse non avranno luogo per ora, e pur ciò non gli accenno.'

313. 28. Grabar, III, 410–11.

29. This building, to which Catherine II's school for the daughters of the nobility was soon transferred from Rastrelli's convent, is the 'Smolny Institute', Lenin's headquarters in 1917 during and after the October Revolution.

CHAPTER 22

314. 1. See Grimm's letter to Catherine of 4 November 1782 recounting the amusing episode he witnessed in Paris, when at a reception the Comte du Nord Clérisseau tried to make amends to Paul for his past difficulties with Catherine.

2. Maria Feodorovna's inventory in French has been published as 'Description du Grand Palais de Pavlovsk, rédigée et écrite par la Grande-Duchesse

Marie Feodorovna en 1795' (1903), 371–82, with many illustrations showing the French character of the interiors and furnishings at Pavlovsk.

3. Grabar, III, chapter 23. Brenna's designs for the Michael Palace were gradually evolved from his first idea of imitating the Villa Farnese at Caprarola. See S. M. Zemtsov, 'Documents pour l'histoire du Château des Ingénieurs', *Arkhitektura SSSR* (1935), no. 9, 63–70 (in Russian).

315. 4. F. F. Vigel (1786–1856), *Zapiski*, I (Moscow, 1864–5), 180. See also Grabar, III, 406; T. Talbot Rice, 'The St Petersburg of Alexander I', *Architectural Review*, LXXVII (1935), 245–9.

5. See the collections of designs by A. A. Mikhailov, *Sobranie fasadov ... dlya chastnykh stroenii v gorodakh rossiiskoi imperii*, parts I–II (1809), III–IV (1812), reproduced in V. M. Vladimirov, *Starye arkhitekturnye proekty* (St Petersburg, 1913), 2 vols.

316. 6. Russian Neo-Classicism (although scantily represented by actual objects) may be studied within the framework of contemporary European developments in *The Age of Neo-classicism* (London, 1972), the catalogue of the fourteenth exhibition of the Council of Europe. See also H. Honour, *Neo-classicism* (Harmondsworth, 1969), passim.

7. W. Kurbatov, 'Le Classicisme et le style de l'Empire', *Starye gody* (July–Sept., 1912), 105–19 (in Russian).

8. For Ledoux's influence on Russian architecture see I. Grabar, 'Les Débuts du classicisme sous Alexandre et ses sources françaises', *Starye gody* (July–Sept., 1912), 68–96.

9. L. Réau, *L'Art russe de Pierre le grand à nos jours* (Paris, 1922), 90.

317. 10. Grabar, III, 470; *Istoriya*, VI, 187–8.

11. Grabar, III, 418–19.

12. Grabar, III, chapter 26; *Istoriya*, VIII (part I), 62–85; V. A. Panov, *Arkhitektor A. N. Voronikhin* (Moscow, 1937); A. Krusetski and E. Lundberg, *Zodchii A. N. Voronikhin* (Sverdlovsk, 1937).

318. 13. A. P. Aplaksin, *Kazanskii Sobor* (St Petersburg, 1911). An obelisk which originally stood in the centre of the square increased the resemblance to St Peter's.

319. 14. N. Tarassoff, 'L'École des Mines, à St-Pétersbourg', *Starye gody* (March, 1909), 139–45 (in Russian).

320. 15. Grabar, III, chapter 27; *Istoriya*, VIII (part I), 106–27.

16. Odessa was once an interesting example of an integrated Neo-classical city. It was founded by Catherine II in 1794, and by 1814 the town plan had been developed on a geometrical scheme. A considerable number of buildings erected in these

years gave it a prevailing classical character. See M. Sinyaver, *Arkhitektura staroi Odessy* (Leningrad, 1935).

17. Grabar, III, chapter 28; *Istoriya*, VIII (part I), 86–105; N. Lancere, 'Adrien Zakharoff et l'Amirauté à St Pétersbourg', *Starye gody* (Dec., 1911), 3–64 (in Russian).

322. 18. For later Russian ceramics, see M. C. Ross, *Russian Porcelains* (Norman, Oklahoma, 1968), an account of Mrs Merriweather Post's extensive collection at Hillwood in Washington, D.C. Various aspects of the decorative arts through the centuries are briefly discussed in T. T. Rice, *A Concise History of Russian Art* (London, 1963). R. Hare, *The Art and Artists of Russia* (New York, 1965), has excellent colour plates. See also the catalogue, *Treasures from the Kremlin* (New York, 1979).

323. 19. I. E. Bondarenko, *Arkhitektor M. F. Kazakov* (Moscow, 1912); *idem, Arkhitektor M. F. Kazakov, 1738–1813* (Moscow, 1938). For further examples of Neo-classical architecture in Moscow see I. Fomin, 'Moskovskii klassizism', *Mir Iskusstva* (1904), no. 7, 147–98; *Istoriya*, VI, 130–64.

324. 20. Grabar, III, chapter 30; *Istoriya*, VIII (part I), 165–80; Akademiya arkhitektury SSSR, *Arkhitektor V. P. Stasov* (Moscow, 1950).

326. 21. The Transfiguration is reproduced, Grabar, III, 532; the Trinity, Grabar, III, 533, and *Istoriya*, VIII (part I), 177. The latter church is no less original even if account is taken of the fact that the plan is essentially a reproduction of the previous wooden church of 1754 which was burned in 1828. This was on the familiar cross plan of the wooden churches of the north, but had five domes and was painted in imitation of stone. See the water-colour drawings in A. S. Drenyakin, *Istoricheskoe opisanie tserkvei leibgvardii Izmailovskago polka, 1730–1850* (St Petersburg, 1851). The appearance of a wooden church of the early Petersburg period can be studied in photographs of the Cathedral of the Holy Trinity near the Peter-Paul Fortress. It was built in 1710, remodelled in 1756, and burned in 1913. See *Starye gody* (March, 1913), 48–9.

22. Grabar, III, chapter 32; *Istoriya*, VIII (part I), 128–65; V. A. Panov, *Arkhitektor Carlo Rossi* (Moscow, 1937).

327. 23. Grabar, III, 544.

24. Augustin de Béthencourt y Molina (1758–1824), a distinguished civil and military engineer, left Spain during the Napoleonic War and reached Russia in 1808, where he was promptly commissioned as a lieutenant-general in the Russian army. For the work of the Committee on Construction and Hydraulic Works, see I. A. Egorov, *The Archi-tectural Planning of St Petersburg* (Athens, Ohio, 1969), *passim*.

25. Reproduced, *Istoriya*, VIII (part I), 131–3. See also Société impériale des architectes de St Pétersbourg, *Le Palais Yélaguine* (St Petersburg, n.d.).

329. 26. Towards the end of the Time of Troubles (1598–1613), Prince D. M. Pozharsky, with the merchant Kuzma Minin, organized an army, drove the Poles from Moscow, and summoned an assembly which elected Mikhail Romanov tsar. They are represented in classical dress by Martos in the sculpture in Red Square [265]. See also N. V. Veinert, 'La Rue de l'architecte Rossi', *Arkhitektura SSSR* (1935), no. 7, 44–50 (in Russian); C. Derzhavin, *A Century of the State Dramatic Theatre, 1832–1932* (Leningrad, 1932), 18.

331. 27. Grabar, III, chapters 33–5; *Istoriya*, VIII (part I), 186–284.

28. Grabar, III, chapter 35; L. Réau, ed., 'Lettres inédites de l'architecte Ricard de Montferrand à son ami Favart (1834–1843)', *Archives de l'art français*, nouv. pér., XVII (1932), 207–33.

29. The complicated procedure of the competition, and many of the plans, as well as Montferrand's several revisions, are analysed and reproduced, N. P. Nikitin, *Ogiust Monferran* (Leningrad, 1939).

30. Montferrand's *L'Église cathédrale de Saint-Isaac, description architecturale, pittoresque, et historique* (St Petersburg, 1845), is illustrated with sixty imposing lithographs showing various stages of construction. Montferrand preserved the four piers and vaults at the crossing of Rinaldi's church in compliance with Nicholas I's command that the three consecrated altars should not be disturbed.

332. 31. As a result of these 'augmentations', and in spite of the thousands of piles driven for the foundations, the weight of the cathedral proved too heavy for the gravelly soil. Within a few years large cracks appeared in the walls. The measurements published by N. P. Nikitin, *op. cit.*, indicate the serious and unequal settling of the fabric.

333. 32. A. R. Montferrand, *Plans et détails du monument consacré à la mémoire de l'empereur Alexandre* (Paris, 1836); P. Hofer, 'Montferrand and the Alexandrine Column at Leningrad', *Gazette des beaux-arts*, 6e pér., XXVI (1944), 333–48.

CHAPTER 23

334. 1. The origin and development of this attitude have been studied by C. Hussey, *The Picturesque* (London, 1927). Russian parks and gardens may be examined in relation to European landscaping in V. Ya. Kurbatov, *Sady i parki* (St Petersburg, 1916).

2. W. F. Reddaway, ed., *Documents of Catherine the Great*, 163. Catherine's alterations extended to Moscow. Archdeacon Coxe described the gardens at the Annenhof: 'In some parts the grounds were laid out in a pleasing and natural manner, but in general the old style of gardening prevailed, and presented rows of clipped yew-trees, long straight canals, and a profusion of preposterous statues. . . . The reign of these deities was however doomed to be short; under the auspices of Catherine, all these instances of grotesque taste will be removed, and give place to more natural ornaments.' He also commented on Prince Panin's park at Miakulka: 'We could not avoid feeling extreme satisfaction that the English style of gardening had penetrated into these distant regions. The English taste, indeed, can display itself in this country to great advantage, where the parks are extensive, and the verdure, during the short summer, uncommonly beautiful. Most of the Russian nobles have gardeners of our nations, and resign themselves implicitly to their direction' (W. Coxe, *Travels*, I, 270, 287).

3. For illustrations of the buildings in the park of Tsarskoe Selo see A. Benois, *Tsarskoe Selo* (1910); S. N. Vilchkovski, *Tsarskoe Selo* (St Petersburg, 1911, German ed., Berlin, 1911); S. S. Bronstein, *Arkhitektura goroda Pushkina* (Moscow, 1940). In the last year of her life Catherine called these little buildings her 'caprices' (*Souvenirs de Mme (M.L.E.) Vigée Le Brun*, I (Paris, 1869), 316).

335. 4. This was the best-known Russian artificial ruin of the time and was painted by Hubert Robert in 1783 after drawings made on the spot. Reproduced, L. Réau, 'L'Œuvre d'Hubert Robert en Russie', *Gazette des beaux-arts*, 4ᵉ pér. XI (1914), 185. In the early nineteenth century an artificial ruined gateway in the classical style was built at Arkhangelskoe, the estate of Prince Yusupov, near Moscow, reproduced, S. V. Bezsonov, *Arkhangelskoe podmoskovnaya usadba* (Moscow, 1937), with many illustrations.

5. Ilya Neelov (b. 1745) was the son of an architect and studied at the Petersburg Academy (1761–70). In 1771 he visited England, where he may have acquired his appreciation of garden architecture. He worked almost exclusively at Tsarskoe Selo. Velten's, Neelov's, and Quarenghi's pavilions are reproduced in S. S. Bronstein, *Arkhitektura goroda Pushkina* (Moscow, 1940), plates 110–43.

6. A drawing of the farm at Pavlovsk by the poet V. A. Zhukovsky (1783–1852) is reproduced by the Grand Duke Constantine Constantinovich in his *Pavlovsk: dvorets, park, zhivopis*, III (St Petersburg, 1899–1904), plate 5 d. Paul and his wife were entertained in the park at Versailles and supplied with a number of plans and engravings of the royal residences. But since they left France in June 1782 they could only have discussed with Marie Antoinette the project for the *Petit Hameau*, which was not undertaken until December of that year. Most probably they saw the earlier *Hameau* at Chantilly. The Grand Duchess professed considerable interest in Gothic architecture, preferring Notre Dame to St Peter's in Rome. See P. Morane, *Paul Ier de Russie avant l'avènement, 1754–96* (Paris, 1907), *passim*; L. de Montbrison, ed., *Mémoires de la baronne d'Oberkirch*, I (Paris, 1869), 213. Several of the rustic buildings at Pavlovsk are reproduced, *Khudozh. sokrov.*, V (1905), plates 38–9.

7. The palace and church are reproduced, Grabar, III, 320–1. For an interesting view of the church in colour, see A. Kennett, *The Palaces of Leningrad* (London, 1973), plate VI.

336. 8. See D. Arkin, 'Bazhenov i Kazakov', *Obrazy arkhitektury* (Moscow, 1941), 169–216; N. A. Kozhin, *Osnovy russkoi psevdo-gotiki XVIII veka* (Leningrad, 1927). Soviet attributions to Bazhenov of most of the early Gothic work at Znamenki, Krasnoe Selo, and elsewhere are summarized in V. L. Snegirev, *Znamentii zodchii V. I. Bazhenov* (Moscow, 1950). See also *Istoriya*, VI, 88–92.

337. 9. A. Mazon, 'Cathérine II, historienne de la Russie médiévale', Académie des inscriptions et belles-lettres, *Comptes-rendus* (Paris, 1944), 458–72. From 1783 to 1794 Catherine published regular instalments of her *Notes sur l'histoire de Russie* in the Petersburg *Interlocuteur*.

338. 10. See D. Arkin, *op. cit.*, 208.

11. See G. C. Williamson, *The Imperial Russian Dinner Service* (London, 1909); A. Kelly, 'Wedgwood's Catherine Services', *Burlington Magazine*, CXXII (Aug., 1980), 554–61. For Bazhenov's original drawings for Tsaritsyno and good photographs of the ruins see E. G. Chernov and A. V. Shishko, *Bazhenov* (Moscow, 1949).

339. 12. L. Rusca, *Recueil des dessins de differens batimens construits à Saint-Pétersbourg et dans l'intérieur de l'empire de Russie* (St Petersburg, 1810).

13. Reproduced, G. G. Grimm, *Arkhitektor A. Zakharov* (Moscow, 1940), figures 1–4.

14. Reproduced, N. Veinert, *Rossi* (Moscow and Leningrad, 1939), figures 95–6.

15. The admiration which the Arsenal and the collections of arms and armour excited can be seen in the lavish photographs published by Théophile Gautier in the second part of his *Trésors d'art de la Russie ancienne et moderne* (Paris, 1859).

340. 16. Horace Vernet, who visited Russia in 1842,

painted an episode from the carnival. A mezzotint after his painting is reproduced *Pridvornaya zhizn, 1613–1913* (St Petersburg, 1913), facing 88.

341. 17. F. Vitberg, 'Alexander Vitberg et son projet d'église à Moscou', *Starye gody* (Feb., 1912), 3–19 (in Russian); V. Snegirev, 'A. L. Vitberg et ses travaux architecturaux', *Arkhitektura SSSR* (1939), no. 7, 79–82 (in Russian).

CHAPTER 24

343. 1. In this connection one can distinguish, as in the history of American painting, between work executed by foreigners of less than first-class talent, and work by gifted but uninstructed native painters attempting an alien mode. Examples of such primitive anonymous portraits are reproduced, G. Lebedev, *Russkaya zhivopis pervoi poloviny XVIII veka* (Leningrad and Moscow, 1938), 22.

2. For information on these and other early engravers see D. A. Rovinski, *Podrobnyi, slovar russkikh graverov, XVI–XIX vv.* (St Petersburg, 1895), 2 vols.

3. For reproductions of works by Danhauer and other early-eighteenth-century masters, see G. Lebedev, *op. cit.*; *Istoriya*, v, 294–339.

344. 4. A. Savinov, *I. Nikitin, 1688–1741* (Moscow and Leningrad, 1945), the most recent essay on this painter, attributes to him a large 'Battle of Kulikovo'. It is known that Nikitin executed a large painting of the genealogy of the Tsars for Anna Ioannovna, so it is possible that he also attempted battle scenes.

5. W. Weretennikoff, 'Le Peintre Louis Caravacque en Russie', *Starye gody* (June, 1908), 323–32 (in Russian).

6. For Torelli, see S. Ernst, 'Stefano Torelli in Russia', *Arte Veneta*, XXIV (1970), 173–84. His portrait of Catherine II in Russian dress, and his sketch of her coronation in the Cathedral of the Assumption in the Moscow Kremlin (State Tretyakov Gallery, Moscow), are curious interpretations of old Russian themes in terms of Italian Late Baroque vision and technique.

345. 7. L. Réau, *Histoire de l'expansion de l'art français moderne: Le Monde slave et l'orient* (Paris, 1924). For the French artists see also W. Graf Kalnein and Michael Levey, *Art and Architecture of the Eighteenth Century in France* (Pelican History of Art) (Harmondsworth, 1973).

8. For reproductions of these icons see S. P. Yaremich, 'Zhivopis Andreevskoi tserkvi v Kiev', *Iskusstvo v iuzhnoi Rossii*, I (1912), 1–14.

347. 9. See J. Hasselblatt, *Historischer Überblick der*

Entwicklung der kaiserlichen russischen Akademie der Künste in St Petersburg (St Petersburg and Leipzig, 1886); S. N. Kondakov, *Iubileinyi spravochnik imperatorskoi akademii khudozhestv, 1764–1914* (St Petersburg, 1914–15), 2 vols., with valuable historical surveys by various contributors; N. Pevsner, *Academies of Art, Past and Present* (Cambridge, 1940), 181–3; *Russkaya akademicheskaya khudozhestvennaya shkola v XVIII veke* (Moscow and Leningrad, 1937); S. K. Isakov, ed., *Akademiya khudozhestv* (Leningrad and Moscow, 1940), a short historical survey.

10. L. Réau, 'Les Artistes russes à Paris au XVIIIe siècle', *Revue des études slaves*, III (1923), 286–98. The obstreperous behaviour of young Russians in Paris was the subject of a *mémoire* from Diderot to Catherine II urging the establishment of a special hostel for them. See M. Tourneux, *Diderot et Catherine II* (Paris, 1899), 424–7.

11. Russian themes had appeared as early as 1766 as subjects for the annual competition in the painting classes of the Academy, but these were student programmes and not known to the general public, such as it was. Losenko's 'Vladimir and Rogneda' is reproduced, M. Aptekar, *Russkaya istoricheskaya zhivopis* (Moscow and Leningrad, 1939), 22.

349. 12. S. P. Diaghilev, *Russkaya zhivopis v XVIII veke, D. G. Levitskii* (St Petersburg, 1902); D. Roche, 'Un Portraitiste petit-russien au temps de Catherine II, D.-G. Levitski', *Gazette des Beaux-arts*, 3e pér., XXIX (1903), 494–507; XXX, 317–32; N. M. Gershenzon-Chegodaeva, *Dmitrii Grigorievich Levitskii* (Moscow, 1964).

13. Engravings by the older Levitsky are reproduced by K. Ladyzhenko, 'Zhizn i deyatelnost G. K. Levitskago', *Iskusstvo v iuzhnoi Rossii* (1914), nos. 5–6, 175–89.

350. 14. This portrait, now in the Public Library, Geneva, was the first important modern Russian painting to enter a public collection in the West.

351. 15. Levitsky may also have studied the portraits in Catherine's collections. The only significant English painting was Reynolds's 'Infant Hercules Strangling the Serpents' (1788), but influences from the several Van Dycks acquired by Catherine from the Walpole Collection, including portraits of Charles I and Henrietta Maria, can be seen in Levitsky's portrait of F. P. Makerovsky (1789), Diaghilev, *op. cit.*, no. 49. The artist may even have dressed the young man, then eighteen years of age, in seventeenth-century costume to disguise his extremely small stature.

16. D. Roche, 'Un peintre petit-russien à la fin du XVIIIe siècle et au commencement du XIXe siècle,

V.-L. Borovikovski', *Gazette des beaux-arts*, 3e pér., XXXVI (1906), 367–81, 485–501.

353. 17. Shchedrin's 'View of the Park and Gardens at Gatchina' is reproduced, N. Kovalenskaya, *Istoriya russkago iskusstva XVIII veka* (Moscow and Leningrad, 1940), 217. For other eighteenth-century academic painters see the catalogue of the Academy of Fine Arts by S. K. Isakov, *Imperatorskaya akademiya khudozhestv muzei, russkaya zhivopis* (Petrograd, 1915).

18. Reproduced, Kovalenskaya, *op. cit.*, 215.

19. For reproductions of Russian wooden sculpture see B. Dunaev, 'Derevyannoe zodchestvo severovostoka Kostromskoi gubernii', MAO, *Drevnosti, Trudy kom.*, VI (1915), 313–32; N. N. Serebrennikov, *Permskaya dereviannaya skulptura* (Perm, 1928).

20. Reproduced Grabar, V, chapters 4–5.

354. 21. For Rastrelli's earlier work see D. Roche, 'Le Monument du marquis de Pomponne par Rastrelli', *Starye gody* (Dec., 1912), 37–40; for further reproductions, Grabar, V, chapter 6; *Istoriya*, V, 460–74.

22. Paul's contempt for his mother's memory can be read in the inscription: 'From great-grandson to great-grandfather', mocking Catherine's haughty words on Falconet's statue 'Catherine II to Peter I'.

23. Reproduced, Grabar, V, 212–13.

24. Catherine described the sculptor in a letter to Mme Geoffrin, 21 October 1766, as 'L'ami de Mme de Diderot'. This, with Catherine's lively correspondence with Falconet on all manner of topics, has been published by L. Réau, *Correspondance de Falconet avec Catherine II, 1767–1778* (Paris, 1921).

25. The transport of the boulder was considered an engineering wonder. See Carburi de Ceffalonie, *Le Monument élevé à la gloire de Pierre le grand.... Relation des moyens méchaniques qu'ont été employés pour transporter à Pétersbourg, un rocher*, etc. (Paris, 1777).

26. D. Roche, 'Les Sculpteurs russes élèves de N.-F. Gillet', *Revue de l'art ancien et moderne*, XXIX (1911), 33–48.

27. S. K. Isakov, *Fedot Shubin* (Moscow, 1938); S. A. Ukhtomski, 'F. I. Shubin', *Materialy po russkomu iskusstvu* (Leningrad, 1928), 185–208.

355. 28. This and other works mentioned in this chapter are reproduced in Grabar, V, chapters 9–30; *Istoriya*, VI, 330–65. See also N. N. Vrangel, 'Katalog starrinykh proizvedenii iskusstva khranyashikhsya v Imperatorskoi akademii khudzhestv', *Starye gody*, special issue (1908); S. K. Isakov, *Imperatorskaya akademiya khudozhestv muzei, russkaya skulptura* (Petrograd, 1915).

356. 29. N. Kovalenskaya, *I. P. Martos* (Moscow and Leningrad, 1938); G. Presnov, 'Antichnye re-

ministsentsii v novom russkom iskusstve', *Materialy po russkom iskusstvom*, 221–33. See also *Istoriya*, VIII (part 1), 287–316.

30. Moscow funeral sculpture is discussed and reproduced, Iu. Shamurim, 'Moskovskaya kladbishcha', *Moskva v eya proshlom i nastoyashchem*, VIII, 89–124.

357. 31. The group has since been re-erected on an even less appropriate site, in front of St Basil on the Red Square [139].

32. Grabar, V, chapter 31.

CHAPTER 25

359. 1. In this and the following chapters a distinction is to be understood between realism in the narrower sense, as the use of exact natural detail as a means of expression, and naturalism as the philosophical and stylistic interpretation of nature and contemporary life dominant in European art in the second half of the nineteenth century.

2. The distinction between *iconography*, the identification of the subject, and *iconology*, the meaning of the subject in a particular work of art, has been proposed and examined at length by E. Panofsky in his *Studies in Iconology* (New York, 1939).

3. N. N. Vrangel, *O. A. Kiprenski v chastnykh sobraniyakh* (St Petersburg, 1912), a catalogue of an exhibition of little-known works from private collections; G. Lebedev, *Kiprenskii* (Moscow and Leningrad, 1937), a collection of plates; *Istoriya*, VIII (part 1), 396–470.

362. 4. Reproduced in colour, M. Aptekar, *Russkaya istoricheskaya zhivopis* (Moscow and Leningrad, 1939), opp. 26.

5. O. Lyaskovskaya's *Karl Briullov* (Moscow and Leningrad, 1940) is a well-documented study with many reproductions, catalogue, and bibliography. See also *Istoriya*, VIII (part 1), 43–103.

363. 6. Scott, in the last months of his life, might have seen Briullov's painting while he was in Rome in April and May 1832 (he had already visited Pompeii in February but seemed little interested in the ruins). His difficulty in walking, the result of a series of strokes, may, more than Briullov's artistry, have kept him so long immobilized. However, there appears to be no authentic record of his having visited Briullov's studio. Bulwer Lytton's *Last Days of Pompeii* (1834) was in part inspired by Briullov's picture.

7. The painting contains several references to Raphael's 'Fire in the Borgo'. One of Briullov's first tasks in Rome had been to copy 'The School of Athens' for the Petersburg Society for the

Encouragement of Art, an organization founded in 1820 which supplemented the academic premiums and assisted many artists in the nineteenth century. See P. N. Stolpyanski, *Staryi Peterburg i obshchestvo pooshchreniya khudozhestv* (Leningrad, 1928).

365. 8. M. P. Botkin, *A. A. Ivanov, ego zhizn i perepiska* (St Petersburg, 1880). See also *Istoriya*, VIII (part I), 156–230.

9. For the origin of this painting, and preliminary drawings, see N. Romanoff, ' "Apollon, Hyacinthe, et Cyparisse", by A. Ivanoff', *Starye gody* (Jan.–Feb., 1916), 36–49 (in Russian).

366. 10. For reproductions see N. Romanov, 'Eskizy genr'a i etiudy A. Ivanova', *Apollon* (1912), no. 8, 5–19.

367. 11. For charts of Ivanov's concordances see V. Zummer, 'Sistema bibleiskikh kompozitsii A. A. Ivanova', *Iskusstvo v iuzhnoi Rossii* (1914), no. 7–12, 1–111. Ivanov, like the contemporary New England Transcendentalists, read Iamblichus's and Porphyry's lives of Pythagoras.

369. 12. 'The Appearance of Rurik before the Walls of Novgorod' was the first Russian subject chosen for the painting competition in 1766. In 1763 the sculptors had worked on an episode from Peter's expedition to Azov in 1696. See *Russkaya akademicheskaya khudozhestvennaya shkola*, 110, 80.

13. The paintings are in the State Tretyakov Gallery in Moscow; the second is reproduced, Kovalenskaya, *op. cit.*, 215.

14. Reproduced, Kovalenskaya, *op. cit.*, 216; O. Wulff, *Die neurussische Kunst*, figure 264. The difference between the cosmopolitan and native attitude towards Russian customs can be seen by comparing the drawings of J.-B. Le Prince (1734–81), who travelled in Russia in 1758–62, and idealized the peasants in the style of Boucher, with the truthful and unprepossessing drawings of Ivan Ermenev (active after 1790), who portrayed rural and urban types in poverty and squalor. Reproductions, *Russkaya akademicheskaya khudozhestvennaya shkola*, 106–7; Kovalenskaya, *op. cit.*, 216. See also L. Réau, 'L'Exotisme russe dans l'œuvre de J.-B. Le Prince', *Gazette des beaux-arts*, 5ᵉ pér., III (1924), 147–65.

15. N. N. Vrangel, *A. G. Venetsianov v chastnykh sobraniyakh* (St Petersburg, 1911), a catalogue of little-known works from private collections.

371. 16. F. I. Bulgakov, *P. A. Fedotov i ego proizvedeniya* (St Petersburg, 1893); V. Dmitriev, 'P. A. Fedotov', *Apollon* (1916), nos. 9–10, 1–36.

CHAPTER 26

374. 1. For reproductions of nineteenth-century painting see G. K. Lukomsky, *History of Modern Russian Painting, 1840–1940* (London, 1945); N. I. Sokolova, ed., *Russkoe iskusstvo, XVIII–XIX vv.* (Moscow and Leningrad, 1938). An interesting collection of essays on the ideological tendencies of nineteenth-century painting has been edited by V. M. Friche as *Russkaya zhivopis XIX veka* (Moscow, 1929). Perov's works are reproduced by N. P. Sobko, *V. G. Perov, ego zhizn i proizvedeniya* (St Petersburg, 1892). Unless otherwise noted, the paintings mentioned in this chapter are in the State Tretyakov Gallery, Moscow.

375. 2. The point of the satire was sharpened by the fact that the landlord and his wife were seated, although in Russia it was customary to remain standing throughout the service. Perov's anticlericalism is closer to such western symptoms as Vibert's flippant irony than to Courbet's forthright denunciation of ecclesiastical impropriety in his 'Retour de la conférence' (1863).

376. 3. The exhibitions of the Society continued until 1920, although its artistic effectiveness diminished in the later 1890s with the emergence of *Mir Iskusstva*. See I. A. Sikorskii, *Uspekhi russkago khudozhestvennago tvorchestva peredvizhnykh khudozhestvennykn vystavok, 1872–97* (Kiev, 1900); A. Novitskii, *Peredvizhniki i vliyanie ikh na russkoe iskusstvo* (Moscow, 1897); L. R. Varshavskii, *Peredvizhniki* (Moscow, 1937), with Kramskoy's account of the episode of 1863; E. Valkenier, *Russian Realist Art. The State and Society. The Peredvizhniki and Their Tradition* (Ann Arbor, 1977).

4. The extremes of such art extend from Repin's 'They Did Not Expect Him' [283] to N. A. Yaroshenko's 'Everywhere there is Life', portraying convicts in a prison van throwing crumbs to birds beyond their bars. More typical of such ideological realism at its best is G. G. Myasoedov's 'The Zemstvo Dines' (1872), showing the peasant delegates to the provincial assembly eating their few crusts outside the town hall, while the gentry dine in comfort within. Reproduced, Sokolova, *Russkoe Iskusstvo*, 118. See also *Russischer Realismus, 1850–1900* (Baden-Baden, Staatliche Kunsthalle, 1972), catalogue of an exhibition of paintings lent by the Tretyakov Gallery and Russian Museum, with commentary.

5. Sokolova, *op. cit.*, 126. See also Kramskoy's letter to F. A. Vasiliev, 10 October 1872, in the artist's *Pisma*, I (Moscow, 1937), 119–23. See also *Istoriya*, IX, 176–216.

378. 6. As a painter of almost exclusively religious subjects Ge of all the nineteenth-century masters has been least studied by Soviet scholars. His correspondence with Tolstoy has been published, *L. N. Tolstoi i N. N. Ge* (Moscow and Leningrad, 1930).

See V. Dmitriev, '*N. N. Ge*', *Apollon* (1913), no. 10, 5–43, with catalogue.

7. E. J. Simmons, *Leo Tolstoy* (Boston, 1946), 362, 450–1, 493.

380. 8. The episode is retold by C. Marsden in *Palmyra of the North*, 95–9.

381. 9. Many others could be added to this list of pictures of implicit political comment, e.g. F. E. Burov's 'Peter III's Visit to Ivan VI' (recalling Elizabeth's and Catherine's cruel imprisonment of their legal predecessor), or K. V. Lebedev's 'Destruction of the Novgorod Veche' (now in the Joseph E. Davies Collection, University of Wisconsin).

10. Surikov's considerable talent can be gauged by his sensitive drawings, reproduced, Ya. Tepin, 'Surikov', *Apollon* (1916), nos. 4–5, 21–39.

11. Musicians matched painters in the exploitation of Russian history. To Moussorgsky's familiar *Boris Godunov* (1870) and *Khovanshchina* (1872) may be added Rimsky-Korsakov's *Sadko* (1867, revised 1891) and *Maid of Pskov* (1870–2); Borodin's *Prince Igor* (published posthumously, after 1887); and Serov's *Rogneda* (1865), to mention only the most important.

382. 12. V. V. Vereshchagin, *Exhibition of the Works of V. Verestchagin* (New York, American Art Galleries, 1888), 6–8; 'These subjects I have treated in a fashion far from sentimental, for having myself killed many a poor fellow-creature in different wars, I have not the right to be sentimental. . . . My intention was to examine war in its different aspects, and transmit these faithfully. Facts laid upon canvas without embellishment must speak for themselves.'

13. This and the other works by Repin discussed in this chapter are reproduced in the admirable biography by I. Grabar, *Repin* (Moscow, 1937), 2 vols., and in the interesting collection of documents edited by Grabar and I. S. Zilbershtein, *Repin* (Moscow and Leningrad, 1948), 2 vols. See also *Istoriya*, IX, 445–563.

383. 14. The earlier drawings and studies from life have a crude power which was lost to some extent in the artificially contrived final composition. For reproductions, Grabar, *Rêpin*, I, chapter 6, and I. Repin, *Burlaki na Volge* (*vospominaniya*) (Moscow and Leningrad, 1944).

385. 15. In 1884 Repin repainted the face of the exile, emphasizing his haunted and hesitant expression.

386. 16. Among the curious paintings are a 'Noli Me Tangere' (1922), and a 'Child Christ Preaching in the Temple' (of the 1920s), reproductions, Grabar and Zilbershtein, *op. cit.*, 299, 307. They are astonishing developments in the light of his only other important religious painting, the painfully realistic 'St Nicholas Staying an Execution' (1888).

387. 17. *V. N. Baksheev* (Moscow, Sovetski khudozhnik, 1949).

CHAPTER 27

388. 1. For further synopses of the history of this research see L. Réau, *L'Art russe des origines à Pierre le grand*, chapter 1; D. V. Ainalov, *Vormoskov.*, v–ix.

2. A. de Demidov, *Album du voyage pittoresque et archéologique en Russie* (Paris, *c.* 1845).

3. See especially *Russkaya starina v pamyatnikakh tserkovnago i grazhdanskago zodchestva* (Moscow, 1851), folio, with text by Snegirev and lithographs by Martynov. There were several earlier and later collections by the same authors with illustrations on a smaller scale.

4. *Drevnosti rossiiskago gosudarstva* (Moscow, 1849–53), 6 vols.

389. 5. The most useful publications of the Moscow Archaeological Society are its *Trudy* ('Works'), the reports of the fifteen congresses held between 1869 and 1915; *Drevnosti* ('Antiquities'), twenty-five volumes of reports issued between 1865 and 1916; and the publication, also entitled *Drevnosti*, of the *Kommissii po sokhraneniiu drevnikh pamyatnikov* (Commission for the Preservation of Ancient Monuments), in six volumes (1907–15). Material on post-Kievan archaeology will also be found in the *Izvestiya* of the St Petersburg Imperial Archeological Commission, I–XXXII (1901–15).

6. V. V. Suslov, *Pamyatniki drevnyago russkago zodchestva* (St Petersburg, 1895–1901), seven parts; *idem*, *Pamyatniki drevne-russkago iskusstva* (St Petersburg, 1908–12), four parts.

7. D. A. Rovinskii, *Istoriya russkikh shkol ikonopisaniya do kontsa XVII veka* (St Petersburg, 1856).

8. See especially N. P. Likhachev, *Materialy dlya istorii russkago ikonopisaniya* (Leipzig and St Petersburg, 1906), 2 vols.; N. P. Kondakov, *Russkaya ikona* (Prague, 1929), 4 vols.

9. I. Grabar, *Istoriya russkago iskusstva* (Moscow, 1909–17), 6 vols. Among the contributors were A. Shchusev, V. Pokrovskii, G. Pavlutskii, V. V. Suslov, F. Gornostaev (architecture); N. N. Vrangel (sculpture); P. P. Muratov, A. I. Uspenskii (painting). Grabar himself wrote many chapters, including the third volume on the eighteenth-century architecture of St Petersburg.

390. 10. The changed attitude towards medieval art appears as early as 1824 in a popular guide to Moscow. G. Lecointe de Laveau remarked of St Basil: 'C'est sans contredit l'édifice le plus extraordinaire qu'ait pu produire l'imagination d'un architecte' (*Putevoditel v Moskve* (Moscow, 1824), 187). In his earlier *Moscou avant et après l'incendie* (Paris, 1814) he had not mentioned the church.

11. The art collection of Alexander III in the Anichkov Palace, his residence in St Petersburg, was indistinguishable from the accumulation of genrepainting, Italian antiques, and oriental bric-à-brac gathered by wealthy middle-class collectors throughout the western world. It can be studied in A. Prakhov, 'Imperator Aleksandr tretii kak deyatel russkago khudozhestvennago prosveshcheniya', *Khudozh. sokrov.*, III (1903), nos. 4–8, plates 46 ff.

12. For illustrations of these and the work at Peterhof see A. Benois and N. Lanceray, 'Les Palais élevés par Nicolas I', *Starye Gody* (July–Sept., 1913), 173–95 (in Russian).

391. 13. An earlier although less accurate reproduction of Russian wooden peasant architecture had occurred in the Alexandrovsky Colony at Potsdam, built after 1825 to house a group of Russian prisoners of war who had remained as singers at the Prussian Court. In 1827 each of the remaining twelve families had its own cottage in the Russian style. See M. Hürlimann, *Die Residenzstadt Potsdam* (Berlin, 1933), 293.

392. 14. An example of Ton's formula modified only in detail is the Church of the Annunciation in St Petersburg, where the same imitation of the massing of St Isaac is topped by five octagonal lanterns with pyramidal cupolas.

393. 15. For the architecture of the Slavic Revival see the brief accounts by Yu. I. Shamurin, 'Arkhitektura Moskva', *Moskva v eya proshlom i nastoyashchem*, XI (1912), 117–25; I. Anterov, 'Russkoe arkhitekturnoe nasledstvo i ego razvitie v noveishei arkhitekture', *Arkhitektura SSSR* (1941), no. 2, 46–52. Among the curious water-colours by an obscure architect, Victor Hartmann, which inspired Moussorgsky's *Pictures at an Exhibition*, there was a project for a monumental gate at Kiev, which is an extreme example of the fantastic effects conceived in Slavic Revival architecture. See A. Frankenstein, 'Victor Hartmann and Modeste Musorgsky', *Musical Quarterly*, XXV (1939), 268–91.

16. Another imitation of seventeenth-century Moscow architecture in St Petersburg was the Church of the Kievan Lavra on Vasily Ostrov (1898), reproduced, E. Zabel, *St Petersburg* (Leipzig, 1905), 14.

394. 17. I. E. Zabelin, *Domashnii byt russkago naroda v XVI i XVII st.* (Moscow, 1872), 2 vols.; *Istoriya russkoi zhizni s drevneishikh vremen* (Moscow, 1876–9), 2 vols.

18. International expositions were showcases for Russian Revivalism. The Russian Pavilion in the Manufacturers' Building at the World's Columbian Exposition in Chicago (1893) was a conglomeration of sixteenth-century decorative elements topped by a miniature Kremlin tower. At Glasgow in 1901 the pavilion was a modification of the Church of the Transfiguration at Kizhy [124]. See below, pages 408–10.

19. Grabar, V, chapter 33.

395. 20. The Slavic Revival was encouraged by such national occasions. The nine-hundredth anniversary of the conversion of Russia was celebrated in 1889, and the tercentenary of the Romanov dynasty in 1913.

21. This church was only the most publicized of the many examples of the Byzantine revival of the 1870s. See also the first prize designs by Schröter and Huhn for the colossal Garrison Cathedral in Tiflis, *Zodchii* (1878), plates 45–6.

22. The official character of the whole undertaking was marked by the dedication of the church in 1896 in the presence of the imperial family, and its commemoration in a *de luxe* folio of photographs, *Kievskii Vladimirskii Sobor* (Kiev, c. 1896). See also S. V. Kulzhenko, *Sobor Sv. Kn. Vladimira v Kiev* (Kiev, 1899).

23. The artist's work, except for his religious painting, is adequately reproduced, N. Morgunov, *V. Vasnetsov* (Moscow and Leningrad, 1941). The Kievan murals are described and reproduced by O. Wulff, *Neurussische Kunst* (Augsburg, 1932), chapter 28.

24. The revival of interest in early Russian poetry, particularly in the *Tale of the Armament of Igor*, had been marked a decade before by Borodin's posthumous opera, *Prince Igor*, and by Perov's 'Yaroslavna's Grief' showing the princess mourning for Igor.

398. 25. E. Mahler, *Michail Nesterov, ein Maler des Gläubigen Russlands* (Lucerne, 1938), with good reproductions.

399. 26. S. Yaremich, 'Vrubel', *Mir Iskusstva*, X (1903), 143–90; idem, *M. A. Vrubel* (Moscow, 1911).

27. For Mamontov's colony at Abramtsevo see T. T. Rice, *A Concise History of Russian Art* (London, 1963), 243–5. The simple wooden country house is reproduced in colour, figure 223.

401. 28. For the artistic conditions in St Petersburg and the formation of the Mir Iskusstva group see A. Benois, *Reminiscences of the Russian Ballet* (London, 1941), parts I–II; N. Sokolova, *Mir Iskusstva* (Moscow and Leningrad, 1934); S. R.

Ernst, *A. Benois* (Petrograd, 1942), with bibliography and catalogue; A. Benois, *Voznikiovenie 'Mira Iskusstva'* (Leningrad, 1928). To the members discussed above may be added K. Somov, a painter of witty Rococo themes, and M. Dobuzhinsky, whose theatrical designs are well known. See also the chapter by V. N. Petrov, 'Mir Iskusstva', *Istoriya*, x (part 1), 341–499.

403. 29. The results of Benois's scrupulous historical research appeared in his book on Tsarskoe Selo, *Tsarskoe Selo v tsarstvovanie imperatritsy Elisavety Petrovny* (St Petersburg, 1910). For Lanceray, who remained in Russia to become a 'social realist' painter, see M. V. Babenchikov, *E. E. Lancere* (Moscow, 1949).

30. V. Diaghilev, ed., *Katalog istoriko-khudozhestvennoi vystavki russkikh portretov v Tavricheskom dvortsie* (St Petersburg, 1905), 8 vols.

31. *Exposition d'art russe* (Paris, Salon d'automne, 1906). The bulk of the exhibition consisted of eighteenth- and nineteenth-century painting; only thirty-six icons were exhibited, all but one from the Likhachev collection.

404. 32. The *Mir Iskusstva* 'tone' can be seen in the photographs of the Pskov Monastery [20], one of several such views which appeared in early issues of *Mir Iskusstva*. The oblique perspective and appreciation of contrast of textures are typical of this fresh point of view towards old Russian architecture.

33. Benois and Golovin were so determined that the production should be historically authentic that they scoured the Tartar junk-shops for antique materials, shawls, head-dresses, etc., although they were obliged to admit that on the stage these were less effective than other costumes which had been newly designed. See Benois, *Reminiscences*, 268.

34. V. N. Soloviev, 'A. Ya. Golovin, kak teatralnyi master', *Apollon* (1917), no. 1, 24–30.

405. 35. *Ballets russes de Diaghilew, 1909–1929* (Paris, Musée des Arts Décoratifs, 1939). See also 'L'Art décoratif au théâtre', *Zolotoe Runo* (1909), nos. 7–9, 5–36; R. Fülöp-Miller and J. Gregor, *The Russian Theatre* (Philadelphia, n.d.), chapter 7 and figures 37–174.

36. V. Ya. Ivchenko, *Le Ballet contemporain* (St Petersburg, 1912); A. Ya. Levinson, *Bakst, the story of the artist's life* (London, 1923).

406. 37. Historical retrospection was pushed even further by S. Prokoviev in his *Scythian Suite*, originally commissioned by Diaghilev as a ballet in 1914, but performed only as an orchestral composition in 1916. The same tendency occurred in architecture. S. I. Vachkov's apartment house for the Church of

the Trinity in the Mire (*c.* 1905) had relief ornament of symbolic beasts based on the twelfth-century sculpture of St Dmitry in Vladimir [27]. The glazed tile designs on the Pertsov apartment house (1905–7) by S. V. Mayutin and N. K. Zhukov included pre-Kievan symbols of solar deities and other pagan devices. Both buildings are illustrated in E. Kirichenko, *Moskva. Pamyatniki arkhitektury 1880–1910–x godov* (Moscow, 1977), plates 73–93.

38. The historical trilogy by Alexey Tolstoy (1817–75) can be counted one of the prime movers of the Slavic Revival. It included *The Death of Ivan the Terrible* (1866), *Tsar Feodor* (1868), and *Tsar Boris* (1870). Only the second play enjoyed a lasting success.

39. C. Stanislavsky, co-founder of the Moscow Art Theatre, described the opening performance of *Tsar Feodor* (14 October 1898) in *My Life in Art* (Boston, 1924), 335. For photographs, a little dim, of these productions see *Moskovskii Khudozhestvennyi Teatr v illiustratsiyakh i dokumentakh, 1898–1938* (Moscow, 1938), 44–57, 76, 216–23.

40. A. Gidoni, 'Tvorcheskii put Rerikha', *Apollon* (1915), nos. 4–5, 1–39; Iu. K. Baltrushaitis, *et al.*, *Roerikh* (St Petersburg, 1916), with good colour plates. His sets for *Prince Igor* are reproduced, 140–3.

41. For the history of Art Nouveau in the seminal centres of western Europe, see R. Schmutzler, *L'Art Nouveau* (London, 1964). A distinction must be made, however, between work executed in the spirit of Mir Iskusstva and Art Nouveau objects or designs imported from abroad which of course were without any specifically Russian character. For works of applied art, see the exhibition catalogue, *Prikladnoe iskusstvo kontsa XIX- nachala XX veka* (Leningrad, Hermitage Museum, 1974). A generous survey of Art Nouveau architecture in Moscow can be found in E. Kirichenko, *Moskva. Pamyatniki arkhitektury 1880–1910–x godov* (Moscow, 1977).

407. 42. M. K. Tenisheva, *Khram svyatogo dukha v Talashkine* (Paris, 1938); *eadem, Broderies des paysannes de Smolensk exécutées sous la direction de la princesse Marie Ténichev* (Paris and Chicago, n.d.). For illustrations of other work executed at Talashkino see S. Diaghilev, 'G. V. Maliutin i ego raboty v imenii kn. M. K. Tenishevoi "Talashkino" ', *Mir Iskusstva*, IX (1903), 157–92.

43. Her work is reproduced, *Mir Iskusstva*, XI (1904). For the revival of peasant industries see *Russkoe narodnoe iskusstvo na vtoroi vserossiiskoi kustarnoi vystavke v Petrograde v 1913* (Petrograd, 1914); Réau, *L'Art russe des origines à Pierre le Grand*, chapter 5.

408. **44.** Grabar, v, chapter 37; *Catalogue of Sculpture by Prince Paul Trubetzkoi* (New York, American Numismatic Society, 1911).

45. For the work of this revival see G. Lukomski, 'Novyi Peterburg', *Apollon* (1913), no. 2, 5–38. A. I. Nekrasov, in *Russkii ampir* (Moscow, 1935), 118–22, has interpreted the revival as part of a bourgeois reaction after the Revolution of 1905.

409. **46.** The pavilion is reproduced, *Mir Iskusstva*, IV (1900), 98–109, and the *Art Journal* (supplement, 1901), 141.

47. The yearbooks of the St Petersburg Society of Artists-Architects, *Ezhegodnik obshchestva arkhitektorov-khudoznikov* (1906–15), contain numerous illustrations of projects and completed buildings in the Slavic and modern classical revival styles. Our Saviour on the Waters is reproduced, v (1910), 101–4; the Leipzig church, VII (1912), 104–5, IX (1914), 111.

48. M. K. Tenisheva, *op. cit.*, 5.

49. The Schlüsselberg church in the style of the sixteenth-century tent churches, and Roerich's murals and mosaics, are reproduced, *Ezhegodnik*, II (1907), 94–124.

411. **50.** The resemblances between Wright's houses and the Ryabushinsky house are generic, rather than specific. They may be traced from Wright's Husser residence (1899) through at least the Kier, Ross, and Kissam houses of 1915 in Glencoe, Illinois. One should note that Wright's second-storey windows are often treated as a single group and never extend into the wall below the frieze. The houses are reproduced in W. A. Storrer, *The Architecture of Frank Lloyd Wright. A Complete Catalogue* (Cambridge, Mass., and London, 1974).

414. **51.** For these collections, the contents of which were subsequently incorporated into the Museum of Modern Western Art in Moscow, see S. Makovski, 'Frantsuzskie khudozhniki iz sobraniya I. A. Morozova', *Apollon* (1912), nos. 3–4, 5–16; Ya. Tugendkhold, 'Frantsuzskoe sobranie S. I. Shchukina', *Apollon* (1914), nos. 1–2, 5–46. The progress of French painting in Russia can also be traced in the pages of *Zolotoe runo* in the accounts of the exhibitions of 1908, which included most of the Post-Impressionists, and 1909, when contemporary paintings by Matisse and Braque were reproduced.

52. For Stelletsky's clever but mannered parodies of older Russian painting see A. Benois, 'Iskusstvo Stelletskago', *Apollon* (1911), no. 4, 5–16. Stelletsky also designed sets for A. Tolstoy's *Tsar Feodor*.

53. For advanced currents in Russian art after 1900 see C. Gray-Prokofieva, *The Great Experiment: Russian Art 1863–1922* (London, 1962); J. E. Kennedy, *The 'Mir Iskusstva' Group and Russian Art, 1898–1912* (New York and London, 1977); J. E. Bowlt, ed. and transl., *Russian Art of the Avant-Garde. Theory and Criticism, 1902–34* (New York, 1976); S. Barron and M. Tuchman, eds., *The Avant-Garde in Russia, 1910–1930. New Perspectives* (Los Angeles County Museum of Art, 1980), with catalogue of an exhibition.

BIBLIOGRAPHY

Since the annotation of the text contains references to the principal Russian sources, this bibliography includes works useful for the student who reads only Western European languages. The Russian works included are helpful for their illustrations, bibliographies, or summaries of recent research.

1. BIBLIOGRAPHIES OF RUSSIAN ART

AUTY, R., and OBOLENSKY, D. (eds.). *An Introduction to Russian Art and Architecture*, 109–11, 173–81. Cambridge, 1980.

BOWLT, J. E. (ed.). *Russian Art of the Avant-Garde. Theory and Criticism 1902–1934*, 309–48. New York, 1976.

BRUNOV, N. I., and ALPATOV, M. 'Altrussische Kunst in der wissenschaftlichen Forschung seit 1914', *Zeitschrift für slavische Philologie*, II (1925), 474–505; III (1926), 387–408.

Encyclopedia of World Art, XIII. New York, 1967.
See article on 'Slavic Art' with extensive bibliography, pp. 107–13, arranged chronologically (1858–1963).

Encyclopedia of World Art, XIV. New York, 1967.
See article, 'Union of Soviet Socialist Republics' with extensive bibliography, pp. 483–6, arranged chronologically (1863–1967).

ETTLINGER, A., and GLADSTONE, J. M. *Russian Literature, Theatre, and Art; a Bibliography of Works in English, Published 1900–1945*. London, 1947.

EVDOKIMOV, I. *Sever v istorii russkago iskusstva*. Vologda, 1921.
Extensive bibliography on northern Russian art, pp. 164–76.

HORECKY, P. L. (ed.). *Basic Russian Publications. An annotated Bibliography on Russia and the Soviet Union*, 237–44. Chicago, 1962.

HORECKY, P. L. (ed.). *Russia and the Soviet Union. A bibliographic Guide to Western-language Publications*, 371–8. Chicago, 1965.

LAZAREV, V. N. *Iskusstvo Novgoroda*, 143–51. Moscow, 1947.

MILLET, G. (ed.). *L'Art byzantin chez les slaves*, II, 'L'Ancienne Russie, les slaves catholiques'. Paris, 1932.
Lists periodicals, publications of learned societies, catalogues of museums and private collections.

2 GENERAL HISTORIES OF RUSSIAN ART

AINALOV, D. V. *Geschichte der russischen Monumentalkunst der vormoskovitischen Zeit*. Berlin and Leipzig, 1932.

AINALOV, D. V. *Geschichte der russischen Monumentalkunst zur Zeit des Grossfürstentums Moskau*. Berlin and Leipzig, 1933.

ALPATOV, M. V. *Trésors de l'art russe*. Paris, 1966.

ALPATOV, M., and BRUNOV, N. *Geschichte der altrussischen Kunst*. 2 vols. Augsburg, 1932.

L'Art russe des Scythes à nos jours. Trésors des musées soviétiques. Paris, Grand Palais, 1967.
Catalogue of the most extensive exhibition of Russian art to be held in Western Europe. With 618 illustrations.

BAEDEKER, K. *Russia with Teheran, Port Arthur, and Peking*. Leipzig, London, and New York, 1914 (reprint, New York, 1970).
Invaluable for the location and description of monuments before the demolitions after 1917 and destruction during World War II.

BEHRENS, E. *Kunst in Russland. Ein Reiseführer zu russischen Kunststätten*. Cologne, 1969.
A guide to the existing monuments in Leningrad, Moscow, Kiev, Vladimir, and Suzdal.

BUNT, C. G. E. *Russian Art from Scyths to Soviets*. London and New York, 1946.

CHERNOV, V., and GIRARD, M. *Splendours of Moscow and its Surroundings*. Cleveland, 1967.

FABRITSKII, B. B. *Sokrovishche Drevnei Rusi. Treasures of Mediaeval Russia*. Moscow, 1974.

GRABAR, I. (ed.). *Istoriya russkogo iskusstva*. 6 vols. Moscow, 1909–16.
Grabar's monumental history, although interrupted by World War I and superseded by the new enlarged edition (see below), remains indispensable for the clarity of the reproductions.

GRABAR, I. E., LAZAREV, V. N., and KEMENOV, V. S. (eds.). *Geschichte der russischen Kunst*. 6 vols. Dresden, 1957–76.
A German translation of the first five volumes

of the following work (from Pre-Christian Russia to 1750).

GRABAR, I. E., LAZAREV, V. N., and KEMENOV, V. S. (eds.). *Istoriya russkogo iskusstva.* 13 vols. in 16. Moscow, 1953–68.
Revised and enlarged edition of Grabar's history of 1909–16. Indispensable for contemporary Soviet scholarship. Contains extensive bibliographies.

KAGANOVICH, A. L. *Arts of Russia, 17th and 18th Centuries.* Cleveland and New York, 1968.
Colour reproductions of unfamiliar works of art and architecture.

KORNILOVICH, K. *Arts of Russia, from the Origins to the End of the 16th Century.* Cleveland and New York, 1967.
Colour reproductions of unfamiliar works of art and architecture.

KOVALENSKAYA, N. N. *Istoriya russkago iskusstva XVIII veka.* Moscow, 1940.
With bibliography.

KOVALEVSKY, P. *Atlas historique et culturel de la Russie et du monde slave.* Paris, 1961.
Useful for historical and geographical reference.

LAZAREV, V. N. *Iskusstvo Novgoroda.* Moscow, 1947.

MATTHEY, W. von. *Russische Kunst.* Zurich, 1948.
Short survey.

MILIUKOV, P. *Outlines of Russian Culture*, part III. Philadelphia, 1942.
Extracts from his comprehensive history.

MONGAIT, A. L. *Archaeology in the U.S.S.R.* Harmondsworth (Penguin Books), 1961.
Useful summary of pre-Christian and pre-Slavic discoveries in European and Asiatic Russia. The last chapter treats of medieval Russian towns.

MYERS, B., and COPPLESTONE, T. (eds.). *Art Treasures in Russia. Monuments, Masterpieces, Commissions and Collections.* London and Sydney, 1970.
Essays on Russian art and culture from 2500 B.C. to the present. Many unusual illustrations in colour, but a few of the earlier icons are printed in reverse.

NEWMARCH, R. *The Russian Arts.* New York, 1916.
The first survey in English.

NIKOLSKII, V. A. *Istoriya russkago iskusstva.* Moscow, 1915.

NOVITZKII, A. *Istoriya russkago iskusstva s drevneishikh vremen.* 2 vols. Moscow, 1903.
The first adequate Russian general history. Interesting illustrations.

RÉAU, L. *L'Art russe des origines à Pierre le Grand.* Paris, 1921.

This and the following works by Réau are admirably ordered, but written with a pronounced French bias.

RÉAU L. *L'Art russe de Pierre le Grand à nos jours.* Paris, 1922.

RÉAU, L. *L'Art russe.* Paris, 1945.
A one-volume summary of his earlier work, brought up to date.

RICE, T. T. *A Concise History of Russian Art.* London, 1963.
Interesting survey, including the decorative arts, with many small but good colour reproductions.

TOLSTOI, I. I., and KONDAKOV, N. P. *Russiya drevnosti v pamyatnikakh iskusstva.* 6 vols. St Petersburg, 1889–99.
A monumental work of early archaeological scholarship. Many valuable illustrations.

VIOLLET-LE-DUC, E. E. *L'Art russe.* Paris, 1877.
The first monograph in a Western European language. Concerned with the oriental derivation of Russian architecture and ornament.

VORONIN, N. N., and others. *Istoriya kultury drevnei Rusi do mongolskii period.* Moscow, 1948.
The first volume of a popular survey, extensively illustrated.

WINKLER, M. 'Das Wesen der altrussischen Kunst', *Osteuropa*, I (1926), 306–32.
An interesting synthesis.

WULFF, O. *Die neurussische Kunst im Rahmen der Kulturentwicklung Russlands von Peter dem Grossen bis zur Revolution.* 2 vols. Augsburg, 1932.
Art in relation to the history of the period. Many illustrations.

ZOTOV A. I. *Narodnye osnovy russkogo iskusstva.* 2 vols. Moscow, (1964?).

3. ARCHITECTURE, PRINCIPALLY BEFORE 1700

ALPATOV, M. *The Dormition Cathedral in the Moscow Kremlin.* Moscow, 1971.

BARTENEV, I. A. *North Russian Architecture.* Moscow, 1972.

BERTON, K. *Moscow. An Architectural History.* London, 1977.

BUXTON, D. R. *Russian Mediaeval Architecture, with an Account of the Transcaucasian Styles and their Influence in the West.* Cambridge, 1934.

CROSS, S. H. *Mediaeval Russian Churches.* Cambridge, Mass., 1949.

EDING, B. von. *Rostov Velikii. Uglich. Pamyatniki khudozhestvennoi stariny.* Moscow, 1913.

DUNCAN, D. D. *The Kremlin.* Greenwich, Conn., 1960.

Superior colour reproductions of the buildings and of the more important decorative objects in the Kremlin museums.

ELIASBERG, A. *Russische Baukunst*. Munich, 1922.

FEDOROV, B. N. *Architecture of the Russian North, 12th–19th Centuries*. London, *c.* 1976.

HOOTZ, R. *Kunstdenkmäler in der Sowjetunion, Ein Bildhandbuch*. Munich, 1978.
Good illustrations of the principal buildings in Moscow and its environs with succinct historical notes.

ILIN, M. A. *Kamennaya letopis Moskovskoi Rusi . . .* Moscow, 1966.

ILIN, M. A. *Zagorsk, Trinity-Sergius Monastery*. Moscow, 1967.
Text in English.

Izvestiya, imperatorskoi arkheologicheskoi kommissii, I–LXIV (1908–17). Voprosy restavratsii, parts 1–18.
An inventory of architectural monuments and reports of restorations in progress. Many illustrations.

KARGER, M. K. *Drevnii Kiev. Ocherki po istorii materialnoi kultury drevnerusskogo goroda*. 2 vols. Leningrad, 1958–61.

KARGER, M. K. *Novgorod Velikii. Arkhitekturnye pamyatniki*. Leningrad, 1966.

KARGER, M. K. *Novgorod the Great, Architectural Guidebook*. Moscow, 1973.

KRASOVSKII, M. V. *Kurs istorii russkoi arkhitektury*. Moscow, 1911.
Wooden architecture.

KRASOVSKII, M. V. *Ocherk istorii moskovskago perioda drevnerusskago tserkovnago zodchestva*. Moscow, 1911.
Admirable plans and sections.

LO GATTO, E. *Gli artisti italiani in Russia*. 2 vols. Rome, 1934–5.

LOGVIN, H. *Kiev's Hagia Sophia, State Architectural–Historical Monument*. Kiev, 1971.

NEKRASOV, A. I. *Ocherki po istorii drevnerusskago zodchestva XI–XVII veka*. Moscow, 1936.
For Soviet theory.

Pskov. Art Treasures and Architectural Monuments, 12th–17th Centuries. London, 1976.

PURISHEV, I. B. *Pereslavl-Zalesskii*. Moscow, 1970.

RZYANIN, M. I. *Arkhitekturnye ansambli Moskvy i Podmoskoviya, XIV–XIX veka*. Moscow, 1950.

RZYANIN, M. I. *Pamyatniki russkogo zodchestva*. Moscow, 1950.

SERVINSKY, S. 'Über die Auffassungen der Wandfläche in der Entwicklung der altrussischen Steinbaukunst', *Belvedere*, IX–X (1926), 257–68.

SUSLOV, V. V. *Pamyatniki drevne-russkago iskusstva*. 4 parts. St Petersburg, 1908–12.
Drawings and water-colour renderings of architecture and painting.

SUSLOV, V. V. *Pamyatniki drevnyago russkago zodchestva*. 7 parts. St Petersburg, 1895–1901.
Drawings of wooden and masonry architecture.

VOEIKOVA, I. N. *Yaroslavl*. Leningrad, 1973.

VORONIN, N. N. *Zodchestvo severo-vostochnoi Rusi, XII–XV vekov*. 2 vols. Moscow, 1961–2.

VORONIN, N. N. (ed.). *Palaces and Churches of the Kremlin*. London, Prague, Moscow, 1965.
With photographs by Karel Neubert.

VOYCE, A. *The Art and Architecture of Mediaeval Russia*. Norman, Okla., 1967.

VOYCE, A. *The Moscow Kremlin. Its History, Architecture and Art Treasures*. Berkeley, Calif., 1954.

VZDORNOV, G. I. *Vologda*. Leningrad, 1972.

WEIDHAAS, H. *Formenwandlung in der russischen Baukunst*. Halle, 1935.

ZABELLO, S. Ya., and others. *Russkoe derevyannoe zodchestvo*. Moscow, 1942.
Comprehensive Soviet study of wooden architecture. Many illustrations.

4. ARCHITECTURE, PRINCIPALLY AFTER 1700

BONDARENKO, I. Ye. *Arkhitekturnye pamyatniki Moskvy*, parts I, II–III. Moscow, 1904–5.
Splendid gravure plates of 18th- and 19th-century buildings.

BUNIN, A. V. *Arkhitekturnaya kompozitsya gorodov*. Moscow, 1940.
Chapters on Russian city-planning.

BUTIKOV, G. P. *St Isaac's Cathedral*. Leningrad, 1974.

GOSLING, N. *Leningrad. History, Art and Architecture*. New York, 1965.
Photographs by Colin Jones with interpretative text.

GRABAR, I. E. (ed.). *Russkaya arkhitektura pervoi poloviny XVIII veka. Issledovaniya i materialy*. Moscow, 1954.

GIBELLINO-KRASCENINNICOWA, M. *L'Architettura russa nel passato e nel presente*. Rome, 1963.

HAUTECOEUR, L. *L'Architecture classique à Saint-Pétersbourg à la fin du XVIIIᵉ siècle*. Paris, 1912.

ILIN, M. A. *Moscow. Monuments of Architecture, 18th – the First Third of the 19th Century*. Moscow, 1975.

Imperial Society of Architects, St Petersburg, *Ezhegodnik* (Yearbook), 1– (1906–).
With many illustrations of modern architectural projects.

Imperial Society of Architects, *Istoricheskaya vystavka arkhitektury*. St Petersburg, 1911.
Illustrated catalogue, edited by A. Benois, of an important exhibition of old St Petersburg architecture.

KAGANOVICH, A. L. *Splendors of Leningrad*. New York, 1969.
With photographs by Gérard Bertin.

KENNETT, A. *The Palaces of Leningrad*. London, 1973.
With excellent photographs by V. Kennett. The best-illustrated work on the subject with an informative historical text.

KIRICHENKO, E. I. *Moscow. Architectural Monuments of the 1830–1910s*. Moscow, 1977.

LO GATTO, E. *Gli Architetti a Mosca e nelle province*. Rome, 1934.

MILLS, A. R. *Portrait of Leningrad*. London, 1966.
With photographs by K. and J. Neubert.

PILYAVSKII, V. I. *Arkhitektura Leningrada*. Leningrad, 1953.

PILYAVSKII, V. I. *Ermitazh. Istoriya i arkhitektura zdanii*. Leningrad, 1974.

USPENSKII, A. I., and others. *Istoricheskaya Panorama Sanktpeterburga i ego okrestnostei*. 10 vols. Moscow, 1911–14.
With numerous illustrations.

5. PAINTING TO 1700

ALPATOV, M. V. *Drevnerusskaya ikonopis. Early Russian Icon Painting*. Moscow, 1974.

AVINOFF, A. (ed.). *Russian Icons and Objects of Ecclesiastical and Decorative Arts from the Collection of George R. Hann*. Carnegie Institute, Pittsburgh, Pa., 1944.
With an introduction.

FARBMAN, M. (ed.). *Masterpieces of Russian Painting*. London, 1930.
Catalogue of the exhibition of icons circulated by the Central State Restoration Workshop, Moscow. With contributions by A. J. Anisimov, R. Fry, and I. Grabar. Colour plates.

FELICETTI-LIEBENFELS, W. *Geschichte der russischen Ikonenmalerei in den Grundzügen dargestellt*. Graz, 1972.

KONDAKOV, N. P. *The Russian Icon*. Oxford, 1927.
Translated by E. H. Minns.
Summary of the following work.

KONDAKOV, N. P. *Russkaya ikona*. 4 vols. Prague, 1928–33.
The culminating study in the iconographical tradition. The first two volumes contain excellent plates in colour and black and white.

LAZAREV, V. N. *Moscow School of Icon Painting*. Moscow, 1971.

LAZAREV, V. N. *Novgorodskaya ikonopis. Novgorod Icon Painting*. Moscow, 1976.

LAZAREV, V. N. *Old Russian Murals and Mosaics from the XI to the XVI Century*. London, 1966.
With extensive bibliography for the surviving monuments.

LAZAREV, V. N., and DEMUS, O. *USSR Early Icons*. Greenwich, Conn., 1958.
UNESCO World Art Series, with good colour plates.

LAZAREV, V. N. *Russkaya srednevekovaya zhivopis. Stati i issledovanniya*. Moscow, 1970.

MURATOV, P. P. *L'Ancienne Peinture russe*. Rome and Prague, 1925.
A French translation of his chapters in Grabar's *Istoriya*, VI.

MURATOV, P. P. *Les Icones russes*. Paris, 1927.

NEKRASOV, A. I. *Drevne-russkoe izobrazitelnoe iskusstvo*. Moscow, 1937.
Summary of Soviet scholarship to that date, with bibliography.

ONASCH, K. *Icons*. London, 1963.
With excellent large colour plates and extensive bibliography.

RICE, D. T., and RICE, T. T. *Icons and Their Dating*. London, 1974.

SCHWEINFURTH, P. *Geschichte der russischen Malerei im Mittelalter*. The Hague, 1930.

SOBKO, N. P. *Slovar russkikh khudozhnikov*. 3 vols. St Petersburg, 1893–9.
A biographical dictionary, complete only for the letters A, I, P.

USPENSKII, A. I. *Tsarskie ikonopitsy i zhivopistsy XVII veka*. 4 vols. Moscow, 1910–16.
Monumental study of 17th-century Moscow painting, with numerous illustrations.

WULFF, O., and ALPATOV, M. *Denkmäler der Ikonenmalerei*. Hellerau bei Dresden, 1925.
With annotated catalogue of Byzantine and Russian icons.

6. PAINTING AFTER 1700

APTEKAR, M. *Russkaya istoricheskaya zhivopis*. Moscow, 1939.

BELYAVSKAYA, V. *Rospisi russkogo klassitsizma*. Leningrad and Moscow, 1940.
Interesting Neo-classic mural painting of the early 19th century.

BENOIS, A. *The Russian School of Painting*. New York, 1916.

An enlarged version of the author's earlier essay on 18th- and 19th-century painting written for R. Muther's *History of Modern Painting*, English tr. (London, 1895–6), III, ch. xliii, with an interesting bibliography.

BENOIS, A. *Russkaya shkola zhivopisi*. St Petersburg, 1904.
10 folios of plates of 18th- and 19th-century painting.

BOWLT, J. E. (ed.). *Russian Art of the Avant-Garde. Theory and Criticism 1902–1934*. New York, 1976.

BULGAKOV, F. I. *Nashi khudozhniki*. 2 vols. St Petersburg, 1890.
A biographical dictionary of later 19th-century painters, sculptors, engravers, etc. Numerous illustrations, poorly reproduced.

FEDOROV-DAVYDOV, A. A. *Russkii peizazh XVIII – nachala XIX veka*. Moscow, 1953.

FIALA, V. *Russian Painting of the 18th and 19th Centuries*. Prague, 1956.

ISAKOV, S. K. *Russkaya zhivopis*. Petrograd, 1915.
Catalogue of paintings in the Academy of Fine Arts.

MARCADÉ, V. *Le Renouveau de l'art pictural russe 1863–1914*. Paris, 1971.
Important bibliography and catalogue lists.

MOLEVA, N. M. *Russkaya khudozhestvennaya shkola pervoi poloviny XIX veka*. Moscow, 1963.

NICHOLAS MIKHAILOVICH, Grand Duke (ed.). *Russkie portrety XVIII i XIX vekov*. 5 vols. St Petersburg, 1905–9.
Portraits by Russian and foreign artists, including miniatures.

NIKOLSKII, V. A. *Russkaya zhivopis, istoriko-kriticheskie ocherki*. St Petersburg, 1904.
Illustrated study of 19th-century academic painting.

La Peinture russe à l'époque romantique. Paris, Grand Palais, 1976.

Russische Malerei 1890–1917. Bilder aus Museen des UdSSR. Hamburg, Kunsthalle, 1977.

Russischer Realismus 1850–1900. Baden-Baden, Staatliche Kunsthalle, 1972–3.
Exhibition catalogue with many important as well as unfamiliar late-19th-century paintings.

SARABIANOV, D. V. *Narodno-osvoboditelnia idei russkoi zhivopisi vtoroi poloviny XIX veka*. Moscow, 1955.
Social Realist criticism of the 19th-century realist painters (Perov, Ge, Repin, etc.).

SARABIANOV, D. V. *Russkaya zhivopis kontsa 1900-kh–nachala 1900-kh godov*. Moscow, 1971.

VALKENIER, E. *Russian Realist Art. The State and Society. The Peredvizhniki and Their Tradition*. Ann Arbor, Mich., 1977.

VRANGEL, N. N. *Katalog vystavki russkoi portretnoi zhivopisi za 150 let*. St Petersburg, 1902.
Biographical and bibliographical catalogue of an exhibition of portraits, 1700–1850.

7. SCULPTURE AND THE DECORATIVE ARTS

BARSHCHEVSKII, I. F. *Russkiya drevnosti*. Moscow, *c*. 1895.
150 plates of decorative arts.

BOBRINSKOI, A. A. *Narodnyya russkiya derevyannyya izdeliya*. Moscow, 1911.
200 plates of wood carving and furniture.

BOBRINSKOI, A. A. *Reznoi kamen v Rossii*. Moscow, 1916.
41 excellent photographs of Suzdalian architecture and sculpture.

BOUTOVSKY, V. de. *Histoire de l'ornement russe du Xᵉ au XVIᵉ siècle, d'après les manuscrits*. 2 vols. Paris, 1870–3.

BUNT, C. G. E. *Russian Art from Scyths to Soviets*. London, 1946.
Considerable information on the decorative arts. *Drevnosti rossiiskago gosudarstva*. 6 vols. Moscow, 1849–53.
Coloured lithographs of objects of religious art.

DUNCAN, D. D. *Great Treasures of the Kremlin*. New York, 1968.
Revised and enlarged edition of the same author's *The Kremlin*, New York, 1960.

GAGARIN, G. G. *Sobranie vizantiiskikh, gruzinskikh, i drevne-russkikh ornamentov*. 3 vols. St Petersburg, 1897–1903.
Byzantine, Georgian, and old Russian ornament.

GEORGIEVSKI, G. P. *Drevne-russkaya miniatiura*. Leningrad, 1933.
Medieval manuscript illumination. English ed., Moscow, 1934.

GUSHCHIN, A. S. *Pamyatniki khudozhestvennogo remesla drevnei Rusi X–XIII veka*. Moscow, 1936.
Industrial arts, old Russian.

HALLE, F. *Die Bauplastik von Wladimir-Ssusdal*. Berlin, 1929.
The best available account of medieval sculpture.

HARE, R. *The Art and Artists of Russia*. London, 1965.

HOLME, C. (ed.). *Peasant Art in Russia*. London, 1912.

ISAKOV, S. K. *Russkaya skulptura*. Petrograd, 1915.
Catalogue of sculpture in the Academy of Fine Arts, Leningrad.

LUKOMSKI, G. K. *Alt-Russland, Architektur und Kunstgewerbe.* Munich, 1923.
108 plates.

LUKOMSKI, G. K. *L'Art décoratif russe.* Paris, 1928.
192 plates.

LUKOMSKI, G. K. *Le Kreml de Moscou, ses cathédrales, ses palais et ses trésors d'art.* 3 vols. Paris, 1928.
120 plates, chiefly of the decorative arts.

LUKOMSKI, G. K. *Mobilier et décoration des anciens palais impériaux russes.* Paris, 1928.
84 plates, principally interiors of the Great Palace at Tsarskoe Selo.

LUKOMSKI, G. K. *Russisches Porzellan, 1744–1923.* Berlin, 1924.
62 plates.

NEKRASOV, A. I. *Russkoe narodnoe iskusstvo.* Moscow, 1924.
Peasant crafts.

NIKOLSKII, V. A. *Drevne-russkoe dekorativnoe iskusstvo.* Petrograd, 1923.

OLSUFIEV, I. A. *Opis drevnyago tserkovnogo serebra v. Troitsko-Sergievskoi Lavre (do XVIII veka).* Sergiev, 1926.
Ancient ecclesiastical silver.

ROSS, M. C. *Russian Porcelains. The Gardner, Iusupov, Batenin Factories.* Norman, Okla, 1968.
The collections of Marjorie Merriweather Post in Washington, D.C.

ROVINSKII, D. A. *Podrobnyi slovar russkikh graverov.* 2 vols. St Petersburg, 1895.
Biographical dictionary of engravers.

ROVINSKII, D. A. *Materialy dlya russkoi ikonografii.* 13 vols. St Petersburg, 1884–91.
480 fascimile reproductions of early engravings.

SHCHEKOTOV, N. M. 'Drevne-russkoe shitie', *Sofiya*, no. 1, 5–32.
Embroideries.

SHCHEKOTOV, N. M. *Russkaya krestyanskaya zhivopis.* Moscow, 1923.
Peasant painting.

SVIRIN, A. N. 'Une Broderie du XVᵉ siècle de style pittoresque, représentant le "Cin"', *L'Art byzantin chez les slaves*, 11, 282–91.

SYREISHCHIKOV, N. P., and TRENEV, D. K. *Ornamenty na pamyatnikakh drevne-russkago iskusstva.* 3 vols. Moscow, 1904–16.
Old Russian ornament.

TOLL, N. 'La Broderie populaire russe et les tissus du moyen age', *L'Art byzantin chez les slaves*, I, 387–92.

USPENSKII, A. I. *Slovar khudozhnikov v XVIII veke pisavshikh v imperatorskikh dvortsakh.* Moscow, 1913.
Dictionary of decorative artists working in the imperial palaces in the 18th century.

LIST OF ILLUSTRATIONS

90. Novgorod: St Paraskeva (Pyatnitsa; Good Friday), *c.* 1500. *Leningrad, Russian Museum (Russkaya ikona)*

91. Novgorod: SS. Florus and Laurus, late fifteenth century. *Moscow, Tretyakov Gallery (Kondakov, i)*

92. Moscow, after an icon by Andrey Rublev and Daniil Cherny: The Ascension, *c.* 1450. *Moscow, Tretyakov Gallery (Kondakov)*

93. Moscow: St Varlaam of Khutyn and Scenes from his Life, sixteenth century. *Present location unknown* (MMA)

94. Dionisy and his sons: The Parable of the Widow's Mite, fresco in the Church of the Nativity of the Virgin, Ferapontov Monastery, 1500–2 (V. T. Georgievski, *Freski Therapontova Monastyrya*, St Petersburg, 1911)

95. Dionisy and his sons: Christ Enthroned with the Virgin and St John the Baptist, from the Last Judgement fresco in the Church of the Nativity of the Virgin, Ferapontov Monastery, 1500–2 (Georgievski)

96. Dionisy or a close follower: The Incredulity of St Thomas, *c.* 1500. *Moscow, Tretyakov Gallery* (MMA)

97. Moscow: The Vision of St Eulogius, *c.* 1530–40. *Leningrad, Russian Museum* (J. Myskivec, *Ikona*, Prague, 1947)

98. Moscow: The Entry into Jerusalem, late sixteenth century. *Leningrad, Russian Museum (Russkaya ikona)*

99. Moscow: SS. Zosima and Savva at the Solovetsky Monastery, late sixteenth century. *Moscow, Tretyakov Gallery (Kondakov, i)*

100. Wooden storehouses, northern Russia, eighteenth century (Zabello)

101. Terentiev house, northern Russia, eighteenth century (Zabello)

102. Tavern between Kostroma and Yaroslavl, eighteenth century. Lithograph by André Durand, 1839 (Demidov)

103. Tsivozero, bell tower, 1658 (Buxton)

104. Tsaritsyn (now Volgograd), on the Volga, in the seventeenth century (Olearius)

105. The outskirts of Moscow in the seventeenth century (From 'The Book of the Election as Tsar of the Sovereign, Tsar, and Great Prince Mikhail Romanov', Moscow, 1672)

106. The village of Yadrovo, west of Moscow, in 1661–2 (Meyerberg)

107. The Iversky Monastery, on an island in Lake Vladai, in 1661–2 (Meyerberg)

108. Moscow: Border scene from the icon of the Virgin of Tikhvin, 1680. *Moscow, Rublev Museum of Early Russian Art*

109 and 110. Olonets, St Lazarus, before 1391(?),

exterior (*Russkoe derevyannoe zodchestv*, Moscow, 1965) and plan (from Suslov)

111. Suzdal, St Nicholas from Glotovo, 1766

112. Panilovo, St Nicholas, consecrated 1600 (SCR)

113. Nizhny Uftiug, Church of the Dormition, plan (from Suslov)

114. Vologda, Church of the Dormition from Ustye, after 1519

115. Rostovskoe, SS. Florus and Laurus, 1755 (Novosti)

116 and 117. Nenoksa, Church of the Trinity, 1727, exterior (SCR) and plan

118. Varzug, Church of the Dormition, 1674 (Grabar, i, 391)

119 and 120. Kondopoga, Church of the Dormition, 1774, exterior and interior (SCR)

121. Berezovets, St Nicholas, early eighteenth century (Grabar, i, 432)

122 and 123. Podporozhye (Lake Onega), Church of the Virgin of Vladimir, 1741, exterior (Suslov, i) and plan (after Suslov)

124. Kizhy, Church of the Transfiguration, 1714 (SCR)

125 and 126. Moscow, Cathedral of the Annunciation in the Kremlin, 1484–9, exterior (SCR) and plan (after Rzyanin)

127 and 128. Aristotele Fioravanti: Moscow, Cathedral of the Dormition in the Kremlin, completed in 1479, exterior and plan (after Nekrasov)

129. Aristotele Fioravanti: Moscow, Cathedral of the Dormition in the Kremlin, completed in 1479, interior

130 and 131. Alevisio Novi: Moscow, Cathedral of St Michael the Archangel in the Kremlin, 1505–9, exterior and plan (after Nekrasov)

132. Zagorsk, Cathedral of the Dormition in the Trinity-Sergius Monastery, 1559–85 (SCR)

133 and 134. Kolomenskoe, Church of the Ascension, probably 1530–2, exterior (Novosti) and plan (after Nekrasov)

135. Ostrov, Church of the Transfiguration, lower part sixteenth century, octagon and roof 1646 (Grabar, ii, facing 64)

136 and 137. Dyakovo, Church of the Decapitation of St John the Baptist, from 1555, exterior (Grabar, ii, 39) and plan (after Nekrasov)

138. Zagorsk, Church of the Descent of the Holy Spirit in the Trinity-Sergius Monastery, 1476 (*Masterpieces of Russian Architecture*, Moscow, 1968)

139–41. Barma and Posnik: Moscow, Cathedral of St Basil, 1555–60, exterior views (Novosti) and plan (after Nekrasov)

142. Moscow, Cathedral of St Basil in the seven-

191. Yaroslavl, St Elias, frescoed wall, late seventeenth century (N. G. Pervukhin, *Tserkov Ilii proroka*, Moscow, 1915)
192. St Petersburg in 1737 (J. D. Schumacher, *Palaty Sankt Peterburgskoi*, 1741)
193. St Petersburg, central section, showing the principal buildings in 1753 (From an engraving by M. I. Makhaev)
194. Domenico Tressini: St Petersburg, Cathedral of SS. Peter and Paul in the fortress, 1712–33. From a lithograph by André Durand, 1839 (Demidov)
195. Domenico Tressini: St Petersburg, the Twelve Colleges on Vasily Ostrov, 1722–33 (From an engraving by M. I. Makhaev, 1761)
196. Georg Johann Mattarnovy: St Petersburg, Peter the Great's Kunstkamera (now the Museum of Anthropology and Ethnology), 1718–25 (Shumacher)
197. Domenico Tressini and B. F. Rastrelli: St Petersburg, the third Winter Palace, 1732–6; and the Old Admiralty (From an engraving by M. I. Makhaev, 1761)
198. Gottfried Schädel: Oranienbaum (Lomonosov), Prince Menshikov's Palace, 1713–25 (From an engraving by M. I. Makhaev, 1761)
199. Wooden model for the Cathedral of the Trinity in the Alexander Nevsky Lavra, St Petersburg, by Domenico Tressini and Theodor Schwertfeger, built in 1720–32 (Grabar, III, 91)
200. M. G. Zemtsov: St Petersburg, Library of the Academy of Sciences in the Kunstkamera, c. 1730 (Shumacher)
201. B. F. Rastrelli: St Petersburg, the Summer Palace on the Fontanka, 1741–4 (From an engraving by M. I. Makhaev, 1761)
202. B. F. Rastrelli: St Petersburg, the Anichkov Palace on the Nevsky Prospekt, looking north towards the Admiralty; begun by Zemtsov in 1742, finished by Rastrelli after 1744 (From an engraving by M. I. Makhaev, 1761)
203. Peterhof, J.-B.-A. Le Blond's palace of 1716–17 as remodelled by Rastrelli in 1747–52 (From an engraving by M. I. Makhaev, 1761)
204. Peterhof. The centre of the palace in modern times (Novosti)
205. B. F. Rastrelli: St Petersburg, Smolny Cathedral, 1748–57 (SCR)
206. B. F. Rastrelli: Wooden model of the proposed belfry for the Smolny Convent, St Petersburg, c. 1750 (*Starye gody*, December 1910, facing 3)
207. B. F. Rastrelli: Tsarskoe Selo, Great Palace, 1749–52, forecourt (From an engraving by M. I. Makhaev, 1761)

208. B. F. Rastrelli: Tsarskoe Selo, Great Palace, 1749–52 (Novosti)
209. B. F. Rastrelli: Tsarskoe Selo, the pavilion of Monbezh ('Mon Bijou') in the park, c. 1750 (From an engraving by M. I. Makhaev, 1761)
210 and 211. B. F. Rastrelli: St Petersburg, the Winter Palace, 1754–62 (Grabar, III, 225, and SCR)
212. B. F. Rastrelli: St Petersburg, the Winter Palace, Jordan Staircase, 1757, reconstructed by V. P. Stasov after 1837 (Audrey Kennett, *The Palaces of Leningrad*, London, 1973)
213. J.-B.-M. Vallin de la Mothe and A. F. Kokorinov: St Petersburg, Academy of Fine Arts, 1765–72 (*Istor. panor.*, 11)
214 and 215. Antonio Rinaldi: Oranienbaum (Lomonosov), Katalnaya Gorka (Sliding Hill), 1760–8, and the Chinese Palace, 1762–8, the Large Chinese Room (Kennett)
216. Antonio Rinaldi: St Petersburg, the Marble Palace, 1768–85 (SCR)
217. V. I. Bazhenov: St Petersburg, Arsenal (demolished), 1769, principal entrance (*Istor. panor.*, 11)
218 and 219. V. I. Bazhenov: Design for a new Kremlin Palace in Moscow, 1769–72 (after Rzyanin), with detail of the wooden model (D. Arkin, *Obrazy arkhitektury*, Moscow, 1941, 203)
220. V. I. Bazhenov and M. F. Kazkov(?): Moscow, the Pashkov Palace (later the Rumyantsov Museum, now the old building of the Lenin Library), 1784–6 (SCR)
221. I. E. Starov: Nikolskoe, church and belfry, 1773–6 (Grabar, III, 343)
222. I. E. Starov: Wooden model of the Cathedral of the Trinity, Alexander Nevsky Lavra, St Petersburg, 1776 (Grabar, III, 346)
223. I. E. Starov: St Petersburg, Cathedral of the Trinity, Alexander Nevsky Lavra, 2778–90, plan
224 and 225. I. E. Starov: St Petersburg, Tauride Palace, 1783–9, plan (after Rzyanin) and Catherine Hall (Novosti)
226 and 227. Charles Cameron: Tsarskoe Selo, Green Dining Room, 1780–3 (Novosti), and Catherine II's bedroom, 1782–4 (*Istor. panor.*, VII)
228 and 229. Charles Cameron: Pavlovsk, palace, 1782–6 (Rzyanin), and Grecian Hall (Kennett)
230. Giacomo Quarenghi: Peterhof, the English Palace (destroyed), 1781–9 (SCR)
231. Giacomo Quarenghi: St Petersburg, State Bank, 1783–90 (*A Picture of St Petersburg*, London, 1815)
232. Giacomo Quarenghi: St Petersburg, Hermitage Theatre, 1783–7 (on the Neva Quay, by Y. M. Velten) (SCR)

281. I. E. Repin: Bargemen, 1870–3. *Leningrad, Russian Museum* (Benois)
282. I. E. Repin: Tsar Ivan IV with the Body of his Son, 1881–5. *Moscow, Tretyakov Gallery*
283. I. E. Repin: They Did Not Expect Him, 1883–98. *Moscow, Tretyakov Gallery*
284. V. N. Baksheev: The Prose of Life, 1892–3. *Moscow, Tretyakov Gallery*
285. André Durand: The Kremlin, Moscow, lithograph, 1843 (Demidov)
286. A. I. Shtakenshneider: Peterhof, The Nicholas Cottage, 1834 (*Starye gody*, July–September, 1913, facing 177)
287. K. A. Ton: Moscow, Church of the Redeemer, 1839–83 (*Moskva*, XI)
288. V. O. Shervud: Moscow, Historical Museum, 1874–83 (Sidorov, *Moskau*, Berlin, 1929)
289. A. A. Parland: St Petersburg, Church of the Ascension, 1883–1907
290. B. V. Freidenberg: Moscow, the Shchukin Museum, *c.* 1890 (SCR)
291. N. V. Nikitin: Moscow, Pogodinsky house, 1850s
292. The Russian Pavilion at the Paris Exhibition of 1878
293. V. M. Vasnetsov: After Prince Igor's Battle with the Polovtsy, 1880. *Moscow, Tretyakov Gallery*
294. V. M. Vasnetsov: Setting for the third act of Ostrovsky's drama *Snegurochka*, 1885. *Moscow, Tretyakov Gallery*
295. A. M. Vasnetsov: Old Moscow – the Crossroads on the way to Kitai-Gorod, 1902. *Moscow, Historical Museum* (*Moskva*, 11)
296. M. V. Nesterov: The Vision of St Bartholomew, 1889–90. *Moscow, Tretyakov Gallery*
297. M. A. Vrubel: A Boyar, 1886. *Kiev, Museum of Russian Art* (S. P. Yaremich, *M.A. Vrubel*, Moscow, 1911)

298. M. A. Vrubel: Valerian Briussov (unfinished), 1905. *Moscow, Tretyakov Gallery*
299. E. E. Lansere: St Petersburg in the Days of Peter the Great, 1906. *Leningrad, Russian Museum*
300. L. Bakst: Costume study for the ballet *L'Oiseau de feu*, 1910 (V. A. Ivchenko, *Le Ballet contemporain*, St Petersburg, 1912)
301. A. N. Benois: Design for the first act of the ballet *Petrouchka*, 1911. *Hartford, Conn., Wadsworth Atheneum*
302. L. Bakst: Costume study for the ballet *Narcisse*, 1911 (Ivchenko)
303. M. V. Yakunchikova: The Cemetery, coloured woodcut (*Mir Iskusstva*, XI, 80)
304. S. T. Konenkov: Stribog, before 1914. *Moscow, Tretyakov Gallery*
305. P. P. Trubetskoy: S. Yu. Vitte, 1901. Bronze. *Leningrad, Russian Museum*
306. I. E. Bondarenko: Moscow, Old Believers' Church, 1909 (*Moskva*, XII)
307. V. M. Vasnetsov: Design for the Tretyakov Art Gallery, Moscow, 1900–2 (*Mir Iskusstva*, IV, 128)
308. A. V. Shchusev: Moscow, Kazan Railway Station, 1913–26 (Sidorov, *Moskau*)
309. F. O. Shekhtel: Moscow, Ryabushinsky house, 1900–2
310. F. O. Shekhtel: Moscow, Ryabushinsky house, 1900–2, staircase
311. F. O. Shekhtel: Moscow, Yaroslavl Railway Station, 1902–4
312. F. O. Shekhtel: Moscow, Utro Rossii Printing House, 1907
313. D. S. Stelletsky: Dawn, 1910 (*Apollon*, 1911)
314. Vasily Kandinsky: Russian Woman in a Landscape, *c.* 1905. *Munich, Städtische Galerie* (© by A.D.A.G.P. Paris, 1975)

INDEX

Churches and other buildings are indexed under the name of the town or other place at which they are located: thus St Basil's Cathedral, Moscow, will be found under the heading Moscow. The dates given for Tsars and other rulers indicate their regnal years. References to notes are given to the page on which the note occurs, followed by the number of the chapter to which it belongs and the number of the note: thus 423(7)[8].